GLENCOE SPANISH 1A

Bienvenidos

Conrad J. Schmitt

Protase E. Woodford

GLENCOE

McGraw-Hill

New York, New York   Columbus, Ohio   Mission Hills, California   Peoria, Illinois

About the Cover

Machu Picchu, the "Lost City of the Incas", was discovered in 1911 by the American, Hiram Bingham. The steep slopes on which the Incas built this majestic city, and its remote location high in the Andes Mountains of Peru, made it impossible for the Spaniards to discover its whereabouts. Even today, no one knows for sure whether this was a sacred city, or a hidden fortress designed to protect the Incan nobility. Machu Picchu is an impressive monument to the great Incan Empire that ruled the Andean area of South America for centuries prior to the coming of the Spaniards.

Printed in the United States of America.

Send all inquiries to:
Glencoe/McGraw-Hill
15319 Chatsworth Street
P.O. Box 9609
Mission Hills, CA 91346-9609

ISBN 0-02-641011-7 (Student Edition)
ISBN 0-02-641012-5 (Teacher's Wraparound Edition)

3 4 5 6 7 8 9   AGH   01 00 99 98 97

Acknowledgments

We wish to express our deep appreciation to the numerous individuals throughout the United States who have advised us in the development of these teaching materials. Special thanks are extended to the people whose names appear here.

Kristine Aarhus
Northshore School District
Bothell, Washington

Kathy Babula
Charlotte Country Day School
Charlotte, North Carolina

Veronica Dewey
Brother Rice High School
Birmingham, Michigan

Anneliese H. Foerster
Oak Hill Academy
Mouth of Wilson, Virginia

Sharon Gordon-Link
Antelope Valley Unified High School
Lancaster, California

Leslie Lumpkin
Prince George's County Public Schools
Prince George's County, Maryland

Loretta Mizeski
Columbia School
Berkeley Heights, New Jersey

Robert Robison
Columbus Public Schools
Columbus, Ohio

Rhona Zaid
Los Angeles, California

T = top M = middle B = bottom L = left R = right

Bienvenidos

CONTENTIDO

BIENVENIDOS

CAPÍTULO 1

UN AMIGO O UNA AMIGA

CAPÍTULO 2

¿HERMANOS O AMIGOS?

CAPÍTULO 3

EN LA ESCUELA

CAPÍTULO 4

PASATIEMPOS DESPUÉS DE LAS CLASES

CAPÍTULO 5

ACTIVIDADES DEL HOGAR

CAPÍTULO 6

LA FAMILIA Y SU CASA

CAPÍTULO 7

LOS DEPORTES DE EQUIPO

CAPÍTULO 8

UN VIAJE EN AVIÓN

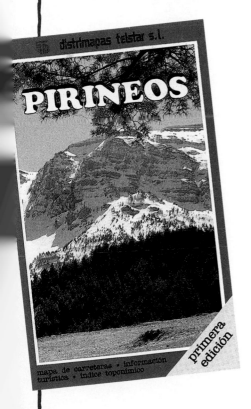

APÉNDICES

Oaxaca, México

Cuzco, Perú

Sevilla, España

En la Costa Brava, España

República Dominicana

Cuzco, Perú

Salinas, Puerto Rico

Andalucía, España

BIENVENIDOS

A
BUENOS DÍAS

—Hola, Manolo.
—Hola, Maricarmen.

—Buenos días, Juan.
—Buenos días, Emilio.

When greeting a friend in Spanish, you say *Hola* or *Buenos días*. *Hola* is a less formal way of saying hello.

Actividad

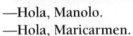 **¡Hola!** Choose a partner. Greet each other. Be sure to shake hands.

—Buenos días, señor.

—Buenas tardes, señora.

—Buenas noches, señorita.

1. When greeting an adult in Spanish, you say *Buenos días* in the morning, *Buenas tardes* in the afternoon, and *Buenas noches* in the evening, with the person's title. You do not use the person's name with the title.

2. The following are abbreviations for these titles.

Sr. señor   Sra. señora   Srta. señorita

Actividades

A **Buenos días.** Greet your Spanish teacher.

B **Señor, señora, señorita.** Choose a partner. Greet the following people. Your partner will answer for the other person.

1. the principal of your school
2. your English teacher
3. a young saleswoman at a record shop
4. your neighbor, Mr. Smith
5. your parents' friend, Mrs. Jones

B

¿QUÉ TAL?

—Hola, Felipe.
—Hola, Susana. ¿Qué tal?
—Bien, ¿y tú?
—Muy bien, gracias.

1. When you want to find out from a friend how things are going, you ask:

   ¿Qué tal?

2. Responses to *¿Qué tal?* include:

   Bien, gracias.
   Muy bien. ¿Y tú?

Actividades

A **¡Hola!** Greet a classmate with the following expressions. Then reverse roles.

1. ¡Hola!   2. ¿Qué tal?

B **¿Qué tal?** You are walking down the street in Guadalajara, Mexico, when you run into one of your Mexican friends.

1. Greet each other.   2. Ask each other how things are going.

C
ADIÓS

—Adiós, Manolo.
—Adiós, Maricarmen.

—Chao, Gerardo.
—¡Chao! ¡Hasta luego!

1. The usual expression to use when saying "good-bye" is:

    ¡Adiós!

2. If you plan to see the person again soon, you can say:

    ¡Hasta pronto!   **¡Hasta luego!**

3. An informal expression that you will hear frequently is:

    ¡Chao!

Chao is an Italian expression, but it is used in Spanish and French.

4. If you plan to see someone the next day, you say:

¡Hasta mañana!

—¡Adiós! Hasta mañana.
—¡Adiós, señora! ¡Hasta mañana!

Conversación

—Hola, Paco.
—Hola, Teresa. ¿Qué tal?
—Bien, ¿y tú?
—Muy bien, gracias.

—Chao, Paco.
—Chao, Teresa. ¡Hasta luego!

Actividades

A ¡Hola! Say the following to a classmate. Your classmate will answer.

1. Hola.   2. ¿Qué tal?   3. ¡Adiós!   4. ¡Chao!

B ¡Adiós!

1. Say good-bye to your Spanish teacher. Indicate that you will see him or her tomorrow.
2. Say good-bye to a friend. Indicate that you will see him or her again soon.

D
¿QUIÉN ES?

Conversación

MUCHACHO 1: ¿Quién es?	(*She comes up to them.*)
MUCHACHO 2: ¿Quién? ¿La muchacha?	MUCHACHO 2: Casandra, Felipe.
MUCHACHO 1: Sí, ella.	MUCHACHA: Hola, Felipe.
MUCHACHO 2: Pues es Casandra López.	MUCHACHO 1: Hola, Casandra. Mucho gusto.

1. When you want to know who someone is, you ask:

    ¿Quién es?

2. When you want to identify a person, you use the name or *Es* with the person's name.

    (Es) Pablo Torres.

3. If you are pleased to meet the person you were introduced to, you can say:

    Mucho gusto.

Actividades

A **¿Quién es?** Ask a classmate who someone else in the class is.

B **Es…** Introduce someone you know to another person in the class.

C **¿Quién?** Prepare the following conversation with two classmates.

1. Greet your classmate.
2. Ask him or her who someone else is in the class.
3. Say hello to the new person.
4. Ask him or her how things are going.
5. Say good-bye to one another.

E

¿QUÉ ES?

una pizarra

una tiza

una c

una mochila

una computadora

un cuaderno

una hoja de papel

un libro

una goma

una calculadora

un bolígrafo

un banco

una silla

1. When you want to know what something is, you ask:

   ¿Qué es?

2. When you want to identify the object, you use *es* + the name of the object.

   Es un bolígrafo. Es una calculadora.

Actividad

Es… Work with a classmate. Your classmate will hold up or point to five of the items above. He or she will ask you what each one is. You will respond.

F

¿CUÁNTO ES?

—¿Cuánto es el cuaderno, señora?
—Ochenta pesos.
—Gracias, señora.

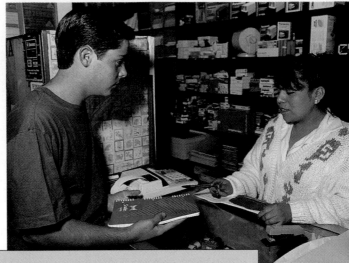

1. When you want to find out how much something is, you ask:

    ¿Cuánto es?

2. Here are the numbers in Spanish from zero to two thousand.

0	cero				
1	uno	21	veinte y uno	31	treinta y uno
2	dos	22	veinte y dos	42	cuarenta y dos
3	tres	23	veinte y tres	53	cincuenta y tres
4	cuatro	24	veinte y cuatro	64	sesenta y cuatro
5	cinco	25	veinte y cinco	75	setenta y cinco
6	seis	26	veinte y seis	86	ochenta y seis
7	siete	27	veinte y siete	97	noventa y siete
8	ocho	28	veinte y ocho	143	ciento cuarenta y tres
9	nueve	29	veinte y nueve		
10	diez	30	treinta	200	doscientos
11	once			300	trescientos
12	doce	40	cuarenta	400	cuatrocientos
13	trece	50	cincuenta	500	quinientos
14	catorce	60	sesenta	600	seiscientos
15	quince	70	setenta	700	setecientos
16	dieciséis	80	ochenta	800	ochocientos
17	diecisiete	90	noventa	900	novecientos
18	dieciocho	100	cien, ciento	1 000	mil
19	diecinueve			2 000	dos mil
20	veinte				

3. Note that 100 is *cien* or *ciento*. You use *cien* before a noun and *ciento* with numbers from 101 to 199.

    cien pesos   **ciento cinco pesos**

Actividades

A **¿Cuánto es?** Tell how many *pesos* are in the picture.

1.

2.

B **En la tienda.** You are in a store. Find out how much each item costs. A classmate will play the part of the salesperson. He or she will give you the price in *pesos*.

1. el cuaderno
2. el bolígrafo
3. la calculadora
4. la mochila
5. el libro

2.000 pesos

75 pesos

100 pesos

250 pesos

1,000 pesos

PUEBLOS DE ESPAÑA

G

UNA LIMONADA, POR FAVOR

—Buenos días.
—Una limonada, por favor.
—Gracias.
—De nada.
—¿Cuánto es, por favor?
—Cien pesos, señorita.

1. Expressions of politeness are always appreciated. Below are the Spanish expressions for "please," "thank you," and "you're welcome."

   Por favor.   Gracias.   De nada.

2. Another way to express "you're welcome" is:

   No hay de qué.

Actividades

A **Por favor.** You're in a Mexican restaurant. Order the following foods. Be polite and add *por favor* to your request.

un taco

una enchilada

una tostada

un burrito

B **Una hoja de papel, por favor.** Ask a friend in class for the following items. Be polite. Thank your friend. He or she will be polite and say you're welcome.

> —**Una hoja de papel, por favor.**
> —**Gracias.**
> —**De nada.** (**No hay de qué.**)

1. una hoja de papel
2. una goma
3. un cuaderno
4. una calculadora
5. un bolígrafo
6. un libro

H

¿CUÁL ES LA FECHA DE HOY?

—Sandra, ¿qué día es hoy?
—Hoy es miércoles.
—¿Y cuál es la fecha?
—El veinte y cinco.

1. The days of the week and the months of the year usually are not capitalized in Spanish.

> **Hoy es martes.**
> **Hoy es martes, veinte y cinco de septiembre.**

2. For the first day of the month *el primero* is used.

> **el primero de enero**
> **el dos de agosto**

Actividades

A **¿Qué día?** Answer the following questions.

1. ¿Qué día es hoy?
2. ¿Cuál es la fecha de hoy?

B **La fecha.** Give the date of the following.

1. your birthday
2. Independence day
3. Christmas

Vocabulario

SUSTANTIVOS	junio	ADJETIVOS	de nada
señor	julio	primero(a)	no hay de qué
señora	agosto		¿quién es?
señorita	septiembre	OTRAS PALABRAS Y EXPRESIONES	¿qué es?
el muchacho	octubre		¿cuánto es?
la muchacha	noviembre	hola	¿cuál es la fecha de hoy?
una limonada	diciembre	buenos días	
la fecha	un cuaderno	buenas tardes	
lunes	un bolígrafo	buenas noches	
martes	un libro	¿qué tal?	
miércoles	una mochila	bien	
jueves	una goma	gracias	
viernes	una hoja de papel	adiós	
sábado	un banco	chao	
domingo	una silla	hasta pronto	
enero	una pizarra	hasta luego	
febrero	una tiza	hasta mañana	
marzo	una computadora	mucho gusto	
abril	una calculadora	por favor	
mayo			

Calendar showing months: DICIEMBRE, NOVIEMBRE, OCTUBRE, SEPTIEMBRE, AGOSTO, JULIO, JUNIO, MAYO, ABRIL, MARZO, FEBRERO, ENERO.

ENERO calendar:

LUNES	MARTES	MIÉRCOLES	JUEVES	VIERNES	SÁBADO	DOMINGO
						1
2	3	4	5	6	7	8
9	10	11	12	13	14	15
16	17	18	19	20	21	22
23/30	24/31	25	26	27	28	29

1

UN AMIGO
UNA AMIGA

OBJETIVOS

In this chapter you will learn to do the following:

1. ask what someone is like
2. ask or tell where someone is from
3. describe yourself or someone else
4. tell some differences between Hispanic and American schools

PALABRAS 1

¿QUIÉN ES?

la escuela

el colegio

el muchacho
el alumno

Manolo

la muchacha   la amiga
la alumna

Elena

el amigo

Guadalajara •

¿Quién es mexicano?
Pablo es mexicano.
Pablo es de Guadalajara.
Él es alumno en un colegio.
Es alumno en el Colegio Hidalgo.
Pablo es amigo de José Luis.

¿Cómo es el muchacho?

alto

bajo

rubio

moreno

divertido

aburrido

¿Cómo es la muchacha?

alta

baja

rubia

morena

divertida

aburrida

Elena es alta. No es baja.
Ella es muy divertida.
Ella es alumna en una
escuela secundaria.

José es amigo de Elena.
Él es alto también.
No es bajo.
José es rubio.

Nota: Some words do not have a precise translation from one language to another. *Simpático* is such a word. *Simpático* conveys the meaning "nice," "pleasant," "warm," "understanding," "friendly," "congenial," all in one word. Its opposite is *antipático*. Frequently, Spanish speakers add the expressions *¿no?, ¿verdad?* or *¿no es verdad?* at the end of statements to change them into questions. If the person answering agrees, he or she will say *sí*, but if he or she disagrees, the answer will be *no*. For total disagreement one may add, *de ninguna manera.*

Teresa es bastante tímida, ¿no?
No, no. De ninguna manera.
Es bastante divertida.

Ejercicios

A Un muchacho mexicano. Contesten. (*Answer.*)

1. ¿Es Pablo mexicano o colombiano?
2. ¿Él es de Bogotá o de Guadalajara?
3. ¿Él es alumno en el Colegio Hidalgo?
4. ¿Es el Colegio Hidalgo un colegio mexicano?
5. ¿Es Pablo amigo de José Luis?

La catedral de Guadalajara, México

B Una muchacha americana. Contesten. (*Answer.*)

1. ¿Es Elena una muchacha americana?
2. ¿Es ella de Los Ángeles?
3. ¿Es ella alumna en una escuela secundaria americana?
4. ¿Es alumna en una escuela en Los Ángeles?
5. ¿Es amiga de Bárbara Andrews?

C **¿Quién, Pablo o Elena?** Contesten. (*Answer.*)

1. ¿Quién es de Guadalajara?
2. ¿Quién es de Los Ángeles?
3. ¿Quién es alumno en un colegio mexicano?
4. ¿Quién es alumna en una escuela secundaria americana?

D **¿Cómo es Manolo?** Contesten. (*Answer.*)

1. ¿Cómo es Manolo? ¿Es alto o bajo?
2. ¿Cómo es Manolo? ¿Es rubio o moreno?
3. ¿Cómo es Manolo? ¿Es divertido o aburrido?
4. ¿Cómo es Manolo? ¿Es simpático o antipático?

E **De ninguna manera.** Contesten según el modelo. (*Answer according to the model.*)

> **¿Es alta Elena?**
> *No, no. De ninguna manera.*
> *Ella es baja.*

1. ¿Es mexicana Elena?
2. ¿Es rubia Elena?
3. ¿Es ella aburrida?
4. ¿Es antipática?

Bogotá, Colombia

PALABRAS 2

¿DE DÓNDE SOY?

Teresa es una amiga fantástica.
Ella es una amiga muy buena.

Carlos es un amigo fantástico.
Él es un amigo muy bueno.

Es Roberto Collins.
Roberto es americano.
Él es de California.

Es Teresa.
Teresa es una amiga de Roberto.

¿Quién soy y de dónde soy?

¡Hola!
Yo soy Roberto Collins.
Soy de California.
Soy amigo de Teresa.
Ella es una amiga fantástica.
Es una amiga muy buena.

Nota: Many words that are similar or identical in Spanish and English are called cognates. Although they look alike and mean the same thing, they are pronounced differently. It is easy to guess the meaning of cognates. Here are some Spanish cognates.

fantástico	fantástica
tímido	tímida
atractivo	atractiva
sincero	sincera
serio	seria
honesto	honesta

Ejercicios

A **Roberto Collins.** Contesten. (*Answer.*)

1. ¿Quién es americano, Roberto Collins o Manolo Salas?
2. ¿De dónde es Roberto Collins? ¿Es de California o es de Guadalajara, México?
3. ¿De qué nacionalidad es Roberto? ¿Es americano o mexicano?
4. ¿Dónde es alumno Roberto? ¿En un colegio mexicano o en una escuela secundaria americana?

B **¿Cómo es la muchacha?** Describan a la muchacha. (*Describe the girl.*)

1. ___.   4. ___.
2. ___.   5. ___.
3. ___.

C **Isabel Torres.** Completen. (*Complete.*)

1. Isabel Torres es de México. Ella es ___.
   No es ___.
2. Isabel es alumna en un ___ mexicano.
   No es alumna en una ___ secundaria
   americana.
3. Isabel es ___. No es rubia.
4. ¿Es Isabel seria y aburrida? De ninguna
   manera. Ella es muy ___.
5. Ella es una amiga ___.

La misión de San José, San Antonio, Tejas

Comunicación
Palabras 1 y 2

A **¿Cómo es…?** Using words you have learned, describe a classmate without saying his or her name. Have your partner guess who the person is. Reverse roles.

B **¿Es aburrido?** Ask your partner what the following people are like, using the words in parentheses. If your partner agrees, he or she will add another word to describe the person. If not, he or she will use a word that describes the person in the opposite way.

> Juan (aburrido)
> Estudiante 1: ¿Es Juan aburrido?
> Estudiante 2: Sí. Es aburrido y antipático.
> (No, de ninguna manera. Es divertido.)

1. Elena (alta)
2. José Luis (moreno)
3. Roberto (tímido)
4. Teresa (simpática)
5. Isabel (seria)
6. Arturo (honesto)
7. Bárbara (rubia)
8. Pedro (sincero)

C **¿Quién es el amigo de…?** Find out from your partner all you can about his or her friend: who the person is, where he or she is from, what he or she is like, where he or she is a student. Then reverse roles.

D **Una persona famosa.** You and your partner each make a list of very famous people (no more than ten), including entertainers, sports figures, politicians, scientists, etc. Try to include people from different countries. Show your lists to each other. Then, tell as much as you can about a person on your list and see if your partner can guess whom you are describing. Take turns, and see how many of your guesses are correct.

> Gloria Estefan
> Estudiante 1: Es morena, simpática y de Cuba.
> Estudiante 2: ¿Es María Conchita Alonso? ¿Es Gloria Estefan?
> Estudiante 1: No. / Sí. Muy bien.

ESTRUCTURA

Los artículos definidos e indefinidos
Formas singulares

Talking about One Person or Thing

LOS ARTÍCULOS DEFINIDOS

1. The name of a person, place, or thing is called a noun. In Spanish every noun has a gender, either masculine or feminine. Almost all nouns that end in *o* are masculine and almost all nouns that end in *a* are feminine.

2. You use the definite article *the* in English when referring to a definite or specific person or thing: *the girl, the boy.* Study the following examples with the definite article.

MASCULINO	FEMENINO
el muchacho	la muchacha
el alumno	la alumna
el colegio	la escuela

3. You use the definite article *el* before a masculine noun. You use the definite article *la* before a feminine noun.

Ejercicios

A **El muchacho mexicano y la muchacha americana.** Completen. (*Complete with* el *or* la.)

1. ___ muchacho no es americano. ___ muchacho es mexicano. ___ muchacha es americana.
2. ___ muchacho mexicano es Raúl y ___ muchacha americana es Sandra.
3. ___ muchacha es morena y ___ muchacho es rubio.
4. ___ muchacha es alumna en ___ Escuela Thomas Jefferson en Houston.
5. Y ___ muchacho es alumno en ___ Colegio Hidalgo en Guadalajara.

En un colegio en Barcelona, España

LOS ARTÍCULOS INDEFINIDOS

1. The Spanish words *un* and *una* are indefinite articles. They correspond to *a* (*an*) in English.

2. You use an indefinite article when speaking about a non-specific person or thing: *a boy, a school*. Study the following examples with the indefinite article.

MASCULINO	FEMENINO
un muchacho	una muchacha
un alumno	una alumna
un colegio	una escuela

3. You use the indefinite article *un* before all masculine nouns. You use the indefinite article *una* before all feminine nouns.

B **Un muchacho y una muchacha.** Completen. (*Complete with* un *or* una.)

1. Roberto es ___ muchacho americano y Lupita es ___ muchacha colombiana.
2. Roberto es ___ alumno muy serio.
3. Él es alumno en ___ escuela secundaria en Nueva York.
4. Lupita es ___ alumna muy seria también.
5. Ella es alumna en ___ colegio colombiano en Cali.

La concordancia de los adjetivos   *Describing a Person or Thing*
Formas singulares

1. A word that describes a noun is an adjective. The italicized words in the
   following sentences are adjectives.

El muchacho es *rubio.*	**La muchacha es** *rubia.*
El alumno es *serio.*	**La alumna es** *seria.*

2. In Spanish, an adjective must agree in gender (masculine or feminine) with
   the noun it describes or modifies. If the noun is masculine, then the adjective
   must be in the masculine form. If the noun is feminine, the adjective must be
   in the feminine form. Many adjectives end in *o* in the masculine and *a* in the
   feminine.

   un muchacho tímido   **una muchacha tímida**

Ejercicios

A **Elena y Roberto.** Contesten. (*Answer.*)

1. ¿Es Elena americana o colombiana?
2. Y Roberto, ¿es él americano o colombiano?
3. ¿Es moreno o rubio el muchacho?
4. Y la muchacha, ¿es rubia o morena?
5. ¿Es Elena una alumna seria?
6. ¿Es ella alumna en un colegio colombiano?
7. Y Roberto, ¿es él un alumno serio también?
8. ¿Es él alumno en una escuela secundaria americana?

B **¿Quién es?** Here are some adjectives that describe
people. Select a class member and an adjective that
describes that person. Then make up a sentence about
him or her.

1. moreno	6. divertido
2. alto	7. bajo
3. rubio	8. simpático
4. serio	9. fantástico
5. americano	10. sincero

El presente del verbo *ser*
Formas singulares

Identifying People and Things

1. The verb "to be" in Spanish is *ser*. Note that the form of the verb changes with each person. Study the following.

SER	
yo	soy
tú	eres
él	es
ella	es

2. You use *yo* to talk about yourself. You use *tú* to address a friend. You use *él* to talk about a boy. You use *ella* to talk about a girl.

3. Since each form of the verb changes in Spanish, the subject pronouns *yo, tú, él,* and *ella* can be omitted. They are not always needed to clarify who performs the action.

> Soy Juan.
> Eres colombiano.
> Es un alumno serio.
> Es María.

4. To make a sentence negative in Spanish, put the word *no* before the verb.

> Yo soy americano.   No soy cubano.
> Ella es simpática.   No es antipática.

Ejercicios

A **¿Quién es ?** Lean o escuchen. (*Read or listen.*)

¡Hola!
Yo soy Susana Márquez.
Soy colombiana.
Yo soy de Bogotá.
Soy alumna en el Colegio Bolívar.

B **Susana Márquez.** Hablen de Susana. (*Talk in your own words about Susana.*)

C **¿Quién eres?** Practiquen la conversación. (*Practice the conversation.*)

MARTA: ¡Hola!
CARLOS: ¡Hola! ¿Quién eres?
MARTA: ¿Quién? ¿Yo?
CARLOS: Sí, tú.
MARTA: Pues, soy Marta. Marta González. ¿Y tú? ¿Quién eres?
CARLOS: Yo soy Carlos. Carlos Príncipe.
MARTA: ¿Eres americano, Carlos?
CARLOS: No, no soy americano.
MARTA: Pues, ¿de dónde eres?
CARLOS: Soy de México.
MARTA: ¡Increíble! Yo soy de México también.

D **Marta y Carlos.** Hablen de Marta y Carlos. (*Tell what you know about Marta and Carlos.*)

1. Marta…
2. Carlos…

E **Una entrevista.** Preguntas personales. (*Answer with* yo.)

1. ¿Eres americano(a) o cubano(a)?
2. ¿Eres alto(a) o bajo(a)?
3. ¿Eres moreno(a) o rubio(a)?
4. ¿Eres alumno(a)?
5. ¿Eres alumno(a) en una escuela secundaria?

F **Hola, Felipe.** Pregúntenle a Felipe Orama si es… (*Ask Felipe Orama if he is…*)

1. puertorriqueño
2. rubio
3. alumno
4. de Ponce

G **¿Eres chilena?** Pregúntenle a Catalina García si es… (*Ask Catalina García if she is…*)

1. de Chile
2. de Santiago
3. alumna
4. alumna en una escuela secundaria
5. amiga de Felipe Orama

H **Yo.** Digan. (*Give the following information about yourself.*)

1. name
2. nationality
3. profession
4. place you come from
5. physical description

La Casa de España en el viejo San Juan, Puerto Rico

CONVERSACIÓN

Escenas de la vida   *¡Hola!*

DAVID: Hola. Eres Maricarmen
Torres, ¿no?
MARICARMEN: Sí, soy yo. Y tú eres
David Davis, ¿verdad?
DAVID: Sí, soy David.

MARICARMEN: Tú eres amigo de
Inés Figueroa, ¿no?
DAVID: Sí, sí. Ella es una amiga
fantástica, muy buena.

MARICARMEN: Es verdad. Es una
persona muy sincera. ¿De dónde
eres, David?
DAVID: Pues, soy de Chicago.
MARICARMEN: Ah, eres americano.

¿Sí o no? Contesten. (*Answer sí or no.*)

1. Maricarmen Torres es de Chicago.
2. David es amigo de Maricarmen Torres.
3. David es amigo de Inés Figueroa.
4. Inés Figueroa es una persona antipática.
5. David es colombiano.

Pronunciación *Las vocales* a, o y u

When you speak Spanish, it is very important to pronounce the vowels carefully. The vowel sounds in Spanish are very short, clear, and concise. The vowels in English have several different pronunciations, but in Spanish they have only one sound. Imitate carefully the pronunciation of the vowels **a**, **o**, and **u**. Note that the pronunciation of **a** is similar to the **a** in *father*, **o** is similar to the **o** in *most,* and **u** is similar to the **u** in *flu*.

a	o	u
Ana	o	uno
Aldo	no	mucha
amiga	Paco	mucho
alumno	amigo	muchacho

Repeat the following sentences.

Ana es alumna.
Aldo es alumno.
Ana es amiga de Aldo.

alumna

Comunicación

A **¿De dónde es?** Ask your partner who each person below is. He or she will tell you the person's name and school. Ask where the person is from. Your partner will tell you the city. You then have to figure out and say what country the person is from.

1. Juan Pablo / Colegio Cervantes / México D.F.
2. Sandra / Instituto Ponce de León / San Juan
3. Isidro / Colegio Libertad / La Habana
4. Carlos / Colegio Colón / Madrid
5. Gloria / Academia Internacional / San Salvador

B **¿Cómo es tu amigo(a)?** Work with a classmate. You will each prepare a list of three friends. Then prepare a conversation about each of your friends. Use the model as a guide.

Estudiante 1: **María es una amiga.**
Estudiante 2: **¿Y cómo es María? ¿Es muy seria?**
Estudiante 1: **¿Quién? ¿María? No, de ninguna manera. Es muy divertida.**

¿UNA ESCUELA SECUNDARIA O UN COLEGIO?

Elena Ochoa es una muchacha colombiana. Ella es de Bogotá, la capital. Elena es alta y morena. Ella es muy simpática. Elena es una alumna muy buena y seria. Ella es alumna en el Colegio Simón Bolívar en Bogotá. Un colegio en Latinoamérica es una escuela secundaria en los Estados Unidos.

Estudio de palabras

Palabras. Busquen cinco palabras afines en la lectura. (*Find five cognates in the reading selection.*)

Simón Bolívar

Comprensión

A **¿Quién es?** Contesten. (*Answer.*)

1. ¿Quién es colombiana?
2. ¿De dónde en Colombia es ella?
3. ¿Qué es Bogotá?
4. ¿Cómo es Elena?
5. ¿Qué tipo de alumna es ella?
6. ¿Es alumna en qué escuela?
7. ¿Qué es un colegio en Latinoamérica?

B **Información.** Busquen la información en la lectura. (*Find the information in the reading.*)

1. a Latin American country
2. the name of your country
3. the capital of Colombia
4. the name of a Latin American hero
5. the term for the group of Spanish-speaking countries in Central and South America

C **Es colombiana.** Escojan la respuesta correcta. (*Choose the correct answer.*)

1. Elena Ochoa es ___.
   a. una muchacha
   b. un muchacho
   c. americana

2. Ella es ___.
   a. de México
   b. americana
   c. de la capital de Colombia

3. La capital de Colombia es ___.
   a. Cali
   b. Bolívar
   c. Bogotá

4. Elena es ___.
   a. un muchacho
   b. americana
   c. alumna

5. Ella es alumna en ___.
   a. una escuela secundaria americana
   b. un colegio colombiano
   c. una escuela americana en Bogotá

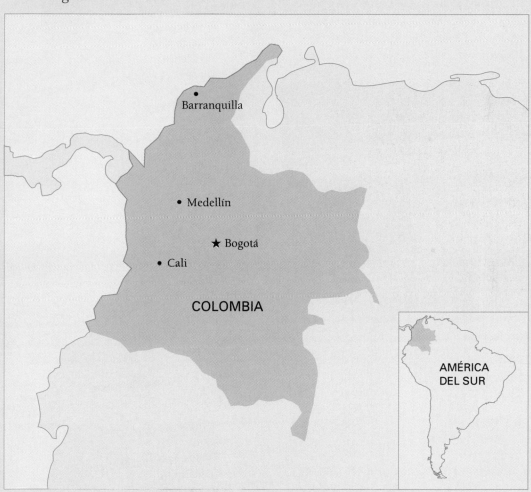

DESCUBRIMIENTO CULTURAL

EN LOS ESTADOS UNIDOS	EN ESPAÑA Y LATINOAMÉRICA
la escuela primaria	la escuela primaria
la escuela intermedia	el liceo
la escuela superior	el colegio, el instituto, la academia
la escuela vocacional	el instituto técnico o vocacional
el colegio o la universidad	la universidad

La educación es obligatoria en los Estados Unidos. ¿Es obligatoria también en España y en Latinoamérica? Sí, es obligatoria. ¿Hasta qué grado? Depende, ¿en qué país? ¿En Chile, en Venezuela, o en Puerto Rico? Es diferente en cada país.

Un colegio en Puerto Rico

LICENCIATURAS
Administración de Empresas
Sistemas Computacionales y Administrativos
Relaciones Internacionales
Comunicación Humana
Psicología Industrial
Psicología de la Conducta Social (Clínica)

BACHILLERATOS
Educación
Psicología General
Estudios de Política Internacional
Administración de Empresas

MAESTRÍAS
Economía
Estudios Latinoamericanos
Economía Política Internacional
Educación
Tutelaje y Terapia Familiar
Administración de Empresas
Psicopedagogía

DIPLOMADOS
Administración Financiera
Administración de Recursos Humanos

IDIOMAS
Inglés, Español, Francés

Aquí tienes los datos para cualquier cosa:
Taxco 432, Col. Juárez, o
Av. Hidalgo 823, Col. Juárez,
C.P. 55320, México, D. F.
Tel. 81 (3) 328 79 42

El Paseo del Río, San Antonio, Texas

Y AQUÍ EN LOS ESTADOS UNIDOS

Enrique Cárdenas es de Texas. Es texano. Es de la ciudad de San Antonio. San Antonio es una ciudad muy histórica. Enrique Cárdenas, como mucha gente en San Antonio, es de ascendencia mexicana. San Antonio es una ciudad bilingüe.

1

Es María Teresa Grávalos **1**. Ella es mexicana. Es de la Ciudad de México, la capital. Ella es de Lomas de Chapultepec. Lomas de Chapultepec es una colonia muy bonita de la Ciudad de México. En México una colonia es una zona o región de una ciudad. Lomas de Chapultepec es una colonia residencial.

Es Felipe Irizarry **2**. Felipe es de Puerto Rico. Es puertorriqueño. Puerto Rico es una isla en el mar Caribe. Es una isla tropical. Felipe es de Santa María. Santa María es un suburbio de San Juan, la capital.

¡Hola! Yo soy Adela Santiago **3**. Sí, Santiago. Pero no soy de Santiago de Chile. No soy chilena. Soy peruana. Soy de San Isidro. San Isidro es un sector residencial de Lima, la capital. Yo soy alumna en una academia en Lima. Es una escuela privada. No es una escuela pública.

¡Hola! Yo soy Enrique, Enrique Cárdenas **4**. Yo soy de los Estados Unidos. Soy texano. Soy de San Antonio. Yo soy de ascendencia mexicana. Soy méxico-americano. Soy alumno en una escuela secundaria de San Antonio.

2

3

4

Comunicación oral

A **Características personales.** Make a list of characteristics you look for in a friend. Get together with up to four classmates and compile your lists. What three characteristics did most people want in a friend? The group secretary will report to the class.

B **En un café de Madrid.** You are seated at an outdoor café on the Gran Vía in Madrid, practicing the art of "people watching," when another tourist (your partner) sits next to you and starts a conversation. You introduce yourselves and say where each of you is from. You tell each other in what school you are a student and if it is fun or boring.

Comunicación escrita

A **Una carta.** You receive the following letter from a new pen pal. Following the example of your pen pal's letter, write him a reply.

B **¿Quién es?** On a piece of paper, write down five things about yourself. Your teacher will collect the descriptions and choose students to read the sentences to the class. Try to guess who is being described.

> Yo soy morena y alta. No
>   soy rubia.
> Yo soy divertida y sincera.
> ¿Quién soy yo?
> Eres ___.

¡Hola!

Soy Jorge Pérez Navarro. Soy de Madrid, la capital de España. Soy español. También soy alumno en el Colegio Sorolla. Es una escuela secundaria.

¿Cómo eres tú? Yo soy alto y rubio. También soy muy divertido. No soy muy serio. Y no soy tímido. ¡De ninguna manera!

Hasta pronto,

Jorge

Reintegración

■ **Un poco de cortesía.** Completen. (*Complete.*)

1. Una Coca-cola, ___.
2. Mucho ___, Elena.
3. ___, Roberto.
4. ¿ ___ tal?, María.
5. Muy bien, ___. ¿Y tú?

Vocabulario

SUSTANTIVOS

el muchacho
la muchacha
el amigo
la amiga
el alumno
la alumna
el colegio
la escuela

ADJETIVOS

alto(a)
bajo(a)
rubio(a)
moreno(a)
divertido(a)
aburrido(a)
simpático(a)
antipático(a)
fantástico(a)
atractivo(a)
sincero(a)
serio(a)
honesto(a)
tímido(a)
bueno(a)
malo(a)
secundario(a)
mexicano(a)
colombiano(a)
americano(a)

VERBOS

ser

OTRAS PALABRAS Y EXPRESIONES

también
bastante
¿verdad?
¿no es verdad?
de ninguna manera
quién
cómo
de dónde
de qué nacionalidad

CAPÍTULO

2

¿HERMANOS O
AMIGOS?

OBJETIVOS

In this chapter you will learn to do the following:

1. describe people and things
2. talk about more than one person or thing
3. tell what subjects you take in school and express some opinions about them
4. tell time
5. tell at what time an event takes place
6. learn some things about Puerto Rico

PALABRAS 1

¿CÓMO SON?

Juan y Paco
rubios

argentinos

Marta y Sarita
rubias

argentinas

los alumnos

las alumnas

los amigos

las amigas

los hermanos

las hermanas

Marta y Sarita son argentinas.
Juan y Paco también son argentinos.
Los cuatro amigos son de Buenos Aires.
Ellos son alumnos en un colegio.

la clase

una clase
pequeña

el profesor

una clase
grande

Nota: Once again, you will see how many Spanish words you already know because they are cognates. You should have no trouble guessing at the meaning of these words.

inteligente   amable
interesante   popular
la clase   el curso

Some cognates are not obvious. *Fácil*, for example, means "easy." Its English cognate is "facile," a word related to "facilitate." The opposite of *fácil* is *difícil*.

la profesora

La avenida 9 de julio, Buenos Aires, Argentina

Ejercicios

A **Unos amigos argentinos.** Contesten. (*Answer.*)

1. ¿Son hermanos o amigos Juan y Paco?
2. ¿Son hermanas o amigas Marta y Sarita?
3. ¿Son de Argentina o de Puerto Rico los cuatro amigos?
4. ¿Son argentinos o puertorriqueños?
5. ¿Son de Buenos Aires o de San Juan?
6. ¿Son ellos alumnos en un colegio o en una escuela secundaria?

B **La clase de español.** Preguntas personales. (*Give your own answers.*)

1. ¿Quién es el profesor o la profesora de español?
2. ¿De qué nacionalidad es él o ella?
3. ¿Es grande o pequeña la clase de español?
4. ¿Cómo es el curso de español? ¿Es interesante o aburrido?
5. El español, ¿es fácil o difícil?
6. ¿Son muy inteligentes los alumnos de español?
7. ¿Son ellos serios?
8. ¿Es la clase de español una clase fantástica?

C **Lo contrario.** Busquen la palabra contraria. (*Match the opposite.*)

1. fácil
2. moreno
3. aburrido
4. grande
5. la hermana
6. el alumno
7. amable
8. alto

a. pequeño
b. el profesor
c. difícil
d. antipático
e. bajo
f. rubio
g. el hermano
h. interesante

D **¿No? Entonces, ¿cómo son?** Contesten según el modelo.
(*Answer according to the model.*)

—Son muy amables, ¿no?
—No. De ninguna manera.
—Entonces, ¿cómo son?
—Pues, son antipáticos.

1. Son muy pequeños, ¿no?
2. Son muy aburridos, ¿no?
3. Son fáciles, ¿no?
4. Son divertidos, ¿no?
5. Son hermanos, ¿no?

VOCABULARIO

PALABRAS 2

LOS CURSOS ESCOLARES

¡Hola!
Nosotros somos americanos.
Uds. son americanos también, ¿no?
Somos alumnos. Somos alumnos de español.
Somos alumnos buenos en español.

Otros cursos, otras materias o disciplinas
Las ciencias

la biología

la química

$$E = MC^2$$

la física

Las matemáticas

$$2 + 2 = 4$$

la aritmética

$$2x + 3 = 9$$

el álgebra

la geometría

$$\sin \theta = \frac{\pi}{2}$$

la trigonometría

Las lenguas

el inglés

el francés

el español

el italiano

Salve!

el latín

Las ciencias sociales

la historia

la geografía

la sociología

Otras asignaturas

la educación cívica

la educación física
los deportes

la música

el arte

la economía doméstica

Ejercicios

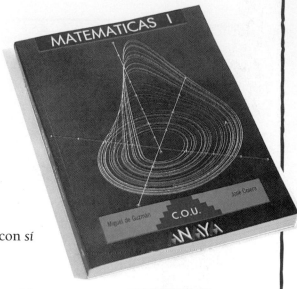

A Alumnos americanos. Contesten. (*Answer.*)

1. ¿Son americanos los alumnos?
2. ¿Son alumnos en una escuela secundaria?
3. ¿Son alumnos de español?
4. ¿Son alumnos buenos o malos en español?
5. ¿Es fácil o difícil el curso de español?
6. ¿Es grande o pequeña la clase de español?

B ¿Ciencias, lenguas o matemáticas? Contesten con *sí* o *no*. (*Answer yes or no.*)

1. La biología es una ciencia.
2. La geometría y la trigonometría son partes de las matemáticas.
3. La química es una lengua.
4. El francés y el español son ciencias.
5. El arte y la música son cursos obligatorios.

C Cursos fáciles y cursos difíciles. Preguntas personales. (*Give your own answers.*)

1. ¿Es grande o pequeña la clase de español?
2. ¿Es el español un curso difícil o fácil?
3. ¿Qué es el español, una lengua o una ciencia?
4. ¿Qué cursos son fáciles?
5. ¿Y qué cursos son difíciles?
6. ¿Cómo es la historia, interesante o aburrida?

D ¿Qué curso o asignatura es? Identifiquen. (*Identify the course.*)

1. el problema, la ecuación, la solución, la multiplicación, la división
2. la literatura, la composición, la gramática
3. un microbio, un animal, una planta, el microscopio, el laboratorio
4. el círculo, el arco, el rectángulo, el triángulo
5. el piano, el violín, la guitarra, el concierto, la ópera
6. las montañas, los océanos, las capitales, los productos
7. la pintura, la estatua, la escultura
8. el gobierno, la nación, la comunidad, el municipio, el Congreso, el Senado, el partido político
9. el fútbol, el básquetbol, el béisbol, el vólibol, la gimnasia

Comunicación

Palabras 1 y 2

A **Las asignaturas.** Using the list of suggestions below, ask your partner if the subjects are as described. Your partner may agree, or disagree and describe them differently. Reverse roles.

> **sociología / interesante**
> **Estudiante 1: ¿Es interesante la sociología?**
> **Estudiante 2: Sí, es interesante. (No, no es interesante. No.**
> **De ninguna manera. Es aburrida.)**

1. la gimnasia / divertida
2. la historia / difícil
3. la música / interesante
4. la educación física / opcional
5. la biología / fácil
6. la geometría / aburrida

B **Los profesores.** You and your partner make separate lists in Spanish of your daily classes. Add to your list of classes the names of your teachers. Swap lists. Then, taking turns, ask what your respective classes and teachers are like and give your opinions.

> **Estudiante 1: ¿Cómo es la clase de historia?**
> **Estudiante 2: Es muy interesante.**
> **Estudiante 1: ¿Cómo es el/la profesor(a)?**
> **Estudiante 2: Es amable y divertido(a).**

C **¡Qué clase tan difícil!** Divide into groups of three or four. In each group rate the courses you take as *fácil, difícil, regular*. After the ratings are tallied, report your results to the class.

D **En España.** You are spending the summer with a Spanish family in Córdoba. Your Spanish "brother" asks about your Spanish teacher. Describe your Spanish teacher to him.

ESPAÑA

• Córdoba

La Gran Mezquita de Córdoba, España

ESTRUCTURA

Los sustantivos, artículos y adjetivos
Formas plurales

Describing More than One Person or Thing

1. Plural means more than one. In Spanish, the plural of most nouns is formed by adding *s* to the noun.

SINGULAR	PLURAL
el muchacho	los muchachos
el colegio	los colegios
la amiga	las amigas
la escuela	las escuelas

2. The plural forms of the definite articles *el, la* are *los, las.* The plural forms of the indefinite articles *un, una* are *unos, unas.*

SINGULAR	PLURAL
el hermano	los hermanos
la alumna	las alumnas
un amigo	unos amigos
una alumna	unas alumnas

3. To form the plural of adjectives that end in *o, a,* or *e,* you add *s* to the singular form.

> El alumno es serio.
> Los alumnos son serios.
>
> La alumna es seria.
> Las alumnas son serias.
>
> La lengua es interesante.
> Las lenguas son interesantes.

4. To form the plural of adjectives that end in a consonant, you add *es.*

> El curso es fácil.
> Los cursos son fáciles.
>
> La lengua es fácil.
> Las lenguas son fáciles.

Ejercicios

A Los dos muchachos. Contesten. (*Answer.*)

1. ¿Son nuevos amigos los dos muchachos?
2. ¿Son ellos alumnos serios?
3. ¿Son inteligentes?
4. ¿Son alumnos buenos o malos en español?
5. ¿Son muchachos populares?

B ¿Cómo son? Describan a las personas. (*Describe the people.*)

1.

2.

3.

4.

C La clase de la señora Ortiz. Completen. (*Complete.*)

1. La señora Ortiz es una profesora muy ___. (bueno)
2. Las clases de la señora Ortiz son ___ y ___. (interesante, divertido)
3. Los alumnos son muy ___ con la señora Ortiz. (amable)
4. La señora Ortiz es muy ___ y muy ___. (simpático, inteligente)
5. Las clases de la señora Ortiz no son ___. Son ___. (pequeño, grande)

El presente del verbo *ser*
Formas plurales

Talking about More than One Person or Thing

1. You have already learned the singular forms of the irregular verb *ser* "to be." Review them.

SER	
yo	soy
tú	eres
él	es
ella	es

2. Now study the plural forms of the verb *ser*.

SER	
nosotros(as)	somos
ellos	son
ellas	son
Uds.	son

3. You use *nosotros(as)* ("we") when you speak about yourself and other people.

Nosotros somos rubios.

4. You use *ellas* when referring to two or more females.

Ellas son simpáticas.

5. You use *ellos* when referring to two or more males, or when referring to a group of males and females.

Ellos son americanos.

6. When speaking to more than one person, you use *ustedes*, usually abbreviated as *Uds*.

¿Ustedes son amigos?

No, nosotros somos hermanos.

Ejercicios

A Son amigos. Contesten según se indica. (*Answer according to the cues.*)

1. ¿Son hermanos o amigos Jorge y José? (amigos)
2. ¿Son alumnos? (sí)
3. ¿Dónde son alumnos ellos? (en el Colegio Alfonso el Sabio)
4. ¿Son amigos de Laura y Teresa? (sí)
5. ¿Cómo son ellas? (divertidas)
6. ¿Son alumnas en la misma escuela? (no)
7. ¿Dónde son ellas alumnas? (en la Academia de Santa María del Pilar)

B ¿Qué son Uds.? Practiquen la conversación. (*Practice the conversation.*)

LAS MUCHACHAS: ¿Son Uds. americanos?
LOS MUCHACHOS: Sí, somos americanos.
LAS MUCHACHAS: ¿Son Uds. alumnos?
LOS MUCHACHOS: Sí, somos alumnos. Y somos alumnos serios.
LAS MUCHACHAS: ¿En qué escuela son Uds. alumnos?
LOS MUCHACHOS: Somos alumnos en la Escuela George Washington.

Completen según la conversación. (*Complete according to the conversation.*)

1. Los muchachos ___ americanos.
2. Ellos ___ alumnos.
3. ___ alumnos muy serios.
4. ___ alumnos buenos.
5. ___ alumnos en la Escuela George Washington.
6. ¿___ americanas las muchachas?
7. ¿En qué escuela ___ alumnas las muchachas?
8. ¿Las muchachas ___ alumnas serias también?

C Él, ella y yo. Contesten. (*With a classmate, answer the following questions.*)

1. ¿Son Uds. hermanos(as) o amigos(as)?
2. ¿Son Uds. alumnos(as) serios(as)?
3. ¿En qué escuela son Uds. alumnos(as)?
4. ¿Son Uds. alumnos(as) en la misma clase de español o en clases diferentes?
5. ¿Son alumnos(as) buenos(as) en español?
6. ¿De qué nacionalidad son Uds.?

D ¿Y Uds.? Formen preguntas. (*Ask your classmates questions as in the model.*)

   americanos o cubanos
     —María y José, ¿son Uds. americanos o cubanos?
     —Somos cubanos.

1. americanos o mexicanos
2. bajos o altos
3. hermanos o amigos
4. morenos o rubios
5. divertidos o aburridos

E **El amigo de Carlos.** Completen con *ser.* (*Complete with* ser.)

Yo ___ un amigo de Carlos. Carlos ___ muy simpático. Y él ___ muy
     1   2   3
divertido. Carlos y yo ___ dominicanos. Nosotros ___ de la República
                        4   5
Dominicana.

   La República Dominicana ___ parte de una isla en el mar Caribe.
                            6
Nosotros ___ alumnos en un liceo en Santo Domingo, la capital. ___ alumnos
          7   8
de inglés. La profesora de inglés ___ la señora Robbins. Ella ___ americana.
                                   9   10
La clase de inglés ___ bastante interesante. Nosotros ___ muy buenos en
                   11   12
inglés pero la verdad es que (nosotros) ___ muy inteligentes, ¿no? ¿Y Uds.?
                                         13
Uds. ___ americanos, ¿no? ¿Uds. ___ de dónde? ¿ ___ Uds. alumnos en una
     14   15   16
escuela secundaria? ¿ ___ Uds. alumnos de español?
                      17

La hora   *Telling Time*

---

1. Observe the following examples of how to tell time.

   ¿Qué hora es?

Es la una.

Son las dos.

Son las diez.

Son las doce.
Es el mediodía.
Es la medianoche.

**Es la una
y cinco.**

**Son las dos
y diez.**

**Son las cuatro y
veinte y cinco.**

**Son las doce
y cuarto.**

**Son las cinco
menos cinco.**

**Son las seis
menos diez.**

**Son las diez
menos veinte.**

2. To indicate A.M. and P.M. in Spanish, you use the following expressions.

> Son las ocho de la mañana.
> Son las tres de la tarde.
> Son las once de la noche.

3. Note how to ask and tell what time something (such as a party) takes place.

> ¿A qué hora es la fiesta?
> La fiesta es a las nueve.

4. Note how to give the duration of an event (to indicate from when until when).

> La clase de español es *de* las diez *a* las once menos cuarto.

Ejercicios

A **El horario escolar.** Look at the following schedule and give the time of each class.

B **La hora.** Give the time on each clock.

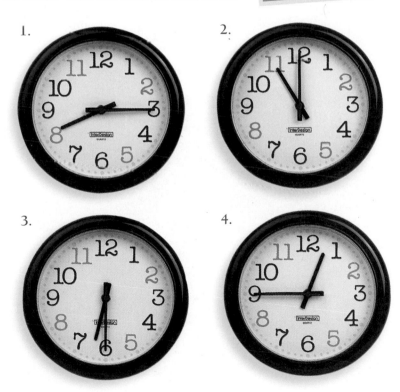

HORARIO ESCOLAR

Nombre: Luisa Morales Pérez   Año: 19—

Horas	Lunes	Martes	Miércoles	Jueves	Vierne
7-8	Español				
8-9	Inglés				
9-10	Educación Físca				
10-11	Música				
11-12	////	////	////	////	//
12-1	Biología				
1-2	Química				
2-3	Trigonometría				

1.

2.

3.

4.

CONVERSACIÓN

Escenas de la vida ¿De qué nacionalidad son Uds.?

SAMUEL: ¿Uds. son americanos?
MARK: Sí, somos americanos. Y Uds. son mexicanos, ¿no?

DANIEL: Sí, somos de Coyoacán.
SARA: ¿Coyoacán?

DANIEL: Sí, es un suburbio de la Ciudad de México. Y Uds., ¿de dónde son?
SARA: Somos de Arlington, un suburbio de Washington.

¿De dónde son? Contesten.
(*Answer.*)

1. ¿De dónde son los mexicanos?
2. ¿Y de dónde son los americanos?
3. ¿Son Coyoacán y Arlington suburbios o ciudades grandes?
4. ¿Cuál es la capital de México?
5. ¿Cuál es la capital de los Estados Unidos?
6. ¿Cuál es un suburbio de la Ciudad de México?
7. ¿Cuál es un suburbio de Wáshington?

Coyoacán, MEXICO

Pronunciación   *Las vocales* e *e* i

The sounds of the Spanish vowels **e** and **i** are short, clear, and concise. The pronunciation of **e** is similar to the **a** in *mate* and the pronunciation of **i** is similar to the **ee** in *bee* or *see*. Imitate the pronunciation carefully.

e	i
Elena	Isabel
peso	Inés

Repeat the following sentences.

> **Elena es amiga de Felipe.**
> **Inés es tímida.**
> **Sí, Isabel es italiana.**

tímido

Comunicación

A **En Antigua.** Work in groups of four. Two of you are visiting Central America. In the lovely little city of Antigua, Guatemala, you strike up a friendship with two other students. Get the following information from them.

1. their nationality
2. where they are from
3. if they are high school or junior high school students
4. what the students are like in their school
5. what their teachers are like
6. if their classes are easy or difficult

B **¿A qué hora es la clase?** Write down your school schedule showing when each of your classes begins. Swap schedules with your partner. Then take turns asking each other when each of your classes is. Decide who has the best schedule.

> **matemáticas 8:00**
> **Estudiante 1: ¿A qué hora es la clase de matemáticas?**
> **Estudiante 2: Es a las ocho.**

SOMOS DE PUERTO RICO

¿Quiénes somos? Pues, somos Ángel y Suso. Nosotros no somos hermanos pero somos muy buenos amigos. Somos puertorriqueños. Somos de San Juan, la capital de Puerto Rico. Puerto Rico es una isla tropical en el mar Caribe. Puerto Rico es una parte de los Estados Unidos. Es un estado libre asociado[1]. Así que nosotros somos ciudadanos[2] americanos como Uds.

Las escuelas en Puerto Rico son como[3] las escuelas en los Estados Unidos. Somos alumnos en una escuela secundaria, la Escuela Asenjo. La Escuela

Asenjo es una escuela pública. Nosotros somos alumnos de inglés. Y somos alumnos de español. Pero para nosotros el español no es una lengua extranjera[4]. Para nosotros el inglés es una segunda[5] lengua.

[1] estado libre asociado   *commonwealth*
[2] ciudadanos   *citizens*
[3] como   *like*
[4] extranjera   *foreign*
[5] segunda   *second*

Estudio de palabras

A **Palabras afines.** Busquen cinco palabras afines. (*Find five cognates in the reading.*)

B **¿Cuál es la palabra?** Den la palabra correcta. (*Give the word being defined.*)

1. de Puerto Rico
2. de los trópicos
3. la ciudad principal de una nación o de un país
4. una institución educativa
5. de otro país o nación
6. lo contrario de privado

El área del Condado, San Juan, Puerto Rico

Comprensión

A **Ángel y Suso.** Contesten según la lectura. (*Answer according to the reading.*)

1. ¿Quiénes son Ángel y Suso?
2. ¿De dónde son ellos?
3. ¿Cuál es la capital de Puerto Rico?
4. ¿Es Puerto Rico una península?
5. ¿Qué es Puerto Rico?
6. ¿Puerto Rico es parte de qué país o nación?
7. ¿Qué son los puertorriqueños?
8. ¿Cómo son las escuelas en Puerto Rico?
9. ¿Dónde son alumnos Ángel y Suso?
10. Para ellos, ¿cuál es una lengua extranjera?

B **La geografía.** ¿Sí o no? (*Yes or no?*)

1. Puerto Rico es una península.
2. Puerto Rico es una parte de España.
3. Puerto Rico es un país independiente.
4. La lengua de los puertorriqueños es el español.
5. Los puertorriqueños son ciudadanos de España.

Una calle en el viejo San Juan, Puerto Rico

DESCUBRIMIENTO CULTURAL

*L*a hora no es la misma en todas partes. La hora en una ciudad es diferente de la hora en otra ciudad. Es el mediodía en Nueva York. Es la una de la tarde en San Juan y son las seis de la tarde en Madrid. La diferencia entre la hora de Nueva York y la hora de Madrid es de seis horas. Es el huso horario.

En Latinoamérica muchas escuelas son privadas. La mayoría de los muchachos de las familias de la clase media y de la clase alta son alumnos en escuelas privadas. Muchas escuelas privadas en los países latinoamericanos son religiosas —católicas o protestantes. Hay escuelas coeducacionales o mixtas, para muchachos y muchachas; pero muchas escuelas son solamente para muchachos o solamente para muchachas.

La situación es diferente en Puerto Rico. Hay escuelas privadas en Puerto Rico pero hay también muchas escuelas públicas. Las escuelas públicas en Puerto Rico son como las escuelas públicas de los Estados Unidos.

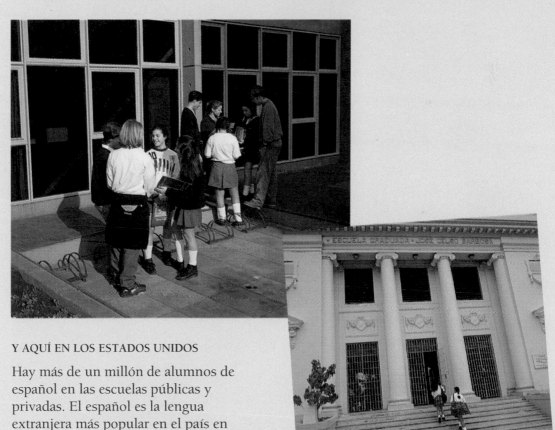

Y AQUÍ EN LOS ESTADOS UNIDOS

Hay más de un millón de alumnos de español en las escuelas públicas y privadas. El español es la lengua extranjera más popular en el país en las escuelas y en las universidades.

REALIDADES

Es una escuela intermedia en Puerto Rico **1**. Es una escuela pública.

Es una escuela privada en la Argentina **2**. Todas las alumnas de la escuela son muchachas. Los uniformes son obligatorios.

Es **3** el Instituto Tecnológico de Monterrey. Los cursos son profesionales.

Es la Universidad de Puerto Rico **4**.

Comunicación oral

A **Es tarde.** Ask your partner if the following classes are at the times listed. Unfortunately, your times are always thirty minutes late! Your partner will give you the correct class time by adding on thirty minutes.

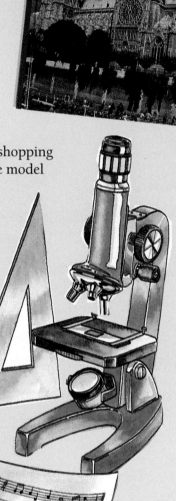

> física/8:45
> Estudiante 1: ¿Es la clase de física a las nueve menos cuarto?
> Estudiante 2: No. Es a las nueve y cuarto.

1. arte/2:00
2. historia/1:10
3. francés/9:30
4. música/10:45
5. geometría/12:20
6. inglés/8:00
7. biología/11:10
8. español/9:55

B **Son chilenos.** You and your partner see a new classmate at the shopping mall with a boy or a girl. Make up a conversation about them using the model below as a guide.

> dos muchachos/Cuba
> Estudiante 1: ¿Son hermanos los dos muchachos?
> Estudiante 2: No. Son amigos. Y no son americanos.
> Estudiante 1: ¿No? ¿De dónde son?
> Estudiante 2: De Cuba.

1. dos muchachos/Colombia
2. un muchacho y una muchacha/Puerto Rico
3. dos muchachos/México
4. dos muchachas/Chile

Comunicación escrita

A **Una carta de un amigo.** In a letter, your friend asks you about your classes and teachers this year. Write the answers to your friend's questions.

1. ¿A qué hora es la clase de inglés?
   ¿Quién es el/la profesor(a)?
   ¿Cómo es?
2. ¿Cuántos alumnos hay en la clase de español?
   ¿Cómo es el/la profesor(a)? ¿Es serio(a) o divertido(a)?
   ¿A qué hora es la clase?
3. ¿Es obligatoria la clase de ciencia?
   ¿Cómo es la clase?
   ¿Quién es el/la profesor(a)?

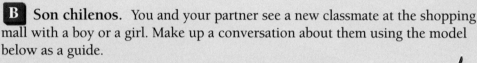

B **Otra carta.** Using the information from Actividad A, write a paragraph about your classes, teachers, and schedule that you could include in your letter of response to your friend.

Reintegración

El amigo. Cambien a la forma singular. (*Change to the singular.*)

1. Los amigos son americanos.
2. Ellos son de Nueva York.
3. Y las muchachas son de Santo Domingo.
4. Ellas son dominicanas.
5. Nosotros somos de Montevideo.
6. Somos alumnos en el Colegio Latinoamericano en Cartagena.

Vocabulario

SUSTANTIVOS
el hermano
la hermana
la clase
el profesor
la profesora
el curso
la materia
la disciplina
las ciencias
la biología
la química
la física
las matemáticas
la aritmética
el álgebra
la geometría
la trigonometría
las lenguas
el inglés
el español
el francés
el italiano
el latín
las ciencias sociales
la historia
la geografía

la sociología
la educación cívica
la educación física
el deporte
el arte
la música
la economía doméstica

ADJETIVOS
pequeño(a)
grande
inteligente
interesante
fácil
difícil
amable
popular
otro(a)
argentino(a)
puertorriqueño(a)

OTRAS PALABRAS
Y EXPRESIONES
¿Qué hora es?
¿A qué hora?
el mediodía
la medianoche

Cartagena, Colombia

3

EN LA ESCUELA

OBJETIVOS

In this chapter you will learn to do the following:

1. talk about going to school
2. talk about some school activities
3. ask for information
4. speak to people formally and informally
5. learn some differences between schools in the United States and Spanish-speaking countries

PALABRAS I

LA ESCUELA

llegar a la escuela

la profesora   el profesor

llegar en el bus escolar
llegar en autobús

una mochila

en carro
en coche

llevar los libros
en una mochila

a pie

entrar en la sala de clase

la sala de clase
el salón de clase

hablar con el profesor

¿A qué hora o cuándo llega Juan a la escuela?
Juan llega a la escuela a las ocho.
¿A las ocho en punto?
No, él llega a eso de las ocho.
¿Cómo llega Juan a la escuela?
Él llega en el bus escolar.

Ejercicios

A **¡A la escuela!** Contesten. (*Answer.*)

1. ¿Llega Juan a la escuela a las ocho?
2. ¿Llega a pie o en el bus escolar?
3. ¿Lleva los libros en una mochila?

4. ¿Entra Juan en la sala de clase?
5. ¿Habla con el profesor?
6. ¿Habla español o inglés con el profesor?

B **¡A la clase de español!** Contesten según se indica. (*Answer according to the cues.*)

1. ¿Cómo llega Teresa a la escuela? (a pie)
2. ¿Cuándo llega? (a eso de las ocho)
3. ¿En qué lleva los libros? (en una mochila)
4. ¿Lleva uniforme a la escuela? (no)
5. ¿En dónde entra Teresa? (en la sala de clase)
6. ¿Qué clase? (la clase de español)
7. ¿Cómo es la clase de español? (interesante)
8. ¿A qué hora es la clase? (a las ocho y media)
9. ¿Quién es la profesora de español? (la señora García)
10. ¿Cómo es ella? (simpática)
11. ¿Cuántas lenguas habla? (dos)
12. ¿Qué habla Teresa con la señora García? (español)

PALABRAS 2

EN LA SALA DE CLASE

el libro

el cuaderno
el bloc
la libreta

el examen

el pizarrón   la pizarra

una nota buena   una nota mala
una nota alta   una nota baja

El alumno estudia la lección.

Mira el libro.

Mira la pizarra.

La alumna toma apuntes en el cuaderno.

Ella toma un examen.

Saca una nota buena.

La profesora enseña. Ella enseña bien.

Ejercicios

A **Paco estudia mucho.** Contesten. (*Answer.*)

1. ¿Estudia mucho Paco?
2. ¿Toma cinco cursos?
3. ¿Estudia español?
4. ¿Toma apuntes Paco en la clase de español?
5. ¿Toma un examen?
6. ¿Es difícil o fácil el examen?
7. ¿Saca Paco una nota buena o mala en el examen?

B **Palabras interrogativas.** Escojan la respuesta correcta. (*Choose the correct response.*)

1. ¿Cómo llega Roberto a la escuela?
   a. a pie   **b.** a las ocho
2. ¿Cuándo llega a la escuela?
   a. en el bus escolar   **b.** a eso de las ocho
3. ¿Cómo es la clase de español?
   a. interesante   **b.** a las ocho y media
4. ¿Quién enseña?
   a. español   **b.** el profesor
5. ¿Qué enseña?
   a. español   **b.** el profesor
6. ¿Cuántos cursos toma Roberto?
   a. a las ocho   **b.** cinco

Una escuela privada en Buenos Aires, Argentina

C **¿Qué? ¿Quién? ¿Cuándo? ¿Dónde? ¿Cuántos? ¿Cómo?** Formen preguntas. (*Make up questions.*)

> <u>Rosita</u> estudia francés en la Escuela Horace Mann.
> <u>¿Quién</u> estudia francés en la Escuela Horace Mann?

1. <u>Rosita</u> estudia español en la Escuela Horace Mann.
2. Rosita estudia <u>español</u> en la Escuela Horace Mann.
3. Rosita estudia español <u>en la Escuela Horace Mann</u>.
4. Rosita llega a la escuela <u>a eso de las ocho</u>.
5. Ella toma <u>cinco</u> cursos.
6. La clase de español es <u>muy interesante</u>.

D **Es lo mismo.** Busquen la palabra que significa lo mismo. (*Find the word that means the same.*)

1. en coche
2. el cuaderno
3. la nota buena
4. la pizarra
5. la nota
6. a eso de

a. la nota alta
b. la calificación
c. en carro
d. aproximadamente
e. la libreta, el bloc
f. el pizarrón

Comunicación

Palabras 1 y 2

A **¿Quién enseña…?** Prepare a school schedule by asking a classmate the number of courses he or she takes, the time of each course, and the teacher.

B **Mi horario.** Based on the schedule done above, ask a classmate if he or she gets good or bad grades, which courses are easy, and which ones are hard. After you interview your classmate have him or her ask you about your schedule.

C **La clase de inglés.** You are thinking about transferring into some of your friend's classes, but first you want to get your facts straight. Find out from your partner who the English teacher is and if the teacher teaches well. Your partner will tell you who the teacher is and how the class really is. Follow the model. Then continue the conversation using other subjects, like math, science, or history.

> Estudiante 1: ¿Quién es tu profesor(a) de inglés?
> Estudiante 2: Es el señor Burton.
> Estudiante 1: ¿Enseña bien?
> Estudiante 2: Sí. La clase es fantástica. (No, de ninguna manera.
>   La clase es bastante aburrida.)

ESTRUCTURA

El presente de los verbos en -ar
Formas singulares

Describing People's Activities

1. A verb is a word that expresses an action or a state of being. Words such as *llevar, llegar, entrar,* and *hablar* are verbs. In Spanish all verbs belong to a family or conjugation. Verbs that end in *-ar* are called first conjugation verbs because the infinitive form (*hablar,* "to speak") ends in *-ar.* The infinitive is the basic form of the verb that you find in the dictionary. These are called regular verbs because they follow the same pattern and have the same endings.

>   llegar   entrar   estudiar
>   tomar   hablar   mirar

2. To form the present tense, you drop the *-ar* of the infinitive to form the stem.

>   hablar   habl-
>   entrar   entr-

3. To this stem you add the appropriate endings for each person. Study the following chart.

INFINITIVE	HABLAR	ENTRAR	ENDINGS
STEM	habl-	entr-	
yo	hablo	entro	-o
tú	hablas	entras	-as
él	habla	entra	-a
ella	habla	entra	-a

4. Since the verb ending shows who is performing the action, the subject pronoun is often omitted.

>   (Yo) Hablo inglés.
>   (Tú) Estudias español.

5. To make a sentence negative, you put *no* in front of the verb.

>   No hablo francés. Hablo español.

Ejercicios

A ¿Estudias español? Practiquen la conversación. (*Practice the conversation.*)

ANDRÉS: Oye, Enrique. Tú hablas español, ¿no?
ENRIQUE: Sí, amigo, hablo español.
ANDRÉS: Pero tú no eres español, ¿verdad?
ENRIQUE: No, hombre. Pero estudio español en la escuela.
ANDRÉS: Hablas muy bien.
ENRIQUE: Pues, gracias. Tomo un curso de español con la señora Ortiz.

Contesten según la conversación. (*Answer according to the conversation.*)

1. ¿Habla español Enrique?
2. ¿Cómo habla español?
3. ¿Es español?
4. ¿Estudia español?
5. ¿Dónde estudia español?
6. ¿Con quién toma un curso de español?
7. ¿Quién es la profesora de español?
8. ¿Qué opinas? ¿Enseña bien la señora Ortiz o no?

B Entrevista. Preguntas personales. (*Give your own answers.*)

1. ¿A qué hora llegas a la escuela?
2. ¿Qué estudias en la escuela?
3. ¿Tomas un curso de español?
4. ¿Hablas con la profesora cuando entras en la sala de clase?
5. ¿Hablas español o inglés en la clase de español?
6. ¿Hablas bien?
7. ¿Estudias mucho?
8. ¿Qué nota sacas en español?

C ¿Sí o no? Sigan el modelo. (*Follow the model.*)

biología
Sí, yo tomo un curso de biología. Estudio biología con (el profesor).
    Saco una nota ___ en biología.
(No, no tomo un curso de biología. No estudio biología.)

1. geometría   4. ciencias
2. historia   5. español
3. inglés

D **¡Hola, Rosita! ¿Hablas inglés?** Rosita Martínez is from Buenos Aires. Find out the following about her. Use *tú* in your questions.

1. if she speaks English
2. if she takes a course in English
3. if she studies a lot
4. if she gets a good grade in English
5. in what school she studies English

E **Yo estudio español.** Completen. *(Complete.)*

¡Hola! Yo ___ (ser) Roberto. Yo ___ (ser) alumno en la Escuela ___ en ___ .
     1   2

En la escuela yo ___ (tomar) un curso de español. Yo ___ (estudiar) español
            3   4

con la señora Ortiz. Ella ___ (ser) muy simpática y ___ (enseñar) muy bien.
                      5   6

Yo ___ (hablar) mucho con la señora Ortiz. Yo ___ (ser) un alumno bastante
   7   8

serio y ___ (sacar) una nota buena en español.
       9

   Tú también ___ (ser) alumno(a), ¿no? ¿En qué escuela (estudiar) ___?
              10   11

¿(Tomar) ___ (tú) un curso de español como yo? ¿Qué nota ___ (sacar) en
         12   13

español?

Tú y usted

Talking to People Formally or Informally

1. In Spanish there are two ways to say "you." You use *tú* when talking to a friend, a person your own age, or to a family member. *Tú* is called the informal or familiar form of address.

José, ¿estudias español?

Catalina, ¿a qué hora llegas a la escuela?

Roberto, hablas español muy bien.

2. You use *usted* when talking to an older person, a person you do not know well or anyone to whom you wish to show respect. The *usted* form is polite or formal. *Usted* is usually abbreviated to *Ud. Ud.* takes the same verb ending as *él* or *ella*.

Señor, ¿habla Ud. inglés?

Señora, Ud. enseña español, ¿no?

3. The *Ud.* form of the irregular verb *ser* that you learned in Chapter 2 is *es*.

Señorita, Ud. es muy amable.

Ejercicios

A **Señor, señora o señorita.** Pregúntenle al profesor o la profesora. (*Ask your Spanish teacher.*)

1. if he or she speaks French
2. if he or she teaches history
3. at what time he or she gets to school

B **¿Tú o Ud.?** Formen preguntas. (*Look at each picture. Ask each person his or her nationality, and if he or she speaks English and studies French. Use* tú *or* Ud. *as appropriate.*)

1.

2.

4.

3.

CONVERSACIÓN

Escenas de la vida *¡Qué bien hablas!*

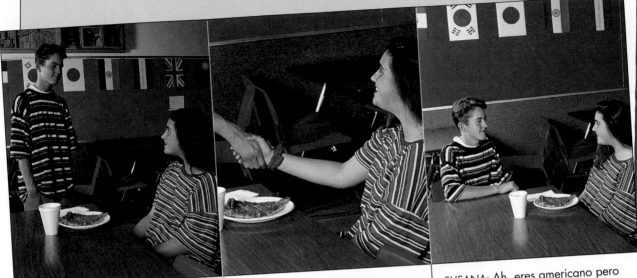

ROBERTO: ¡Hola!
SUSANA: ¡Hola! ¿Quién eres?
ROBERTO: Yo soy Roberto, Roberto Davidson.
SUSANA: Y yo soy Susana del Río.

ROBERTO: Mucho gusto, Susana.
SUSANA: ¿De dónde eres, Roberto?
ROBERTO: Soy de Miami.

SUSANA: Ah, eres americano pero hablas muy bien el español.
ROBERTO: Pues, no hablo muy bien. Sólo hablo un poco. Estudio español en la escuela.
SUSANA: No, no. La verdad es que hablas muy bien, Roberto.
ROBERTO: Gracias, Susana. Eres muy amable.

A **¡Qué bien hablas!** Contesten. (*Answer.*)

1. ¿Con quién habla Roberto?
2. ¿De qué nacionalidad es él?
3. ¿Habla Roberto español?
4. ¿Cómo habla Roberto español?
5. ¿Y qué opinas? ¿Es americana Susana?
6. ¿Habla ella español?

B **Usted habla español.** The language Roberto and Susana used in their conversation was rather familiar. Repeat the conversation in a more formal style using *Ud.* rather than *tú.*

Pronunciación   *Las consonantes* l, f, p, m, y n

The pronunciation of the consonants l, f, p, m, and n is quite similar in both Spanish and English. However, the p is not followed by a puff of breath as it often is in English. When you make the p sound in Spanish you round your lips.

la	le	li	lo	lu

La sala de Lolita es elegante.

ma	me	mi	mo	mu

El amigo de Manolo toma un momento.

na	ne	ni	no	nu

Ana no es una alumna nueva.

fa	fe	fi	fo	fu

Felipe es profesor de física.

pa	pe	pi	po	pu

Pepe pasa por la puerta.

Repeat the following sentences.

Elena es la amiga de Lupita.
La sala es elegante.
El profesor de física es famoso.
El papá de Pepe no fuma una pipa.

La mesa es un monumento.

Comunicación

A **¿Qué clase toma?** Using just two words as your cue, make up a story about each person. Use this model as your guide.

Roberto/historia

Roberto toma un curso de historia. En la clase de historia Roberto habla inglés con el profesor. No habla español. Roberto es un alumno serio y estudia mucho. Él saca una nota buena en historia.

1. María/matemáticas
2. Yo/español
3. Tú/biología
4. Yo/inglés

B **El día escolar.** Exchange class schedules with a classmate. Ask each other questions about your courses and the school day. Find out when each of you arrives at school; the times for different courses; the teachers who teach the courses; and whether the courses are difficult or easy, interesting, or boring.

DOS ESCUELAS DE LAS AMÉRICAS

Daniel es un muchacho americano. Él estudia en una escuela secundaria en Chicago. Es una escuela pública. En la escuela Daniel toma un curso de español. La profesora de español es la señora Ortiz. Ella enseña muy bien y Daniel habla mucho en la clase de español. Él siempre[1] practica el español con otro alumno de la escuela, José Luis Delgado. José Luis es de Puerto Rico. José Luis y Daniel son buenos amigos. Daniel saca notas buenas en español. Pero la verdad es que él es un alumno serio. Estudia mucho. Toma cinco cursos: inglés, español, historia, biología y álgebra.

Maricarmen es una muchacha ecuatoriana. Ella estudia en un colegio en Quito, la capital. El colegio de Maricarmen no es una escuela pública. Es una escuela privada. Es solamente para muchachas y las muchachas siempre llevan uniforme a la escuela. Maricarmen, como Daniel, es una alumna seria y estudia mucho. Pero ella no toma cinco cursos. ¿Cuántos cursos toma? Toma nueve. ¿Cómo es posible tomar nueve cursos en un año[2] o en un semestre?

Una escuela secundaria en los Estados Unidos

Pues, en la escuela de Maricarmen, no todos los cursos son diarios[3]. Por eso[4] Maricarmen toma nueve cursos en un semestre.

[1] siempre *always*
[2] año *year*
[3] diarios *daily*
[4] por eso *therefore*

Estudio de palabras

A **Palabras afines.** Busquen diez palabras afines. (*Find ten cognates in the reading.*)

B **¿Cuál es la palabra?** Busquen la palabra. (*Find the word being defined.*)

1. la asignatura, la materia, la disciplina
2. la persona que enseña
3. no privado, lo contrario de privado
4. un alumno que estudia mucho
5. del Ecuador
6. medio año escolar, división del año escolar

Comprensión

A **¿Quién? ¿El americano o la ecuatoriana?** Identifiquen a la persona. (*Identify the person.*)

1. Estudia en una escuela pública.
2. Estudia en una escuela privada.
3. No estudia en una escuela mixta.
4. Estudia en una escuela que es exclusivamente para muchachas.
5. Es de Quito.
6. Es de Chicago.
7. Las clases son diarias.
8. Estudia en la capital.
9. Lleva uniforme a la escuela.
10. Toma nueve cursos en un semestre.
11. Toma cinco cursos en un semestre.

B **La idea principal.** Escojan la idea principal de la lectura. (*Select the main idea of the story.*)

a. Daniel es un muchacho.
b. El alumno latinoamericano toma más cursos en un semestre que el alumno norteamericano.
c. La muchacha ecuatoriana estudia también.

La Plaza Mayor, Quito, Ecuador

DESCUBRIMIENTO CULTURAL

Valparaíso, Chile

*E*l alumno norteamericano saca notas y el alumno latinoamericano saca notas. En los Estados Unidos, la nota es a veces un número, 90, y a veces es una letra, B. Pues, es igual en el mundo hispano.

En el colegio de Carlos en Valparaíso, Chile, Carlos saca "siete" en el curso de inglés. ¿Qué opinas? ¿Es una nota buena o mala? Pues, en la escuela de Carlos es una nota muy buena. Dos es una nota mala. Y en la escuela de Maripaz, una alumna argentina en Buenos Aires, diez es la nota más alta y cuatro es una nota mala, muy baja. Varía de país en país.

A veces, y sobre todo en España, la nota no es un número. No es una letra. Es una palabra—un comentario.

Sobresaliente
Bueno, Notable
Aprobado, Regular
Suspenso, Desaprobado, Cate, Insuficiente

¿Qué opinas? ¿Sobresaliente es A o F? ¿Suspenso es A o F?

Y AQUÍ EN LOS ESTADOS UNIDOS

En las grandes ciudades de los Estados Unidos algunas escuelas llevan el nombre de importantes figuras hispanas. Hostos Community College es una institución de Nueva York. Eugenio María de Hostos es una figura muy importante en la historia de la educación en Puerto Rico. En Chicago hay escuelas que llevan nombres de Benito Juárez, José Martí, Luis Muñoz Marín, Roberto Clemente, Lázaro Cárdenas, José de Diego, Francisco Madero, José Clemente Orozco, el Padre Miguel Hidalgo y Costilla, y Pablo Casals. ¿Quiénes son estas grandes figuras?

Roberto Clemente (Puerto Rico)

Benito Juárez (México)

Pablo Casals (España)

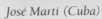

José Martí (Cuba)

R E A L I D A D E S

1

Es una escuela en San José, Costa Rica **1**. Es una clase de historia. ¿En qué lengua enseña la profesora? ¿Es una clase grande o pequeña?

Es la clase del señor Irizarry en Caguas, Puerto Rico **2**. Él enseña inglés como segundo idioma en una escuela secundaria de Caguas. ¿Cuál es la lengua materna de los alumnos del señor Irizarry?

Es la Universidad Nacional Autónoma de México **3**. Es una universidad muy importante en México. Es muy grande.

Es el patio de un colegio **4**. Los alumnos hablan.

84

Comunicación oral

A **Las notas.** In Spanish tell your partner about your last report card. Then reverse roles.

B **Llego a tiempo.** Ask your partner at what time he or she arrives at the following places. After your partner has answered all the questions, reverse roles.

> **a la escuela**
> Estudiante 1: **¿A qué hora llegas a la escuela?**
> Estudiante 2: **Llego a las ocho menos cuarto.**

1. a la escuela
2. a la clase de educación física
3. a la cafetería
4. a la clase de matemáticas

C **Una entrevista.** Work with a classmate. Find out the following information. Then compare his or her responses with your own.

1. qué cursos toma
2. qué clase(s) considera aburrida(s)
3. qué clase(s) considera interesante(s)
4. en qué clase estudia mucho
5. en qué clase estudia poco
6. en qué clase(s) saca buenas notas
7. en qué clase saca notas malas

Comunicación escrita

A **Los amigos.** You and your partner each think of a friend (preferably one who studies at a different school). Then write notes to each other inquiring about this friend. Answer each others' notes. They should include the following questions.

1. Who is the friend?
2. What is he or she like?
3. Where is he or she from?
4. Where does he or she study?
5. What foreign language does he or she study?
6. What kind of grades does he or she receive?

B **De Costa Rica.** You have just received a note from a pen pal in San José, Costa Rica. He or she wants to know about your school life. Write him or her a note telling all you can about life at school.

Reintegración

A ¿Cómo es que hablas español? Completen. (*Complete.*)

1. Yo ___ americano(a) pero ___ español. (ser, hablar)
2. Si tú ___ americano(a), ¿cómo es que ___ español? (ser, hablar)
3. Pues, yo ___ un curso con un profesor que ___ muy bueno. (tomar, ser)
4. ¿Con quién ___ (tú)? (estudiar)
5. Yo ___ con el señor Romero. (estudiar)
6. ¿De qué nacionalidad ___ él? ¿ ___ bien? (ser, enseñar)

B ¿Usted habla español? Cambien *tú* a *Ud.* y *yo* a *ella* en el Ejercicio A. (*Change* tú *to* Ud. *and* yo *to* ella *in Exercise A.*)

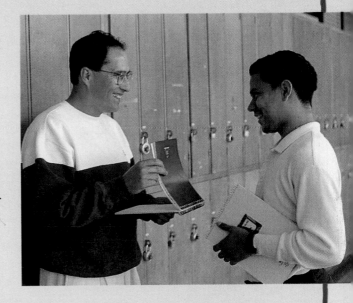

C Los alumnos de la clase de español.
Completen con *ser.* (*Complete with* ser.)

1. Los alumnos de la clase de español ___ muy inteligentes.
2. Todos nosotros ___ alumnos buenos.
3. Yo ___ alumno(a) en la clase de la señora Salas.
4. Ella ___ una profesora muy buena.
5. Y ella ___ simpática.
6. ¿Tú ___ alumno(a) en qué escuela?
7. Tú también ___ alumno(a) de español, ¿no?
8. ¿Uds. ___ alumnos buenos?

Vocabulario

SUSTANTIVOS

la sala de clase
el salón de clase
el profesor
la profesora
la lección
el examen
los apuntes
el libro
el cuaderno
el bloc
la libreta
la mochila
la pizarra
el pizarrón
la nota
la calificación

el coche
el carro
el autobús
el bus

ADJETIVOS

escolar

VERBOS

llegar
entrar
hablar
estudiar
mirar
tomar
sacar
llevar
enseñar

OTRAS PALABRAS Y EXPRESIONES

cuándo
cuánto
en punto
a eso de
a pie

PASATIEMPOS DESPUÉS DE LAS CLASES

OBJETIVOS

In this chapter you will learn to do the following:

1. describe some of your after-school activities
2. greet people and ask how they feel
3. tell how you feel
4. tell where you or others are
5. tell where you or others go
6. compare some of your after-school activities with those of students in the Hispanic countries

VOCABULARIO

PALABRAS 1

DESPUÉS DE LAS CLASES

la cinta

el teléfono

el disco

la televisión

la cocina

la casa

la sala

Después de las clases…

Los amigos van a casa.

Están en la sala. Escuchan discos.
Miran la televisión.

Preparan una merienda.

Toman un refresco.

Hablan por teléfono.

Estudian en la biblioteca.

el centro comercial

la tienda

Van al centro comercial.

Trabajan en una tienda.

Ejercicios

A Todos van a la casa de Emilio. Contesten. (*Answer.*)

1. Después de las clases, ¿van los amigos a la casa de Emilio?
2. ¿Van a la casa de Emilio a pie o toman el autobús?
3. En la casa, ¿miran la televisión?
4. ¿Miran la televisión en la sala?
5. ¿Escuchan discos?
6. ¿Escuchan discos de jazz, de rock, de música popular o de música clásica?
7. ¿Qué clase de cintas escuchan?
8. ¿Toman un refresco?
9. ¿Hablan por teléfono?

B Todos no van a casa. Completen. (*Complete.*)

1. ___ las clases, Elena y José no van a casa.
2. ¿Adónde van? Pues, van al ___ comercial.
3. En el ___ comercial, hay una ___ de discos.
4. Elena y José ___ en la tienda.
5. Luis y Sandra son alumnos muy serios. Después de las clases, ellos no van a casa. No van al centro comercial. Van a ___.
6. Ellos ___ en la biblioteca.

C **¿Dónde…?** ¿Cuál es la palabra? (*What's the word?*)

1. donde miran los amigos la televisión
2. donde preparan una merienda
3. donde estudian después de las clases
4. donde hay muchas tiendas

Acérquese a Moda Shopping.

Espacios serenos, confortables, seguros,
de cómodo acceso, en los que "ir de compras"
es un paseo relajante.

100 TIENDAS, 3 RESTAURANTES, SALA DE EXPOSICIONES.

CENTRO COMERCIAL.

El corazón de la Gran Manzana.

Avda. General Perón, 40. Edificio Mapfre Vida. 900 plazas de aparcamiento, primer nivel de AZCA.

PALABRAS 2

UNA FIESTA

María da una fiesta.
Ella invita a los amigos.

Los amigos van a la fiesta.
Ellos llegan a la casa de María.

Durante la fiesta todos…

bailan

cantan

Están en la sala.

José toca el piano…

la guitarra   el violín   la trompeta

Ejercicios

A La fiesta de María. Contesten. (*Answer.*)

1. ¿Da María una fiesta?
2. ¿Ella invita a los amigos a la fiesta?
3. ¿Da la fiesta en casa, en un restaurante o en un café?
4. ¿Llegan los amigos a la casa de María?
5. Durante la fiesta, ¿cantan y bailan todos?
6. ¿Toca José el piano? ¿La trompeta? ¿El violín?
7. ¿Prepara María refrescos para la fiesta?
8. ¿Toman los amigos los refrescos?

B ¿Adónde y dónde? Contesten. (*Answer.*)

1. ¿Dónde da María la fiesta?
2. ¿Adónde van los amigos?
3. ¿Adónde llegan?
4. ¿Dónde bailan los amigos durante la fiesta?
5. ¿Dónde prepara María los refrescos?

C ¡A casa de Emilio! Contesten. (*Answer.*)

1. ¿Adónde van los amigos?
2. ¿Cuándo van a casa de Emilio?
3. ¿Qué escuchan?
4. ¿Qué miran?
5. ¿Dónde preparan una merienda?

D Después de las clases. Escojan la respuesta correcta. (*Choose the correct answer.*)

1. Después de las clases los alumnos __.
   a. entran en la escuela   **b.** van a casa
2. En casa, ellos __.
   a. hablan con el profesor   **b.** miran la televisión
3. Miran la televisión __.
   a. en la tienda   **b.** en la sala
4. Escuchan __.
   a. la televisión   **b.** discos
5. Luego preparan una merienda __.
   a. en la sala   **b.** en la cocina
6. María y Teresa no van a casa. Ellas __.
   a. trabajan en una tienda de discos   **b.** toman el autobús a la escuela

Comunicación

Palabras 1 y 2

A **En clase o después de las clases.** Tell five daily activities of some of your friends. Your partner will decide whether your friends do these things in class or after school.

> Estudiante 1: **Ellos miran la televisión.**
> Estudiante 2: **Miran la televisión después de las clases.**

B **¿Dónde…?** Tell your partner what you do in each of the following places. Then your partner will report this information to the class.

> Estudiante 1: **En la cocina preparo una merienda.**
> Estudiante 2: **Él/ella prepara una merienda en la cocina.**

1. En la cocina…
2. En la sala…
3. En la escuela…
4. En la fiesta…
5. En el autobús…

C **Eres diferente.** Ask your partner the following questions. Your partner will always say *no*, and then answer something different. Reverse roles.

> Estudiante 1: **¿Escuchas discos?**
> Estudiante 2: **No. Escucho cintas.**

1. ¿Vas a la escuela en autobús?
2. ¿Hablas mucho en clase?
3. ¿Escuchas discos de rock?
4. ¿Trabajas en casa?
5. ¿Hablas español en clase?

D **En casa o en la escuela.** With a classmate make a list of as many activities as you can. Then decide if each one takes place *en casa*, *en la escuela*, or *durante una fiesta*.

Miguel Bosé, cantante y actor español

Chayanne, cantante puertorriqueño

ESTRUCTURA

El presente de los verbos en –ar Formas plurales
Describing People's Activities

1. You have learned the singular forms of regular *-ar* verbs. Study the plural forms.

INFINITIVE	HABLAR	CANTAR	TRABAJAR	ENDINGS
STEM	habl-	cant-	trabaj-	
nosotros(as)	hablamos	cantamos	trabajamos	-amos
ellos, ellas, Uds.	hablan	cantan	trabajan	-an

2. In most parts of the Spanish-speaking world, except for some regions of Spain, there is no difference between formal and informal address in the plural. Whenever you are speaking to more than one person you use the *ustedes* form of the verb.

   Ustedes hablan mucho en clase.

3. *Vosotros(as)* is the plural form of *tú*. It is used in much of Spain. Since *vosotros(as)* is not used in Latin America, you only have to recognize this verb form.

   ¿Cantáis y bailáis en la fiesta de Susana?

4. Review all the forms of the present tense of regular *-ar* verbs.

INFINITIVE	HABLAR	CANTAR	TRABAJAR	ENDINGS
STEM	habl-	cant-	trabaj-	
yo	hablo	canto	trabajo	-o
tú	hablas	cantas	trabajas	-as
él, ella, Ud.	habla	canta	trabaja	-a
nosotros(as)	hablamos	cantamos	trabajamos	-amos
vosotros(as)	habláis	cantáis	trabajáis	-áis
ellos, ellas, Uds.	hablan	cantan	trabajan	-an

Ejercicios

A En la escuela. Formen oraciones. (*Form sentences.*)

> Los alumnos…
> **tomar el bus escolar**
> *Los alumnos toman el bus escolar.*

1. llegar a la escuela a eso de las ocho
2. entrar en la sala de clase
3. tomar cuatro o cinco cursos
4. hablar con el profesor
5. estudiar mucho
6. sacar notas buenas

B Una entrevista. Preguntas personales. (*Give your own answers.*)

1. Tú y tus amigos, ¿estudian Uds. español?
2. ¿Con quién estudian Uds. español?
3. ¿Sacan Uds. buenas o malas notas?
4. ¿Hablan Uds. mucho en la clase de español?
5. ¿Hablan Uds. español o inglés?
6. ¿Y qué lengua hablan Uds. en casa?
7. Después de las clases, ¿preparan Uds. una merienda?
8. ¿Toman Uds. un refresco?
9. ¿Miran Uds. la televisión?

C ¿Y Uds.? Formen preguntas con *Uds.* (*Make up questions with* Uds.)

1.

2.

4.

3.

D **Un muchacho en un colegio de Madrid.** Completen. (*Complete.*)

Emilio ___ (ser) un muchacho español. Él ___ (estudiar) en un colegio de
1   2
Madrid, la capital de España. Emilio ___ (ser) un muchacho muy inteligente.
                                      3
Él ___ (trabajar) mucho en la escuela. Él ___ (estudiar) inglés. Los alumnos
   4   5
___ (hablar) mucho en la clase de inglés. La profesora de inglés ___ (ser)
6   7
muy interesante y ella ___ (enseñar) muy bien.
                       8

   Yo ___ (estudiar) español en una escuela secundaria de los Estados Unidos.
      9
Yo también ___ (trabajar) mucho en la escuela y ___ (sacar) muy buenas
           10   11
notas. En la clase de español nosotros ___ (hablar) mucho con la profesora de
                                        12
español. Siempre ___ (hablar) con ella en español. Ella ___ (ser) de Cuba.
                 13   14
Después de las clases los amigos ___ (tomar) un refresco. A veces
                                 15
nosotros ___ (mirar) la televisión o ___ (escuchar) discos o cintas.
        16   17

El presente de los verbos ir, dar y estar

Describing People's Activities

1. The verbs *ir* "to go," *dar* "to give," and *estar* "to be," are irregular. An
   irregular verb does not conform to the regular pattern. Note the similarity in
   the irregular *yo* form of these verbs.

       yo   voy   doy   estoy

2. The other forms of these verbs are the same as those you have learned for
   regular -*ar* verbs.

INFINITIVE	IR	DAR	ESTAR
yo	voy	doy	estoy
tú	vas	das	estás
él, ella, Ud.	va	da	está
nosotros(as)	vamos	damos	estamos
vosotros(as)	*vais*	*dais*	*estáis*
ellos, ellas, Uds.	van	dan	están

3. The verb *estar* is used to express how you feel and where you are.

How you feel:

¿Cómo estás? **Muy bien, gracias. ¿Y tú?**
       No estoy bien.   I'm not well.
       Estoy enfermo(a). I'm ill.

Location:

  Nosotros estamos en la escuela.
  Armando y Rosario están en casa.
  Pero no están en la sala. Están en la cocina.

Ejercicios

A **Voy a la escuela.** Contesten. (*Answer.*)

1. ¿Vas a la escuela?
2. ¿A qué hora vas a la escuela?
3. ¿Estás en la escuela ahora?
4. ¿En qué escuela estás?
5. ¿En qué clase estás?
6. Después de las clases, ¿vas a casa?
7. En casa, ¿vas a la cocina? ¿Preparas una merienda?
8. ¿Das un sándwich a José?
9. A veces, ¿das una fiesta?
10. ¿Das una fiesta para los amigos?
11. ¿Das la fiesta en casa?

B **Perdón, ¿adónde vas?** Sigan el modelo.
(*Follow the model.*)

  Voy a la escuela.
  Perdón, ¿adónde vas?

1. Voy a la clase de español. 4. Voy al laboratorio.
2. Voy a la clase de biología. 5. Voy al gimnasio.
3. Voy a la cafetería.

C **¿Dónde están Uds.?** Preparen una mini-conversación. (*Prepare a mini-conversation.*)

  Miramos la televisión. (en la sala)
  —*¿Dónde están Uds.? ¿En la sala?*
  —*Sí, estamos en la sala.*

1. Escuchamos discos. (en la sala) 4. Trabajamos. (en la tienda)
2. Preparamos un refresco. (en la cocina) 5. Tomamos un refresco. (en el café)
3. Tomamos un examen. (en la escuela) 6. Estudiamos biología. (en el laboratorio)

D **La escuela.** Contesten. (*Answer.*)

1. ¿A qué hora van Uds. a la escuela?
2. ¿Cómo van?
3. ¿Están Uds. en la escuela ahora?
4. ¿En qué clase están?

5. ¿Está el/la profesor(a)?
6. ¿Da él o ella muchos exámenes?
7. ¿Da él o ella exámenes difíciles?
8. ¿Qué profesores dan muchos exámenes?

Las contracciones *al* y *del*   *Expressing Location and Possession*

1. The preposition *a* means "to" or "toward." *A* contracts with the article *el* to form one word, *al.* The preposition *a* does not change when used with the other articles *la, las,* and *los.*

   > **a + el = al**

   En la escuela voy al laboratorio.
   Después de las clases voy al café.
   Y después voy a la biblioteca.

2. The preposition *a* is also used before a direct object that refers to a specific person or persons. It is called the personal *a* and has no equivalent in English.

Miro la televisión.	**Miro al profesor.**
Escucho el disco.	**Escucho a los amigos.**

3. The preposition *de* can mean "of," "from," or "about." Like *a*, the preposition *de* contracts with the article *el* to form one word, *del.* The preposition *de* does not change when used with the articles *la, las,* and *los.*

   > **de + el = del**

   Él habla del profesor de español.
   El profesor es del estado de Nueva York.
   Es de la ciudad de Nueva York.
   Él es de los Estados Unidos.

4. You also use the preposition *de* to indicate possession.

   Es el libro del profesor.
   Son las mochilas de Lourdes y de Sofía.

Ejercicios

A ¿A quién…? Contesten. (*Answer.*)

1. ¿Invitas a Juan y a María a la fiesta?
2. ¿Invitas a otros amigos a la fiesta?
3. ¿Miras a los amigos?
4. ¿Escuchas a los amigos?

B ¿Adónde vas? Preparen una conversación. (*Make up a mini-conversation based on the illustrations.*)

> ¿Adónde vas?
> ¿Quién? ¿Yo?
> Sí, tú.
> *Voy al café.*

1.
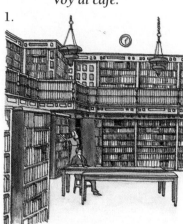

2.

3.

4.

5.

6.

C ¿De qué habla Roberto? Contesten. (*Answer.*)

1. ¿Es Roberto del estado de Nueva York?
2. ¿Es de la ciudad de Nueva York?
3. ¿Habla Roberto del curso de biología?
4. ¿Habla del profesor de biología?
5. Después de las clases, ¿habla Roberto con los amigos?
6. ¿Hablan de la escuela?
7. ¿Hablan de los cursos que toman?
8. ¿Hablan de los profesores?

Escenas de la vida   *Al trabajo o a la fiesta*

ALFREDO: ¿Cómo estás?
TOMÁS: Bien, ¿y tú?
ALFREDO: Muy bien. Oye, ¿adónde vas el viernes?
TOMÁS: ¿El viernes? Voy al trabajo como siempre.

ALFREDO: ¿Al trabajo? ¿Dónde trabajas?
TOMÁS: Pues, Clarita y yo trabajamos en una tienda de discos.

ALFREDO: Clarita también, ¿eh? Entonces, ¿Uds. no van a la fiesta de María?
TOMÁS: Sí, vamos. Pero después del trabajo.

 ¿Adónde vas? Contesten. (*Answer.*)

1. ¿Con quién habla Alfredo?
2. ¿Cómo están los dos muchachos?
3. ¿Adónde va Tomás el viernes?
4. ¿Quién trabaja con él en la tienda de discos?
5. ¿Quién da una fiesta el viernes?
6. ¿Adónde va Alfredo?
7. ¿Van a la fiesta Tomás y Clarita?
8. ¿Cuándo van?

OCTUBRE

LUNES	MARTES	MIÉRCOLES	JUEVES	VIERNES	SÁBADO	D
				1	2	
4	5	6	7	8	9	
11	12 Fiesta Nacional de España	13	14	15	16	
18	19	20	21	22	23	24
25	26	27	28	29	30	31

Pronunciación   *La consonante* t

The **t** in Spanish is pronounced with the tip of the tongue pressed against the upper teeth. Like the Spanish **p**, it is not followed by a puff of air. The Spanish **t** is extremely clear.

ta	te	ti	to	tu
taco	Teresa	tienda	toma	tú
fruta	televisión	tiempo	tomate	estudia
está	teléfono	latín	Juanito	estupendo

Repeat the following sentences.

Tito toca la trompeta durante la fiesta.
Tú estudias latín.
Teresa invita a Tito a la fiesta.

Teresa toca la trompeta.

Comunicación

A **Después de las clases.** Interview classmates about what they do after school. Then make a list of the most popular activities and report them to the class. Some verbs you may want to use in the interviews are:

ir	tomar
llegar	preparar
mirar	tocar
escuchar	cantar
estudiar	hablar
trabajar	dar

B **¡Qué pachanga!** Are your classmates *pachangueros*, real party types? Ask some of your classmates what they do when they go to a party.

1. ¿Bailan? ¿Qué bailan? el merengue, la rumba, la salsa, la samba, el mambo
2. ¿Escuchan discos? ¿Qué tipo de discos escuchan? jazz, rock, rap, música popular, música romántica, música clásica
3. ¿Hablan? ¿De qué hablan? de la política, de la escuela, de los profesores, de los muchachos (las muchachas), de los deportes, del fútbol, de la música
4. ¿Tocan un instrumento musical? ¿Qué tocan? el piano, el violín, la guitarra, la trompeta, la flauta

C **Vamos a estudiar.** With a classmate play the roles of two acquaintances and tell each other where you study, practice Spanish, work, and do other things. Decide on a place to meet later to study together.

EL TRABAJO A TIEMPO PARCIAL, ¿DÓNDE?

En los Estados Unidos muchos alumnos de las escuelas secundarias trabajan después de las clases. Trabajan a tiempo parcial[1] en una tienda, en un restaurante o en una gasolinera. Ganan dinero[2], y con el dinero que ganan compran cositas[3] personales—discos, blue jeans, un T shirt o ¡un carro!

En muchos países de Latinoamérica muy pocos alumnos trabajan a tiempo parcial. Las clases en los colegios no terminan hasta las cuatro y media de la tarde. Y los sábados las clases no terminan hasta el mediodía. Los alumnos de las escuelas latinoamericanas trabajan mucho, pero trabajan en la escuela. No trabajan en una tienda o en una gasolinera.

La mayor parte de los jóvenes[4] que trabajan en los países de Latinoamérica no son alumnos. Y no trabajan a tiempo parcial. Trabajan a tiempo completo. Son muchachos que terminan con la educación después de la escuela primaria. Hoy en día, muchos jóvenes continúan los estudios en clases nocturnas.

[1] a tiempo parcial *part time*
[2] ganan dinero *earn money*
[3] compran cositas *buy things*
[4] los jóvenes *young people*

Estudio de palabras

■ **Los trabajos.** Busquen ocho palabras afines en la lectura.
(*Find at least eight cognates in the reading.*)

Comprensión

A **¿Qué hacen los alumnos?** Completen. (*Complete.*)

1. Muchos alumnos de las escuelas secundarias en los Estados Unidos…
2. Ellos trabajan en…
3. Trabajan a…
4. Con el dinero que ganan…
5. Las clases en muchos colegios latinoamericanos no terminan…
6. Los alumnos de las escuelas latinoamericanas…
7. Los jóvenes que trabajan en los países latinoamericanos…

B **¿Dónde?** Indiquen dónde: en los Estados Unidos o en Latinoamérica.
(*Indicate where: in the United States or in Latin America.*)

1. Muchos alumnos trabajan a tiempo parcial.
2. Los alumnos ganan dinero y compran cosas personales con el dinero que ganan.
3. Las clases terminan a las cuatro y media de la tarde.
4. Los alumnos no van a la escuela los sábados.
5. Muchos jóvenes trabajan a tiempo completo cuando terminan la escuela primaria.

DESCUBRIMIENTO CULTURAL

¿Los jóvenes en España y en Latinoamérica hablan por teléfono con los amigos? Sí, claro. Hablan por teléfono. Pero no como aquí en los Estados Unidos. Los jóvenes en España y en Latinoamérica no pasan horas al teléfono. ¿Qué opinan Uds.? ¿Nosotros pasamos horas al teléfono o no?

La televisión, ¿es popular en España y en Latinoamérica? Sí, la televisión es un pasatiempo popular como aquí en los Estados Unidos. Y los programas de los Estados Unidos

son muy populares. También son populares las telenovelas. ¿Qué son las telenovelas? Las telenovelas tratan de historias románticas.

Y el televisor, ¿dónde está? Está en la sala. Los miembros de la familia miran la televisión juntos.

Manuela
POR LA CADENA TELEMUNDO

El Fantasma de un pasado empeñado en opacar la felicidad del presente.

CON
GRECIA COLMENARES • JORGE MARTINEZ

7 PM Este

TELEMUNDO
Únete a Telemundo. Tu mundo.

Y AQUÍ EN LOS ESTADOS UNIDOS

En muchas partes de los Estados Unidos
es posible mirar la televisión en español.
Muchos programas son de Univisión.
Univisión es una compañía mexicana de
televisión. *Sábado Gigante* es uno de los
programas más populares. Univisión
presenta programas en español en Nueva
York, Chicago, Miami, San Antonio, Los
Ángeles—en todas partes del país.

REALIDADES

Es un grupo de alumnos de un colegio de Madrid **1**. Están en un café en la Plaza Mayor. En el café los amigos toman un refresco. Mientras toman el refresco, hablan de otros amigos, de los cursos que toman, de los profesores, etc. Cuando tú estás con un grupo de amigos, ¿de qué hablan Uds.? ¿Uds. van a cafés o no? ¿Adónde van Uds. después de las clases?

Es un teléfono público en Argentina **2**. Antonio habla por teléfono con un amigo. ¿Qué opina Ud.? ¿Es una conversación agradable o no? ¿Es una conversación seria o divertida?

Es Gabriel Suárez **3**. Es de Miami. Él prepara una merienda después de las clases. ¿Qué prepara? Después de la merienda, ¿va a trabajar en una tienda o va a estudiar en la biblioteca?

Telefónica de Argentina

111

CULMINACIÓN

Comunicación oral

A **Un alumno de intercambio.** You are spending a school vacation living with the Sánchez family in San José, Costa Rica. Eduardo Sánchez is your "brother." He wants to know the following things about you.

1. if you work part time
2. if you listen to music and if so, what kind
3. a few things you and your friends do when you're not in school
4. what you and your friends talk about
5. what American teenagers talk about on the phone with their friends

B **Tú y yo.** Work with a classmate. Ask your classmate about each topic below. He or she will respond. Indicate if you do the same thing or not.
Use the model as a guide.

> música
> Estudiante 1: ¿Qué tipo de música escuchas?
> Estudiante 2: Yo escucho discos de jazz.
> Estudiante 1: ¿Ah, sí? Yo también. Tú y
> yo escuchamos jazz.
> (¿Ah, sí? Yo, no. Yo escucho música popular.)

1. música
2. el teléfono
3. fiestas
4. escuela
5. instrumentos musicales

Comunicación escrita

A **Un amigo muy bueno.** You are writing in your diary about a very good friend. Include the following.

1. who the person is
2. where he or she is from
3. a description of your friend
4. his or her favorite class
5. if he or she is a good student
6. why you like this person

B **Una fiesta divertida.** Write a paragraph about a fun party. Tell what you do, who you talk to, and what kind of music you listen to.

Reintegración

A **Dos amigos.** Here is a photo of two friends. They are from Miami. They are of Cuban background. Describe these two friends and say as much about them as you can.

B **Una entrevista.** Preguntas personales. (*Give your own answers.*)

1. ¿Hablas mucho por teléfono?
2. ¿Con quién hablas por teléfono?
3. ¿De qué hablan Uds.?
4. ¿Escuchas discos?
5. ¿Qué tipo de música escuchas?

Vocabulario

SUSTANTIVOS

la casa
la cocina
la sala
la televisión
el teléfono
la merienda
el refresco
la fiesta
la música
el piano
la guitarra
el violín
la trompeta
la cinta
el disco
la biblioteca
la tienda
el centro comercial

VERBOS

preparar
trabajar
invitar
bailar
cantar
escuchar
tocar
mirar

ir
dar
estar

ADJETIVOS

clásico(a)
popular

OTRAS PALABRAS Y EXPRESIONES

adónde
a casa
después de
durante
por teléfono
todos
de jazz
de rock

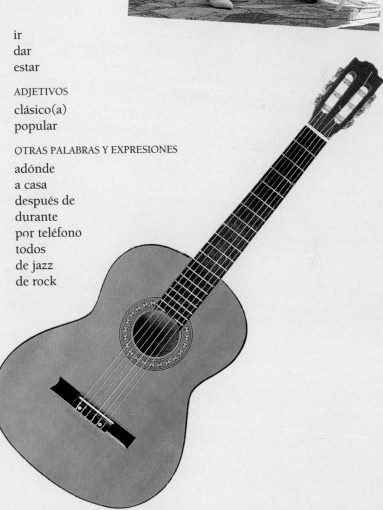

NUESTRO MUNDO

Here is an actual "report card" for a student in Latin America.

REPÚBLICA DE CHILE
MINISTERIO DE EDUCACIÓN PÚBLICA
DIRECCIÓN DE EDUCACIÓN
SECRETARÍA REGIONAL MINISTERIAL
DE EDUCACIÓN

INFORME EDUCACIONAL
EDUCACIÓN GENERAL BÁSICA

Decreto Evaluación
_146/88-_
(Régimen _TRIMESTRAL_)

NOMBRE _NURIA RODRÍGUEZ_

CURSO _____ AÑO ESCOLAR

ESTABLECIMIENTO _____
COMUNA _NUÑOA_ PROVINCIA _SA_

PROFESOR JEFE
O DE CURSO _MIRTA SALINAS_

ASISTENCIA	Nº DE DÍAS TRABAJADOS	Nº DE DÍAS DE INASISTENCIAS
1º		
2º		
ANUAL		

B. ÁREAS DE DESARROLLO

	CONCEPTO	
ÁREA PSICO-BIOLÓGICA		
– Cuida de su higiene y presentación personal	S	S
– Se recrea de acuerdo a su etapa de desarrollo	S	S
– Desarrolla el trabajo escolar en forma sistemática y continua	S	S
– Trata de resolver los problemas que se le presentan	S	S
ÁREA SOCIAL		
– Participa en actividades de grupo	S	S
– Actúa con responsabilidad en las actividades en que se compromete	S	S
– Mantiene buenas relaciones con sus compañeros	S	S
– Manifiesta una actitud deferente y respetuosa con los miembros de su comunidad	S	S
ÁREA AFECTIVA		
– Demuestra preocupación por los problemas de los demás	S	S
– Manifiesta sentimientos de agrado frente a las diferentes actividades que le ofrece la Unidad Educativa	S	S
– Trata de superar sus limitaciones	S	S
– Reconoce sus errores y trata de corregirlos	S	S
– Reconoce los aspectos positivos de su personalidad	S	S
– Manifiesta disposición para acatar las normas establecidas en la Unidad Educativa	S	S

ÁREA VOCACIONAL O PROFESIONAL
– INTERESES.
Se interesa por el área
– APTITUDES y/o HABILIDADES.
Manifiesta Aptitudes y/o Habilidades para
– Existe congruencia entre los intereses y habilidades manifestados
SÍ ☐ NO ☐
– Aspiraciones de prosecución de estudios relacionados con su futuro profesional y/o laboral

OTRAS OBSERVACIONES:

ESCALA DE EVALUACIÓN ÁREAS DE DESARROLLO
SIEMPRE : Permanencia y continuidad en la evidencia del rasgo. El alumno se destaca.
GENERALMENTE : En forma frecuente manifiesta el rasgo.
OCASIONALMENTE : Sólo a veces manifiesta el rasgo.
NUNCA : No se manifiesta el rasgo. El alumno requiere de un apoyo directo del Profesor Jefe y del Orientador.

OBSERVACIONES:

_____ PROFESOR(A) JEFE _____ UNIDAD DE ORIENTACIÓN

114 NUESTRO MUNDO

A Las calificaciones. Contesten. (*Answer the questions.*)

1. From what country is the report?
2. What is the student's name?
3. In what grade or year is the student?
4. What is the teacher's name?
5. How many subjects does the student take?
6. What is the highest grade obtainable?
7. What is the lowest possible passing grade?
8. In what subject did the student get the highest final average?
9. What was her "worst" subject?

B ¿Qué quiere decir…? Adivinen. (*Guess.*)

1. What might "establecimiento" mean in this context?
2. How do you say "general average" or "overall average"?
3. How do you say "academic achievement"?
4. What grade does everyone avoid?
5. What course is "optional"?

C Observaciones. Under *observaciones* it says:

> Queda promovida a 5° año de Educación General Básica.
> Obtiene el primer lugar en rendimiento escolar entre 47 alumnos.

Please explain what you think that means.

D Los cursos. Contesten. (*Answer.*)

Why do you think the "optional" course is "optional"?

A. RENDIMIENTO ESCOLAR: (Plan de Estudios) R.B.D. _ _ _ _ _ _ _

ASIGNATURAS	PRIMER.				Promedio	CALIF. FINAL
			6.8 70 60 67 70 70 70 70 6.4		6.7	6.8
CASTELLANO	70 70 70 70 70 68 70 69	6.9 64 70 70 70 70			6.6	6.7
HISTORIA Y GEOGRAFÍA	65 70 70	6.8 66 70 70	6.8 64 70 61		7.0	6.8
I. EXT.	70 60 70	6.6 70 67 70	6.9 70 70			
I. EXT.			6.6 70 66 70 63 70 65		6.7	6.6
MATEMÁTICA	65 60 70 70 65 70 70	6.6 70 66 70 68 70 65	6.7 70 70 70 70		70	6.8
CIENCIAS NATURALES	65 70 70	6.8 70 63 70	7.0 70 70 70 70		70	6.9
ARTES	70 50 70 70 70 70 70	6.7 70 70 70 70	6.8 70 65 70 70		6.8	6.8
EDUC. TEC. MAN. Y HUERTOS ESC.	70 70 70 70 70	70 65 70 70 65 70	6.8 70 70 70 70		70	6.8
ED. MUSICAL	70 70 70 55	6.6 70 65 70	6.3 70 65 70 70		6.8	6.3
ED. FÍSICA	45 50 70 70	5.8 60 70 55 70			MB	MB
RELIGIÓN (Optativo)	70 70 70	MB 70 70 63	MB 70 65 70		6.8	6.7
PROMEDIO GENERAL		6.6	6.7			

% DE ASISTENCIA		FIRMAS	DIRECTOR	PROFESOR DE CURSO O JEFE	APODERADO	FECHA
ESCALA DE EVALUACIÓN. DECRETO		**1** TRIMESTRE		M.S	M.Rodriguez	08-05-93
		2		M.S	M.Rodriguez	19-06-93
MUY BUENO 6.0 a 7.0 SUFICIENTE 4.0 a 4.9				M.S	M.Rodriguez	10.09-93
BUENO 5.0 a 5.9 INSUFICIENTE 1.0 a 3.9						

OBSERVACIONES Queda promovida a 5° año de Educación General Básica. Obtiene el 1° lugar en rendimiento escolar entre 47 alumnos.

CAPÍTULOS 1–4

Lectura   *La familia Avilés*

Yo soy Josefina Avilés. Somos seis en la familia: papá, mamá, tres hermanos, y yo. Somos de la Argentina, de Buenos Aires, la capital. Papá y mamá son profesores. Él enseña matemáticas en un colegio, y ella enseña inglés en la universidad. Los tres hermanos y yo somos estudiantes. Yo estoy en el colegio. Estudio mucho y soy una alumna buena. Saco muy buenas notas en inglés y en matemáticas. Soy alta y rubia, pero mis hermanos son bajos y morenos, como mamá.

 La familia de Josefina. Contesten. (*Answer.*)

1. ¿Quién es la muchacha?
2. ¿Cuántas personas hay en la familia?
3. ¿Quiénes son profesores?
4. ¿Quién enseña matemáticas?
5. ¿Qué enseña la madre?
6. ¿Dónde enseña el padre?
7. ¿Qué son los hermanos?
8. ¿Josefina está en la universidad?
9. ¿Quién es buena alumna?
10. ¿En qué asignaturas saca buenas notas?
11. ¿Cómo es ella?
12. ¿Quiénes son bajos y morenos?

Estructura

El presente de los verbos en *-ar* y los verbos *ser, ir, dar* y *estar*

1. Review the following forms of regular *-ar* verbs.

INFINITIVE	HABLAR	CANTAR
yo	hablo	canto
tú	hablas	cantas
él, ella, Ud.	habla	canta
nosotros(as)	hablamos	cantamos
vosotros(as)	*habláis*	*cantáis*
ellos, ellas, Uds.	hablan	cantan

2. The irregular verbs *ir, dar*, and *estar* follow a common pattern. Review the forms of these verbs.

INFINITIVE	IR	DAR	ESTAR
yo	voy	doy	estoy
tú	vas	das	estás
él, ella, Ud.	va	da	está
nosotros(as)	vamos	damos	estamos
vosotros(as)	*vais*	*dais*	*estáis*
ellos, ellas, Uds.	van	dan	están

3. Review the forms of the irregular verb *ser.*

ser	yo soy, tú eres, él/ella/Ud. es, nosotros(as) somos, *vosotros(as) sois,* ellos/ellas/Uds. son

A **Después de las clases.** Completen. (*Complete.*)

Esta tarde, a las cinco y media, después de las clases, yo ___1
(ir) a casa de Sara. Sara ___2 (ser) una amiga. Yo ___3
(ser) un amigo de Sara. Ella ___4 (dar) una fiesta hoy.
Allí nosotros ___5 (bailar) y ___6 (cantar). Marcos
Rosales ___7 (tocar) la guitarra. Jorge Campos y
Teresa Ruiz ___8 (preparar) una merienda. Y tú, ¿ ___9
(ir) a la fiesta también?

Los sustantivos y los artículos

1. Spanish nouns are classified as masculine or feminine. Most nouns ending in *o* are masculine, and most ending in *a* are feminine. To make any noun plural that ends in a vowel, simply add an *s*. To form the plural of nouns that end in a consonant, add *es*.

alumno	alumnos	clase	clases
alumna	alumnas	profesor	profesores

2. Review the following forms of the indefinite and definite articles.

el alumno	los alumnos	un alumno	unos alumnos
la alumna	las alumnas	una alumna	unas alumnas

B **En la escuela.** Cambien *un(a)* en *dos*. (*Change* un(a) *to* dos *and make any other necessary changes.*)

1. La Sra. Ramírez enseña una clase de matemáticas.
2. Ella enseña a diez muchachos y a una muchacha.
3. Solamente un profesor de español enseña en la escuela.
4. Yo tomo un curso de ciencias y un curso de matemáticas.
5. Yo estudio una lengua y una ciencia.

C **José Luis.** Completen. (*Complete with the appropiate form of the definite or indefinite article.*)

Son ___ tres de la tarde. Estamos en
      1
___ colegio. Estamos en ___ clase
  2   3
de español. ___ Sra. Cortés es ___
              4   5
profesora. Todos ___ alumnos estudian
                   6
mucho, pero José Luis, no. Él no es ___
                                      7
alumno muy serio. José Luis saca notas muy
malas en muchas asignaturas. Pero en ___
                                        8
cosa José Luis es muy bueno. En ___ deportes.
                                 9

Los adjetivos

Adjectives agree with the nouns they modify. Adjectives ending in *o* have four forms. Adjectives ending in *e* or in a consonant have only two forms.

el alumno bueno	los alumnos buenos
la alumna buena	las alumnas buenas
el alumno inteligente	los alumnos inteligentes
la alumna inteligente	las alumnas inteligentes
el alumno popular	los alumnos populares
la alumna popular	las alumnas populares

D **En la clase de español.** Contesten. (*Answer.*)

1. ¿Quiénes son inteligentes?
2. ¿Quién es popular?
3. ¿Qué es aburrido?
4. ¿Quiénes son altas?
5. ¿Quién es rubio?
6. ¿Quiénes son simpáticos?
7. ¿Qué es difícil?
8. ¿Quién es morena?
9. ¿Qué son fáciles?
10. ¿Qué es interesante?

Comunicación

A **Mi familia.** Describe each member of your family to a classmate. Reverse roles.

B **Mi horario.** An exchange student (your partner) wants to know about your school and your schedule. Explain both in as much detail as you can.

Un instituto en México

LAS CIENCIAS NATURALES

Antes de leer

1. The natural sciences are grouped under major categories—physics, chemistry, biology—and each of those into subcategories. List as many of the specialties and subspecialties as you can.
2. You will now learn the names of the most common ones in Spanish, as well as some science terminology with which you are already familiar in English.

Lectura

En las escuelas enseñan las ciencias naturales. Los cursos típicos son la biología, la física y la química. La biología es el estudio de la vida[1]. En biología, las dos importantes categorías son la zoología y la botánica. En zoología estudian los animales. Estudian los animales microscópicos como las amebas y los paramecios. Estudian los animales primates como los chimpancés y los orangutanes. Y estudian los animales enormes como los elefantes, y los hipopótamos. En botánica estudian las plantas microscópicas como las algas y las bacterias, y los enormes árboles[2] secuoyas de California. Los especialistas estudian las plantas y la vegetación de las zonas del desierto, de las junglas o selvas[3] tropicales y de las regiones polares.

La física es el estudio de la materia y la energía. La química es el estudio de las características de elementos o substancias simples. Las dos categorías importantes son la química orgánica, que trata sólo de los compuestos[4] de carbono, y la inorgánica que trata de los compuestos de todos los otros elementos. Todos los científicos, los biólogos, los químicos y los físicos trabajan en laboratorios. Uno de los instrumentos más importantes que usan es el microscopio.

29 Cu 63,5 Cobre	30 Zn 65,4 Cinc	31 Ga 69,7 Galio	32 Ge 72,6 Germanio	33 As 74,9 Arsénico	34 Se 79,0 Selenio	35 Br 79,9 Bromo	36 Kr 83 Criptó
47 Ag 107,9 Plata	48 Cd 112,4 Cadmio	49 In 114,8 Indio	50 Sn 118,7 Estaño	51 Sb 121,8 Antimonio	52 Te 127,6 Telurio	53 I 126,9 Yodo	54 Xe 131 Xenó
79 Au 197,2 Oro	80 Hg 200,6 Mercurio	81 Tl 204,4 Talio	82 Pb 207,2 Plomo	83 Bi 209,0 Bismuto	84 Po 210 Polonio	85 At 210 Astato	86 Rn 2 Rad

[1] la vida *life*
[2] árboles *trees*
[3] selvas *rainforests*
[4] los compuestos *compounds*

Tabla periódica de los elementos (fragmento)

Un hipopótamo

El desierto, Baja California, México

Los secuoyas

Un tucán

La selva en la frontera entre la Argentina y Brasil

Después de leer

A **Las ciencias.** Escojan la respuesta correcta.

1. La biología es el estudio de la ___.
   a. vida   b. ameba   c. categoría

2. El microscopio es un ___ importante para los científicos.
   a. laboratorio   b. instrumento
   c. estudio

3. El ___ es un ejemplo de un animal enorme.
   a. insecto   b. alga   c. hipopótamo

4. La persona que estudia las algas es ___.
   a. biólogo   b. químico   c. físico

5. El nitrógeno, el potasio y el sodio son substancias ___.
   a. biológicas   b. físicas
   c. químicas

B **En la lectura.** ¿Dónde dice lo siguiente?

1. the name of a microscopic plant
2. the names of microscopic animals
3. three of the geographic areas where botanists study plant-life

C **Seguimiento.** Preparen una lista de animales que comen (*eat*) algas.

LAS CIENCIAS SOCIALES

Antes de leer

The social sciences or social studies are those that deal with history and related areas—human behavior, social customs and interactions, etc. List in English, as many of the social sciences as you can think of, then see if you can recognize their names in Spanish below.

la antropología   la historia
la psicología   la ciencia política
la geografía   la sociología
la demografía   la economía

Lectura

Las ciencias sociales estudian al hombre, su historia, sus instituciones y su comportamiento[1]. En la historia estudiamos el pasado. Algunos historiadores son especialistas en épocas específicas como las antiguas Grecia y Roma; la época medieval; el siglo XIII; el siglo XIX, o la época contemporánea—hoy. Otros historiadores son especialistas en áreas geográficas específicas, por ejemplo: los Estados Unidos, Europa, Centroamérica, China, el Medio Oriente, etc.

    La sociología es el estudio de la sociedad humana, del comportamiento de individuos en sus relaciones con otros, y sus instituciones y grupos. Los sociólogos estudian la familia. Estudian las instituciones: el matrimonio, la educación, la religión, el divorcio y mucho

El Partenón de la Acrópolis, Atenas, Grecia

Ruinas mayas, Copán, Honduras

más. La antropología es el estudio del hombre. Los antropólogos estudian al hombre físico, sus costumbres, su trabajo, su idioma, sus ceremonias. La ciencia política estudia las instituciones políticas y cómo funcionan. La psicología es el estudio de la conducta y de los procesos mentales. La geografía es la ciencia que describe y analiza la superficie^2 de la tierra. Dos especialidades de la geografía son la geografía física y la geografía económica.

^{1} el comportamiento   *behavior*
^{2} la superficie   *surface*

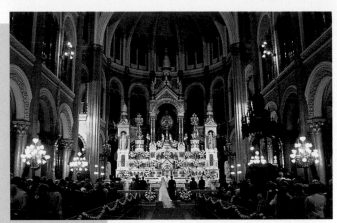
Una boda en España

El Alcázar de Segovia, España

La Gran Muralla, China

Después de leer

A **Las ciencias sociales.** Contesten.

1. ¿Quiénes estudian el pasado?
2. ¿Cuál es una época histórica que estudian los historiadores?
3. ¿Cuál es una de las áreas que los historiadores estudian?
4. ¿Qué estudian los sociólogos?
5. ¿Cuáles son dos instituciones que los sociólogos estudian?
6. ¿Cuáles son dos especialidades de la geografía?

B **¿Quién estudia qué…?** ¿Dónde dice lo siguiente?

1. which science studies the surface of the earth
2. what sociologists study

C **Seguimiento.** Comparen la sociología con la geografía.

LAS BELLAS ARTES

Antes de leer

The arts cover the plastic arts such as painting, sculpture and architecture; the performing arts such as theater, music and dance, and letters, or literature. The Spanish-speaking countries have provided artists in all these fields. Make a list of Spanish-speaking artists in any of the disciplines above.

Lectura

Algunos artistas pintan o dibujan[1]. Los artistas que pintan son pintores, como Velázquez y Goya. Las personas miran los cuadros[2] de los pintores famosos en los importantes museos del mundo como el Prado de Madrid y el Louvre de París. Muchos pintores dibujan primero y después pintan a una persona, una escena, un objeto o figura. La pintura y la escultura son artes plásticas. Diego Velázquez es un importante pintor clásico. Francisco de Goya es un gran pintor del siglo XIX. Los dos son pintores españoles.

Familia de Carlos IV *de Francisco de Goya*

El Dos de Mayo *de Francisco de Goya*

Plácido Domingo, tenor español

Alicia de Larrocha, pianista española

Las figuras hispanas en la música son muchas. Hay pianistas y cantantes[3]. El gran tenor Plácido Domingo canta en Roma, Londres, París y Nueva York. La famosa pianista, Alicia de Larrocha, toca en Europa, Asia y las Américas.

[1] dibujan   *sketch*
[2] el cuadro   *the painting, picture*
[3] el cantante   *singer*

PABLO PICASSO
EL GRECO
DIEGO VELÁZQUEZ
DIEGO RIVERA
FRIDA KAHLO
MANUEL DE FALLA
ISAAC ALBÉNIZ
ERNESTO LECUONA
CLAUDIO ARRAU
ALICIA DE LARROCHA
XAVIER CUGAT
JOSÉ ITURBI
FERNANDO SOR
RUFINO TAMAYO
DAVID ALFARO SIQUEIROS
PABLO CASALS
ANDRÉS SEGOVIA
FRANCISCO DE GOYA

Después de leer

A **Las artes.** Escojan la respuesta correcta.

1. Velázquez y Goya son ___.
   a. cantantes   **b.** músicos
   c. pintores
2. Alicia de Larrocha es una ___ famosa.
   a. pianista   **b.** compositora
   c. cantante
3. Un gran cantante de ópera es ___.
   a. Francisco Goya
   b. Diego Velázquez
   c. Plácido Domingo
4. El Prado de Madrid es ___.
   a. una ópera   **b.** un pintor
   c. un museo
5. Un famoso pintor clásico es ___.
   a. Goya   **b.** Velázquez
   c. Domingo

B **Pianistas y pintores.** ¿Dónde dice lo siguiente?

1. the name of a famous pianist
2. where a famous opera star performs
3. the name of a famous French art museum
4. the name of a great classical painter
5. what many painters do before beginning to paint
6. the name of a great nineteenth-century artist

C **Seguimiento.** Choose an artist from the list on the left. Prepare a brief report about the artist to present to the class. Get help from the art or music department if necessary. If you choose a painter, get some reproductions of his or her work to show to the class.

5

ACTIVIDADES DEL HOGAR

OBJETIVOS

In this chapter you will learn to do the following:

1. describe your home
2. tell where you live
3. talk about things you do at home
4. express "there is" and "there are"
5. compare some American and Hispanic eating habits
6. talk about housing in the Hispanic world

VOCABULARIO

PALABRAS 1

¿DÓNDE VIVE?

la ciudad

el pueblo

el campo

los suburbios

las afueras

la ciudad

el edificio

a la izquierda

a la derecha

la avenida   la calle

el quinto piso

el cuarto piso

el tercer piso

el segundo piso

el primer piso

la planta baja

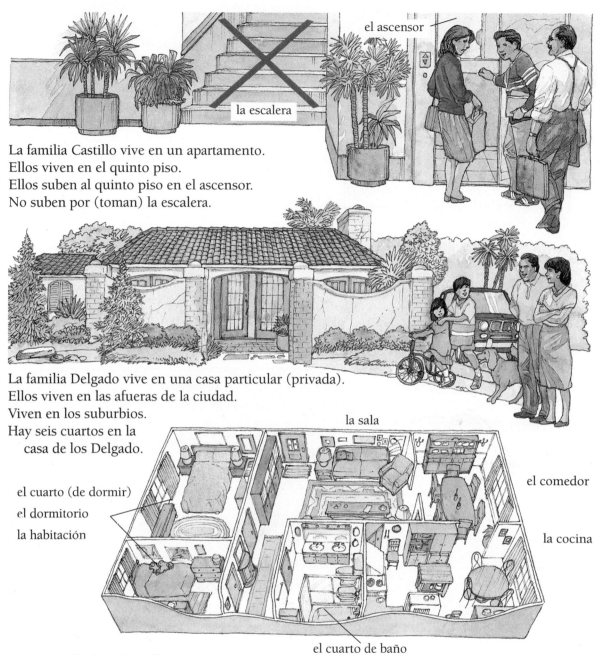

el ascensor

la escalera

La familia Castillo vive en un apartamento.
Ellos viven en el quinto piso.
Ellos suben al quinto piso en el ascensor.
No suben por (toman) la escalera.

La familia Delgado vive en una casa particular (privada).
Ellos viven en las afueras de la ciudad.
Viven en los suburbios.
Hay seis cuartos en la
    casa de los Delgado.

la sala

el comedor

el cuarto (de dormir)
el dormitorio
la habitación

la cocina

el cuarto de baño

Note the ordinal numbers (first, second, etc.).

primer(o)	**sexto**
segundo	**séptimo**
tercer(o)	**octavo**
cuarto	**noveno**
quinto	**décimo**

Primero and *tercero* shorten to *primer* and *tercer* before a singular masculine noun.

el tercer piso	**la tercera calle a la derecha**
el primer piso	**la primera calle a la izquierda**

Ejercicios

A **La familia Castillo.** Contesten. (*Answer.*)

1. ¿Vive la familia Castillo en una casa particular o en un apartamento?
2. ¿Está en un edificio alto el apartamento?
3. ¿Está en el tercer piso o en el quinto piso?
4. ¿Suben ellos al quinto piso en el ascensor o toman la escalera?
5. Cuando llegan al quinto piso, ¿van a la derecha o a la izquierda?
6. ¿Está el edificio en la Avenida Moreto?
7. ¿Viven los Castillo en la ciudad o en las afueras de la ciudad?

B **La familia Delgado.** Contesten según se indica. (*Answer according to the cues.*)

1. ¿Quiénes viven en una casa particular? (los Delgado)
2. ¿En qué viven ellos? (en una casa particular)
3. ¿Dónde está la casa? (en un suburbio, en las afueras)
4. ¿Cuántos cuartos hay en la casa? (seis)

Apartamentos en Viña del Mar, Chile

C **Una casa particular.** Contesten según el dibujo. (*Answer according to the illustration.*)

1. ¿Cuántos cuartos hay en la planta baja?
2. ¿Cuántos cuartos hay en el primer piso?
3. ¿Qué cuartos están en la planta baja?
4. ¿Qué cuartos están en el primer piso?

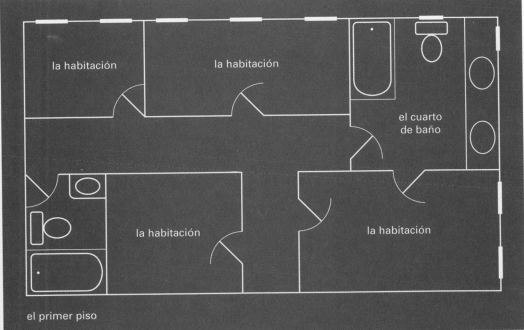

el primer piso

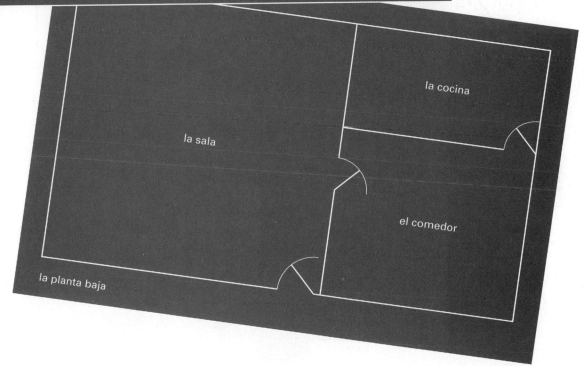

la planta baja

PALABRAS 2

ACTIVIDADES EN CASA

las comidas

el desayuno   el almuerzo   la cena

Joselito come.
¿Qué come?

Teresita bebe.
¿Qué bebe?

una gaseosa

las papas

la sopa

la ensalada

la carne

un vaso
de leche

un café

el helado

el sándwich
el bocadillo

una limonada

el postre

Papá (papi) lee.
¿Qué lee?

un libro

una novela

una
revista

HOGAR

Eva Luna

LA PRENSA LIBRE

un periódico

una tarjeta postal

ABRIL

el lápiz

siempre

una carta

el bolígrafo

Mamá escribe.
¿Qué escribe?
¿Con qué escribe?

una invitación

una telenovela

una película

siempre no, a veces

La familia ve la televisión.
¿Qué ven?

una emisión deportiva

las noticias

Nota: Not all Spanish and English cognates have exactly the same meaning. The verb *asistir*, for example, can mean "to assist", but more frequently it means "to attend." *Asistir* can be a false cognate.

Los alumnos asisten a la escuela.

When learning a language you should attempt to take educated guesses at the meaning of words through the context of the sentence. Try to guess at the meaning of the words in italics.

En la escuela la profesora *enseña*.
Los alumnos no enseñan. Los alumnos *aprenden*.
La profesora enseña y los alumnos *aprenden*.
Los alumnos *comprenden*. ¿Qué *comprenden*?
Comprenden las instrucciones de la profesora.
El señor no compra helados. El *vende* helados.
El *vende* los helados a los clientes que compran los helados.

Ejercicios

A Siempre o a veces.
Contesten con *siempre* o *a veces*. (*Answer with siempre or a veces.*)

1. ¿Cuándo tomas el desayuno en casa?
2. ¿Cuándo tomas el almuerzo en la escuela?
3. ¿Cuándo cenas en un restaurante?
4. ¿Cuándo estudias en la biblioteca?
5. ¿Cuándo subes en el ascensor?

B Comer y beber.
Contesten. (*Answer.*)

1. ¿A qué hora toma la familia el desayuno?
2. ¿A qué hora toma la familia el almuerzo?
3. ¿A qué hora cena la familia?
4. ¿Come Diego frutas y cereal para el desayuno?
5. ¿Toma un vaso de leche con el almuerzo?
6. ¿Bebe mucha leche Diego?
7. ¿Come una ensalada con la cena?
8. De postre, ¿come helado?
9. ¿Come helado de vainilla o de chocolate?

C Teresita.
Contesten según la foto. (*Answer according to the photo.*)

1. ¿Qué lee Teresita?
2. ¿Qué escribe Teresita?
3. ¿Con qué escribe ella?
4. ¿Qué ve Teresita en la televisión?

D Palabras relacionadas.
Busquen una palabra relacionada. (*Find a related word.*)

1. comer
2. beber
3. aprender
4. comprender
5. vender
6. leer
7. escribir
8. asistir
9. vivir
10. subir

a. la comprensión
b. la asistencia
c. la escritura
d. la bebida
e. la comida
f. la subida
g. la lectura
h. la venta
i. el aprendizaje
j. la vivienda

Comunicación

Palabras 1 y 2

A **En la escuela.** Work with a classmate. Prepare a list of activities. Compare your activities with those of your classmate. Then decide in which of the categories below to place each activity.

> **en la escuela con los amigos**
> **después de las clases**
> **con la familia en casa**

B **La familia.** Work with two classmates. Each of you will do the following.

1. make up the name of a family
2. tell where they live
3. tell at what time they get back home each day
4. tell who prepares dinner
5. tell at what time they eat
6. tell some things they eat
7. tell what they do after dinner

C **Un juego.** Write the words that follow on small slips of paper. Put them in a stack. You and a classmate will take turns picking from the stack. Write a sentence with the word you picked. Help each other if you can't do it right away.

> **el periódico**
> **Juan lee el periódico.**

1. una novela
2. una carta
3. un bolígrafo
4. un vaso de leche
5. una ensalada
6. el desayuno
7. la televisión
8. la película

ESTRUCTURA

El presente de los verbos en *-er* e *-ir*

Describing People's Activities

1. You have already learned that many Spanish verbs end in *-ar*. These verbs are referred to as first conjugation verbs. Most regular Spanish verbs belong to the *-ar* group. The other two groups of regular verbs in Spanish end in *-er* and *-ir*. Verbs whose infinitives end in *-er* are second conjugation verbs. Verbs whose infinitive ends in *-ir* are third conjugation verbs. Study the following forms. Note that the endings of *-er* and *-ir* verbs are the same except for the *nosotros* and *vosotros* forms.

-ER VERBS				
INFINITIVE	COMER	LEER	APRENDER	ENDINGS
STEM	com-	le-	aprend-	
yo	como	leo	aprendo	-o
tú	comes	lees	aprendes	-es
él, ella, Ud.	come	lee	aprende	-e
nosotros(as)	comemos	leemos	aprendemos	-emos
vosotros(as)	*coméis*	*leéis*	*aprendéis*	*-éis*
ellos, ellas, Uds.	comen	leen	aprenden	-en

-IR VERBS				
INFINITIVE	VIVIR	SUBIR	ESCRIBIR	ENDINGS
STEM	viv-	sub-	escrib-	
yo	vivo	subo	escribo	-o
tú	vives	subes	escribes	es
él, ella, Ud.	vive	sube	escribe	-e
nosotros(as)	vivimos	subimos	escribimos	-imos
vosotros(as)	*vivís*	*subís*	*escribís*	*-ís*
ellos, ellas, Uds.	viven	suben	escriben	-en

La UNICA Manera de Vivir

2. The verb *ver* "to see" follows the same pattern as other *-er* verbs except the *yo* form.

VER	
yo	veo
tú	ves
él, ella, Ud.	ve
nosotros(as)	vemos
vosotros(as)	*véis*
ellos, ellas, Uds.	ven

Ejercicios

A **¿A quién escribes?** Practiquen la conversación. (*Practice the conversation.*)

RENÉ: Oye, Carmen. ¿Qué escribes?
CARMEN: Escribo una carta.
RENÉ: ¿A quién escribes?
CARMEN: Pues, a un amigo, Jesús Orjales.
RENÉ: ¿Jesús Orjales? ¿Dónde vive él?
CARMEN: Vive en Madrid. Él y yo somos buenos amigos.

Contesten según la conversación. (*Answer based on the conversation.*)

1. ¿Dónde vive Jesús Orjales?
2. ¿Vive Carmen en Madrid también?
3. ¿Escribe Carmen una tarjeta postal a Jesús?
4. ¿Qué escribe?
5. ¿Escribe Carmen la carta o recibe ella la carta?

B **¿Qué aprenden los alumnos en la escuela?** Formen oraciones. (*Make up sentences.*)

En la escuela los alumnos…

1. aprender mucho
2. aprender el español
3. leer muchas novelas en la clase de inglés
4. escribir muchas composiciones
5. recibir notas o calificaciones buenas

C **Entrevista.** Preguntas personales. (*Give your own answers.*)

1. ¿Dónde vives?
2. ¿Vives en un apartamento o en una casa particular?
3. ¿Vives en una ciudad, en un pueblo pequeño, en un suburbio o en el campo?
4. ¿En qué calle vives?
5. En casa, ¿comes con la familia?
6. ¿Comes en el comedor o en la cocina?
7. Después de la cena, ¿lees el periódico?
8. ¿Qué periódico lees?
9. A veces, ¿lees un libro?
10. A veces, ¿escribes una carta a un(a) amigo(a)?

D **Preferencias.** Formen oraciones según el modelo. (*Make up sentences according to the model.*)

> **¿Yo? Yo leo muchas novelas. (¿Yo? Yo leo pocas novelas.)**

1. novelas
2. poesías
3. comedias
4. novelas de ciencia ficción
5. novelas históricas
6. novelas policíacas
7. biografías
8. autobiografías

E **Más preferencias.** Formen oraciones según el modelo. (*Make up sentences according to the model.*)

> **¿Yo? Siempre como frutas.**
> **¿Yo? Como frutas a veces.**

1. frutas
2. tomates
3. sándwiches (bocadillos)
4. papas
5. hamburguesas
6. ensalada
7. postre
8. helado

F **¿Y para beber?** Preparen una conversación según el modelo. (*Make up a conversation according to the model.*)

> **—¿Bebes té?**
> **—Sí, bebo té. (No, no bebo té.)**

1. té
2. café
3. leche
4. Coca cola
5. Pepsi
6. Fanta
7. gaseosa
8. limonada

G Oye, ¿qué…? Formen preguntas según el modelo. (*Make up questions according to the model.*)

Oye, Catalina. ¿Qué lees?

1.

2.

3.

4.

H ¡Y Uds. también! Sigan el modelo. (*Follow the model.*)

Vivimos en los Estados Unidos.
Y Uds. también viven en los Estados Unidos, ¿no?

1. Vivimos en los Estados Unidos.
2. Vivimos en una ciudad grande.
3. Recibimos el periódico todos los días.
4. Leemos el periódico todos los días.
5. Aprendemos mucho cuando leemos el periódico.

I Vivimos en los Estados Unidos. Contesten. (*Answer.*)

1. ¿Dónde viven Uds.?
2. ¿Viven Uds. en una casa particular?
3. ¿Viven Uds. en un apartamento?
4. ¿Escriben Uds. mucho en la clase de español?
5. Y en la clase de inglés, ¿escriben Uds. mucho?
6. ¿Comprenden Uds. cuando la profesora habla en español?
7. ¿Reciben Uds. buenas notas en español?
8. ¿Aprenden Uds. mucho en la escuela?
9. ¿Leen Uds. muchos libros?
10. ¿Comen Uds. en la cafetería de la escuela?

J ¿Qué ve? Completen con *ver*. (*Complete with* ver.)

1. Muchas veces yo ___ una película en la televisión.
2. Yo ___ la película con la familia.
3. Las películas que nosotros ___ son interesantes.
4. Yo ___ las noticias en la televisión.
5. ¿___ tú las noticias también?
6. ¿Qué películas ___ Uds.?

Sustantivos en *-dad, -tad,* y *-ión*   *The Gender of Nouns*

1. Most nouns that end in *-dad* and *-tad* are feminine. Almost all of these nouns are cognates. The *-dad* or *-tad* endings in Spanish correspond to the ending *-ty* in English.

la universidad	la capacidad
la oportunidad	la realidad
la popularidad	la responsabilidad

2. Most nouns that end in *-ión* are also feminine. The *-ión* ending in Spanish corresponds to the *-ion* ending in English.

la región	la opinión
la nación	la división

3. Note that all nouns that end in *-dad, -tad,* and *-ión* form their plural by adding an *-es.*

la ciudad	las ciudades
la universidad	las universidades
la solución	las soluciones
la administración	las administraciones

Ejercicios

A **Una universidad muy buena.**
Completen. (*Complete with an appropriate word.*)

Asistir a una ___ como Princeton o Harvard es una buena ___. La ___ de los profesores y de la ___ es enseñar a los estudiantes.

B **El plural por favor.** Den el plural. (*Give the plural.*)

1. la ciudad
2. la nación
3. la oportunidad
4. la calificación

La entrada de la Universidad de Salamanca, España

La expresión impersonal *hay*   *Telling What There is Around You*

The expression *hay* means "there is" or "there are."

> **Hay muchos edificios altos en una ciudad grande.**
> **Hay un cuarto de baño en la planta baja de la casa.**

Ejercicio

 ¿Cuántos hay? Contesten. (*Answer.*)

1. ¿Cuántos cuartos hay en una casa grande?
2. ¿Cuántos cuartos hay en una casa pequeña?
3. ¿Cuántos pisos hay en un edificio alto?
4. ¿Cuántos alumnos hay en la clase de español?
5. ¿Cuántos profesores o cuántas profesoras hay en la clase de español?
6. ¿Cuántas cafeterías hay en la escuela?
7. ¿Cuántos gimnasios hay en la escuela?
8. ¿Hay un gimnasio para muchachos y otro para muchachas?

aquí hay
ORLANDO

CONVERSACIÓN

Escenas de la vida *¿Dónde vives?*

FELIPE: Oye, Casandra. Tú vives en
Madrid, ¿no?
CASANDRA: Sí, soy madrileña y
muy castiza.
FELIPE: ¿Dónde vives en Madrid?
CASANDRA: Vivo en Goya,
cuarenta y ocho.

FELIPE: ¿En Goya?
CASANDRA: Sí, en la calle Goya.

FELIPE: ¿Uds. viven en la planta
baja?
CASANDRA: No, vivimos en el
segundo izquierda.

Nota: No es fácil explicar la palabra
castizo. Es como la palabra simpático.
Significa "puro, legítimo". En Madrid,
significa muy madrileño.

A **¿Dónde vive Casandra?** Contesten. (*Answer.*)

1. ¿Vive Casandra en Madrid?
2. ¿Es ella madrileña?
3. ¿En qué calle vive?
4. ¿Qué número?
5. ¿Vive con la familia?
6. ¿Viven ellos en la planta baja?
7. ¿En qué piso viven?

B **¿Y tú?** Preguntas personales.
(*Give your own answers.*)

1. ¿En qué ciudad o pueblo vives?
2. ¿En qué calle vives?
3. ¿Cuál es el número de la casa?
4. ¿Cuál es la zona postal?

Pronunciación   *La consonante* d

The pronunciation of the consonant **d** in Spanish varies according to its position in the word. When a word begins with **d** (initial position) or follows the consonants **l** or **n**, the tongue gently strikes the back of the upper front teeth.

da	de	di	do	du
da	de	Diego	donde	duque
tienda	derecha	disco	segundo	

When **d** appears within the word between vowels (medial position), the **d** is extremely soft. To pronounce this **d** properly, your tongue should strike the lower part of your upper teeth, almost between the upper and lower teeth. Listen and imitate carefully.

da	de	di	do	du
privada	Adela	estudio	helado	educación
ensalada	modelo	media	estado	

helado

When a word ends in **d** (final position), the **d** is either extremely soft or omitted completely, not pronounced.

    ciudad   nacionalidad

Repeat the following sentences.

> **Diego da el dinero a Donato en la ciudad.**
> **El empleado vende helado y limonada.**
> **Adela compra la merienda en la tienda.**

Comunicación

A **¿Verdad?** Assume that your partner does the following things, and say so, using *¿verdad?* (right). Your partner says *mentira* and corrects you.

> **vivir en las afueras**
> **Estudiante 1: Tú vives en las afueras, ¿verdad?**
> **Estudiante 2: Mentira. Vivo en la ciudad.**

1. beber un vaso de leche
2. comer helado de vainilla
3. escribir con lápiz
4. leer un periódico
5. ver una telenovela

B **A Sevilla.** On the train from Madrid to Sevilla you meet a Spanish student (your partner). He or she wants to know something about you. Provide the following information.

1. where you live
2. where you work or study
3. if you live in an apartment or a private home
4. if you live in a city, suburb, or the country

VIVIENDAS

*E*n los países hispanos gran parte de la población vive en las grandes ciudades. Por eso, mucha gente vive en apartamentos. En algunos[1] casos son propietarios del apartamento y en otros son inquilinos[2].

Chabolas en Valparaíso, Chile

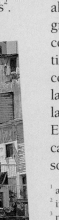

Como mucha gente vive y también trabaja en la misma ciudad, hay muchos que van a casa al mediodía. Toman el almuerzo en casa con la familia. El almuerzo típico es una comida bastante grande con varios platos. Pero hoy día como hay tanto[5] tráfico, toma mucho tiempo para ir a casa. Por eso la gente come al mediodía en un restaurante o en la cafetería (cantina) de la escuela o de la empresa (compañía) donde trabajan. En todas partes del mundo hay muchos cambios[6] en la manera de vivir. Es la sociedad moderna.

[1] algunos *some*
[2] inquilinos *renters*
[3] pobres *poor*
[4] chabolas, chozas *shacks*
[5] tanto *so much*
[6] cambios *changes*

Hay también suburbios con casas particulares en las afueras de las ciudades. Algunos suburbios son muy elegantes con grandes casas de lujo. Pero en las afueras de las ciudades también hay zonas pobres[3] donde la gente vive en chabolas o chozas[4] humildes.

Casas particulares en la Ciudad de México

Estudio de palabras

A **Palabras afines.** Busquen diez palabras afines en la lectura. (*Find ten cognates in the reading.*)

B **¿Sí o no?** ¿Verdad o no? (*Answer* sí *or* no.)

1. Una persona pobre es una persona con mucho dinero.
2. Un suburbio es un pueblo en las afueras de una ciudad.
3. El propietario es la persona que compra una casa o un apartamento.
4. El inquilino es la persona que compra una casa o un apartamento.
5. El total de habitantes de una ciudad o de un país es la población.
6. El desayuno es la comida del mediodía.
7. Una chabola o choza es una casa elegante.
8. Mucha gente pobre vive en chabolas o chozas.

Comprensión

A **¿Cómo es?** Escojan la respuesta correcta. (*Choose the correct completion.*)

1. En los países hispanos gran parte de la gente vive en ___.
   a. hoteles en los suburbios
   b. apartamentos en las grandes ciudades
   c. casas elegantes en el campo
2. Muchas familias viven en apartamentos porque ___.
   a. viven en las grandes ciudades
   b. viven en las afueras de las ciudades
   c. no hay suburbios
3. La mayoría de la gente que vive en apartamentos son ___.
   a. propietarios
   b. inquilinos
   c. pobres

4. La gente rica vive en ___.
   a. chabolas
   b. las zonas pobres
   c. casas grandes y lujosas
5. Una chabola es ___.
   a. una casa lujosa y elegante
   b. una pequeña casa pobre
   c. una zona pobre

B **Información cultural.** Según la lectura, escojan la diferencia cultural más importante. (*According to the reading, select the most important cultural difference.*)

a. Las ciudades son muy importantes en Latinoamérica.
b. En los países hispanos más gente vive en apartamentos en ciudades grandes que en los Estados Unidos.
c. No hay suburbios en Latinoamérica.

LOS CIPRESES DEL MAR

MEMORIA CALIDADES

Gran lujo
Aire acondicionado
Sofisticado sistema de seguridad
Cocina equipada con aparatos BOSCH
Bañera JACUZZI con hidromasaje
Antena parabólica
Televisión ✳ Video

MILLA DE ORO
Km. 0,00 MARBELLA (Junto Hotel Don Pepe)
desde: 200.000 Ptas. m²
Telf. 942-837586

DESCUBRIMIENTO CULTURAL

*A*quí ves la dirección de un madrileño.

Emilio Iglesias Herrera
Calle de Serrano 74, 5° Izda[1].
28006 Madrid,
España

interesante—la gente no bebe leche ni agua con la comida. En España beben agua mineral. En algunos países, sobre todo, en España, la Argentina, Chile y el Uruguay, la gente toma vino[2] con la comida—vino blanco o vino tinto.

¿En qué calle vive el señor Herrera? ¿En qué piso vive? ¿Cuál es la zona postal? ¿El apartamento o piso en Madrid está a la derecha o a la izquierda? ¿Cuál es la abreviatura de izquierda?

Casandra, la muchacha castiza en la conversación, vive en la calle Goya. La calle Goya es una calle en la zona o barrio Salamanca. Salamanca es una zona elegante de Madrid. Otra calle en Salamanca es la calle Velázquez. Goya y Velázquez son pintores o artistas muy famosos de España. Hay una colección fantástica de sus pinturas en el Museo del Prado. El Museo del Prado es un museo famoso de Madrid.

En muchos países hispanos la cena es a las ocho o a las ocho y media de la noche. Pero en España, la gente no cena hasta las diez o las once de la noche.

En España y Latinoamérica la gente toma café, pero no con la comida. Toman café después de la comida. Y otra cosa

¿Cuándo comen los hispanos la ensalada, antes de la comida, con la comida o después de la comida? Muchos hispanos comen la ensalada después del plato principal. ¿Cuándo comen Uds. la ensalada?

[1] izda., izquierda *left*
[2] vino *wine*

Y AQUÍ EN LOS ESTADOS UNIDOS

En los Estados Unidos gran número de ciudades llevan nombres españoles, Sacramento, San Antonio, El Paso, Los Ángeles y San Francisco, Monterey y Las Vegas y en Alaska, Valdez. También los nombres de algunos estados son españoles, especialmente en el suroeste del país. California, Colorado, Nevada, Nuevo México, Florida, todos son nombres españoles. Los españoles son los primeros exploradores europeos del continente norteamericano.

La misión de Carmel, California

REALIDADES

El almuerzo en la casa de Juan Pablo Rodriguez, un muchacho español **1**.

Aquí ven Uds. una zona residencial de Guadalajara, México **2**.

Una casa particular en Caracas, Venezuela **3**. Es una casa moderna.

Apartamentos en Sevilla, España **4**.

Apartamentos en venta en Puerto Rico **5**.

148

3 APARTAMENTOS
SE VENDE
INF. OSVALDO VELEZ
REAL ESTATE
AVE. ESMERALDA P-10, GUAYNABO, PR
TEL. 789-4279
DIA Y NOCHE
2 MIL PIES² COMERCIAL

5

Comunicación oral

A **De paseo.** While visiting in Chile you meet a student (your partner) who wants to know the following about eating customs in the United States.

1. when you eat your salad at dinner
2. at what time you eat dinner
3. where people eat lunch
4. what people drink with their meals
5. when people drink coffee

B **El apartamento nuevo.** You are looking for an apartment. Tell the real estate agent (your partner) the type of apartment you need and the features you want it to have. The real estate agent will tell you what apartments he or she has available.

Comunicación escrita

A **En el campo.** You and your family have rented a condo in the country. Write a letter to a Spanish-speaking friend describing the condo. Include the following information.

1. where it is located
2. which floor you are on
3. if it is big or small
4. how many rooms it has
5. if it has stairs or an elevator
6. if it has a television and how many
7. your general impression of the condo

B **Otra carta.** Write a letter to a friend in Puerto Rico. Tell him or her where you live; some things you do at home after school; when you eat; what you eat for dinner; what you talk about with your friends on the telephone; what types of things you read or watch on TV.

Reintegración

A **Entrevista.** Preguntas personales. (*Give your own answers.*)

1. ¿De dónde eres?
2. ¿Dónde vives?
3. ¿En qué escuela eres alumno(a)?
4. ¿Estudias español?
5. ¿Quién es el/la profesor(a) de español?
6. ¿Qué notas sacas en español?
7. ¿Lees mucho en español?
8. ¿Comprendes cuando el/la profesor(a) habla español en clase?

B **La clase de español.** Completen con la forma apropiada del verbo. (*Complete with the correct form of the verb.*)

1. La clase de español ___ muy interesante. (ser)
2. La profesora ___ muy buena. (ser)
3. Ella ___ bien. (enseñar)
4. Nosotros ___ mucho en la clase de español. (estudiar)
5. Juan y Carlos ___ la guitarra. (tocar)
6. Ellos ___ la guitarra y nosotros ___. (tocar, cantar)
7. Yo ___ una nota muy buena en español. (sacar)

Vocabulario

SUSTANTIVOS

la ciudad
las afueras
los suburbios
el pueblo
el campo
la calle
la avenida
el edificio
la planta baja
el apartamento
el ascensor
la escalera
el piso
la sala
la cocina
el comedor
el cuarto de dormir
el dormitorio
la habitación
el cuarto de baño

la comida
el desayuno

el almuerzo
la cena
la sopa
la carne
la papa
la ensalada
el sándwich
el bocadillo
el postre
el helado
el vaso
la leche
la gaseosa
el café
la limonada
la televisión
la película
la telenovela
la emisión
las noticias
el libro
la novela
el periódico
la revista

la carta
la tarjeta postal
la invitación
el bolígrafo
el lápiz

ADJETIVOS

primer(o)(a)
segundo(a)
tercer(o)(a)
cuarto(a)
quinto(a)
sexto(a)
séptimo(a)
octavo(a)
noveno(a)
décimo(a)

particular
privado(a)
deportivo(a)

VERBOS

comer
beber

leer
vender
comprender
aprender
ver
vivir
subir
asistir
escribir

OTRAS PALABRAS Y
EXPRESIONES

hay
a la derecha
a la izquierda
siempre
a veces
mucho
poco

6

LA FAMILIA
Y SU CASA

OBJETIVOS

In this chapter you will learn to do the following:

1. talk about your family
2. describe your home
3. give your age and find out someone else's age
4. tell what you have to do
5. tell what you are going to do
6. talk about your belongings and those of others
7. talk about families in Spanish-speaking countries

153

VOCABULARIO

PALABRAS 1

LA FAMILIA

el abuelo   los abuelos   la abuela

los padres   los hijos

el padre   la madre   la hija   el hijo

el esposo   el marido   la esposa   la mujer   la tía   el tío

los tíos

los nietos

el nieto   el primo   la nieta   la sobrina   la prima   el sobrino

el gato   el perro

Es la familia Galdós.
El señor y la señora Galdós tienen dos hijos.
Tienen un hijo y una hija.
Los Galdós tienen un perro.
No tienen un gato.

¿Cuántos años tienen los hijos?
Pepe, el hijo, tiene dieciséis años.
Celia, la hija, tiene catorce años.
Son jóvenes. No son viejos.

Ejercicios

A La familia Galdós. Contesten. (*Answer.*)

1. ¿Tiene la familia Galdós un apartamento en Lima?
2. ¿Tienen dos hijos los Galdós?
3. ¿Es grande o pequeña la familia Galdós?
4. ¿Cuántos años tiene el hijo?
5. ¿Y cuántos años tiene la hija?
6. ¿Los Galdós tienen un perro o un gato?
7. Los hijos de los Galdós, ¿tienen primos?
8. ¿Tienen tíos también?

B Mi familia. Completen. (*Complete.*)

1. El hermano de mi padre es mi ___.
2. La hermana de mi padre es mi ___.
3. El hermano de mi madre es mi ___.
4. La hermana de mi madre es mi ___.
5. El hijo de mi tío y de mi tía es mi ___.
6. Y la hija de mis tíos es mi ___.
7. Los hijos de mis tíos son mis ___.

C ¡Y yo! Escojan la respuesta correcta. (*Choose the correct answer.*)

1. Y yo, yo soy ___ de mis abuelos.
   a. el nieto   b. la nieta

2. Yo soy ___ de mis padres.
   a. el hijo   b. la hija

3. Yo soy ___ de mi tío.
   a. el sobrino   b. la sobrina

4. Yo soy ___ de mi hermana.
   a. el hermano   b. la hermana

5. Yo soy ___ de mi hermano.
   a. el hermano   b. la hermana

VOCABULARIO

PALABRAS 2

LA CASA Y EL APARTAMENTO

la casa

el árbol

la planta

la flor

el jardín

alrededor de

Es la casa de la familia López.
Su casa es bonita.
Alrededor de la casa hay un jardín.
El jardín tiene árboles, plantas y flores.

el ciclomotor

el garaje

el coche

el carro viejo

el carro nuevo

la bicicleta

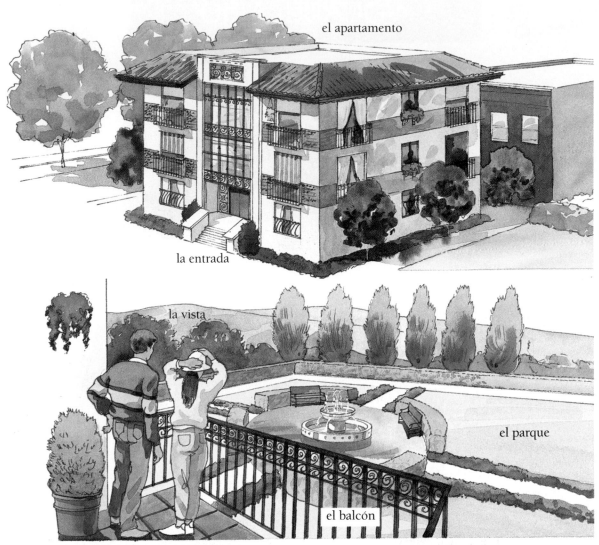

el apartamento

la entrada

la vista

el parque

el balcón

Es el apartamento de la familia Asenjo.
Su apartamento tiene un balcón.
Del balcón hay una vista bonita, preciosa.
Hay una vista del parque.

el cumpleaños

los regalos

la fiesta de cumpleaños

Ejercicios

A La casa de la familia López.
Contesten. (*Answer.*)

1. ¿Es bonita la casa de la familia López?
2. ¿Tiene la casa un jardín?
3. ¿Es bonito el jardín?
4. ¿Tiene flores y árboles el jardín?
5. ¿Tienen los López un coche nuevo?
6. ¿Está en el garaje su coche?
7. ¿Tienen los hijos de los López una bicicleta o un ciclomotor?
8. ¿Tienen televisor? ¿Dónde está?

B El apartamento o la casa. Escojan la respuesta correcta. (*Choose the correct answer.*)

1. Tiene un balcón. (el apartamento/la casa)
2. Está en el quinto piso. (el apartamento/la casa)
3. Hay una vista bonita. (del balcón/del coche)
4. Tiene garaje. (el apartamento/la casa)
5. Del balcón hay una vista preciosa. (del garaje/del parque)
6. ¿Dónde está el coche? (en el jardín/en el garaje)

C El cumpleaños de Luisa López.
Contesten según se indica. (*Answer according to the cue.*)

1. ¿Qué es hoy? (el cumpleaños de Luisa)
2. ¿Cuántos años tiene o cumple? (quince)
3. ¿Qué dan sus padres en su honor? (una fiesta)
4. ¿Qué recibe Luisa? (muchos regalos)
5. ¿Van todos sus parientes a la fiesta? (sí)

Comunicación

Palabras 1 y 2

A **La familia.** You and your partner each prepare a family tree with grand-parents, aunts and uncles, cousins, parents, brothers and sisters, and nieces and nephews (if you have them). Then take turns, identifying and telling something about each relative.

> **Mi abuelo es José Marchena.**
> **Es viejo, y muy simpático.**

B **Mi familia.** Work with a classmate. Tell him or her something about your family. After each statement you make, your classmate will say something about his or her family. Use the model as a guide.

> Estudiante 1: En mi familia hay cuatro personas. (Somos cuatro.)
> Estudiante 2: ¡Cuatro! En mi familia hay cinco personas.
>   (Somos cinco.)
> Estudiante 1: Vivimos en una casa.
> Estudiante 2: Nosotros, no. Vivimos en un apartamento.

C **Mis parientes.** Work with a classmate. Write each of the following words on a slip of paper. Put the papers in a pile. Take turns picking a paper from the pile and give a definition of the word on your slip.

1. mi primo
2. mi abuela
3. mi tío
4. mi sobrina
5. mis tíos
6. mi papá

ESTRUCTURA

El presente del verbo *tener*

*Telling What You and Others Have,
Telling People's Ages*

1. The verb *tener* "to have," is irregular. Study the following forms.

TENER	
yo	tengo
tú	tienes
él, ella, Ud.	tiene
nosotros(as)	tenemos
vosotros(as)	*tenéis*
ellos, ellas, Uds.	tienen

2. You also use the verb *tener* to express age in Spanish.

> ¿Cuántos años tienes?
> ¿Cuántos años tiene Ud.?
> Tengo dieciséis años.

Ejercicios

A **¿Tienes un hermano?** Practiquen la conversación. (*Practice the conversation.*)

TERESA: Reynaldo, ¿tienes un hermano?
REYNALDO: No, no tengo hermano. Tengo una hermana.
TERESA: ¿Cuántos años tiene ella?
REYNALDO: Tiene catorce años.
TERESA: Y tú, ¿cuántos años tienes?
REYNALDO: ¿Yo? Yo tengo dieciséis.
TERESA: ¿Uds. tienen un perrito?
REYNALDO: No, perrito no tenemos. Pero tenemos una gata adorable.

Completen según la conversación. (*Complete according to the conversation.*)

1. Reynaldo no ___ hermano.
2. Pero él ___ una hermana.
3. Su hermana ___ catorce años.
4. Reynaldo ___ dieciséis años.
5. Reynaldo y su hermana no ___ perrito.
6. Pero ellos ___ una gata adorable.

B **Una entrevista.** Preguntas personales. (*Give your own answers.*)

1. ¿Tienes un hermano?
2. ¿Cuántos hermanos tienes?
3. ¿Tienes una hermana?
4. ¿Cuántas hermanas tienes?
5. ¿Tienes un perro?
6. ¿Tienes un gato?
7. ¿Tienes muchos amigos?
8. ¿Tienes primos?
9. ¿Cuántos primos tienes?
10. ¿Cuántos tíos tienes?
11. ¿Cuántas tías tienes?
12. ¿Tienes una familia grande o pequeña?

C **¿Qué tienes?** Formen preguntas con *tienes.* (*Make up questions with* tienes.)

1. un hermano
2. una hermana
3. primos
4. un perro
5. un gato
6. muchos amigos

D **¿Qué tienen Uds.?** Formen preguntas según se indica. (*Make up questions according to the model.*)

> una casa o un apartamento
> *Marcos y Adela, ¿qué tienen Uds.? ¿Tienen una casa o un apartamento?*

1. un perro o un gato
2. un hermano o una hermana
3. un sobrino o una sobrina
4. una familia grande o pequeña
5. una bicicleta o un ciclomotor
6. cintas o discos

E **Nuestra familia.** Contesten según su familia. (*Answer based on your family.*)

1. ¿Tienen Uds. una casa?
2. ¿Tienen Uds. un apartamento?
3. ¿Tienen Uds. un coche?
4. ¿Tienen Uds. un ciclomotor o una bicicleta?
5. ¿Tienen Uds. teléfono?
6. ¿Tienen Uds. televisor?

Un edificio de apartamentos en Madrid

*La plaza en
Chinchón,
España*

F **La familia Sánchez.** Completen con *tener*. (*Complete with* tener.)

Aquí ___ (nosotros) la familia Sánchez. La familia Sánchez ___ un piso
          1   2
(apartamento) muy bonito en Madrid. El piso ___ seis cuartos y está en
                                            3
Salamanca, una zona bastante elegante de Madrid. Los Sánchez ___ una casa de
                                                              4
campo en Chinchón. La casa de campo en Chinchón es un pequeño chalet
donde los Sánchez pasan los fines de semana (*weekends*) y sus vacaciones. La
casa de campo ___ cinco cuartos. Hay cuatro personas en la familia Sánchez.
              5
Carolina ___ diecisiete años y su hermano Gerardo ___ quince años. Gerardo
         6   7
y Carolina ___ un perrito encantador, Chispa. Adoran a su Chispa. ¿Tú ___ un
           8   9
perro? ¿Tú ___ un gato? ¿Tu familia ___ un apartamento o una casa? ¿Uds.
           10   11
también ___ una casa de campo donde pasan los fines de semana como ___ los
        12   13
Sánchez?

Tener que + el infinitivo
Ir a + el infinitivo

Telling What You Have to Do
Telling What You're Going to Do

1. *Tener que* + *infinitive* (-ar, -er, or -ir form of the verb) means "to have to."

   Tengo que comprar un regalo.

2. *Ir a* + *infinitive* means "to be going to." It is used to express what is going to
   happen in the near future.

   Vamos a llegar mañana.
   Ella va a cumplir quince años.

Ejercicios

A ¡Cuánto tengo que trabajar! Preguntas personales. (*Give your own answers.*)

1. ¿Tienes que trabajar mucho en la escuela?
2. ¿Tienes que estudiar mucho?
3. ¿Tienes que leer muchos libros?
4. ¿Tienes que escribir composiciones?
5. ¿Tienes que tomar exámenes?
6. ¿Tienes que sacar buenas notas?

B En la clase de español. ¿Qué tienen que hacer? (*Tell what you have to do in Spanish class.*)

1. hablar
2. pronunciar bien
3. aprender el vocabulario
4. leer
5. escribir un poco
6. comprender una nueva cultura

C Voy a dar una fiesta. Contesten. (*Answer.*)

1. ¿Vas a dar una fiesta?
2. ¿Vas a dar la fiesta en honor de Paco?
3. ¿Va a cumplir diecisiete años Paco?
4. ¿Vas a invitar a los amigos de Paco?
5. ¿Vas a preparar refrescos?
6. ¿Van Uds. a bailar durante la fiesta?
7. ¿Van a cantar?
8. ¿Van a comer?

D No, porque… Sigan el modelo. (*Follow the model.*)

> ver la televisión/preparar la comida
> *No voy a ver la televisión porque tengo que preparar la comida.*

1. escuchar discos/estudiar
2. ver la televisión/escribir una composición
3. ir a la fiesta/trabajar
4. tomar seis cursos/sacar buenas notas
5. tomar apuntes/escuchar al profesor
6. ir al café/escribir una carta a abuelita

Los adjetivos posesivos

Telling What Belongs to You and to Others

1. You use possessive adjectives to show possession or ownership. Like other adjectives, the possessive adjectives must agree with the nouns they modify.

    mi   tu   su   nuestro(a)   *(vuestro[a])*

2. The adjectives *mi*, *tu*, and *su* have only two forms: singular and plural.

mi disco y mi cinta	**mis discos y mis cintas**
tu disco y tu cinta	**tus discos y tus cintas**
su disco y su cinta	**sus discos y sus cintas**

3. The possessive adjective *su* can mean "his," "her," "their," or "your." Its meaning is usually clear by its use in the sentence. If, however, it is not clear, *su* can be replaced by a prepositional phrase.

    el libro $\begin{cases} \text{de él} \\ \text{de ella} \\ \text{de Ud.} \end{cases}$ el libro $\begin{cases} \text{de ellos} \\ \text{de ellas} \\ \text{de Uds.} \end{cases}$

4. The possessive adjective *nuestro* "our" has four forms.

    nuestro apartamento
    nuestros libros
    nuestra casa
    nuestras revistas

5. The possessive adjective *vuestro,* like the subject pronoun *vosotros,* is only used in parts of Spain. *Vuestro,* like *nuestro,* also has four forms.

165

Ejercicios

A Mi casa y mi familia. Preguntas personales. (*Give your own answers.*)

1. ¿Dónde está tu casa o tu apartamento?
2. ¿Cuántos cuartos tiene tu casa o tu apartamento?
3. Tu apartamento o tu casa, ¿es grande o pequeño(a)?
4. Si tienes hermano, ¿cuántos años tiene?
5. Si tienes hermana, ¿cuántos años tiene?
6. ¿Cuántas personas hay en tu familia?
7. ¿Tus tíos viven en la misma ciudad o en el mismo pueblo?
8. Tu casa o tu apartamento, ¿está en una ciudad o en un pueblo pequeño?
9. ¿Tus abuelos viven en la misma ciudad o en el mismo pueblo?
10. Si tienes un perro o un gato, ¿es adorable tu animalito, tu mascota?

B ¿Dónde está tu…? Sigan el modelo. (*Follow the model.*)

la casa
Lupita, ¿dónde está tu casa?

1. el hermano
2. la hermana
3. los primos
4. el padre
5. la madre
6. el perro
7. el gato
8. los libros
9. la escuela
10. el/la profesor(a) de español

C ¿Yo? De ninguna manera. Preparen una conversación. (*Make up a conversation.*)

libro
Estudiante 1: ___, ¿(tú) tienes mi libro?
Estudiante 2: No. De ninguna manera. No tengo tu libro. La verdad es que tú tienes tu libro.

1. libros
2. revista
3. cinta
4. discos
5. dinero

D Su amigo es muy simpático. Sigan el modelo. (*Follow the model.*)

el hermano de Susana
Su hermano es muy simpático.

1. el hermano de Pablo
2. el hermano de Ud.
3. la amiga de Pablo
4. la amiga de Ud.
5. el primo de Carlos y José
6. la tía de Teresa y José
7. los tíos de Teresa y José
8. los padres de Uds.
9. el abuelo de Uds.
10. los amigos de Uds.

E **Nuestra casa.** Preguntas personales. (*Give your own answers.*)

1. Su casa (la casa de Uds.), ¿es grande o pequeña?
2. ¿Cuántos cuartos tiene su casa?
3. ¿Su casa está en la ciudad o en el campo?
4. ¿En qué calle está su escuela?
5. Su escuela, ¿es una escuela intermedia o una escuela superior?
6. ¿Quién es su profesor(a) de español?
7. ¿De qué nacionalidad es su profesor(a) de español?
8. En general, ¿sus profesores son simpáticos?
9. ¿Son interesantes sus cursos?
10. ¿Son grandes o pequeñas sus clases?

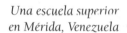

Una escuela superior en Mérida, Venezuela

Una casa en Chile

CONVERSACIÓN

Escenas de la vida   *¿Tú tienes hermana?*

TADEO: Tengo que ir a la tienda.
JAIME: ¿Por qué?
TADEO: Tengo que comprar un regalo para mi hermana. Mañana es su cumpleaños.

JAIME: ¿Tú tienes hermana?
TADEO: Sí.

JAIME: ¿Cuántos años tiene?
TADEO: Mañana va a cumplir quince años.

De compras. Contesten según la conversación. (*Answer according to the conversation.*)

1. ¿Con quién habla Tadeo?
2. ¿Adónde tiene que ir Tadeo?
3. ¿Qué tiene que comprar?
4. ¿Por qué tiene que comprar un regalo para su hermana?
5. ¿Cuántos años tiene su hermana?
6. ¿Cuántos años va a cumplir mañana?

168   CAPÍTULO 6

Pronunciación   *Las consonantes* b y v

There is no difference in pronunciation between a **b** and a **v** in Spanish. The **b** or **v** sound is somewhat softer than the sound of an English **b**. When making this sound, the lips barely touch.

ba	be	bi	bo	bu
bajo	bebé	bicicleta	bonito	bueno
balcón	escribe	bien	recibo	bus
trabaja	recibe	biología	árbol	aburrido

va	ve	vi	vo	vu
va	ve	vista	vosotros	vuelo
vaso	verano	vive	vólibol	vuelta

El bebé vuela
en el verano.

Repeat the following sentences.

El joven vive en la avenida Bolívar en Bogotá.
Bárbara trabaja los sábados en el laboratorio de biología.
El bebé ve la vista bonita del balcón.

Comunicación

A **Las vacaciones.** You are travelling through the Yucatan peninsula in Mexico visiting the wonderful Mayan ruins. You meet Jaime Buenrostro, a Mexican student. He asks you:

1. how old you are
2. how many brothers and sisters you have
3. if you live in a house or apartment
4. when your birthday is
5. if you have a cat or a dog

Answer Jaime's questions.

B **Mañana…** With a classmate prepare a list of things you are going to do tomorrow. Tell your classmate what you are going to do and he or she will let you know if he or she has to do the same thing. Report to the class.

C **Tengo que…** Make a list of things that you're not going to do because you have to do something else. Ask your partner if he or she has to do the same thing. If the answer is *no*, find out what your classmate is going to do.

D **Mis cosas.** Ask your partner questions about the following. Your classmate will answer. Then reverse roles.

1. su carro o su bicicleta
2. su casa o su apartamento
3. el jardín de su casa o el balcón de su apartamento
4. su perro o su gato
5. su hermana o su prima

LA FAMILIA HISPANA

Cuando un joven hispano habla de su familia, no habla solamente[1] de sus padres y de sus hermanos. Habla también de sus abuelos, de sus tíos y de sus primos. En fin, habla de todos sus parientes—incluso sus padrinos[2], el padrino y la madrina. Los padrinos forman una parte íntegra del círculo familiar.

La familia tiene mucha importancia en la sociedad hispana. Cuando hay una celebración como un matrimonio, un bautizo o un cumpleaños, todos los parientes van a la fiesta. Aun[3] los apellidos hispanos reflejan[4] la importancia que tiene la familia de una persona.

Aquí tenemos un ejemplo de los apellidos de una familia.

¡Y otra cosa importante! Los parientes políticos[5] también forman parte de la familia hispana.

[1] solamente *only*
[2] padrinos *godparents*
[3] aun *even*
[4] reflejan *reflect*
[5] políticos *in-laws*

CONTRERAS L. MARTHA

DOCTORA MARTHA CONTRERAS LAURRABAQUIO

CIRUJANO DENTISTA
DE 11 A 3 Y 5 A 9:30

2-16-27

ABOGADOS

**LIC. CARLOS MORALES VILLALOBOS
LIC. JOAQUÍN RENTERÍA DÍAZ**

Asuntos Judiciales y Administrativos

F. Bartolomé de las Casas 139 Sur
(Casi Esq. Con 16 de Sept)   4-11-15

ANTES DEL MATRIMONIO			
		APPELLIDO PATERNO	APPELLIDO MATERNO
EL JOVEN, EL NOVIO	Arturo	Guzmán	Echeverría
LA JOVEN, LA NOVIA	María	Blanco	Robles

DESPUÉS DEL MATRIMONIO	
EL ESPOSO	LA ESPOSA
Arturo Guzmán Echeverría	María Blanco de Guzmán

LOS HIJOS DEL MATRIMONIO	
EL HIJO	LA HIJA
José Guzmán Blanco	Luisa Guzmán Blanco

Estudio de palabras

A **Palabras afines.** Busquen diez palabras afines en la lectura.
(*Find ten cognates in the reading.*)

B **¿Quiénes…?** Escojan la
respuesta correcta. (*Choose the
correct answer.*)

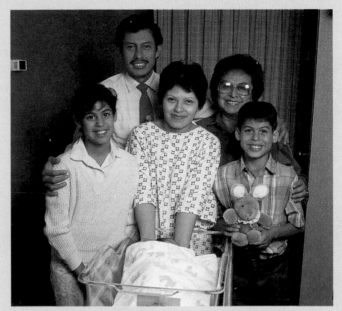

1. ¿Quiénes son los padres?
   a. el padre y la madre
   b. los parientes

2. ¿Quiénes son los parientes?
   a. el padre y la madre
   b. los abuelos, los tíos, los
      primos, etc.

3. ¿Quiénes son los parientes
   políticos?
   a. los parientes del esposo
   b. los parientes de sus
      abuelos o de la esposa

Comprensión

A **La familia.** Contesten. (*Answer.*)

1. Cuando un joven hispano habla de su familia, ¿habla solamente de
   sus padres y de sus hermanos?
2. ¿De quiénes habla?
3. ¿Cómo es la familia en la sociedad hispana?

B **Los apellidos.** Completen. (*Complete.*)

1. Un joven hispano lleva el apellido de su padre y de ___.
2. Una joven hispana también lleva el apellido de su ___ y de su ___.
3. Después del matrimonio, la esposa mantiene el apellido de su ___
   y toma el apellido de su ___.

C **Inferencia.** From this reading, what would you say about the
families in Spain and Latin America in comparison to the families in
the United States?

DESCUBRIMIENTO CULTURAL

*E*n España y en Latinoamérica, ¿hay familias de un sólo padre como aquí en los Estados Unidos? Sí, hay. Y en los países más industrializados del mundo hispano hay más y más. Sin embargo, el divorcio es un fenómeno relativamente nuevo (reciente) en las sociedades hispanas.

En inglés usamos la palabra "step" cuando hablamos, por ejemplo, del esposo de uno de nuestros padres. Hay términos en español también. Son la madrastra, el padrastro, el hijastro, la hijastra, el hermanastro y la hermanastra. Pero no son palabras de uso común. En vez de hablar de su madrastra, un hispano habla de la esposa de su padre. En vez de hablar de su hermanastro, habla del hijo del esposo de su madre o del hijo de la esposa de su padre.

En los Estados Unidos celebramos el "sweet sixteen" de una muchacha con una fiesta especial en su honor. En muchos países hispanos y también entre las familias hispanas de los Estados Unidos festejan a la quinceañera. La quinceañera es la muchacha que cumple quince años. Hay una gran fiesta en su honor. Todos los parientes y amigos asisten a la fiesta. La muchacha recibe

QUINCE AÑOS. Rodeada del afecto de sus seres queridos, celebró sus anhelados quince años la gentil señorita Ivonne de la Caridad Bolaños, hija del señor José Bolaños y señora, Mayra de Bolaños, estimados miembros de la colonia hispanoamericana. A las muchas felicitaciones recibidas, unimos las nuestras muy especiales, más votos por que cumpla muchos más.

Para una Hija muy linda

DOM	LUN	MAR	MIER	JUE	VIER	SAB
	1 San Severo	2 La Candelaria	3 San Blas	4 San Gilberto	5 C Mexicana 1917	6 San Teófilo
7 San Romualdo	8 San Ciriaco	9 San Nicéforo	10 San Guillermo	11 N. S. de Lourdes	12 San Melesio	13 San Benigno
14 San Valentín	15 San Faustino	16 San Onésimo	17 San Teódulo	18 San Heladio	19 San Álvaro	20 San Eleuterio
21 San Severiano	22 San Pascasio	23 Sta. Marta	24 Día de la Bandera	25 San Cesáreo	26 San Néstor	27 San Leandro
28 San Hilario						

muchos regalos. Si la familia de la quinceañera tiene mucho dinero, ella recibe regalos fabulosos, como un viaje a los Estados Unidos o a Europa.

En los países hispanos la gente celebra también el día de su santo. Muchas personas llevan el nombre de un santo. Hay un santo para cada día del calendario. Celebran también el cumpleaños del santo que tiene el mismo nombre. frecuentemente, el cumpleaños y el día del santo son el mismo día. ¿Por qué? Algunas veces los padres dan a su hijo el nombre del santo del día de su nacimiento.

Y AQUÍ EN LOS ESTADOS UNIDOS

En muchas comunidades hispanas de los Estados Unidos todavía se celebran *los quince*. Los americanos de ascendencia cubana, mexicana y puertorriqueña en particular tienen la costumbre de dar una fiesta para la *quinceañera*. Las fiestas de las familias ricas son magníficas, con comida abundante, baile y músicos que tocan música tradicional y moderna. El vestido de la quinceañera también es elegante y caro[1]. Las familias modestas celebran de manera más modesta. Pero también hay mucha comida, baile y música. Si no hay una banda de música, siempre hay discos. Las fiestas son alegres, y toda la familia, jóvenes y viejos, toma parte.

[1]caro   *expensive*

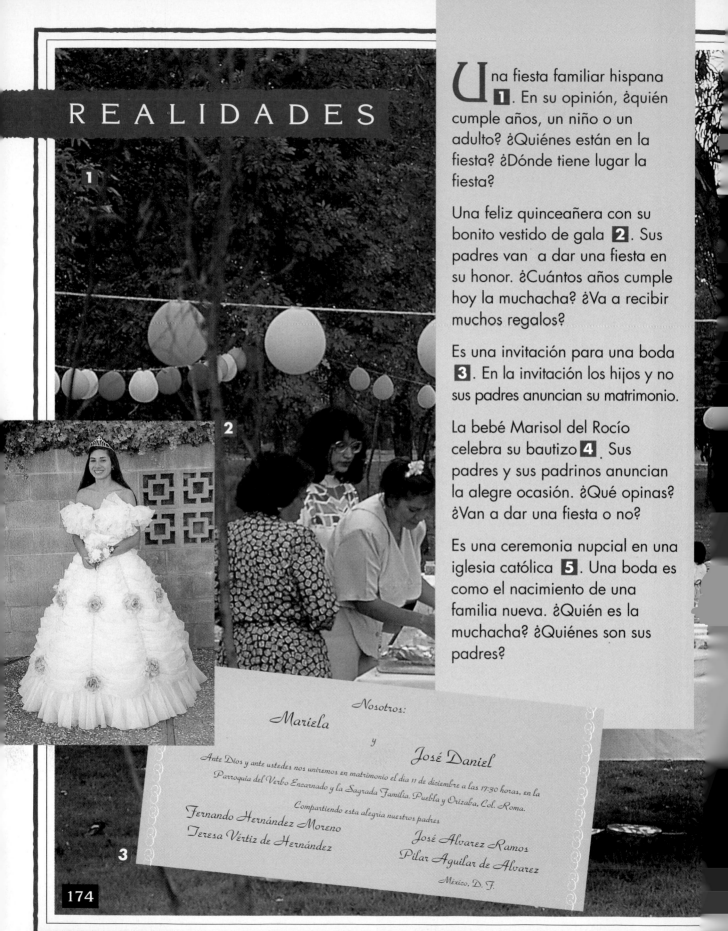

REALIDADES

Una fiesta familiar hispana **1**. En su opinión, ¿quién cumple años, un niño o un adulto? ¿Quiénes están en la fiesta? ¿Dónde tiene lugar la fiesta?

Una feliz quinceañera con su bonito vestido de gala **2**. Sus padres van a dar una fiesta en su honor. ¿Cuántos años cumple hoy la muchacha? ¿Va a recibir muchos regalos?

Es una invitación para una boda **3**. En la invitación los hijos y no sus padres anuncian su matrimonio.

La bebé Marisol del Rocío celebra su bautizo **4**. Sus padres y sus padrinos anuncian la alegre ocasión. ¿Qué opinas? ¿Van a dar una fiesta o no?

Es una ceremonia nupcial en una iglesia católica **5**. Una boda es como el nacimiento de una familia nueva. ¿Quién es la muchacha? ¿Quiénes son sus padres?

Nosotros:

Mariela

y

José Daniel

Ante Dios y ante ustedes nos uniremos en matrimonio el día 11 de diciembre a las 17:30 horas, en la Parroquia del Verbo Encarnado y la Sagrada Familia. Puebla y Orizaba, Col. Roma.

Compartiendo esta alegría nuestros padres

Fernando Hernández Moreno
Teresa Vértiz de Hernández

José Alvarez Ramos
Pilar Aguilar de Alvarez

México, D. F.

174

Marisol del Rocío

Nació en la Ciudad de México el día
9 de julio de 1993 y fué bautizada en
el Santuario Parroquial de Ntra.
Señora de la Piedad el día 14
del mismo mes y año.

Sus padres:

Raúl García Puente

e

Inés Gómez de García

Sus padrinos:

Hugo Magaña Campos

y

Diana Collado de Magaña

4

5

Comunicación oral

A **¿Qué tengo que hacer?** Tell your partner what you have to do to accomplish the following things. Reverse roles.

> **para llegar a la escuela**
> *Para llegar a la escuela, tengo que tomar el autobús.*

1. para ir a la tienda
2. para hablar español bien
3. para sacar una "A" en historia
4. para ir a la universidad
5. para ir a la fiesta
6. para tener buenos amigos

B **Mi casa.** Give your partner a description of your house or apartment. Your partner will write down the information and report it to the class.

C **¿Por qué…?** Tell your partner why you have to go to the following places. Reverse roles.

> **a la tienda**
> *Tengo que ir a la tienda porque tengo que comprar un regalo.*

1. a la tienda
2. a la cocina
3. a la escuela
4. al pueblo
5. al comedor
6. a mi cuarto
7. a la avenida Nueva York
8. al apartamento de mi amigo

Comunicación escrita

A **El árbol genealógico.** Prepare your own family tree using the Hispanic system of last names. Include the following relatives: grandparents, aunts and uncles, your parents, and your brothers and sisters.

B **Voy a vivir en Puerto Rico.** You are going to move to San Juan, Puerto Rico, and need to rent a house or apartment there. You decide to put an ad in the local newspaper. Write an ad describing the kind of house you are looking for.

C **La casa de mis sueños.** Write a paragraph describing the house of your dreams. Include its size, how many rooms it has, what the rooms are, if there is a garage, yard, balcony, trees, plants, flowers, etc. Then exchange papers with a classmate and proofread the paragraphs.

Reintegración

A **La casa.** Completen. (*Complete.*)

1. Preparamos la comida en ___.
2. Comemos en ___.
3. Miramos (vemos) la televisión en ___.
4. La sala, la cocina y el comedor están en ___.
5. Los cuartos de dormir están en ___.
6. Alrededor de la casa hay ___.
7. El jardín tiene ___.
8. El coche está en el ___.

B **¿Qué clase?** Escojan. (*Choose.*)

biología   español   álgebra   inglés

1. Voy al laboratorio donde miro muestras en el microscopio.
2. Hablo mucho.
3. Soluciono ecuaciones.
4. Aprendo una nueva cultura.
5. Tengo que disecar un animal.
6. Aprendo muchas palabras nuevas.
7. Leo muchas novelas, poesías, etc.
8. Escribo composiciones.
9. Estudio las células de los animales y de las plantas.
10. Estudio el binomio de Newton.

C **Los alumnos…** Rewrite all the sentences from Ejercicio B, beginning with *Los alumnos…*

Alumnos en una escuela en Madrid

Vocabulario

SUSTANTIVOS

la familia
el padre
la madre
la mujer
la esposa
el marido
el esposo
los padres
el hijo
la hija
el abuelo
la abuela
el nieto
la nieta
el tío
la tía
el primo
la prima

el sobrino
la sobrina
el perro
el gato
la casa
el apartamento
el balcón
la entrada
la vista
el parque
el jardín
el árbol
la flor
la planta
el garaje
el coche
el carro
la bicicleta
el ciclomotor

el cumpleaños
la fiesta
el regalo

ADJETIVOS

nuevo(a)
viejo(a)
joven
bonito(a)
precioso(a)

VERBOS

tener
recibir

OTRAS PALABRAS Y EXPRESIONES

tener… años
tener que
ir a…
alrededor de

CAPÍTULO

7

LOS DEPORTES DE EQUIPO

OBJETIVOS

In this chapter you will learn to do the following:

1. talk about team sports and other physical activities
2. tell what you want to do or prefer to do
3. tell what you can do
4. identify people's nationalities
5. discuss differences between football as it is played in the U.S. and in Hispanic countries
6. discuss the role of sports in Hispanic society

PALABRAS 1

EL FÚTBOL

el estadio

el tablero indicador

PERU
ARGENTINA

el árbitro

el portero
la portera

la portería

el campo de fútbol

la cabeza

la mano

el equipo

el balón

el pie

el jugador

el otoño

Los jugadores juegan al fútbol en el otoño.
Un jugador lanza el balón.
Tira el balón con el pie.

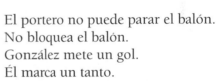

El segundo tiempo empieza.
Los dos equipos vuelven al campo.
El tanto queda empatado en cero.

El portero no puede parar el balón.
No bloquea el balón.
González mete un gol.
Él marca un tanto.

Perú gana el partido.
Argentina pierde.

A **Un juego de fútbol.** Contesten. (*Answer.*)

1. ¿Cuántos equipos de fútbol hay en el campo de fútbol?
2. ¿Y cuántos jugadores hay en cada equipo?
3. ¿Qué tiempo empieza, el primero o el segundo?
4. ¿Vuelven los jugadores al campo cuando empieza el segundo tiempo?
5. ¿Tiene un jugador el balón?
6. ¿Lanza el balón con el pie o con la mano?
7. ¿Para el balón el portero o entra el balón en la portería?
8. ¿Mete el jugador un gol?
9. ¿Marca un tanto?
10. ¿Queda empatado el tanto?
11. ¿Quién gana, el Perú o la Argentina?
12. ¿Qué equipo pierde?

B **El fútbol.** Contesten según se indica. (*Answer according to the cues.*)

1. ¿Cuántos jugadores hay en el equipo de fútbol? (once)
2. ¿Cuántos tiempos hay en un partido de fútbol? (dos)
3. ¿Quién guarda la portería? (el portero)
4. ¿Cuándo mete un gol el jugador? (cuando el balón entra en la portería)
5. ¿Qué marca un jugador cuando el balón entra en la portería? (un tanto)
6. En el estadio, ¿qué indica el tanto? (el tablero indicador)
7. ¿Cuándo queda empatado el tanto? (cuando los dos equipos tienen el mismo tanto)

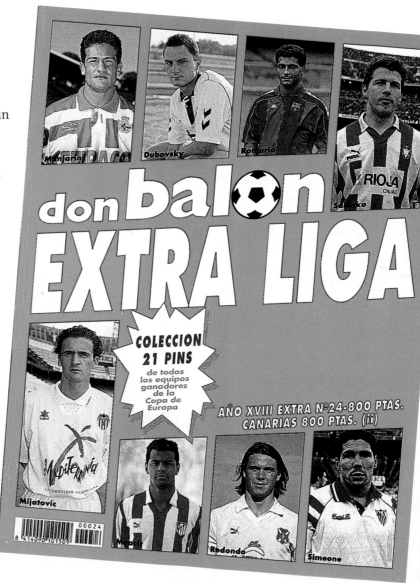

VOCABULARIO

PALABRAS 2

OTROS DEPORTES

el tablero

el aro

el cesto
el canasto

el baloncesto, el básquetbol

la cancha   driblar con el balón

encestar

meter en el cesto

pasar el balón

tirar el balón

el vólibol

la red

devolver el balón por encima de la red

CAPÍTULO 7   **183**

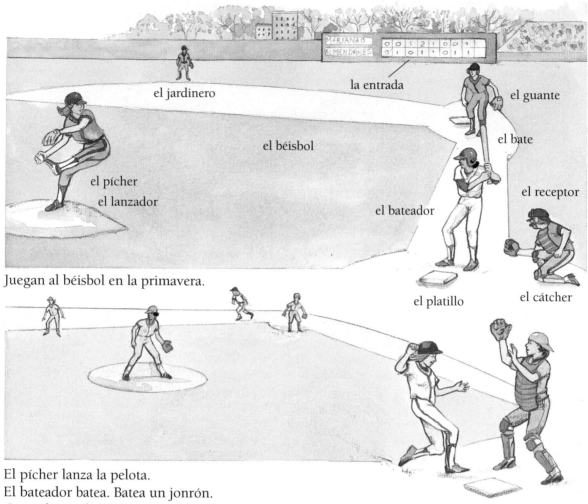

el jardinero

la entrada

el guante

el béisbol

el bate

el pícher
el lanzador

el receptor

el bateador

el platillo

el cátcher

Juegan al béisbol en la primavera.

El pícher lanza la pelota.
El bateador batea. Batea un jonrón.
Corre de una base a otra.

La jugadora atrapa la pelota.
Atrapa la pelota con el guante.

la base

El jugador puede robar una base.

Nota: Here are some English words used in Spanish.

el cátcher   **el hit**   **el out**

Ejercicios

A **El baloncesto.** Contesten. (*Answer.*)

1. ¿Es el baloncesto un deporte de equipo o un deporte individual?
2. ¿Hay cinco u once jugadores en el equipo de baloncesto?
3. Durante un partido de baloncesto, ¿los jugadores driblan con el balón o lanzan el balón con el pie?
4. ¿El jugador tira el balón en el cesto o en la portería?
5. ¿Marca un tanto cuando dribla o cuando encesta?
6. ¿El encestado (canasto) vale dos puntos o seis puntos?

B **El vólibol.** ¿Verdad o no? (*¿True or false?*)

1. El equipo de vólibol tiene seis jugadores.
2. En el vólibol los jugadores driblan con el balón.
3. El balón tiene que pasar por encima de la red.
4. El balón puede tocar la red.
5. Cuando el balón toca el suelo, los jugadores no pueden devolver el balón al campo contrario.

C **El béisbol.** Escojan la respuesta correcta. (*Choose the correct answer.*)

1. Juegan al béisbol en ___ de béisbol.
   a. un campo   b. una cancha   c. una red
2. El pícher ___ la pelota.
   a. lanza   b. encesta   c. batea
3. El receptor atrapa la pelota en ___.
   a. una red   b. un cesto   c. un guante
4. El jugador ___ de una base a otra.
   a. tira   b. devuelve   c. corre
5. En el béisbol el jugador ___ robar una base.
   a. puede   b. tiene que   c. necesita
6. En un partido de béisbol hay ___ entradas.
   a. dos   b. nueve   c. once

D **¿Qué deporte es?** Escojan. (*Choose.*)

el fútbol   el vólibol   el baloncesto

1. El jugador lanza el balón con el pie.
2. Hay cinco jugadores en el equipo.
3. El balón no puede tocar el suelo.
4. El jugador devuelve el balón por encima de la red.
5. El portero para o bloquea el balón.
6. El jugador tira el balón y encesta.
7. Los jugadores marcan tantos.

Comunicación

Palabras 1 y 2

A **En nuestro colegio.** With a classmate make a list of all your school's teams. Ask your classmate how each team is doing. Your friend will answer. Then decide if each team is good or not. Compile a list of your school's good and bad teams.

> Estudiante 1: El equipo de béisbol, ¿gana muchos partidos o pierde muchos partidos?
> Estudiante 2: Pierde muchos partidos. No juega bien.
> Estudiante 1: ¿Es un equipo bueno o malo?
> Estudiante 2: Es un equipo malo.

B **¿Qué deporte es?** Make up a sentence about a sport. Your partner will tell you what sport it is. Reverse roles.

C **Adivina quién es.** You and your partner each write down the name of your favorite sports hero. Do not show the name to each other. Ask your partner yes or no questions until you think you can name the player. You can only try to guess the name once. If you are wrong, you lose. You also lose if you have to ask more than ten questions. Then switch, and let your partner ask you the questions.

El presente de los verbos con el cambio *e* > *ie*

Describing People's Activities

1. There are certain groups of verbs in Spanish that have a stem change in the present tense. The verbs *empezar*, *comenzar* "to begin," *querer* "to want," *perder* "to lose," and *preferir* "to prefer" are stem-changing verbs. Note that the *e* of the stem changes to *ie* in all forms except *nosotros* and *vosotros*. The endings are the same as those of regular verbs. Study the following chart.

INFINITIVE	EMPEZAR	QUERER	PREFERIR
yo	empiezo	quiero	prefiero
tú	empiezas	quieres	prefieres
él, ella, Ud.	empieza	quiere	prefiere
nosotros(as)	empezamos	queremos	preferimos
vosotros(as)	empezáis	queréis	preferís
ellos, ellas, Uds.	empiezan	quieren	prefieren

2. The verbs *empezar, comenzar, querer,* and *preferir* are often followed by an infinitive.

> **Ellos quieren ir al gimnasio.**
> **¿Por qué prefieres jugar al fútbol?**

Before an infinitive *empezar* and *comenzar* require the preposition *a*.

> **Ellos empiezan (comienzan) a jugar.**

Ejercicios

A Queremos ganar. Contesten. (*Answer.*)

1. ¿Empiezan Uds. a jugar?
2. ¿Empiezan Uds. a jugar a las tres?
3. ¿Quieren Uds. ganar el partido?
4. ¿Quieren Uds. marcar un tanto?
5. ¿Pierden Uds. a veces o ganan siempre?
6. ¿Prefieren Uds. jugar en el parque o en la calle?

B El segundo tiempo empieza. Formen oraciones según el modelo. (*Make up sentences according to the model.*)

> el segundo tiempo/empezar
> *El segundo tiempo empieza.*

1. los jugadores/empezar a jugar
2. los dos equipos/querer ganar
3. ellos/preferir marcar muchos tantos
4. Toral/querer meter un gol
5. el portero/querer parar el balón
6. el equipo de Toral/no perder

C ¿Eres muy deportista? Preguntas personales. (*Give your own answers.*)

1. ¿Prefieres jugar al béisbol o al fútbol?
2. ¿Prefieres jugar con un grupo de amigos o con un equipo?
3. ¿Prefieres jugar o participar en el partido o prefieres mirar el partido?
4. ¿Prefieres ser jugador(a) o espectador(a)?
5. ¿Siempre quieres ganar?
6. ¿Pierdes a veces?

LA GRAN REVANCHA

LA SALSA PROFESSIONAL SOCCER CLUB

vs.

CLUB DEPORTIVO GUADALAJARA

DOMINGO
18 JULIO 6:05PM

ESTADIO CAL STATE DE FULLERTON

Compre anticipadamente su boleto para el domingo 18 y asista GRATIS al juego del Sábado 17 de Julio

PRECIO DE BOLETOS: ADULTOS $15.00 NIÑOS (M-14) $5.00
Estacionamiento del Estadio: $3.00

D **¿Quién va a ganar o triunfar?** Completen. (*Complete.*)

Rosita ____ (querer) jugar al baloncesto. Yo ____ (querer) jugar al béisbol. Y tú,
¿ ____ (preferir) jugar al baloncesto o ____ (preferir) jugar al béisbol? Si tú ____
(querer) jugar al béisbol, tú y yo ____ (ganar) y Rosita ____ (perder). Pero si
tú ____ (querer) jugar al baloncesto, entonces tú y Rosita ____ (ganar) y
yo ____ (perder).

El presente de los verbos con el cambio *o* > *ue*

Describing People's Activities

1. The verbs *volver* "to return to a place," *devolver* "to return a thing," *poder* "to be able," and *dormir* "to sleep" are also stem-changing verbs. The *o* of the stem changes to *ue* in all forms except *nosotros* and *vosotros*. Study the following chart.

INFINITIVE	VOLVER	PODER	DORMIR
yo	vuelvo	puedo	duermo
tú	vuelves	puedes	duermes
él, ella, Ud.	vuelve	puede	duerme
nosotros(as)	volvemos	podemos	dormimos
vosotros(as)	*volvéis*	*podéis*	*dormís*
ellos, ellas, Uds.	vuelven	pueden	duermen

2. Note that the *u* in the verb *jugar* changes to *ue* in all forms except *nosotros* and *vosotros*.

JUGAR	
yo	juego
tú	juegas
él, ella, Ud.	juega
nosotros(as)	jugamos
vosotros(as)	*jugáis*
ellos, ellas, Uds.	juegan

Jugar is sometimes followed by *a* when a sport is mentioned. Both of the following are acceptable.

Juegan al fútbol.
Juegan fútbol.

Ejercicios

A **Un partido de béisbol.** Contesten. (*Answer.*)

1. ¿Juegan Uds. al béisbol?
2. ¿Juegan Uds. al béisbol en la primavera?
3. ¿Juegan Uds. con amigos o con el equipo de la escuela?
4. ¿Vuelven Uds. al campo después de cada entrada?
5. ¿Pueden Uds. jugar una entrada más si el partido queda empatado después de la novena entrada?
6. ¿Duermen Uds. bien después de un buen partido de béisbol?

B **En la clase de español.** Contesten. (*Answer.*)

1. ¿Juegas al bingo en la clase de español?
2. ¿Juegas al loto en la clase de español?
3. ¿Puedes hablar inglés en la clase de español?
4. ¿Qué lengua puedes o tienes que hablar en la clase de español?
5. ¿Duermes en la clase de español?
6. ¿Devuelve el profesor o la profesora los exámenes pronto?

C **Sí, pero ahora no puede.** Completen. (*Complete.*)

Yo ＿＿ (jugar) mucho al fútbol y Diana ＿＿
﹍﹍1 ﹍﹍2
(jugar) mucho también, pero ahora ella no

＿＿ (poder).
﹍﹍3
　—Diana, ¿por qué no ＿＿ (poder) jugar
﹍﹍4
　ahora?

　—No ＿＿ (poder) porque ＿＿ (querer)
﹍﹍5 ﹍﹍6
　ir a casa.

　Sí, Diana ＿＿ (querer) ir a casa porque
﹍﹍7
ella ＿＿ (tener) un amigo que ＿＿ (volver) hoy de Puerto Rico y ella ＿＿
﹍﹍8 ﹍﹍9 ﹍﹍10
(querer) estar en casa. Pero mañana todos nosotros ＿＿ (ir) a jugar. Y el amigo
﹍﹍11
puertorriqueño de Diana ＿＿ (poder) jugar también. Su amigo ＿＿ (jugar)
﹍﹍12 ﹍﹍13
muy bien.

D **Puedo.** Tell all the things you can do.

E **Quiero.** Tell all the things you want to do.

F **Quiero y puedo.** Tell what you want to do and can do.

G **No quiero, prefiero…** Tell some things you don't want to do and tell what you prefer to do instead.

H **Quiero pero no puedo porque tengo que…** Tell what you want to do but can't do because you have to do something else.

I **No quiero y no voy a…** Tell some things you don't want to do and aren't going to do.

Los adjetivos de nacionalidad   *Identifying Nationalities*

1. Adjectives of nationality that end in *-o* or *-e* follow the same pattern as any other adjective. Those that end in *-o* have four forms and those that end in *-e* have two forms.

el muchacho cubano	los muchachos cubanos
la muchacha cubana	las muchachas cubanas
el muchacho nicaragüense	los muchachos nicaragüenses
la muchacha nicaragüense	las muchachas nicaragüenses

2. Adjectives of nationality that end in a consonant have four forms rather than two. Note the following.

el muchacho español	los muchachos españoles
la muchacha española	las muchachas españolas

3. Adjectives of nationality that end in *-s* or *-n* have a written accent in the masculine singular. The accent is dropped in all other forms.

francés	franceses
francesa	francesas
alemán	alemanes
alemana	alemanas

    Other common adjectives of nationality like the above are: *inglés, portugués, japonés, holandés, irlandés, finlandés.*

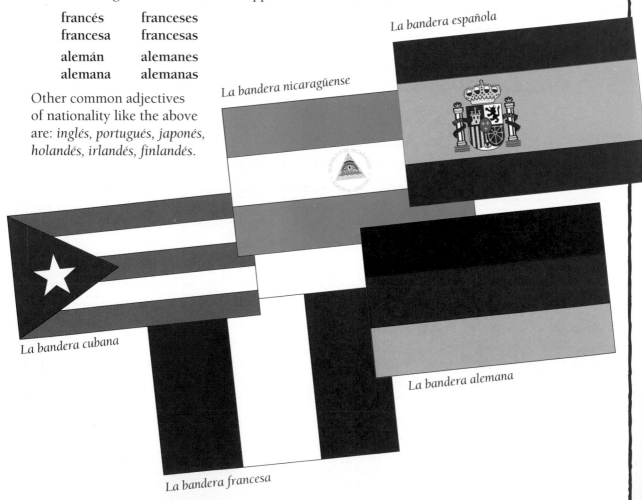

La bandera española

La bandera nicaragüense

La bandera cubana

La bandera alemana

La bandera francesa

Ejercicios

A ¿De qué nacionalidad es?
Completen. (*Complete.*)

1. Carlos es ___. (español)
2. Teresa y Carmen son ___. (mexicano)
3. Ellos son ___. (argentino)
4. Isabel es ___. (portugués)
5. Las alumnas son ___. (francés)
6. Los señores son ___. (irlandés)
7. Ella es ___. (canadiense)
8. Él es ___. (inglés)

B ¿Qué país juega contra el otro?
Sigan el modelo. (*Follow the model.*)

> El Japón vs. el Canadá.
> *Ah, los japoneses juegan contra los canadienses.*

1. Alemania vs. España
2. Francia vs. Italia
3. Portugal vs. Inglaterra
4. Holanda vs. Irlanda

C ¿De dónde es el equipo?
Sigan el modelo. (*Follow the model.*)

> El equipo es del Perú.
> *Ah, el equipo es peruano.*
> *¿Son todos los jugadores peruanos?*

1. El equipo es de la Argentina.
2. El equipo es de Colombia.
3. El equipo es de México.
4. El equipo es de Francia.
5. El equipo es de España.
6. El equipo es de Alemania.

DEPORTES

Futbolista argentino juega en club chileno

José Zamora, súper técnico del club porteño, Fonseca, firmó un contrato para jugar con el equipo Casa Blanca de Santiago. Zamora se destaca por sus espectaculares saltos y sus potentes cabezazos, su movilidad, el espíritu de lucha, la habilidad en carrera y su remate con la derecha. Zamora fue el delantero centro titular de la selección en los dos últimos partidos.

DEPORTES

El equipo español gana la liga europea

El pasado 30 de mayo, el Estadio fue el escenario donde el Valenciano se proclamó campeón del fútbol europeo por tercera ocasión en su historia, tras 10 años de no conseguirlo, luego de una victoria de tres goles a cero sobre los holandeses.

---

25   **DEPORTES**

Los americanos pueden ganar la Copa Mundial dice el entrenador

En una entrevista exclusiva para este diario el entrenador del equipo americano declaró que el equipo estadounidense aunque con poca experiencia en las arenas internacionales puede ganar el Mundial. Los americanos son un equipo joven pero con gran temple y sin miedo de pelear como locos para ganar una victoria, dijo el entrenador.

FÚTBOL

El equipo mexicano juega contra los ingleses hoy

El delantero Javier Marín piensa llevar al equipo mexicano a una victoria contra el equipo inglés en el Estadio Azteca. Marín ha sido internacional en cinco ocasiones con los Blancos y cuatro con la olímpica.

CONVERSACIÓN

Escenas de la vida   *¿Qué quieres jugar?*

ANITA: ¿Prefieres el fútbol o el béisbol?
TOMÁS: Prefiero el fútbol.

ANITA: ¿Juegas al fútbol?
TOMÁS: Sí, juego, pero prefiero ser espectador y no jugador.

ANITA: ¿Tiene tu escuela un equipo bueno?
TOMÁS: Estupendo. Tenemos un equipo que no pierde.

■ **¿Qué prefiere?** Contesten según la conversación. (*Answer according to the conversation.*)

1. ¿Prefiere Tomás el fútbol o el béisbol?
2. ¿Juega al fútbol?
3. ¿Juega mucho?
4. ¿Qué prefiere ser?
5. ¿Qué opinas? ¿Va Tomás a los partidos de fútbol?
6. ¿Tiene su escuela un equipo bueno?
7. ¿Pierde muchos partidos el equipo?

Pronunciación   *Las consonantes* s, c y z

The consonant **s** is pronounced the same as the **s** in sing.

sa	se	si	so	su
sala	clase	sí	peso	su
casa	serio	simpático	sopa	Susana
saca	seis	siete	sobrino	suburbio

The consonant **c** in combination with **e** or **i** (*ce, ci*) is pronounced the same as an **s** in all areas of Latin America. In many parts of Spain, **ce** and **ci** are pronounced **th**. Likewise the pronunciation of *z* in combination with **a, o, u** (*za, zo, zu*) is pronounced the same as an **s** throughout Latin America and as a **th** in most areas of Spain.

za	ce	ci	zo	zu
cabeza	cero	cinco	zona	zumo
empieza	encesta	ciudad	almuerzo	Zúñiga

Repeat the following.

> **González enseña en la sala de clase.**
> **El sobrino de Susana es serio y sincero.**
> **La ciudad tiene cinco zonas.**
> **Toma el almuerzo a las doce y diez en la cocina.**

Zúñiga, sí encesta.

Comunicación

A **Un fanático del deporte.** A real sports fan from Santo Domingo (your partner) wants to know if you are a real fan too, and asks you the following:

1. if you prefer to play in a game or to watch
2. which sport is your favorite
3. if your school has a football team
4. if your school has a baseball team
5. if the teams are any good
6. if you play with a team

B **Una entrevista.** With a classmate prepare a TV talk show. One of you is the interviewer, the other is the "school celebrity." In the interview find out information such as follows:

> qué cursos prefiere y por qué
> qué deportes juega
> si quiere ir a la universidad
> en qué universidad quiere estudiar
> qué quiere estudiar

C **Ahora y en el futuro.** Tell your partner all the things you want to do either now or in the future. He or she will do the same. Then make a list of your common interests and make up conclusions.

> **Queremos ___ y vamos a ___ porque ___.**

EL PERÚ CONTRA LA ARGENTINA

*E*stamos en el estadio Nacional en Lima. ¡Qué emoción! El Perú juega contra la Argentina. Quedan[1] dos minutos en el segundo tiempo. El partido está empatado en cero. ¿Qué va a pasar?[2] Toral tiene el balón. Lanza el balón con el pie izquierdo. El balón vuela[3]. El portero quiere parar el balón. ¿Puede o no? No, no puede. El balón entra en la portería. Toral mete un gol y marca un tanto. En los últimos dos minutos del partido, el equipo de Toral gana. El Perú derrota[4] a la Argentina uno a cero. Los peruanos son triunfantes, victoriosos. Y Toral es su héroe.

Pero el fútbol que juegan en el Perú y en los otros[5] países de Latinomérica y España no es el fútbol americano. El balón es redondo[6], no ovalado, y los jugadores tienen que lanzar el balón con los pies o con la cabeza. No pueden tocar el balón con las manos. El partido tiene dos tiempos, no cuatro. Sin embargo[7] hay algunas cosas que no son diferentes—el número de jugadores, por ejemplo. Hay once jugadores en cada equipo.

El fútbol es un deporte muy popular en todos los países hispanos. Pero el béisbol es popular en relativamente pocos países. ¿Dónde tiene o goza de popularidad el béisbol? En Cuba, en Puerto Rico, en la República Dominicana, en Venezuela, en Nicaragua, en México y en Panamá. Como el béisbol es un deporte norte-americano, la mayoría del vocabulario del béisbol es inglés—la base, el pícher, el hit, el out.

[1] quedan *remain*
[2] pasar *happen*
[3] vuela *flies*
[4] derrota *defeat*
[5] otros *other*
[6] redondo *round*
[7] sin embargo *nevertheless*

Estudio de palabras

A **Definiciones.** Escojan la palabra equivalente. (*Choose an equivalent term.*)

1. la mayoría
2. el vocabulario
3. lanzar
4. redondo
5. triunfante
6. el jugador
7. parar

a. victorioso
b. tirar
c. de forma circular
d. la mayor parte
e. el miembro del equipo
f. las palabras
g. no permitir pasar, bloquear

B **Lo contrario.** Escojan lo contrario. (*Choose the opposite.*)

1. la mayoría   a. primeros
2. contra   b. derecho
3. izquierdo   c. pro
4. gana   d. pierde
5. redondo   e. la minoría
6. últimos   f. ovalado

Comprensión

A **¿Dónde?** Contesten. (*Answer.*)

1. ¿A qué juegan los dos equipos?
2. ¿Cuántos minutos quedan en el segundo tiempo?
3. ¿Quién lanza el balón?
4. ¿Cómo lanza el balón?
5. ¿Puede parar el balón el portero?
6. ¿Qué mete Toral?
7. ¿Qué marca?
8. ¿Qué equipo es victorioso?

B **Los deportes.** Escojan. (*Choose.*)

1. ¿Dónde es popular el fútbol?
   a. No es un deporte popular.
   b. En todos los países hispanos.
   c. Solamente en los Estados Unidos.

2. ¿Es el fútbol como el fútbol norteamericano?
   a. No. Hay solamente once jugadores en el equipo.
   b. No. Los jugadores tienen que lanzar el balón.
   c. No. Los jugadores no pueden tocar el balón con las manos.

3. ¿Es popular el béisbol en los países latinoamericanos?
   a. Sí, en todos.
   b. No. Solamente los norteamericanos juegan al béisbol.
   c. Sí, pero solamente en algunos países.

C **Datos.** Contesten. (*Answer.*)

1. el número de jugadores en un equipo de fútbol
2. el número de tiempos en un juego de fútbol
3. los países latinoamericanos donde es popular el béisbol

DESCUBRIMIENTO CULTURAL

*L*os deportes son populares en Latinoamérica y en España—sobre todo el
fútbol. Las grandes ciudades tienen su
equipo y los países tienen un equipo
nacional. Los equipos nacionales juegan
en los campeonatos internacionales.
La competencia entre los países es muy
fuerte. Todos los equipos quieren ganar
la Copa Mundial[1].

Pero hay una cosa interesante. Aquí
en los Estados Unidos, casi todas las
escuelas tienen su equipo de béisbol, de
fútbol, de baloncesto, etc. Hay mucha
competencia entre una escuela y otra.
Todos los viernes o sábados en el otoño
hay un partido de fútbol entre dos
escuelas y mucha gente va a ver el partido. Pero en Latinoamérica y España,
la mayoría de las escuelas no tienen
equipos deportivos. Los muchachos
juegan al fútbol, al vólibol, etc., pero
no en equipos que compiten con otras
escuelas. El objetivo de las escuelas es
mayormente académico—la enseñanza
y el aprendizaje.

Y AQUÍ EN LOS ESTADOS UNIDOS

El béisbol es muy popular en el Caribe,
México, Centroamérica y Venezuela.
Algunos de los jugadores más famosos
en las Grandes Ligas son hispanos.
Adolfo Luque, cubano, es uno de los
píchers de los Rojos de Cincinnati
contra los Medias Blancas de Chicago
en la Serie Mundial de 1919. Entre
1919 y 1993 más de cien jugadores
latinos se presentan en la Serie Mundial; 32 puertorriqueños, 28 dominicanos, 22 cubanos, 10 venezolanos,

PROGRAMA DE LA COPA MUNDIAL FIFA 1994
SEDE POR SEDE

BOSTON
Estadio Foxboro
Junio 21	Primera ronda
Junio 23	Primera ronda
Junio 25	Primera ronda
Junio 30	Primera ronda
Julio 5	Ronda de los 16
Julio 9	Cuartos de final

CHICAGO
Soldier Field
Junio 17	Primera ronda
(CEREMONIAS DE APERTURA)	
Junio 21	Primera ronda
Junio 26	Primera ronda
Junio 27	Primera ronda
Julio 2	Ronda de los 16

DALLAS
Cotton Bowl
Junio 17	Primera ronda
Junio 21	Primera ronda
Junio 27	Primera ronda
Junio 30	Primera ronda
Julio 3	Ronda de los 16
Julio 9	Cuartos de final

DETROIT
Silverdome
Junio 18	Primera ronda
Junio 22	Primera ronda
Junio 24	Primera ronda

**NUEVA YORK/
NEW JERSEY**
Estadio Giants
Junio 18	Primera ronda
Junio 23	Primera ronda
Junio 25	Primera ronda
Junio 28	Primera ronda
Julio 5	Ronda de los 16
Julio 10	Cuartos de final
Julio 13	Semifinal

ORLANDO
Citrus Bowl
Junio 19	Primera ronda
Junio 24	Primera ronda
Junio 25	Primera ronda
Junio 29	Primera ronda
Julio 4	Ronda de los 16

SAN FRANCISCO
Stanford
Junio 20	Primera ronda
Junio 24	Primera ronda
Junio 26	Primera ronda
Junio 28	Primera ronda
Julio 4	Ronda de los 16
Julio 10	Cuartos de final

WASHINGTON D.C.
Estadio RFK
Junio 19	Primera ronda
Junio 20	Primera ronda

8 panameños, 7 mexicanos y 2 nicaragüenses. Algunos nombres de jugadores latinos forman parte de la historia del béisbol americano, nombres como Orlando Cepeda, Tony Pérez, José Canseco, Juan Marichal, Fernando Valenzuela, Luis Aparicio, "Sandy" Alomar, Benito Santiago y Roberto Clemente.

[1] la Copa mundial   *World Cup*

Orlando Cepeda

Fernando Valenzuela

Tony Pérez

E s un juego de fútbol en el Estadio Azteca de la Ciudad de México **1**. El fútbol es muy popular en México y en otros países.

Es un artículo de la sección de deportes del periódico español ABC **2**. ¿Puedes leer el artículo?

Es Jorge Campos, un jugador de fútbol méxicano **3**. Aquí él juega contra el equipo canadiense en un partido de la Copa Mundial. ¿Juegas tú al fútbol?

Son los jugadores del equipo de fútbol Club Barcelona **4**. Casi todas las ciudades grandes de España tienen un equipo de fútbol.

DEPORTES

28 DE OCTUBRE

El Barcelona pierde ante el Unicaja imbatibilidad en la Liga de baloncesto

El Estudiante es el único equipo que continúa invicto

Madrid. **S. D.**

Lo más destacable de la octava jornada de la Liga ACB es que el Barcelona ha perdido su calidad de invicto al caer ante el Unicaja por 91-93. El único equipo que continúa imbatido, despúes de su victoria ante el Argal Huesca por 82-00 es el Estudiantes. El Real Madrid por su parte solventó sin dema... su compromiso liguero ante el Juver (95-8... impuso al TDK por un aplas...

FUTBOL
CLUB BARCELONA

3

4

MÉXICO

Comunicación oral

 **A** **¿Qué tipo eres?** With a classmate make up a list of fun things to do. Decide if each is a sport or party activity. List them in order starting with your favorite. Then decide if you are a party type or a sports type.

B **Los atletas.** You will pretend to be a famous athlete and two classmates will try to guess who you are. They will ask you questions about what, where, and when you play, your other activities, your family, and your personality. All three of you take turns asking and answering questions.

Comunicación escrita

A **Y aquí los deportes.** Write a brief article for the sports page of a paper about a football game between two Latin American countries.

B **Un juego de béisbol.** Write a paragraph about a baseball game using the following expressions.

> el pícher/lanzar o tirar la pelota
> el bateador Gómez/batear la pelota, tomar tres bases, correr a tercera
> el bateador Salas/pegar un fly
> el jardinero/atrapar la pelota
> Salas/estar out
> el receptor/tirar la pelota al pícher
> Gómez/robar una base, llegar al platillo, batear otra vez, batear un
> jonrón, anotar una carrera

C **Mi deporte favorito.** Write a paragraph about your favorite team sport. First, tell why it is your favorite sport. Then describe the game. Tell how many players are on a team and what each player (or position) has to do. Tell how you win the game. Finally, include whether you prefer to play the sport, watch it, or both.

Reintegración

A **Mi familia.** Contesten. (*Answer.*)

1. ¿Tienes una familia grande?
2. ¿Dónde vive tu familia?
3. ¿Cuántas personas hay en tu familia?
4. ¿Cuántos hermanos tienes?
5. ¿Cuántos años tienen?
6. Y tú, ¿cuántos años tienes?
7. ¿A qué escuela vas?
8. Tus hermanos y tú, ¿van Uds. a la misma escuela?
9. ¿Cómo van a la escuela?
10. ¿A qué hora llegan Uds. a la escuela?

B **¿Quién es?** Identifiquen. (*Identify.*)

1. la hermana de mi padre
2. la hija de mi tío
3. el padre de mi padre
4. el hijo de mi hermano
5. el hermano de mi madre

Vocabulario

SUSTANTIVOS
el fútbol
el campo de fútbol
el estadio
el partido
el tiempo
el tanto
el gol
el tablero indicador
el equipo
el jugador
la jugadora
el/la espectador(a)
el portero
la portera
el árbitro
la árbitra
la portería
el balón
la cabeza
la mano
el pie

el baloncesto
el básquetbol
el cesto
el canasto
el tablero
el aro
el vólibol
la cancha
la red
el suelo
el béisbol
la base
el platillo
el hit
el out
el jonrón
la pelota
la entrada
el pícher
el lanzador
el receptor
el cátcher

el/la bateador(a)
el jardinero
el guante
la pelota

el otoño
la primavera

ADJETIVOS
individual
contrario(a)
empatado(a)

VERBOS
tirar
lanzar
parar
pasar
driblar
encestar
bloquear
atrapar
batear
tocar

robar
marcar
ganar
meter
correr
empezar(ie)
comenzar(ie)
querer(ie)
perder(ie)
preferir(ie)
jugar(ue)
poder(ue)
volver(ue)
devolver(ue)
dormir(ue)

OTRAS PALABRAS Y
EXPRESIONES
por encima
de equipo
quedar empatado

CAPÍTULO

8

UN VIAJE
EN AVIÓN

OBJETIVOS

In this chapter you will learn to do the following:

1. check in for a flight
2. talk about some services on board the plane
3. get through the airport after deplaning
4. describe travel-related activities
5. tell what you or others are presently doing
6. discuss the importance of air travel in South America

Salida Internacional
International Departures
Dèpart International

D

205

VOCABULARIO

PALABRAS 1

EN EL AEROPUERTO

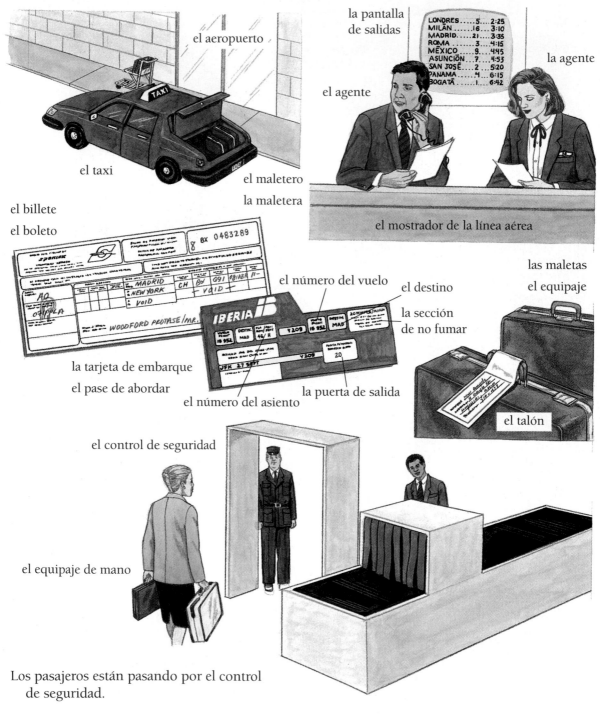

la pantalla de salidas

LONDRES	5	2:25
MILÁN	16	3:10
MADRID	21	3:35
ROMA	3	4:15
MÉXICO	9	4:45
ASUNCIÓN	7	4:53
SAN JOSÉ	2	5:20
PANAMÁ	4	6:15
BOGATÁ	1	6:42

la agente

el agente

el aeropuerto

el taxi

el maletero
la maletera

el mostrador de la línea aérea

el billete
el boleto

BX 0483289

MADRID
NEW YORK
VOID
WOODFORD PROTASE/MR.

la tarjeta de embarque
el pase de abordar

IBERIA

el número del vuelo
el número del asiento

el destino
la sección de no fumar
la puerta de salida

las maletas
el equipaje

el talón

el control de seguridad

el equipaje de mano

Los pasajeros están pasando por el control de seguridad.

LLEGADAS				SALIDAS			
ROMA	423	5	3:40	BOGOTÁ	760	22	3:20
MADRID	670	12	4:56	SAN JOSÉ	444	8	3:55
MÉXICO	482	7	5:20	PANAMÁ	287	14	4:30
ASUNCIÓN	512	9	5:54				

el tablero de llegadas y salidas

la báscula

Clarita Gómez hace un viaje.
Hace un viaje a la América del Sur.
Va a Bogotá.
Hace el viaje en avión.
En este momento Clarita está facturando su equipaje.
Pone sus maletas en la báscula.

El avión va a salir de la puerta número cinco.
El vuelo sale a tiempo. No sale tarde.

Están subiendo al avión.

Ejercicios

A **En el aeropuerto.** Contesten. (*Answer.*)

1. ¿Hace Clarita un viaje a la América del Sur?
2. En este momento, ¿está en el aeropuerto?
3. ¿Está hablando con la agente de la línea aérea?
4. ¿Dónde pone sus maletas?
5. ¿Está facturando su equipaje a Bogotá?
6. ¿Pone el agente un talón en cada maleta?
7. ¿Revisa el agente su boleto?
8. ¿Tiene Clarita su tarjeta de embarque?
9. ¿De qué puerta va a salir su vuelo?

B **El billete.** Den la información siguiente. (*Give the following information.*)

1. nombre de la línea aérea   4. aeropuerto de salida
2. número del vuelo   5. hora de salida
3. destino del vuelo   6. fecha del vuelo

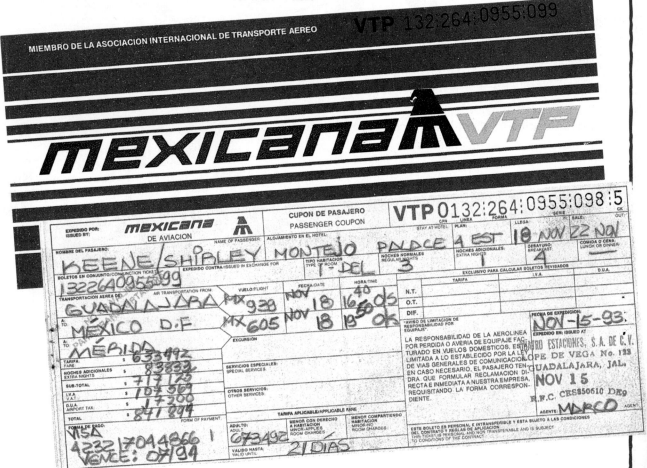

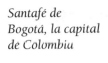

*Santafé de
Bogotá, la capital
de Colombia*

TARJETA DE EMBARQUE

**CUETA
ALGECIRAS**

TURISTA

SERIE P

TARJETA DE EMBARQUE N° 283967

ESTA TARJETA SOLO ES VÁLIDA
PARA EMBARCAR EN EL DÍA Y HORA QUE SE INDICAN

FECHA Y HORA DE SALIDA

10·OCT. 13³⁰ 22C
NO FUMAR

CONSERVE ESTA TARJETA DURANTE TODO EL TRAYECTO

C **El asiento.** Contesten según la tarjeta. (*Answer according to the boarding pass.*)

1. ¿Cuál es la letra del asiento que tiene el pasajero?
2. ¿En qué fila está el asiento?
3. ¿A qué hora es la salida?
4. ¿Tiene que conservar el pasajero la tarjeta durante el viaje?
5. ¿Está su asiento en la sección de fumar o de no fumar?

D **Antes de la salida.** Escojan. (*Choose.*)

1. ___ indica el asiento que tiene el pasajero a bordo del avión.
   a. El talón   b. La tarjeta de embarque   c. El boleto

2. Bogotá es ___ del vuelo.
   a. el embarque   b. la ciudad   c. el destino

3. Inspeccionan el equipaje de los pasajeros en ___.
   a. el mostrador de la línea aérea   b. el control de seguridad
   c. la puerta de salida

4. El vuelo para Bogotá sale ___ número cinco.
   a. del mostrador   b. del control   c. de la puerta

5. Los pasajeros están ___ el avión.
   a. saliendo   b. facturando   c. abordando

PALABRAS 2

EN EL AVIÓN

la tripulación

el asistente de vuelo   la copiloto   el comandante   la asistenta de vuelo

el piloto

Inmigración

el control de pasaportes

el reclamo de equipaje

Los pasajeros están reclamando (recogiendo) su equipaje.

la aduana

Salida →

la ropa

Está abriendo las maletas.
La agente de aduana está inspeccionando el equipaje.

Un avión está despegando.

Otro avión está aterrizando.

A **La llegada.** Contesten. (*Answer.*)

1. Cuando el avión aterriza, ¿abordan o desembarcan los pasajeros?
2. ¿Tienen que pasar por el control de pasaportes cuando llegan a un país extranjero?
3. ¿Van los pasajeros al reclamo de equipaje?
4. ¿Reclaman su equipaje?
5. ¿Tienen que pasar por la aduana?
6. ¿Abre el agente las maletas?

B **¿Sí o no?** ¿Verdad o no? (*True or false?*)

1. El avión aterriza cuando sale.
2. El avión despega cuando llega a su destino.
3. Los agentes de la línea aérea que trabajan en el mostrador en el aeropuerto son miembros de la tripulación.
4. Los asistentes de vuelo y el comandante son miembros de la tripulación.
5. La tripulación consiste en los empleados que trabajan a bordo del avión.

C **Pareo.** Busquen una palabra relacionada. (*Match the verb with its noun form.*)

1. asistir   a. la llegada
2. controlar   b. la salida
3. reclamar   c. el asistente, la asistenta
4. inspeccionar   d. el despegue
5. despegar   e. el aterrizaje
6. aterrizar   f. el control
7. salir   g. la inspección
8. llegar   h. el reclamo
9. embarcar   i. el vuelo
10. volar   j. el embarque

Comunicación

Palabras 1 y 2

A **En el mostrador.** You are speaking with an airline agent (your partner) at the airline counter at the airport. Answer the agent's questions.

1. ¿Adónde va Ud.?
2. ¿Tiene Ud. su boleto?
3. ¿Cuántas maletas tiene Ud.?
4. ¿Tiene Ud. equipaje de mano?
5. ¿Prefiere Ud. un asiento en la sección de no fumar o en la sección de fumar?

B **En el aeropuerto.** You and your classmate make up a list of things passengers must do at an airport. Combine your lists and put the activities in a logical order.

C **La agente.** You are an agent at an airline check-in counter. Your partner is a Spanish-speaking passenger buying a ticket at the last minute. Develop a conversation using the following words.

boleto	clase
pasaporte	maletas
equipaje de mano	asiento
puerta de salida	

El presente de los verbos *hacer, poner, traer, salir* y *venir*

Describing People's Activities

1. The verbs *hacer, poner, traer,* "to bring", and *salir* have an irregular *yo* form. The *yo* has a *g.* Note that the endings are the same as those of regular *-er* and *-ir* verbs.

INFINITIVE	HACER	PONER	TRAER	SALIR
yo	hago	pongo	traigo	salgo
tú	haces	pones	traes	sales
él, ella, Ud.	hace	pone	trae	sale
nosotros(as)	hacemos	ponemos	traemos	salimos
vosotros(as)	*hacéis*	*ponéis*	*traéis*	*salís*
ellos, ellas, Uds.	hacen	ponen	traen	salen

2. The verb *venir* also has an irregular *yo* form. Note that in addition it has a stem change *e > ie* in all forms except *nosotros* and *vosotros*.

VENIR	
yo	vengo
tú	vienes
él, ella, Ud.	viene
nosotros(as)	venimos
vosotros(as)	*venís*
ellos, ellas, Uds.	vienen

3. The verb *hacer* means "to do" or "to make."

Hago un sándwich.	I'm making a sandwich.
¿Qué haces?	What are you doing?

Note that the question *¿Qué haces?* or *¿Qué hace Ud.?* means "What are you doing?" or "What do you do?" In Spanish, you will almost always answer questions with a completely different verb.

¿Qué haces?	**Trabajo en el aeropuerto.**
¿Qué hace Teresa?	**Mira la pantalla de salidas.**

4. The verb *hacer* is also used in many idiomatic expressions. An idiomatic expression is one that does not translate directly from one language to another. The expression *hacer un viaje* is an idiomatic expression because in Spanish the verb *hacer* is used whereas in English we use the verb "to take." Another idiomatic expression is *hacer la maleta* which means to pack a suitcase or *poner la ropa en la maleta*.

Ejercicios

A **Hago un viaje en avión.** Contesten. (*Answer.*)

1. ¿Haces un viaje?
2. ¿Haces un viaje a la América del Sur?
3. ¿Haces el viaje a Bogotá?
4. ¿Sales para el aeropuerto?
5. ¿Sales en coche o en taxi?
6. ¿Traes equipaje?
7. ¿Pones el equipaje en la maletera del taxi?
8. En el aeropuerto, ¿pones el equipaje en la báscula?
9. ¿En qué vuelo sales?
10. ¿Sales de la puerta de embarque número ocho?

B **Ellos y nosotros también.** Sigan el modelo. (*Follow the model.*)

> Ellos hacen un viaje…
> *Ellos hacen un viaje y nosotros también hacemos un viaje.*

1. Ellos hacen un viaje en avión.
2. Ellos salen para el aeropuerto.
3. Ellos salen en taxi.
4. Ellos traen mucho equipaje.
5. Ellos ponen las maletas en la maletera del taxi.
6. Ellos salen a las seis.

Una calle en Santafé de Bogotá, Colombia

C ¿Qué hace Ud.? Preparen una conversación. (*Make up a conversation.*)

—¿Qué hace Ud.?
—Yo miro mi boleto.

1.

2.

3.

4.

5.

D Un viaje a Marbella. Completen. (*Complete.*)

Yo ___ (hacer) un viaje a Marbella. Marbella ___ (estar) en la Costa del Sol en
    1   2
el sur de España. Mi amiga Sandra ___ (hacer) el viaje también. Nosotros(as)
                                   3
___ (hacer) el viaje en avión hasta Málaga y luego ___ (ir) a tomar el autobús
4   5
a Marbella.

—¡Dios mío, Sandra! Pero tú ___ (traer) mucho equipaje.
                                  6

—No, (yo) no ___ (traer) mucho. ___ (tener) sólo dos maletas. Tú exageras.
               7   8

—¡Oye! ¿A qué hora ___ (salir) nuestro vuelo?
                   9

—No ___ (salir) hasta las seis y media. Nosotros(as) ___ (tener) mucho
    10   11
tiempo.

E **¿De dónde vienes, amigo?** Completen. (*Complete.*)

ENRIQUE: ¡Hola, Carlos! ¿De dónde ___ (venir) tú?
                                           ₁

CARLOS: ___ (venir) de mi trabajo.
    ₂

ENRIQUE: ¿Tus amigos ___ (venir) de San Francisco hoy?
                      ₃

CARLOS: No, no ___ (venir) hoy. ___ (venir) mañana.
          ₄   ₅

ENRIQUE: Entonces, ¿por qué no ___ (venir) (tú) con
                                  ₆
nosotros? Vamos a un partido de fútbol.

CARLOS: Gracias pero no ___ (poder). ___ (tener) que
                       ₇   ₈
ir a casa.

ENRIQUE: ¿Por qué ___ (tener) que ir a casa si tus amigos
            ₉
no ___ (venir) hasta mañana?
    ₁₀

CARLOS: Porque yo ___ (tener) un montón de (muchas)
           ₁₁
cosas que hacer.

El puente Golden Gate, San Francisco, California

El presente progresivo

Describing an Action in Progress

1. The present progressive is used in Spanish to express an action that is presently going on, an action that is in progress. The present progressive is formed by using the present tense of the verb *estar* and the present participle. To form the present participle of most verbs you drop the ending of the infinitive and add *-ando* to the stem of *-ar* verbs and *-iendo* to the stem of *-er* and *-ir* verbs. Study the following forms of the present participle.

INFINITIVE	HABLAR	LLEGAR	COMER	HACER	SALIR
STEM PARTICIPLE	habl- hablando	lleg- llegando	com- comiendo	hac- haciendo	sal- saliendo

2. Note that the verbs *leer* and *traer* have a *y* in the present participle.

    leyendo   trayendo

3. Study the following examples of the present progressive.

    ¿Qué está haciendo Elena?
    En este momento está esperando
        el avión.
    Ella está mirando y leyendo su
        tarjeta de embarque.
    Y yo estoy buscando mi boleto.

Ejercicios

A ¿Qué están haciendo en el aeropuerto? Contesten según se indica. (*Answer according to the cues.*)

1. ¿Adónde están llegando los pasajeros? (al aeropuerto)
2. ¿Cómo están llegando? (en taxi)
3. ¿Adónde están viajando? (a Europa)
4. ¿Cómo están haciendo el viaje? (en avión)
5. ¿Dónde están facturando el equipaje? (en el mostrador de la línea aérea)
6. ¿Qué está revisando la agente? (los boletos y los pasaportes)
7. ¿De qué puerta están saliendo los pasajeros para Madrid? (número siete)
8. ¿Qué están abordando? (el avión)

B Yo (no) estoy… Formen oraciones. (*Make up a sentence telling whether you are or are not doing each of the following.*)

1. comer
2. hablar
3. estudiar
4. bailar
5. escribir
6. aprender
7. trabajar
8. hacer un viaje
9. leer
10. salir para España

C ¿Qué están haciendo ahora? Digan lo que están haciendo. (*Tell what the following members of your family or friends are doing now.*)

1. Mi madre
2. Mi padre
3. Mis primos
4. Mis hermanos
5. Yo
6. Mis amigos
7. Mi novio(a) y yo

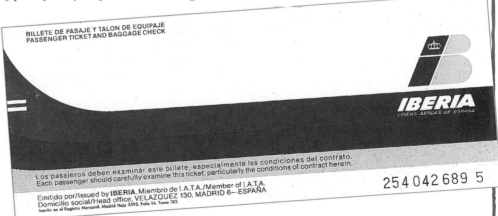

CONVERSACIÓN

Escenas de la vida   *Está saliendo nuestro vuelo*

Señores pasajeros. Su atención por favor. La compañía de aviación anuncia la salida de su vuelo ciento seis con destino a Santiago de Chile. Embarque inmediato por la puerta de salida número seis.

ROBERTO: ¡Chist! Están anunciando la salida de nuestro vuelo.
MARTA: Sí, sí. ¡Pero Dios mío! ¿Dónde está Andrés?
ROBERTO: Llega tarde como siempre. Todavía está facturando su equipaje.

MARTA: Hablando de equipaje, ¿tienes los talones para nuestras maletas?
ROBERTO: Sí, sí. Aquí están.

MARTA: ¿De qué puerta sale nuestro vuelo?
ROBERTO: De la puerta número seis. Primero tenemos que pasar por el control de seguridad.
MARTA: ¡Vamos ya! No voy a esperar a Andrés. Él puede perder el vuelo si quiere. Pero yo no.

A **El vuelo sale.** Den algunos informes. (*Based on the conversation say something about each of the following.*)

1. el vuelo 106
2. la puerta 6
3. Andrés
4. los talones
5. el control de seguridad
6. Santiago de Chile

B **El pobre Andrés.** Contesten. (*Answer.*)

1. ¿Andrés está en la puerta de salida?
2. ¿Qué está haciendo?
3. ¿Qué va a perder?
4. ¿Qué significa *perder*?

Pronunciación   *La consonante* c

You have already learned that **c** in combination with **e** or **i** (*ce, ci*) is pronounced like an **s**. The consonant **c** in combination with **a, o, u** (*ca, co, cu*) has a hard **k** sound. Repeat the following.

ca	co	cu
casa	come	cubano
cabeza	cocina	báscula
saca	comandante	película

Since **ce, ci** have the soft **s** sound, **c** changes to **qu** when it combines with **e** or **i** (*que, qui*) in order to maintain the hard **k** sound.

Pone el equipaje en la báscula.

que	qui
que	aquí
parque	química
embarque	equipaje
pequeño	equipo

Repeat the following sentences.

> Carmen come una comida cubana en casa.
> ¿Quién come una comida pequeña aquí en el parque pequeño?
> El equipo pone su equipaje aquí en la báscula.

Comunicación

A **¿Dónde está mi equipaje?** You have just arrived in Madrid but your two suitcases did not make it. Your partner is the agent for missing baggage. You have to file a lost baggage report. The agent needs to know the following information.

1. the number of suitcases that are missing
2. a description of the suitcases
3. the flight number
4. your baggage tickets
5. your address in Madrid
6. the time at which suitcases can be sent to your home tomorrow

B **¿A qué hora sale?** You are a passenger at the airport and your partner is an agent. In the following conversation, ask the time and gate number for each flight. Your partner will answer by using the cues. Reverse roles.

> vuelo 202/14:00/puerta #21
> Estudiante 1: ¿A qué hora sale el vuelo dos cero dos?
> Estudiante 2: Sale a las dos de la tarde.
> Estudiante 1: ¿De qué puerta sale?
> Estudiante 2: Sale de la puerta número veinte y uno.

1. vuelo 18/17:00/puerta #3
2. vuelo 156/10:00/puerta #11
3. vuelo 99/8:00/puerta #15
4. vuelo 7/21:30/puerta #8

EL AVIÓN EN LA AMÉRICA DEL SUR

*E*l avión es un medio de transporte muy importante en la América del Sur. ¿Por qué? Pues vamos a mirar un mapa del continente sudamericano. Si en este momento están mirando el mapa, van a ver que el continente sudamericano es inmenso. Por consiguiente[1], toma mucho tiempo viajar de una ciudad a otra, sobre todo por tierra[2]. Y en la mayoría de los casos es imposible viajar de un lugar a otro por tierra. ¿Por qué? Porque es imposible cruzar[3] los picos de los Andes o las junglas de la selva tropical del río Amazonas. Por eso, a todas horas del día y de la noche, los aviones de muchas líneas aéreas están sobrevolando[4] el continente. Hay vuelos nacionales (de cabotaje) que enlazan (comunican) una ciudad con otra en el mismo país. Y hay vuelos internacionales que enlazan un país con otro.

Los vuelos entre los Estados Unidos y Europa son largos[5], ¿no? El Atlántico es un océano grande. Pero los vuelos dentro de la América del Sur pueden ser muy largos también. Vamos a comparar. En este momento Linda Conover está abordando un jet en el aeropuerto de John F. Kennedy en Nueva York para ir a Madrid. Es un vuelo sin escala[6] y después de siete horas, el avión va a estar aterrizando en el aeropuerto de Barajas en Madrid.

A la misma hora, José Dávila está saliendo de Caracas, Venezuela con destino a Buenos Aires, Argentina. Está haciendo un vuelo sin escala también. ¿Y cuánto tiempo va a estar volando José? Un poco menos de siete horas. Como ven Uds. hay muy poca diferencia. No es difícil comprender que debido a las largas distancias y la tierra inhóspita[7], el avión es un medio de transporte tan importante en el continente sudamericano.

[1] por consiguiente   *consequently*
[2] tierra   *land*
[3] cruzar   *cross*
[4] sobrevolando   *flying over*
[5] largo   *long*
[6] sin escala   *non stop*
[7] inhóspita   *inhospitable*

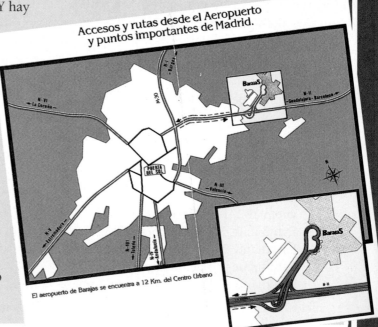

Accesos y rutas desde el Aeropuerto y puntos importantes de Madrid.

El aeropuerto de Barajas se encuentra a 12 Km. del Centro Urbano

Estudio de palabras

A **Palabras afines.** Busquen doce palabras afines en la lectura. (*Find twelve cognates in the reading.*)

B **Algunos términos geográficos.** Den la palabra. (*Give the word defined.*)

1. una población grande donde vive mucha gente y donde hay industria y comercio
2. una gran extensión de tierra—Europa, Sudamérica, Norteamérica, Asia, África, Australia, Antártida
3. una zona o selva tropical donde hay mucha vegetación, una vegetación muy densa
4. una corriente de agua considerable que desemboca en el mar—el Misisipí, el Amazonas, el Orinoco
5. elevaciones considerables de tierra—los Andes, los Pirineos

El Río Amazonas

Comprensión

A **Informes.** Busquen la siguiente información. (*Find the following information in the reading.*)

1. el nombre de un océano
2. el nombre de una cadena de montañas
3. el nombre de un país
4. el nombre de una ciudad
5. el nombre de un río
6. duración del vuelo entre Nueva York y Madrid
7. duración del vuelo entre Caracas y Buenos Aires

B **Análisis.** Contesten. (*Answer.*)

1. ¿Por qué es el avión un medio de transporte importante en la América del Sur?
2. ¿Por qué es imposible viajar por tierra de una ciudad a otra en muchas partes de la América del Sur?

C **Un problema.** Contesten. (*Answer.*)

Vamos a solucionar o resolver un problema. Cuando es el mediodía en Nueva York son las seis de la tarde en Madrid. El huso horario es de seis horas. Linda Conover sale de Nueva York para Madrid en un vuelo sin escala. La duración del vuelo es de siete horas con cinco minutos. Linda sale de Nueva York a las ocho y media de la noche. ¿A qué hora va a llegar a Madrid, hora local?

DESCUBRIMIENTO CULTURAL

Un vuelo muy interesante en la América Central es el vuelo de la ciudad de Guatemala a Tikal. Es un vuelo corto[1] que los pasajeros hacen en una avioneta de dos motores, no en un jet. ¿Por qué es interesante? Pues Tikal está en una selva tropical muy densa. Y en la selva, entre una vegetación densa de árboles y plantas exóticas están las famosas ruinas de los templos de los mayas. Muchos años antes de la llegada de los españoles los mayas tienen una civilización muy avanzada en las áreas que hoy son la península de Yucatán en México, Guatemala, Honduras y El Salvador.

Otro vuelo impresionante y espectacular es el vuelo de Lima a Iquitos en el Perú. El vuelo sale del aeropuerto internacional de Lima, Jorge Chávez, cerca del océano Pacífico. Sube rápido para poder cruzar en seguida los Andes. Los pasajeros miran con asombro los picos y valles de los Andes. A veces el avión brinca bastante porque en las zonas montañosas hay mucha turbulencia. Después de una hora de vuelo los picos andinos desaparecen[2] y aparece la selva tropical amazónica. Iquitos es un puerto del río Amazonas. Está en el Perú cerca de la frontera con el Brasil.

Y otro viaje para los aventureros. El vuelo de Buenos Aires a Ushuaia en la Argentina. Ushuaia está al sur de la Patagonia en la Tierra del Fuego. Es la ciudad más austral (al sur) del mundo entero. A causa de los vientos antárticos, el aterrizaje en Ushuaia puede ser muy turbulento. Cerca del pueblo hay un glaciar gigantesco y durante el aterrizaje el avión tiene que descender rápidamente.

[1] corto *short*
[2] desaparecen *disappear*

Ruinas mayas en Tikal, Guatemala

Glaciar cerca de la ciudad de Ushuaia

Iquitos, Perú

Ushuaia, la ciudad más austral del mundo entero

Y AQUÍ EN LOS ESTADOS UNIDOS

Día y noche los aviones están despegando y aterrizando en los aeropuertos internacionales de Miami, Houston y Los Ángeles. Aeroméxico, LanChile, Viasa, Aerolíneas Argentinas, LACSA, SAHSA y TACA y tantas compañías más, sin contar las compañías norteamericanas, conectan estos aeropuertos con las capitales de la América Central y Sudamérica. Los agentes de mostrador y los asistentes de vuelo son, casi todos, bilingües. Hablan inglés y español para poder servir a todos sus clientes. Y todos los pilotos comerciales en el mundo tienen que comprender y hablar inglés. Es porque el idioma de la aviación internacional es el inglés. En todas las torres de control[3], en todas partes del mundo, los controladores de tráfico aéreo[4] dan sus instrucciones a los vuelos internacionales en inglés. Es obvio que la comunicación clara y precisa entre controladores y pilotos es de máxima importancia.

[3] torres de control   *control towers*
[4] controladores de tráfico aéreo   *air traffic controllers*

REALIDADES

E s la selva amazónica cerca de Iquitos, Perú **1**. ¿Te gusta el lugar?

Es el menú de Viasa, una aerolínea venezolana **2**. ¿Qué quieres comer?

Es un billete de exceso de equipaje **3**. ¿Cuántas maletas quiere llevar el pasajero?

Aquí puedes ver los picos de los Andes **4**. ¿Dónde están estas montañas?

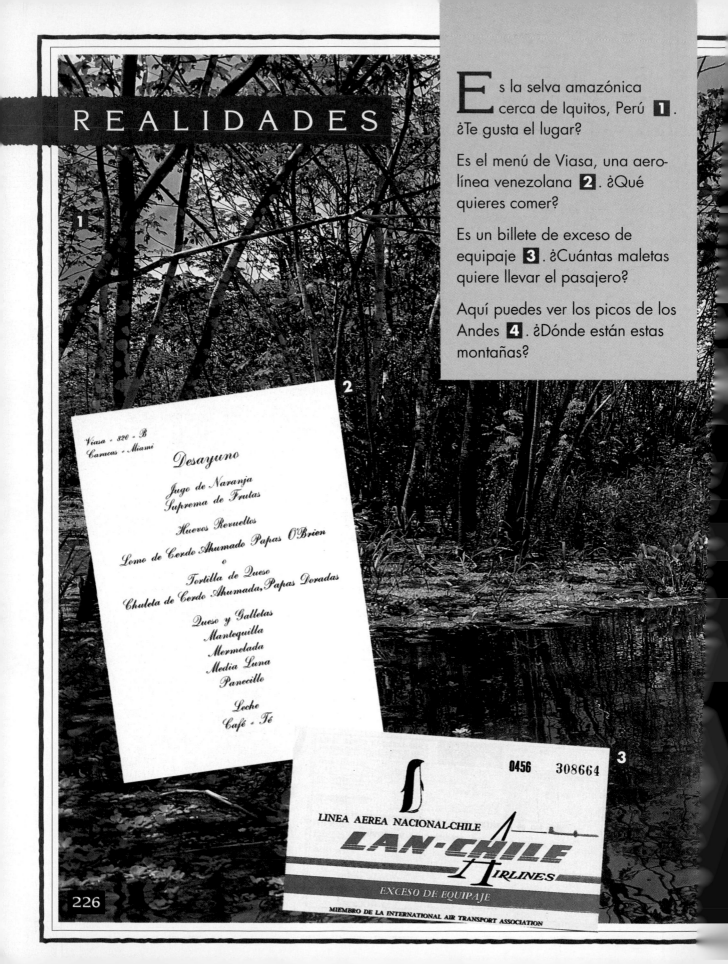

Viasa - 820 - B
Caracas - Miami

Desayuno

Jugo de Naranja
Suprema de Frutas

Huevos Revueltos
Lomo de Cerdo Ahumado Papas O'Brien
o
Tortilla de Queso
Chuleta de Cerdo Ahumada, Papas Doradas

Queso y Galletas
Mantequilla
Mermelada
Media Luna
Panecillo

Leche
Café - Té

0456   308664

LINEA AEREA NACIONAL-CHILE
LAN·CHILE
AIRLINES
EXCESO DE EQUIPAJE
MIEMBRO DE LA INTERNATIONAL AIR TRANSPORT ASSOCIATION

4

Comunicación oral

A **Una conferencia importante.** You and your partner have to leave in three weeks for an important conference in Barcelona. First make a list of all the things you have to do in preparation for the trip. Then make a list of things you need to take with you. Work together to make two comprehensive lists.

Tengo que comprar el billete.   **Necesito llevar el pasaporte.**

B **¿Qué estás haciendo?** Work in pairs. Give the names of several friends or family members. Tell each other what you think each person is doing at this very moment. Decide if many of your friends or relatives are doing the same thing.

C **En el parque.** You and your partner are at the following places. People there are doing different things, but since you forgot your glasses, you can't see them very well. So, you ask your partner what they are doing. Reverse roles.

el parque/los muchachos
Estudiante 1: ¿Qué están haciendo los muchachos?
Estudiante 2: Están jugando fútbol.

1. en el parque/los primos
2. en el autobús escolar/los alumnos
3. en la cafetería/los profesores
4. en la escuela/los hermanos
5. en la sala/la familia
6. en la aduana/los agentes

Hacemos del volar, una obra de arte.

MEXICANA ✈

Comunicación escrita

A **El concurso.** In order to win an all-expense-paid vacation to the Spanish-speaking country of your choice, you must write a letter to the company that sponsors the contest. Your letter should include the following: where you want to go and why; with whom you want to go; under what conditions you want to travel.

B Tienes que… Imagine that your good friend from Costa Rica has never taken an airplane trip. Leave a note explaining what he or she has to do at the airport. Do the following:

1. Write a list of words that you need to describe what you do at an airport.
2. Form complete sentences with the words.
3. Put the sentences in a logical order.
4. Polish the sentences and develop a coherent paragraph explaining what your friend has to do at the airport.

Reintegración

A Un partido en Los Ángeles. Completen. (*Complete.*)

1. Los Tigres ____ a jugar en Los Ángeles. (ir)
2. Ellos ____ contra los Dodgers. (jugar)
3. Ellos ____ ganar el partido. (querer)
4. El equipo ____ muy bueno. (ser)
5. Pero los Dodgers ____ muy buenos también. (ser)
6. Los Tigres ____ que ir a Los Ángeles. (tener)
7. ¿Cómo ____ ellos el viaje a Los Ángeles? (hacer)
8. Ellos ____ a tomar el avión. (ir)
9. ¿Cuándo ____ ellos? (salir)
10. ¿Y cuándo ____ ellos? (volver)

B ¿Qué deporte es? Identifiquen el deporte. (*Identify.*)

1. Hay once jugadores en el equipo.
2. No pueden tocar el balón con la mano.
3. Driblan con el balón.
4. El pícher tira la pelota.
5. Los jugadores corren de una base a otra.
6. El portero bloquea el balón.

Vocabulario

SUSTANTIVOS

el aeropuerto
la línea aérea
el mostrador
el/la agente
el boleto
el billete
el pasaporte
la maleta
el talón
el equipaje
el equipaje de mano
la ropa
la báscula
la tarjeta de embarque
el pase de abordar
el destino
el vuelo

el número del vuelo
el asiento
la fila
la sección de no fumar
el control de seguridad
el control de pasaportes
el tablero
la pantalla
la llegada
la salida
la puerta de salida
el reclamo de equipaje
la aduana
el taxi
el maletero
la maletera
el avión

la tripulación
el/la comandante
el/la piloto
el/la copiloto
el asistente de vuelo
la asistenta de vuelo

VERBOS

hacer
traer
poner
salir
venir
facturar
revisar
inspeccionar
abordar
despegar

aterrizar
desembarcar
reclamar
recoger
abrir
subir

OTRAS PALABRAS Y EXPRESIONES

hacer la maleta
hacer un viaje
en avión
en este momento
a tiempo
tarde
a bordo

Futura estrella Softball femenino

La única niña participante de las ligas infantiles y juveniles de Ponce (LIJUPO), es Debora Seilhamer, y participa con el equipo de béisbol del Club Deportivo de Ponce, 5-6 años Liga Pedrín Zorrilla.

Debora juega en la posición de segunda base y "out field". Batea a la derecha y es sexta en la posición de bateo. Actualmente tiene un promedio de .625 y es una futura estrella del softball.

Sus padres, el Ing. Larry Seilhamer y Linda, sus hermanos Dennis, David y Dissiree, son fanáticos número uno de Debora, y los mejores testigos de sus hazañas en el terreno de juego.

Además de poseer habilidad para jugar béisbol, Debora es una niña muy activa en todos los deportes de su colegio, también tiene notas sobresalientes.

¡Arriba, Debora!

Look at the ticket and answer the questions.

A **¡Qué partido!** Escojan la respuesta correcta. (*Choose the correct answer.*)

1. Este boleto es una entrada para un partido de ___.
   a. fútbol   **b.** béisbol   **c.** baloncesto
2. El nombre de uno de los equipos es ___.
   a. Sudamericana   **b.** Boliviano   **c.** Cobreloa
3. La fecha del partido es ___.
   a. el tres de septiembre   **b.** el nueve de marzo
   c. el cuatro de agosto
4. El precio de la entrada es ___.
   a. 40 dólares   **b.** 40 pesos   **c.** 40 bolivianos

Now read the newspaper article and do the exercises.

B **¡A jugar!** Contesten. (*Answer the questions.*)

1. ¿Con qué equipo juega Debora?
2. ¿Qué son todos los otros participantes en las ligas infantiles y juveniles, excepto Debora?
3. ¿Cuántos años tiene la niña aproximadamente?
4. ¿Cuál es el nombre de la liga en que juega Debora?
5. ¿Cuál es el deporte favorito de la niña?
6. ¿Qué posición juega ella?
7. ¿Cómo batea Debora?
8. ¿Es el béisbol el único deporte que juega Debora?

C **¿Dónde dice...?** Escriban la frase que dice lo siguiente. (*Write the phrase that says the following.*)

1. que Debora es estudiante
2. cuál es su promedio de bateo
3. qué clase de notas saca en sus estudios
4. quiénes son los fánaticos de Debora

D **La familia de Debora.** Escojan la respuesta correcta. (*Choose the correct answer.*)

1. La niña tiene ___ hermanos.
   a. uno   **b.** dos   **c.** tres
2. El nombre de su padre es ___.
   a. David   **b.** Dennis   **c.** Larry
3. El padre de Debora es ___.
   a. estudiante   **b.** ingeniero   **c.** profesor
4. Dissiree es la ___ de Debora.
   a. madre   **b.** amiga   **c.** hermana

E **¿Cómo se dice...?** Escriban en español. (*Give the Spanish for the following.*)

1. a future star
2. women's softball
3. batting average
4. baseball playing ability

REPASO

CAPÍTULOS 5–8

Conversación   *Hugo y Marta conversan*

HUGO: ¿Dónde vives? ¿En una casa o en un apartamento?

MARTA: Vivimos en un apartamento grande. ¿Y tú, ¿dónde vives?

HUGO: Ahora, en la universidad, donde estoy aprendiendo mucho.

MARTA: ¿Sólo estudias? ¿No haces otra cosa?

HUGO: Claro que sí. Juego (al) tenis y (al) baloncesto, y hago
         unos viajes durante las vacaciones. Y tú, ¿qué estudias?

MARTA: Estoy estudiando medicina. Pero prefiero jugar (al) tenis.
         Casi siempre gano. ¿Quieres jugar mañana?

HUGO: Pues no puedo. Tengo que asistir a una fiesta familiar.

■ **¿Qué hacen?** Contesten. (*Answer according to the conversation.*)

1. ¿Quién vive en la universidad?
2. ¿A qué juega el muchacho?
3. ¿Cuándo viaja el muchacho?
4. ¿Qué estudia la muchacha?
5. ¿A qué juega ella?
6. ¿El muchacho va a jugar (al) tenis mañana?
7. ¿Por qué, o por qué no?

Estructura

Los verbos que terminan en *-er* y en *-ir*

Review the following forms of regular *-er* and *-ir* verbs.

beber	yo bebo, tú bebes, él/ella/Ud. bebe, nosotros(as) bebemos, *vosotros(as) bebéis,* ellos/ellas/Uds. beben
vivir	yo vivo, tú vives, él/ella/Ud. vive, nosotros(as) vivimos, *vosotros(as) vivís,* ellos/ellas/Uds. viven

A **En nuestro pueblo.**   Completen. (*Complete.*)

Leonardo y yo ____ (vivir) en una ciudad pequeña. Trabajamos para el
1
periódico. Leonardo ____ (escribir) artículos de deportes. Yo ____ (escribir)
2   3
artículos de cocina. Yo ____ (aprender) los secretos de la cocina cuando visito
4
los restaurantes. Yo ____ (comer) comidas deliciosas todos los días. Pobre
5
Leonardo ____ (comer) hamburguesas y ____ (beber) limonada en el estadio.
6   7

Los adjetivos posesivos

Review the possessive adjectives.

> mi, mis
> tu, tus
> su, sus
> nuestro, nuestros
> nuestra, nuestras
> *vuestro, vuestros*
> *vuestra, vuestras*
> su, sus

B **Nuestro hogar.** Completen con un adjetivo posesivo. (*Complete with a possessive adjective.*)

Vivimos en un apartamento. ＿＿ apartamento tiene seis cuartos. El cuarto
           1
de ＿＿ hermana es grande. El cuarto de ＿＿ hermanos es pequeño. En ＿＿
  2   3   4
cuarto mis hermanos tienen todos ＿＿ libros, ＿＿ televisor y otras cosas. ＿＿
                                  5   6   7
cocina es bastante grande y también la sala y el comedor. Tenemos muchos
amigos. Cuando ＿＿ amigos vienen a casa, ellos traen ＿＿ videos. Miramos los
           8   9
videos en el cuarto de ＿＿ hermanos. Y tú, ¿miras videos en ＿＿ casa?
                  10   11

El presente del verbo *tener*

1. Review the following forms of the irregular verb *tener*.

> **tener**   yo tengo, tú tienes, él/ella/Ud. tiene, nosotros(as) tenemos,
> *vosotros(as) tenéis,* ellos/ellas/Uds. tienen

2. Remember that the expression *tener que* means "to have to," and is always
   followed by an infinitive.

   Tengo que comer.   **Tenemos que estudiar.**

C **¿Qué tienes?** Preguntas personales. (*Give your own answers.*)

1. ¿Cuántos años tienes?
2. ¿Cuántos años tienen los muchachos en tu clase de español?
3. ¿Tienen Uds. un profesor o una profesora?
4. ¿Qué días tienes clases de español?
5. ¿Tienes que leer mucho en clase?
6. ¿Quiénes tienen que trabajar más, los profesores o los alumnos?

Los verbos con cambio en la raíz

1. Review the forms of the following verbs with the stem changes *e > ie, o > ue*.

PERDER (E > IE)		PODER (O > UE)	
yo	pierdo	yo	puedo
tú	pierdes	tú	puedes
él, ella, Ud.	pierde	él, ella, Ud.	puede
nosotros(as)	perdemos	nosotros(as)	podemos
vosotros(as)	*perdéis*	*vosotros(as)*	*podéis*
ellos, ellas, Uds.	pierden	ellos, ellas, Uds.	pueden

2. Remember that the *u* of *jugar* changes to *ue*.

jugar	yo juego, tú juegas, él/ella/Ud. juega, nosotros(as) jugamos, *vosotros(as) jugáis*, ellos/ellas/Uds. juegan

D **El partido de béisbol.** Completen. (*Complete.*)

Los Leones de Ponce _____ (jugar) hoy el partido más duro del año. Tienen que
ganar. Si _____ (perder) el partido con los Cangrejeros no _____ (poder) ganar
el campeonato. El partido de hoy _____ (empezar) a la una de la tarde. Ellos
van a jugar en el estadio de los Cangrejeros. El mánager de los Leones no _____
(querer) jugar allí, él _____ (preferir) jugar en Ponce. El pícher, Guzmán _____
(empezar) a lanzar hoy después de sólo dos días de descanso. Mis amigos y
yo nunca _____ (poder) dormir antes de un juego importante. Estamos muy
nerviosos. ¡Nosotros _____ (querer) otra victoria para nuestros Leones!

Los verbos con g en la primera persona

1. Remember that the verbs *hacer, poner, traer,* and *salir* have a g in the *yo* form.

hacer	yo hago
poner	yo pongo
traer	yo traigo
salir	yo salgo

The other forms are the same as regular *-er* and *-ir* verbs.

2. Remember that *venir* is a stem-changing, *e > ie*, verb.

venir	yo vengo, tú vienes, él/ella/Ud. viene, nosotros(as) venimos, *vosotros(as) venís*, ellos/ellas/Uds. vienen

E **De regreso a casa.** Preguntas personales. (*Give your own answers.*)

1. ¿A qué hora sales de casa para ir a la escuela?
2. ¿Cómo haces el viaje a la escuela, en autobús o a pie?
3. ¿Quién más hace el viaje?
4. ¿Vienes a casa solo(a) por la tarde, o alguien te trae a casa?
5. ¿Qué traes cuando vienes a casa por la tarde?
6. ¿Pones la televisión cuando llegas a casa?
7. ¿Qué hacen tus padres y tus hermanos cuando vienen a casa por la tarde?

El presente progresivo

1. The present progressive is used to describe an action or an event that is happening right now. It is formed with the present tense of *estar* and the present participle of the verb.

2. Review the present participles of the following regular verbs:
   revisar-revisando   hacer-haciendo   subir-subiendo

   The participles of *leer* and *traer* have a *y*: *leyendo, trayendo.*

F **En el aeropuerto.** Completen con el presente progresivo. (*Complete with the present progressive.*)

Los pasajeros ⎯⎯ (salir) por la puerta número dos. Ellos ⎯⎯ (subir) al avión.
        1   2
El avión no puede despegar todavía porque otro avión ⎯⎯ (aterrizar). Los
                                                      3
aviones que ⎯⎯ (aterrizar) tienen preferencia sobre los aviones que ⎯⎯
            4   5
(despegar). Todos están a bordo y un asistente de vuelo ⎯⎯ (cerrar) las puertas
                                                        6
del avión. El capitán ⎯⎯ (dar) la bienvenida a bordo a los pasajeros.
                      7

Comunicación

■ **El concurso.** Your local real estate office is giving away a house to the person who writes the best and most original description of his or her dream house. You want to enter the contest. Write two paragraphs describing your dream house.

LAS CIENCIAS NATURALES

Antes de leer

We inherit certain characteristics from our parents. Our race, our height, the color of our eyes and hair are all determined by the genes we inherit from our parents and grandparents. This inheritance is not totally random.

1. Look up "Mendel's Law" and review the principles of heredity.
2. Prepare a family tree for yourself or, if you prefer, for a classmate, going back as far as you can. Next to each person jot down all the physical characteristics known about him or her. All labels should be in Spanish.
3. Make a list of all the physical characteristics you wrote down in the family tree. Which characteristics turn up most often? Explain your findings.

Lectura

Gregor Johann Mendel (1822–1884)

GREGOR JOHANN MENDEL (1822-1884)

Mendel es de Austria. Es naturalista. Cuando tiene veintiún años entra en el convento de Brno donde continúa estudiando y practicando la botánica. Mendel cruza plantas para ver cómo cambian las sucesivas generaciones. Sus investigaciones científicas resultan en la formulación de las leyes[1] de Mendel. Las leyes de Mendel son publicadas en 1865 en un libro titulado *Experimentos de hibridación en plantas*.

Ya conocemos la forma de reproducción de las amebas. Simplemente se dividen. Las células nuevas heredan[2] los rasgos o características de la célula original, y son idénticas. En los organismos superiores hay que tener dos padres. Los hijos heredan rasgos de los dos padres. Es obvio que los rasgos se mezclan[3] de alguna manera. Cada individuo tiene algunos rasgos del padre y otros de la madre. Es Mendel quien descubre cómo los rasgos se combinan.

[1] las leyes   *laws*
[2] heredan   *inherit*
[3] mezclan   *mix*

Mendel experimenta con la hibridación de las plantas.

Después de leer

A **Mendel.** Contesten.

1. ¿De qué país es Mendel?
2. ¿Dónde trabaja Mendel?
3. ¿Qué clase de científico es Mendel?
4. ¿Qué libro escribe Mendel y cuándo publica el libro?
5. ¿Cuál es un sinónimo de *rasgo*?

B **Investigaciones.** ¿Dónde dice lo siguiente?

1. how amoebas reproduce
2. what Mendel studied
3. where Mendel's law first appeared
4. from whom offspring inherit their traits
5. with what Mendel experimented

C **Seguimiento.** Prepare a brief resume in English of the passage about Gregor Mendel.

Los hijos heredan los rasgos de sus padres.

LAS CIENCIAS SOCIALES: LA GEOGRAFÍA FÍSICA

Antes de leer

In North America, it is common to consider North and South America as two continents. In the Spanish-speaking world, the two continents are considered one, *la América*. In the following passage, you will find out about the major regions of America, their location and size.

1. On a topographical map of the Americas locate and identify: the highest peak, two desert regions, and the country in South America with the longest coastline.
2. One of the republics of South America is totally landlocked. In 1879, it lost its only access to the sea. Name the country, indicate how it lost its seaport, and on a map show a location of the port.

Lectura

El continente americano se extiende desde Alaska, en el extremo Norte, hasta la Tierra del Fuego, en el extremo Sur. Su límite al este es el Océano Atlántico, y al oeste es el Océano Pacífico. Está completamente separado de los otros continentes. La distancia desde el norte hasta el sur es de 19.000 kilómetros. Es el continente más largo en latitud. El continente americano se divide en tres partes. la América del Norte, que cubre 24 millones de kilómetros cuadrados[1]; la América del Sur, que cubre 18 millones de kilómetros cuadrados; y la América Central, un istmo largo que une la América del Norte con la América del Sur que cubre 500 mil kilómetros cuadrados.

Debido a que es tan largo, el continente tiene una gran variedad climática. Hay cuatro climas que se representan en el continente: el clima subpolar; el clima continental; el clima tropical; y el clima ecuatorial.

[1] cuadrados   *square*

Glacial Moreno, Tierra del Fuego, Argentina

Los Andes

El desierto de Atacama, Chile

Salto de Ángel, Venezuela

Las cataratas de Iguazú entre Paraguay y la Argentina

Después de leer

A La geografía. Contesten.

1. ¿Cuál es la extensión, en kilómetros, del continente americano?
2. ¿Con qué limita el continente al este?
3. ¿En cuántas partes se divide el continente?
4. ¿Cuántos kilómetros cuadrados cubre la América Central?
5. ¿Cuántos climas hay en el continente americano?
6. ¿Cuáles son los climas del continente americano?

B Las Américas. ¿Dónde dice lo siguiente?

1. the area of North America
2. what is at the southernmost point of America

C Seguimiento. Describan la extensión y el clima del estado o provincia donde Uds. van a la escuela.

LAS ARTES

Antes de leer

Probably the greatest of Spain's classical painters was the seventeenth-century artist Velázquez. Familiarize yourself with some of his major works: *Las Meninas*, *Vulcan's Forge*, and the *Surrender of Breda*. Breda is a city in Flanders. Flanders, today a part of Belgium, once was a Spanish colony.

Lectura

Diego Rodríguez de Silva y Velázquez nace[1] en Sevilla en 1599, y muere en Madrid en 1660. Velázquez empieza a pintar en Sevilla, pero en 1623 va a Madrid como pintor de cámara del rey Felipe IV. En Madrid su estilo cambia. Velázquez es famoso por su uso de la luz[2] en sus cuadros.

Las Meninas

La fragua de Vulcano

Dos de las obras más importantes de Velázquez son de gran interés histórico. En el cuadro *Las Meninas* aparece la familia del rey don Felipe IV. Es curioso porque el artista está en el cuadro también. La otra gran obra es *La rendición de Breda*. Breda es una ciudad de Flandes. En el siglo XVII Flandes es parte del imperio español. Los flamencos quieren ser independientes y entran en una guerra[3] con España. El general que gana la batalla y ocupa la ciudad de Breda es Ambrosio de Spínola, un italiano al servicio del rey de España, Felipe IV. El cuadro también tiene el nombre de *Las lanzas*[4].

[1] nace   *is born*
[2] luz   *light*
[3] guerra *war*
[4] lanzas *spears*

La rendición de Breda

Después de leer

A Velázquez.   Completen.

1. Es pintor de cámara del rey ___.
2. Velázquez va de Sevilla a Madrid en ___.
3. Una característica de su arte es su uso de la ___.
4. Las personas que están en el cuadro *Las Meninas* son ___.
5. En el siglo XVII los españoles tienen una guerra con los ___ .
6. El general que gana la batalla no es español, es ___.
7. Breda está en ___.

B Los cuadros.   ¿Dónde dice lo siguiente?

1. that his use of light was extraordinary
2. the name of a seventeenth-century Spanish colony in Europe
3. where Velázquez was born and where he died
4. why there was a war in Flanders
5. the subject of the painting *Las Meninas*

C Seguimiento.

1. Describe, en español, *Las Meninas*.
2. *La rendición de Breda* también tiene el nombre *Las Lanzas*. ¿Por qué?
3. En *Las Lanzas*, ¿quién es Ambrosio de Spínola?
4. ¿Quiénes crees que son "las meninas"?
5. En *Las Meninas*, ¿dónde está Velázquez?
6. ¿Qué relación existe entre *Las Meninas* y *Las Lanzas*?

APÉNDICES

MAPAS

ESPAÑA

FRANCIA

ANDORRA

Océano Atlántico

Mar Cantábrico

Golfo de Vizcaya

PORTUGAL

Lisboa ✪

Santiago de Compostela

Oviedo

Santander

San Sebastián

Bilbao

CORDILLERA CANTÁBRICA

León

Burgos

Pamplona

PIRINEOS

Zaragoza

Barcelona

Río Ebro

Río

Río Duero

Valladolid

Salamanca

Segovia

Ávila

SIERRA DE GUADARRAMA

Madrid ✪

Toledo

ESPAÑA

Río Tajo

Guadiana

SIERRA MORENA

Río

Guadalquivir

Córdoba

Sevilla

Granada

SIERRA NEVADA

Málaga

Jerez de la Frontera

Cádiz

Gibraltar (R.U.)

Ceuta (Esp.)

Tánger

Peñón de Vélez de la Gomera (Esp.)

Peñón de Alhucemas (Esp.)

Melilla (Esp.)

Islas Chafarinas (Esp.)

MARRUECOS

ÁFRICA

ARGELIA

Mar Mediterráneo

ISLAS BALEARES

Menorca

Mallorca

Palma de Mallorca

Formentera

Ibiza

Valencia

Alicante

Murcia

40°

0°

10°

40°

0°

N E S O

0   100   200
Kilómetros

ISLAS CANARIAS

La Palma

Santa Cruz de Tenerife

Tenerife

Gomera

Hierro

Lanzarote

Fuerteventura

Las Palmas

Gran Canaria

ÁFRICA

245

LA AMÉRICA DEL SUR

20°   90°   80°   20°   30°

Mar Caribe   *Océano Atlántico*

Maracaibo   Caracas
10°   GUYANA
          VENEZUELA
                         Georgetown   SURINAM
                Medellín   Cayena
                Bogotá   Paramaribo
          COLOMBIA   GUAYANA
                                              FRANCESA
Islas
Galápagos
(Ecuador)   Quito
0°   *Río Amazonas*
          ECUADOR
          Guayaquil
                    Iquitos

10°   BRASIL
          PERÚ
                                        Brasilia
     Lima   Cuzco
          CORDILLERA DE LOS ANDES
                    BOLIVIA
                La Paz
                    Sucre

Océano Pacífico   São Paulo
                    PARAGUAY
20°   Asunción   Río de Janeiro

                         Córdoba
                    Rosario   URUGUAY
          Valparaíso   Buenos Aires   Montevideo
          Santiago
30°   ARGENTINA   Mar del Plata
          CHILE
          CORDILLERA DE LOS ANDES
          Puerto Montt   Bariloche

                    Islas
                    Malvinas
                    (R.U.)

     0   500   1000   N
     Kilómetros   O   E
40°
                    Punta Arenas   S

110°   100°   90°   80°   70°   60°   50°   40°   30°   20°

MÉXICO, LA AMÉRICA CENTRAL Y EL CARIBE

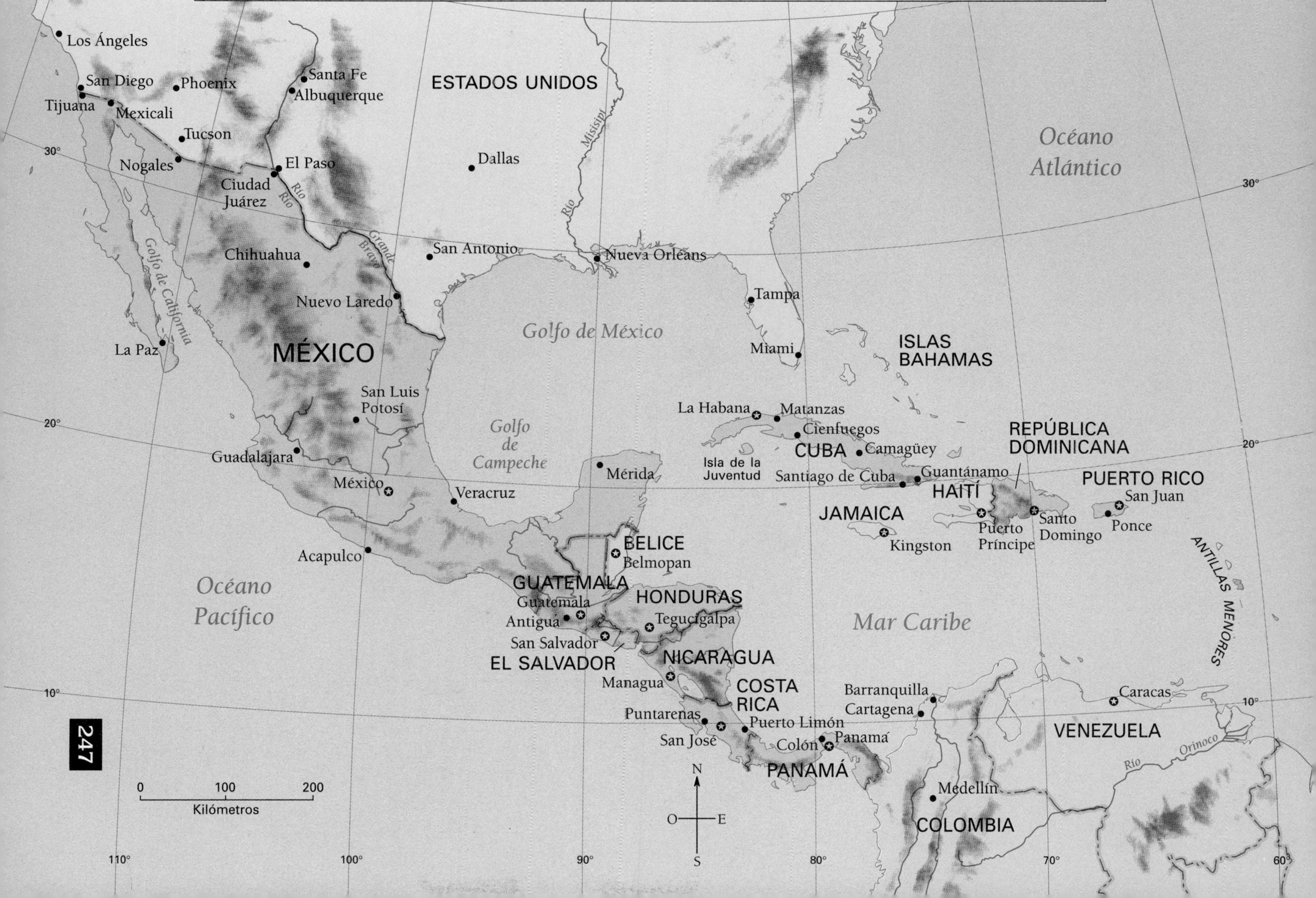

Océano Atlántico

Océano Pacífico

Golfo de México

Golfo de Campeche

Golfo de California

Mar Caribe

ESTADOS UNIDOS

MÉXICO

ISLAS BAHAMAS

CUBA

JAMAICA

HAITÍ

REPÚBLICA DOMINICANA

PUERTO RICO

ANTILLAS MENORES

BELICE

GUATEMALA

EL SALVADOR

HONDURAS

NICARAGUA

COSTA RICA

PANAMÁ

VENEZUELA

COLOMBIA

Los Ángeles
San Diego
Tijuana
Mexicali
Nogales
Phoenix
Tucson
La Paz
Santa Fe
Albuquerque
El Paso
Ciudad Juárez
Chihuahua
Nuevo Laredo
San Antonio
Dallas
Nueva Orleans
Misisipí
Río Grande
Río Bravo
Guadalajara
Acapulco
México
San Luis Potosí
Veracruz
Mérida
Tampa
Miami
La Habana
Matanzas
Cienfuegos
Isla de la Juventud
Camagüey
Santiago de Cuba
Guantánamo
Kingston
Puerto Príncipe
Santo Domingo
San Juan
Ponce
Caracas
Medellín
Barranquilla
Cartagena
Panamá
Colón
Puerto Limón
San José
Puntarenas
Managua
Tegucigalpa
San Salvador
Antigua
Guatemala
Belmopan
Río Orinoco

N
E
S
O

0   100   200
Kilómetros

247

VERBOS

A. Verbos regulares

INFINITIVO	**hablar** *to speak*	**comer** *to eat*	**vivir** *to live*
PRESENTE PROGRESIVO	estar hablando	estar comiendo	estar viviendo
PRESENTE	yo hablo tú hablas él, ella, Ud. habla nosotros(as) hablamos *vosotros(as) habláis* ellos, ellas, Uds. hablan	yo como tú comes él, ella, Ud. come nosotros(as) comemos *vosotros(as) coméis* ellos, ellas, Uds. comen	yo vivo tú vives él, ella, Ud. vive nosotros(as) vivimos *vosotros(as) vivís* ellos, ellas, Uds. viven

B. Verbos regulares con cambio en la primera persona singular
(Regular verbs with stem change in the first person singular)

INFINITIVO	**ver** *to see*	**hacer** *to do*	**poner** *to put*
PRESENTE PROGRESIVO	estar viendo	estar haciendo	estar poniendo
PRESENTE	yo veo	yo hago	yo pongo

INFINITIVO	**traer** *to bring*	**salir** *to leave*	
PRESENTE PROGRESIVO	estar trayendo	estar saliendo	
PRESENTE	traigo	salgo	

C. Verbos con cambio radical *(Stem-changing verbs)*

INFINITIVO	**preferir (e>ie)** *to prefer*	**volver (o>ue)** *to return*	
PRESENTE PROGRESIVO	estar prefiriendo	estar volviendo	
PRESENTE	yo prefiero tú prefieres él, ella, Ud. prefiere nosotros(as) preferimos *vosotros(as) preferís* ellos, ellas, Uds. prefieren	yo vuelvo tú vuelves él, ella, Ud. vuelve nosotros(as) volvemos *vosotros(as) volvéis* ellos, ellas, Uds. vuelven	

D. Verbos irregulares

INFINITIVO	**dar** *to give*	**estar** *to be*	**ir** *to go*
PRESENTE PROGRESIVO	estar dando		estar yendo
PRESENTE	yo doy tú das él, ella, Ud. da nosotros(as) damos vosotros(as) dais ellos, ellas, Uds. dan	yo estoy tú estás él, ella, Ud. está nosotros(as) estamos *vosotros(as) estáis* ellos, ellas, Uds. están	yo voy tú vas él, ella, Ud. va nosotros(as) vamos *vosotros(as) vais* ellos, ellas, Uds. van
INFINITIVO	**ser** *to be*	**tener** *to have*	**venir** *to come*
PRESENTE PROGRESIVO	estar siendo	estar teniendo	estar viniendo
PRESENTE	yo soy tú eres él, ella, Ud. es nosotros(as) somos *vosotros(as) sois* ellos, ellas, Uds. son	yo tengo tú tienes él, ella, Ud. tiene nosotros(as) tenemos *vosotros(as) tenéis* ellos, ellas, Uds. tienen	yo vengo tú vienes él, ella, Ud. viene nosotros(as) venimos *vosotros(as) venís* ellos, ellas, Uds. vienen

VOCABULARIO
ESPAÑOL-INGLÉS

The *Vocabulario español-inglés* contains all productive and receptive vocabulary from the text.

The reference numbers following each productive entry indicate the chapter and vocabulary section in which the word is introduced. For example **3.2** means that the word first appeared in *Capítulo 3, Palabras 2*. **BV** refers to the introductory *Bienvenidos* lesson.

Words without a chapter reference indicate receptive vocabulary (not taught in the *Palabras* sections).

A

¿A qué hora? At what time?, **2**
a veces sometimes, **5.2**
abordar to board, **8.1**
   el pase de abordar boarding
    pass, **8.1**
la **abreviatura** abbreviation
abril April, **BV**
abrir to open, **8.2**
el/la **abuelo(a)** grandfather
   (grandmother), **6.1**
los **abuelos** grandparents, **6.1**
abundante abundant
aburrido(a) boring, **1.1**
la **academia** academy
académico(a) academic
la **actividad** activity, **5.2**
adiós good-bye, **BV**
adivinar to guess
¿adónde? (to) where?, **4**
la **aduana** customs, **8.2**
el **aeropuerto** airport, **8.1**
las **afueras** outskirts, **5.1**
el/la **agente** agent, **8.1**
agosto August, **BV**
agradable pleasant
el **agua** (f.) water
   el agua mineral mineral
    water
ahora now
al (a + el) to the
alegre happy
el **alga** seaweed
el **álgebra** algebra, **2.2**
alguno(a) some, any
el **almuerzo** lunch, **5.2**
alrededor de around, **6.2**
alto(a) tall, **1.1**; high, **3.2**
el/la **alumno(a)** student, **1.1**
amable kind, **2.1**
amazónico(a) Amazon,
   Amazonian
la **ameba** amoeba
la **América del Sur** South
   America, **8.1**
americano(a) American, **1.2**
el/la **amigo(a)** friend, **1.1**
el **análisis** analysis
analizar to analyze
el **animal** animal
antártico(a) antarctic
antes before
antiguo(a) ancient
antipático(a) unpleasant

(person), **1.1**
la **antropología** anthropology
el/la **antropólogo(a)** anthropologist
el **anuncio** advertisement,
   announcement
el **año** year
aparecer (zc) to appear
el **apartamento** apartment, **5.1**
el **apellido** last name
aprender to learn, **5.2**
el **aprendizaje** learning
aprobado(a) passing
los **apuntes** notes, **3.2**
   tomar apuntes to take notes,
    3.2
aquí here
el/la **árbitro(a)** referee, **7.1**
el **árbol** tree, **6.2**
   el árbol genealógico family
    tree
el **área** (f.) area
argentino(a) Argentinian, **2.1**
la **aritmética** arithmetic, **2.2**
el **aro** hoop, **7.2**
el **arte** (f.) art, **2.2**
el/la **artista** artist
la **ascendencia** ancestry
el **ascensor** elevator, **5.1**
así thus
el **asiento** seat, **8.1**
   el número del asiento seat
    number, **8.1**
la **asignatura** subject, **2.2**
el **asistente (la asistenta) de**
   vuelo flight attendant, **8.2**
asistir to attend, to assist, **5.2**
el **asombro** amazement
el **aterrizaje** landing
aterrizar to land, **8.2**
Atlántico: Océano Atlántico
   Atlantic Ocean
el/la **atleta** athelete
atractivo(a) attractive, **1.2**
atrapar to catch, **7.2**
aun even
austral southern
el **autobús** bus, **3.1**
avanzado(a) advanced
la **avenida** avenue, **5.1**
el/la **aventurero(a)** adventurer
el **avión** airplane, **8.1**
   en avión by plane, **8.1**
la **avioneta** small airplane

B

la **bacteria** bacterium
bailar to dance, **4.2**
el **baile** dance
bajo(a) short (person), **1.1**;
   low, **3.2**
el **balcón** balcony, **6.2**
el **balón** ball, **7.1**
el **baloncesto** basketball, **7.2**
el **banco** bench, **BV**
la **banda** (music) band
el **barrio** neighborhood
la **báscula** scale, **8.1**
la **base** base, **7.2**
el **básquetbol** basketball, **7.2**
bastante rather, quite, **1.1**
la **batalla** battle
el **bate** bat, **7.2**
el/la **bateador(a)** batter, **7.2**
batear to hit (baseball), **7.2**
el **bautizo** baptism
beber to drink, **5.2**
el **béisbol** baseball, **7.2**
bello(a) beautiful
la **biblioteca** library, **4.1**
la **bicicleta** bicycle, **6.2**
bien fine, well, **BV**
bilingüe bilingual
el **billete** ticket, **8.1**
la **biología** biology, **2.2**
el/la **biólogo(a)** biologist
blanco(a) white
el **bloc** writing pad, **3.2**
bloquear to block, **7.1**
el **bocadillo** sandwich, **5.2**
el **boleto** ticket, **8.1**
el **bolígrafo** ballpoint pen, **BV**
bonito(a) pretty, **6.2**
la **botánica** botany
brincar to bounce
bueno(a) good, **1.2**
   buenas noches good
    evening, good night, **BV**
   buenas tardes good
    afternoon, **BV**
   buenos días hello, good
    morning, **BV**
el **bus** bus, **3.1**

C

la **cabeza** head, **7.1**
cabotaje: de cabotaje domestic, **8**

cada each
el café coffee, **5.2**; cafe
la cafetería cafeteria
la calculadora calculator, **BV**
el calendario calendar
la calificación grade, **3.2**
la calle street, **5.1**
la cámara: de cámara court, royal
cambiar to change
el cambio change
el campeonato championship
el campo country, **5.1**; field, **7.1**
   el campo de fútbol soccer
     field, **7.1**
canadiense Canadian
el canasto basket, **7.2**
la cancha court (sports), **7.2**
el/la cantante singer
cantar to sing, **4.2**
la cantina lunchroom
la capital capital
la característica characteristic
Caribe Caribbean
la carne meat, **5.2**
caro(a) expensive
el carro car, **3.1**
la carta letter, **5.2**
la casa house, **4.1**
   la casa particular private
     house
   en casa at home, **4.2**
   ir a casa to go home, **4.1**
casi almost
el caso case
castizo(a) real, legitimate,
   genuine
el/la cátcher catcher, **7.2**
cate failing (grade)
la categoría category
católico(a) Catholic
la causa cause
   a causa de because of
la celebración celebration
celebrar to celebrate
la célula cell
la cena dinner, **5.2**
cenar to dine, to have dinner
el centro comercial shopping
   center, **4.1**
Centroamérica Central
   America
cerca de near
la ceremonia ceremony
cero zero
el cesto basket, **7.2**

la chabola shack
chao good-bye, **BV**
el chimpancé chimpanzee
la choza shack
el ciclomotor motorbike, **6.2**
cien(to) one hundred, **BV**
la ciencia science, **2.2**
   la ciencia política political
     science
   las ciencias naturales
     natural sciences
   las ciencias sociales social
     sciences, **2.2**
el/la científico(a) scientist
científico(a) scientific
cinco five, **BV**
cincuenta fifty, **BV**
la cinta tape, **4.1**
el círculo circle
la ciudad city, **5.1**
el/la ciudadano(a) citizen
la civilización civilization
claro of course
la clase class, **2.1**; type
clásico(a) classical, **4**
el/la cliente customer, **5.2**
el clima climate
climático(a) climatic
la cocina kitchen, **4.1**
el coche car, **3.1**
coeducacional coeducational
el colegio high school, **1.1**
la colección collection
colombiano(a) Colombian, **1**
el/la comandante captain, **8.2**
combinar to combine
el comedor dining room, **5.1**
el comentario commentary
comenzar (ie) to begin, **7**
comer to eat, **5.2**
la comida meal, **5.2**
como as, like
¿cómo? what?; how?, **1.1**
la compañía company
comparar to compare
la competencia competition
competir to compete
completamente completely
el comportamiento behavior
comprar to buy, **5.2**
comprender to understand, **5.2**
el compuesto compound
la computadora computer, **BV**
común common
comunicar to communicate

la comunidad community
con with
el concurso contest
la conducta conduct
conocer to know
contar to count
contemporáneo(a)
   contemporary
el continente continent
continuar to continue
contra against
contrario(a) opposite
el control inspection, **8.1**
   el control de seguridad
     security inspection, **8.1**
   el control de pasaportes
     passport inspection, **8.2**
el convento convent
la conversación conversation
la copa cup
   la Copa Mundial World
     Cup
el/la copiloto copilot, **8.2**
correr to run, **7.2**
corto(a) short
la cosa thing
la costumbre custom
cruzar to cross
el cuaderno notebook, **BV**
cuadrado(a) square
el cuadro painting, picture
¿cuál? what?, which?, **BV**
   ¿Cuál es la fecha de hoy?
     What is today's date?, **BV**
cuando when
¿cuándo? when?, **3.1**
¿cuánto(a)? how much?, **BV**
   ¿Cuánto es? How much is it?,
     BV
cuarenta forty, **BV**
cuarto fourth, **5.1**
   menos cuarto a quarter to
     (the hour), **2**
   y cuarto a quarter past (the
     hour), **2**
el cuarto room, **5.1**
   el cuarto de dormir
     bedroom, **5.1**
   el cuarto de baño bathroom,
     5.1
cuatro four, **BV**
cubano(a) Cuban
cubrir to cover
la cultura culture
el cumpleaños birthday, **6.2**

cumplir to be (so many years) old
curioso(a) curious
el **curso** course, **2.1**

D

dar to give, **4.2**
el **dato** fact
de of, from, for, **1.1**
    de equipo (adj.) team, **7**
    de jazz jazz, **4**
    De nada. You're welcome., **BV**
    de rock rock, **4**
debido a due to
décimo tenth, **5.1**
la **definición** definition
del (de + el) from the, of the
la **demografía** demography
denso(a) thick
dentro de in; inside, within
depender to depend
el **deporte** sport, **2.2**
deportivo(a) related to sports
la **derecha** right, **5.1**
    a la derecha to the right, **5.1**
derrotar to defeat
desaparecer (zc) to disappear
desaprobado(a) failing
el **desayuno** breakfast, **5.2**
descender to descend
describir to describe
el **descubrimiento** discovery
descubrir to discover
desde from; since
el **desierto** desert
despegar to take off (airplane), **8.2**
después de after, **4.1**
el **destino** destination, **8.1**
    con destino a to, **8**
devolver (ue) to return, **7.2**
el **día** day
diario(a) daily; diary
dibujar to sketch
el **dibujo** drawing, sketch
diciembre December, **BV**
diez ten, **BV**
la **diferencia** difference
diferente different
difícil difficult, **2.1**
el **dinero** money
la **dirección** address
la **disciplina** subject, **2.2**

el **disco** record, **4.1**
la **distancia** distance
divertido(a) fun, **1.1**
dividir to divide
el **divorcio** divorce
el **domingo** Sunday, **BV**
dominicano(a) Dominican
¿dónde? where?, **1.2**
dormir (ue) to sleep, **7**
el **dormitorio** bedroom, **5.1**
dos two, **BV**
driblar (con) to dribble, **7.2**
durante during, **4.2**

E

la **economía** economy
    economía doméstica home economics, **2.2**
ecuatorial equatorial
ecuatoriano(a) Ecuadorean
el **edificio** building, **5.1**
la **educación** education
    la educación cívica social studies, **2.2**
    la educación física physical education, **2.2**
el **ejemplo** example
    por ejemplo for example
el the (m. sing.), **1.1**
él he, **1.1**
el **elefante** elephant
elegante elegant
el **elemento** element
ella she, her, **1.2**
ellos(as) they, them
la **emisión deportiva** sports broadcast, **5.2**
la **emoción** emotion; excitement
empatado(a) tied, **7**
empezar (ie) to begin, **7.1**
la **empresa** company
en in, **1.1**
    en autobús by bus, **3.1**
    en avión by plane, **8**
    en carro by car, **3.1**
    en este momento right now, **8.1**
encestar to put in a basket, **7.2**
la **energía** energy
enero January, **BV**
enlazar to join, connect

enorme enormous
la **ensalada** salad, **5.2**
la **enseñanza** teaching
enseñar to teach, **3.2**
entero(a) whole
la **entrada** entrance, **6.2**; inning, **7.2**
entrar to enter, **3.1**
entre between
la **entrevista** interview
la **época** epoch, age
el **equipaje** baggage, **8.1**
    el equipaje de mano carry-on luggage, **8.1**
    el reclamo de equipaje baggage claim, **8.2**
el **equipo** team, **7.1**
eres you (sing. fam.) are
es he/she/it is, **1.1**
la **escalera** stairway, **5.1**
la **escena** scene
escolar (adj.) school, **3.1**
escribir to write, **5.2**
escrito(a) written
escuchar to listen, **4.1**
la **escuela** school, **1.1**
    la escuela intermedia junior high, middle school
    la escuela primaria elementary school
    la escuela secundaria high school, **1.1**
    la escuela superior high school
    la escuela vocacional vocational school
la **escultura** sculpture
eso: a eso de about, **3.1**
España Spain
el **español** Spanish (language), **2.2**
español(a) Spanish
la **especialidad(a)** specialty
el/la **especialista** specialist
especialmente especially
específico(a) specific
espectacular spectacular
el/la **espectador(a)** spectator, **7**
el/la **esposo(a)** husband (wife), **6.1**
el **estadio** stadium, **7.1**
el **estado** state
    el estado libre asociado commonwealth
los **Estados Unidos** United States
están they/you (pl. form.) are, **4.1**

estar to be, **4.1**

estás you (sing. fam.) are

el este east

este(a) this

el estilo style

estoy I am

el/la estudiante student

estudiar to study, **3.2**

el estudio study

estupendo(a) terrific

la Europa Europe

europeo(a) European

la evaluación evaluation

el examen examination, test, **3.2**

exótico(a) exotic

el experimento experiment

el/la explorador(a) explorer

extenderse to extend

extranjero(a) foreign

extremo(a) extreme

F

fabuloso(a) fabulous

fácil easy, **2.1**

facturar to check (luggage), **8.1**

facultativo(a) optional

la familia family, **5.1**

familiar family

famoso(a) famous

fantástico(a) fantastic, **1.2**

febrero February, **BV**

la fecha date, **BV**

¿Cuál es la fecha de hoy?
What is today's date?, **BV**

el fenómeno phenomenon

festejar to celebrate

la fiesta party, **4.2**

la fila row, **8**

el fin end

en fin finally

la física physics, **2.2**

el/la físico physicist

físico(a) physical

el/la flamenco(a) Flemish

la flor flower, **6.2**

formar to form

la formulación formation

francés(a) French, **2.2**

frecuentar to frequent

frecuentemente frequently

la frontera border

fuerte strong

funcionar to function

el fútbol soccer, **7.1**

el campo de fútbol soccer field, **7.1**

G

ganar to win, **7.1**; to earn

el garaje garage, **6.2**

la gaseosa soft drink, soda, **5.2**

la gasolinera gas station

el gato cat, **6.1**

la generación generation

el/la general general

por lo general in general

la gente people

la geografía geography, **2.2**

geográfico(a) geographic

la geometría geometry, **2.2**

gigantesco(a) gigantic, huge

el glaciar glacier

el gol goal, **7.1**

meter un gol to score a goal (soccer), **7.1**

la goma eraser, **BV**

gozar to enjoy

gracias thank you, **BV**

gran, grande big, **2.1**

las Grandes Ligas Major Leagues

el grupo group

el guante glove, **7.2**

la guerra war

la guitarra guitar, **4.2**

H

la habitación room, **5.1**

hablar to speak, **3.1**

hacer to do, to make, **8.1**

hacer un viaje to take a trip, **8.1**

hacer la maleta to pack one's suitcase, **8**

hasta until, **BV**

Hasta luego. See you later., **BV**

Hasta mañana. See you tomorrow., **BV**

Hasta pronto. See you soon., **BV**

hay there is, there are, **5.1**

el helado ice cream, **5.2**

heredar to inherit

el/la hermanastro(a) stepbrother (stepsister)

el/la hermano(a) brother (sister), **2.1**

el/la héroe hero

la hibridación hybridization

el/la hijastro(a) stepson (stepdaughter)

el/la hijo(a) son (daughter), **6.1**

los hijos children (sons and daughters), **6.1**

el hipopótamo hippopotamus

hispánico(a) Hispanic

hispano(a) Hispanic

la historia history, **2.2**; story

el/la historiador(a) historian

histórico(a) historic

el hit hit (baseball), **7.2**

la hoja sheet, **BV**

la hoja de papel sheet of paper, **BV**

hola hello, **BV**

holandés, holandesa Dutch, **BV**

el hombre man

honesto(a) honest, **1.2**

el honor honor

la hora hour; time

el horario schedule

hoy today

hoy en día nowadays

¿Cuál es la fecha de hoy? What is today's date?, **BV**

humano(a) human

humilde humble

el huso horario time difference

I

la idea idea

idéntico(a) identical

el idioma language

igual equal; the same

el imperio empire

la importancia importance

importante important

imposible impossible

impresionante amazing, impressive

incluso including

independiente independent

individual individual, **7**

el individuo individual

industrializado(a)

industrialized
el **inglés** English, (language), **2.2**
inglés, inglesa English
la **información** information
el **informe** report
inhóspito(a) inhospitable
inmenso(a) immense
el/la **inquilino(a)** renter
inspeccionar to inspect, **8.2**
la **institución** institution
el **instituto** institute
las **instrucciones** instructions, **5.2**
el **instrumento** instrument
insuficiente failing (grade)
íntegro(a) integral
inteligente intelligent, **2.1**
intercambio exchange
el **interés** interest
interesante interesting, **2.1**
internacional international
interrogativo(a) interrogative
la **investigación** investigation
la **invitación** invitation, **5.2**
invitar to invite, **4.2**
ir to go, **4.1**
ir a (+inf.) to be going
(+inf.), **6**
la **isla** island
el **istmo** isthmus
el/la **italiano(a)** Italian, **2.2**
la **izquierda** left, **5.1**
a la izquierda to the left, **5.1**

J

el **jardín** garden, **6.2**
el/la **jardinero(a)** outfielder
(baseball), **7.2**
el **jonrón** home run, **7.2**
joven young, **6.1**
el/la **joven** young person
el **juego** game
el **jueves** Thursday, **BV**
el/la **jugador(a)** player, **7.1**
jugar (ue) to play, **7.1**
julio July, **BV**
la **jungla** jungle
junio June, **BV**
juntos(as) together

K

el **kilómetro** kilometer

L

la the (f. sing.), **1.1**
el **laboratorio** laboratory
la **lanza** spear
el/la **lanzador(a)** pitcher, **7.2**
lanzar to throw, **7.1**
el **lápiz** pencil, **5.2**
largo(a) long
las the (f. pl.)
el **latín** Latin, **2.2**
la **Latinoamérica** Latin America
latinoamericano(a) Latin
American
la **latitud** latitude
la **lección** lesson, **3.2**
la **lectura** reading
la **leche** milk, **5.2**
leer to read, **5.2**
la **lengua** language, **2.2**
lengua materna
native language
la **ley** law
la **libreta** notebook, **3.2**
el **libro** book, **BV**
el **liceo** (primary school in
Mexico, but high school in
most places)
el **límite** limit; boundary
la **limonada** lemonade, **BV**
la **línea aérea** airline, **8.1**
la **llegada** arrival, **8.1**
**el tablero de llegadas y
salidas** arrival and
departure board, **8.1**
llegar to arrive, **3.1**
llevar to carry, **3.2**; to wear
los the (m. pl.)
luego: Hasta luego., See you
later., **BV**
el **lugar** place
lujo: de lujo deluxe
el **lunes** Monday, **BV**
la **luz** light

M

la **madre** mother, **6.1**
el/la **madrileño(a)** native of Madrid
la **madrina** godmother
magnífico(a) magnificent
la **maleta** suitcase, **8.1**
hacer la maleta to pack
one's suitcase, **8**
el/la **maletero(a)** trunk (of a car),
8.1
malo(a) bad, **1**
la **mamá** mom, **5.2**
manera way, manner, **1.1**
de ninguna manera by no
means, **1.1**
la **mano** hand, **7.1**
el equipaje de mano hand
(carry-on) luggage, **8.1**
la **mañana** morning, **2**
mañana tomorrow
el **mapa** map
el **mar** sea
marcar to score (sports), **7.1**
el **marido** husband, **6.1**
el **martes** Tuesday, **BV**
marzo March, **BV**
más more, most
las **matemáticas** mathematics, **2.2**
la **materia** subject matter, **2.2**
materno(a) maternal
la lengua materna native
language
el **matrimonio** wedding; marriage
el/la **maya** Maya, Mayan
mayo May, **BV**
mayor great, greater, greatest
la **mayoría** majority
mayormente principally, mainly
las **medias** stockings, pantihose
la **media: y media** half past the
hour, **2**
la **medianoche** midnight, **2**
medieval medieval
el **medio** mean, way
medio(a) middle
el **mediodía** midday, noon, **2**
menos less
menos cuarto a quarter to
(the hour), **2**
mental mental
la **merienda** snack, **4.1**
meter to put in, **7.1**
meter en el cesto to make a
basket, **7.2**
meter un gol to score a goal,
7.1
mexicano(a) Mexican, **1.1**
mezclar to mix

mi my

microscópico(a) microscopic

el **microscopio** microscope

el/la **miembro(a)** member

mientras while

el **miércoles** Wednesday, **BV**

mil (one) thousand, **BV**

el **millón (de)** million

mirar to look at, **3.2**

mismo(a) same

mixto(a) mixed

la **mochila** bookbag, knapsack, **BV**

moderno(a) modern

modesto(a) of modest means

el **momento** moment

  en este momento right now

montañoso(a) mountainous

moreno(a) brown, dark-haired, **1.1**

morir (ue, u) to die

el **mostrador** counter, **8.1**

el **motor** motor

el/la **muchacho(a)** boy (girl), **BV**

mucho(a) a lot; many, **5**

  Mucho gusto. Nice to meet you., **BV**

la **mujer** wife, **6.1**

mundial worldwide

  la Copa Mundial World Cup

  la Serie Mundial World Series

el **mundo** world

el **museo** museum

la **música** music, **2.2**

el/la **músico** musician

muy very, **BV**

N

nacer to be born

el **nacimiento** birth

nacional national

la **nacionalidad** nationality, **1**

el/la **naturalista** naturalist

ni... ni neither... nor

nicaragüense Nicaraguan

el/la **nieto(a)** grandchild, **6.1**

los **nietos** grandchildren, **6.1**

ninguno(a): de ninguna manera by no means, **1.1**

no no

  No hay de qué. You're welcome., **BV**

nocturno(a) (adj.) night

el **nombre** name

norteamericano(a) North American

nosotros(as) we, **2.2**

la **nota** grade, **3.2**

notable outstanding

las **noticias** news, **5.2**

la **novela** novel, **5.2**

noveno(a) ninth, **5.1**

noventa ninty, **BV**

noviembre November, **BV**

el/la **novio(a)** boyfriend (girlfriend); fiancé(e)

nuestro(a) our

nueve nine, **BV**

nuevo(a) new, **6.2**

el **número** number, **8.1**

  el número del vuelo flight number, **8.1**

  el número del asiento seat number, **8.1**

nunca never

O

o or

el **objetivo** objective

el **objeto** object

obligatorio(a) required

obvio(a) obvious

el **océano** ocean

  el Océano Atlántico Atlantic Ocean

  el Océano Pacífico Pacific Ocean

octavo(a) eighth, **5.1**

octubre October, **BV**

ocupar to occupy

ochenta eighty, **BV**

ocho eight, **BV**

el **oeste** west

oír to hear

opinar to think

el **orangután** orangutan

orgánico(a) organic

el **organismo** organism

original original

el **otoño** autumn, **7.1**

otro(a) other, **2.2**

el **out** out (baseball), **7.2**

ovalado(a) oval

oye hey, listen

P

el **padre** father, **6.1**

los **padres** parents, **6.1**

el **padrino** godfather

los **padrinos** godparents

el **país** country

la **palabra** word

panameño(a) Panamanian

la **pantalla** screen, **8.1**

la **papa** potato, **5.2**

el **papá** dad, **5.2**

el **papel** paper, **BV**

  la hoja de papel sheet of paper, **BV**

para for; to

el **paramecio** paramecium

parar to stop, **7.1**

el/la **pariente** relative

el **parque** park, **6.2**

la **parte** part

particular private; particular, **5.1**

el **partido** game, **7.1**

el **pasado** past

el/la **pasajero(a)** passenger, **8.1**

el **pasaporte** passport, **8.1**

  el control de pasaportes passport inspection, **8.2**

pasar to pass, **7.2**; to happen

el **pasatiempo** pastime, hobby

el **pase de abordar** boarding pass, **8.1**

el **paseo** stroll, walk

paterno(a) paternal

el **patio** patio, courtyard

pegar un fly to hit a fly

la **película** movie, **5.2**

la **pelota** ball, **7.2**

pequeño(a) small, **2.1**

perder (ie) to lose, **7.1**

perdón excuse me

el **periódico** newspaper, **5.2**

pero but

el **perro** dog, **6.1**

la **persona** person

personal personal

el/la **pianista** pianist

el **piano** piano, **4.2**

el **pico** peak

el/la **pícher** pitcher, **7.2**

el **pie** foot, **7.1**

  a pie on foot, **3.1**

el/la **piloto** pilot, **8.2**

pintar to paint

el/la **pintor(a)** painter
la **pintura** painting
el **piso** floor, **5.1**
la **pizarra** chalkboard, **BV**
el **pizarrón** chalkboard, **3.2**
el **plan** plan
la **planta** floor; plant, **6.2**
    la planta baja ground floor, **5.1**
   plástico(a) plastic
el **platillo** home plate (baseball), **7.2**
el **plato** plate; dish
la **población** population
pobre poor
poco(a) little, small (amount), **5.2**
poder (ue) to be able, **7.1**
polar polar
político(a) political
los **políticos (parientes)** in-laws, **6**
poner to put, **8.1**
popular popular, **2.1**
la **popularidad** popularity
por about, for, by
   por consiguiente consequently
   por ejemplo for example
   por encima over, **7.2**
   por eso therefore
   por favor please, **BV**
¿por qué? why?
porque because
la **portería** goal, **7.1**
el/la **portero(a)** goalkeeper, goalie **7.1**
posible possible
el **postre** dessert, **5.2**
practicar to practice
precioso(a) beautiful, **6.2**
la **preferencia** preference
preferir (ie) to prefer, **7**
preparar to prepare, **4.1**
presentar to present
la **presente** present
la **primavera** spring, **7.2**
primer, primero(a) first, **BV**
el/la **primo(a)** cousin, **6.1**
principal main
privado(a) private, **5.1**
el **problema** problem
el **proceso** process
profesional professional
el/la **profesor(a)** teacher, **2.1**
el **programa** program

el/la **propietario(a)** owner
protestante Protestant
publicado(a) published
público(a) public
el **pueblo** town, **5.1**
la **puerta** gate, **8.1**
   la puerta de salida departure gate, **8.1**
el **puerto** port
puertorriqueño(a) Puerto Rican, **2**
pues well
el **punto: en punto** on the dot, **3.1**

Q

que that
¿qué? what; how, **BV**
   ¿Qué es? What is it?, **BV**
   ¿Qué tal? How are you?, **BV**
   ¿Qué hora es? What time is it?, **2**
quedar to remain
   quedar empatado(a) to be tied (sports), **7.1**
querer (ie) to want, **7**
¿quién? who?, **BV**
   ¿Quién es? Who is it (she, he)?, **BV**
la **química** chemistry, **2.2**
el/la **químico** chemist
la **quinceañera** young woman's fifteenth birthday
quinientos five hundred
quinto fifth, **5.1**

R

rápidamente quickly
rápido fast
el **rasgo** feature
el/la **receptor(a)** catcher (baseball), **7.2**
recibir to receive, **5.2**
reciente recent
reclamar to claim, **8.2**
el **reclamo de equipaje** baggage claim, **8.2**
recoger to pick up, collect, **8.2**
la **red** net, **7.2**
redondo(a) round
reflejar to reflect

el **refresco** soft drink, **4.1**
el **regalo** gift, **6.2**
la **región** region
el **regreso** return
   regular fair; passing (grade)
la **relación** relationship
relativamente relatively
religioso(a) religious
representar to represent
la **reproducción** reproduction
residencial residential
el **restaurante** restaurant
resultar to result
revisar to inspect, **8**
la **revista** magazine, **5.2**
el **rey** king
rico(a) rich
el **río** river
robar to steal, **7.2**
rojo(a) red
romántico(a) romantic
la **ropa** clothes, **8.2**
rubio(a) blond(e), **1.1**
la **ruina** ruin

S

el **sábado** Saturday, **BV**
sacar to get, receive, **3.2**
   sacar notas buenas (malas) to get good (bad) grades, **3.2**
la **sala** living room, **4.1**
   la sala de clase classroom, **3.1**
la **salida** departure, **8.1**
   la puerta de salida departure gate, **8.1**
   el tablero de llegadas y salidas arrival and departure board, **8.1**
salir to leave, **8.1**
el **salón de clase** classroom, **3.1**
el **sándwich** sandwich, **5.2**
el/la **santo(a)** saint
la **sección de no fumar** no smoking section, **8.1**
el **sector** section
secundario(a) secondary, **1.1**
   la escuela secundaria high school, **1.1**
segundo(a) second, **5.1**
secuoya sequoia
la **seguridad** security, **8.1**

el control de seguridad security control, **8.1**

seis six, **BV**

la **selva** rainforest

el **semestre** semester

el **señor** Mr., sir, **BV**

la **señora** Mrs., ma'am, **BV**

la **señorita** Miss, Ms., **BV**

separado(a) separated

septiembre September, **BV**

séptimo(a) seventh, **5.1**

ser to be, **1**

la **serie** series

la **Serie Mundial** World Series

serio(a) serious, **1.2**

el **servicio** service

sesenta sixty, **BV**

setenta seventy, **BV**

sexto sixth, **5.1**

sí yes

siempre always, **5.2**

siete seven, **BV**

el **siglo** century

la **silla** chair, **BV**

simple simple

simplemente simply

sin without

sin embargo nevertheless

sin escala nonstop

sincero(a) sincere, **1.2**

la **situación** situation

sobre above, over

sobre todo especially

sobresaliente outstanding

sobrevolar to fly over

el/la **sobrino(a)** nephew (niece), **6.1**

los **sobrinos** niece(s) and nephew(s), **6.1**

la **sociedad** society

la **sociología** sociology, **2.2**

el/la **sociólogo(a)** sociologist

solamente only

sólo only

somos we are, **2.2**

son they/you (pl. form.) are, **2.1**

la **sopa** soup, **5.2**

soy I am, **1.2**

su his, her, your (form.), their

subir to go up, **5.1**

subir a to get on, to board, **8.1**

la **substancia** substance

los **suburbios** suburbs, **5.1**

sucesivo(a) successive

sudamericano(a) South American

el **suelo** ground, **7**

tocar el suelo to touch the ground

el **sueño** dream

la **superficie** surface

superior superior

el **sur** south

La America del Sur South America, **8.1**

el **suroeste** southwest

suspenso(a) failing

T

el **tablero** backboard (basketball), **7.2**

el **tablero de llegadas y salidas** arrival and departure board, **8.1**

el **tablero indicador** scoreboard, **7.1**

el **talón** luggage claims ticket, **8.1**

también also, too, **1.1**

tan so

el **tanto** score; point, **7.1**

tarde late, **8.1**

la **tarde** afternoon

la **tarjeta** card

la **tarjeta de embarque** boarding pass, **8.1**

la **tarjeta postal** postcard, **5.2**

el **taxi** taxi, **8.1**

técnico(a) technical

el **teléfono** telephone, **4.1**

por teléfono on the phone, **4.1**

la **telenovela** soap opera, **5.2**

la **televisión** television, **4.1**

el **televisor** television (set)

el **templo** temple

temprano early

tener to have, **6.1**

tener... años to be... years old, **6.1**

tener que to have to, **6**

tercer(o) third, **5.1**

terminar to end

el **término** term, word

el **tiempo** half (of a soccer game), **7.1**

a tiempo on time, **8.1**

a tiempo completo full time

a tiempo parcial part time

la **tienda** store, **4.1**

la **tierra** earth

tímido(a) timid, shy, **1.2**

tinto(a) red

el/la **tío(a)** uncle (aunt), **6.1**

los **tíos** aunt(s) and uncle(s), **6.1**

típico(a) typical

el **tipo** type

tirar to throw, **7.2**

tirar con el pie to kick, **7.2**

titulado(a) entitled

la **tiza** chalk, **BV**

tocar to play (an instrument), **4.2**; to touch, **7**

todavía yet, still

todo(a) every, all, **4.2**

sobre todo especially

todos everyone

tomar to take, **3.2**; to drink, **4.1**

tomar apuntes to take notes, **3.2**

trabajar to work, **4.1**

el **trabajo** work, job

el trabajo a tiempo parcial part-time work

tradicional traditional

traer to bring, **8**

el **tráfico** traffic

el **transporte** transportation

tratar to deal with

tratar de to be about

treinta thirty, **BV**

tres three, **BV**

la **trigonometría** trigonometry, **2.2**

la **tripulación** crew, **8.2**

triunfante triumphant

triunfar to win, triumph

la **trompeta** trumpet, **4.2**

tropical tropical

tú you (sing. fam.)

tu your (sing. fam.)

la **turbulencia** turbulence

turbulento(a) turbulent

U

Uds., ustedes you (pl. form.), **2.2**

último(a) last

un(a) a, an, **BV**

el **uniforme** uniform

llevar uniforme to wear a

uniform
unir to unite
la **universidad** university
uno one, **BV**
usar to use
el **uso** use

V

va he/she/it goes, is going
las **vacaciones** vacation
el **valle** valley
vamos we go, we are going
van they/you (pl. form.) go, are going, **4.1**
variar to vary
la **variedad** variety
varios(as) several
vas you (sing. fam.) go, you are going
el **vaso** glass, **5.2**
veces: a veces sometimes
la **vegetación** vegetation
veinte twenty, **BV**
vender to sell, **5.2**
venezolano(a) Venezuelan
venir to come, **8**
venta: en venta for sale

ver to see, to watch, **5.2**
el **verbo** verb
la **verdad** truth, **1.1**
  ¿**no es verdad?** isn't it true?, **1.1**
  ¿**verdad?** right?, **1.1**
el **vestido** dress
la **vez** time
  en vez de instead of
el **viaje** trip, **8.1**
  hacer un viaje to take a trip, **8.1**
victorioso(a) victorious
la **vida** life
viejo(a) old, **6.1**
el **viento** wind
el **viernes** Friday, **BV**
el **vino** wine
el **violín** violin, **4.2**
la **vista** view, **6.2**
la **vivienda** housing
vivir to live, **5.1**
el **vocabulario** vocabulary
volar (ue) to fly
el **vólibol** volleyball, **7.2**
volver (ue) to go back, **7.1**
vosotros(as) you (pl. fam.)
voy I go, I am going

el **vuelo** flight, **8.1**
  el asistente, la asistenta de vuelo flight attendant, **8.2**
  el número del vuelo flight number, **8.1**
vuestro(a) your (pl. fam.)

Y

y and, **1.2**
yo I, **1.2**

Z

la **zona** district, zone
  la zona postal ZIP code
la **zoología** zoology

VOCABULARIO
INGLÉS-ESPAÑOL

The *Vocabulario inglés-español* contains all productive vocabulary from the text.

The reference numbers following each entry indicate the chapter and vocabulary section in which the word is introduced. For example **2.2** means that the word first appeared actively in *Capítulo 2, Palabras 2*. Boldface numbers without a *Palabras* reference indicate vocabulary introduced in the grammar section of the given chapter. **BV** refers to the introductory *Bienvenidos* lesson.

A

a, an un(a), **BV**
about (time) a eso de, **3.1**
activity la actividad, **5.2**
after después de, **4.1**
afternoon la tarde
  good afternoon buenas tardes, **BV**
agent el/la agente, **8.1**
airline la línea aérea, **8.1**
airplane el avión, **8.1**
  by plane en avión, **8.1**
airport el aeropuerto, **8.1**
algebra el álgebra, **2.2**
also también, **1.1**
always siempre, **5.2**
  not always siempre no, **5.2**
am soy, **1.2**
American americano(a), **1.2**
and y, **1.2**
apartment el apartamento, **5.1**
April abril (m.), **BV**
are son, **2.1**; están, **4.1**
Argentinian argentino(a), **2.1**
arithmetic la aritmética, **2.2**
around alrededor de, **6.2**
arrival la llegada, **8.1**
  arrival and departure board el tablero de llegadas y salidas, **8.1**
to **arrive** llegar, **3.1**
art el arte, **2.2**
to **assist** asistir, **5.2**
At what time? ¿A qué hora?, **2**
at home en casa, **4.2**
to **attend** asistir, **5.2**
attractive atractivo(a), **1.2**
August agosto (m.), **BV**
aunt la tía, **6.1**
aunt(s) and uncle(s) los tíos, **6.1**
autumn otoño, **7.1**
avenue la avenida, **5.1**

B

backboard (basketball) el tablero, **7.2**
backpack la mochila, **BV**
bad malo(a), **1**
baggage el equipaje, **8.1**
  baggage claim el reclamo de equipaje, **8.2**
balcony el balcón, **6.2**

ball el balón, **7.1**; la pelota, **7.2**
ballpoint pen el bolígrafo, **BV**
base la base, **7.2**
baseball el béisbol, **7.2**
basket el cesto, el canasto, **7.2**
  to make a basket encestar, meter en el cesto, **7.2**
basketball el baloncesto, el básquetbol, **7.2**
bat el bate, **7.2**
bathroom el cuarto de baño, **5.1**
batter el/la bateador(a), **7.2**
to **be** ser, **1**; estar, **4.1**
  to be... years old tener... años, **6.1**
to **be able** poder (ue), **7.1**
to **be going to** ir a, **6.1**
to **be tied (sports)** quedar empatado(a), **7.1**
beautiful precioso(a), **6.2**
bedroom el cuarto de dormir, el dormitorio, **5.1**
to **begin** empezar (ie), comenzar (ie), **7.1**
bench el banco, **BV**
bicycle la bicicleta, **6.2**
big grande, **2.1**
biology la biología, **2.2**
birthday el cumpleaños, **6.2**
blackboard la pizarra, el pizarrón, **3.2**
to **block** bloquear, **7.1**
blond(e) rubio(a), **1.1**
to **board** abordar, subir a, **8.1**
board el tablero, **8.1**
  arrival and departure board el tablero de llegadas y salidas, **8.1**
boarding pass la tarjeta de embarque, el pase de abordar, **8.1**
book el libro, **BV**
bookbag la mochila, **BV**
boring aburrido(a), **1.1**
boy el muchacho, **BV**
breakfast el desayuno, **5.2**
to **bring** traer, **8**
brother el hermano, **2.1**
building el edificio, **5.1**
bus el autobús, el bus, **3.1**
to **buy** comprar, **5.2**
by no means de ninguna manera, **1.1**
by bus, car en autobús, en carro (coche), **3.1**
by plane en avión, **8**

C

calculator la calculadora, **BV**
captain el/la comandante, **8.2**
car el coche, el carro, **3.1**
to **carry** llevar, **3.2**
carry-on luggage el equipaje de mano, **8.1**
cat el gato, **6.1**
to **catch** atrapar, **7.2**
catcher el/la cátcher, el/la receptor(a), **7.2**
chair la silla, **BV**
chalk la tiza, **BV**
chalkboard la pizarra, **BV**; el pizarrón, **3.2**
to **check (luggage)** facturar, **8.1**
chemistry la química, **2.2**
children los hijos, **6.1**
city la ciudad, **5.1**
civic education la educación cívica, **2.2**
to **claim** reclamar, **8.2**
class la clase, **2.1**
classical clásico(a), **4**
classroom la sala de clase, el salón de clase, **3.1**
clothes la ropa, **8.2**
coffee el café, **5.2**
to **collect** recoger, **8.2**
Colombian colombiano(a), **1**
computer la computadora, **BV**
control: security control el control de seguridad, **8.1**
copilot el/la copiloto, **8.2**
counter el mostrador, **8.1**
country el campo, **5.1**
course el curso, **2.1**
court (sports) la cancha, **7.2**
cousin el/la primo(a), **6.1**
crew la tripulación, **8.2**
customer el/la cliente, **5.2**
customs la aduana, **8.2**

D

dad el papá, **5.2**
to **dance** bailar, **4.2**
date la fecha, **BV**
  What is today's date? ¿Cuál es la fecha de hoy?, **BV**
daughter la hija, **6.1**
day el día
December diciembre (m.), **BV**

departure la salida, **8.1**
  arrival and departure board el tablero de llegadas y salidas, **8.1**
  departure gate la puerta de salida, **8.1**
dessert el postre, **5.2**
destination el destino, **8.1**
difficult difícil, **2.1**
to **dine** cenar, **5**
  dining room el comedor, **5.1**
  dinner la cena, **5.2**
    to have dinner cenar, **5**
  dog el/la perro(a), **6.1**
  domestic de cabotaje, **8**
  dot: on the dot en punto, **3.1**
to **dribble** driblar (con), **7.2**
to **drink** tomar, **4.1**; beber, **5.2**
  during durante, **4.2**

E

early temprano
easy fácil, **2.1**
to **eat** comer, **5.2**
  eight ocho, **BV**
  eighth octavo(a), **5.1**
  eighty ochenta, **BV**
  elevator el ascensor, **5.1**
  English (language) el inglés, **2.2**
  English inglés, inglesa, **2.2**
to **enter** entrar, **3.1**
  entrance la entrada, **6.2**
  eraser la goma, **BV**
  evening la noche
    good evening buenas noches, **BV**
  everyone todos, **4.2**
  examination el examen, **3.2**

F

failing (grade) insuficiente, cate
family la familia, **5.1**
fantastic fantástico(a), **1.2**
father el padre, **6.1**
February febrero (m.), **BV**
field el campo, **7.1**
  soccer field el campo de fútbol, **7.1**
fifth quinto(a), **5.1**
fifty cincuenta, **BV**
fine bien, **BV**

first primer, primero(a), **BV**
five cinco, **BV**
five hundred quinientos
flight el vuelo, **8.1**
  flight attendant el asistente (la asistenta) de vuelo, **8.2**
  flight number el número del vuelo, **8.1**
floor el piso, **5.1**
flower la flor, **6.2**
foot el pie, **7.1**
  on foot a pie, **3.1**
for de, **1.1**
forty cuarenta, **BV**
four cuatro, **BV**
fourth cuarto(a), **5.1**
French francés (francesa), **2.2**
Friday el viernes, **BV**
friend el/la amigo(a), **1.1**
from de, **1.1**
fun divertido(a), **1.1**

G

game el partido, **7.1**
garage el garaje, **6.2**
garden el jardín, **6.2**
gate la puerta, **8.1**
  departure gate la puerta de salida, **8.1**
geography la geografía, **2.2**
geometry la geometría, **2.2**
to **get on** subir a, **8.1**
to **get** sacar, **3.2**
    to get good (bad) grades sacar notas buenas (malas), **3.2**
  gift el regalo, **6.2**
  girl la muchacha, **BV**
to **give** dar, **4.2**
  glass el vaso, **5.2**
  glove el guante, **7.2**
to **go** ir, **4.1**
    they go, they are going van, **4.1**
    to go home ir a casa, **4.2**
to **go back** volver (ue), **7.1**
to **go up** subir, **5.1**
  goal el gol, la portería, **7.1**
  goalie el/la portero(a), **7.1**
  goalkeeper el/la portero(a), **7.1**
  good bueno(a), **1.2**
    good evening, good night buenas noches, **BV**
    good afternoon buenas tardes,

BV
  good morning buenos días, **BV**
good-bye adiós, chao, **BV**
grade la nota, **3.2**; la calificación
grandchild el/la nieto(a), **6.1**
grandfather el abuelo, **6.1**
grandmother la abuela, **6.1**
grandparents los abuelos, **6.1**
ground floor la planta baja, **5.1**
ground el suelo, **7**
to **guard** guardar, **7**
  guitar la guitarra, **4.2**

H

half el tiempo (soccer), **7.1**
hand la mano, **7.1**
to **have** tener, **6.1**
    to have to tener que, **6**
  he él, **1.1**
  head cabeza, **7.1**
  hello hola, buenos días, **BV**
  history la historia, **2.2**
to **hit (baseball)** batear, **7.2**
  hit (baseball) el hit, **7.2**
  home la casa, **4.2**
    at home en casa, **4.2**
  home economics la economía domestica, **2.2**
  home plate el platillo, **7.2**
  home run el jonrón, **7.2**
  honest honesto(a), **1.2**
  hoop aro, **7.2**
  house la casa, **4.1**
  how much? ¿cuánto(a)?, **BV**
    How much is it? ¿Cuánto es?, **BV**
  how? ¿qué?, **BV**; ¿cómo?, **1.1**
    How are you? ¿Qué tal?, **BV**
  husband el marido, el esposo, **6.1**

I

I yo, **1.2**
ice cream el helado, **5.2**
in en, **1.1**
individual individual, **7**
inning la entrada, **7.2**
to **inspect** revisar, **8**; inspeccionar, **8.2**
  inspection el control, **8.1**
    passport inspection el control de pasaportes, **8.1**

security inspection el control de seguridad, 8.1
instruction la disciplina, 2.2
instructions las instrucciones, 5.2
intelligent inteligente, 2.1
interesting interesante, 2.1
invitation la invitación, 5.2
to **invite** invitar, 4.2
is es, 1.1
Italian el/la italiano(a), 2.2

J

January enero (m.), BV
jazz (adj.) de jazz, 4
July julio (m.), BV
June junio (m.), BV

K

kind amable, 2.1
kitchen la cocina, 4.1
knapsack la mochila, BV

L

to **land** aterrizar, 8.2
language la lengua, 2.2
late tarde, 8.1
Latin el latín, 2.2
to **learn** aprender, 5.2
to **leave** salir, 8.1
left la izquierda, 5.1
   to the left a la izquierda, 5.1
lemonade la limonada, BV
lesson la lección, 3.2
letter la carta, 5.2
library la biblioteca, 4.1
to **listen** escuchar, 4.1
little poco(a), 5.2
to **live** vivir, 5.1
living room la sala, 4.1
to **look at** mirar, 3.2
to **lose** perder (ie), 7.1
low bajo, 3.2
luggage el equipaje, 8.1
   carry-on (hand) luggage el equipaje de mano, 8.1
lunch el almuerzo, 5.2

M

ma'am señora, BV
magazine la revista, 5.2
to **make** hacer, 8.1
   to make a basket encestar, meter en el cesto, 7.2
manner la manera, 1.1
many muchos(as), 5
March marzo (m.), BV
mathematics las matemáticas, 2.2
May mayo (m.), BV
meal la comida, 5.2
means: by no means de ninguna manera, 1.1
meat la carne, 5.2
Mexican mexicano(a), 1.1
midday el mediodía, 2
midnight la medianoche, 2
milk la leche, 5.2
Miss señorita, BV
mom la mamá, 5.2
moment el momento, 8.1
Monday el lunes, BV
morning la mañana
mother la madre, 6.1
motorbike el ciclomotor, 6.2
movie la película, 5.2
Mr. señor, BV
Mrs. señora, BV
music la música, 2.2

N

nationality la nacionalidad, 1
nephew el sobrino, 6.1
net la red, 7.2
new nuevo(a), 6.2
news las noticias, 5.2
newspaper el periódico, 5.2
Nice to meet you. Mucho gusto., BV
niece la sobrina, 6.1
niece(s) and nephew(s) los sobrinos, 6.1
night la noche
   good night buenas noches, BV
nine nueve, BV
ninety noventa, BV
ninth noveno(a), 5.1
noncarbonated soft drink el refresco, 4.1
no smoking section la sección de no fumar, 8.1

noon el mediodía, 2
not any ninguno(a), 1.1
   by no means de ninguna manera, 1.1
notebook el cuaderno, BV; la libreta, 3.2
notes los apuntes, 3.2
   to take notes tomar apuntes, 3.2
novel la novela, 5.2
now ahora
November noviembre (m.), BV
number el número, 8.1
   flight number el número del vuelo, 8.1
   seat number el número del asiento, 8.1

O

October octubre (m.), BV
of de, 1.1
old viejo(a), 6.1
one hundred cien(to), BV
one uno, BV
to **open** abrir, 8.2
opposite contrario(a), 7
other otro(a), 2.2
out (baseball) out, 7.2
outfielder (baseball) el/la jardinero(a), 7.2
outskirts las afueras, 5.1
over por encima, 7.2

P

to **pack one's suitcase** hacer la maleta, 8
paper el papel, BV
   sheet of paper la hoja de papel, BV
parents los padres, 6.1
park el parque, 6.2
party la fiesta, 4.2
to **pass** pasar, 7.2
passenger el/la pasajero(a), 8.1
passport el pasaporte, 8.1
   passport inspection el control de pasaportes, 8.1
pencil el lápiz, 5.2
physical education la educación física, 2.2
physics la física, 2.2

piano el piano, **4.2**
to **pick up** recoger, **8.2**
pilot el/la piloto, **8.2**
pitcher el/la pícher, el/la lanzador(a), **7.2**
plant la planta, **6.2**
plate: home plate el platillo, **7.2**
to **play (an instrument)** tocar, **4.2**
to **play** jugar (ue), **7.1**
player el/la jugador(a), **7.1**
please por favor, **BV**
point (score) tanto, **7.1**
popular popular, **2.1**
postcard la tarjeta postal, **5.2**
potato la papa, **5.2**
to **prefer** preferir (ie), **7**
to **prepare** preparar, **4.1**
pretty bonito(a), **6.2**
private particular, privado(a), **5.1**
Puerto Rican puertorriqueño(a), **2**
to **put in** meter, **7.1**
to **put** poner, **8.1**

Q

quarter: a quarter to, a quarter past (the hour) menos cuarto, y cuarto, **2**
quite bastante, **1.1**

R

rather bastante, **1.1**
to **read** leer, **5.2**
to **receive** sacar, **3.2**; recibir, **6**
record el disco, **4.1**
referee el/la árbitro(a), **7.1**
to **return** devolver (ue), **7.2**
right la derecha, **5.1**
to the right a la derecha, **5.1**
right? ¿verdad?, **1.1**
right now en este momento, **8.1**
rock (adj.) de rock, **4**
room el cuarto, la habitación, **5.1**
classroom la sala de clase, el salón de clase, **3.1**
row la fila, **8**
to **run** correr, **7.2**

S

salad la ensalada, **5.2**
sandwich el sándwich, el bocadillo, **5.2**
Saturday el sábado, **BV**
scale la báscula, **8.1**
school el colegio, la escuela, **1.1**
high school la escuela secundaria, **1.1**
school (adj.) escolar, **3.1**
science la ciencia, **2.2**
to **score (sports)** marcar, **7.1**
scoreboard el tablero indicador, **7.1**
screen la pantalla, **8.1**
seat el asiento, **8.1**
seat number el número del asiento, **8.1**
second segundo(a), **5.1**
secondary secundario(a), **1.1**
security la seguridad, **8.1**
security control el control de seguridad, **8.1**
to **see** ver, **5.2**
See you later. Hasta luego., **BV**
See you tomorrow. Hasta mañana., **BV**
See you soon. Hasta pronto., **BV**
to **sell** vender, **5.2**
September septiembre (m.), **BV**
serious serio(a), **1.2**
seven siete, **BV**
seventh séptimo(a), **5.1**
seventy setenta, **BV**
she ella, **1.2**
sheet la hoja, **BV**
sheet of paper la hoja de papel, **BV**
shopping center el centro comercial, **4.1**
short bajo(a), **1.1**
shy tímido(a), **1.2**
sincere sincero(a), **1.2**
to **sing** cantar, **4.2**
sir señor, **BV**
sister la hermana, **2.1**
six seis, **BV**
sixth sexto(a), **5.1**
sixty sesenta, **BV**
to **sleep** dormir (ue), **7**
small pequeño(a), **2.1**; **(amount)** poco(a), **5.2**
smoking (no smoking) section la sección de (no) fumar, **8.1**,

snack la merienda, **4.1**
soap opera la telenovela, **5.2**
soccer el fútbol, **7.1**
soccer field el campo de fútbol, **7.1**
social science las ciencias sociales, **2.2**
social studies la educación cívica, **2.2**
sociology la sociología, **2.2**
soda la gaseosa, **5.2**
soft drink la gaseosa, **5.2**
sometimes a veces, **5.2**
son el hijo, **6.1**
soup la sopa, **5.2**
South America la América del Sur, **8.1**
Spanish el español (language), **2.2**; español(a)
to **speak** hablar, **3.1**
spectator el/la espectador(a), **7**
sport el deporte, **2.2**
sports broadcast la emisión deportiva, **5.2**
spring la primavera, **7.2**
stadium el estadio, **7.1**
stairway la escalera, **5.1**
to **steal** robar, **7.2**
to **stop** parar, **7.1**
store la tienda, **4.1**
street la calle, **5.1**
student el/la alumno(a), **1.1**
to **study** estudiar, **3.2**
subject la asignatura, la disciplina, **2.2**
suburbs los suburbios, **5.1**
suitcase la maleta, **8.1**
to pack one's suitcase hacer la maleta, **8**
Sunday el domingo, **BV**

T

to **take** tomar, **3.2**
to take a trip hacer un viaje, **8.1**
to **take off (airplane)** despegar, **8.2**
tall alto(a), **1.1**
tape la cinta, **4.1**
taxi el taxi, **8.1**
to **teach** enseñar, **3.2**
teacher el/la profesor(a), **2.1**
team el equipo; (adj.) de equipo, **7.1**
telephone el teléfono, **4.1**

on the phone por teléfono, **4.1**
television la televisión, **4.1**
ten diez, **BV**
tenth décimo(a), **5.1**
test el examen, **3.2**
thank you gracias, **BV**
the el, la, **1.1**
there is/are hay, **5.1**
third tercer(o)(a), **5.1**
thirty treinta, **BV**
thousand mil, **BV**
three tres, **BV**
to **throw** tirar, lanzar, **7.1**
Thursday el jueves, **BV**
ticket el boleto, el billete **8.1**
tied empatado(a), **7**
time: on time a tiempo, **8.1**
At what time? ¿A qué hora?, **2**
timid tímido(a), **1.2**
to a; con destino a, **8**
today hoy, **BV**
too también, **1.1**
to **touch** tocar, **7**
town el pueblo, **5.1**
tree el árbol, **6.2**
trigonometry la trigonometría, **2.2**
trip el viaje, **8.1**
to take a trip hacer un viaje, **8.1**
trumpet la trompeta, **4.2**
trunk el/la maletero(a), **8.1**
truth la verdad, **1.1**
isn't it true? ¿no es verdad?, **1.1**
Tuesday el martes, **BV**
twenty veinte, **BV**
two dos, **BV**

U

uncle el tío, **6.1**
to **understand** comprender, **5.2**
unpleasant antipático(a), **1.1**
until hasta, **BV**

V

very muy, **BV**
view la vista, **6.2**
violin el violín, **4.2**
volleyball el vólibol, **7.2**

W

to **want** querer (ie), **7**
to **watch** ver, **5.2**
way la manera, **1.1**
we are somos, **2.2**
we nosotros(as), **2.2**
Wednesday el miércoles, **BV**
well bien, **BV**
what? ¿cuál?, ¿qué?, **BV**; ¿cómo?, **1.1**
What is it? ¿Qué es?, **BV**
What time is it? ¿Qué hora es?, **2**
What is today's date? ¿Cuál es la fecha de hoy?, **BV**
when? ¿cuándo?, **3.1**
where? ¿dónde?, **1.2**; ¿adónde?, **4**
which? ¿cuál?, **BV**
who? ¿quién?, **BV**
Who is it (he, she)? ¿Quién es?, **BV**
wife la esposa, la mujer, **6.1**
to **win** ganar, **7.1**
to **work** trabajar, **4.1**
to **write** escribir, **5.2**
writing pad el bloc, **3.2**

Y

you are son (pl. form.), **2.1**; están (pl. form.), **4.1**
you go van (pl. form.), **4.1**
you Uds., ustedes (pl. form.), **2.2**
You're welcome. De nada., No hay de qué., **BV**
young joven, **6.1**

Z

zero cero, **BV**

ÍNDICE GRAMATICAL

PREHISTORIC TIMES

Readings from
**SCIENTIFIC
AMERICAN**

PREHISTORIC TIMES

With Introductions by
Brian M. Fagan
University of California, Santa Barbara

W. H. Freeman and Company
New York San Francisco

Some of the SCIENTIFIC AMERICAN articles in *Prehistoric Times* are available as separate Offprints. For a complete list of articles now available as Offprints, write to W. H. Freeman and Company, 660 Market Street, San Francisco, California 94104.

Library of Congress Cataloging in Publication Data
Main entry under title:

Prehistoric times.

   Bibliography: p.
   Includes index.
   1. Man, Prehistoric—Addresses, essays, lectures.
I. Fagan, Brian M.   II. Scientific American, Inc.
GN766.P73   1983   573.3   82-24235
ISBN 0-7167-1490-6
ISBN 0-7167-1491-4 (pbk.)

Printed in the United States of America

2 3 4 5 6 7 8 9 KP 1 0 8 9 8 7 6 5 4 3

PREFACE

*P*rehistoric Times is a collection of articles from the pages of *Scientific American* that provides a summary of the major developments of human prehistory. My introduction identifies these major developments and surveys the basic principles, methods, and theories that archaeologists use to study the past. Each of the four parts focuses on a single aspect of prehistory: Part I covers the origins of humanity and what we know about the early evolution of human behavior. Part II describes hunter-gatherer cultures and the peopling of the world after the emergence of more modern forms of human beings. Part III deals with the origins of agriculture and animal domestication, perhaps the most revolutionary developments in our history. Part IV takes us on a brief journey through the first civilizations, describing some of the ways archaeologists have approached the study of early complex societies.

This Reader brings up to date the material presented in an earlier *Scientific American* Reader, *Avenues to Antiquity* (W. H. Freeman and Company, 1976). It reflects state-of-the-art archaeology, fieldwork, and laboratory analysis as they combine to provide detailed interpretations of sites, artifacts, and food remains. The objective is not just to describe what happened in prehistory, but also to explain why it happened. To many people, archaeology is a world of romantic discovery, buried treasure, and lost civilizations—an escapist adventure story that bears little resemblance to historical reality. The irony is that the most exciting stories archaeologists are writing about the prehistoric past are based not on rich graves and great temples, but on the tiniest and most inconspicuous of finds and a battery of ingenious scientific techniques. These discoveries and methods enable archaeologists to reconstruct such information as the direction of the wind on the day of an 8000-year-old hunt, and to glean statistics on crop yields from long buried Mycenaean clay tablets.

Prehistoric Times covers all areas of the world but gives necessarily superficial coverage to many sites and cultures. Readers seeking more specific information on either Old or New World archaeology should consult two other *Scientific American* Readers: *Hunters, Farmers, and Civilizations* and *Pre-Columbian Archaeology*.

This book is designed to serve as a mirror to prehistory, as an insight into the long millennia of the human experience that served as the catalyst for the extraordinary biological and cultural diversity of modern humanity. An understanding of this diversity is essential to anyone living in modern industrial civilization, when it is possible for us to communicate instantaneously with any nation on the globe.

January 1983   Brian M. Fagan

CONTENTS

PREHISTORIC TIMES

INTRODUCTION

A SURVEY OF PREHISTORY

"In the beginning God created the heavens and the earth . . . ." The magnificent words of Genesis thunder across the centuries, a story of the creation of humankind that has been an object of faith for millions. Some people still believe that the Old Testament is the literal historical truth and that the world was created in six days, while on the seventh God rested. A seventeenth-century archbishop named James Ussher used the genealogies in the Old Testament to date the Creation to 4004 BC. Another scholar went so far as to declare that the world was created at nine in the morning on October 23, 4004 BC! This long-accepted chronology allowed but 6000 years for all of human history. In contrast, archaeologists now accept a date of at least three million years ago for the origins of humankind.

Lost Civilizations and Insoluble Mysteries

Speculation about the past is nothing new. Ancient Mesopotamian clay tablets reveal that the biblical legend of the Creation and the story of the Great Flood probably originated in ancient Sumerian folktales recited at least five thousand years ago. The Greeks and Romans philosophized about the remote past. Chinese sages thought in terms of Stone, Bronze, and Iron ages. One Aztec ruler in Mexico sent an expedition to find the original homeland of his people. His emissaries were lucky. A demon obligingly turned them into birds and flew them to a remote lake where they found their ancestors.

Until the Age of Discovery in the fifteenth century, few Western scholars were much concerned about human origins or about the riddles of human diversity. The discovery of the American Indian was a watershed in Western intellectual experience and changed the way Europeans looked at other societies, ancient and modern. At first the Spaniards did not believe the Indians were human at all. It took a papal bull in 1537 to settle the matter once and for all. Then the intellectuals had a field day speculating about Indian origins. The Indians became descendants of Carthaginians and Ancient Egyptians, of the Ten Lost Tribes of Israel, even citizens of the Lost Continent of Atlantis that had supposedly sunk beneath the waters of the Atlantic thousands of years before. Only a few more serious scholars argued that the American Indian had reached the Americas from Asia, across the Bering Strait, the hypothesis that is accepted by most archaeologists today.

The nineteenth century was an age of heroic archaeological discovery that started with the decipherment of the Rosetta Stone and Ancient Egyptian hieroglyphs in 1822. In the 1840s, French diplomat Paul Botta and Englishman Austen Henry Layard unearthed the palaces of the Assyrian kings in northern Iraq. Their spectacular finds of sculpture and clay tablets clothed a shadowy biblical civilization in historical clothes. These finds came when interest in the historical veracity of the Scriptures was at its height. Frenzied writers piled speculation upon speculation. Where had civilization begun, they wondered. Did the Garden of Eden exist in distant Mesopotamia? How had civilization spread to Egypt, China, and the Americas? When Heinrich Schliemann excavated ancient Hissarlik, the site of Homeric Troy, in the 1870s, popular interest in lost civilizations and ancient history reached fever pitch. The remarkable discoveries of the early archaeologists filled for many people a need for vicarious adventure and romance. When John Lloyd Stephens and Frederick Catherwood returned from the Yucatán in the 1840s with details of the Maya civilization, they became celebrities. The nineteenth-century archaeologist was a folk hero, an adventurer who found buried treasure in remote places. The stereotype persists into the 1980s.

The excitement of lost civilizations and unsolved mysteries of the past attracted not only serious scholars but the eccentric as well. They found the past a convenient outlet for their harmless lunacies and bizarre faiths. One such eccentric was Augustus Le Plongeon (1826–1908), who thought that the Maya of Mexico had sailed all the way to Egypt to found colonies on the banks of the Nile. He claimed that the Maya had told him their secret history, which linked them not only with the pharaohs but with Atlantis as well. Le Plongeon thought of himself as a Maya god and believed the Maya invented the electric telegraph! His successors flourish, for the rich diversity of our past is a happy hunting ground for cultists, minor prophets, and facile writers out for a quick profit at the cost of science.

Even today, there are many people who believe that the world was created only six thousand years ago, that Chinese settled in America long before Columbus, and that Egyptians and Phoenicians colonized the United States centuries ahead of the Vikings. To such folk, archaeology is a great adventure story of lost tribes and sunken continents, of epic voyages, great heroes, and buried treasure. Buried cities emerge from swirling mists (an essential ingredient for any prehistoric riddle), unexplained mysteries abound. A highly profitable literary industry has grown up around the search for Noah's Ark and the prehistoric journeys of ancient astronauts who came to earth to found civilization in Egypt and Mexico. Adventurers of lively imagination claim to have found Atlantis in the Bahamas and off the coast of Spain.

All of this is, of course, scientific nonsense. Not that the cultists are deterred. Their fantasies follow a familiar pattern. A theory is advanced that cuts against the weight of a scientific evidence and established hypotheses. The reader is made to feel that he or she has joined the author in a "Great Adventure," in seeing "The Light." Experts are consulted, scattered "archaeological" evidence from all over the world assembled to clothe the tale in a semblance of coherence. Those experts who agree are quoted (or misquoted). Those who disagree are either ignored or abused for their narrow-mindedness. The entire saga becomes a narrative epic, a lesson in "the triumph of Truth over science." Many such books pursue their theories with an almost religious frenzy, dismissing generations of meticulous archaeological research as sheer irrelevance. It is hardly surprising that they sell briskly, for they tell their stories well.

It is very easy to dismiss such theories as cynical exploitation of a gullible audience, as the research of mere amateurs pitted against professional science. In fact, archaeologists are themselves divided about such issues or long-distance voyaging and the origins of early civilization. There are many respected scholars who believe, for example, that there were at least some sporadic contacts between the Old World and the New long before the Vikings or Columbus. Unfortunately, the physical evidence for such contacts, if they did occur, is likely to be extremely sparse. Indeed, the chances of uncovering evidence for such sporadic events are minimal. The search for such evidence continues unabated, and so it should, for no scientists rejects a legitimate hypothesis out of hand. But such a search for rigorously excavated data is quite different from wild theories that are presented as substantiated when in fact they are neither testable nor even falsifiable. Such unsubstantiated hypotheses are based more on religious faith and ardently held beliefs than they are on hard information.

One of the fascinations of the past is that it does contain some unexplained mysteries, riddles that have long defied science. Why, for example, did Maya civilization collapse so suddenly? There are two ways of attacking such challenging problems—through plodding scientific research, or by taking a quick fix through wild speculation, faith and inspiration. Many people prefer the wild fables, simply because they do not understand what archaeologists do, and also because they are looking for some lesson from the past that will enable them to understand today's confusing world. They are impatient with uncertainties and question marks, with the huge gaps in our knowledge of prehistory.

Archaeologists suffer from the peculiar problem that much of their research is conducted under the merciless eye of public scrutiny. Archaeology is conceived of as a romantic, exciting subject, not as a methodical discipline that can take years to work out even trivial problems. Scientists prefer to tell the scientific truth and to give cautious and tentative answers that may seem unromantic and at times dull. The myths and fantasies are appealingly simple explanations of complex events. They appeal to the "there is always a remote possibility" school of thought that tempts all of us when we think about the past, about the possibility of life on other planets, or ponder other unexplained phenomena. Actually, the scientific story of the past is even more fascinating than the space fiction. It is a pity that some of archaeology's most interesting, indeed spectacular, recent advances have been reported only in the scientific literature and never exposed to the public eye. In a special sense, archaeology is like a dramatic script: it comes to life only when performed for a wider audience.

A century after Heinrich Schliemann electrified the world with his discovery of Homeric Troy, the scientific discoveries of archaeologists have modified even the wildest theories about the past. Today, one can gaze back at a prehistoric landscape that extends back more than 3000 millennia. We live in a century when scientific discovery is accepted as a routine part of our lives. Scientists have landed astronauts on the moon, explored the profoundest depths of the oceans, split the atom, and traced the most intricate details of mammalian evolution. The exploration of prehistory is one of the great intellectual achievements of the nineteenth and twentieth centuries, yet the scientific achievements of arachaeologists remain surprisingly little known. Their voyage of discovery has revolutionized the way we think about the past and given us totally new perceptions of the extraordinary biological and cultural diversity of humankind. The archaeologist has come up with evidence and interpretations that are completely different from the wildest theories. *Prehistoric Times* takes you on a journey through the long millennia of our remote past and shows how archaeologists have used not only spectacular finds but what might appear to be the most insignificant of small finds to reconstruct the prehistoric past.

Prehistory Begins: Hunter-Gatherers

Three million years ago, the world's human population probably numbered in the hundreds and consisted of small bands of hominids living in the savannah woodlands of East and southern Africa. As recently as 15,000 years

TIME	SITES, CULTURES, CIVILIZATIONS	CULTURAL AND TECHNOLOGICAL DEVELOPMENTS
AD 1500	SPANISH CONQUEST AZTECS INCA	
AD 1	ROMAN EMPIRE TEOTIHUACÁN M	EMERGENCE OF WESTERN CIVILIZATION
1000 BC	ASSYRIANS MYCENAEANS A	
1500 BC	SHANG MINOANS OLMEC Y	
2500 BC	HARAPPANS CUELLO A	WHEELED TRANSPORT
3000 BC	SUMERIANS ANCIENT EGYPTIANS	FIRST CITIES
5000 BC	CATAL HÜYÜK TEHUACÁN	WRITING
	JERICHO	
10,000 BC	EARLY AGRICULTURE IN THE NEAR EAST	ORIGINS OF FOOD PRODUCTION
15,000 BC	LASCAUX ? EARLY CULTIVATION IN EGYPT	
35,000 BC		ART
		BLADE TECHNOLOGY
		EMERGENCE OF MODERN HUMANS
100,000 BC		NEANDERTHALS
		FIRST BURIALS
250,000 BC		EMERGENCE OF EARLY *HOMO SAPIENS*
400,000 BC	TERRA AMATA CHOUKOUTIEN	
1.5 MILLION BC		EMERGENCE OF *HOMO ERECTUS*
	OLDUVAI GORGE	
2 MILLION BC		EARLIEST DOCUMENTED STONE TOOLMAKING
	EAST TURKANA	*HOMO*
		AUSTRALOPITHECUS
3.5 MILLION BC	LAETOLI HADAR	
4 MILLION BC	MIDDLE AWASH	UPRIGHT WALKING HOMINIDS IN ETHIOPIA

Figure 1 Major developments in prehistory. Sites and areas are underlined; cultures and civilizations are not.

ago, when everyone lived as hunters and gatherers, the biosphere supported a population of no more than 10 million—less than that of London or Tokyo. Then came agriculture, animal domestication, urban civilization, and the industrial revolution. Today, more than 4 billion people live on planet earth and our numbers increase dramatically every year. We added the fourth billion in only 15 years, between 1950 and 1965. This dramatic acceleration in human population is a recent phenomenon. At first, the pace of human cultural evolution was glacially slow (Washburn, Leakey, Isaac, articles 1, 2, 3).

The first hominids flourished in East Africa more than 3 million years ago, walking upright, using the simplest of stone, wood, and bone artifacts, and living by gathering, scavenging and occasional hunting. For more than 2 millions years, our ancestors lived in tropical regions where game and wild vegetable foods were relatively plentiful. Their simple technology consisted of little more than flaked pebbles, sharpened sticks, and fractured bones. Sometime between 1,500,000 and 400,000 years ago, more advanced humans (*Homo erectus*) began to use fire and a slightly more sophisticated technology that helped them adapt to much greater extremes of climate, ranging from more temperate environments in western Europe to distinctly cold regimens in China.

Homo sapiens, modern people, began to emerge some 250,000 years ago. They developed far more specialized toolkits that helped them exploit a far wider range of environments than their predecessors could (Howells and Trinkaus, article 5). Starting about 70,000 years ago, we find the first burials that we take to be signs of a belief in life after death. The world's first artists were living in southwestern France by 30,000 BC, by which time hunters and gatherers had peopled most regions of the world, including Australia, the Americas, and Siberia (Leroi-Gourhan, article 6). Everyone still lived by hunting and gathering, a way of life that has survived in some parts of the world to this day. The Australian aborigines, the Eskimo of the far north, the Indians of Tierra del Fuego, and the San of the Kalahari Desert in Southern Africa have provided anthropologists with valuable insights into the most enduring, and perhaps most viable, of all human adaptations.

With the emergence of *Homo sapiens* and the peopling of the world, the pace of cultural evolution accelerated rapidly. As people adapted to increasingly diverse environments, their toolkits became more specialized and more elaborate. Some hunter-gatherer societies like the Paleo-Indians of the Great Plains of North America seem to have concentrated on big-game hunting (Wheat, article 7). Others, like the salmon fishers of the Pacific Northwest, relied heavily on maritime resources and annual salmon runs. They lived in much more sedentary settlements and developed complex societies characterized by powerful chieftains and elaborate ceremonials. But most hunter-gatherer societies were more transitory in their habits; small bands of several families exploited a well-defined territory with a very low population density per square mile. All hunter-gatherer societies, whether small mobile bands or more settled groups, enjoyed an intimate relationship with their natural environment. They observed the seasons of game and vegetable foods, the cycles of germination and growth, and could schedule their activities to take advantage of each resource as it came into season throughout the year.

Farmers and Herders

Some 15,000 years ago, some hunter-gatherer communities on the Nile were experimenting with the planting of wild cereals and grasses that grew in abundance on the banks of the river. Perhaps population pressure and other as yet little understood ecological factors caused them to experiment with growing rather than gathering food. In any case, the experiments were successful in several areas. By 8000 BC many societies in the Near East were probably cultivating the soil and experimenting with crops of wheat and barley (Moore, article 8; Mellaart, article 9; Figure 2). At about the same time, goats and sheep were domesticated, probably in the hilly flanks overlooking the lowlands of what are now Syria and Iraq. The gradual change from hunting and gathering to food production was a process that began not only in the Near East, but in Southeast Asia, northern China, Mexico, and Peru, and later in North America and Africa. Agriculture and animal domestication appear on the face of it to have been revolutionary inventions. In fact, they were probably simple steps for those people already engaged in the intensive exploitation of, say, wild sheep or cereal grasses flourishing in dense natural stands. It was not the changeover from food gathering to food production that was the revolution; it was rather the consequences of that shift that were to alter the course of human history for ever.

The new economies caught on gradually. Within four millennia, agricultural societies were flourishing not only in Egypt and Mesopotamia, but as far afield as western Europe and deep in India (Daniel, article 10). A few millennia after its first domestication, probably in Mexico, some 7500 years

Figure 2   Aerial view of an early farming village in the Zagros mountains of Iraq. The site is 3.2 acres. About one-third of the original area has eroded away. Archaeologists dug the square trenches in their effort to trace the village plan. [From The Oriental Institute, University of Chicago Museum, photograph by Robert J. Braidwood.]

ago (MacNeish, article 11), maize had become the staple of hundreds of American Indian communities. Farmers spread far afield into Melanesia and Polynesia, reaching such outlying island groups as Hawaii and New Zealand in the late first millennium AD. Food production spread to all corners of the world, except where extremes of heat, aridity, or cold rendered agriculture or herding impracticable, or where people chose to remain hunter-gatherers. Most human societies adopted the new economies but remained at subsistence-level food production until the industrial power of nineteenth- and twentiety-century Europe led them into the machine era. In some placcs, however, food production was the economic base for urbanization and literate civilization, for cultural changes that were unimagined just a few short millennia earlier.

Food production resulted in higher population densities, for the domestication of plants and animals can result in an economic strategy that both increases and stabilizes available food supplies. Farmers used concentrated tracts of land for agriculture and for grazing cattle or smaller animals, if they practiced mixed farming. Their more densely populated territory was much smaller than that of hunger-gatherers (although pastoralists need huge areas of grazing land for seasonal pasture). Within a smaller area of farming land, property lines were more sharply delineated as individual ownership of land came into being and questions of inheritance arose. Farmers used less portable toolkits, lived in more substantial, effectively permanent settlements. New social institutions came into being, reflecting ownership and inheritance of land and also the constant association of family groups, which previously had been separated during much of the hunting year. Now people

Figure 3   The scribal quarter of the Sumerian city of Nippur. Nippur was excavated in 1951 and 1952 by a joint expedition of the University Museum of the University of Pennsylvania and the Oriental Institute of the University of Chicago. [From the University Museum, University of Pennsylvania.]

stored their food and altered their environment by felling trees and burning vegetation to clear the the ground for planting. Their animals stripped pastures of their grass cover, then heavy rainfalls denuded the hillsides of their valuable soil and the pastures were never the same again.

In many respects the new agricultural societies were less secure than their hunter-gatherer predecessors. Their fields supported far more people. In lean years when the rains failed or crops withered, the people would fall back on the same game and vegetable resources that had sustained their ancestors, but with one difference: although the cushion of wild edible foods available to them was the same as their predecessors had used, there were many more mouths to feed. So famine, together with disease, the limitations of water supplies, and available food surpluses, helped control the burgeoning growth of farming populations. In many parts of the Third World, you can still see people living by subsistence methods developed thousands of years ago and modified but little in the intervening centuries. The traveler up the Nile can see farming communities still cultivating the fertile floodplain in much the same ways as their ancestors did when the Ancient Egyptian pharaohs ruled from Thebes.

Cities and Civilizations

Civilizations rose and fell, but the undercurrent of farming life, with its eternal cycles of planting and harvest, of life and death, persisted. Every civilization, however spectacular or far-reaching, depended for its survival not on the power of its gods nor the shrewdness of its traders, but on a firm subsistence base of food surpluses that supported thousands of nonfarmers— rulers, merchants, nobles, priests, and hundreds of officials. Like agriculture, civilization was not so much an invention as a quantum jump in the complexity of human society (Adams, article 12). The anthropologist Robert Redfield made a sharp distinction between "folk society," where the moral order is more important than the technical order, and civilization, a state of society in which the community is much larger and less self-sufficient. The simple division of labor between males and females is replaced by more complex, impersonal relationships. Family and kin relationships give way to larger affiliations of social class or religious belief.

Civilization is, of course, mostly things added to society: writing, public works, cities, markets, long-distance trading, and so on. A whole new and elaborate social structure comes into being, based on a state organized into social or economic classes, with power in the hands of an aristocratic elite and, often, a divine ruler or a group of military leaders and priests. The leaders of the new civilizations had to create new organizational structures to feed more mouths and to handle the increased political and economic complexities of the city-state. Soon even more complex societies emerged, with political, economic, and military leadership overshadowing kin and clan ties. The distinctive cultural styles of such early civilizations developed either from thousands of years of earlier cultural evolution or from contacts with other civilizations.

Old World Civilizations

The story of civilization begins more than 5000 years ago. The earliest cities developed in the sandy delta of southern Mesopotamia, by the banks of the rivers Tigris and Euphrates. There, the Sumerians created a series of city-states, each based on simple irrigation systems that harnessed the seasonal floods of the great rivers. The people themselves were turbulent, practical folk, born innovators and traders, who created one of the world's first written scripts, used metals, developed sailboats, wheeled carts, and a host of humbler inventions that we take for granted (Schmandt-Besserat, article 13). The quarrelsome, warlike Sumerians ruled over Mesopotamia for more than a millennium after 3000 BC, until power passed northward to the Babylonians, and later the Assyrians, who ruled over an empire that extended from the Mediterranean to the Persian Gulf.

The vigorous Sumerian civilization contrasted dramatically with that of the pharaohs of the Nile. The Ancient Egyptians lived in a land of predictable phenomena, a land where rainfall was virtually nonexistent, where the annual inundations of the great river provided a measure of natural irrigation for the land. They were lively, peaceful, hardworking people, who believed that death was merely an incident in eternal life. They strove to achieve a state of *ma'et,* "rightness," a feeling that everything was in satisfactory equilibrium, a philosophical concept in dramatic contrast to the more violent passions of the Sumerians. Ancient Egyptian civilization flourished in various forms from about 3200 BC right up to the time of Christ. Like the Sumerian civilization, this long-lived society originated from cultural traditions that had begun thousands of years earlier.

Originally, scholars believed that all civilizations originated from Egyptian or Mesopotamian roots. In fact, most early states were of indigenous origins, the result of adaptive responses to a variety of complex environmental factors. One can see these factors at work on the islands and mainland of Greece, where the Minoans and Mycenaeans developed distinctive maritime civilizations that flourished on trade that ranged the length and breadth of the Aegean between about 2000 and 1200 BC. Their rulers lived not in great cities but in sprawling palaces that were as much commercial centers and shrines as they were royal residences (Chadwick, article 14). In the final analysis, however, the early Greek civilizations were not based on conquest or trade, but on the unique ecology of the commodities they traded. The olive and vine can be cultivated together in the hillside landscape, for they enjoy different, and complementary, adaptations.

The Minoans were immortalized in the Greek legend of the Athenian prince Theseus and the intricate Cretan labyrinth of King Minos, where the dreaded Minotaur skulked. In 1900, British archaeologist Arthur Evans discovered the Palace of Minos at Knossos and a legend was suddenly clothed in a semblance of historical truth. A quarter century before, German-businessman-turned-excavator Heinrich Schliemann was so entranced with Homer's epics recounting the siege of Troy that he went in search of that ancient city; he found it deep under a mound named Hissarlik in northern Turkey. Homer's stirring verses are now thought to perpetuate folk memories of the Mycenaeans and other Bronze Age civilizations of Greece.

Far to the west, the Harappan civilization dominated the Indus Valley of Pakistan from before 2500 to around 1600 BC. This civilization was excavated by Sir John Marshall not until the 1920s, and later by Sir Mortimer Wheeler in the late 1940s. The great cities of Harappa and Moenjo-daro ruled over a vast region of the Indus Valley and controlled over 700 miles of coastline. Each boasted a fortified citadel overlooking a teeming city of standardized brick houses laid out along a grid of narrow streets. The Harappan civilization is characterized by a depressing standardization. Its anonymous rulers led unostentatious lives marked by a complete lack of priestly pomp or lavish public display. There is nothing of the ardent militarism displayed by the Assyrian kings, nor of the slavish glorification that the Egyptian pharaohs enjoyed.

The unquestioning hands of thousands of farmers and menial workers supported the apparatus of Harappan civilization. Behind every one of them stood an extended family of several generations providing a network of kinship ties and other benefits, such as communal ownership of property. Perhaps, too, the Harappan people were organized in a hierarchy of castes that restricted upward social mobility and provided a wider identity outside the confines of the family. If the evidence of figurines and seals is to be believed, the symbolism of Harappan religion bears some similarities to that of modern Hinduism. These parallels suggest that the deeply ingrained conservatism of Indian society derives from the very earliest moments of Harappan civilization.

Civilization would never have been possible anywhere without the unswerving loyalty of the country farmer. The village crops might change from rice to other cereals, the fertility of the soils respond to radically different rainfall patterns, building materials alter from brick and tile to mud, sticks, or bamboo—but what never varied was the unquestioning acceptance of an emerging social order that imposed an almost alien, privileged society of great wealth on the shoulders of the peasant. Nowhere can this conservatism be seen more clearly than in northern China, where civilization emerged well before 2000 BC. Chinese legends tell us that the celebrated Yellow Emperor Huang Ti founded civilization in the north about 2700 BC. He set for centuries the pattern of the repressive, harsh government that was the hallmark of early Chinese civilization.

Three dynasties of local rulers dominated the north between 2200 and 1000 BC, the Hsia, Shang, and Chou, grouped by historians under the general label "Shang." Each ruler was related to his competitors by intricate kin ties, each sought dominance over his neighbors. For all the political changes, the Shang civilization continued more or less unchanged, a loosely unified confederacy of competing small kingdoms that quarreled and fought incessantly. Only a tiny minority of the population enjoyed the full fruits of civilization. They were the ruler and his immediate relatives, some prominent priests and officials, and the few traders and warriors who achieved rank through sheer ability. Most of the population were petty artisans and farmers, whose unquestioning loyalty made the entire exploitative fabric of civilization work.

Warfare was endemic in early China, as competing states vied for supremacy in both the north and south. It was not until 221 BC that the great Ch'in emperor Huang Ti unified China into a single empire. He was buried under a monumental funeral mound that still awaits excavation, but archaeologists have found over 3000 terracotta replicas of the soldiers of his royal regiment and bronze figures of his courtiers by the sides of the grave—one of the most spectacular archaeological discoveries ever made. By Roman times, Chinese civilization had been flourishing for more than 2000 years, a distinctive and highly nationalistic culture that differed sharply from its Western contemporaries in its ability to assimilate conquerors and conquered into its own traditions. The Roman Empire, built on the groaning back of the slave, collapsed into the Dark Ages when attacked by barbarian nomads. The Chinese, by contrast, simply assimilated their nomadic conquerors—which is why the essential fabric of their civilization survived into modern times.

Pre-Hispanic Civilizations in the New World

When Hernando Cortés and his gold-hungry Spanish *conquistadores* gazed down on the Valley of Mexico in AD 1519, they were amazed to see great cities and temples, an Indian civilization rivaling the greatest splendors of Rome and Seville. The Aztec civilization was the culmination of more than three millennia of intense cultural development in Mexico that probably began in the steamy lowlands of Veracruz, the Yucatán, and Belize, where Norman Hammond has found traces of Maya occupation dating to earlier than 2500 BC (Hammond, article 16). In Veracruz, the Olmec ("rubber") people flourished as early at 1500 BC, building elaborate ceremonial centers and creating new religious beliefs and a magnificent art tradition that were to influence thousands of Mexicans in the centuries ahead. The Olmec traded with the lowlands of the Yucatán and had contacts with obsidian-rich communities on the highlands of the interior. Their religious beliefs spread with their trade.

Soon the basic patterns of Mesoamerican civilization were established in the highlands and the lowlands: highly symbolized religious beliefs that centered on militaristic nature gods with an increasing penchant for human sacrifice; distinctive monumental architecture designed to overwhelm the worshipper with the power of the gods; elaborate public ceremonies; and a highly stratified society preoccupied with trade, war, and ceremonial life. The magnificent cities of Monte Albán in Oaxaca and Teotihuacán in the Basin of Mexico flourished from around 200 BC well into the first millennium AD. Teotihuacán covered more than eight square miles in AD 600 and housed well over 125,000 people (Millon, article 15). Its vast temples, palaces, and avenues are still impressive today. The foodstuffs and luxury goods sold in its markets came from all over Mesoamerica.

The Maya civilization of the Yucatán and Petén areas of the lowlands developed during the last millennia before Christ, a civilization based on sophisticated cultivation of swamps, rain-forest gardens, and dry agriculture. The Maya nobility lived in towns and cities like El Mirador and Tikal, which boasted high pyramids and elaborately carved and painted stucco temples and palaces. They traded with the highlands, exchanging luxury goods like tropical bird feathers for essentials like grinding stones and obsidian for knives. This hierarchical and militaristic society suddenly collapsed at the end of the eighth century and the focus of political and economic power passed to those living in the highlands.

The Toltecs ruled briefly over the Basin of Mexico, but their civilization collapsed about AD 1160 when drought and repeated nomadic incursions undermined their political authority. In the centuries that followed, an obscure tribe of Mexica people (often called Aztecs) gradually gained mastery over the Basin. In about 1325, landless and decimated by war, they founded a tiny hamlet named Tenochtitlán in the remote swamps of Lake Texcoco. Less than two centuries later, Tenochtitlán was the largest city in pre-Hispanic America, an imperial capital surrounded by dozens of square miles of intensively cultivated swamp gardens that fed its estimated 250,000 inhabitants. The Aztec empire was more of a tribute-gathering machine than a state, a loose confederacy of often rebellious vassals who were kept in line by a carefully orchestrated policy of terror and military force. The insatiable Aztec gods were fed an estimated 20,000 human hearts a year, most of them acquired through conquest or ceremonial wars in which warriors fought to the death or became sacrificial victims.

By the time the *conquistadores* arrived in 1519, the Aztecs were living in a xenophobic, frenzied world of terror and bloodshed. They thought Cortés was a returning god: they had no precedent in their world to explain white strangers who arrived on mountains that moved on the sea. Cortés played on the fears and discontent of their allies and subjects. He made maximum psychological use of his cavalry and cannons, both weapons totally unfamiliar to Indian warriors. He destroyed the Aztec civilization less than two years after landing in Mexico.

In 1532 Spaniard Francisco Pizarro landed in Peru, far to the south. He found himself confronted by a powerful civilization ruled from a city named Cuzco high in the Andes. The Inca civilization was the culmination of more than 3000 years of slowly evolving Peruvian culture. The first sedentary agriculture settlements developed on the arid coast before 2500 BC. By 1500

Figure 4 The founding of the Aztec capital of Tenochtitlán depicted on a codex painted after the Spanish Conquest. An eagle perches on the cactus, where the war god Huitzilopochli ordained that his temple was to be built. The cactus is surrounded by ten leaders. Less than two centuries later, Tenochtitlán was the largest city in pre-Hispanic America. [From *Codex Mendoza*, photograph by Lesley Newhart.]

BC maize was being cultivated in irrigated plots in inland river valleys watered by Andes runoff, and the cereal diet combined with the abundant maritime resources of the Pacific fed relatively high population densities in large villages and towns.

Soon small states were flourishing in isolated river valleys, states that extended their influence over neighboring estuaries. By 200 BC the Moche civilization was flourishing in northern coastal Peru. Their rulers are depicted on finely modeled clay pots as aristocratic, calm men who ruled over a hierarchical society of priests, artisans, and peasants. The potters modeled warriors dressed in padded helmets and colorful cotton uniforms, women giving birth, domesticated llamas straining under heavy loads. The Moche artisans worked gold and manufactured superb textiles preserved in graves desiccated by the dry climate of the coast. The Chimu state followed in the footsteps of the Moche after AD 1000. Its rulers controlled and irrigated twelve river valleys and more than 125,000 acres.

The Incas were humble mountain people when Chimu rose to prominence in the lowlands. They first became a significant group around AD 1200. Two centuries later, a series of brilliant Inca rulers embarked on long-term campaigns of military conquest that gave them mastery over both highlands and lowlands. At the time of the Spanish Conquest the Inca ruled over vast domains extending from Ecuador to northern Chile. They had annexed the Chimu state and incorporated its irrigation systems and state roads into a much greater empire, linked by courier systems and highways that enabled the ruler to move his armies hundreds of miles in a few days. Pizarro landed at a time when the Inca nobility was quarreling over the succession. He captured the major contestant, and the last of the prehistoric civilizations soon vanished into historical obscurity.

The final chapter of prehistory was still to be played out. It began with the unification of Near Eastern city-states into larger empires by such powerful and ambitious leaders as Sargon of Akkad, Alexander the Great, Cyrus, and Julius Caesar. Their efforts led ultimately to the emergence of Western Civilization. By then, centuries of trade and violent warfare and precipitated technological change and had brought an awareness of a wider world unknown in prehistoric times. After the Dark Ages, the focus of Western Civilization passed to the maritime nations of the West. In the fifteenth century, Prince Henry of Portugal ushered in the Age of Discovery that sent ships to Africa, India, and America. These voyages brought an exploitative, technologically sophisticated civilization into confrontation not only with elaborate civilizations like those of the Aztecs and Incas, but with dozens of simpler societies—all of them unique adaptations to their own environments and all living in the expectation that life would continue in the future much as it had in the past. Sometimes the voyagers came with disinterested motives, in pursuit of knowledge. More often they came in search of gold or to save souls. They brought exotic diseases and alien values, sometimes stayed to settle on age-old tribal lands. The societies they displaced were decimated and disrupted, their homelands taken over, the people sometimes set to work in mines and plantations. By 1890, the tentacles of Western Civilization had penetrated to the remotest corners of Africa and New Guinea.

Today, few peoples still lead a truly prehistoric life: the world is simply too small and too well known to the all-seeing eyes of the civilized nations. No corner of the inhabited globe is too remote for European settlement. The Industrial Revolution of the nineteenth century brought unprecedented changes in world population patterns. It has been estimated that more than 52 million Europeans migrated overseas between 1840 and 1930, quite apart from the millions of blacks, Indians, Chinese, and others, who were transported to remote colonies in the eighteenth and nineteenth centuries as indentured laborers or slaves. Yet we all live with the legacy of prehistory, with cultural precedents and values that have been honed over 3 million years of collective human experience.

Many of our contemporary problems—famine, endemic warfare, despotism, slavery, and chronic disparities in wealth—have been pressing concerns of humanity for thousands of years. Sometimes we look at the future, at our awesome ability to destroy our planet, and wonder if we will survive. Our prehistory is reassuring. Civilizations may rise and fall, tribal societies vanish into oblivion. But somehow the survivors, and humanity as a whole, has so far always managed to rise to the challenge, to adapt, and to carry on. We shall survive.

ARCHAEOLOGY INTERPRETS PREHISTORY

Some grasp of the basic principles of archaeology is essential to an understanding of the *Scientific American* articles that form the main body of this Reader. This chapter attempts to summarize these principles and to give you—as fully as these few pages permit—an account of archaeological method and theory. First we examine the basic processes and principles, then we look at ways in which archaeologists have tried to interpret major developments of world prehistory.

Archaeology and Archaeologists

Archaeology is the application of scientific techniques and theoretical concepts to the study of the material remains of human cultures. This broad definition of archaeology includes not only its subject matter but also the techniques used to describe and explain that subject matter. Archaeologists use the term *culture* in many ways, but most commonly to refer to the unique system that all humans use to adapt to their natural environment. Polar bears are endowed with thick fur, seals with fins for swimming. Only humans manufacture thick clothes and build snowhouses in the Arctic and invent sunglasses to protect their eyes from the glare. Thus, human cultures are made up of human behavior and its results, most commonly expressed in archaeological terms in the form of surviving artifacts and food remains. Culture is our buffer against our environment. Remove our culture and we would be helpless, probably unable to survive.

To understand scientific archaeology requires some knowledge of the material evidence it examines. In most archaeological sites, only the most durable of inorganic materials survive. Stone implements and clay vessels are commonly discovered, because they are virtually indestructible. Dry climates like that of the American Southwest or of the Nile Valley allow much more complete preservation. When Howard Carter and Lord Carnarvon uncovered the pharaoh Tutankhamun's tomb in 1922, they recovered not only the mummy but the most delicate of organic objects: bone and ivory ornaments, wooden furniture, even leather reins and sandals. Arctic cold literally refrigerates the past (Figure 5), preserving such perishable items as Persian rugs in ancient burial mounds. Swamps and waterlogged deposits are environments favorable to the survival of wood. A famous example is the 500-year old Makah Indian vilalge at Ozette, Washington, whose wooden plank houses were overwhelmed by a prehistoric mudslide that preserved the entire contents of the dwellings—basketry, fishing hooks, and all.

There are many types of archaeologists. *Prehistoric archaeologists* study the long millennia of human history from our beginnings over 3 million years ago right up to the advent of written records. The articles in this Reader are all the work of such scholars. The first writing was developed in the Near East about 5500 years ago, but many parts of the world acquired literacy only in recent centuries with the arrival of European settlers. So prehistoric archae-

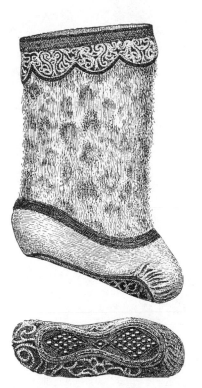 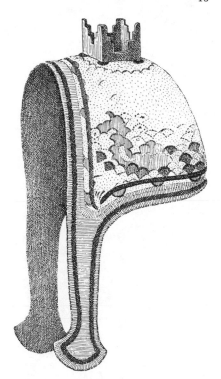

Figure 5 The preservation of archaeological finds: hat and boots from a frozen Scythian tomb at Pazyryk, U.S.S.R. These artifacts demonstrate a high level of craftsmanship in furs and skins. The crested hat is a man's, the fur boot a woman's. The sole of a second boot (bottom left) is embroidered with glass beads and pyrite crystals—it was obviously not for walking. [From "Frozen Tombs of the Scythians" by M. I. Artamonov. Copyright © 1965 by Scientific American, Inc. All rights reserved.]

ologists (prehistorians) work in every time period of the past, from millions of years ago right up to the nineteenth century AD. Some call themselves palaeoanthropologists (Greek: "ancient anthropology"). Glynn Isaac and Mary Leakey (articles 2 and 3), for example, are experts in the campsites and artifacts of the earliest humans. Others specialize in prehistoric technologies, domesticated grains, ancient settlement systems, animal bones, even symbolic behaviors. Since modern prehistoric archaeology is global in its coverage, there are both New and Old World archaeologists, each focusing on specific regions, such as western Europe, Mexico, or Japan. *Classical archaeologists* study the remains of the great Mediterranean civilizations of Greece and Rome, while Egyptologists concentrate on the land of the pharaohs, and so on. *Historical archaeologists* use archaeological data to amplify historical documents. They study medieval European towns, colonial settlements in the eastern United States, western missions and frontier forts.

Prehistoric archaeology is not only an extension of history; it is a form of anthropology. *Anthropology* is the scientific study of humankind in the broadest possible sense. *Physical anthropologists* study human beings as biological organisms and also as people with a distinctive and unique characteristic—culture. They engage in research not only on contemporary societies, but on human evolution and biological variation as well. *Cultural anthropologists* analyze human cultural life past and present: the archaeologist is a special type of anthropologist, one who studies people of the past. The only difference between anthropologists and archaeologists is the type of evidence they search for in their study of human behavior. One of the most exciting areas of anthropology is the study of living peoples, such as the Australian aborigines, to gather data for interpreting prehistoric sites in their region. This is "Living Archaeology."

Prehistoric archaeology has three broad goals: (1) The study of sites and their contents in a context of time and space, from which one derives long sequences of human culture; this descriptive activity is the reconstruction of culture history. (2) The reconstruction of past modes of life. (3) The study of the processes of cultural change.

Is archaeology a science? In the sense that archaeology studies human societies in the past by scientifically recovering and analyzing material data from ancient societies, it is a science. But in the sense that archaeologists as anthropologists examine intangible philosophies and religious beliefs, they are not scientists. Science is a disciplined and carefully ordered search for knowledge, carried out in a systematic manner. It advances by disproof, proposing the most adequate explanation for the moment, knowing that new and better explanations will later be found.

Scientific archaeology is based on the formulation of specific research designs that refine the problems to be studied in order to generate highly specific hypotheses that can be tested against data acquired in the field. The researcher creates the design before going out into the field. Surveys, excavations, and many months of detailed laboratory analysis comprise the task of data collection; the processing, analysis, and interpretation of the information collected leads to the final testing of the original hypotheses. From these tests emerge models for the reconstruction and explanation of the prehistory of the site or region under investigation. Like chemistry or physics, archaeological research is a cumulative process. Ever self-correcting, ever seeking to refine and improve our detailed knowledge of the past, modern archaeology bears little resemblance to the spectacular digging campaigns of yesteryear that uncovered entire cities in a few short months.

Data Acquisition: Context

The cartoon archaeologist of *New Yorker* fame is often depicted as a bearded, pith-helmeted eccentric, supervising an army of laborers in the shadow of a mighty pyramid. After moving acres of soil, he uncovers the long lost treasure of an ancient king. The stereotype dies hard. Many believe that archaeological excavation is a spectacular pastime, with the diggers constantly on the alert for buried treasure. The days when archaeologists used regiments of workers are long gone, the victims not only of inflation, but of much more rigorous excavation and recording methods. We stress recording, for both archaeological survey and excavation are fundamentally processes of recording as much as they are of discovery.

Archaeological sites, any places where traces of past human activity are to be found, are the equivalent of the historian's archives, and form, with their contents, what is known as the *archaeological record*. But, unlike official archives, an archaeological site is a finite resource of information; it yields not only artifacts and other traces of human behavior, but also the temporal and spatial context of the finds—perhaps the most vital information of all. Because the process of excavation destroys the archive forever, archaeologists have the heavy responsibility of meticulously recording the archaeological findings; the site can never be put together again; it is a nonrenewable (cultural) resource.

Context: Time. "How old is it?" This is perhaps the question most commonly asked of archaeologists. Sometimes the query is easily answered—if historical records are available to date a find, or if an excavated coin bears a date. But most prehistoric finds belong in the long, seemingly featureless landscape of the remote past, and have to be dated by other methods. Archaeologists have made use of the basic laws of stratigraphic geology, the study of layers of the earth, to examine the *relative chronology* of archae-

Figure 6   Historical archaeology: excavations in the shadow of Winchester Cathedral, England. [From Winchester Research Unit.]

18

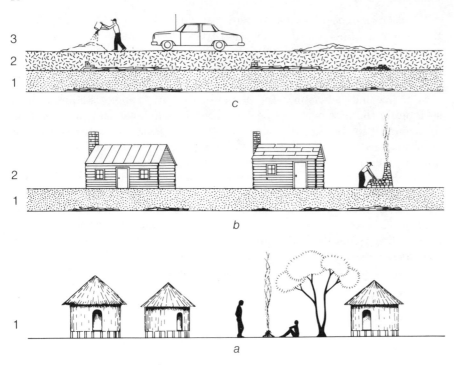

Figure 7   The Law of Superposition. (a) A farming village built on virgin subsoil. After a time, the village is abandoned, and the huts fall into disrepair. Their ruins are covered by accumulating soil and vegetation. (b) After an interval, a second village is built on the same site, with different architectural styles. Ths in turn is abandoned; the houses collapse into piles of rubble and are covered by accumulating soil. (c) Twentieth-century people park their cars on top of both village sites and drop litter and coins which, when uncovered, reveal to the archaeologist that the top layer is modern. An archaeologist digging this site would find that the modern layer is underlaid by two prehistoric occupation levels; that square houses were in use in the upper of the two, which is the later (Law of Superposition); and that round huts are stratigraphically earlier than square ones here. Therefore, village 1 is earlier than village 2, but when either was occupied or how many years separate village 1 from 2 cannot be known without further data. [From Brian M. Fagan, *In the Beginning: An Introduction to Archaeology*, 4th ed. Copyright © 1981 by Brian M. Fagan. Reprinted by permission of the publisher, Little, Brown and Company.]

ological sites. The law of Superposition (that which is lower is earlier) (Figure 7) and the Law of Association (objects found associated in the same layer are contemporary) (Figure 8) are fundamental to all archaeological research. For example, the bison carcasses found at the Olsen-Chubbuck site (article 7) are all from the same contemporary layer, so that we can be sure they were killed at the same time.

Chronometric or *absolute* chronology is dating in calendar years, by means of a variety of ingenious scientific methods (Figure 9). The earliest millennia of prehistory are dated by the *potassium argon method*, by measuring the decay over time of radioactive potassium-40 atoms in volcanic rocks that crystallize upon formation. Since many of the earliest archaeological sites are found in volcanic areas of East Africa, it is possible to establish for such famous locations as Mary Leakey's Laetoli footprints at 3.25 million years ago (article 2) and Olduvai Gorge in Tanzania dates between 1 and 3 million years ago. Postassium argon dating is too inaccurate for sites much more recent than 500,000 years, but it is possible to use the fission tracks in some minerals—volcanic glass (obsidian) is an example—to establish the ratio between the density of the tracks and the uranium content of the rock. This method can be used to date artifacts between about 1,000,000 and 100,000 years old, but it is still experimental.

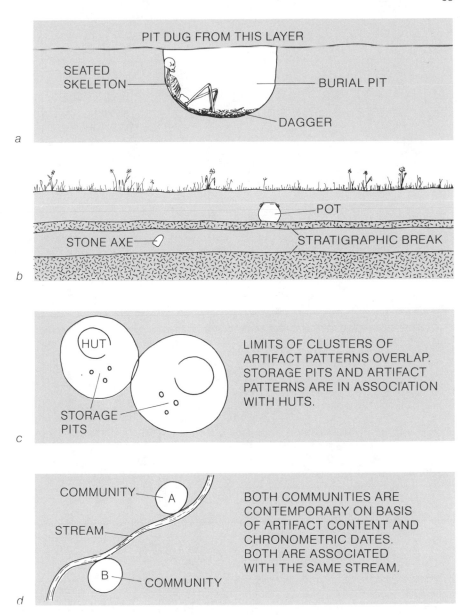

Figure 8 The Law of Association: some examples. (a) The burial pit, dug from the uppermost layer, contains not only a skeleton but also a dagger that lies close to its foot. The dagger is associated with the skeleton, and both finds are associated with the burial pit and the layer from which the grave pit was cut into the subsoil. (b) In contrast, a pot and a stone axe are found in two different layers, separated by a sterile zone, a zone with no finds. The two objects are not in association. (c) Two different household clusters with associated pits and scatters of artifacts. These are in association with each other. (d) An association of two contemporary communities. [From Brian M. Fagan, *In the Beginning: An Introduction to Archaeology*, 4th ed. Copyright © 1981 by Brian M. Fagan. Reprinted by permission of the publisher, Little, Brown and Company.]

Radiocarbon dating, perhaps the most widely known of all archaeological dating methods, can be applied to sites about 75,000 to 500 years old. Cosmic radiation produces neutrons that enter the earth's atmosphere and react with nitrogen. They produce the carbon isotope carbon-14 contained in all living things. From the moment that any organism dies, this decays gradually to carbon-12 until after 5568 years (the half-life of C-14) only half of the original amount is left, and so on. Radiocarbon samples can be taken from organic materials like wood charcoal, burnt bone, shell, and skin. The sample is converted to gas, then purified and counted in a proportional counter. The

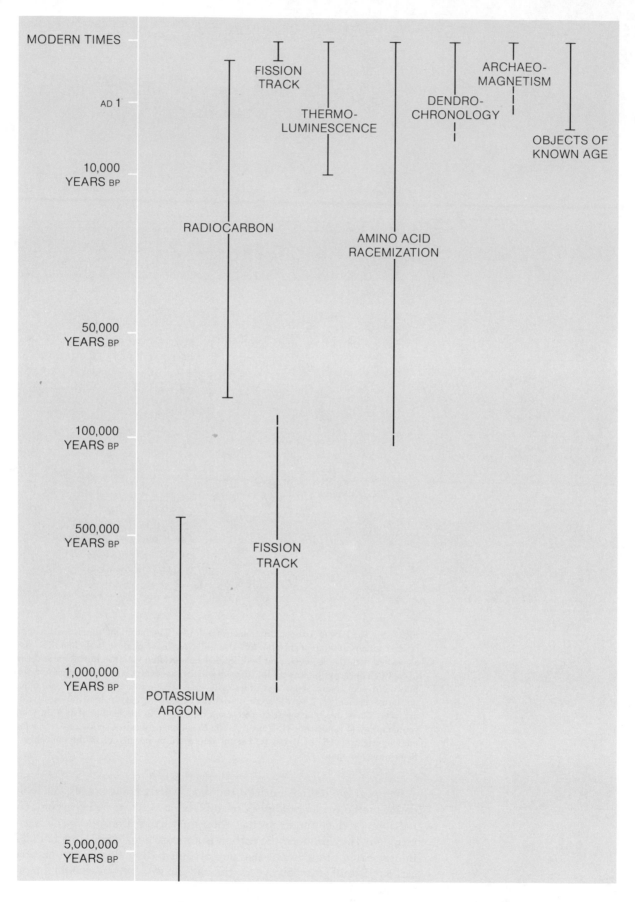

Figure 9   Chronological spans of major chronometric methods in archaeology. [From Brian M. Fagan, *In the Beginning: An Introduction to Archaeology*, 4th ed. Copyright © 1981 by Brian M. Fagan. Reprinted by permission of the publisher, Little, Brown and Company.]

count is then compared to that from a modern sample and the radiocarbon date and its statistical limit of error computed by a formula. To correct for variations in the concentration of radiocarbon in the atmosphere and in living things, radiocarbon dates are calibrated where possible with extremely accurate calendar dates obtained from tree-ring counts from ancient trees.

Radiocarbon dating has provided the chronology for most of the sites in Parts II, III, and IV of this Reader. It has established dates for the spread of the first *Homo sapiens sapiens* throughout the world (article 5), the first settlement of the Americas, the beginnings of agriculture and animal domestication, as well as the earliest civilizations. A variety of dating methods can be applied to the more recent millennia of prehistory. Archaeologists have used annual tree-growth rings to date archaeological sites in the American Southwest. They have also used imported artifacts like dated coins or pottery of known age to extend the limits of historical chronologies—say, artifacts from Ancient Egypt to develop chronologies for more remote areas of western Europe. But radiocarbon dating remains the most commonly used prehistoric dating method for cultures more recent than some 35,000 to 40,000 years old.

Context: Space.   Space to the mariner is a set of coordinates, measurements of latitude and longitude that establish the position of a ship on the globe. Space to the archaeologist is a similar set of coordinates that place a site, an artifact, or an association of tools and other finds in a precise spatial context. The dimension of space invokes both the Law of Association which associates artifacts with other artifacts in the same layer, and grave furniture with a grinning skeleton, and the "settlement pattern," the placement of ancient settlements on the prehistoric landscape. William Sanders of Pennsylvania State University has spent much of his career studying the changing settlement patterns in the Basin of Mexico between about 1500 BC and the Spanish Conquest in AD 1519. He has shown how the rise and fall of great Mexican cities like Teotihuacán (article 15) affected the distribution of population for hundreds of miles around. The sixteeenth-century Aztec capital, Tenochtitlán, was an island city surrounded by hundreds of acres of swamp gardens that provided food for over 600,000 people. The Aztecs may have boasted of their prowess as conquerors but their real strength was in their agriculture, something that could only be established by studying the distribution of Tenochtitlán's satellite villages, towns, and thousands of acres of field systems that fed its population.

Survey and Excavation

Archaeological sites can be located by simple observation, by walking over the ground, or by sophisticated methods combining remote sensing techniques, aerial photography, even electronic detection methods. (The Teotihuacán research in article 15 is an admirable example of large-scale surface survey applied to a prehistoric city.) But surface investigations yield only limited information about chronology or subsurface features such as houses or fortifications. Excavation adds an additional dimension to surface survey, provided it is conducted in a systematic and scientific manner. The early archaeologists worked on a massive scale, using a small army of workers. In these inflationary days of highly problem-oriented research, most excavation is on a much reduced scale, involving perhaps a small team of expert scholars and a handful of students. Sophisticated sampling methods may be employed to locate trenches and ensure that the desired sample of artifacts or features is obtained from the excavation. No dig is undertaken except with the objective of testing specific hypotheses. Vertical excavations (Figure 10) are used to test smaller sites, to establish basic chronological sequences, and to obtain

Figure 10 Vertical excavation at Moenjo-daro, Pakistan, showing the ancient city wall extending down to the water table. [Photograph by George Dales.]

Figure 11 Horizontal excavation of an Iroquois long house at Howlett Hill, New York. The stakes show the outline of the house walls and inner structures that once supported the roof. [Photograph by James A. Tuck.]

artifact samples. Much larger, horizontal excavations are used to uncover entire campsites or to study the layout of towns or villages (Figure 11). The excavations described in this Reader cover the entire spectrum of prehistoric sites, from tiny camps occupied for a few days (article 3), to kill sites (article 7), rockshelters, peasant villages, and entire cities (Parts III and IV).

Whatever the hypotheses to be tested or othe size of the site, the same basic principles of excavation apply: precise recording of stratigraphy and context and accurate reporting of the unique archive that is being destroyed during the excavation. Every artifact is labeled, its stratigraphic coordinates determined, the processes by which the site was formed—and later buried—established. Once the finds have been analyzed and interpreted, the entire site is written up in a detailed report that becomes the permanent record of a site that has been dissected, and destroyed, by excavation. The finite nature of the archaeological site places a unique responsibility on the archaeologist to excavate with accuracy and precision. Unlike physics experiments, these experiments cannot be replicated.

Analyzing the Finds

Archaeologists call on specialists from many disciplines to analyze the finds unearthed in their excavations. Botanists study the minute pollen grains from ancient vegetation found in many prehistoric sites. These make it possible to reconstruct the environment at the time the site was occupied, even to establish the moments at which people began to clear forests and cultivate the soil. Some botanists are experts in prehistoric seeds. They spend their careers examining early cereal crops like maize or wheat, using tiny vegetable remains found in early farming villages (articles 8 and 11).

Some archaeologists have special training in vertebrate zoology and are expert at identifying the bones of animals hunted or herded, even when later butchered literally to ribbons. They not only identify the animals, but look at butchery techniques and fix the ages at which cattle and other species were slaughtered; they even spend months examining tiny rodent bones that may provide evidence of ancient plagues. The physical sciences have not only developed dating methods for the past, they provide opportunities for sophisticated spectrographic analyses of trace elements in minerals and volcanic rocks like obsidian. The trace elements in obsidian are so idiosyncratic that it has proved possible to identify the specific sources from which hundreds of early farming villages obtained this rock in early Mexico and the Near East, thereby providing a way of studying the dynamics of early trade in both areas.

British archaeologist Stuart Piggott once called archaeology "the science of rubbish." In some respects he is right, for archaeologists use thousands upon thousands of surviving artifacts to study cultural change in the past. The culture history of most areas of the world is based on the study of thousands of those most durable of all artifacts: stone tools and pottery fragments (Figure 12). Thousands upon thousands of archaeological reports describe minute details of stone types and pottery decoration that tell us, alas, relatively little about human behavior except as it is evident in ancient technology and the evolution of various tool forms. Often these efforts seem somewhat like taking a handful of miscellaneous objects—say two spark plugs, an electrical switch plate, a spoon, a candleholder, and some china plates—and trying to reconstruct the culture of the makers of these diverse objects on the basis of this miscellaneous collection alone. The culture history obtained from such limited sources is related to a body of theoretical concepts that provide both a framework and a means for archaeologists to look beyond the facts and material objects for the explanation of developments that took place during our long history.

Figure 12   Stone artifacts: two scrapers made by Neanderthal stoneworkers in southwestern France about 50,000 years ago. Length of the scrapers is about 5 inches. [Photograph by Brian M. Fagan.]

Interpreting the Past:
Analogy and Living Archaeology

No archaeologist works in a complete vacuum, for the great diversity of humankind provides us with a vital source of information about societies that were until quite recently—or, indeed, still are—living in much the same way as prehistoric peoples. For well over a century, anthropologists have been working among non-Western societies to acquire a mass of information that is of enormous value for interpreting the archaeological record. In the 1960s, anthropologist Richard Lee worked among the San hunter-gatherers of the Kalahari desert in southern Africa. He took an archaeologist along with him to record abandoned modern San camps as a basis for interpreting prehistoric scatters of artifacts, house foundations, and other archaeological features in behavioral terms. This type of "living archaeology" has become increasingly fashionable in recent years, replacing an older form of interpretation by analogy, where archaeologists compared isolated modern artifacts, even entire cultures, with prehistoric finds. This latter approach is fine if there is some direct, historic continuity between past and present, but it provides limited opportunities for understanding the relationships between extinct prehistoric societies and their natural environment.

The techniques of living archaeology can be applied to modern artifacts as well. Some fascinating experiments have been carried out at the Tucson city garbage dump, where William Rathje has been using sophisticated archaeological methods to study random samples of modern suburban garbage. He is examining contemporary waste-utilization patterns, not only for the purposes of studying modern resource management, but also to construct a statistical basis for interpreting prehistoric middens and waste heaps. He found, for example, that the average middle-class Tucson household wasted $100 worth of edible beef per year. This provisional study revealed that middle-class families were the most wasteful group in the population.

Interpretation by analogy goes hand in hand with experimental archaeology—controlled experiments where scholars try to replicate ways in which prehistoric peoples manufactured stone artifacts, practised metallurgy, even cleared forests with stone axes, and cultivated maize. These are no casual experiments, but carefully designed tests under which, say, Bronze Age shields are made with replicas of prehistoric tools, in the original materials, and then tested against bronze-edged swords. Such controlled experiments are very different from the much publicized voyages of adventure like Thor Heyerdahl's *Ra* expedition, which claimed to prove that the Ancient Egyptians crossed the Atlantic in reed boats. In fact, all this uncontrolled experiment proved was that almost any craft can cross from Morocco to the West Indies down the trade wind route. Scientific proof of such voyaging would require discovery of Egyptian artifacts in the New World.

Interpreting World Prehistory:
Early Hypotheses

Both archaeology and anthropology are children of the social sciences, academic disciplines that emerged during the great expansion of intellectual inquiry in the nineteenth century. The first scholars to puzzle over the major developments of prehistory were strongly influenced by Charles Darwin's theories of evolution and natural selection. They believed that human societies had evolved just like living organisms, from the simple to the complex, with Victorian civilization at the very pinnacle of human achievement. Civilization was, they felt, a state to which all human societies aspired, a notion that gave credence to the ethnocentric and racist beliefs that served as justification for the great empires of three quarters of a century ago. Anthropologist Lewis Morgan (1837–1881) was an ardent evolutionist. He declared in 1877 that human societies had developed through no less than seven stages, beginning with savagery and culminating in civilization. Morgan's views had a strong influence on Karl Marx, who believed that people shared communal resources until this type of sharing was eroded by the forces of industrial civilization. Morgan's type of single-line (unilinear) evolution is, of course, far too simple to accommodate what we now know about prehistory.

The diffusionists followed close on the heels of the evolutionists. They believed that all the great ideas of prehistory had originated in one place, say the Near East, and then spread far and wide. One such scholar was British anatomist Elliot Grafton Smith (1871–1937), who acquired a fixation on Ancient Egyptian civilization. He wrote a series of books in which he argued that the "Children of the Sun," the Ancient Egyptians, had voyaged all over the world, planting the institutions of civilization in foreign lands, even in Mexico and the Pacific. This world of high adventure and epic voyaging was far too simple an explanation to fit even the limited archaeological information available in the 1920s. One reason for these simple, and often wild, hypotheses was that there simply was not enough archaeological information, even from areas like Europe and the Near East. The past was still full of mysteries and unknowns.

Two scholars, Franz Boas (1858–1942) and Vere Gordon Childe (1892–1957), turned archaeology away from wild speculation toward science. Boas trained dozens of students to collect meticulous data about prehistoric and living American cultures, while Childe, a brilliant linguist, was an authority on the prehistory of Europe and Near East. A cultural materialist who believed in Marxism, Childe used artifacts and cultures to write a coherent "history" of prehistoric times, to chronicle thousands of years of European prehistory, in which simple hunter-gatherers and peasants were influenced by two great cultural developments, the Agricultural (Neolithic) and Urban Revolutions. V. Gordon Childe painted a beguiling picture of inventions and migrations based much more on artifacts than on the ecological concepts that inform archaeology today. His explanations for the rise of civilization, for example, listed a number of prime movers that were the "cause" of urban life, among them metallurgy, the invention of writing, the emergence of specialist artisans and social classes, and, of course, the city itself.

Childe wrote a series of brilliant accounts of Old World prehistory that influenced a whole generation of popular historians, among them the Durants and Arnold Toynbee. His "revolutions" haunt the pages of some history books to this day, assumptions that do not stand up against the vast body of new archaeological information that has accumulated from all over the world since World War II. We now know that agriculture and civilization developed not only in the Near East, but quite independently in several parts of the Old and New Worlds. The latest researches seek explanations not in terms of simple, linear causes, but argue that major developments like food production and civilization occurred as a result of many constantly interacting cultural and ecological factors that led to cultural change. It is these minute changes that the archaeologist of today examines with a battery of sophisticated scientific methods and theoretical concepts totally unknown in Childe's time.

Cultural Ecology and Systems

The advent of the digital computer, the widespread use of statistical methods, and the influence of the latest theories of philosophers of science have coincided with a tremendous explosion of archaeological data. Perhaps the most pervasive influence has been that of *cultural ecology*, the study of interrelationship between environment and cultural change. Archaeologists first took an interest in ancient environments in the 1930s, when the technique of palynology, the analysis of prehistoric pollen grains, was first applied to archaeological sites in Britain and Scandinavia. Soon botanists were able to reconstruct the changing vegetational surroundings of sites over hundreds, even thousands, of years of occupation. In a classic example of environmental reconstruction, British archaeologist Grahame Clark excavated a 10,000-year-old hunting camp at Star Carr in northwest England in the late

1940s and used pollen analysis of surviving vegetal remains to show that the site flourished by the shores of a shallow lake lined by birch trees.

This classic excavation was one of the first digs to alert archaeologists to the possibilities of cultural ecology, a body of theory developed by American anthropologist Julian Steward in the 1950s. He argued that similar adaptations may be found in different cultures in similar environments throughout the world and that no culture ever achieved an adaptation to its environment that remained unchanged for any length of time. He also hypothesized that during periods of cultural development differences and changes in any area can either lead to the increased complexity of society or can result in completely new cultural patterns. In other words, the study of cultural change includes the study of not only human cultures, but of changing environmental conditions as well.

It follows that human cultures throughout the world have evolved through time, sometimes through hundreds upon thousands of slow, cumulative changes, changes sometimes so imperceptible that the people involved barely noticed them. These alterations modified cultures living in broadly similar environments in basically similar ways, even when they were separated by thousands of miles. We find, as an example of a common response to environmental stress, that many societies experimented with cultivation or with animal domestication, or adopt irrigation when faced with the need to feed more people. Such developments account for the chance resemblances between civilizations in Egypt and Mexico, for the fact is that many societies in the Near East, Asia, and the Americas turned to food production at about the same time. No one genius invented agriculture or civilization; these were cultural responses to all manner of external and internal stimuli, responses so complex that a single cause for the rise of civilization or the peopling of the Americas is a ludicrously simplistic way to look at evolving human behavior. This type of *multilinear* cultural evolution is very different from the simple, *unilinear* schemes favored by Edward Tylor and the other pioneer evolutionists of the nineteenth century.

Until the 1950s, the main thrust of archaeology was descriptive, toward the ordering of artifacts and chronological sequences. It was in this environment that archaeologists like V. Gordon Childe flourished. They developed hypotheses about world prehistory that saw Old World agriculture, civilization, and other major inventions and cultural changes developing in one place and slowly spreading from this primary area into neighboring regions. This form of "modified diffusionism" was completely outmoded by the theories of cultural ecology and the development of radiocarbon dating in 1949. Carbon-14 dates provided the first opportunities to compare the chronologies of prehistoric cultures in widely separated parts of the world and to develop a truly global chronology for prehistoric times.

In 1948, archaeologist W. W. Taylor wrote a classic essay, *The Study of Archaeology*, in which he argued that in studying their sites archaeologists should pursue every possible line of evidence, not only artifacts, but ecological evidence, architecture, food remains, even architecture, and then focus on the people who lived there and the changes of their culture. This essay was a preliminary to a period of intense controversy in American archaeology during the 1960s, a consequence not only of the advent of cultural ecology, computers, and an explosion of data, but also of the fact that archaeologists were for the first time reading the literature of the philosophy of science. Lewis Binford and others argued for much more rigorous scientific method in archaeology. They challenged the widespread assumption that much of the past was unknowable merely because the data did not survive: the archaeologist's task was to devise the methods for extracting such information from the soil and to ask the questions about the past.

The furor of this so-called new archaeology has largely died down, for much of the newness has worn off. The archaeology of the 1980s is new in the sense that it is based on rigorously tested hypotheses, scientifically collected evidence, and a body of theory that replaces the less explicit generalizations of earlier scholars. The big differences are not so much in the use of scientfic method, but in the strong emphasis on ecological studies. As archaeologists have moved away from simple explanations like unlinear evolution and diffusion, they have begun to examine the delicate and ever changing relationships between human societies and their environments. In this approach, human cultures are thought of as complicated systems of interacting elements, such as technology and social organization, which in turn interact with the ecological systems of which they are part. At issue is a society's total adaptation to both its natural and cultural environments; a development such as the adoption of irrigation agriculture can trigger changes throughout the culture, not only in crops and in the implements of tillage, but in social organization, politics, and governance—even in clothes worn to cultivate the soil.

General Systems Theory is a body of theoretical concepts developed as a way of searching for general relationships in the empirical world. A "system" is best defined as a whole which functions as a whole because its various parts depend on one another to operate. Systems theory has been widely applied in physics and other hard sciences, where relationships between different parts of a system can be defined with a high degree of precision. It has great appeal to archaeologists, for it assumes that any organization, however simple or complex, can be studied as a system of interrelated components. Archaeologists use systems theory in thinking of human cultures as sophisticated systems of interacting variables—subsistence, material culture, religious beliefs, and many others. The cultural system in turn is part of a wider ecological system, the natural environment in which it flourishes.

The systems approach to human culture argues that such conditions as geographical distance between settlements, differences in activities conducted at various sites, and changes in subsistence have affected human culture as deeply as the progress of time. Because of this, many archaeologists take systems approaches to cultural systems that are constantly changing in response to both external stimuli like the natural environment, and internal stimuli. Under this rubric, human organizations are adaptive systems that can react to their environment in ways that are favorable to the continued operation of the cultural system. They achieve their direction not only from preprogrammed instructions, but also from decisions made by their members. When the behavior resulting from these decisions is more adaptive to new conditions, changes in organization will occur. The advantage of the systems approach is that it enables one to look not at single agents of cultural change, but instead at the regulatory mechanisms, at the relationships among different components of the cultural system, at the system as a whole, and at its environment.

This systems-ecological approach is but the beginning of a new chapter in the study of prehistoric times, in which archaeologists are making use of far more comprehensive and complex data than ever before. Kent Flannery of the University of Michigan has used such an approach to study the ecology of early agriculture in highland Mexico. He assumed that the southern highlands were part of a single, complex system consisting of many subsystems— economic, botanical, social among others—which interacted with one another. He found that between 8000 and 2000 BC the highland peoples used no less than five different food-collecting systems, each with its own distinctive artifacts, each carefully scheduled for the different seasons. The people so conducted their collecting activities that they never overexploited the available resources of the environment. After 5000 BC, they began experimenting with the deliberate planting of maize and other foods and intentionally expanded the areas where certain plants were found in the wild. These experiments were so successful that they triggered positive feedback within the cultural system. A whole series of cumulative changes in the cultural system resulted, reflected at first in changing scheduling patterns, and eventually in sedentary settlement and a full agricultural economy. By 2000 BC, the Indians had developed a self-perpetuating food procurement system with entirely different scheduling demands—those of planting, constant crop care, and harvest.

Systems-ecological studies can be conducted only if there is detailed background knowledge of the specific environment in which the culture flourished, changed, and eventually died. The articles reprinted in this Reader give some insights into the complexities of modern archaeological research. They show that we can discern some regularities and trends in the course of world prehistory. But the more general relationships and cultural processes that led to these regularities and trends are still little understood. The fascination or archaeology lies not in simplistic explanations of the great developments of the past but in exploring the ways in which people made decisions about living within the natural environment where their ancestors had lived, where they themselves existed, and where they reasonably expected their children to live. Modern science has given archaeologists new and sophisticated tools of awesome power. *Prehistoric Times* shows how we are beginning to use some of them to understand the millennia of evolving human behavior that have shaped our own world and will help shape our own future.

Is There a Future for the Past?

A century and a half ago, an ambitious traveler could go forth to a remote part of the world and find a lost city, even a forgotten civilization in a few weeks. Even today, the headlines sometimes announce a dramatic new archaeological discovery—a royal tomb, a long-buried metropolis, or a cache of gold objects. But it is safe to say that the major civilizations of the world are now known to the archaeologist, even if many details remain to be filled in. The early adventurers excavated as much for spectacular objects as they did for information. Their finds were sold to the major museums of Europe and America, or to the highest private bidder, which is why some of the world's most spectacular artifacts are now housed thousands of miles from their homelands, removed from their contexts.

Great numbers of people now collect prehistoric artifacts and pay enormous prices for them. A huge illegal antiquities trade flourishes throughout the world—an industry that literally supports entire villages of illegal grave diggers who ravage pre-Hispanic tombs in Peru, dig up Ancient Egyptian burial sites, and chisel sculptures from Maya ceremonial centers. No archaeological site is safe from the depredations of tomb robbers and collectors, for to possess artifacts appears to be one of humanity's most basic urges. Collecting, remarked one French psychologist, is a "passion and often so violent that it is inferior to love and ambition only in the pettiness of its aims." Thousands of North American sites have been damaged beyond repair by irresponsible pot hunters and antiquities dealers who care nothing for the priceless and irreplaceable information stored in the sites they ravage.

The archaeological record is under siege from the industrial society as well, from massive mining operations, deep plowing, and ever expanding urban sprawl. Despite desparate efforts by archaeologists and the enactment of some legislation, much of the world's prehistoric heritage has vanished under the bulldozer and plow within this century—unrecorded and unexcavated. In some areas like Los Angeles County, it is estimated that less than five percent of the known archaeological sites remain undisturbed and many of these are threatened. Unless the tide of destruction is checked, there is a real chance that there will be no undisturbed archaeological sites left for our descendants to study. And that would be a cultural, intellectual, and global tragedy of the first magnitude.

Is there a future for the past? Yes, if we all learn to respect the finite sites of the archaeological record as much as we respect virgin forest and clear water. The survival of archaeology as something for us all to enjoy demands that we suppress our urges to own and possess the past, and learn to live responsibly with the archaeological record, the unique and glorious heritage of all humankind.

REFERENCES

Ceram, C. W. 1951. *Gods, Graves, and Scholars*. New York: Knopf.

Daniel, Glyn. 1981. *A Short History of Archaeology*. London: Thames and Hudson.

Fagan, Brian M. 1981. *In the Beginning*, 4th ed. Boston: Little, Brown. 1983. *Archaeology: A Brief Introduction*, 2nd ed. Boston: Little, Brown.

Fagan, Brian M. 1980. *World Prehistory: A Brief Introduction*. Boston: Little, Brown. 1983. *People of the Earth*, 4th ed. Boston: Little, Brown.

Rathje, William, and Michael Schiffer. 1982. *Archaeology*. New York: Harcourt, Brace, Jovanovich.

Sharer, Robert, and Wendy Ashmore. 1979 *Fundamentals of Archaeology*. Menlo Park, Calif: Benjamin Cummings.

Wauchope, Robert. 1962. *Lost Tribes and Sunken Continents*. Chicago: University of Chicago Press.

Wenke, Robert. 1979. *Patterns in Prehistory*. New York: Oxford University Press.

Willey, Gordon R., and Jeremy A. Sabloff. 1980. *A History of American Archaeology*. San Francisco: W. H. Freeman and Company.

HUMAN ORIGINS

HUMAN ORIGINS

I

INTRODUCTION

"The question of questions," the great Victorian biologist Thomas Huxley called it in 1863, four years after Charles Darwin published *The Origin of Species*. Was the ancestry of humankind to be found among the apes? Was there a "Missing Link," a long extinct creature that had once been the critical bridge between the chimpanzees and human beings? Who were the more recent ancestors of modern humanity? Huxley himself was in no doubt of our close anatomical relationship to living apes. His classic essay *Man's Place in Nature* (1863) compared the anatomy of apes and *Homo sapiens* and described a primitive skull that had been found in a cave at Neanderthal, western Germany, in 1856. The Neanderthal skull has beetling, bony eyebrow ridges and a bun-shaped cranium quite unlike that of a modern person. Some scientists dismissed the find as the remains of pathological idiot, or even as one of Napoleon's soldiers. But Huxley and other scientists realized that the Neanderthal cranium was indeed an ancestor of modern humans. The sciences of palaeoanthropology was born with this discovery.

In 1891, a Dutch surgeon named Eugene Dubois, with a fixation about missing links, discovered a primitive-looking fossil skull and long bones in some river gravels in Java where he had deliberately sought evidence of transitional forms between humans and apes. He claimed they belonged to the "Missing Link." Dubois was ridiculed and his finds forgotten until 1929, when Chinese archaeologists unearthed some fossil remains in the deposits of Choukoutien Cave near Peking. These human bones were associated with broken animal bones, hearths, and stone tools. The Chinese and Javanese finds were found to belong to the same human form named *Homo erectus* (Figure 13). They were estimated to be at least 250,000 years old. But by this time even earlier fossil remains were coming to light.

Australopithecus and *Homo*

In 1924 a young Johannesburg anatomist named Raymond Dart was handed some fossil skulls embedded in a hard, limestone breccia from a quarry near the small town of Taung in the Cape Province of South Africa. At first he thought they were prehistoric baboons, then discovered they were apelike creatures with small teeth and somewhat rounded, almost humanlike skulls. Dart named them *Australopithecus africanus* ("Southern Ape of Africa") and claimed they were intermediate between apes and humans. Few anthropologists agreed with him at the time, considering them another form of prehistoric ape. Hundreds more australopithecine fragments have come to light in the Transvaal area of northern South Africa since the 1930s, including

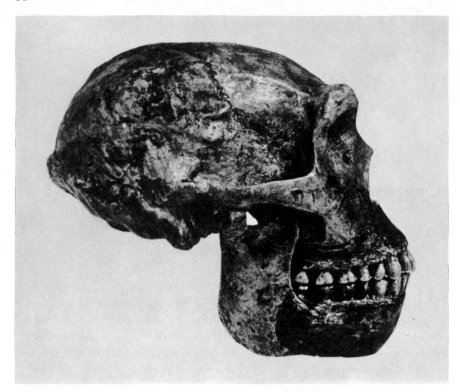

Figure 13 *Homo erectus* from Java. [Courtesy of W. W. Howells, photograph by G. H. R. von Koenigswald.]

fossils from a much more robust australopithecine (*Australopithecus robustus*), with a thick skull and massive jaw musculature. For years, the only australopithecines known were from South Africa. Then, in 1959, the Leakey family found a robust *Australopithecus* at Olduvai Gorge in Tanzania, and Dart was vindicated. His ape-humans were indeed close to the ancestry of humankind.

Louis S. B. Leakey (1903–1972), the son of a pioneer Kenya missionary, developed an interest in fossil hunting and archaeology while an undergraduate at Cambridge University. After several successful expeditions to East Africa in the 1920s, Leakey developed a fascination with fossil-rich Olduvai Gorge, a jagged gash in the game-rich Serengeti Plains of northern Tanzania (Figure 14). Between 1931 and 1959 he and his wife Mary worked the deep strata of the gorge, searching for traces of human fossils and artifacts, and for the actual campsites where the early hominids once lived (hominid: a member of the family *Hominidae*, represented today by a single species, *Homo sapiens*).

The Leakeys realized that the key to understanding the earliest millennia of human evolution would be found not only by examining artifacts and bones, but by studying human behavior through meticulous excavations of long abandoned living sites. Olduvai was an ideal site for finding such locations, for the gorge cut through the shores of a now vanished lake that had once been a favored hunting spot for Stone Age folk, literally exposing millions of years of geological strata like a many-layered cake. The hominids had camped for a few days by this lake, then moved on, leaving a scatter of broken-up bones, seeds, and artifacts behind them. Later, the waters of the lake rose and covered the abandoned campsite, preserving it for the Leakeys to discover. In 1959 the Leakeys found the skull of a robust australopithecine on a "floor" at the very base of Olduvai Gorge, dated by potassium-argon samples to about 1.75 million years ago, a date far earlier than anyone had suspected. The 1960s produced more fossils from Olduvai that only served to confuse the evolutionary picture: a gracile, lightweight australopithecine

Figure 14 Excavation of a fossil hominid skull at Olduvai Gorge, Tanzania. [From the *Illustrated London News.*]

and another hominid allegedly more anatomically advanced than *Australopithecus*. This Leakey named *Homo habilis* ("handy person"), believing that he had found the earliest toolmaking human being.

Louis Leakey was a controversial figure, a brilliant fieldworker with an eye for sites and a vast experience of Africa. But his interpretations of human evolution often suffered from hasty judgments based on inadequate data. His claims for *Homo habilis* were hotly contested by his scientific colleagues, who argued (rightly) that he was working with far too few fossils. One result of Leakey's work was an expansion of research into new areas, to fossil-bearing beds in southern Ethiopia and on the eastern shores of Lake Turkana in northern Kenya. In these two areas, American and French scholars, as well as Leakey's son Richard, discovered australopithecines and a more advanced form of hominid similar to *Homo habilis* dating back to perhaps as early as two million years ago, and, in East Turkana, a *Homo erectus* fossil at least a million years old. There were scattered campsites in the same area, too, tiny concentrations of flaked stone tools and animal bones only a few feet across, where hominids had once camped and sheltered in the shade of trees by dry streams. Some of the East Turkana artifacts were more than 2 million years old. Recent researches have centered on Ethiopia, where even earlier hominids have been found.

Due in part to the Leakeys and their association with the National Geographic Society, palaeoanthropology has become a glamorous subject, thwart with controversy and colorful personalities, whose clashes sometimes tend to cloud the scientific issues. Each of the major figures has his or her pet evolutionary scheme, all of which agree on only one point: there was far more variability among hominid populations 2 to 4 million years ago than was formerly believed. So the search for a "Missing Link" is really a search for large assemblages of hominid fossils that will enable us to detect the ranges of variation between nonhuman primates and the earliest human beings.

In recent years, some of the most sensational discoveries have come from the Hadar area of Ethiopia, a desolate region that is difficult of access but incredibly rich in early human fossils. At Hadar, Don Johanson and Maurice Taieb found the remarkably complete skeleton of a creature dated to between 3 and 3.75 million years old. They named it Lucy, a female hominid less than 4 feet tall and 19 to 21 years old. Nearby they found the remains of at least 13 individuals—males, females, and children. The Hadar hominids display extraordinary variation in size and weight; some weigh perhaps as much as 150 pounds. All were powerful, heavily muscled creatures, standing fully upright, with arms longer in proportion to body size than the arms of humans. They had brains about the size of chimpanzees, ape-shaped heads, and forward-thrusting jaws. Apparently they did not make tools. The Hadar fossils have generated considerable debate. Were they direct ancestors of humanity, the predecessors of the australopithecines? Johanson and physical anthropologist Tim White consider them to be a primitive form of *Australopithecus* and have given them a new species name (*A. afarensis*). Despite continuing finds as old as 4 million years, the debate still rages about the biological and evolutionary relationships among these fossil hominids.

The Early Evolution of Humankind

Sherwood Washburn's article, "The Evolution of Man," reviews the scattered evidence for human evolution, not only the story told by the fossils, but the information gleaned from molecular biology and the study of living apes and monkeys as well. He points out that the old notion that Africa was the cradle of humankind may be false, for the new science of plate tectonics has shown that Africa and Eurasia were much closer between 18 million and some 5 to 6 million years ago. The older our toolmaking, upright-walking ancestors prove to be, the more likely it is that they lived on other continents as well.

Washburn also surveys the powerful new analytical tools that palaeo-anthropologists use to amplify the sketchy fossil record, notably, a possible molecular time clock for measuring rates of primate evolution, and the results of studies of apes and monkeys, including efforts to teach apes to converse. He argues that our ancestors walked upright and used objects just as chimpanzees do long before they made tools, and that hunting and the use of tools evolved before our brains became enlarged to their present size. He also hypothesizes that there was evolutionary feedback from the successful way of life made possible by the earliest simple tools to the growing brain: the anatomy of the human brain reflects a selection for success in manual skills.

By no means every palaeoanthropologist would agree with Washburn's conclusions, but, as he himself points out, many of today's theories are based on very sketchy information. It is for this reason that many scientists, Washburn among them, prefer a simple evolutionary picture at this stage in research.

Laetoli

When did the first toolmaking humans live on earth? Current research suggests between 2 and 3 million years ago, at the very beginning of the great Ice Age that affected later human societies so radically. We know little of their appearance or how they lived, except from bones, stone tools, and occasional human fossils. This makes Mary Leakey's recent Laetoli discoveries of the greatest importance. The Laetoli fossil beds in northern Tanzania have been potassium-argon dated to between 3.59 and 3.75 million years ago. They have yielded the bones of long extinct animals and also the fragmentary remains of at least twenty hominids with some resemblances to the Hadar creatures.

In her article, Mary Leakey reports that excavations uncovered game trails across the ancient savannah that were buried by a volcanic eruption that preserved not only fossilized animal dung and twigs, but also the footprints of animals that had used the tracks some 3.5 million years ago. Seventeen different animal families left footprints on the buried track, prints probably made during the transition from the dry to the rainy season. These include the earliest hominid footprints ever found, impressions left by a creature with a rounded heel, uplifted arch, and forward-pointing big toe typical of a human foot. Leakey estimates two of the three individuals were between 3 feet 10 inches and 4 feet 7 inches tall. The Laetoli footprints prove that hominids were walking upright at least 3.5 million years ago, a posture that freed the hands for carrying, toolmaking, and tool use. So farm, Mary Leakey has found no tools at Laetoli, so this site and Hadar may well date to those critical millennia immediately before the moment at which humankind began making tools and creating its most unique and distinctive attribute: culture.

Opportunism

The tiny campsites of the first hominids provide us with a unique window into early human existence. We are lucky that their artifacts and broken bones remained sealed from the ravages of time. The excavation of even the smallest living site takes months of meticulous work. Every artifact, however small and apparently insignificant, has to be excavated individually, then its position recorded in place. This enables the palaeoanthropologist to make a precise map of the clusters of finds on the site as a basis for interpreting the behavior of the people who lived there.

Archaeologist Glynn Isaac has spent his career studying such campsites in East Africa. "The Food-Sharing Behavior of Protohuman Hominids" describes some of these early human bases. Isaac believes that the first phase of human cultural evolution involved major shifts in the basic patterns of subsistence and locomotion, as well as new ingredients—food sharing and toolmaking. These developments led to enhanced communication, exchange of information, and economic and social insight—as well as to cunning and restraint. And human anatomy was augmented with tools. Culture became an inseparable part of humanity.

Glynn Isaac argues that opportunism is the restless hallmark of humankind, a process like mutation and natural selection. The normal pressures of ecological competition were enough to transform the versatile behavior of the ancestral primates into the new and distinctive early hominid pattern. The changes required constant feedback between such activities as hunting and sharing food. Weapons and tools made it possible to kill and butcher larger and larger animals. Vegetable foods were a staple, a protection against food shortages. Foraging provided stability and may also have led to division of labor between men and women. The savannah was an ideal and available ecological niche for hominids who lived on hunting and gathering combined.

Were the first toolmakers human in the sense that we are? The most striking thing about prehistory between the earliest times and about 400,000 years ago is the simple nature of human technology, with its basically opportunistic tools, like stone choppers, that performed simple functions effectively. After 400,000, toolkits become far more elaborate and specialized, human adaptations more sophisticated and flexible. These elaborations can, one suspects, be connected to the great expansion of language and the ability to communicate, and to the cognitive and cultural capabilities integrally related to speech and language.

REFERENCES

Campbell, Bernard. 1982. *Humankind Emerging*. Boston: Little Brown.

Cole, Sonia. 1975. *Leakey's Luck*. New York: Harcourt Brace Jovanovich.

Howell, F. Clark. 1973. *Early Man*. Rev. edition. New York: Time-Life Books.

Isaac, Glynn, and Elizabeth R. McCown, eds. 1979. *Human Origins*. Menlo Park, Calif.: Benjamin/Cummings.

Johanson, Donald, and Maitland, Edey. 1981. *Lucy: The Beginnings of Humankind*. New York: Simon and Schuster.

Leakey, R. E., and Roger Levin. 1977. *Origins*. New York: Dutton.

Pfeiffer, John. 1973. *The Emergence of Man*, 2nd ed. New York: Harper and Row.

Reader, John. 1981. *Missing Links*. Boston: Little, Brown.

Washburn, S. L., and Ruth Moore. 1981. *Ape into Man*, 2nd ed. Boston: Little, Brown.

The Evolution of Man

by Sherwood L. Washburn
September 1978

*A wealth of new fossil evidence indicates that manlike
creatures had already branched off from the other
primates by four million years ago. Homo sapiens
himself arose only some 100,000 years ago*

Perhaps the most significant single fact about human evolution has a paradoxical quality: the brain with which man now begins to understand his own lengthy biological past developed under conditions that have long ceased to exist. That brain evolved both in size and in neurological complexity over some millions of years, during most of which time our ancestors lived under a daily obligation to act and react on the basis of exceedingly limited information. What is more, much of the information was wrong.

Consider what that meant. Before the information being fed to man's evolving brain began to be refined by an advancing technology our ancestors lived in a world that seemed to them small and flat and that they could assess only in very personal terms. Sharing the world with them were divine spirits, ghosts and monsters. Yet the brain that developed these concepts was the same brain that today deals with the subtleties of modern mathematics and physics. And it is this same technological progress that allows us to recognize human evolution.

One relevant example of the paradox is the extraordinary expansion over the past two centuries of man's perception of time. As Ernst Mayr points out in his article *Evolution*, SCIENTIFIC AMERICAN Offprint 1400, at the beginning of the 18th century the accepted view was that the time that had elapsed between the creation of the earth and the present was no more than a few thousand years. At the end of the 19th century the perceived interval had been enlarged a thousandfold and stood at about 40 million years. With the discovery that the slow and constant decay of certain radioactive isotopes constitutes a clock it became necessary to enlarge the interval another hundredfold, so that today we reckon the age of the earth to be about 4.6 billion years.

The human mind cannot literally comprehend such an interval; it is as ineffable as the trillions and quadrillions of dollars that are juggled in world economics. Man's common sense perceives time as being short: a rhythm of birth,

growth and death. To this sense of biological time can be added a sense of social time: a less tangible interval of three to five generations that is important to the actors in the drama of human society. Longer intervals do not have the same emotional impact. The real time scale of the universe that has been developed by science can be regarded as having liberated the perception of time from the limitations of the human mind.

The modern perception of time is of course only one in a series of mental emancipations that have led man to a deeper understanding of his own evolutionary history. In what follows I shall review information bearing on human evolution that has been gathered by workers in several fields of study, and I shall also assess the contribution of each field to our overall grasp of the subject today. No one can be an expert in all these fields, and this article might better be regarded as a personal evaluation than as an objective summary.

Few things defy common sense more than the concept that the continents of the earth are constantly in motion and that their positions have shifted drastically on a time scale short compared with the age of the earth. One consequence of yesterday's common sense is that all traditional theories of human evolution have assumed that the positions of the continents are fixed. To be sure, "land bridges" between continents and shallow seas that invaded continents were postulated, but the positions of the great continental plates were not affected. Although it has been nearly 70 years since Alfred Wegener proposed that continental drift was a reality, it is only over the past 20 years, as the mechanism of plate tectonics has been developed

and the movement of continents has actually been measured, that the concept of moving continents has become accepted and even respectable.

The combined data from radioactive-isotope dating and plate tectonics have fundamentally changed the background of human evolutionary studies. For example, everyone used to think that the monkeys of the New World had evolved directly from the primitive prosimians that had once flourished in North America. (The prosimians are the least advanced of the order Primates, which includes the apes and man. All living prosimians are confined to the Old World.) We now know, however, that 35 to 40 million years ago Africa was as close to South America as North America was. Some of the primates that were ancestral to the New World monkeys might just as easily have been accidentally rafted (perhaps on a tree felled by a flood) to South America from Africa as from North America. The propinquity of the three continents, which was unthinkable before continental drift was accepted, does not prove that the ancestral stock of the New World monkeys emigrated from Africa; nevertheless, it does present that entirely new and important possibility.

Another example of the effect of plate tectonics on human evolutionary hypotheses has to do with recent and repeated assertions that Africa was the focus of human origins. What the history of continental drift indicates is that there were broad connections between Africa and Eurasia from the time of their collision some 18 million years ago (when some ancestral elephants left Africa and spread over Eurasia) until the flooding of the Mediterranean basin five or six million years ago. It happens that

IMMUNOLOGICAL DISTANCES between selected mammals are indicated by the separation, as measured along the horizontal axis, between the branches of this "divergence tree." For example, the monotremes (primitive egg-laying mammals) are removed from the marsupials by a distance (in arbitrary units) of only 1.5 but are removed from the chimpanzee by a distance of nearly 17. The distance between man and the Old World monkeys is a little more than 3, between man and the Asiatic gibbons 2, and between man and the gorillas and the chimpanzees of Africa less than 1. The data are from Morris Goodman of Wayne State University.

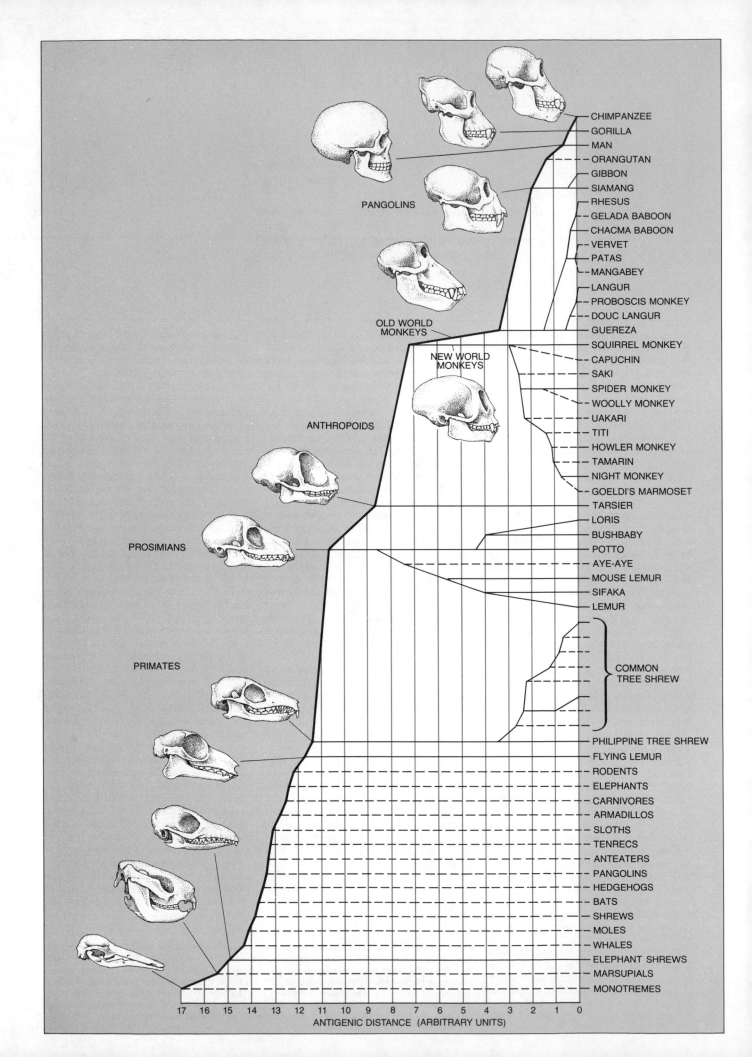

PANGOLINS

OLD WORLD
MONKEYS

NEW WORLD
MONKEYS

ANTHROPOIDS

PROSIMIANS

PRIMATES

CHIMPANZEE
GORILLA
MAN
ORANGUTAN
GIBBON
SIAMANG
RHESUS
GELADA BABOON
CHACMA BABOON
VERVET
PATAS
MANGABEY
LANGUR
PROBOSCIS MONKEY
DOUC LANGUR
GUEREZA
SQUIRREL MONKEY
CAPUCHIN
SAKI
SPIDER MONKEY
WOOLLY MONKEY
UAKARI
TITI
HOWLER MONKEY
TAMARIN
NIGHT MONKEY
GOELDI'S MARMOSET
TARSIER
LORIS
BUSHBABY
POTTO
AYE-AYE
MOUSE LEMUR
SIFAKA
LEMUR

COMMON
TREE SHREW

PHILIPPINE TREE SHREW
FLYING LEMUR
RODENTS
ELEPHANTS
CARNIVORES
ARMADILLOS
SLOTHS
TENRECS
ANTEATERS
PANGOLINS
HEDGEHOGS
BATS
SHREWS
MOLES
WHALES
ELEPHANT SHREWS
MARSUPIALS
MONOTREMES

17 16 15 14 13 12 11 10 9 8 7 6 5 4 3 2 1 0
ANTIGENIC DISTANCE (ARBITRARY UNITS)

the fossil remains of *Ramapithecus*, the Miocene-Pliocene ape commonly believed to be an ancestor of the hominid line, that is, the line of man and his extinct close relatives, are found from India and Pakistan through the Near East and the Balkans to Africa. The continuity in the distribution of these fossils suggests that the geography of Eurasia and Africa then was substantially different from what it is today. Moreover, the list of identical Indian and African faunas can be extended far beyond this single extinct ape: both regions harbor macaque monkeys, lions, leopards, cheetahs, jackals, wild dogs and hyenas. The possibility that man originated solely in Africa therefore seems less likely than it once did. In other words, the longer man's ancestors existed as intelligent, upright-walking, tool-using hunters, the less likely it is that their distribution was confined to any one continent.

Comparative anatomy is a field of study considerably older than plate tectonics. Its roots are in the 19th century, and it has been the discipline most concerned with the similarities and differences between man and his fellow primates. Its basic assumption has been that a sufficiently large quantity of information will inevitably lead to a correct conclusion; it gives little attention to questions of how anatomical data are related to evolutionary theory or to phylogeny. For example, the shape of one human tooth, the lower first premolar, has been cited as proof that man never went through an apelike stage in the course of his evolution. As late as 1972 this datum was offered as evidence that man and his ancestors had been separated from the other primates for at least 35 million years. Since then late Pliocene hominid fossils have been found that are about 3.7 million years old, and their lower first premolars show moderately apelike characteristics. It was not the description of the tooth that was wrong but the conclusions drawn from it (not to mention the belief that it is reasonable to base major phylogenetic determinations on the anatomy of a single tooth).

Comparative anatomy nonetheless makes many valuable connections. For example, the bones of the human arm are much like those of an ape's arm but are very different from the comparable bones of a monkey. Monkey arm bones are very similar to those of many other primates and indeed to those of many other mammals; their form is basic to quadrupedal locomotion. In contrast, the form of human and ape arm bones is basic to the motions of climbing. This finding is a significant one, but it can lead to two quite opposite conclusions: (1) man and apes are related or (2) man and apes have followed a parallel course of evolution, that is, the structures of the arm evolved in the same way even though the two evolutionary lines had long since separated. Deciding between the two alternatives is made all the more difficult by the fact that the comparison is being made between two living animals, each of which has evolved to an unknown degree since its divergence from a common ancestry. Fortunately powerful new analytical tools have come into existence that are a great help in resolving such dilemmas. To these I shall return, under the heading of molecular anthropology; for the moment it is necessary only to say that when the patterns of primate biology being compared are functional ones, the fit between the conclusions drawn from comparative anatomy and those drawn from molecular anthropology is quite close.

Until a few decades ago the fossil record of the primates was poor and that of the hominids, including man, was even poorer. For example, when Sir Arthur Keith undertook to array the existing hominid fossils along their probable lines of descent some 50 years ago, he had to deal with only three genera in the Miocene epoch, and he was able to spread the five (at that time) hominid genera across a later Pliocene-to-Recent time interval of less than half a million years. (Between the Pliocene and the Recent epochs was the Pleistocene; to it and the Recent combined was allotted 200,000 years.) The five genera were *Homo erectus* (then represented only by specimens from Java named *Pithecanthropus*), Neanderthal man, Piltdown man (then still accepted as a valid genus named *Eoanthropus*), Rhodesian man (*Homo rhodesiensis,* a form no longer considered a distinct species) and finally the genus and species *Homo sapiens* (from which, as can be seen, Keith excluded the Neanderthals). Keith had Java man branching off from the main human stem in Miocene times and indicated the extinction of the line at the start of the Pleistocene. The Neanderthals, today classified as *Homo sapiens neanderthalensis,* he saw as branching off in the mid-Pliocene, shortly before the appearance of Rhodesian man and well before that of Piltdown man; he had all three genera extinct in Pleistocene times.

Keith's arrangement was marvelous in its simplicity: each fossil that had to be accounted for stood at the end of its own evolutionary branch, and the time of branching was deduced from its anatomy. (Piltdown man was a problem: its genuinely modern cranium put this faked specimen's branching point higher up on the tree than Rhodesian man's, but its genuinely nonhuman jawbone demanded that the branching be put in the Pliocene.) This kind of typological thinking died slowly with the discovery of many new hominid fossils and the rise of radioactive-isotope dating, which have extended the duration of the Pleistocene from about 200,000 years to about two million. Theodosius Dobzhansky's 1944 paper "On Species and Races of Living and Fossil Man" ushered in the new era and ended nearly a

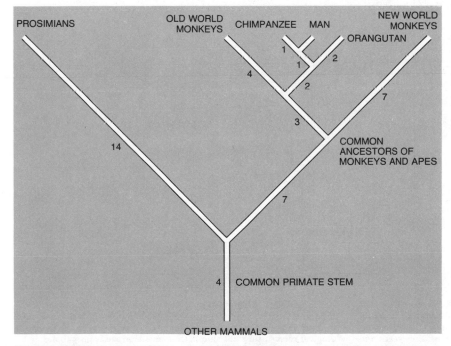

CLOSER VIEW of primate divergence is afforded by this schematic structure. The distance between man and the chimpanzee has a value of 1; this places both man and chimpanzee at a remove of 4 from the orangutan, and the orangutan and the Old World monkeys at a remove of 7 from the ancestor that both have in common with the New World monkeys. All anthropoids are at a remove of 7 from the ancestor they have in common with all prosimians (less advanced primates such as the lemurs) and at a remove of 11 from the most primitive primates.

42

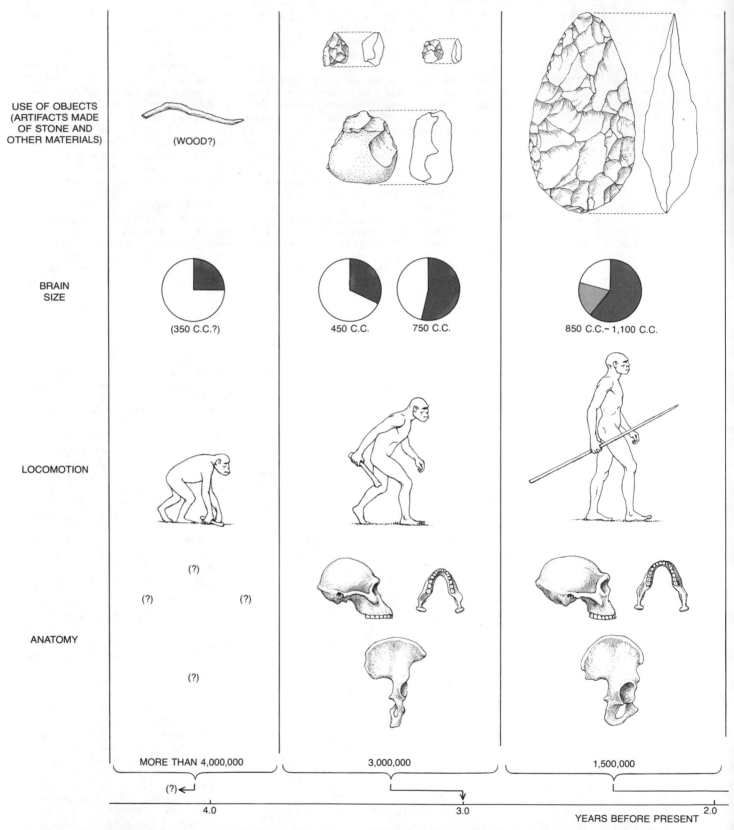

| USE OF OBJECTS (ARTIFACTS MADE OF STONE AND OTHER MATERIALS) | (WOOD?) | | |
| BRAIN SIZE | (350 C.C.?) | 450 C.C. | 750 C.C. | 850 C.C.–1,100 C.C. |

USE OF OBJECTS (ARTIFACTS MADE OF STONE AND OTHER MATERIALS)

(WOOD?)

BRAIN SIZE

(350 C.C.?)   450 C.C.   750 C.C.   850 C.C.–1,100 C.C.

LOCOMOTION

(?)

(?)   (?)

ANATOMY

(?)

MORE THAN 4,000,000   3,000,000   1,500,000

(?)

4.0   3.0   2.0

YEARS BEFORE PRESENT

HUMAN EVOLUTION, projected over a possible span of 10 million years, begins at a slow pace when a still undiscovered hominid branches off from the hominoid stock ancestral to man, the chimpanzee and the gorilla at some time more than four million years ago (*far left*). It is assumed that the ancestral hominid had a small brain and walked on its knuckles. This mode of locomotion enables a quadruped to move about while holding objects in its hands, leading to the further assumption that the hominid outdid living chimpanzees in manipulating sticks and other objects. By four million years ago the African fossil record reveals the presence of an advanced hominid:

Australopithecus. This subhuman had a pelvis that allowed an upright posture and a bipedal gait. The size of the brain had increased to some 450 cubic centimeters. Stone tools soon appear in the archaeological record; they are simple implements made from pebbles and cobbles. The tools may have been made by a second hominid group, chiefly notable for having a much larger brain: 750 c.c. Next, about 1.5 million years ago, the first true man, *Homo erectus,* appeared. Still primitive with respect to the morphology of its cranium and jaw, *H. erectus* had an essentially modern pelvis and a striding gait. Its brain size approaches the modern average in a number of instances.

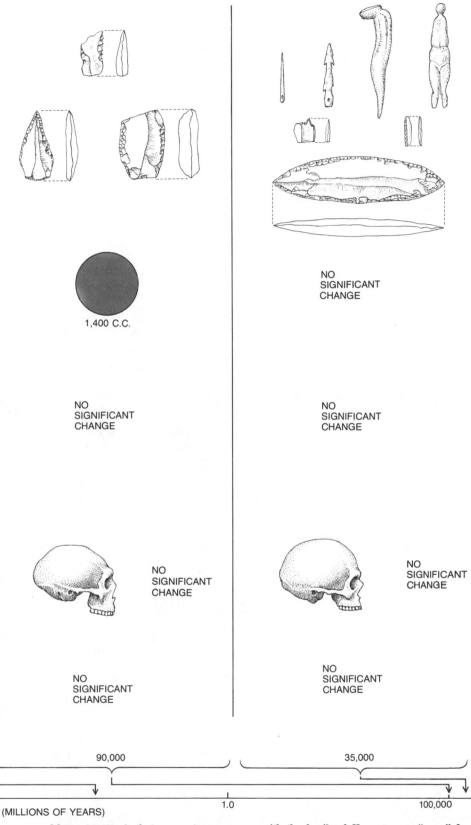

1,400 C.C.

NO
SIGNIFICANT
CHANGE

NO
SIGNIFICANT
CHANGE

NO
SIGNIFICANT
CHANGE

NO
SIGNIFICANT
CHANGE

NO
SIGNIFICANT
CHANGE

NO
SIGNIFICANT
CHANGE

NO
SIGNIFICANT
CHANGE

90,000   35,000

1.0   100,000   0

(MILLIONS OF YEARS)

Many stone tools that are contemporaneous with the fossils of _H. erectus_ are "cores" from which flakes have been removed on two sides; they are representative of the Acheulian tool industry. Not until some 100,000 years ago did _Homo sapiens_ appear, in the form of Neanderthal man. The shape of Neanderthal's skull is not quite modern but the size of its brain is. Most of the tools found at Neanderthal sites represent the Mousterian industry; they are made from flakes of flint rather than cores. Only 40,000 years ago modern man, _Homo sapiens sapiens,_ arrived on the scene. His skull is less robust than that of Neanderthal and his brain is slightly smaller. Many of his stone tools are slender blades; some, known as laurel-leaf points, appear to be ceremonial rather than utilitarian. Among his bone artifacts are needles, harpoon heads, awls and statuettes. About 10,000 years ago man's transition from hunting to farming began.

century of analysis that had been primarily typological.

Today there are hundreds of primate fossils. Many of them are accurately dated and more are being discovered every year. It is no longer even practical to list the individual specimens, which was the custom until a few years ago. Problems still remain with respect to the hominid fossil record, perhaps in part because human beings are obsessively curious about the details of their own ancestry. If any animal other than the human one were involved, the hominid fossil record over the past four million years would be considered adequate and even generous.

How is the evidence of those four million years to be read? To begin with, it can now be said with some certainty that hominids have walked upright for at least three million years. That is the age of a pelvis of the early hominid _Australopithecus_ recently unearthed in the Afar region of Ethiopia by Donald C. Johanson of Case Western Reserve University. Prior to Johanson's find the best evidence of upright walking was a younger _Australopithecus_ pelvis uncovered at Sterkfontein in South Africa. The two fossils are nearly identical. The inference is inescapable that bipedal locomotion is not just another human anatomical adaptation but the most fundamental one. The early bipeds all had small brains (average: 450 cubic centimeters).

Not much later, perhaps about 2.5 million years ago, the bipeds were making stone tools and hunting animals for food. By about two million years ago hominid craniums with a larger capacity appeared; by 1.5 million years ago _Homo erectus_ was on the scene, the brains had doubled in size and the stone tools now include bifaces, tools that have been flaked on both sides. These bifaces belong to the core-tool industry known as the Acheulian. (The characteristic form was first recognized at a French Paleolithic site, St.-Acheul.) From about two million to one million years ago another kind of early biped was also present; its robust anatomy identifies it as a separate species of _Australopithecus_. It is readily distinguishable from the less robust bipeds by its massive jaw and molar teeth that are very large compared with the incisors.

This summary of the hominid fossil record is undoubtedly oversimplified, but I think the evidence supports the main outline. What difficulties there are arise mainly from the fragmentary nature of many of the fossils. For example, Johanson has found one skeleton in the Afar region complete enough to allow reconstruction of that hominid's general proportions. The reconstruction shows that it had relatively long arms, a fact that could not be determined from the hundreds of previously discovered fragmentary remains of _Australopithecus_.

Dating also causes problems. For example, there are no radioactive-isotope dates for the hominid fossils found in South Africa. There is disagreement among specialists about the date of a particularly important marker layer of volcanic tuff in the East Turkana region of Kenya, where many important hominid fossils are currently being found. My response (or my bias) is to try to see the general order and to add complications only when they are absolutely inescapable.

The first conclusion I draw from this simplified picture is that upright walking evolved millions of years before a large brain, stone tools or other characteristics we think of as being human. If one accepts this conclusion, the problem of tracing human origins is primarily one of unearthing fossil evidence for that complex locomotor adaptation. How much time the adaptation required and what its intermediate stages may have been cannot be determined as long as the fossil leg bones are missing. The adaptation may have begun at any time from five to 10 million years ago. Fossil-bearing deposits of that age exist, and so all that is needed to clarify this aspect of human evolution is money for the search and a bit of luck.

The second conclusion I draw from my simplified outline is that stone tools and hunting long antedate the appearance of a large brain. Excavating in East Turkana, Glynn Isaac of the University of California at Berkeley and his colleagues uncovered a scatter of crude stone tools including both flakes and the cores that had yielded the flakes, and together with the tools were bits of animal bone. Unfortunately the creatures that deposited this material, which may be as much as 2.5 million years old, left no evidence of their own anatomy.

The East Turkana tools are very early but it is most unlikely that they are the earliest. For example, at Olduvai in neighboring Tanzania many of the stone tools from Bed I are unworked stones. They could not have been identified as tools except for the fact that they were found in a layer of volcanic ash otherwise free of stones, so that someone must have brought them there from somewhere else. In the absence of some similar circumstance the earliest stone tools are likely to go unrecognized.

My third conclusion stems both from the fossil record and from what is known about the anatomy of the human brain. As I have indicated, in my view large brains follow long after stone tools. Tools that are hard to make, such as those of the Acheulian industry, follow the earlier simple tools only after at least a million years have passed. It looks as if the successful way of life the earlier tools made possible acted in some kind of feedback relation with the evolution of the brain. What can be seen in the cortex of the human cerebrum

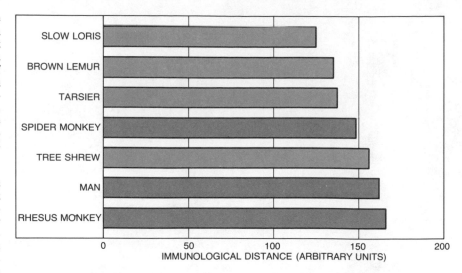

RATE OF EVOLUTION appears to be independent of the number of generations per unit time according to immunological-distance data. Bars show the distances, calculated by Vincent M. Sarich of the University of California at Berkeley, separating the carnivores from various primates. Man and the rhesus monkey were the most distant, respectively 162 and 166 units removed, although each human generation is five times longer than a rhesus generation. Four prosimians (color), also far shorter-lived than man, were even less distant from the carnivores.

mirrors this evolutionary success. Just as the proportions of the human hand, with its large and muscular thumb, reflect a selection for success in the use of tools, so does the anatomy of the human brain reflect a selection for success in manual skills.

Here a further point arises that is often forgotten. The only direct evidence for the importance of increasing brain size comes from the archaeological record. The hypothesis of a correlation between tool use and a large brain argues that the archaeological progression (from no stone tools to simple stone tools to tools of increasing refinement) is correlated with the doubling of hominid brain size. If the hypothesis is correct, the brain should not only have grown in size but also have increased in complexity. The fact remains that the fossil record contains no clues bearing on this neurological advance. Nevertheless, increasing brain size does seem to be correlated with the increasing complexity of stone tools over hundreds of thousands of years in a way that is not evident during the past 100,000 years of human evolution.

Students of the fossil record rely almost entirely on description, just as students of comparative anatomy do. When a fossil is discovered, the first requirement is to determine its geological context, its associations and its probable age. Once the fossil has been brought to the laboratory it is described and compared with similar fossils, and conclusions are drawn on the basis of the comparisons. The anatomical structures that are compared are complex ones and the work is arduous, so that a great deal of analysis remains to be completed on fossils first discovered many years ago. The method has other limitations. For exam-

ple, teeth are traditionally compared in isolation one at a time. In nature, of course, upper and lower teeth interact where they meet. Comparisons that take this functional factor into account, as the anatomist W. E. Le Gros Clark has shown, give results quite different from those yielded by the traditional tooth-by-tooth method.

Comparative methods are further complicated by the simple fact that a face is full of teeth. The form of the face is related both to the teeth and to the chewing muscles; functional patterns of this kind are not well described by linear measurements. What is more, the descriptive tradition even sets limits on what is observed. For example, the lower jaw of the robust species of *Australopithecus* from East Africa has a very large ascending ramus, the part of the lower jaw that projects upward to hinge with the skull. At the top of the ascending ramus is what is called the mandibular condyle. As this species' lower jaw opened and its mandibular condyle moved forward, the teeth of its upper and lower jaws must have moved farther apart than they do in any other primate. When one considers all that has been written about the possible diet of *Australopithecus* and about this hominid's teeth, it is surprising to find a fact as fundamental as the size of its bite is not discussed.

The same jaw provides another example of the weakness of such descriptive systems. In the robust species of *Australopithecus* the inside of the ascending ramus has features unlike those found in any other primate. This fact is not mentioned in the formal descriptions because it is not traditional to study the inside of the ramus. I could give a number of other examples, but the point at issue is the same in all of them: there are no clearly defined rules that state how fossils should be compared or how anatomy should be understood.

Having sketched what the traditional disciplines have to suggest on the subject of man's evolution, we can now turn to the suggestions that stem from work in two relatively new disciplines: molecular anthropology and the observation of primate behavior in the wild. The first of these disciplines actually has a longer history than plate tectonics: whereas Wegener first proposed his theory in 1912, George H. F. Nuttall demonstrated that the biochemical classification of animals was a possibility in 1904. Nuttall's method was immunological. If blood serum from an animal is injected into an experimental animal, the experimental animal will manufacture antibodies against proteins in the foreign serum. If serum from the experimental animal is added to serum from a third animal, the antibodies will combine with similar proteins in that serum to form a precipitate. The stronger the precipitation reaction, the closer the relation of the first animal to the third.

Nuttall's method was successfully applied in a number of investigations, but he attracted no more disciples than Wegener did. Not until the past decade, when findings based on immunological methods were seen to agree with those based on the similarity of amino acid sequences in proteins and the similarity of nucleotide sequences in DNA, did the concept of molecular taxonomy gain acceptance. As with the radioactive-isotope methods for determining absolute dates, the new molecular methods are objective and quantitative; they yield the same results when the tests are conducted by different workers.

The capacity of molecular taxonomy to define the relations among primates is perhaps the most important development in the study of human evolution over the past several decades. The great strength of the method is of course its objectivity. For example, data from the fossil record and from comparative anatomy have been cited to demonstrate that man's closest relative is variously the tarsier, certain monkeys, certain extinct apes, the chimpanzee or the gorilla, and to suggest that the time separating man from the last ancestor he shares with each of these candidates is variously from 50 million to four million years.

What do the data of molecular taxonomy show? The primary finding is that the molecular tests indicate little "distance" between man and the African apes. For example, when the distance separating the Old World monkeys from the New World monkeys is given a value of 1 and other distances are expressed as fractions of that value, then the distance between man and the Old World monkeys, as Vincent M. Sarich of the University of California at Berkeley has shown, is more than half a unit (.53 to .61). The distance between man and the Asian great ape the orangutan is about a quarter of a unit (.25 to .33) and the distance between man and the chimpanzee is about an eighth of a unit (.12 to .15).

The short distance between man and the African apes can be compared with similar distances among other related mammals. The relationship is about as close as that between horses and zebras and closer than that between dogs and foxes. Mary-Claire King and Allan C. Wilson of the University of California at Berkeley estimate (on the basis of comparisons between human and chimpanzee polypeptides, or protein chains) that man and the chimpanzee share more than 99 percent of their genetic material.

It might be thought such a wealth of new information about primate relationships would have been welcomed by students of human evolution. This has not been the case. The problem is that whereas the molecular data prove that man and the African apes are very closely related, the data appear to measure relationship and not time. It may be, however, that they do both. The overall picture seems clear: animals that are phylogenetically distant relatives are separated by large molecular distances and those that are close relatives are separated by small distances. This suggests that time and molecular distance are correlated. Unfortunately when it comes to the primates, the molecular distance between the New World and Old World monkeys is much too small to fit in with conventional phylogeny. What is worse, the distance between man and the African apes is startlingly less than convention demands. I suspect

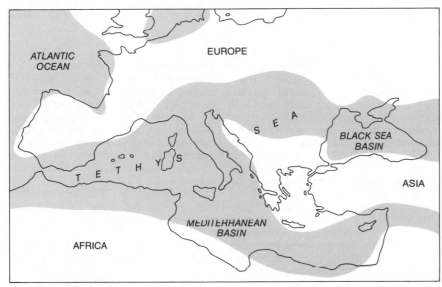

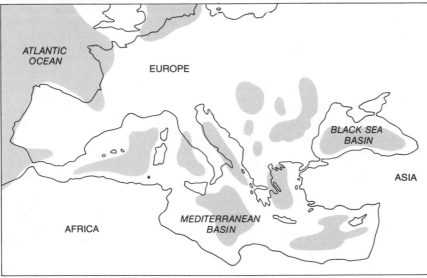

SEPARATION OF ASIA AND AFRICA, now joined by a narrow land bridge, was absolute some 20 million years ago (top), when the Tethys Sea reached from the Atlantic to the Persian Gulf. Later and until five million years ago (bottom) the Tethys was reduced to a network of lakes; the Old World primates were thus free at the time to move between the two continents.

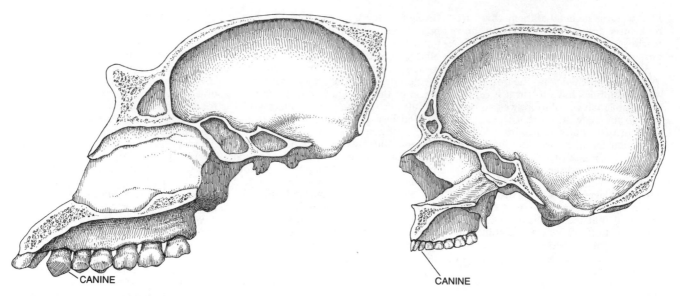

CANINE

CANINE

SKULLS OF MAN AND THE GORILLA, seen here in centerline section, have in common upper canine teeth that are much reduced in size. The gorilla is a female; male gorillas bare their very large canines when threatening to fight. The suggestion by Charles Darwin that man's use of weapons relieved him of the need for large canines seems to be supported by fossil evidence: the oldest human canines known are quite small compared with the canines of male African apes. This implies man's use of weapons for hundreds of millenniums.

that if molecular anthropology had shown man and apes to be very far apart, the concept of a correlation between genetic difference and time would have been accepted without debate.

The validity of a molecular clock is being argued at present, but I believe the problems will be worked out over the next few years. The chemical techniques are being improved and the fund of relevant information is being enlarged by work in many laboratories. Meanwhile the fossil evidence makes it highly unlikely that the ape and human lines separated less than five million years ago, and the molecular evidence makes it highly unlikely that they separated more than 10 million years ago. I have friends and colleagues who violently attack both dates, and they may be right! I am impressed by the degree of emotion that still surrounds the study of human evolution.

Studies of monkeys and apes under natural conditions have increased in number over the past few years. It is noteworthy in this connection that the heyday of evolutionary speculation was in the 19th century and that almost all the primate field studies began after 1960. The brutish, stooped Neanderthal and the monogamous chimpanzee have both proved to be products of the 19th-century imagination. Perhaps the most pertinent revision of preconceived views has to do with locomotion. All the traditional theories of human origins carefully considered how it was that a tree-dwelling ancestor became a ground-dwelling upright walker. The field studies have shown that our closest primate relatives, the African apes, are primarily ground dwellers. Moreover, their locomotor patterns suggest that the ancestor we share in common with them, howev-

er long ago, was also a ground dweller.

In the quadrupedal locomotion of most primates the hand and the foot are both placed flat on the ground; the animal cannot carry anything in them and move at the same time. Gorillas and chimpanzees (and the men who play some of the forward positions in American football), however, have developed a form of locomotion called knuckle walking that enables the apes (if not the football players) to walk normally as they carry objects between their fingers and their palm. If knuckle walking is an ancient trait, it neatly gets around the problem of how the handling and using of objects could have become a common habit. Of all living mammals except man the knuckle-walking chimpanzee is the most habitual user of objects. As Jane Goodall and her colleagues at the Gombe Stream Research Centre in Tanzania add to their observations year after year, the record of the number of objects handled by chimpanzees and the number of ways they are employed steadily increases. The chimpanzees use sticks for bluffing and attack, for poking, teasing and exploring. They use twigs and blades of grass to collect termites and ants. They use leaves to clean themselves. They use stones to crack nuts and also throw stones with moderate accuracy.

Our incredulity dies hard. When Peking man (now classified as *Homo erectus*) was first found, he was declared to be far too primitive to have made the stone tools found in association with his remains. The next unjustified victim of incredulity was *Australopithecus;* surely, the consensus had it, no one with such a small brain could have made tools. Even today many believe only one form of early biped, the form ancestral to man, could have made tools. Chimpan-

zee behavior is therefore enlightening: it shows that a typical ape is able to use objects in far greater variety and with greater effectiveness than anyone had suspected. There is no longer any reason not to suppose all the early bipeds also used objects, and probably used them far more than chimpanzees do, from a time far earlier than the time when stone tools first appear in the archaeological record.

Darwin suggested that the reason men had small canine teeth and the gorilla had huge ones was that man's possession of weapons had eliminated the need for fangs. It is clear that the large canine of the male gorilla has nothing to do with efficient chewing; the canine of the female gorilla is small but she is as well nourished as the male. Is the male canine part of an adaptation for bluffing and fighting? Before such an anatomical feature could have been reduced in the course of evolution its offensive function would have had to have been transferred to some other structure or mechanism. On this view the evolution of small human canine teeth would, as Darwin surmised, have depended on the use of weapons. The chimpanzee field studies, with their evidence for the frequent use of objects, support Darwin's interpretation. Sticks are seldom fossilized and unworked stones can rarely be proved to be artifacts, but teeth are the commonest of all hominid fossils and the earliest bipeds already had small canines. They had probably been using tools for many hundreds of thousands of years.

Not all behavioral information comes from studies in the field. Consider speech. The nonhuman primates cannot learn to speak even though great efforts have been made in the laboratory to teach them to do so. The recent remarkable successes in teaching apes how to communicate by symbols have been achieved in ways other than verbal ones. There is a lesson here, since human beings learn to speak with the greatest of ease.

The sounds made by monkeys primarily convey emotions and are controlled by brain systems more primitive than the cerebral cortex; removal of the cortex does not affect the production of sounds. In man the cortex of the dominant side of the brain is very important in speech. Speech is of course the form of behavior that more than any other differentiates man from other animals. Yet in spite of many ingenious attempts at investigation the origins of human speech remain a mystery. There is no clue to its presence or absence to be found in the fossils.

The archaeological record, however, does offer clues. What we see in the last 40,000 years of prehistory may have been triggered by the development of speech as we know it today. This is to say that although man was surely not mute for most of his development, an increased capacity for verbal communication may have been the ability that led to the extraordinary spread of modern man, *Homo sapiens sapiens.*

For most of the past million years the progress of human evolution, both biological and technological, was slow. Traditions of stone-tool manufacture, as reflected in the rise of successive stone-tool industries, persisted for hundreds of thousands of years with little change. Then came the great acceleration of about 40,000 years ago. Men who were anatomically modern now dominated the scene. Primitive forms of man disappeared; there are not enough fossils to make it possible to decide whether the disappearance was by evolution, hybridization or extinction. Then, in far less than 1 percent of the

time that bipeds are present in the fossil record, came a technological revolution. Its fruits included entirely new and complex tools and weapons, the construction of shelters, the invention of boats, the addition of fish and shellfish to the human diet, deep-water voyages (to Australia, for example), the peopling of the Arctic, the migration to the Americas and the proliferation of a lively variety of arts and a wide range of personal adornment.

The rate of change continued to accelerate. Agriculture and animal husbandry appeared at roughly the same time around the globe. Technological progress, the mastery of new materials (such as metals) and new energy sources (such as wind and water power) led in an amazingly short time to the Industrial Revolution and the world of today. The acceleration of human history cannot be better illustrated than by comparing the changes of the past 10,000 years with those of the previous four million.

Language, that marriage of speech and cognitive abilities, may well have been the critical new factor that provided a biological base for the acceleration of history. Just as upright walking and toolmaking were the unique adaptation of the earlier phases of human evolution, so was the physiological capacity for speech the biological base for the later stages. Without this remarkably effective mode of communication man's technological advance would perforce have been slow and limited. Given an open system of communication rapid change becomes possible and social systems can grow in complexity. Human social systems are all mediated by language; perhaps this is why there are no forms of behavior among the nonhuman primates that correspond to religion, politics or even economics.

If all this seems too pat, I should remind the reader that some of the

oldest and most troublesome questions about human evolution remain unanswered. Looking to the future, I expect that molecular biology will determine the relationships between man and the other living primates and the times of their mutual divergence more accurately than any other discipline can. But there will still be other major problems, particularly in determining the rates of evolution. As in the past, the present proponents of various hypotheses may be wrong on the very points on which they are surest they are right.

At this stage, then, it is probably wise to entertain more than one hypothesis and to state opinions in terms of the odds in favor of their being right rather than presenting them as conclusions. On this basis I would guess from the present evidence that the odds are 100 to one (in favor) that man and apes do in fact form a closely related group. I would also guess that a very recent separation of man and the apes, say five to six million years ago, was not nearly as probable; there my odds are only two to one in favor.

Perhaps by presenting opinions in this way we might demonstrate that all views of human evolution are built on seeming facts that vary widely in their degree of reliability. For example, if it is accepted that man is particularly close in his relationship to the African apes, it does not necessarily follow that man and the apes separated in Africa. At the time when the ape and human lines separated there were apes in the Near East and India; man may be descended from the apes of those areas. Perhaps the reason there are no longer any apes in India is that those apes evolved into men. Both the African and the non-African theories of the evolution of the earliest upright walkers are reasonable; only the discovery of more fossils will determine which theory is correct.

2

The Fossil Footprints of Laetoli

by Richard L. Hay and Mary D. Leakey
February 1982

*At this site in Tanzania thousands of animal tracks,
including those of predecessors of man, are found
in volcanic ash that fell some 3.5 million years ago*

Near Lake Eyasi in Tanzania is a series of layers of volcanic ash notable for having yielded the remains of early hominids that are among the oldest known: they date back between 3.5 and 3.8 million years. The layers of ash hold an even more unusual example of preservation: fossil footprints. Several tens of thousands of animal tracks have now been discovered in these ash deposits. The survival of these normally ephemeral traces, ranging from early hominid footprints to the trail of a passing insect, gives a vivid glimpse of life on the African savanna well before the Pleistocene epoch. How did they escape obliteration?

The extensive formation known to geologists as the Laetolil Beds is exposed over some 1,500 square kilometers on the Eyasi Plateau, an uplifted fault block northwest of Lake Eyasi. The beds overlie ancient basement rocks of Precambrian age and are themselves bordered and overlain to the east by several large volcanoes. The exposures richest in fossils are found in the smaller area called Laetoli, about 70 square kilometers in extent, that lies at an elevation of 1,700 to 1,800 meters on and near the drainage divide that runs between Lake Eyasi and Olduvai Gorge to the north.

Fossils are found mainly in the upper 45 to 60 meters of the beds, which at Laetoli are at least 130 meters thick. About three-fourths of the upper part of the formation consists of eolian tuffs: beds of volcanic ash that was redeposited by the wind after it had fallen. Most of the other ash beds, which alternate with the eolian tuffs, are "air fall" tuffs, that is, deposits of ash that remained essentially undisturbed after it had settled out of the eruptive cloud. Consisting largely of particles the size of fine sand grains (.125 to .25 millimeter) and medium-size sand grains (.25 to .5 millimeter), the eolian ash buried animal bones and teeth, bird eggs, land snails and other objects exposed on the ground. All the ash, eolian and air-fall came from one volcano: Sadiman, about 20 kilometers east of Laetoli.

In 1935 the area was explored by Louis Leakey, the geologist Peter Kent and one of us (Mary Leakey). The party found that the fossil animal remains at Laetoli were older than those discovered in the lowest level (Bed I) at Olduvai Gorge. In 1938–39 an expedition headed by Ludwig Kohl-Larsen of the University of Tübingen collected a large number of fossils in the area, including a fragment of a hominid upper jaw. In 1974 one of us (Mary Leakey) found additional hominid remains in a better state of preservation. As a result systematic investigations of the area have continued from 1975 to the present. They have yielded numerous hominid fossils, chiefly lower jaws and teeth, and a wide variety of other animal remains.

In 1976 Andrew Hill of Harvard University first came on animal tracks in a bed of tuff that since then has been called the Footprint Tuff. The next year Peter Jones of the University of Oxford and Philip Leakey found rather poorly preserved footprints, probably of hominid origin, in the same bed, and in 1978 Paul I. Abell of the University of Rhode Island discovered an unmistakably hominid footprint in the tuff at another place. Clearing of the surface layer there revealed more hominid footprints in two long parallel trails.

Several of the tuff beds contain the mineral biotite, which is rich in potassium. This makes it possible to date those beds by the potassium-argon method, which is based on the decay of the radioactive isotope potassium 40 into the no-ble gas argon. Working with samples of biotite from a bed under the lowest fossil-bearing deposits at the site and other samples from near the top of the formation, Garniss H. Curtis and Robert Drake of the University of California at Berkeley obtained potassium-argon dates that bracketed the Footprint Tuff. The samples from below it indicated that the tuff there was 3.8 million years old; the ages of samples from the Footprint Tuff itself and from above it clustered closely around 3.5 million years.

In general the animals preserved as fossils at Laetoli are similar in type to the animals found in the area today. Listed in order of their decreasing abundance, the commonest vertebrate remains are those of bovids (antelopes and related forms), lagomorphs (specifically hares), giraffes, rhinoceroses, horses, pigs and two kinds of proboscideans (elephants and dinotheres, a form now extinct). Significantly absent from the tuff deposits are the remains of crocodiles, hippopotamuses and other water-dwelling animals.

The air-fall tuffs that alternate with the eolian tuffs in the Laetolil Beds number about 50. Many of them are found throughout the fossil-rich area and can thus serve for stratigraphic correlations. Most of the air-fall tuffs range from one centimeter to 10 centimeters in thickness and are unlaminated; each tuff was evidently the product of a single eruption of Sadiman. Three of them, however, are laminated. They range from 12 to 30 centimeters in thickness and are evidently the result of a series of

PARALLEL TRACKS of hominid footprints extend for 25 meters across cemented volcanic ash at Site *G,* one of 16 localities at Laetoli where the tracks of various animals are found in the ancient series of ash layers known collectively as the Footprint Tuff. The tracks to the right of of the hominid trails are those of an extinct three-toed horse, *Hipparion.* The hominid trail at the left was made by the smallest of the three upright walkers; the other was made by a large individual whose prints were partially obliterated by a smaller individual who stepped in them. Whether the hominids walked together or at different times cannot be judged. The photograph appears through the courtesy of John Reader, © National Geographic Society.

PORTABLE SUNSHADE offered some protection to Mary Leakey (*left*), R. J. Clarke of the National Museum of Bloemfontein (*center*) and two technicians as they cleared overlying tuff from the hominid trails at Site *G* in 1979. Trails were discovered in 1978.

PARALLEL LINES, some six centimeters long, mark the passage of an insect across Laetoli ash. The insect may have been a dung beetle.

PAW PRINT, measuring 3.5 centimeters from front to back, is another of the thousands of tracks at Laetoli. It was made by a cat.

closely spaced eruptions. Whereas the ash particles forming the eolian tuffs are the size of fine sand to medium sand, the particles in the air-fall tuffs range in size from fine sand to coarse sand (.5 to one millimeter). Consisting of fragments of glassy lava, the particles are low in silica and contain the calcium-rich mineral melilite.

An additional constituent of most of the air-fall tuffs and perhaps all of them is carbonatite ash. This igneous material consists of calcium carbonate, with or without sodium carbonate. Carbonatite ash is highly unusual. Only one volcano in the world, Oldoinyo Lengai, 90 kilometers north of Laetoli, is known to have erupted carbonatite in recent times. The Oldoinyo Lengai carbonatite and the carbonatite of the Laetolil Beds are of the type that is rich in sodium carbonate. This fact provides a clue to the preservation of the tracks in the Footprint Tuff.

A carbonatite that contains both calcium carbonate and sodium carbonate reacts with water in a characteristic way. The calcium carbonate becomes a fine precipitate and the sodium carbonate goes into solution. When the solution evaporates, crystals of the mineral trona form; the crystals provide an instant cement for the ash layers.

The Footprint Tuff is one of the three laminated air-fall tuffs in the Laetolil Beds. Fossil footprints have now been found in all three of the laminated tuffs, and they are particularly abundant and widespread in this one. Generally between 12 and 15 centimeters thick, the Footprint Tuff lies near the top of the fossil-bearing zone and is overlain by a more massive deposit of ash, 50 centimeters thick in places. The thin ash layers that make up the Footprint Tuff accumulated in the early stages of an eruptive episode; the thicker overlying tuff represents the culmination of the same episode.

The Footprint Tuff is divisible into two major units. The lower of the two is seven to 10 centimeters thick; the upper is four to six centimeters thick. The contact between the units is sharp, and the top of the lower unit is eroded in places. The two units differ in their lithology, in their structure and in the footprints they contain.

The lower unit is subdivided into 14 thin layers, ranging from two to 15 millimeters in thickness. The layers are generally recognizable over the entire Laetoli area; each is very likely the product of a single volcanic eruption. Most of the layers cover surface irregularities such as footprints with little change in thickness. This shows that they remained essentially undisturbed where they were deposited.

The surfaces of five layers are widely pockmarked by the impact of drops of rain; three others are only locally rain-

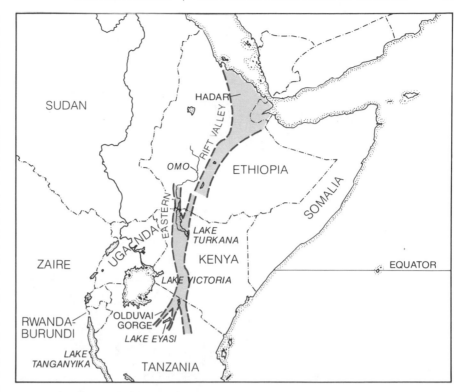

LAKE EYASI, southeast of Lake Victoria in Tanzania, is near the southern end of the Eastern Rift valley, which runs through Kenya and Ethiopia to the Red Sea. Early hominid remains have been found in large numbers in or near the valley. Some of the better-known hominid localities are at Hadar and Omo in Ethiopia, east of Lake Turkana in Kenya and at Olduvai Gorge and nearby Laetoli in Tanzania. Animal fossils and tracks abound in the Laetoli tuffs.

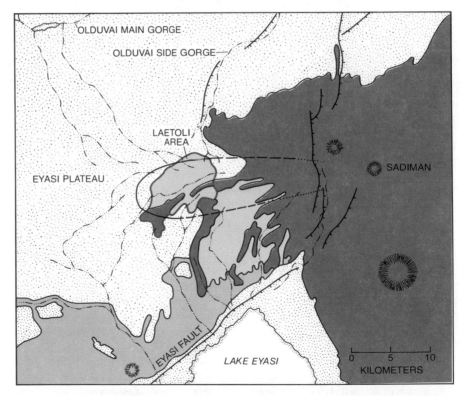

LAETOLIL BEDS, volcanic-ash deposits north of Lake Eyasi, are exposed over an area of 1,500 square kilometers (light color). They overlie Precambrian basement rocks (gray) to the west and are covered by volcanic rock (dark color) to the east. The beds richest in fossils are in the 70-square-kilometer Laetoli area, outlined in color. The Footprint Tuff, which lies near the top of the fossil-bearing strata, is generally more than 12 centimeters thick inside the black oval line. The volcanic ash deposited in the Laetolil Beds came from the volcano Sadiman.

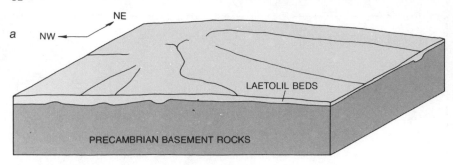

a

NE

NW

LAETOLIL BEDS

PRECAMBRIAN BASEMENT ROCKS

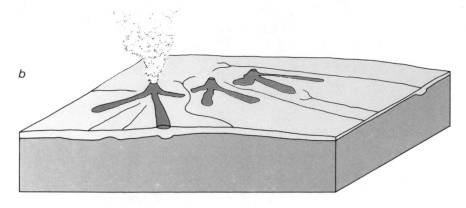

b

c

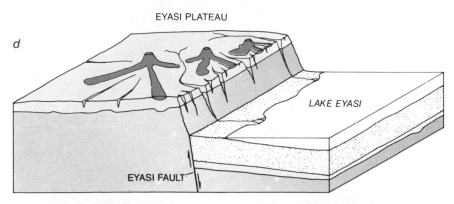

EYASI PLATEAU

d

LAKE EYASI

EYASI FAULT

FOUR BLOCK DIAGRAMS show the development of the Eyasi region. At the time when the ash of the Laetolil Beds was being deposited, between 3.8 and 3.5 million years ago (*a*), the region was relatively flat grassland savanna. Some 1.2 million years later (*b*) the region went through a period of major volcanic activity. After another 1.2 million years (*c*), when rift-valley faulting had begun, came the uplifting of the Eyasi plateau and the development of a lake below it. Further uplift and erosion (*d*) made the landscape of the Eyasi region as it is today.

printed. The rainprints are close together and well defined. They were evidently made by showers that were heavy enough to dampen the ash but not heavy enough to erode it. Footprints indent the surface of the topmost layer (No. 14) and the surfaces of seven of the 13 layers below it; they are particularly abundant and widespread on layers No. 9 and No. 14. Very few footprints are found within individual ash layers.

The upper unit of the Footprint Tuff presents a somewhat different picture. It consists of only four layers, each one representing either a single volcanic eruption or a closely spaced series of eruptions. Each of the layers has been extensively redeposited by water action: the runoff associated with heavy rainfall. The two lower layers cover surface irregularities, but together they are thicker over depressions such as hoofprints than they are over raised areas such as the rims of footprints. Most of the raised areas are truncated at the base of the third layer, which in many places is an erosional surface. Where the layers have been redeposited they are laminated, and the laminated tuff of each layer can fill the broad, shallow channels that have been scoured into the layers below it. Footprints in the upper unit are widespread on the surfaces of layers No. 1 and No. 2. Rainprints have been found at one place on the surface of layer No. 2.

As we noted above, most of the ash in the Footprint Tuff consists of particles of lava that contain the calcium-rich mineral melilite. The particles are ovoid or spheroidal in shape and mostly the size of fine to medium grains of sand (.1 to .3 millimeter). Particles of coarsely crystalline calcite, ranging in shape from rounded to flattish and generally between .02 to .01 millimeter in length, are widespread and locally abundant in the bottom layer of the lower unit (layer No. 1). Similar particles of calcite are found in a few places in layers No. 2 through No. 5.

The calcite contains relatively high concentrations of strontium and barium (a chemical "signature" of carbonatite). Textural evidence visible under the microscope, however, shows that the calcite has replaced what was originally a sodium-rich carbonatite mineral such as nyererite. The calcite particles undoubtedly represent only a small fraction of the carbonatite ash particles originally present; most of the ash would have disappeared in reacting with water (as it does, for example, in the process that leads to the formation of trona crystals).

Trona, being a water-soluble mineral, was long ago dissolved away; the Footprint Tuff layers are now cemented by calcite and, less commonly, by the mineral phillipsite (an aluminosilicate). Some layers consist largely of cement in which the ash particles appear to float. These layers are interpreted as being ash deposits where much of the space now filled with cement was originally occupied by carbonatite. The cement-rich layers are common in the lower unit of the tuff and are rare in the upper unit, which presumably received a smaller proportion of carbonatite ash.

The land surface buried under the Footprint Tuff was nearly flat. Its largest irregularities were trenchlike depressions, some 10 centimeters in depth. They are interpreted as being game trails across the Pliocene savanna. The presence of grass is suggested by small fossilized rootlets under the Footprint Tuff. The ground must, however, have been essentially bare when the first layers of the Footprint Tuff were deposited; upright blades of grass would have disrupted the delicate layering of the ash. Most probably the savanna herbivores had grazed the grass down to a stubble.

The fossilized dung of hares, giraffes and the miniature antelope called the dik-dik is abundant at the base of the Footprint Tuff. Also found are the fossilized twigs and branches of trees and shrubs. A few fossilized sticks, thorns and leaves of the acacia, a typical savanna tree, have been found in overlying layers of the lower unit; one of these layers contains the dung of hares and possibly that of giraffes.

The Footprint Tuff was deposited over a short span, perhaps in a few weeks beginning near the end of the savanna dry season and extending into the early part of the rainy season. The excellent preservation of footprints and rainprints alike shows that the tuff layers must have been buried by fresh ash falls soon after the prints were made. Further evidence that the burial process was quick is provided by the continuity of layers, some only a few millimeters thick, over an area 70 square kilometers in extent.

There is other evidence of the short span of the event. The absence of grass blades at the base of the tuff suggests that the first volcanic eruptions came in the dry season. The rainprints in the lower unit were most probably made by brief showers as the dry season neared its end. In contrast, the redeposition of ash falls in the upper unit by runoff water points to a period of heavier rains, presumably the early part of the rainy season. Moreover, the widespread erosion at the base of the upper unit and between layers No. 2 and No. 3 of the upper unit is clearly attributable to heavy rainfall. Finally, the scarcity of rainprints on the surface of the upper-unit layers can be laid to the fact that rain-saturated sediments do not preserve such prints.

Since the Footprint Tuff is well ce-

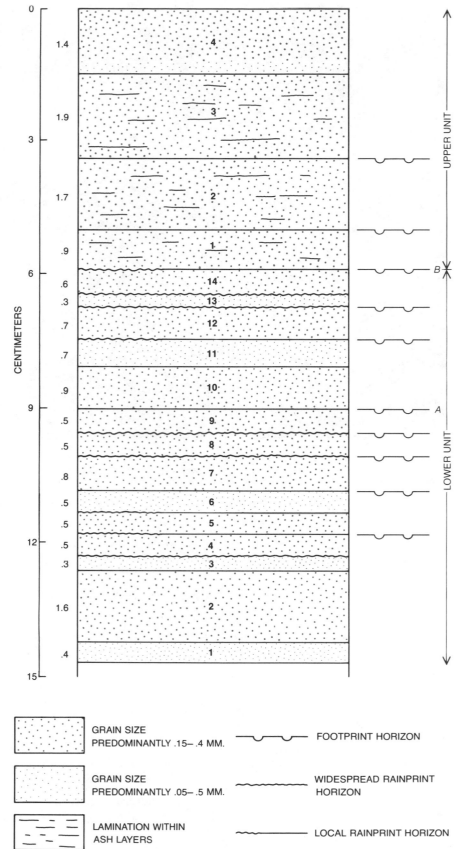

FOOTPRINT TUFF is seen in section at a point where it is almost 15 centimeters thick. Of the 14 subdivisions of the lower unit eight are imprinted with tracks; the tracks are most abundant on horizons A and B. Two of the upper-unit subdivisions also bear tracks. The hominid tracks appear on horizon B. Numerals indicate the average thickness of the layers at Site A.

ELEPHANT FOOTPRINT is the large, shallow circular depression in this exposure of Upper Unit No. 1, a wet-season horizon. Additional footprints can be seen within the large one; they were probably made by small animals such as hares. The scale is 20 centimeters long.

Site *G*. The tracks are 25 centimeters apart and have been exposed over a distance of 25 meters. The best-defined of the footprints are from one centimeter to three centimeters deep and have clear margins. They show the rounded heel, uplifted arch and forward-pointing big toe typical of the human foot. One of the tracks was made by a single small individual. The other is a composite: the original prints were made by a comparatively large individual, and a second set of prints was superposed on the first set by a smaller individual who stepped in the original prints.

The hominid tracks are clear proof that 3.5 million years ago these East African precursors of early man walked fully upright with a bipedal human gait. This was at a time when both in stature and in brain size the hominids of Africa were still small by later human standards. Assuming that, as is true of modern human populations, the length of the Laetoli hominids' feet was about 15 percent of their height, then the smallest of the three who left their tracks at Site *G* was 1.2 meters tall (about three feet 10 inches). The next-largest would have been 1.4 meters tall (four feet seven inches). The length of the footprints made by the third and largest individual cannot be measured because they are overprinted and partly obliterated by the tracks of the next-largest.

An upright posture this early in the course of human evolution is of great importance. It freed the hands both for carrying and for toolmaking and tool use. In spite of diligent searching, no stone tools have been found in the Laetolil Beds. Hence it seems likely that the hominids who left their tracks in the Footprint Tuff had not arrived at the stage of making stone tools. The fact remains that their upright posture gave them full-time use of the first of all primate tools: unencumbered hands.

The nonhominid footprints preserved in the Footprint Tuff range from the very large to the minuscule. The large prints include those of elephants, dinotheres, giraffes and rhinoceroses. The smaller ones represent a small cat, hares, guinea fowl, francolins (birds somewhat smaller than guinea fowl) and one insect (possibly a dung beetle).

Both the making and the preservation of fossil footprints call for a rather special set of circumstances. First, the ground must be sufficiently soft and cohesive to retain clear prints. Second, the prints must be buried before destructive processes such as erosion can modify or obliterate them. Finally, the material covering them up must later separate cleanly from the surface that holds the prints. Most prints preserved in the fossil record were made in muddy sediments that became hard on drying and

mented and more resistant to erosion than the underlying and overlying deposits, it has survived exposure to erosion over wide areas. Where the tuff is weathered it splits readily along the bedding planes between layers, revealing any footprints on the surface of the layer exposed. The footprints have now been examined in 16 localities at Laetoli; the exposures have been labeled sites *A* through *P*.

The largest of the exposures is Site *A*, which preserves clear tracks over an area of about 800 square meters. We counted the number of individual prints in 17 square meters at Site *A* and in 20 square meters at Site *D* (which covers about 113 square meters) to arrive at an estimate of footprint density. The small oval prints of hares (and possibly of dik-diks) averaged 21 per square meter at Site *A* and 30 per square meter at Site *D*. Other prints, most of them larger, respectively averaged 1.8 and 3.6 per square meter. Taking an average of 23 footprints of all sizes per square meter, some 18,400 prints are preserved at Site *A* alone.

The footprints of animals belonging to a total of 17 separate families have

been recognized. The animals make up a majority of those whose fossil remains have been found in the Laetolil Beds. The vertical distribution of the prints in the strata accords with the hypothesis that they were made during a transition from the dry season to the rainy one. Hence the prints in the lower unit are chiefly those of hares, guinea fowl, rhinoceroses and other animals that stay in the grassland savanna during the dry season. In contrast, the prints in the upper unit include those of wet-season visitors: proboscideans, horses, baboons and hominids. None of their prints are found in the lower unit. The prints of large antelopes are also much commoner in the upper unit than they are in the lower. They very probably record the wet-season migrations that are characteristic of the East African savanna. The tracks follow the preexisting game trails and indicate a normal walking gait. From this one may conclude that the ash falls from Sadiman were not heavy enough to disrupt the usual patterns of seasonal movement.

The five footprints found in 1977 that were probably made by hominids are at Site *A*. The two parallel tracks of hominid prints, first uncovered in 1978, are at

were then buried by sand or mud. The volcanic ash of the Footprint Tuff was quite different; it had the texture of fine- to medium-grained sand. For print preservation this is a most unusual surface.

The nature of a footprint made in unconsolidated sand depends to a great extent on how wet the sand is. Loose, dry sand will retain the tracks of small animals nicely. It will not clearly preserve the deep prints of large animals because the steep sides of the prints slump inward. Wet sand will preserve the prints of large animals but will not accept the tracks of small ones. To preserve both kinds of track the sand must be only slightly damp.

The clarity of the smaller animals' tracks in the Footprint Tuff shows that the ash was soft when the tracks were made. At the same time the well-defined vertical margins of some of the larger animals' prints show that the ash was fairly cohesive. (Some of the larger prints do have gentle inward slopes, suggestive of a minor slumping of loose ash.) Most of the larger prints also have a raised rim, squeezed upward by the pressure of the foot. The ash layers must have been firm only a few centimeters down, because the largest footprints, those of the rhinoceroses and the proboscidians, are generally no more than five centimeters deep.

It is difficult to imagine that when the various footprints were made, all 10 of the ash layers that preserve tracks could have been appropriately damp. Would that, however, have been strictly necessary? The answer is no. Just as mixing wood ash or portland cement with dry sand will make the sand more cohesive, so could the carbonatite have made the volcanic ash more cohesive by providing a fine-grained matrix for the ash particles. If the carbonatite had been fine-grained initially, a suitable primary matrix would have been supplied at the very time of deposition, and the subsequent reaction of the carbonatite with water would have provided an even finer-grained secondary matrix of precipitated calcium carbonate. Meanwhile, unless the sodium carbonate dissolved out of the carbonatite was entirely leached away by rainfall, it would crystallize into trona as the water evaporated, weakly cementing the surface layer of ash and stabilizing the footprints until they were buried by the next ash fall.

Over the ensuing thousands of years the ash layers of the Footprint Tuff were modified by a variety of processes. First the reaction of carbonatite with water produced an abundance of calcite that in the early stages would have weakly cemented the ash layers and would also have replaced the dung and the plant material in the ash. At this stage insects and other animals burrowed in the ash. As the tuffs were weathered, ash and melilite were transformed into montmorillonite clay, and the aluminosilicate mineral phillipsite was deposited locally as an additional cementing agent. Thereafter calcite filled nearly all the remaining pore space, leaving the ash layers a well-cemented hard rock. Calcite was also deposited between some ash layers in the form of thin, discontinuous sheets of limestone. Such limestone coated many of the hominid footprints at Site *G*, making it easier to excavate the prints without altering them.

To summarize, a most unusual set of conditions gave rise to the Footprint Tuff. Approximately 3.5 million years ago the Laetoli area supported an abundant and diverse animal population. The showers of volcanic ash that fell in the area were not heavy enough to drive the animals away. The excellent definition of a multitude of footprints, tracks and trails made in the fresh ash was a result of the admixture of carbonatite, an uncommon igneous material, with the more typical particles of volcanic ash; the imprinted ash layers were then buried at frequent intervals by fresh falls. Finally a heavy ash fall deeply buried the Footprint Tuff, protecting it from erosion, and the imprinted layers were cemented and became hard rock. When recent weathering split the layers of tuff along their bedding planes, it opened a unique window on the world of early hominids and the animals with which they lived.

THREE KINDS OF ANIMAL made the imprints seen in this part of the exposed tuff. Tracks of a bird appear at the lower left; those of a small animal, possibly a hare or a dik-dik, appear at the upper left and right. To the left of center is a print of a baboon's hind foot.

3

The Food-Sharing Behavior of Protohuman Hominids

by Glynn Isaac
April 1978

*Excavations at two-million-year-old sites in East Africa
offer new insights into human evolutionary progress
by showing that early erect-standing hominids made
tools and carried food to a home base*

Over the past decade investigators of fossil man have discovered the remains of many ancient protohumans in East Africa. Findings at Olduvai, Laetolil, Koobi Fora, the Omo Valley and Hadar, to name some prominent locations, make it clear that between two and three million years ago a number of two-legged hominids, essentially human in form, inhabited this part of Africa. The paleontologists who have unearthed the fossils report that they differ from modern mankind primarily in being small, in having relatively large jaws and teeth and in having brains that, although they are larger than those of apes of comparable body size, are rarely more than half the size of modern man's.

The African discoveries have many implications for the student of human evolution. For example, one wonders to what extent the advanced hominids of two million years ago were "human" in their behavior. Which of modern man's special capabilities did they share? What pressures of natural selection, in the time since they lived, led to the evolutionary elaboration of man's mind and culture? These are questions that paleontologists find difficult to answer because the evidence that bears on them is not anatomical. Archaeologists, by virtue of their experience in studying prehistoric behavior patterns in general, can help to supply the answers.

It has long been realized that the human species is set apart from its closest living primate relatives far more by differences in behavior than by differences in anatomy. Paradoxically, however, the study of human evolution has traditionally been dominated by work on the skeletal and comparative anatomy of fossil primates. Several new research movements in recent years, however, have begun to broaden the scope of direct evolutionary inquiry. One such movement involves investigations of the behavior and ecology of living primates and of other mammals. The results of

these observations can now be compared with quantitative data from another new area of study, namely the cultural ecology of human societies that support themselves without raising plants or animals: the few surviving hunter-gatherers of today. Another important new movement has involved the direct study of the ecological circumstances surrounding human evolutionary developments. Investigations of this kind have become possible because the stratified sedimentary rocks of East Africa preserve, in addition to fossil hominid remains, an invaluable store of data: a coherent, ordered record of the environments inhabited by these protohumans.

The work of the archaeologist in drawing inferences from such data is made possible by the fact that at a certain stage in evolution the ancestors of modern man became makers and users of equipment. Among other things, they shaped, used and discarded numerous stone tools. These virtually indestructible artifacts form a kind of fossil record of aspects of behavior, a record that is complementary to the anatomical record provided by the fossil bones of the toolmakers themselves. Students of the Old Stone Age once concentrated almost exclusively on what could be learned from the form of such tools. Today the emphasis in archaeology is increasingly on the context of the arti-

facts: for example the distribution pattern of the discarded tools in different settings and the association of tools with various kinds of food refuse. A study of the contexts of the early African artifacts yields unique clues both to the ecological circumstances of the protohuman toolmakers and to aspects of their socioeconomic organization.

Comparing Men and Apes

What are the patterns of behavior that set the species *Homo sapiens* apart from its closest living primate relatives? It is not hard to draw up a list of such differences by comparing human and ape behavior and focusing attention not on the many features the two have in common but on the contrasting features. In the list that follows I have drawn on recent field studies of the great apes (particularly the chimpanzee, *Pan troglodytes*) and on similar studies of the organization of living hunter-gatherer societies. The list tends to emphasize the contrasts relating to the primary subsistence adaptation, that is, the quest for food.

First, *Homo sapiens* is a two-legged primate who in moving from place to place habitually carries tools, food and other possessions either with his arms or in containers. This is not true of the great apes with regard to either posture or possessions.

Second, members of *Homo sapiens* so-

PAST AND PRESENT LANDSCAPES in the Rift Valley region of East Africa, shown schematically on the opposite page, summarize the geological activity that first preserved and later exposed evidence of protohuman life. Two million years ago (*top*) the bones of hominids (*1–4, color*) and other animals (*x's, color*) were distributed across hills and a floodplain (*foreground*) adjacent to a Rift Valley lake. Also lying on the surface were stone tools (*black dots*) made, used and discarded by the protohumans. Layers of sediments then covered the bones and tools lying on the floodplain; burial preserved them, whereas the bones and tools in the hills were eventually washed away. Today (*bottom*), after a fault has raised a block of sediments, erosion is exposing some of the long-buried bones and clusters of tools, including the three types of site shown on the surface in the top block diagram (*A–C*). Sites of Type A contain clusters of stone tools together with the leftover stone cores that provided the raw material for the tools and waste flakes from the toolmaking process, but little or no bone is present. Sites of Type B contain similar clusters of tools in association with the bones of a single large animal. Sites of Type C also contain similar clusters of tools, but the bones are from many different animal species.

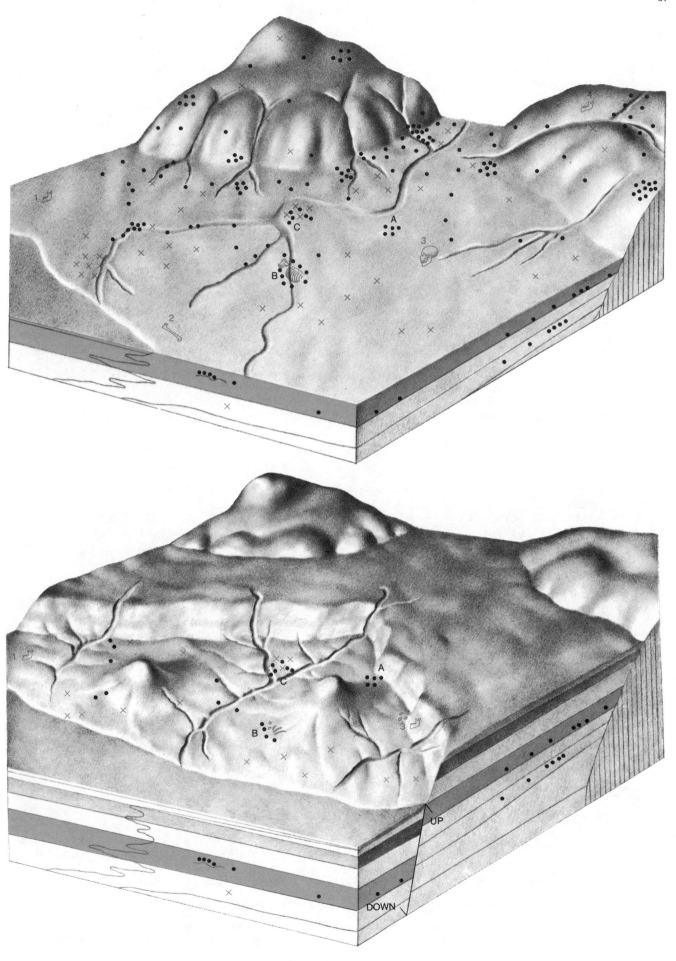

57

cieties communicate by means of spoken language; such verbal communication serves for the exchange of information about the past and the future and also for the regulation of many aspects of social relations. Apes communicate but they do not have language.

Third, in *Homo sapiens* societies the acquisition of food is a corporate responsibility, at least in part. Among members of human social groupings of various sizes the active sharing of food is a characteristic form of behavior; most commonly family groups are the crucial nodes in a network of food exchange. Food is exchanged between adults, and it is shared between adults and juveniles. The only similar behavior observed among the great apes is seen when chimpanzees occasionally feed on meat. The chimpanzees' behavior, however, falls far short of active sharing; I suggest it might better be termed tolerated scrounging. Vegetable foods, which are the great apes' principal diet, are not shared and are almost invariably consumed by each individual on the spot.

Fourth, in human social groupings there exists at any given time what can be called a focus in space, or "home base," such that individuals can move independently over the surrounding terrain and yet join up again. No such home base is evident in the social arrangements of the great apes.

Fifth, human hunter-gatherers tend to devote more time than other living primates to the acquisition of high-protein foodstuffs by hunting or fishing for animal prey. It should be noted that the distinction is one not of kind but of degree. Mounting evidence of predatory behavior among great apes and monkeys suggests that the principal contrast between human beings and other living primates with respect to predation is that only human beings habitually feed on prey weighing more than about 15 kilograms.

The gathering activities of human hunter-gatherers include the collection of edible plants and small items of animal food (for example lizards, turtles, frogs, nestling birds and eggs). Characteristically a proportion of these foodstuffs is not consumed until the return to the home base. This behavior is in marked contrast to what is observed among foraging great apes, which almost invariably feed at the spot where the food is acquired.

Still another contrast with great-ape feeding behavior is human hunter-gatherers' practice of subjecting many foodstuffs to preparation for consumption, by crushing, grinding, cutting and heat-

ing. Such practices are not observed among the great apes.

Human hunter-gatherers also make use of various kinds of equipment in the quest for food. The human society with perhaps the simplest equipment ever observed was the aboriginal society of Tasmania, a population of hunter-gatherers that was exterminated in the 19th century. The inventory of the Tasmanians' equipment included wood clubs, spears and digging sticks, cutting tools made of chipped stone that were used to shape the wood objects, and a variety of containers: trays, baskets and bags. The Tasmanians also had fire. Although such equipment is simple by our standards, it is far more complex than the kind of rudimentary tools that we now know living chimpanzees may collect and use in the wild, for example twigs and grass stems.

In addition to this lengthy list of subsistence-related behavioral contrasts between human hunter-gatherers and living primates there is an entire realm of other contrasts with respect to social organization. Although these important additional features fall largely outside the range of evidence to be considered here, they are vital in defining human patterns of behavior. Among them is the propensity for the formation of long-

DESOLATE LANDSCAPE in the arid Koobi Fora district of Kenya is typical of the kind of eroded terrain where gullying exposes both bones and stone tools that were buried beneath sediments and volcanic ash more than a million years ago. Excavation in progress (*center*) is exposing the hippopotamus bones and clusters of artifacts that had been partially bared by recent erosion and were found by Richard Leakey in 1969. The site is typical of the kind that includes the remains of a single animal and many tools manufactured on the spot.

term mating bonds between a male and one or more females. The bonds we call "marriage" involve reciprocal economic ties, joint responsibility for aspects of child-rearing and restrictions on sexual access. Another such social contrast is evident in the distinctively human propensity to categorize fellow members of a group according to kinship and metaphors of kinship. Human beings regulate many social relations, mating included, according to complex rules involving kinship categories. Perhaps family ties of a kind exist among apes, but explicit categories and rules do not. These differences are emphasized by the virtual absence from observed ape behavior of those distinctively human activities that are categorized somewhat vaguely as "symbolic" and "ritual."

Listing the contrasts between human and nonhuman subsistence strategies is inevitably an exercise in oversimplification. As has been shown by contemporary field studies of various great apes and of human beings who, like the San (formerly miscalled Bushmen) of the Kalahari Desert, still support themselves without farming, there is a far greater degree of similarity between the two subsistence strategies than had previously been recognized. For example, with regard to the behavioral repertories involving meat-eating and tool-using the differences between ape and man are differences of degree rather than of kind. Some scholars have even used the data to deny the existence of any fundamental differences between the human strategies and the nonhuman ones.

It is my view that significant differences remain. Let me cite what seem to me to be the two most important. First, whereas humans may feed as they forage just as apes do, apes do not regularly postpone food-consumption until they have returned to a home base, as human beings do. Second, human beings actively share some of the food they acquire. Apes do not, even though chimpanzees of the Gombe National Park in Tanzania have been observed to tolerate scrounging when meat is available.

From Hominid to Human

Two complementary puzzles face anyone who undertakes to examine the question of human origins. The first relates to evolutionary divergence. When did the primate stock ancestral to the living apes diverge from the stock ancestral to man? What were the circumstances of the divergence? Over what geographical range did it take place? It is not yet established beyond doubt whether the divergence occurred a mere five to six million years ago, as Vincent M. Sarich of the University of California at Berkeley and others argue on biochemical grounds, or 15 to 20 million years ago, as many paleontologists believe on the grounds of fossil evidence.

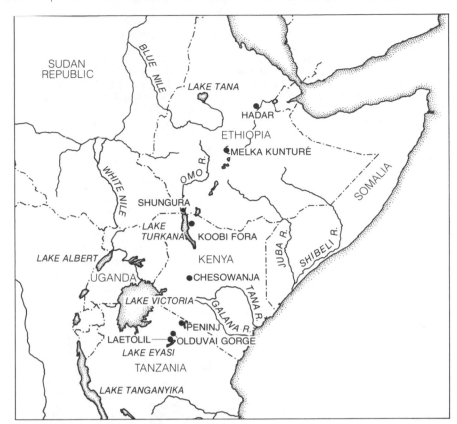

PROMINENT SITES in East Africa include (from north to south) Hadar, Melka Kunturé and Shungura in Ethiopia, the Koobi Fora district to the east of Lake Turkana in Kenya, Chesowanja in Kenya and Peninj, Olduvai Gorge and Laetolil in Tanzania. Dates for clusters of stone tools, some associated with animal bones, uncovered at these sites range from one million years ago (Olduvai Upper Bed II) to 2.5 million (Hadar upper beds). Some sites may be even older.

	OLDUVAI	KOOBI FORA	OMO VALLEY	OTHER
1.0				
1.2	UPPER BED II			PENINJ
	MIDDLE BED II			MELKA KUNTURÉ
1.4		KARARI SITES		CHESOWANJA
	LOWER BED II			
1.6				
	BED I	KBS, HAS		
1.8				
2.0				
2.2			SHUNGURA MEMBER F	
2.4			SHUNGURA MEMBER E	
		?		HADAR UPPER BEDS
2.6				
2.8				
3.0				
3.2				HADAR LOWER BEDS
3.4				
				LAETOLIL
3.6				

YEARS BEFORE PRESENT (MILLIONS)

RELATIVE ANTIQUITY of selected sites in East Africa is indicated in this table. Olduvai Gorge beds I and II range from 1.8 to 1.0 million years in age. The Shungura sites in the Omo Valley are more than two million years old. Two Koobi Fora locales, the hippopotamus/artifact site (HAS) and the Kay Behrensmeyer site (KBS), are at least 1.6 million years old. Initial geological studies of the Koobi Fora sites suggested that they might be 2.5 million years old (*colored line*). Only hominid fossils have been found in the lower beds at Hadar and at Laetolil.

At least one fact is clear. The divergence took place long before the period when the oldest archaeological remains thus far discovered first appear. Archaeology, at least for the present, can make no contribution toward solving the puzzle of the split between ancestral ape and ancestral man.

As for the second puzzle, fossil evidence from East Africa shows that the divergence, regardless of when it took place, had given rise two to three million years ago to populations of smallish two-legged hominids. The puzzle is how to identify the patterns of natural selection that transformed these protohumans into humans. Archaeology has a major contribution to make in elucidating the second puzzle. Excavation of these protohuman sites has revealed evidence suggesting that two million years ago some elements that now distinguish man from apes were already part of a novel adaptive strategy. The indications are that a particularly important part of that strategy was food-sharing.

The archaeological research that has inspired the formulation of new hypotheses concerning human evolution began nearly 20 years ago when Mary Leakey and her husband Louis discovered the fossil skull he named "Zinjanthropus" at Olduvai Gorge in Tanzania. The excavations the Leakeys undertook at the site showed not only that stone tools were present in the same strata that held this fossil and other hominid fossils but also that the discarded artifacts were associated with numerous broken-up animal bones. The Leakeys termed these concentrations of tools and bones "living sites." The work has continued at Olduvai under Mary Leakey's direction, and in 1971 a major monograph was published that has made the Olduvai results available for comparative studies.

Other important opportunities for archaeological research of this kind have come to light in the Gregory Rift Valley, at places such as the Koobi Fora (formerly East Rudolf) region of northern Kenya, at Shungara in the Omo Valley

of southwestern Ethiopia and in the Hadar region of eastern Ethiopia. Current estimates of the age of these sites cover a span of time from about 3.2 million years ago to about 1.2 million.

Since 1970 I have been co-leader with Richard Leakey (the son of Mary and Louis Leakey) of a team working at Koobi Fora, a district that includes the northeastern shore of Lake Turkana (the former Lake Rudolf). Our research on the geology, paleontology and paleoanthropology of the district involves the collaboration of colleagues from the National Museum of Kenya and from many other parts of the world. Work began in 1968 and has had the help and encouragement of the Government of Kenya, the National Science Foundation and the National Geographic Society. Our investigations have yielded archaeological evidence that corroborates and complements the earlier evidence from Olduvai Gorge. The combined data make it possible to see just how helpful archaeology can be in answering

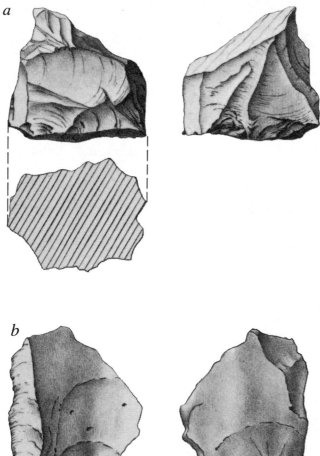

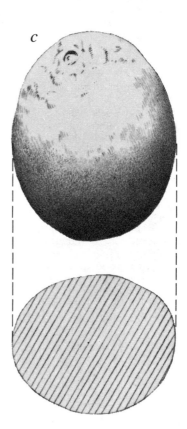

KOOBI FORA ARTIFACTS include four from the HAS assemblage (*left*) and four from the KBS assemblage (*right*). All are shown actual size; the stone is basalt. The HAS core (*a*) shows what is left of a piece of stone after a number of flakes have been struck from it by percussion. The jagged edges produced by flake removal give the core potential usefulness as a tool. The flakes were detached from the core by blows with a hammerstone like the one shown here (*c*). The sharp edges of the flakes, such as the example illustrated (*b*), allow their use as cutting tools. The tiny flake (*d*) is probably an accidental product of the percussion process; the presence of many stone splinters such

questions concerning human evolution.

At Koobi Fora, as at all the other East African sites, deposits of layered sediments, which accumulated long ago in the basins of Rift Valley lakes, are now being eroded by desert rainstorms and transient streams. As the sedimentary beds erode, a sample of the ancient artifacts and fossil bones they contain is exposed at the surface. For a while the exposed material lies on the ground. Eventually, however, the fossil bones are destroyed by weathering or a storm washes away stone and bone alike.

All field reconnaissance in East Africa progresses along essentially similar lines. The field teams search through eroded terrain looking for exposed fossils and artifacts. In places where concentrations of fossil bone or promising archaeological indications appear on the surface the next step is excavation. The digging is done in part to uncover further specimens that are still in place in the layers of sediments and in part to gather exact information about the original stratigraphic location of the surface material. Most important of all, excavation allows the investigators to plot in detail the relative locations of the material that is unearthed. For example, if there are associations among bones and between bones and stones, excavation will reveal these characteristics of the site.

The Types of Sites

The archaeological traces of protohuman life uncovered in this way may exhibit several different configurations. In some ancient layers we have found scatterings of sharp-edged broken stones even though there are no other stones in the sediments. The broken stones come in a range of forms but all are of the kind produced by deliberate percussion, so that we can classify them as undoubted artifacts. Such scatterings of artifacts are often found without bone being present in significant amounts. These I propose to designate sites of Type A.

In some instances a layer of sediment may include both artifacts and animal bones. Such bone-and-artifact occurrences fall into two categories. The first consists of artifacts associated with bones that represent the carcass of a single large animal; these sites are designated Type B. The second consists of artifacts associated with bones representing the remains of several different animal species; these sites are designated Type C.

The discovery of sites with these varied configurations in the sediments at Koobi Fora and Olduvai provides evidence that when the sediments containing them were being deposited some 2.5 to 1.5 million years ago, there was at least one kind of hominid in East Africa that habitually carried objects such as stones from one place to another and made sharp-edged tools by deliberately fracturing the stones it carried with it. How does this archaeological evidence match up with the hominid fossil record? The fossil evidence indicates that

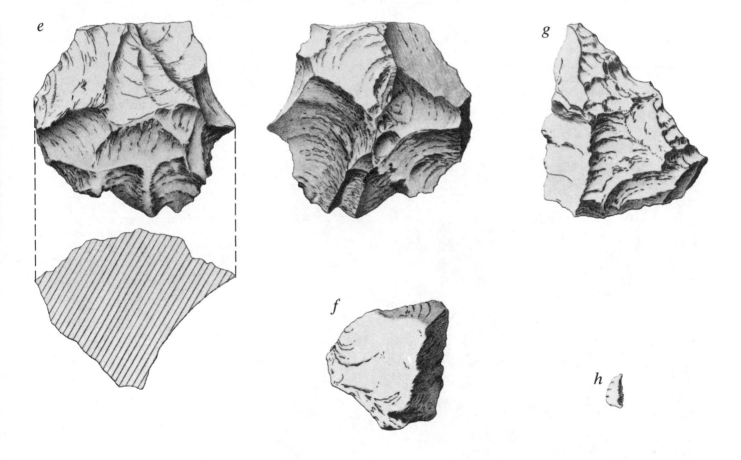

as this one in the HAS tool clusters indicates that the stone tools were made on the spot. At the same time the absence of local unworked stone as potential raw material for tools suggests that the cores were carried to the site by the toolmakers. The artifacts from the second assemblage also include a core (e) that has had many flakes removed by percussion and another small splinter of stone (h). The edges of the two flakes (f, g) are sharp enough to cut meat, hide, sinew or wood. As at the hippopotamus/artifact site, the absence of local raw material for stone tools at the Kay Behrensmeyer site suggests that suitable lumps of lava must have been transported there by the toolmakers.

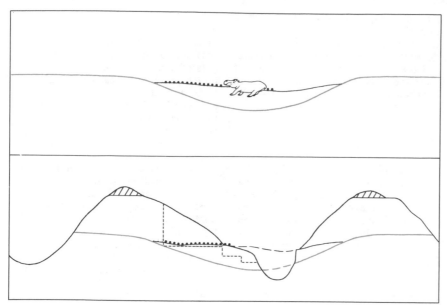

KOOBI FORA LANDSCAPE in the vicinity of the hippopotamus/artifact site consisted of a level floodplain near the margin of a lake (*top section*). Protohuman foragers apparently found the carcass of a hippopotamus lying in a stream-bed hollow and made tools on the spot in order to butcher the carcass. Their actions left a scatter of stone tools among the bones and on the ground nearby. The floodplain was buried under layers of silt and ash and was subsequently eroded (*bottom section*), exposing some bones and tools. Their discovery led to excavation.

two and perhaps three species of bipedal hominids inhabited the area at this time, so that the question arises: Can the species responsible for the archaeological evidence be identified?

For the moment the best working hypothesis seems to be that those hominids that were directly ancestral to modern man were making the stone tools. These are the fossil forms, of early Pleistocene age, classified by most paleontologists as an early species of the genus *Homo*. The question of whether or not contemporaneous hominid species of the genus *Australopithecus* also made tools must be set aside as a challenge to the ingenuity

of future investigators. Here I shall simply discuss what we can discover about the activities of early toolmaking hominids without attempting to identify their taxonomic position (or positions).

Reading the Evidence

As examples of the archaeological evidence indicative of early hominid patterns of subsistence and behavior, consider our findings at two Koobi Fora excavations. The first is a locality catalogued as the hippopotamus/artifact site (HAS) because of the presence of fossilized hippopotamus bones and stone tools.

The site is 15 miles east of Lake Turkana. There in 1969 Richard Leakey discovered an erosion gully cutting into an ancient layer of volcanic ash known as the KBS tuff. (KBS stands for Kay Behrensmeyer site; she, the geologist-paleoecologist of our Koobi Fora research team, first identified the ash layer at a nearby outcrop.) The ash layer is the uppermost part of a sedimentary deposit known to geologists as the Lower Member of the Koobi Fora Formation; here the ash had filled in one of the many dry channels of an ancient delta. Leakey found many bones of a single hippopotamus carcass weathering out of the eroded ash surface, and stone artifacts lay among the bones.

J. W. K. Harris, J. Onyango-Abuje and I supervised an excavation that cut into an outcrop where the adjacent delta sediments had not yet been disturbed by erosion. Our digging revealed that the hippopotamus carcass had originally lain in a depression or puddle within an ancient delta channel. Among the hippopotamus bones and in the adjacent stream bank we recovered 119 chipped stones; most of them were small sharp flakes that, when they are held between the thumb and the fingers, make effective cutting implements. We also recovered chunks of stone with scars showing that flakes had been struck from them by percussion. In Paleolithic tool classification these larger stones fall into the category of core tool or chopper. In addition our digging exposed a rounded river pebble that was battered at both ends; evidently it had been used as a hammer to strike flakes from the stone cores.

The sediments where we found these artifacts contain no stones larger than a pea. Thus it seems clear that the makers of the tools had carried the stones here from somewhere else. The association between the patch of artifacts and the hippopotamus bones further suggests that toolmakers came to the site carrying stones and hammered off the small sharp-edged flakes on the spot in order to cut meat from the hippopotamus carcass. We have no way of telling at present whether the toolmakers themselves killed the animal or only came on it

HAMMERSTONE unearthed at the hippopotamus/artifact site is a six-centimeter basalt pebble; it is shown here being lifted from its position on the ancient ground surface adjacent to the hippopotamus bones. Worn smooth by water action before it caught the eye of a toolmaker some 1.7 million years ago, the pebble is battered at both ends as a result of use as a hammer.

dead. Given the low level of stone technology in evidence, I am inclined to suspect scavenging rather than hunting.

The HAS deposit was formed at least 1.6 million years ago. The archaeological evidence demonstrates that the behavior of some hominids at that time differed from the behavior of modern great apes in that these protohumans not only made cutting tools but also ate meat from the carcasses of large animals. The hippopotamus/artifact site thus provides corroboration for evidence of similar behavior just as long ago obtained from Mary Leakey's excavations at Olduvai Gorge.

This finding does not answer all our questions. Were these protohumans roaming the landscape, foraging and hunting, in the way that a troop of baboons does today? Were they instead hunting like a pride of lions? Or did some other behavioral pattern prevail? Excavation of another bone-and-arti-

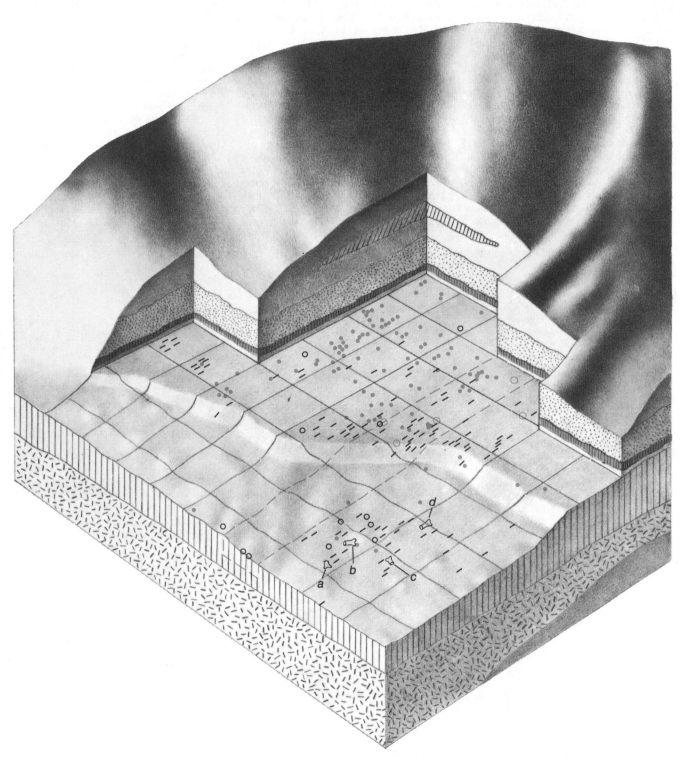

FINDINGS at the hippopotamus/artifact site are shown schematically in this block diagram; squares are one meter to a side. In the foreground are the objects that had been exposed by weathering: hippopotamus limb bones (a–d) and teeth (small open circles), many fragments of bone (short dashes) and a few stone artifacts (colored dots). Trenching (dashed line, color) and hillside excavation over a wide **area exposed an ancient soil surface (color) overlying a deposit of silty tuff. Lying on the ancient surface were stone cores (open circles, color) from which sharp-edged flakes had been struck, more than 100 other stone artifacts and more than 60 additional fragments of teeth and bones. The scatter of tools and broken bones suggests the hypothesis that the toolmakers fed on meat from the hippopotamus.**

fact association, only a kilometer away from the hippopotamus/artifact site, has allowed us to carry our inquiries further.

The second site had been located by Behrensmeyer in 1969. Erosion was uncovering artifacts, together with pieces of broken-up bone, at another outcrop of the same volcanic ash layer that contained the HAS artifacts and bones. With the assistance of John Barthelme of the University of California at Berkeley and others I began to excavate the site. The work soon revealed a scatter of several hundred stone tools in an area 16 meters in diameter. They rested on an ancient ground surface that had been covered by layers of sand and silt. The concentration of artifacts exactly coincided with a scatter of fragmented bones. Enough of them, teeth in particular, were identifiable to demonstrate that parts of the remains of several animal species were present. John M. Harris of the Louis Leakey Memorial Institute in Nairobi recognized, among other

species, hippopotamus, giraffe, pig, porcupine and such bovids as waterbuck, gazelle and what may be either hartebeest or wildebeest. It was this site that was designated KBS. The site obviously represented the second category of bone-and-artifact associations: tools in association with the remains of many different animal species.

Geological evidence collected by A. K. Behrensmeyer of Yale University and others shows that the KBS deposit had accumulated on the sandy bed of a stream that formed part of a small delta. At the time when the toolmakers used the stream bed, water had largely ceased to flow. Such a site was probably favored as a focus of hominid activity for a number of reasons. First, as every beachgoer knows, sand is comfortable to sit and lie on. Second, by scooping a hole of no great depth in the sand of a stream bed one can usually find water. Third, the growth of trees and bushes in the sun-parched floodplains of East Africa is often densest along watercour-

ses, so that shade and plant foods are available in these locations. It may also be that the protohuman toolmakers who left their discards here took shelter from predators by climbing trees and also spent their nights protected in this way.

Much of this is speculative, of course, but we have positive evidence that the objects at the KBS site did accumulate in the shade. The sandy silts that came to cover the discarded implements and fractured bones were deposited so gently that chips of stone small enough to be blown away by the wind were not disturbed. In the same silts are the impressions of many tree leaves. The species of tree has not yet been formally identified, but Jan Gilette of the Kenya National Herbarium notes that the impressions closely resemble the leaves of African wild fig trees.

Carrying Stones and Meat

As at the hippopotamus/artifact site, we have established the fact that stones

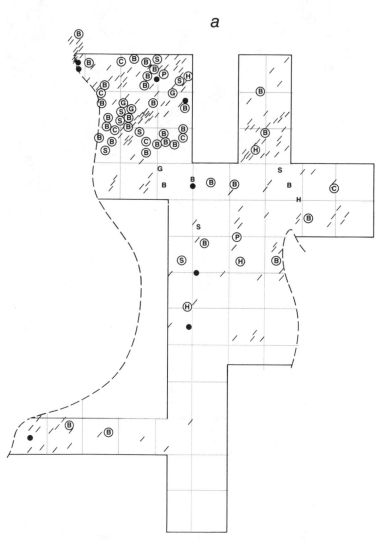
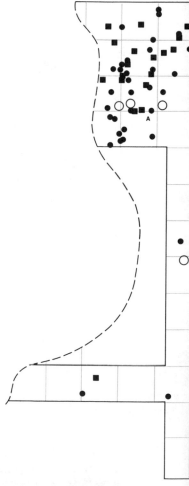

BONES AND STONE TOOLS were also found in abundance at the Kay Behrensmeyer site. As the plot of bone distribution (*a*) shows, the animal remains represent many different species. These are identified by capital letters; if the find was a tooth the letter is circled. Most are small to medium-sized bovids, such as gazelle, waterbuck and hartebeest (*B*). The remains of crocodile (*C*), giraffe (*G*), hippopotamus (*H*), porcupine (*P*) and extinct species of pig (*S*) were also present. Dots and dashes locate unidentified teeth and bone fragments respectively.

larger than the size of a pea do not occur naturally closer to the Kay Behrensmeyer site than a distance of three kilometers. Thus we know that the stones we found at the site must have been carried at least that far. With the help of Frank Fitch and Ron Watkins of the University of London we are searching for the specific sources.

It does not seem likely that all the animals of the different species represented among the KBS bones could have been killed in a short interval of time at this one place. Both considerations encourage the advancement of a tentative hypothesis: Like the stones, the bones were carried in, presumably while there was still meat on them.

If this hypothesis can be accepted, the Kay Behrensmeyer site provides very early evidence for the transport of food as a protohuman attribute. Today the carrying of food strikes us as being commonplace, but as Sherwood Washburn of the University of California at Berkeley observed some years ago such an

action would strike a living ape as being novel and peculiar behavior indeed. In short, if the hypothesis can be accepted, it suggests that by the time the KBS deposit was laid down various fundamental shifts had begun to take place in hominid social and ecological arrangements.

It should be noted that other early sites in this category are known in East Africa, so that the Kay Behrensmeyer site is by no means unique. A number of such sites have been excavated at Olduvai Gorge and reported by Mary Leakey. Of these the best preserved is the "Zinjanthropus" site of Olduvai Bed I, which is about 1.7 million years old. Here too a dense patch of discarded artifacts coincides with a concentration of broken-up bones.

There is an even larger number of Type A sites (where concentrations of artifacts are found but bones are virtually or entirely absent). Some are at Koobi Fora; others are in the Omo Valley, where Harry V. Merrick of Yale Uni-

versity and Jean Chavaillon of the French National Center for Scientific Research (CNRS) have recently uncovered sites of this kind in members E and F of the Shungura Formation. The Omo sites represent the oldest securely dated artifact concentrations so far reported anywhere in the world; the tools were deposited some two million years ago.

One of the Olduvai sites in this category seems to have been a "factory": a quarry where chert, an excellent tool material, was readily available for flaking. The other tool concentrations, with very few associated bones or none at all, may be interpreted as foci of hominid activity where for one reason or another large quantities of meat were not carried in. Until it is possible to distinguish between sites where bone was never present and sites where the bones have simply vanished because of such factors as decay, however, these deposits will remain difficult to interpret in terms of subsistence ecology.

What, in summary, do these East Af-

b

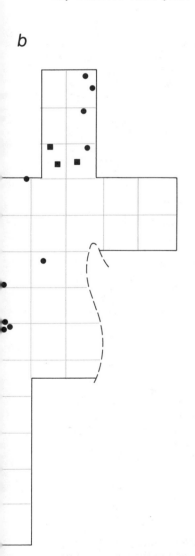

c

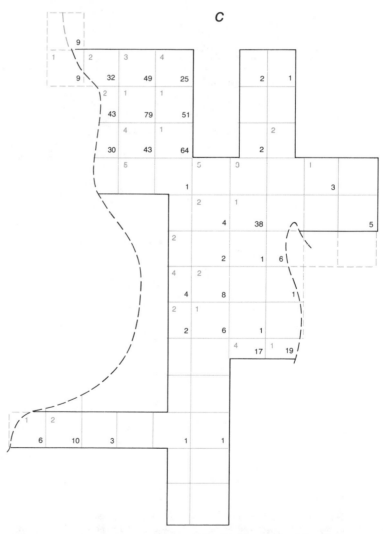

The plot of artifact distribution (*b*) shows that three of four stone cores (*open circles*), most waste stone (*squares*) and flakes and fragments of flakes (*dots*) were found in 12 adjacent squares. Also found here was an unworked stone (*A*) that, like the cores, must have been carried to the site from a distance. Plotting of all tools and bones unearthed at the site was not attempted. Numbers in grid squares (*c*) show how many flakes and bits of waste stone (*color*) and fragments of bone (*black*) were recorded without exact plotting in each square.

rican archaeological studies teach us about the evolution of human behavior? For one thing they provide unambiguous evidence that two million years ago some hominids in this part of Africa were carrying things around, for example stones. The same hominids were also making simple but effective cutting tools of stone and were at times active in the vicinity of large animal carcasses, presumably in order to get meat. The studies strongly suggest that the hominids carried animal bones (and meat) around and concentrated this portable food supply at certain places.

Model Strategies

These archaeological facts and indications allow the construction of a theoretical model that shows how at least some aspects of early hominid social existence may have been organized. Critical to the validity of the model is the inference that the various clusters of remains we have uncovered reflect social and economic nodes in the lives of the toolmakers who left behind these ancient patches of litter. Because of the evidence suggestive of the transport of food to certain focal points, the first question that the model must confront is why early hominid social groups departed from the norm among living subhuman primates, whose social groups feed as they range. To put it another way, what ecological and evolutionary advantages are there in postponing some food consumption and transporting the food?

Several possible answers to this question have been advanced. For example, Adrienne Zihlman and Nancy Tanner of the University of California at Santa Cruz suggest that when the protohumans acquired edible plants out on the open grasslands, away from the shelter of trees, it would have been advantageous for them to seize the plant products quickly and withdraw to places shel-

tered from menacing predators. Others have proposed that when the early hominids foraged, they left their young behind at "nest" or "den" sites (in the manner of birds, wild dogs and hyenas) and returned to these locales at intervals, bringing food with them to help feed and wean the young.

If we look to the recorded data concerning primitive human societies, a third possibility arises. Among extant and recently extinct primitive human societies the transport of food is associated with a division of labor. The society is divided by age and sex into classes that characteristically make different contributions to the total food supply. One significant result of such a division is an increase in the variety of foodstuffs consumed by the group. To generalize on the basis of many different ethnographic reports, the adult females of the society contribute the majority of the "gathered" foods; such foods are mainly plant products but may include shellfish, amphibians and small reptiles, eggs, insects and the like. The adult males usually, although not invariably, contribute most of the "hunted" foodstuffs: the flesh of mammals, fishes, birds and so forth. Characteristically the males and females range in separate groups and each sex eventually brings back to a home base at least the surplus of its foraging.

Could this simple mechanism, a division of the subsistence effort, have initiated food-carrying by early hominids? One cannot dismiss out of hand the models that suggest safety from competitors or the feeding of nesting young as the initiating mechanisms for food-carrying. Nevertheless, neither model seems to me as plausible as one that has division of labor as the primary initiating mechanism. Even if no other argument favored the model, we know for a fact that somewhere along the line in the evolution of human behavior two patterns became established: food-sharing and a division of labor. If we include both patterns in our model of early hominid society, we will at least be parsimonious.

Other arguments can be advanced in favor of an early development of a division of labor. For example, the East African evidence shows that the protohuman toolmakers consumed meat from a far greater range of species and sizes of animals than are eaten by such living primates as the chimpanzee and the baboon. Among recent human hunter-gatherers the existence of a division of labor seems clearly related to the females being encumbered with children, a handicap that bars them from hunting or scavenging, activities that require speed afoot or long-range mobility. For the protohumans too the incorporation of meat in the diet in significant quantities may well have been a key factor in the development not only of a division

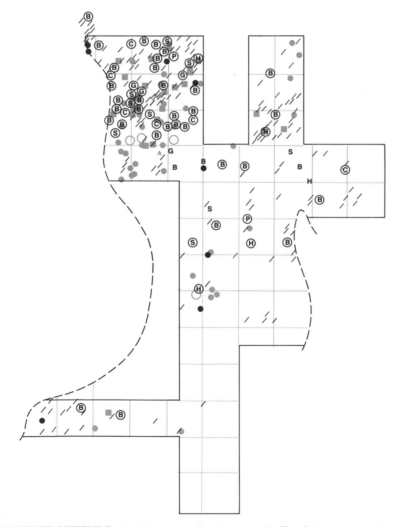

CLUSTERED MIXTURE of artifacts and animal bones at the Kay Behrensmeyer site is evident when the stone (*color*) and bone (*black*) plots are superposed. Combinations of this kind are sometimes produced by stream action, but such is not likely to be the case here, as is attested by the preservation of leaf impressions and other readily washed-away debris such as fine splinters of stone. It appears instead that the protohumans who made and discarded their tools here were also responsible for the bone accumulation because they met here to share their food.

of labor but also of the organization of movements around a home base and the transport and sharing of food.

The model I propose for testing visualizes food-sharing as the behavior central to a novel complex of adaptations that included as critical components hunting and/or scavenging, gathering and carrying. Speaking metaphorically, food-sharing provides the model with a kind of central platform. The adaptive system I visualize, however, could only have functioned through the use of tools and other equipment. For example, without the aid of a carrying device primates such as ourselves or our ancestors could not have transported from the field to the home base a sufficient amount of plant food to be worth sharing. An object as uncomplicated as a bark tray would have served the purpose, but some such item of equipment would have been mandatory. In fact, Richard Borshay Lee of the University of Toronto has suggested that a carrying device was the basic invention that made human evolution possible.

What about stone tools? Our ancestors, like ourselves, could probably break up the body of a small animal, as chimpanzees do, with nothing but their hands and teeth. It is hard to visualize them or us, however, eating the meat of an elephant, a hippopotamus or some other large mammal without the aid of a cutting implement. As the archaeological evidence demonstrates abundantly,

the protohumans of East Africa not only knew how to produce such stone flakes by percussion but also found them so useful that they carried the raw materials needed to make the implements with them from place to place. Thus whereas the existence of a carrying device required by the model remains hypothetical as far as archaeological evidence is concerned, the fact that tools were used and carried about is amply attested to.

In this connection it should be stressed that the archaeological evidence is also silent with regard to protohuman consumption of plant foods. Both the morphology and the patterns of wear observable on hominid teeth suggest such a plant component in the diet, and so does the weight of comparative data on subsistence patterns among living nonhuman primates and among nonfarming human societies. Nevertheless, if positive evidence is to be found, we shall have to sharpen our ingenuity, perhaps by turning to organic geochemical analyses. It is clear that as long as we do not correct for the imbalance created by the durability of bone as compared with that of plant residues, studies of human evolution will tend to have a male bias!

As far as the model is concerned the key question is not whether collectable foods—fruits, nuts, tubers, greens and even insects—were eaten. It is whether these protohumans carried such foods about. Lacking any evidence for the

consumption of plant foods, I shall fall back on the argument that the system I visualize would have worked best if the mobile hunter-scavenger contribution of meat to the social group was balanced by the gatherer-carrier collection of high-grade plant foods. What is certain is that at some time during the past several million years just such a division of labor came to be a standard kind of behavior among the ancestors of modern man.

A final cautionary word about the model: The reader may have noted that I have been careful about the use of the words "hunter" and "hunting." This is because we cannot judge how much of the meat taken by the protohumans of East Africa came from opportunistic scavenging and how much was obtained by hunting. It is reasonable to assume that the carcasses of animals killed by carnivores and those of animals that had otherwise died or been disabled would always have provided active scavengers a certain amount of meat. For the present it seems less reasonable to assume that protohumans, armed primitively if at all, would be particularly effective hunters. Attempts are now under way, notably by Elizabeth Vrba of South Africa, to distinguish between assemblages of bones attributable to scavenging and assemblages attributable to hunting, but no findings from East Africa are yet available. For the present I am inclined to accept the verdict of J. Desmond

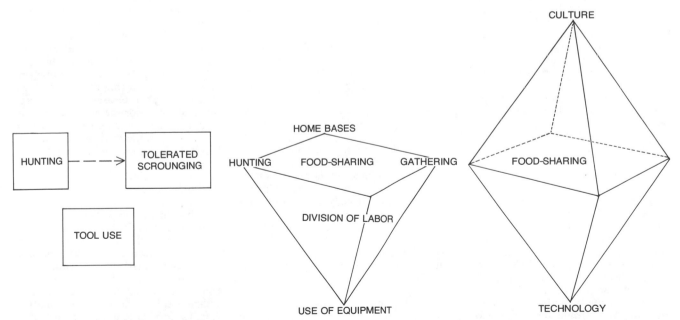

BEHAVIOR PATTERNS that differ in degree of organization are contrasted in these diagrams. Living great apes, exemplified here by the chimpanzee, exhibit behavior patterns that became important in human evolution but the patterns (*left*) exist largely as isolated elements. Hunting occurs on a small scale but leads only to "tolerated scrounging" rather than active food-sharing; similarly, tools are used but tool use is not integrated with hunting or scrounging. The author's model (*center*) integrates these three behavior patterns and others into a coherent structure. Food-sharing is seen as a central structural element, incorporating the provision of both animal and plant foods, the organization of a home base and a division of labor. Supporting the integrated structure is a necessary infrastructure of tool and equipment manufacture; for example, without devices for carrying foodstuffs there could not be a division of labor and organized food-sharing. In modern human societies (*right*) the food-sharing structure has undergone socioeconomic elaboration. Its infrastructure now incorporates all of technology, and a matching superstructure has arisen to incorporate other elements of what is collectively called culture.

Clark of the University of California at Berkeley and Lewis R. Binford of the University of New Mexico. In their view the earliest meat-eaters might have obtained the flesh of animals weighing up to 30 kilograms by deliberate hunting, but the flesh of larger animals was probably available only through scavenging.

Tools as Testimony

Of course, the adaptive model I have advanced here reflects only a working hypothesis and not established fact. Nevertheless, there is sufficient evidence in its favor to justify looking further at its possible implications for the course of human evolution. For example, the model clearly implies that early toolmaking hominids displayed certain patterns of behavior that, among the patterns of behavior of all primates, uniquely characterize our own species and set it apart from its closest living relatives, the great apes. Does this mean that the toolmaking hominids of 1.5 to two million years ago were in fact "human"?

I would surmise that it does not, and I have been at pains to characterize these East African pioneers as protohumans. In summarizing the contrasts between living men and living apes I put high on the list language and the cultural phenomena that are dependent on it. We have no direct means of learning whether or not any of these early hominids had language. It is my suspicion, however, that the principal evolutionary change in the hominid line leading to full humanity over the past two million years has been the great expansion of language and communication abilities, together with the cognitive and cultural capabilities integrally related to language. What is the evidence in support of this surmise?

One humble indicator of expanding mental capacities is the series of changes that appears in the most durable material record available to us: the stone tools. The earlier tools from the period under consideration here seem to me to show a simple and opportunistic range of forms that reflect no more than an uncomplicated empirical grasp of one skill: how to fracture stone by percussion in such a way as to obtain fragments with sharp edges. At that stage of toolmaking the maker imposed a minimum of culturally dictated forms on his artifacts. Stone tools as simple as these perform perfectly well the basic functions that support progress in the direction of becoming human, for example the shaping of a digging stick, a spear and a bark tray, or the butchering of an animal carcass.

The fact is that exactly such simple stone tools have been made and used ever since their first invention, right down to the present day. Archaeology also shows, however, that over the past several hundred thousand years some assemblages of stone tools began to reflect a greater cultural complexity on the part of their makers. The complexity is first shown in the imposition of more arbitrary tool forms; these changes were followed by increases in the number of such forms. There is a marked contrast between the pure opportunism apparent in the shapes of the earliest stone tools and the orderly array of forms that appear later in the Old Stone Age when each form is represented by numerous standardized examples in each assemblage of tools. The contrast strongly suggests that the first toolmakers lacked the highly developed mental and cultural abilities of more recent humans.

The evidence of the hominid fossils and the evidence of the artifacts together suggest that these early artisans were nonhuman hominids. I imagine that if we had a time machine and could visit a place such as the Kay Behrensmeyer site at the time of its original occupation, we would find hominids that were living in social groups much like those of other higher primates. The differences would be apparent only after prolonged observation. Perhaps at the start of each day we would observe a group splitting up as some of its members went off in one direction and some in another. All these subgroups would very probably feed intermittently as they moved about and encountered ubiquitous low-grade plant foods such as berries, but we might well observe that some of the higher-grade materials—large tubers or the haunch of a scavenged carcass—were being reserved for group consumption when the foraging parties reconvened at their starting point.

To the observer in the time machine behavior of this kind, taken in context with the early hominids' practice of making tools and equipment, would seem familiarly "human." If, as I suppose, the hominids under observation communicated only as chimpanzees do or perhaps by means of very rudimentary protolinguistic signals, then the observer might feel he was witnessing the activities of some kind of fascinating bipedal ape. When one is relying on archaeology to reconstruct protohuman life, one must strongly resist the temptation to project too much of ourselves into the past. As Jane B. Lancaster of the University of Oklahoma has pointed out, the hominid life systems of two million years ago have no living counterparts.

Social Advances

My model of early hominid adaptation can do more than indicate that the first toolmakers were culturally protohuman. It can also help to explain the dynamics of certain significant advances in the long course of mankind's development. For example, one can imagine that a hominid social organization involving some division of labor and a degree of food-sharing might well have been able to function even if it had communicative abilities little more advanced than those of living chimpanzees. In such a simple subsistence system, however, any group with members that were able not only to exchange food but also to exchange information would have gained a critical selective advantage over all the rest. Such a group's gatherers could report on scavenging or hunting opportunities they had observed, and its hunters could tell the gatherers about any plant foods they had encountered.

By the same token the fine adjustment of social relations, always a matter of importance among primates, becomes doubly important in a social system that involves food exchange. Language serves in modern human societies not only for the exchange of information but also as an instrument for social adjustment and even for the exchange of misinformation.

Food-sharing and the kinds of behavior associated with it probably played an important part in the development of systems of reciprocal social obligations that characterize all human societies we know about. Anthropological research shows that each human being in a group is ordinarily linked to many other members of the group by ties that are both social and economic. The French anthropologist Marcel Mauss, in a classic essay, "The Gift," published in 1925, showed that social ties are usually reciprocal in the sense that whereas benefits from a relationship may initially pass in only one direction, there is an expectation of a future return of help in time of need. The formation and management of such ties calls for an ability to calculate complex chains of contingencies that reach far into the future. After food-sharing had become a part of protohuman behavior the need for such an ability to plan and calculate must have provided an important part of the biological basis for the evolution of the human intellect.

The model may also help explain the development of human marriage arrangements. It assumes that in early protohuman populations the males and females divided subsistence labor between them so that each sex was preferentially tapping a different kind of food resource and then sharing within a social group some of what had been obtained. In such circumstances a mating system that involved at least one male in "family" food procurement on behalf of each child-rearing female in the group would have a clear selective advantage over, for example, the chimpanzees' pattern of opportunistic relations between the sexes.

I have emphasized food-sharing as a principle that is central to an understanding of human evolution over the past two million years or so. I have also set forth archaeological evidence that food-sharing was an established kind of behavior among early protohumans. The notion is far from novel; it is implicit in many philosophical speculations and in many writings on paleoanthropology. What is novel is that I have undertaken to make the hypothesis explicit so that it can be tested and revised.

Accounting for Evolution

Thus the food-sharing hypothesis now joins other hypotheses that have been put forward to account for the course of human evolution. Each of these hypotheses tends to maintain that one or another innovation in protohuman behavior was the critical driving force of change. For example, the argument has been advanced that tools were the "prime movers." Here the underlying implication is that in each successive generation the more capable individuals made better tools and thereby gained advantages that favored the transmission of their genes through natural selection; it is supposed that these greater capabilities would later be applied in aspects of life other than technology. Another hypothesis regards hunting as being the driving force. Here the argument is that hunting requires intelligence, cunning, skilled neuromuscular coordination and, in the case of group hunting, cooperation. Among other suggested prime movers are such practices as carrying and gathering.

If we compare the food-sharing explanation with these alternative explanations we see that in fact food-sharing incorporates many aspects of each of the others. It will also be seen that in the food-sharing model the isolated elements are treated as being integral parts of a complex, flexible system. The model itself is probably an oversimplified version of what actually happened, but it seems sufficiently realistic to be worthy of testing through further archaeological and paleontological research.

Lastly, the food-sharing model can be seen to have interconnections with the physical implications of fossil hominid anatomy. For example, a prerequisite of food-sharing is the ability to carry things. This ability in turn is greatly facilitated by a habitual two-legged posture. As Gordon W. Hewes of the University of Colorado has pointed out, an important part of the initial evolutionary divergence of hominids from their primate relatives may have been the propensity and the ability to carry things about. To me it seems equally plausible that the physical selection pressures that promoted an increase in the size of the protohuman brain, thereby surely enhancing the hominid capacity for communication, are a consequence of the shift from individual foraging to food-sharing some two million years ago.

II

HUNTER-GATHERERS

II

HUNTER-GATHERERS

INTRODUCTION

During the first 2.5 million years of the Ice Age (known to geologists as the Pleistocene), the world population of humans was extremely small, being confined for the most part to tropical regions. *Homo erectus* had evolved at least a million years before and had appeared in several parts of the Old World half a million years later. Hunters and gatherers, they could adapt to a far wider range of environmental conditions than their predecessors. *Homo erectus* possessed a larger brain than earlier hominids and stood fully upright, with limbs and hipbones virtually identical to those of modern people. The skull, however, was flatter, with a retreating forehead and prognathous (jutting out) face. Many people believe that *Homo erectus* had vastly improved communication skills, including fully articulate speech. Certainly, traces of fire found in East Africa have been dated as early as 1.5 million years ago, just about the time that the new humans first appeared. They had more sophisticated tools, including fine "handaxes," multipurpose tools probably used for butchering animals and digging up roots as well as for woodworking. These artifacts have been found not only in tropical Africa and India, but in the temperate latitudes of western Europe and China and as far north as the southern U.S.S.R.

Henry de Lumley's excavations at Terra Amata near Nice in the south of France, described in his article "A Paleolithic Camp at Nice," were remarkable for the complete information they yielded on the inhabitants of a temporary camp by the seashore. The hearths and shelters of the hunters could be reconstructed from the archaeological evidence; we even know the time of year the settlement was occupied. Terra Amata is probably typical of many *Homo erectus* campsites: occupied for a few weeks, located in an area whose food supplies were abundant at certain times of the year, it was a locality visited at regular intervals by generations of hunters.

By 100,000 years ago, *Homo erectus* populations had adapted successfully to a wide range of Old World climates and were not afraid of tackling even the biggest game. Memorable excavations at Ambrona-Torralba in Spain have revealed kill sites where several bands of hunters appear to have driven a herd of elephants into a swamp, then butchered parts of the huge carcasses at leisure.

The Neanderthals

The modern world boasts a remarkable diversity of human populations, with distinctive cultures, adaptations, and physical characteristics. Although the concept of different human "races" has been around for at least a century, in reality all humans belong within the same family. The present distribution of world population results in part from massive resettlements in the past 500 years and also from population movements that took place many thousands of years ago, some of them as long ago as 50,000 years before Christ.

We do not have even a rough idea of when the first modern humans appeared (there are several world prehistories that summarize the evidence). But sometime around 150,000 years ago, one group of *Homo sapiens,* the Neanderthals, began to evolve. By 75,000 years ago, *Homo sapiens neanderthalensis* was flourishing from western Europe to central Asia. The Neanderthalers came to light in West Germany in 1856 and were soon recognized as early humans. At first archaeologists depicted them as shambling, brutish primitives, with a short life expectancy and limited hunting skills. Eric Trinkaus and William W. Howells in "The Neanderthals" summarize what we know about these early *Homo sapiens* today. They consider the Neanderthals to be a subspecies of *Homo sapiens,* people with fairly low skulls and prominent brow ridges that show their probable ancestry in *Homo erectus.* Their noses and teeth were further forward than ours, their bodies bulkily built, with massive limbs and great muscular power. The Neanderthalers, competent hunters of large and small game, adapted successfully to the arctic climate of western Europe 70,000 years ago. They used much more complex and more specialized toolkits that the handaxes of *Homo erectus.* Generations of cartoonists have taken traditional views of Neanderthalers as the models for their skin-clad cave people. The Neanderthalers may indeed have lived in caves and worn skins, but it is certain that many bands adapted successfully· to a wide range of conditions in the open. They were also the earliest humans to bury their dead and perhaps to believe in a life after death, as there is some evidence that they did.

Modern Humanity: The Birth of Art

After about 60,000 years, somewhere around 45,000 to 40,000 years ago, anatomically modern people replaced the Neanderthals in the Near East. The same process occurred in western Europe slightly later, perhaps around 35,000 years ago. The changeover everywhere was a rapid one, and is still unexplained. Did the new humans spread from the Near East to new areas within a mere 5000 years? What cultural or adaptive advantages did they enjoy? Did certain societies reach some threshold in the evolution of their sociocultural systems that, once crossed, had a significant influence on the biological evolution of the Neanderthals? We simply do not know at this stage in research.

Certainly, the Neanderthals' successors developed much more sophisticated ways of working stone and bone. They manufactured highly standardized blade tools by striking blanks off carefully shaped stone cores with the aid of sharp punches; stone scrapers, grazing tools, knives, even tiny stone barbs mounted in bone and wood points, are evidence of a technological revolution that produced many specialized artifacts designed for highly specific purposes. These included bows and arrows, spear throwers, and throwing sticks. Some groups, like the reindeer hunters of southwestern France, manufactured fine harpoons, points, and sinew processors from bone and antler. Many bands now lived in much more elaborate shelters, probably used boats, and developed new social institutions that formed part of a sophisticatd, deeply symbolic ritual life. Some people began to specialize in fishing and started to eat shellfish. Others migrated across deep water to Australia, settled in the Americas and in the Arctic for the first time. Lively art traditions and ever more sophisticated speech and symbolism came into being. All this happened in less than one percent of the time it took for humanity to evolve from its very beginnings up to the time of the Neanderthals.

The hunter-gatherers of southwestern France were among the first people we know about to develop their own artistic traditions; they engraved and painted on the walls of caves or rockshelters and carved on small pieces of bone or reindeer antler. This art was first identified in the mid-nineteenth century, but the authenticity of the cave paintings and engravings remained in doubt until French scientists became convinced of the antiquity of the art upon finding long-sealed caves and comparing the style of the wall art they contained with engraved artifacts found in occupation levels in painted rockshelters. Now hundreds of painted and engraved sites are known in southwestern France and northern Spain. The most famous paintings are those from Altamira and Lascaux, where, along the walls of long-abandoned caverns, bison, wild horses, large wild oxen, and stags dance with a sense of life and movement that delights the eye.

Arlette Leroi-Gourhan's "The Archaeology of Lascaux Cave" describes not only the discovery of the site and its remarkable paintings, but 1500 little known engravings found on its walls. Recent researches have established that Lascaux served as a painted shrine for only a few centuries, in "early Magdalenian" times, around 15,000 BC. The excavators have not only dated the paintings, but have recovered traces of scaffolding used by the painters and even the remains of the meals they ate as they decorated the walls. This article shows how modern analytical methods reveal the painting techniques of the artists including the ways in which they mixed their paints.

Separated as we are from these artists by more than 12,000 years, it is impossible for us to comprehend the full significance of their art. No one denies that there was a gradual movement toward greater realism through the millennia, but the details of stylistic change, worked out by close scrutiny of superimpositions of different paintings and by statistical analysis of the clusters of drawings and engravings, remain highly controversial. There are several chronological benchmarks for this art: the first styles evolved after 17,000 BC and it vanished completely after 9000 BC, as ice sheets retreated and the hunting cultures of western Europe became impoverished and more specialized. Both cave paintings and more portable art pieces reveal sophisticated hunting societies, which prized beautifully decorated artifacts and enjoyed a rich symbolism and deep familiarity with the world in which they flourished. Many authorities, Leroi-Gourhan among them, believe that the art had some magico-religious significance, connected with the seasons of game and the chase, an expression of a world view that organized the hunter's life. To judge from Australian aboriginal art, some of the ritual and symbolism connected with the paintings and engravings must have been both elaborate and highly abstract, so much so that we are unlikely ever to recover the details.

Many modern hunter-gatherer groups use ritual and art to give meaning to their existence. Many anthropologists have shown how people manipulate visual forms as an integral part of their daily life. Art, with its symmetry and other principles, underlies every aspect of daily life from social relationships to house architecture and village planning. Margaret Conkey and others have argued that Stone Age art shows obvious continuities between animal and human life and the social world. The artists created their pictures and designs as deliberate symbolic depictions of these continuities. Every fragment of antler, every smooth or contoured area of rock face, was chosen deliberately to paint or engrave a specific animal or geometric form. The study of such choices can provide clues to the significance of the world's earliest artistic traditions.

San and Australians

Many details of the peopling of the world remain unexplained and unexplored, for archaeological research in Africa and Asia has hardly begun.

Sub-Saharan Africa was rich in game and wild vegetable foods, a paradise for the hunter-gatherer. For much of the Ice Age the Sahara Desert was open grassland studded with shallow lakes, a fine homeland for hunters, who left their tools by their shores. By 50,000 years ago, people were living in the dense rain forests of Zaire, using crude woodworking tools and subsisting off the rich vegetable resources of the perennially moist forest. Their neighbors settled throughout the open savannahs and deserts that stretched southwards from the Sudan to the Cape of Good Hope. The ancestors of the modern San (Bushman) hunter-gatherers of the Kalahari Desert in southern Africa were flourishing in East and southern Africa at least 10,000 years ago. Their descendants have left us priceless archives of rock paintings that depict the full richness of their existence in the abundant enviornment of the savannah. We can see them hunting antelope, stalking ostrich in disguise, gathering honey, and seated around their camp fires.

This hunters' paradise was disrupted about 2000 years ago by the arrival of farming peoples, who usurped the best farmland and grazing grounds. The San were forced to come to terms with the newcomers, or to withdraw into marginal areas, where cattle could not graze and cultivation was impracticable. It was in these marginal areas that hunter-gatherers survived until modern times, living descendants of prehistoric societies whose ancestry lies far back in prehistoric times. These peoples have provided a rich source of ethnographic analogy for the archaeologist studying their prehistoric relatives.

The hunter-gatherer way of life survives in Asia, too, in the forests of the southeast, and especially in Australia. In 1774, a French explorer named Marion de Fresne anchored off a sandy beach in southern Tasmania. As his boat landed, a band of aborigines walked out of the trees to greet him. The French seamen were the first strangers the Tasmanians had seen in the 8000 years since their homeland was isolated from mainland Australia by the rising waters of the Bass Strait at the end of the Ice Age. Scientists were astounded at the simplicity of Tasmanian culture. The aborigines possessed only some 24 artifacts, mainly spears and simple digging sticks. They lived off shellfish and wild vegetable foods for the most part, moving around within their territory on a regular seasonal round. The Tasmanians were perceived as the most primitive people on earth, a true relic of the Stone Age. They did not even possess the dog, a domestic animal used by their Australian relatives on the mainland.

While the Tasmanians were driven into extinction within seventy years of European colonization, the Australian aborigines have been somewhat more thoroughly studied before assimilation (Figure 15). The latest archaeological researches reveal that *Homo sapiens* had crossed from Southeast Asia to Australia by at least 32,000 years ago, perhaps much earlier. Except for the introduction of the dog and some minor technological innovations, including the boomerang (a throwing stick), the Australians flourished in complete isolation until European contact in the eighteenth century AD, enabling us to study in considerable detail the dynamics of the way of life that flourished in the Stone Age.

Homo sapiens adapted not only to tropical latitudes, but to the extremes of arctic climate as well. No one knows when humans first settled on the chilly plains of eastern Europe and Siberia, but we can be sure that some Neanderthal bands ventured into this challenging environment well before 50,000 years ago. Their successors adapted successfully to a pattern of life based on the seasonal hunting of big game. The steppe country of the Ukraine supported a rich and varied fauna, including reindeer, wild horse, and bison. Although the hunters exploited a variety of game, they relied on the extinct woolly elephant, the mammoth, for construction materials for their large shelters. The limb bones, tusks, and other carefully selected bones were used for this purpose. The people clothed themselves in the skins

Figure 15   An Australian aborigine depicted by an artist on the Baudin expedition that visited Australia in 1803. Studies of modern Australian bands have provided abundant analogies for interpreting the archaeological record. [From F. Peron, 1803.]

of wolves, arctic foxes, and other animals.

They not only adapted successfully to environmental extremes, but may have developed new social structures to allow the integration of larger, denser populations. Such social innovations would have facilitated intergroup cooperation in the hunting of large mammals, with such formidable beasts as the Ice Age mammoth. The same new social structures may have also encouraged greater intergroup food sharing as a means of tiding people over lean months and temporary local shortages. In areas like the Ukraine, cooperation both in the hunt and in the drying and storage of food may have been indispensable to hunter-gatherers living in an environment of seasonal extremes inhabited by big game with marked seasonal migration patterns.

The First Americans

As long ago as 1856 a Massachusetts archaeologist named Samuel Haven hypothesized that the first humans to settle in the Americas originated in Asia and crossed into the New World via the Bering Strait. Most archaeologists now agree that he was right, and that the first Americans traversed the strait sometime after the emergence of *Homo sapiens* in the Old World. Despite claims to the contrary, no one has yet discovered any indisputable traces of either *Australopithecus, Homo erectus,* or of the Neanderthals—or of their artifacts—in the Americas. Until very recently, the consensus of scientific opinion placed the earliest human settlement at no earlier than about 10,000 BC, largely because few earlier discoveries held scientific water. The search for the earliest Americans is complicated not only by emotion and irresponsible theorizing, but by the sheer difficulty of finding either artifacts and food remains or human fossils. Much of the evidence for the first Americans consists of little more than scatters of stone tools, many of them so simple and undiagnostic that they could have been made by later peoples as well.

Another problem, that of the Bering Land Bridge, is geological. Everyone agrees that the first Americans crossed the Bering Strait during the last great cold snap of the Ice Age, probably at a time when the world's sea levels were locked up in great ice sheets. The low sea levels left much of the strait a flat, swampy plain joining Siberia and Alaska and exposed coastal plains right down the West Coast (and elsewhere of course). The land bridge was dry land around 45,000 years ago, and again for about 15,000 years after 25,000 BP (before present). Theoretically, hunter-gatherers were able to cross dry-shod during these periods. It seems certain that they arrived as early as 20,000 years ago, for a few archaeological sites in eastern North America, Mexico, and highland Peru have yielded radiocarbon dates in that chronological vicinity. Claims for even earlier settlement are far harder to substantiate. The Old Crow site in the Yukon is said to have yielded some worked bones radiocarbon-dated to about 28,000 BC, but even this claim is disputed. As archaeologist Richard Morlan has said, looking for the first Americans is "like looking for a needle in a haystack (and a frozen one at that)!"

The earliest well-attested American Indian settlement occurs after about 16,000 years ago, documented by artifacts so distinctive that they bear no resemblance to any possibly ancestral tools from Asia. The distinctive features of these artifacts may result from isolation that occurred at a time after a much earlier, and as yet poorly documented, first settlement. Toward the end of the Ice Age, the high plains area east of the Rockies supported a browsing and grazing mammalian fauna, which provided subsistence for a large number of hunter-gatherers. Twelve thousand years ago, the plains supported herds of mammoths, bison, camels, and horses. Big-game hunting has long been synonymous with Plains Indians in North America. Mass game drives, enormous bison herds, galloping Indian braves thundering across the plains—all these are familiar phenomena on the movie screen. The first widespread big-game hunting coincides with the appearance of "Paleo-Indian" hunting bands on the Great Plains somewhere before 10,000 BP. Paleo-Indian sites have yielded enormous numbers of carefully flaked projectile heads, a favorite target of artifact collectors.

In a few localities, such as the Olsen-Chubbock site described by Joe Ben Wheat in his article "A Paleo-Indian Bison Kill," these projectile heads have been found in association with the skeletons of bison herds stampeded from narrow arroyos (gullies) to their death. This wasteful destruction of game herds far in excess of meat requirements was undoubtedly a factor in the extinction of large Pleistocene mammals in the Americas. Joe Ben Wheat's account of the Colorado bison kills gives many details of Paleo-Indian hunting and butchery techniques 8000 years ago. He describes in such detail how they hunted, butchered, cooked, and carried meat that the atmosphere of the hunt comes to life in vivid detail. He even calculates the direction of the wind on the day of the hunt.

As the world climate warmed up at the end of the last glaciation, New World environments changed greatly. The western and southwestern United States became drier, the East Coast and much of the Midwest more densely forested. While the bison remained a major food source, other large animals became extinct, perhaps in part as a result of overhunting. The early Americans responded to these environmental changes by adopting more specialized subsistence patterns. The Pacific Northwest peoples became increasingly dependent on maritime resources and migrating salmon, developing elaborate societies whose surplus wealth was distributed through complex winter rituals. The western Paleo-Indians became increasingly adapted to desert life, relying on intensive collecting of wild vegetable foods or coastal fishing and shellfish exploitation. Many societies developed diverse economies based on deer-hunting, collecting, and fishing, and food-gathering activities were carefully scheduled according to the season of the year. It was among such people, in Mexico, Peru, and elsewhere, that the first tentative experiments with cultivation and food production began more than 8000 years ago, just about the time when the last Ice Age big game was becoming extinct.

REFERENCES

Campbell, Bernard. 1982. *Humankind Emerging*. Boston: Little, Brown.

Claiborne, Robert. 1973. *The First Americans*. New York: Time-Life Books.

Constable, George. 1973. *The Neanderthals*. New York: Time-Life Books.

Graziosi, Paolo. 1960. *Paleolithic Art*. New York: Harry N. Abrams.

Lee, Richard B. 1979. *The !Kung San*. New York: Cambridge University Press.

Leroi-Gourhan, Andre. 1965. *Treasures of Prehistoric Art*. New York: Harry N. Abrams.

Mulvaney, Derek. 1975. *The Prehistory of Australia*. Baltimore: Pelican Books.

Pfeiffer, John. 1973. *The Emergence of Man*, 2nd. ed. New York: Harper and Row.

A Paleolithic Camp at Nice

4

by Henry de Lumley
May 1969

Construction work on the French Riviera has uncovered the remains of man's earliest-known construction work: huts put up by hunters who visited the shore of the Mediterranean some 300,000 years ago

A Paleolithic site uncovered recently in the south of France contains traces of the earliest-known architecture: huts that were built some 300,000 years ago. The structures were evidently made by nomadic hunters who visited the Mediterranean shore briefly each year. They left behind artifacts and animal bones that, together with the plant pollen found at the site, yield a remarkably detailed picture of the occupants' activities during their annual sojourn by the sea. Because the discovery of the site and its excavation were unusual, I shall give a brief account of both before describing the new evidence the site provides concerning human life during this very early period of prehistory.

The city of Nice, in southeastern France, stands on a basement formation of limestone and marl. The bedrock is covered by layers of sand, clay and soil that mark the glacial oscillations of the ice age. During the construction of a shipyard some years ago certain glacial strata were exposed to view and attracted the attention of several scholars. In one sandy layer in 1959 Georges Iaworsky of the Monaco Museum of Prehistoric Anthropology found a few stone tools of typical Paleolithic workmanship. Two years later in another sandy section he found a tool of the early Paleolithic type known as Acheulean. Acheulean tools take their name from St. Acheul, a site in France where examples were first discovered, but since then Acheulean implements have been found at many other sites in Europe and in Asia and Africa. It had originally seemed that the sands had been deposited in the warm period between the glaciations called the Riss and the Würm, but Iaworsky pointed out that the age of the Acheulean tool indicated that these deposits were much older.

Then, in the course of foundation work during October, 1965, bulldozers cut a series of terraces into the sloping grounds of the Château de Rosemont, on the shoulder of Mont Boron in the eastern part of the city. The area of excavation, near the corner of Boulevard Carnot and an alley romantically named Terra Amata (beloved land), was scarcely 300 yards from Nice's commercial harbor and not far from the shipyard where Iaworsky and others, myself included, had studied the glacial strata. As the excavation proceeded the bulldozers exposed an extensive sandy deposit containing more Paleolithic implements. The significance of the discovery was quickly realized, and the builders agreed to halt operations temporarily. With the help of the French Ministry of Culture, a major archaeological salvage effort was mounted.

Starting on January 28, 1966, and continuing without interruption until July 5 more than 300 workers, including young students of archaeology from the universities and a number of enthusiastic amateurs, devoted a total of nearly 40,000 man-hours to the excavation of the Terra Amata site. The excavated area covered 144 square yards; in the course of investigating the 21 separate living floors found within the area the workers gradually removed a total of 270 cubic yards of fill, using no tools except trowels and brushes. The digging brought to light nearly 35,000 objects, and the location of each object was recorded on one or another of 1,200 charts. In addition, casts were made of 108 square yards of living floor and the progress of the work was documented in some 9,000 photographs.

In stratigraphic terms the deposits at Terra Amata begin at the surface with a layer of reddish clay that is nine feet thick in places and contains potsherds of the Roman period. Below the clay is a series of strata indicative of glacial advances during the Würm, Riss and Mindel periods and the warmer periods that intervened. The site embraces three fossil beaches, all belonging to the latter part of the Mindel glaciation. The youngest beach, marked by a dune and a sandbar, proved to be the site of human habitation.

When the youngest beach was deposited, the level of the Mediterranean was 85 feet higher than it is today. Soon after the beach was formed the sea level dropped somewhat, exposing the sandbar and allowing the wind to build a small dune inland. The hunters must have visited the area during or soon after a major period of erosion that occurred next. The evidence of their presence is found on or in the sands but not in the reddish-brown soil that later covered the eroded sand surface. Numerous shells of land snails, found at the base of the reddish soil, indicate a period of temperate climate.

The landscape of Terra Amata at the time of the hunters' visits differed in a number of respects from today's. The backdrop of the Alps, dominated by Mont Chauve, was much the same, but the sea covered most of the plain of Nice and even penetrated a short distance into what is now the valley of the Paillon River. The climate, though temperate, was somewhat brisker and more humid than the one we know. Pollen studies, undertaken by Jacques-Louis de Beaulieu of the pollen-analysis laboratory at the University of Aix-Marseilles, indicate that fir and Norway pine on the alpine heights grew farther down the slopes than is now the case, and that heather, sea pine, Aleppo pine and holm oak covered Mont Boron and its coastal neighbors.

In the limestone of Mont Boron's western slope the sea had cut a small cove opening to the south. Within the cove a sandy, pebble-strewn beach extended down to the sea, sheltered from the north and east winds. A small spring to one side provided a source of fresh water. A few seashore plants—grasses, horsetails, short-stemmed plantain and various shrubs—grew in the cove. The stream from the spring held water lilies of the genus *Euryale,* which, as De Beaulieu notes, can be found only in Asia today. All things considered, it appears that nothing was lacking even 300 millenniums ago to make Terra Amata a beloved land.

The superimposed living floors at Terra Amata are located in three separate areas. Four are on the section of beach that had formed the sandbar until the sea level dropped; six are on the beach seaward of the bar, and 11 are on the dune inland. The huts that were built on the living floors all had the same shape: an elongated oval. They ranged from 26 to 49 feet in length and from 13 to nearly 20 feet in width. Their outline can be traced with two kinds of evidence. The first is the imprint of a series of stakes, averaging some three inches in diameter, that were driven into the sand to form the walls of the hut. The second is a line of stones, paralleling the stake imprints, that apparently served to brace the walls. One of the earliest of the huts is perfectly outlined by an oval of stones, some as much as a foot in diameter and some even stacked one on the other. The living floor within the oval consisted of a thick bed of organic matter and ash.

The palisade of stakes that formed the walls was not the huts' only structural element. There are also visible the imprints left by a number of stout posts, each about a foot in diameter. These supports were set in place down the long axis of the hut. Evidence of how the palisade and the center posts were integrated to form the roof of the hut has not survived.

A basic feature of each hut is a hearth placed at the center. These fireplaces are either pebble-paved surface areas or shallow pits, a foot or two in diameter, scooped out of the sand. A little wall, made by piling up cobbles or pebbles, stands at the northwest side of each hearth. These walls were evidently windscreens to protect the fire against drafts, particularly from the northwest wind that is the prevailing one at Nice to this day.

The fact that the hunters built windscreens for their hearths makes it clear that their huts were not draft-free. This suggests that many of the palisade stakes may have been no more than leafy branches. Certainly nothing more permanent was required. As we shall see, the huts were occupied very briefly. As we shall also see, the time of the annual visit can be narrowed down to the end of spring and the beginning of summer, a season when such a building material would have been readily available.

In the huts on the dune the hearths were apparently designed for small fires. If one can judge from the larger amounts of charcoal and ash, the hearths in the huts closer to the sea must have accommodated much bigger fires. It is worth noting that the hearths at Terra Amata, together with those at one other site in Europe, are the oldest yet discovered anywhere in the world. The hearths that

OVAL HUTS, ranging from 26 to 49 feet in length and from 13 to 20 feet in width, were built at Terra Amata by visiting hunters. A reconstruction shows that the hut walls were made of stakes, about three inches in diameter, set as a palisade in the sand and braced on the outside by a ring of stones. Some larger posts were set up along the huts' long axes, but how these and the walls were joined to make roofs is unknown; the form shown is conjectural. The huts' hearths were protected from drafts by a small pebble windscreen.

equal them in age were found by László Vértes in strata of Mindel age at Vértesszölös in Hungary. Like some of the hearths at Terra Amata, those at the Hungarian site are shallow pits a foot or two in diameter.

Also from Vértesszölös comes a significant early human fossil: the occipital bone of a skull that has been assigned to modern man. No such human remains were found in our excavation at Terra Amata, but we came on two indirect sources of information about the site's inhabitants. One is the imprint of a right foot, 9½ inches long, preserved in the sand of the dune. Calculating a human being's height from the length of the foot is an uncertain procedure. If, however, one uses the formula applied to Neanderthal footprints found in the grotto of Toirano in Italy, the individual whose footprint was found at Terra Amata may have been five feet one inch tall.

Our other indirect source of information consists of fossilized human feces found in the vicinity of the huts. De Beaulieu's analysis of their pollen content shows that all of it comes from plants, such as *Genista*, that shed their pollen at the end of spring or the beginning of summer. This is the finding that enables us to state the precise time of year when the hunters came to Terra Amata.

How did the visitors occupy themselves during their stay? The evidence shows that they gathered a little seafood, manufactured stone tools and hunted in the nearby countryside. The animal bones unearthed at Terra Amata include the remains of birds, turtles and at least eight species of mammals. Although the visitors did not ignore small game such as rabbits and rodents, the majority of the bones represent larger animals. They are, in order of their abundance, the stag *Cervus elaphus*, the extinct elephant *Elephas meridionalis*, the wild boar (*Sus scrofa*), the ibex (*Capra ibex*), Merk's rhinoceros (*Dicerothinus merki*) and finally the wild ox *Bos primigenius*. Although the hunters showed a preference for big game, they generally selected as prey not the adults but the young of each species, doubtless because they were easier to bring down.

The visitors did not systematically exploit the food resources available in the Mediterranean. Nevertheless, they were not entirely ignorant of seafood. A few shells of oysters, mussels and limpets at the site show that they gathered shellfish; fishbones and fish vertebrae indicate that on occasion the hunters also fished.

The large majority of all the artifacts found at Terra Amata are stone tools. They represent two different but closely related stone industries. Both appear to be contemporary with the earliest "biface" industries of the Paleolithic period (so named because many of the tools are made out of stone "cores" that are shaped by chipping flakes from both faces rather than from one face only). They bear certain resemblances to the tools of an early Paleolithic biface industry named the Abbevillian (after the site in France where they were first discovered) and to the Acheulean biface industry named the Abbevillian (after the site in France where they were first discovered) and to the Acheulean biface industry, which is somewhat more advanced. On balance, both Terra Amata industries should probably be characterized as early Acheulean.

The more primitive of the two Terra Amata industries is represented by the tools found in the huts closest to the sea. Mainly pebble tools, they include many pieces of the type designated choppers, a few of the type called chopping tools and some crude bifaces made by detaching flakes from one end of an oval cobble but leaving a smooth, unflaked "heel" at the other end. Among the other tools found in the seaside huts are cleavers, scrapers, projectile points of a kind known in France as *pointes de Tayac*

REPRESENTATIVE TOOLS unearthed at Terra Amata include a pebble (*middle*) that has been flaked on one of its faces to form a pick, another stone tool (*left*), flaked on both faces but with one end left smooth, and a bone fragment (*right*) pointed to make an awl.

82

FLOOR OF A HUT at Terra Amata is one of several brought to light by the excavators, revealing the ancient debris left behind by the occupants. The whole pebbles are raw material for tools; the chips and flakes, toolmakers' waste. The antler is from a stag.

and pebble tools flaked on one face only.

The stone industry represented by the tools found in the huts on the dune is more advanced, although it too includes choppers, chopping tools and cobble bifaces with a smooth heel. There are no single-faced pebble tools or cleavers on the dune, however, and tools made from flakes rather than from cores are relatively numerous. The tools made from flakes include those designated scrapers with abrupt retouch, end scrapers with toothed edges and flakes of the kind named Clactonian (after the English site Clacton-on-Sea). Some of the Clactonian flakes have been notched on one edge; others have been made into perforators by chipping out two notches side by side so that a point of stone protrudes. Projectile points from the dunes include, in addition to *pointes de Tayac*, some that are triangular in cross section and others of a kind known in France as *pointes de Quinson*.

Some of the tools found at Terra Amata were probably made on the spot. The hut floors show evidence of tool manufacturing, and the toolmaker needed only to walk along the beach to find workable pebbles and cobbles of flint, quartzite, limestone and other rock. The toolmaker's place inside the huts is easily recognized: a patch of living floor is surrounded by the litter of tool manufacture. The bare patches are where the toolmakers sat, sometimes on animal skins that have left a recognizable impression.

Not all the stone debris represents the waste from finished work. In one instance the excavators found a cobble from which a single chip had been struck. Nearby was a chip that fitted the scar perfectly. In another toolmaker's atelier several flakes had been removed from a cobble by a series of successive blows. Both the core and the flakes were found, and it was possible for us to reassemble the cobble. Scarcely a flake was missing; evidently the toolmaker did not put either the core or the flakes to use.

At least one of the projectile points unearthed at Terra Amata could not have been produced locally. The stone from which it is made is a volcanic rock of a kind found only in the area of Estérel, southwest of Cannes and some 30 miles from Nice. This discovery allows us to conclude that these summer visitors' travels covered at least that much territory in the south of France, although we cannot be sure how much more widely they may have roamed.

A few tools made of bone have been

FIRE PIT (*right*) was protected from drafts and from the prevailing northwest wind in particular by a windscreen built of cobbles and pebbles, seen partially preserved at left.

TOOLMAKER'S ATELIER occupies one section of a hut. It is easily identified by the debris of tool manufacture that surrounds the bare patch of floor where the toolmaker sat.

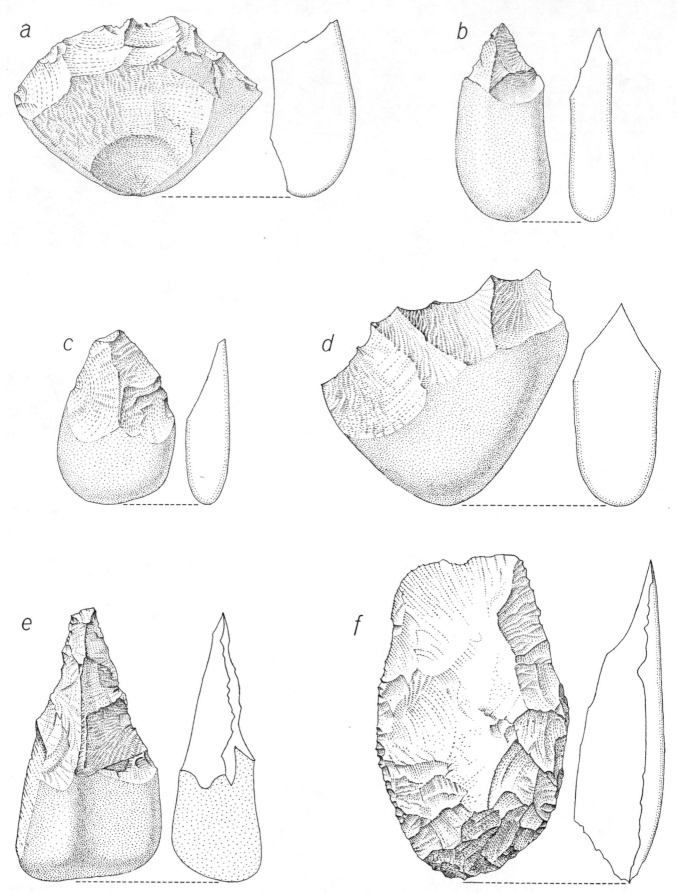

GROUP OF PRIMITIVE TOOLS was found in association with the huts closest to the sea at Terra Amata. They include choppers (a) and picks (b,c), made from pebbles that are flaked on one face only; chopping tools (d) that are flaked on both faces; crude bi-faces (e), made by detaching flakes from one end of a cobble but leaving an unflaked "heel" at the opposite end; cleavers (f), and two other kinds of stone artifacts (illustrated on opposite page): scrapers and projectile points of a kind known as pointes de Tayac.

found at Terra Amata. One leg bone of an elephant has a hammered point at one end. Another bone has a point that was probably hardened in a fire (a technique used today by some primitive peoples to harden the tips of wooden spears). A third bone fragment has one end smoothed by wear; still another may have served as an awl, and some fragments of bone may have been used as scrapers.

As for other kinds of artifacts, there are traces of only two. On the dune a spherical imprint in the sand, filled with a whitish substance, may be the impression left by a wooden bowl. Some pieces of red ocher found at the site obviously belonged to the visitors: the ends are worn smooth by wear. They recall the red ocher found at sites belonging to the much later Mousterian period, which François Bordes of the University of Bordeaux suggests were used for body-painting.

Let us see if the pattern of the hunters' annual visits to Terra Amata can be reconstructed. We know from the pollen evidence that they arrived in the late spring or early summer, and we can assume that they chose the sheltered cove as their camping ground as much because of its supply of fresh water as for any other reason. On arrival they set up their huts, built their hearths and windscreens, hunted for a day or two, gathered some seafood, rested by their fires, made a few tools and then departed. How do we know that their stay was so short? First, the living floors show no sign of the compaction that would characterize a longer occupation. Second, we have independent evidence that the huts collapsed soon after they were built. A freshly chipped stone tool that is left in the sun will quickly become bleached on the exposed side whereas the bottom side retains its original coloring. Many of the tools on the living floors at Terra Amata are bleached in this way. For the implements to be exposed to the full force of the Mediterranean summer sun the huts must have fallen apart soon after they were abandoned.

In the fall the winds covered the living floors, the leveled palisades and the rest of the camp debris with a layer of sand perhaps two inches deep. The rains then spread out the sand and packed it down, so that when the hunters returned to the cove the following year the evidence of their earlier stay had been almost obliterated. Only a few objects, such as the windscreens for the hearths, still protruded from the sand. The visi-

tors then built new huts, often digging the hearth pit exactly where the preceding year's had been and rekindling their fires on the ashes of the previous season. After a day or two of hunting, gathering seafood and making tools the annual visit was ended. The 11 living floors on the dune at Terra Amata are so precisely superimposed that they almost certainly represent 11 consecutive yearly visits, probably involving many of the same individuals.

There is no older evidence of man-

made structures than that at Terra Amata. Until this site was excavated the record for antiquity was held by the traces of construction discovered at Latamne, an open-air site in Syria, by J. Desmond Clark of the University of California at Berkeley. An early Acheulean site, Latamne is believed to be as old as the Mindel-Riss interglacial period. Terra Amata, which evidently was inhabited at the end of the Mindel glacial period, is therefore even earlier.

The evidence indicating that the hunt-

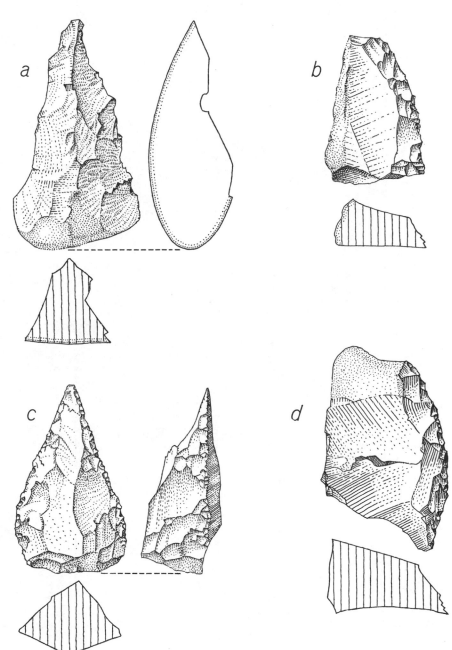

LESS PRIMITIVE TOOLS were found in the huts on the dune at Terra Amata. There were no cleavers or single-faced pebble tools and many more of the tools were made from flakes rather than from cores. Tools common to both areas are *pointes de Tayac* (*a*) and flakes made into simple scrapers (*b*), choppers, chopping tools and bifaces like those on the opposite page. Flakes were also made into projectile points (*c*) and more elaborate scrapers (*d*).

YEARS BEFORE PRESENT	GLACIAL STAGES	STONE INDUSTRY	SITES IN SOUTHEAST FRANCE	CULTURAL ADVANCES
				FIRST AGRICULTURE
10,000	WÜRM	UPPER PALEOLITHIC		
		MOUSTERIAN	GRIMALDI CAVES	OLDEST BURIALS
100,000				
	RISS	ACHEULEAN	LAZARET CAVE	
200,000				
	MINDEL		TERRA AMATA	OLDEST MAN-MADE DWELLINGS
		ABBEVILLIAN		
500,000				OLDEST EVIDENCE OF FIRE
				OLDEST BIFACE TOOLS
1,000,000	GÜNZ	PEBBLE CULTURE	VALLONNET CAVE	
			UPPER TERRACES ROUSSILLON VALLEY	
				OLDEST STONE TOOLS
2,000,000	DONAU			

CHRONOLOGICAL POSITION of Terra Amata in prehistory is indicated on this chart, which shows (*left to right*) the time, given in thousands of years before the present, of the major glacial advances and retreats in Europe, the successive stone industries of the Paleolithic period, sites in southeastern France where the industries have been found and early man's progress in technology.

ers came to Terra Amata at about the same time year after year, together with the likelihood that the dune huts sheltered some of the same individuals for more than a decade, suggests that the visitors possessed stable and even complex social institutions. It is thus appropriate to conclude with the words of the French historian Camille Jullian, written soon after the Terra Amata living floors had been exposed. "The hearth," Jullian wrote, "is a place for gathering together around a fire that warms, that sheds light and gives comfort. The toolmaker's seat is where one man carefully pursues a work that is useful to many. The men here may well be nomadic hunters, but before the chase begins they need periods of preparation and afterward long moments of repose beside the hearth. The family, the tribe will arise from these customs, and I ask myself if they have not already been born."

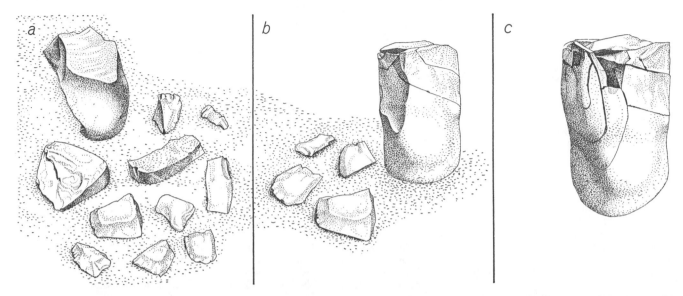

UNUTILIZED RAW MATERIAL was found in one Terra Amata toolmaker's atelier. Near the shattered half of a large cobble lay most of the fragments that had been struck from it (*a*). They could be reassembled (*b*) so that the cobble was almost whole again (*c*).

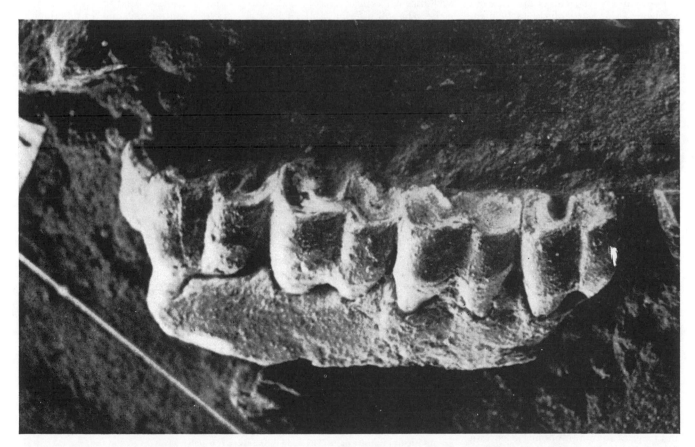

ANIMAL BONE, photographed *in situ* near one corner of an excavation unit, is a fragment of rhinoceros mandible, complete with teeth. The visitors preferred large mammals to other game. Along with rhinoceros they hunted stag, elephant, boar, ibex and wild ox.

5

The Neanderthals

by Erik Trinkaus and William W. Howells
December 1979

*They flourished from western Europe to central Asia
between 75,000 and 35,000 years ago. The differences
between them and later peoples are not as great as was
once thought but still call for an explanation*

The Neanderthals were first recognized in 1856, when workmen uncovered fossil human bones in the Neander Valley near Düsseldorf in Germany. At the time and for some time thereafter the idea of early men, of men different from those now living, was so unfamiliar that the Neanderthals were regarded either as a freakish variant of modern men or as beings that were not quite human. They came to be classified not as members of our own species, *Homo sapiens,* but as a separate species, *Homo neanderthalensis.*

Today the Neanderthals cannot even be regarded as particularly early men. They arose long after other members of the genus *Homo* and longer still after the hominid genus *Australopithecus.* The Neanderthals belong to a rather late stage of the Pleistocene epoch. Indeed, their lateness is the main reason so much is known about them.

In recent years this knowledge has been simultaneously extended and refined. To look broadly at the new picture, the Neanderthals appear on the scene as competent hunters of large and small game, taking their prey in ways that might seem primitive to us but would nonetheless be familiar. They were able to deal with the rigors of a cold climate during the last phase of the Pleistocene. They flourished from western Europe to central Asia. They must have used animal skins for clothing and shelter, because there is clear evidence that earlier people had used them.

They took shelter in caves, where most of their bones have been found. The reason few Neanderthal bones are uncovered elsewhere, however, is that caves preserve bones as open-air sites rarely do. Neanderthals lived in the open as well, as is indicated by open-air sites with masses of the kind of stone tools that are associated elsewhere with Neanderthal bones. Moreover, hearths and rings of mammoth bones at certain sites point to their occupants' living in skin tents. Indeed, it is probable that Neanderthals lived more in the open than they did in caves.

Most of the Neanderthals' tools were flakes of flint, struck from a "core" and trimmed into the projectile points, knives and scrapers that make up the Mousterian (or Middle Paleolithic) tool complex. This complex is not a uniform assemblage of tools everywhere it is found but manifests itself in local variations on a theme of similar manufacture. François Bordes of the University of Bordeaux has distinguished five such "subcultures" in France alone, and other variant assemblages, all loosely classified as Mousterian, stretch off to the east through central Europe and into Asia. The Mousterian culture was a long-lived one appropriate to this late period in the cultural evolution of the Paleolithic.

It is important to note that whereas all Neanderthals made Mousterian tools, not all Mousterian toolmakers were Neanderthals. The Mousterian tool complex is a general level of achievement in the making of stone tools rather than an expression of a specifically Neanderthal intellect and skill.

From about 40,000 years ago in eastern Europe and about 35,000 in western Europe the Mousterian tool assemblages were succeeded by those of somewhat more varied cultures that belong to what is designated the Upper Paleolithic. When these later tools are found with human fossils, the bones are those not of Neanderthals but of anatomically modern human beings. The basic innovation in the tools is that the flakes struck from the core were long, narrow blades. This made it easy to vary the final form of the tools and thus to have a larger assortment of tools. The innovation was also more economical of flint, often a scarce raw material.

In some early manifestations of the Upper Paleolithic certain technical ideas first seen in the Mousterian persist. In others, such as the Aurignacian, the break from the Middle Paleolithic is more complete. The Upper Paleolithic also introduces art: cave paintings, engravings on bone, statuettes of bone and stone, and such personal decoration as strings of beads. The Middle Paleolithic is devoid of such expressions except possibly for a few rock carvings. The Neanderthals did, however, bury their dead and place grave offerings with them. Goat horns have been found in a boy's grave in central Asia and flowers (identified from their pollen) in a burial at Shanidar Cave in Iraq.

In spite of such distinctions it would be unwarranted to decide on the basis of the Neanderthals' tools that their way of life differed radically from that of hunting peoples living into our own times. If the Neanderthals' stone implements were limited to flakes technically inferior to those of the Upper Paleolithic, the same is true of tools made over a period of perhaps 30,000 years by members of one modern population: the Australian aborigines. Again, whereas the Eskimos have had tools of great refinement and variety, comparable in their development to those of the Upper Paleolithic, the first people to occupy the New World certainly did not. It therefore seems safest to speculate that the Neanderthals were formed into hunting bands similar to those of recent hunting peoples, probably linked loosely into tribal groupings, or at least groups with a common language. To judge by the wide distribution and homogeneity of Neanderthal remains, the Neanderthals formed a distinct and major human population that was not a particularly

FRONT AND SIDE VIEWS of the skull of an adult male Neanderthal appear in the photographs on the opposite page. The skull is Shanidar 1, which was discovered at the Iraq cave site of the same name in 1957 by Ralph S. Solecki of Columbia University and his colleagues. The left side of the individual's head had suffered an injury of the eye socket and the bone around it that had healed before his death. Specimen is in the Iraq Museum in Baghdad. Photographs were made through the courtesy of Muayed Sa'id al-Damirji, Director General of Antiquities.

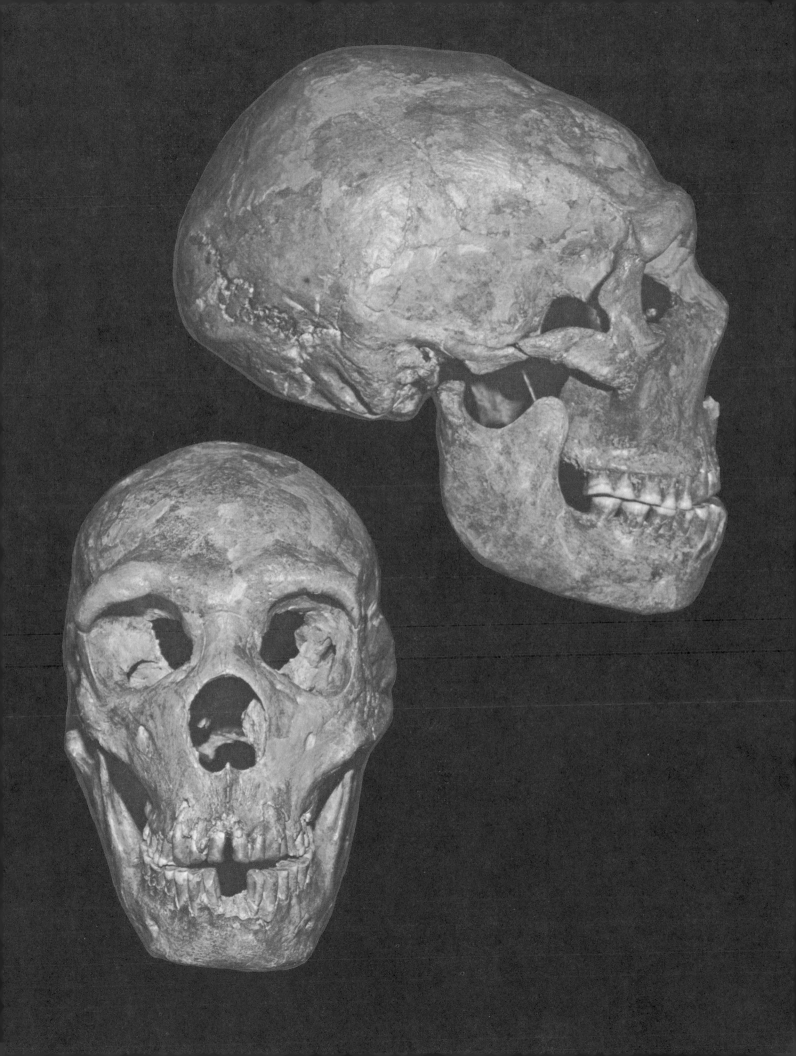

sparse one. Finally, whereas the organization of human populations in the Middle Paleolithic is necessarily a subject of speculation, the evidence of the fossil remains is concrete. Here the question becomes not what is meant by "Mousterian" but what is meant by "Neanderthal."

Although the Neanderthals were first recognized well over 100 years ago, the evolutionary significance of the original Neanderthal discovery and of other human remains uncovered at Paleolithic sites was not apparent until the turn of the 20th century. At that time a number of sites in Europe yielded new Neanderthal fossils, most of them partial skeletons. Among them were the remains of a man aged between 40 and 50 uncovered in a cave near the village of La Chapelle-aux-Saints in France. With this skeleton as a point of departure Marcellin Boule, the leading French anthropologist of his day, published in 1913 a monograph that reviewed all known Neanderthal remains. Boule's monograph included what soon became the standard description and interpretation of the Neanderthals.

At the time no older human fossils were known except those of "Java man," or "Pithecanthropus," which Boule did not regard as being human. He therefore inserted the Neanderthals taxonomically somewhere between chimpanzees and modern men. In this framework the differences between the

Neanderthals and modern men tended to make the Neanderthals seem apelike. Boule was further misled, both by anatomical views then current and by his own evolutionary preconceptions, into seeing the Neanderthals as being somewhat stooped and having knees slightly bent and feet rolled in such a way that the outer edge of the foot, rather than the sole, formed the walking surface. Other experts either did not disagree or enthusiastically agreed, and Boule's view of the Neanderthals as an aberrant branch of humanity prevailed. He gave his stamp of approval to their classification as a species distinct from and not ancestral to *Homo sapiens.*

Some two decades later there was a reaction against this view as many other human fossils were discovered, notably in Java and China. Most of these fossil forms were earlier and more primitive than the Neanderthals. Some anthropologists now inserted the Neanderthals not between men and apes but between modern man and such probable ancestors as the Indonesian and Chinese fossils now classified as *Homo erectus.* The Neanderthals were thus viewed as a stage of human evolution, well up on the scale of time and development: a "Neanderthal phase." By extension some earlier fossils were considered to be representative of the same phase in other areas. For example, the Broken Hill skull from Zambia ("Rhodesian man") was classified as an African Neanderthal and the Solo skulls from Java were

classified as Eastern Neanderthals. The classification was based on their common possession of large, bony brow ridges and a low-vaulted brain case. In addition two important human populations, relatively recent but still making Mousterian tools, were interpreted as being in transition between the Neanderthals and modern men. These populations were represented by skeletal samples from the caves at Mugharet es-Skhūl and Jebel Qafzeh in Israel.

In this picture the populations of the earliest anatomically modern men arose separately from such immediate predecessors in various parts of the Old World and in association with cultural advances such as those of the Upper Paleolithic of Europe. All these predecessors were taken to be "Neanderthals" of one kind or another, and in contrast to Boule's view most if not all of them were accepted as being the ancestors of various living peoples.

Today a more noncommital attitude is conveyed by the practice of classifying the Neanderthals as a subspecies within our own species. Thus they are commonly referred to as *Homo sapiens neanderthalensis,* and all living human beings are referred to as *Homo sapiens sapiens.* Such taxonomic distinctions, however, are merely an aid to grouping related individuals. They are not particularly useful as a guide in exploring the actual relations between the Neanderthals and modern men. To arrive at an

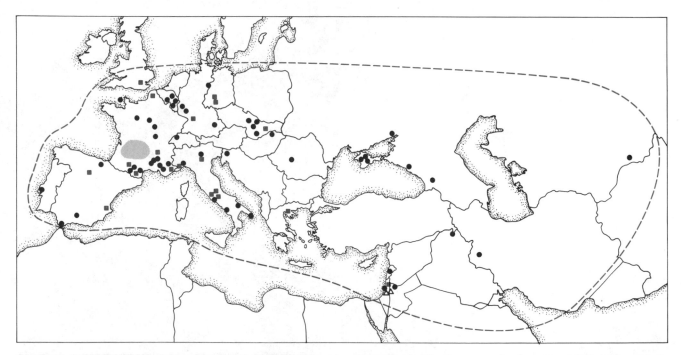

SPATIAL DISTRIBUTION of sites where Neanderthal fossils have been found is plotted on this map. The westernmost site is in Portugal and the easternmost is in Uzbekistan in Soviet Central Asia. The greatest concentration of Neanderthal remains is in the western Massif Central of France (*colored area*), where at least 10 early Neanderthal sites and 25 later Neanderthal ones are situated. Elsewhere on the map early sites appear as colored squares and later sites as black dots. The 19 early sites have yielded the partial remains of some 75 individuals and the 52 later sites the remains of at least 200 more, ranging from a few isolated teeth to complete skeletons. Two open triangles in the Levant locate Mugharet es-Skhūl and Jebel Qafzeh; some of the 30 fossils there were formerly classified as being Neanderthal.

understanding of what the term Neanderthal means one should ignore past controversies and take account of everything that is known today. For example, one can systematically examine the large corpus of Neanderthal fossils in the light of present knowledge of the anatomical functions of bone and muscle. Furthermore, the fossils can be examined against a fuller chronological background based on carbon-14 dating and on recent archaeological work. When this is done, the picture that emerges is quite clear. It reveals a human population complex with a special pattern of anatomical features that extends without interruption from Gibraltar across Europe into the Near East and central Asia. That population complex occupies a span of time from about 100,000 years ago (or at least before the beginning of the last Pleistocene glaciation) down to 40,000 or 35,000 years ago (depending on the locality). Within that space and time only remains recognizable as belonging to this population complex have been found.

The Neanderthal anatomical pattern, or combination of skeletal features, can now be distinguished from that of modern human populations and from the patterns of the European Upper Paleolithic and the Near Eastern late Mousterian. The Neanderthals can also be consistently differentiated from the human beings who lived at the same time in Africa and eastern Asia. Although some of the pattern's individual features grade into those of neighboring populations, its important aspects appear to be distinctively Neanderthal. Moreover, the Neanderthal population is at least as homogeneous as the human populations of today. The people of this anatomical pattern have often been called "classic Neanderthals." In our own view they are the only Neanderthals. To apply the term to specimens of any other time and place is only to invite confusion.

The anatomical pattern must be carefully defined. To begin with, the Neanderthal skull and skeleton exhibit a specific overall pattern. Compared with its modern counterpart the long Neanderthal skull is relatively low but not exceptionally so. The low cranium and the prominent brow ridges give an appearance resembling that of *Homo erectus,* and they are probably derived from such ancestry. Here, then, is the basis for the belief in a "Neanderthal stage" between *Homo erectus* and modern man. The brain encased in the Neanderthal skull, however, was on the average slightly larger than the brain of modern men. This anatomical feature is undoubtedly related to the fact that the musculature of the Neanderthals was more substantial than that of modern men; it does not suggest any difference in intellectual or behavioral capacities.

The Neanderthal face is unique. A

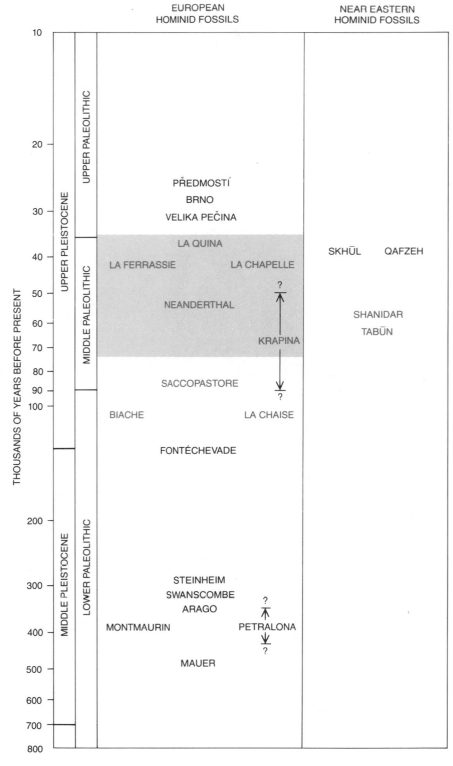

TEMPORAL DISTRIBUTION of the Neanderthals is shown on this chart, which extends from 10,000 years ago to 800,000. The time scale is logarithmic, which expands the space available for the Middle and Upper Paleolithic and the Upper Pleistocene. The last glacial phase of the Upper Pleistocene lasted from 80,000 years ago to 10,000 and was interrupted by a warm interval 35,000 years ago. Although many Neanderthal sites in Europe are not precisely dated, most are between 75,000 and 35,000 years old (*colored band*). The oldest of the fossils from Krapina are slightly older than other European Neanderthals, but most are contemporaneous. These Neanderthal site names appear in color, as do others more than 80,000 years old containing fossils that can be classified as early Neanderthals: Saccopastore, Biache and La Chaise. Still earlier European fossils, from Fontéchevade to Mauer, show varying degrees of affinity with both the Neanderthals and *Homo erectus.* The Upper Paleolithic sites of Velika Pečina, Brno, Předmostí, Skhūl and Qafzeh all contain human fossils of the modern type.

prominence down the midline brings the nose and the teeth farther forward (with respect to the vault of the skull) than they are in any other human fossil, either older or younger. The cheek arches slope backward instead of being angled, as they are in modern "high cheekbones." The forehead slopes instead of rising abruptly as it does over the tucked-in face of modern men. The Neanderthal midfacial prominence may be related to the teeth. The dentition is positioned so far forward with respect to

the face that in a profile view there is a gap between the last molar (the wisdom tooth) and the edge of the ascending branch of the mandible, or lower jawbone. This is something seldom seen except in Neanderthals. A distinct bony chin, supposedly a hallmark of modern men, is variably developed among Neanderthals. Its prominence may have been largely obscured by the forward position of the lower teeth with respect to the mandible below them.

The spectacular forward position of

the teeth in the Neanderthal skull remains unexplained. The cheek teeth were not significantly larger than those of modern men. The front teeth were somewhat bulkier than is common today, with the result that the arch at the front of the jaws is broader and opener. C. Loring Brace of the University of Michigan has suggested that the front teeth were regularly employed for something more than routine biting: for holding objects or perhaps for processing skins. Indeed, the crowns of the

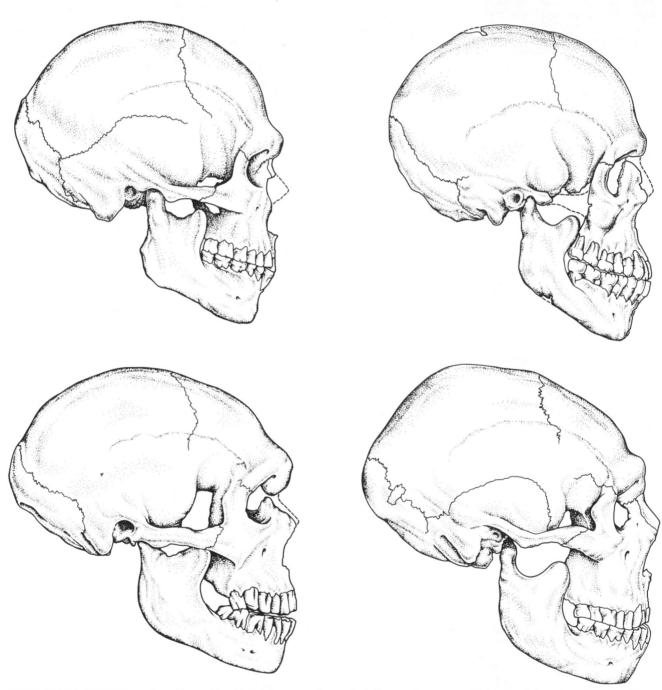

FOUR FOSSIL SKULLS are shown in profile, all slightly restored. The top two, anatomically modern, are Předmostí 3 from Czechoslovakia and Qafzeh 9 from Israel. The bottom two, both Neanderthals, are La Ferrassie 1 from France and Shanidar 1 from Iraq. (A profile photograph of the latter is on page 205.) Compared with the modern skulls the Neanderthal skulls are long, low and massive and their faces project, particularly around the nose and teeth. The anatomically modern skulls have a higher and rounder brain case, and their nose and teeth are more in line with their eye sockets. All should be compared with the Neanderthal precursor illustrated on opposite page.

front teeth of elderly Neanderthals are worn down in an unusual rounded way. Brace's hypothesis is that with the appearance of better tools in the Upper Paleolithic such uses of the front teeth became obsolete, and so the front teeth and jaws became smaller. It would seem, however, that the Mousterian tools were not so inferior as to account for the difference. Furthermore, some Mousterian toolmakers, the Skhūl people, already had front teeth that were like those of Upper Paleolithic populations in size and form.

The Neanderthal face as a whole is large, although it is not as large as the face in earlier members of the genus *Homo*. The front part of the upper jaw was generously proportioned; it accommodated the relatively long roots of the front teeth, particularly the canines. The nasal cavity and the rounded eye sockets are capacious. The sinus cavities are also large. For example, the frontal sinuses fill the brow ridges from above the nose out to the middle of the eye sockets with multichambered "cauliflower" cavities. They do not, however, reach up into the frontal bone above the brows, as is the case in earlier members of the genus *Homo*. In modern skulls the frontal sinuses are flattened, often extend above the brows and are quite irregular in size and shape.

In order to explain the Neanderthals' large, projecting face scholars have invoked a variety of causes, most often adaptation to cold. Carleton S. Coon and others have suggested that the Neanderthal midfacial prominence was such an adaptation. The nasal cavities were placed well away from the temperature-sensitive brain, and at the same time the enlarged size of the cavities may have provided additional space for warming inhaled air. The same Neanderthal facial shape, however, is found in Europe before the last onset of subarctic glacial cold and also in the Near East, where subarctic conditions never arrived. The unique Neanderthal facial configuration is more probably the result of a combination of factors: a highly complex interaction of forces from the chewing apparatus, a response to climatic conditions and a variety of other factors as yet undetermined. Sorting out these factors is one of the principal goals of current research on the Neanderthals. Meanwhile no coherent adaptive explanation for the total Neanderthal cranial pattern has been offered.

For the rest of the skeleton the situation is different. The postcranial skeleton, after all, is the structure that enables a large animal to maintain an erect posture, and *Homo* is a large animal. It is also the structure that allows the muscles to place enormous stresses on the bones while driving the body through the complex characteristic

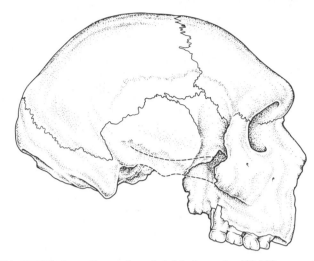

PETRALONA SKULL, from Greece, is undated but may be 400,000 years old. It shows a number of features reminiscent of *Homo erectus:* a low, wide brain case, a large, heavily built face and a large area at back of the skull for attachment of strong neck muscles. Although it has no specific Neanderthal character, it represents Neanderthal ancestral stock in Europe.

movements of the animal. A 150-pound man standing still needs to support only that much weight with his legs, but if he starts to run, the forces generated by muscle contraction and momentum are greatly increased and amount to several times the weight of his body. The bones of the skeleton must sustain these great stresses structurally, and the tendons must be attached to the bones strongly enough to produce the desired motion (or resistance to motion) effectively and efficiently. The tendon attachments leave characteristic marks on the bones that are clues to the power and action of the muscles. Equally significant, living bone under habitual stresses will reshape itself, within limits, to accommodate the stresses more efficiently.

There are many differences between the skeletons of Neanderthals and those of modern men. Some of the differences were formerly interpreted (as, for example, they were by Boule) as evidence of Neanderthal primitiveness. They were easily misinterpreted, and it was not possible to judge which might be more significant and which less so. Today, systematically examined in the light of functional anatomy, the skeletal differences present a coherent and satisfying picture.

To summarize, Boule and others were mistaken: Neanderthals were not less human than modern men, nor were their heads hung forward, their knees bent and their feet rolled over. A touch of arthritis in the neck bones of the La Chapelle-aux-Saints Neanderthal helped to lead Boule astray, but what misled him most was faulty anatomical interpretation. It is now clear that the Neanderthals had the same postural abilities, manual dexterity and range and character of movement that modern men do. They nonetheless differed from modern men in having massive limb bones, often somewhat bowed in the thigh and

forearm. The skeletal robustness evidently reflects the Neanderthals' great muscular power. Everything indicates that for their height both Neanderthal men and Neanderthal women were bulkily built and heavily muscled. Furthermore, signs of this massiveness appeared early in their childhood.

Many skeletal parts testify to this conclusion. For example, the talus, or anklebone, differs slightly in shape from the modern human talus. This difference was once taken to be a sign of primitiveness. It consists, however, only in just such an expansion of the joint surfaces at the ankle as would resist greater stress under load. The bones of the foot arches and the toes show stronger tendon attachments for the muscles that support the arches and propel the body in walking and running. The finger bones show similar attachments for the tendons of the powerful muscles that flexed the fingers. They also show an enlargement of the tuberosities that supported the pads at the fingertips. Both features indicate a much stronger grip than that of modern men, but there was nothing gorillalike in it; the control of movement was evidently the same as ours.

This kind of refined control, coupled with great power, also appears in a curious feature of the scapula, or shoulder blade. The feature has long been recognized but not explained. In modern individuals the outer edge of the scapula usually has a shallow groove on the front, or rib, surface. In Neanderthals a deeper groove characteristically appears on the back surface. This feature seems to reflect the strong development in Neanderthals of the teres minor muscle that runs from the scapula to the upper end of the humerus, or upper-arm bone. Part of the action of the muscle is to roll the arm (with the hand) outward. This action would have balanced and counteracted the major muscles that pull the arm down. In throwing or pounding motions, for example, all these muscles roll the arm inward. In balancing this tendency the teres minor muscle would have made possible a finer control of the arm and the hand in throwing a spear or retouching a flint tool, without any loss in the great muscular strength of the limb.

Other Neanderthal body parts repeat the theme. For example, quantitative analysis of the shape and cross-sectional area of the upper and lower bones of the leg shows that the difference between Neanderthal and modern human bones can also be explained in terms of resistance to the higher stresses of weight and activity in Neanderthals.

One difference still calls for explanation. In Neanderthals the pubic bone, at the front of the pelvis, has a curiously extended and lightened upper branch that forms a part of the rim of the pelvis. This is true of every Neanderthal specimen, male or female, from Europe and the Near East, in which the fragile bone is preserved. Possibly the feature is an adaptation for increasing the size of the birth canal in females. That would have allowed easier passage of an infant's head (which was presumably large) at birth. The presence of the same feature in males as well as females might be explained in terms of close genetic bonding between the two sexes. In any event it is not a trait that lends itself to explanation in terms of patterns of muscle action and movement. The peculiarity seems to be a significant Neanderthal anatomical marker. The pubic bones from Skhūl and Qafzeh are modern in form, as are those of the earliest Upper Paleolithic fossils from Europe. How the feature originated remains an unanswered question, because the pubic bones of earlier members of the genus *Homo* have not been preserved.

It now seems likely that the Neanderthals' antecedents can be traced in at least one section of the Neanderthal range, namely western Europe. Early human fossils from Europe are still few and fragmentary, but their number has increased greatly in recent years. Moreover, certain important specimens were formerly held to be more "progressive," or more modern in appearance, than Neanderthal specimens. These specimens now appear, on reexaminations that include multivariate statistical comparisons, to ally themselves more closely with the Neanderthals than with any other known human type. The specimens include the well-known Swanscombe skull from England, the Fontéchevade skull from France and the Steinheim skull from Germany.

In summarizing the evidence for the origins of the Neanderthals one can begin with the Petralona skull from Greece. It is of uncertain age but is probably as much as 400,000 years old. It shows no specifically Neanderthal character, looking more like an advanced *Homo erectus*. Next in line are the early jaws from Montmaurin in France and from Mauer (near Heidelberg) in Germany. Neither jaw shows any sign of a forward extension of the face such as the Neanderthal postmolar gap. A facial skeleton and two mandibles from Arago, a site in the French Pyrenees, are some 300,000 years old. Like the Swanscombe and Steinheim skulls, the Arago fossils show some suggestions of Neanderthal form, but the projection of the face and the tooth row is not as strongly developed.

From the last interglacial period, which began about 130,000 years ago, come several fossils that show clear signs of the Neanderthal pattern. They include the rear half of a skull, recently found at Biache in northeastern France, that has the lowness of the vault and the protruding rear characteristic of the Neanderthals. A mandible from another French site, the cave of Bourgeois-Delaunay near La Chaise, shows the typical Neanderthal position of the teeth. Two other skulls, from Saccopastore in Italy, clearly approach the typical Neanderthal pattern. Toward the end of the last interglacial the Neanderthal physique is seen in its complete development among the Krapina people. Found in a rock-shelter at Krapina in Yugoslavia, these fossil remains are believed to have accumulated over a considerable span of time both before and after the onset of the last glaciation. All the typical Neanderthal traits are visible: the shape of the skull, the projection of the face, the form of the limbs and the peculiarities of the shoulder blade and the pubic bone.

Why this physical pattern evolved can only be guessed at. The activity of the Neanderthals' massive muscles would have supplied their chunky body with more heat in a chill climate, but the pattern existed before the cold of the last glacial period began in Europe, and it was also present in the more temperate Near East. The robust physique was undoubtedly inherited from populations of *Homo erectus*. Those early men had a massive skull, and the few *H. erectus* limb bones that have been discovered are also massive. Such a heritage does not, however, explain the details of the Neanderthal pattern, particularly the skull pattern.

Whatever the origins of the Neanderthal physique, the fact that it was successful as an evolutionary adaptation is evident from its long stability. From the time of its full establishment perhaps 100,000 years ago down to 40,000 or 35,000 years ago this physical pattern continued without any evidence of evolutionary change. One possible exception is tooth dimensions. The teeth of the Krapina people are larger than those of more recent Neanderthals, which suggests that over a period of time there was a reduction in Neanderthal tooth size. In their details, however, the Krapina teeth are typically Neanderthal, and

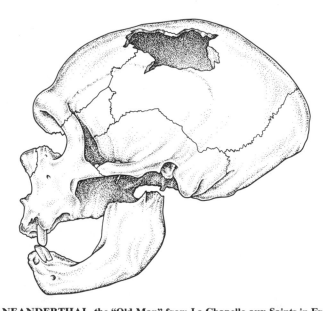

"BRUTISH" NEANDERTHAL, the "Old Man" from La Chapelle-aux-Saints in France, was discovered in 1908. The base of the skull was altered by arthritis and damaged after burial; this led to incorrect conclusions about the head posture of Neanderthals in general. Most of the teeth had been lost before death, so that the lower jaw acquired an abnormal rounded contour. This specimen is one of the longest Neanderthal skulls known and has one of the most projecting faces. Because the "Old Man" was for a long time the most complete and best-described Neanderthal specimen it became the stereotype of subspecies *Homo sapiens neanderthalensis*.

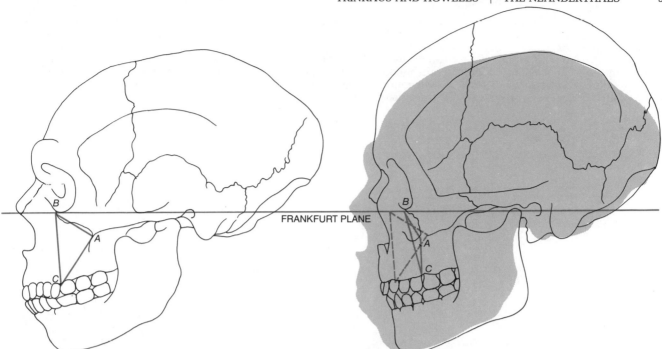

FRANKFURT PLANE

PROJECTING FACE of a Neanderthal (*left*) is annotated by the triangle connecting *A*, *B* and *C*. The forward edge of the first molar tooth (*C*) is well ahead of the lower edge of the cheekbone (*A*) and almost directly below the upper end of the cheekbone (*B*). The horizontal line passing above the triangle defines the Frankfurt plane, a standard orientation. The face of an anatomically modern skull (*right*), with point *B* and the Frankfurt plane superposed on a silhouette of the Neanderthal skull, has a tucked-in appearance; point *A* lies above the first molar tooth, and all three points in the triangle are nearly in the same vertical plane. The Neanderthal specimen used for this comparison is an idealized restoration of the "Old Man" of La Chapelle-aux-Saints. This specimen is shown unrestored on the opposite page.

the evidence of a trend toward a reduction of tooth size elsewhere among the Neanderthals is equivocal. It is possible that the Krapina people merely represent an extreme of tooth size, as the Australian aborigines do among modern populations.

After a stability lasting for perhaps 60,000 years the Neanderthal physical pattern was rapidly replaced by one similar to that of modern men. The first anatomically modern groups showed little difference from the Neanderthals in size. For example, the change in the teeth came not in average size but in details of form. The modern reduction in tooth size began later and has continued down to the present day. In general the anatomically modern people of the Near Eastern late Middle Paleolithic (Skhūl and Qafzeh) and the European early Upper Paleolithic had large bones and robust skulls. Fugitive signs of Neanderthal features appear in some of the Skhūl craniums, but they are rarely found in the Qafzeh group or in Upper Paleolithic specimens. The Neanderthal complex of traits is simply not there; these were ordinary robust representatives of modern humanity, like the Polynesians and northern Europeans of today. Indeed, the Upper Paleolithic skulls are specifically like those of later Europeans, or Caucasoids.

These are not subjective judgments: recent studies based on refined measurements, in particular those of Christopher Stringer of the British Museum (Natural History), make the separation between the cranial pattern of Neanderthals and that of early anatomically modern human beings quite clear. Moreover, both populations have skulls that are distinct from those of other fossil hominids. Other skeletal details, including the features of the scapula and the pubic bone mentioned above, fortify the distinction between the Neanderthals and their successors.

A transition from Neanderthals to their immediate successors undoubtedly took place, but there is little evidence for the actual course of events. The problem is dating. The period of time falls near the limit of accuracy of carbon-14 dating, and in any case samples suitable for carbon-14 analysis have been meager. The problem is particularly difficult in the Near East, and it is only beginning to be solved by the work of Arthur J. Jelinek of the University of Arizona and others. From what is known the most recent Neanderthals at Tabūn Cave in Israel and Shanidar in Iraq are at least 45,000 years old, but they may be considerably older. On the basis of archaeological comparisons the undated Skhūl skeletons are later, being probably no more than 40,000 years old and possibly younger. The Qafzeh remains are undated at the moment, but it seems reasonable to suppose they are about the same age as the Skhūl ones.

We shall therefore assume for the moment, but with no great confidence, that in the Near East anatomically modern men replaced the Neanderthals between 45,000 and 40,000 years ago.

In Europe the dating is a little clearer. Carbon-14 dates for sites that hold late Mousterian artifacts (taken as evidence of Neanderthal occupation) come as close to the present as about 38,000 years ago. A date of 35,250 years ago has been determined for the final Mousterian layer in the rock-shelter of La Quina in France. A frontal bone of modern form, found at Velika Pečina in Yugoslavia, has been dated to about 34,000 years ago. Meanwhile a series of carbon-14 dates obtained at sites across Europe place the beginnings of the culture level known as the Aurignacian (inferentially associated with people of modern physique) at about 33,000 years ago or slightly earlier. Hence in Europe the interval between Neanderthals and anatomically modern populations appears to have been extremely short.

What is important here is to contrast the departure of the Neanderthals with their arrival. The pace is totally different. From what is known about the arrival it can be seen as a gradual evolution. The departure can only be called abrupt; it probably took a tenth as much time as the arrival. Can the two transitions be assessed in the same terms? To answer the question one must accept some guidelines from current knowledge of evolutionary processes. These processes have been notably neglected in the two prevailing explanations of the Neanderthals' disappearance.

One of the two explanations, favored today by anthropologists in the U.S.S.R. and elsewhere in eastern Europe and by many in the U.S., is a restatement of the old "Neanderthal phase" hypothesis. In this view the Neanderthals evolved directly and on the spot into the anatomically modern people of the Upper Paleolithic. Its adherents see Neanderthal or "transitional" anatomical traits in the Skhūl population and in certain Upper Paleolithic specimens such as those from Brno and Předmostí in Czechoslovakia. One of those specimens has not only heavy brow ridges but also a lower jaw with the characteristic gap between the wisdom tooth and the jaw's ascend-

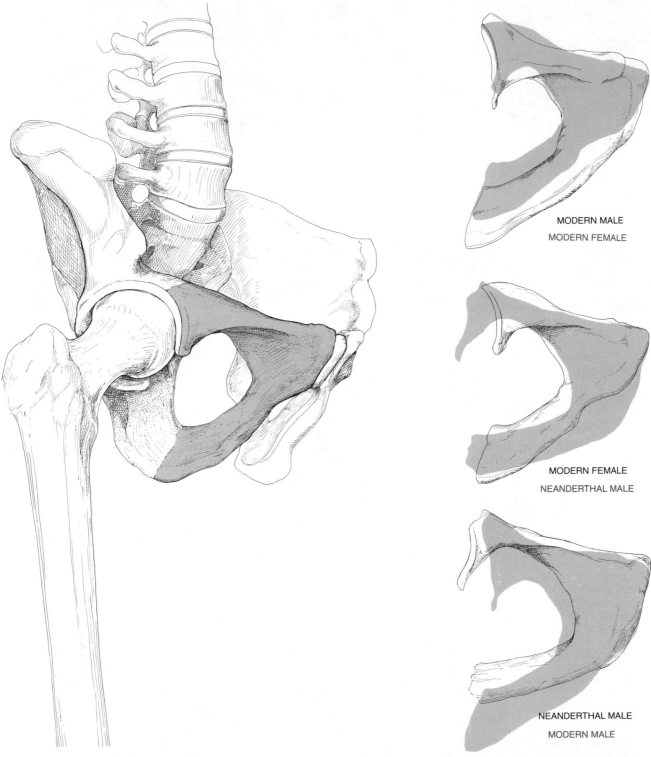

MODERN MALE
MODERN FEMALE

MODERN FEMALE
NEANDERTHAL MALE

NEANDERTHAL MALE
MODERN MALE

PUBIC BONES of a Neanderthal male and an anatomically modern male and female are compared. The pubic bone is the portion of the pelvis (*left*) that extends from the hip socket to the front midline; here the right pubic bone is seen from the front in all instances. First (*top right*) the pubic bone of a modern female is silhouetted in color. It is wider and less massive than the pubic bone of an anatomically mod- ern male (*black*). The pubic bone of a Neanderthal male, Shanidar 1, is silhouetted in color (*center right*). It is even wider and slenderer than that of a modern female (*black*). Finally (*bottom right*) the slenderness of the Neanderthal pubic bone is even more evident when it is compared with that of a modern male (*silhouette in color*). All Neanderthal pubic bones, male and female, show this characteristic.

ing branch. These features do not, however, make up the full Neanderthal pattern. Both are found in some prehistoric skulls from Australia. Moreover, the brow ridges are not Neanderthal in form; they probably represent an extreme among the generally rugged skulls of Upper Paleolithic people in Europe. Finally, when the measurements of the overall skull shape and of several limb-bone features are subjected to statistical analysis, they indicate that the specimens lack any particularly close Neanderthal affinity. In general, then, fossil specimens from the early Upper Paleolithic, although they are robust and rugged, show no convincing sign of a total morphology that is transitional between Neanderthals and modern men. Nor do late Neanderthal fossils show signs of having begun an evolutionary trend in a modern direction.

The second interpretation ascribes the disappearance of the Neanderthals not to local evolution but to invasion by new peoples of modern form. If there were a cave containing the remains of killed Neanderthals in association with Upper Paleolithic tools, one might entertain the hypothesis of replacement. The hypothesis might also be supported if there were evidence of a homeland for the alleged invaders or for their migration route. Current archaeological and paleontological information, however, is far too fragmentary to support the hypothesis. One can only point out that human populations of modern, although not European, anatomical form certainly occupied the distant continent of Australia 32,000 years ago and probably 8,000 years earlier than that. Signs of even older modern men are found in sub-Saharan Africa. Hence if anatomically modern men sprang from a single original main population, a point that many dispute, then it was not a population of Neanderthals, since anatomically modern men were in existence elsewhere when the Neanderthals still inhabited Europe.

Any attempt to choose between these two interpretations is sterile unless evolutionary principles are taken into account. In evolutionary terms a significant change in a physical pattern, such as the one separating the Neanderthals from their Upper Paleolithic successors, normally comes in two steps. First the change arises as a consequence of new selective forces acting on the individuals of a particular population. Then the change somehow becomes established as the norm in all populations of the species. Since the skeletal differences among all living human populations are less than the differences between the living populations and the Neanderthals, there is little doubt that the new pattern has become established throughout *Homo sapiens* today.

More specifically, a widely distrib-

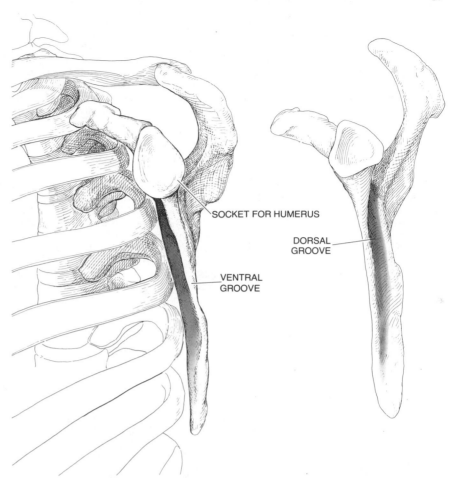

SHOULDER BLADES of a Neanderthal and an anatomically modern man are compared. These are left scapulas seen from the side. The modern scapula, at the left, shows a single groove on the ventral, or rib, side of the outer edge (*color*). This ventral-groove pattern is present in four out of five modern men; it is related to the development of a shoulder muscle, the teres minor, which in anatomically modern men connects the upper arm to the scapula by attaching to a small portion of the dorsal scapular surface (*see illustration below*). The Neanderthal scapula, at the right, has a single large groove on the dorsal, or back, side of the outer border (*color*). This dorsal-groove pattern appears in more than 60 percent of Neanderthal scapulas; the scapula illustrated is that of Shanidar 1. All of outer edge of the bone and part of the dorsal surface provided attachment for the teres minor muscle, indicating that it was well developed.

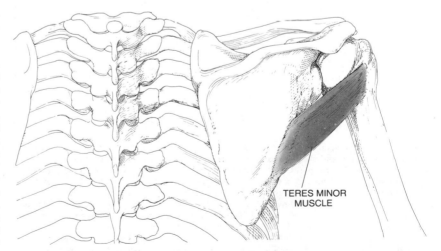

LINE OF ACTION of the teres minor muscle (*color*) is indicated in this dorsal view of the right scapula and part of the right upper arm bone, or humerus. When the muscle contracts, it pulls the humerus in toward the scapula, thereby strengthening the shoulder joint; at the same time it turns the upper arm, forearm and hand outward. All the major muscles of the shoulder that pull the arm downward, as in throwing or striking a blow, tend to turn the arm and hand inward. By countering this rotation the teres minor muscle gave Neanderthals more precise arm control.

uted species that interbreeds freely is likely to be relatively static in the evolutionary sense. It changes quite slowly because the lack of barriers to gene exchange between populations encourages a species-wide genetic homogeneity. Moreover, if the species has a common adaptation, and human culture can be so viewed, then selection will be similar for most of its features, which further promotes its general uniformity.

If, on the other hand, the species is more fragmented, perhaps by various degrees of geographical isolation, an increase in diversity is more likely. In small, isolated populations the substitution of genes under the pressure of natural selection will be faster. Only by some advantage in adaptation, for example a better adaptation to a new ecological situation or a better exploitation of the old one, can a new pattern in one population of a species become the dominant pattern of the species as a whole. The adaptive pattern may be propagated by the flow of genes to other populations or by the simple replacement of part or all of the old populations, with the new population expanding and successfully competing for existing resources. How is Neanderthal history to be seen in the light of such processes?

We have outlined two eventualities: either evolution throughout an entire species (or a large population) because of a common selective pressure or a faster evolution in one element of the population toward a specific adaptation, after which that element of the population replaces other elements because of its adaptive advantage. The two eventualities correspond generally to the two customary interpretations of why after a certain time men of the modern type came to the fore and the Neanderthals disappeared. The two interpretations also imply different degrees of complexity in the genetic basis of the observed anatomical differences. If, on the one hand, the Neanderthals evolved locally into early Upper Paleolithic people, one would expect that relatively few simply coded genetic traits were responsible for the anatomical differences in order for them to appear and spread across the Near East and Europe in a few thousand years. The rate of such evolution within local populations might have been accelerated by the influence of behavioral adaptations on certain aspects of growth, such as the robustness of limb bones; this characteristic is known to be sensitive, within limits, to patterns of individual activity. If, on the other hand, there was significant migration of non-Neanderthal peoples, together with interbreeding and replacement, then a far more complex set of circumstances of genetic substitution and change might be involved.

The fossils themselves furnish some hint of the complexity of the genetic basis for the anatomical differences. First, the Neanderthal pattern seems to have coalesced slowly during the late Middle Pleistocene and the early Upper Pleistocene. This suggests that the kind of complex genetic basis that could build up over many millenniums may well have been responsible for the Neanderthal pattern. Second, the fossil remains of Neanderthal children show that the characteristic Neanderthal morphology had developed by the age of five, and perhaps earlier. Since it is difficult to see how activity could seriously affect the developmental pattern of an infant, it appears likely that there was a complex genetic determination of the development of many details of the Neanderthal morphological pattern.

Broadly, then, the Neanderthal physical pattern evolved in 50 millenniums or more; thereafter it remained relatively constant for about another 50 millenniums. Then came the observed transition, within Neanderthal territory, to an essentially modern human anatomy in about 5,000 years. The various evolutionary and anatomical considerations seem to fit best a model that presents the evolution of populations of anatomically modern men (the early Upper Paleolithic people of Europe and the final Mousterians of the Near East) in partial isolation from the majority of the Neanderthals. These populations may have arisen from a strictly Neanderthal population or a non-Neanderthal one. At any rate they undoubtedly spread, absorbing and replacing various local Neanderthal populations across the Near East and Europe. The time and place of the establishment of these earliest modern people within the Neanderthal area are not yet known.

The main selective force that favored

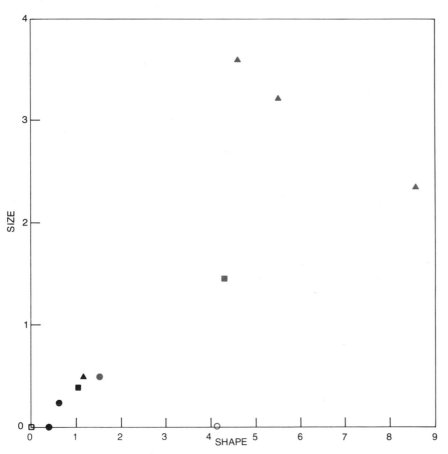

MULTIVARIATE ANALYSIS of fossil and modern skulls compares 18 measurements in terms of size (*ordinate*) and shape (*abscissa*). An average of European Upper Paleolithic skulls (*open square*) is used as the point of departure. Farthest removed from the starting point in terms of shape and well removed in terms of size is the Middle Pleistocene skull from Petralona (*colored triangle at far right*). More removed in terms of size but nearer in terms of shape are the skulls of Rhodesian man (*colored triangle to right of center*) and a Near Eastern Neanderthal, from Amud (*colored triangle at top center*). The colored square near the center represents the average of European Neanderthal skulls; the Middle Pleistocene European fossil from Steinheim (*open colored circle*), although it is smaller than the Neanderthal average, is quite close to the Neanderthal average in shape. The Saccopastore skulls (*colored dot*), most recent of the early Neanderthals, are surprisingly close to the averages of two modern skull samples (*black dots*): Norwegians and Zulus. The same is true of two skulls from Qafzeh (*black triangle*) and another specimen from the Levant, Skhūl 5 (*black square*). The modern and the Levant specimens diverge only trivially from the European Upper Paleolithic average. This Penrose size and shape analysis was done by Christopher Stringer of the British Museum (Natural History).

the modern physique over the Neanderthal one also remains to be discovered. Was it perhaps climatic change? Actually the last glacial period reached its coldest point more than 10,000 years after the transition from the Neanderthal physique to the modern one, and there is no consistent correlation between the transition and any major climatic change. Was it ecology? Both kinds of men hunted the same game and presumably collected the same plant foods.

Was it cultural advance? Here we have the best evidence in the form of the stone tools. It is hard to see that the specific Upper Paleolithic tools have much of an advantage over the Mousterian ones, for hunting, for gathering or for any other subsistence activity. It is more likely that, as the Mousterian tools were beginning to suggest the Upper Paleolithic forms, there arrived a threshold in human subsistence patterns, and that the only indication of the threshold appears in the tools themselves. One might hypothesize that crossing this threshold made the bulky Neanderthal physique both unnecessary and too costly in its food requirements, thereby initiating a rapid reduction in body size and conceivably even a change in all the special Neanderthal traits. Alternatively the improvement in stoneworking techniques and the associated behavioral changes may have given a significant adaptive advantage to the less heavy-bodied Upper Paleolithic people.

It is interesting that between 40,000 and 35,000 years ago there was a marked increase in the complexity of the sociocultural system of these hominids. Soon thereafter various forms of art are a regular feature at archaeological sites, implying the existence of well-established rituals for various kinds of social behavior. Although ritual existed considerably earlier among the Nean-derthals, as is indicated by their burial practices, a rapid increase in its complexity would suggest that some threshold had been reached in the evolution of the sociocultural system. The crossing of such a threshold may well have had significant influence on the biological evolution of these prehistoric human populations.

The problems remain: on the theoretical side the nature of the advantage giving rise to the transition and on the factual side the lack of datable fossils that would make the real story clear. Yet the importance of the Neanderthals is that so much is now known about them, incomparably more than is known about other human populations that lived at the same time. Reconciling this wealth of information with what is known about evolution in general presents by far the best opportunity for the scientific study of human development in the late Pleistocene.

6

The Archaeology of Lascaux Cave

by Arlette Leori-Gourhan
June 1982

*Forty years' work has revealed much about how the
great Paleolithic paintings of Lascaux Cave were created.
It has also focused attention on hundreds of engravings
that rival the paintings in their import*

The cave site of Lascaux, with its magnificent array of some 600 paintings from the Old Stone Age, was discovered more than 40 years ago. Situated in the Dordogne region of southwestern France, the cave has been closed to all but officially sanctioned visitors for the past 20 years. The closing was part of a conservation effort, fortunately successful, aimed at halting further deterioration of these Paleolithic art treasures. Until recently, however, few people other than specialists have been aware that the mighty paintings of Lascaux are only a part of the wealth of archaeological material discovered in the cave over the past four decades.

Among these discoveries are nearly 1,500 engravings on the cave's walls and ceilings. They were all painstakingly copied by Abbé André Glory, who until his untimely death in 1966 was by far the most indefatigable of the scientific investigators at Lascaux. Glory and others have also excavated the flint tools used to make the engravings, have found the stone lamps that provided light for the artists, have found the palettes that held the painters' pigments and most recently have studied the minerals that were ground into pigments. They have even been able to reconstruct the kind of scaffolding that allowed the painters and engravers to work on rock faces far out of normal reach. These findings and others now enable prehistorians to picture in some detail man's activities at Lascaux as the Old Stone Age entered its final stages some 17,000 years ago.

The discovery of the cave in September, 1940, early in World War II, has often been attributed to the actions of some village boys after a dog had fallen into a deep hole. The facts are somewhat different. A boy from the village of Montignac, a kilometer away, did come on a hole in the ground. It was newly made by the uprooting of a pine tree, but no dog had fallen into it. He and some friends began to test the depth of the hole by dropping stones into it. Their curiosity further aroused, the boys enlarged the opening and were able to slide down a steep tunnel of wet clay. They landed a good deal farther underground than they had expected. What they saw by the glimmer of a weak flashlight left them amazed. After they had led the local schoolmaster to the site their discovery was reported in the school paper. Specialists in prehistoric studies were told of the find, and a small ramp was dug to give easier access to the cave. The first professional archaeologist to inspect the site was Abbé Henri Breuil.

The lower end of the ramp opens into a great chamber some 20 meters long. Its ceiling is covered with immense paintings of bulls; some of the animal figures are more than five meters long. At the far end of this "Hall of the Bulls" open two passages. One passage is straight ahead and the other branches off to the right. The ceiling of the passage straight ahead (known as the Axial Alleyway) is also covered with paintings; they depict deer, horses, wild cattle, ibexes and a bison. Access to the branch to the right (known simply as the Passage) was difficult in the early years. Visitors had at first to go on all fours, but they were soon rewarded by another series of animal paintings. A second branching to the right leads to "the Apse," beyond which lies "the Well," a five-meter depression with a curious group of paintings depicting a man, a bird perched on a staff, a rhinoceros and a charging bison with a horse's head above it. Opening to the left of the Apse is "the Nave." Here and in the long, narrow passage farther along are several more animal paintings. The passage leads eventually through "the Cat's Hole" to "the Alleyway of the Felines," where engravings are found not only of felines but also of several other kinds of animal. This final excursion completes the visitor's tour of Lascaux.

Soon after the war ended the cave was fitted out to accommodate visitors; Lascaux was transformed into an underground museum. Then, after two decades of tourism, it became apparent that the dust, the dampness and the fungi that entered the cave along with the visitors were threatening to destroy this unique Paleolithic gallery. The closing of Lascaux to tourism in 1963 has saved the paintings. In what follows I shall briefly recount what the work of Abbé Glory and others over the past four decades has revealed about the contents of the cave.

How can one determine the age of a prehistoric painting? This question was perhaps the most difficult one that faced the scholars at Lascaux from the first. There is no known way of dating such a painting by itself; one must begin by determining the context of the artists' work. That means looking for traces the artists left behind. To find such traces one must dig, first in order to expose the levels of soil that contain artifacts contemporaneous with the artists' work. Next one must establish the sequence of the layers, since not all the layers from top to bottom will be present in all parts of the site. Even when the stratigraphy is known, however, one has the problem of determining which levels are contemporaneous with the paintings.

At Lascaux, fortunately, this problem did not arise. The first stratigraphic in-

TWELVE PIGMENTS applied by the painters at Lascaux range from a pale yellow (*A*) to black (*70A*). All the pigments used at Lascaux, with the exception of those incorporating charcoal, consisted of powdered minerals. The application of a single mineral as a pigment, however, was rare; the minerals were more usually mixed together. The powder labeled *66A* is unusually pure, being a mixture of hematite (70 percent), clay (20 percent), quartz (5 percent) and other substances. Powder labeled *70B*, in contrast, is a black containing 40 percent calcium phosphate, 25 percent quartz and 15 percent manganese dioxide, the chief mineral for blacks.

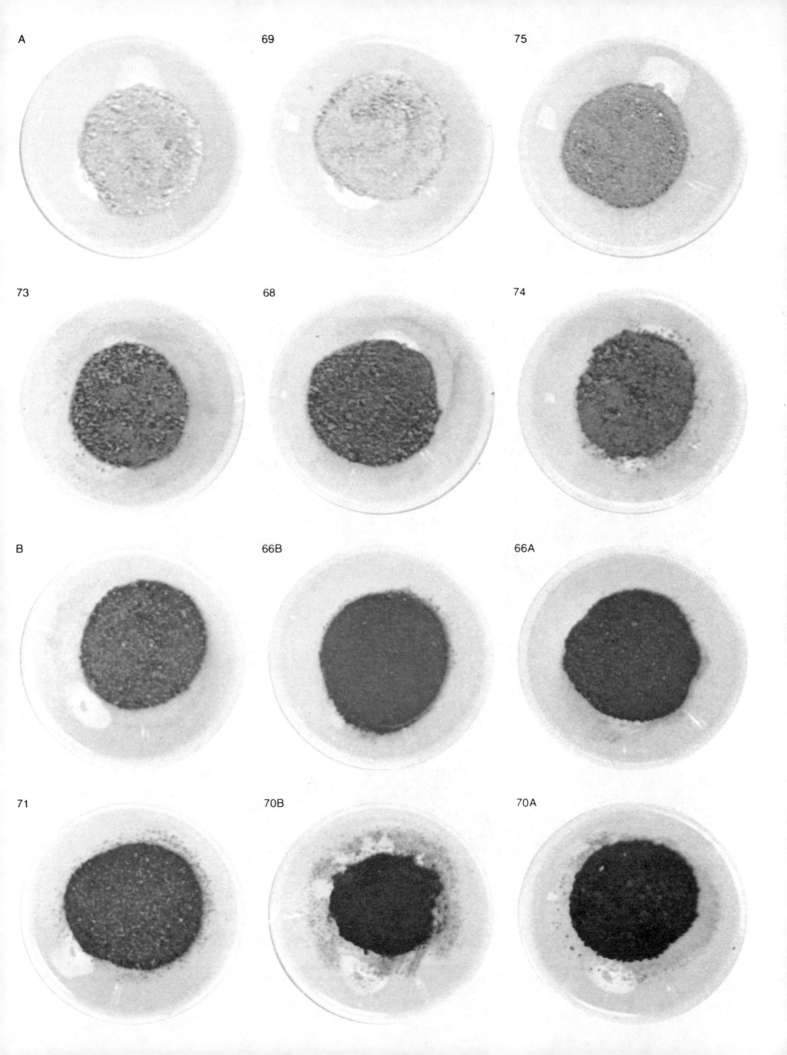

vestigations were conducted by Abbé Glory, who excavated 15 cross-section trenches in different parts of the cave. All the evidence of human activity he found proved to come from the same stratum. No further proof that this layer was contemporaneous with the paintings was needed other than the uncovering, along with the other objects in the layer, of the lamps, the stone palettes and the lumps of mineral coloring matter used by the Lascaux painters.

The archaeological remains unearthed in these excavations indicate that although the cave never served for living purposes, those who made the paintings and engravings worked there for many hours at a time, often eating their meals on the spot. It also seems likely that religious rites were held in the cave. In the Well beyond the Apse are the remains of meals, the finest stone lamp found at Lascaux, ornamental seashells and bone lance heads. Among the shells was a particularly beautiful one that had been pierced for stringing as an ornament. It shows grooves worn by the cord that suspended it and bears traces of red ocher. Since the nearest seashore is 200 kilometers away, the shells must have come from at least that distance. The Well seems to have served as a kind of sanctuary.

The stratigraphic investigations at Lascaux, together with analyses of pollen grains in the strata from contemporaneous plants, show that Paleolithic man used the cave for a relatively brief period, perhaps only a few hundred years. This conclusion is consistent with the fact that the stone and bone artifacts excavated in the cave all belong to a single late Upper Paleolithic culture well known in the Dordogne and elsewhere in France: the Lower Magdalenian. It is also in accord with studies of the many Lascaux paintings and the more numerous engravings demonstrating that their style is homogeneous. Hence everything points toward the utilization of the cave for a single short

STAG'S HEAD, its eye and ear carefully outlined, was engraved on the south wall of the area called "the Apse" at Lascaux Cave. The animal's body was outlined but is not seen in this view. Its exaggerated antlers, also outlined in part, have in addition been painted in black.

period. Carbon-14 dating of charcoal associated with the painters' lamps places that period at about 15,000 B.C.

How did the artists do their work? Their first problem must have been the need for artificial light. In Magdalenian times the entrance to the cave was sizable and the roof stood about three meters above ground level. This means that the front of the Hall of the Bulls did receive some daylight. At the back of the hall, however, the natural light would not have been enough to work by, whereas in the Axial Alleyway and all the other galleries artificial light was an absolute necessity.

It is thus not surprising that stone lamps have been found by the score at Lascaux. Some 130 of the total have been carefully studied. The Magdalenian artists did not have to invest much effort in making the kind of lamp most often used; these lamps were simply stones selected from the rocky hillside around the cave mouth that had natural cup-shaped depressions in them. Indeed, some of the stones have depressions so shallow that one may wonder whether they served as lamps at all. The residue of soot, charcoal and ash found in the depressions, however, along with evidence of heating, leaves no doubt about their function.

To better understand how these simple lamps worked, Brigitte and Gilles Delluc of the Musée des Eyzies collected similar flat stones in the vicinity of the cave and tried some experiments. They found that suitable wicks could be made out of dried lichen, moss or twigs of juniper. (Analysis of the charcoal from seven of the lamps had identified juniper wood as one of the wick materials.) The fuel they found most suitable was tallow; in each lamp they put a 50-gram piece of this animal fat. It burned without smoking, gave as much light as an ordinary candle and the 50 grams lasted for about an hour. If one had wanted more illumination, several wicks could have been put in one lamp.

The handsome lamp that was found in the Well was smoothly carved out of red sandstone and decorated with linear incisions. It was found on the floor of the Well, just below the tip of the tail of the rhinoceros in the painting above it. The refinement of the lamp's workmanship and its presence in this putative sanctuary suggest that it had served some purpose other than mere illumination.

The artists' second problem became apparent as soon as they had decided which parts of the cave were suitable for painting. Paintability depended on the condition of the rock surface. For example, in the Axial Alleyway the surface that is sufficiently smooth for painting is three to four meters above the floor and therefore out of reach. The

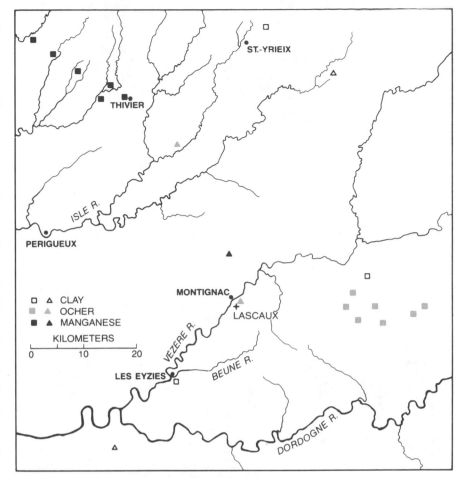

LASCAUX CAVE, near the village of Montignac on the Vézère River 40 kilometers east of Périgueux, lies in a region where deposits of clay, manganese oxide and red and yellow ocher are common (*squares*). The closest source of manganese mapped by geological surveys is at Thivier, 40 kilometers to the northwest of Lascaux, and the closest sources of clay, red ocher and yellow ocher are 20 kilometers to the east. Investigators who sought closer sources (*triangles*) found manganese within six kilometers of the cave and both ochers within 500 meters.

BITS OF PAINT from Lascaux are seen in these scanning electron micrographs. At the left is a red ocher, enlarged 6,000 diameters; the platelike crystals are hematite (Fe_2O_3). At the right is a black manganese, enlarged 7,000 diameters; the needlelike crystals are pyrolusite (MnO_2). The study is being done by Pamela B. Vandiver at the Massachusetts Institute of Technology.

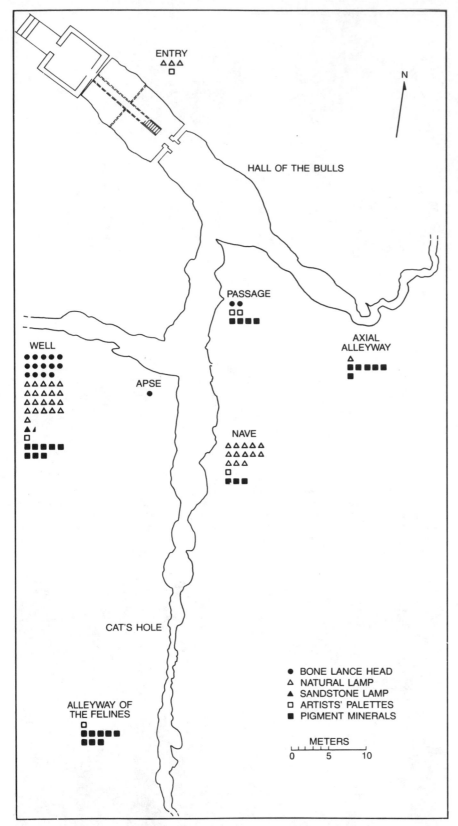

ENTRY

HALL OF THE BULLS

N

PASSAGE

AXIAL
ALLEYWAY

WELL

APSE

NAVE

CAT'S HOLE

● BONE LANCE HEAD
△ NATURAL LAMP
▲ SANDSTONE LAMP
□ ARTISTS' PALETTES
■ PIGMENT MINERALS

METERS
0   5   10

ALLEYWAY OF
THE FELINES

EIGHT PRINCIPAL LANDMARKS in the cave at Lascaux are named on this plan; where some key artifacts were found is also indicated. The richest source of artifacts was "the Well," 55 meters from the entrance to the cave at the left. The Well yielded 21 lamps of unworked stone, one carefully fashioned stone lamp (and a fragment of another), 14 of the 17 bone lance heads found at Lascaux, one of the six artist's palettes and eight of the 29 lumps of minerals the artists powdered to make their pigments. (One hundred and twenty-nine other lumps were found in the cave, but their location was not recorded.) Many stone lamps were also found in "the Nave." Additional minerals were found in the Nave, in "the Passage," in "the Axial Alleyway" and in the remotest gallery, "the Alleyway of the Felines," 100 meters from the entrance.

same is true of many of the best surfaces for painting elsewhere in the cave. In the Hall of the Bulls one can imagine the Magdalenians bringing saplings in and propping them up to form a crude scaffolding for the painter to perch on. Traces of more ambitious scaffolding, however, have been found in the Axial Alleyway. From them it has been possible to reconstruct how the painter was given a level platform close to the ceiling of the passage.

The investigators found a series of recesses cut into the rock on both sides of the passage, all on the same level about two meters above the floor. The recesses had been packed with clay, and holes about 10 centimeters deep can be seen in the soft clay packing. The surface of the wall later became covered by a thin coat of the soluble mineral calcite, so that 17 of the indentations were perfectly preserved. Evidently stout tree branches, long enough to span the passage, were fitted into the recesses on each side and were cemented in place with clay. This array of joists could then support a flooring of additional branches that was high enough to give the painters access to the entire ceiling.

Once the painters were settled on their platform they must have been quite comfortable. Judging from the animal bones found on the floor below, they did not even bother to come down when they ate. Animal bones also indicate that a second area in the cave was a popular eating place: a large rock ledge in the Nave near a painting of a black cow.

Analysis of bone in both deposits suggests that the artists of Lascaux were partial to the meat of young reindeer, but this may have been less a matter of gastronomic preference than one of what game was available. It is of interest in this connection to note that only one of the animal paintings at Lascaux depicts a reindeer. Facts such as this one help to emphasize the hazards facing those who seek to speculate about the "why" of Paleolithic painting.

The mineral pigments applied by the Magdalenian painters at Lascaux have been the subject of three related studies. First, the late Annette Laming-Emperaire of the École Pratique des Hautes Études in Paris and one of her students, Claude Couraud, have analyzed the raw materials used to produce powdered pigments and have determined where in this part of France the sources of these minerals are. Second, at the suggestion of Aimé Bocquet of the Center for the Documentation of Alpine Prehistory and under the direction of R. Bouchez of the Nuclear Research Center at Grenoble, a group of scholars undertook a technical analysis of the powdered pigments and of the Magdalenian methods of preparing them.

Third, Pamela B. Vandiver, a gradu-

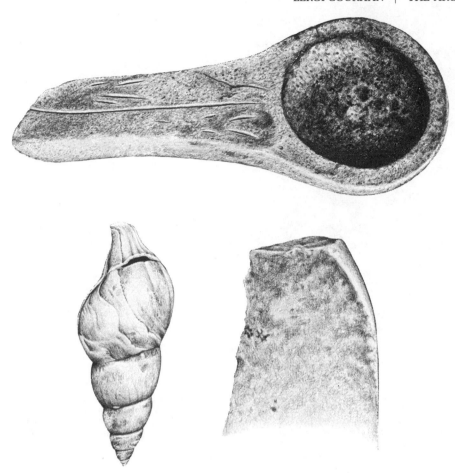

THREE ARTIFACTS among the many discovered at Lascaux are the carefully worked stone lamp found in the Well (*top*), a seashell stained with ocher and pierced for stringing as a personal ornament (*bottom left*), which was also found in the Well, and the worn, work-polished end of one of the 27 flint engraving tools that have been discovered in the cave (*bottom right*).

ate student at the Massachusetts Institute of Technology working under the direction of William D. Kingery, has used scanning electron microscopy to study chips of pigment from several of the Lascaux paintings. The chips were furnished by S. Delbourgo of the Musée du Louvre. Vandiver's findings are about to be published; some of the highlights will be summarized below.

In the first of these studies Laming-Emperaire and Couraud had at their disposal a total of 158 mineral fragments Abbé Glory had found at various places in the cave. Many of the fragments show scratch lines and other evidence of purposeful wear. To judge from the fragments, the colors the Magdalenians most prized were blacks (105 fragments), yellows (26), reds (24) and, as a poor fourth, whites (3). There was substantial variation within the blacks, yellows and reds. For example, the blacks ranged from very dark black to olive gray, the yellows from light yellow to reddish and brownish yellow and the reds from brownish and yellowish red to light red and very pale red. Abbé Glory's collection included some crude pigment-stained stone "mortars" and "pes-

tles" one may assume the painters used in preparing their colors. It also included a number of naturally hollowed stones that still held small amounts of powdered pigment.

To determine the sources of the minerals Laming-Emperaire and Couraud first turned to government geological-survey data on the known deposits in the vicinity of Lascaux of manganese oxide (blacks), iron oxide (reds and yellows) and porcelain clay (white). The closest source of manganese, according to geological-survey maps, was 40 kilometers to the north-northwest of the cave and the closest source of clay was 20 kilometers to the east. Red and yellow ocher were available 20 kilometers to the east. Later field work by the two scholars turned up unmapped sources much closer to Lascaux: a source of manganese oxide five kilometers away and one of ocher only half a kilometer away.

Laming-Emperaire and Couraud next turned their attention to the painting methods of the Magdalenians. Experiments demonstrated that the pigments had been prepared by mixing the ground mineral powders with cave water, which has a naturally high calcium content

that ensures good adhesion and great durability. Further experiments showed how the pigments were applied to the rock surface. Laming-Emperaire and Couraud made paintbrushes by macerating the tips of twigs and by binding bison hair in small bundles. They applied powdered pigments directly to damp stone surfaces and also used fragments of ocher as crayons for initially sketching out a painting.

They soon found the best way to hold the paintbrushes, and they demonstrated the efficiency of transferring colors to the stone with a tamping pad. Finally they applied pigments on top of other pigments to determine the effects of such superpositions. In this way they were able to confirm what infrared photography had already suggested: the red cows in the Hall of the Bulls were painted before the great black bulls.

The group in Grenoble analyzed 10 samples of the powdered pigments recovered by Abbé Glory and a further sample of a black pigment removed from the surface of one mortar. For each sample they determined both the chemical elements present and the specific minerals the elements came from. Bits of pigment from a number of Upper Paleolithic paintings had been subjected to similar analysis in the past, but Lascaux is unique in yielding the powders from which the cave artists prepared their pigments. Hence it is not surprising that the work of the Grenoble group has brought out a number of new facts.

Foremost among them is that the Magdalenian painters not only mixed pigments to achieve the colors and other properties they sought but also processed pigments in unexpected ways. For example, a component of one pigment was calcium phosphate, a substance obtained by heating animal bone to a temperature of about 400 degrees Celsius. The calcium phosphate was then mixed with calcite and heated again, to about 1,000 degrees C., transforming the mixture into tetracalcitic phosphate ($4CaO \cdot P_2O_5$).

A white pigment that at first glance seems reddish because of surface contamination with red ocher proved to be not pure porcelain clay but a mixture of clay (10 percent), powdered quartz (20 percent) and powdered calcite (70 percent). Similarly, whereas manganese oxide was the primary substance of the dark pigments, the black pigment removed from the mortar proved to be a blend of charcoal (65 percent), clay rich in iron (25 percent) and smaller amounts of other minerals, including powdered quartz. Clay had also been added to the powdered red and yellow ochers, in proportions ranging from 20 to 40 percent.

Vandiver's analysis of pigment chips with the scanning electron microscope

ENGRAVED ANIMALS on the west wall of the Passage cover six square meters. A total of 32 animals are shown in part or in their entirety; most of them are horses. Painting has been used to accent three of the horses (Nos. 120, 133 and 135). A few cattle heads and a bull's hindquarters appear to the left of the center. At the center and to the right of the center are the exaggerated tails of three horses. This illustration and the one below are tracings made by Abbé André Glory. His tracings of the engravings covered 117 square meters of paper.

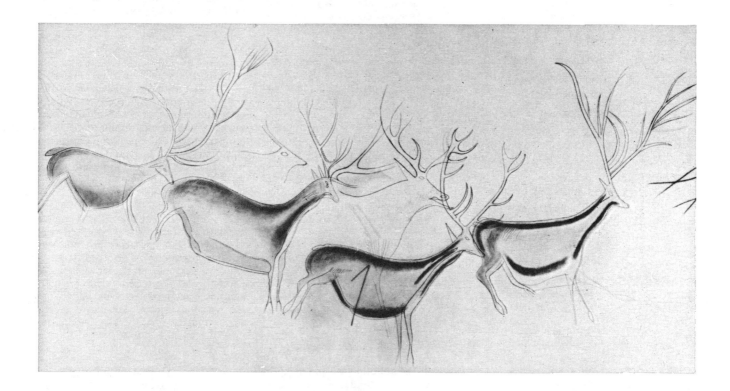

DETAIL OF SIX DEER, all of them engraved but four fully painted and one with paint accents in outline, forms part of a panel four meters square south of the Well. The sixth deer, the head, horns and back of which are faintly visible above the painted deer second from the left, has the least exaggerated antlers. The dark angular lines visible on the painted deer second from the right may represent an arrow.

has yielded more detailed evidence on the preparation and application of pigments at Lascaux. She has also exploited energy-dispersive X-ray analysis, X-ray diffraction and optical petrography to evaluate the technology developed by the Lascaux artists. Such techniques reveal that the microstructure of the red pigments differs from that of the black ones. For example, the hematite crystals of a red ocher pigment are characteristically platy, and the pyrolusite crystals of a black manganese oxide pigment are fibrous or needlelike. An important part of Vandiver's program has been the establishing of a reference collection of natural minerals related to the minerals of the cave-painting pigments. The microstructure and composition of the Lascaux pigments are currently being compared with those of the natural samples in order to learn the nature and extent of Magdalenian processing.

Of Abbé Glory's many contributions to the study of Lascaux none is greater in scope and in importance than his documentation of the 1,500 Magdalenian engravings in the cave. Ranging in complexity from simple straight lines to renderings of entire groups of animals, these incised figures are found in the Passage, in the Nave and particularly in the Apse, where no fewer than 578 of them occupy every available rock surface. It is in these same parts of the cave that 27 flint burins, or engraving tools, have come to light. All of them show identical signs of wear: at the working corner the original sharp angle is worn smooth and round.

The Lascaux paintings, particularly those in the Hall of the Bulls and the Axial Alleyway, were widely reproduced in books and periodicals in the years following World War II. The engravings, however, except for the few that were most clearly visible, attracted little attention. As a result hundreds of significant Upper Paleolithic works of art remained unknown except to specialists. To rectify this neglect was the main task Glory set himself when in 1952 Abbé Breuil, whose eyesight was failing, enlisted Glory's aid. Glory adopted a technique pioneered by Breuil: sheets of transparent plastic were placed over the engravings and the incised lines were traced on the surface of the plastic. The tracings were subsequently transferred to sheets of tracing paper large enough to encompass an entire composition. Eventually Glory's transfers covered 117 square meters of paper.

Glory did much other work at Lascaux: excavation, the collection of artifacts, photography. In the early years he often pursued his researches at night when the flow of tourists, as many as 1,000 per day in season, had ended. Nevertheless, his greatest labor—the record-

PALEOLITHIC ROPE, seven millimeters in diameter, was "fossilized" in the Alleyway of the Felines. Calcite has replaced the plant fibers that had been twisted together to form the rope, but the 30-centimeter fragment preserves details of the twisting. Bone needles are common late Paleolithic artifacts, and it has been assumed they were used to pull some kind of "thread." It has not been clear, however, whether the thread was plant fiber or animal sinew or both. Discovery of the plant-fiber rope at Lascaux suggests that fiber was in common use by 15,000 B.C.

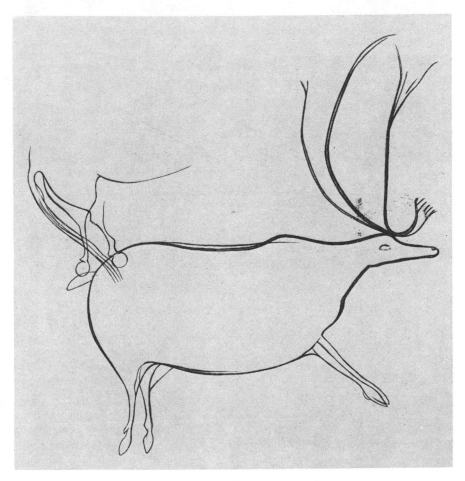

ENGRAVED REINDEER, 70 centimeters long from its muzzle to the tip of its stubby tail, stands at one edge of a composition in the Apse that includes a painted yellow horse. Two rear hooves and a small part of the tail of an engraved horse overlap the reindeer's rump and tail. This copy of another of Abbé Glory's tracings is somewhat simplified for the sake of clarity.

108

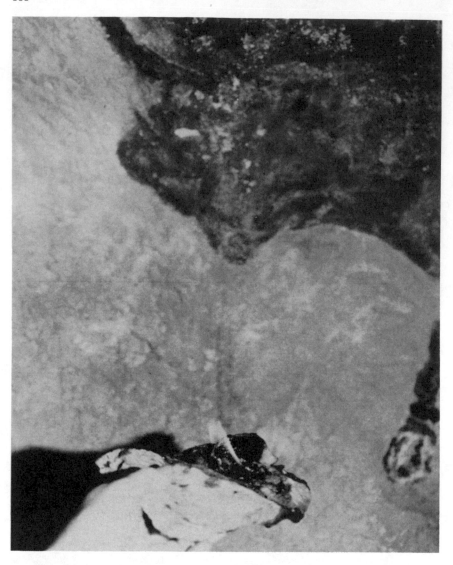

ing of the engravings—was also his most important. From the closing of the cave in 1963 to the time of his death Glory continued to prepare this great mass of graphic material for publication. In so doing he has given prehistorians a base for the study of Upper Paleolithic cave art and symbolism that exists nowhere else and may never be surpassed.

REPLICA OF A LASCAUX LAMP, consisting of a fieldstone with a natural hollow, has juniper twigs as a wick and animal tallow as a fuel. Here it illuminates one painting in the cave.

A Paleo-Indian Bison Kill

By Joe Ben Wheat
January 1967

Some 8,500 years ago a group of hunters on the Great Plains stampeded a herd of buffaloes into a gulch and butchered them. The bones of the animals reveal the event in remarkable detail

When one thinks of American Indians hunting buffaloes, one usually visualizes the hunters pursuing a herd of the animals on horseback and killing them with bow and arrow. Did the Indians hunt buffaloes before the introduction of the horse (by the Spanish conquistadors in the 16th century) and the much earlier introduction of the bow? Indeed they did. As early as 10,000 years ago Paleo-Indians hunted species of bison that are now extinct on foot and with spears. My colleagues and I at the University of Colorado Museum have recently excavated the site of one such Paleo-Indian bison kill dating back to about 6500 B.C. The site so remarkably preserves a moment in time that we know with reasonable certainty not only the month of the year the hunt took place but also such details as the way the wind blew on the day of the kill, the direction of the hunters' drive, the highly organized manner in which they butchered their quarry, their choice of cuts to be eaten on the spot and the probable number of hunters involved.

The bison was the most important game animal in North America for millenniums before its near extermination in the 19th century. When Europeans arrived on the continent, they found herds of bison ranging over vast areas, but the animals were first and foremost inhabitants of the Great Plains, the high, semiarid grassland extending eastward from the foothills of the Rocky Mountains and all the way from Canada to Mexico. Both in historic and in late prehistoric times the bison was the principal economic resource of the Indian tribes that occupied the Great Plains. Its meat, fat and bone marrow provided them with food; its hide furnished them with shelter and clothing;

its brain was used to tan the hide; its horns were fashioned into containers. There was scarcely a part of the animal that was not utilized in some way.

This dependence on big-game hunting probably stretches back to the very beginning of human prehistory in the New World. We do not know when man first arrived in the Americas, nor do we know in detail what cultural baggage he brought with him. The evidence for the presence of man in the New World much before 12,000 years ago is scattered and controversial. It is quite

clear, however, that from then on Paleo-Indian hunting groups, using distinctive kinds of stone projectile point, ranged widely throughout the New World. On the Great Plains the principal game animal of this early period was the Columbian mammoth [see "Elephant-hunting in North America," by C. Vance Haynes, Jr., in June 1966 issue of SCIENTIFIC AMERICAN Magazine]. Mammoth remains have been found in association with projectile points that are usually large and leaf-shaped and have short, broad grooves on both sides of the base. These points are

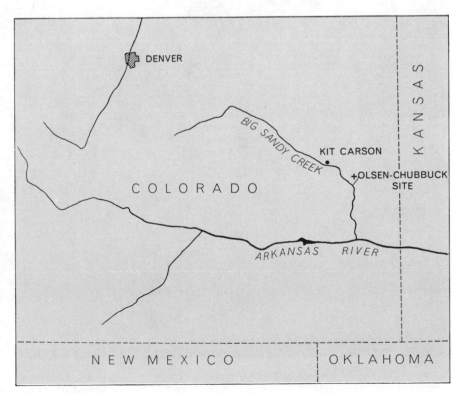

SITE OF THE KILL is 140 miles southeast of Denver. It is named the Olsen-Chubbuck site after its discoverers, the amateur archaeologists Sigurd Olsen and Gerald Chubbuck.

PROJECTILE POINTS found at the site show a surprising divergence of form in view of the fact that all of them were used simultaneously by a single group. In the center is a point of the Scottsbluff type. At top left is another Scottsbluff point that shows some of the characteristics of a point of the Eden type at top right. At bottom left is a third Scottsbluff point; it has characteristics in common with a point of the Milnesand type at bottom right. Regardless of form, all the points are equally excellent in flaking.

typical of the complex of cultural traits named the Clovis complex: the tool kit of this complex also included stone scrapers and knives and some artifacts made of ivory and bone.

The elephant may have been hunted out by 8000 B.C. In any case, its place as a game animal was taken by a large, straight-horned bison known as *Bison antiquus*. The first of the bison-hunters used projectile points of the Folsom culture complex; these are similar to Clovis points but are generally smaller and better made. Various stone scrapers and knives, bone needles and engraved bone ornaments have also been found in Folsom sites.

A millennium later, about 7000 B.C., *Bison antiquus* was supplanted on the Great Plains by the somewhat smaller *Bison occidentalis*. The projectile points found in association with this animal's remains are of several kinds. They differ in shape, size and details of flaking, but they have some characteristics in common. Chief among them is the technical excellence of the flaking. The flake scars meet at the center of the blade to form a ridge; sometimes they give the impression that a single flake has been detached across the entire width of the blade [*see the illustration on opposite page*]. Some of the projectile points that belong to this tradition, which take their names from the sites where they were first found, are called Milnesand, Scottsbluff and Eden points. The last two kinds of point form part of what is called the Cody complex, for which there is a fairly reliable carbon-14 date of about 6500 B.C.

Paleo-Indian archaeological sites fall into two categories: habitations and kill sites. Much of our knowledge of the early inhabitants of the Great Plains comes from the kill sites, where are found not only the bones of the animals but also the projectile points used to kill them and the knives, scrapers and other tools used to butcher and otherwise process them. Such sites have yielded much information about the categories of projectile points and how these categories are related in time. Heretofore, however, they have contributed little to our understanding of how the early hunters actually lived. The kill site I shall describe is one of those rare archaeological sites where the evidence is so complete that the people who left it seem almost to come to life.

Sixteen miles southeast of the town of Kit Carson in southeastern Colorado, just below the northern edge of the broad valley of the Arkansas River, lies a small valley near the crest of a low divide. The climate here is semiarid; short bunchgrass is the main vegetation and drought conditions have prevailed since the mid-1950's. In late 1957 wind erosion exposed what appeared to be five separate piles of bones, aligned in an east-west direction. Gerald Chubbuck, a keen amateur archaeologist, came on the bones in December, 1957; among them he found several projectile points of the Scottsbluff type. Chubbuck notified the University of Colorado Museum of his find, and we made plans to visit the site at the first opportunity.

Meanwhile Chubbuck and another amateur archaeologist, Sigurd Olsen, continued to collect at the site and ultimately excavated nearly a third of it. In the late spring of 1958 the museum secured permission from the two discoverers and from Paul Forward, the owner of the land, to complete the excavation. We carried out this work on summer expeditions in 1958 and 1960.

The Olsen-Chubbuck site consists of a continuous bed of bones lying within the confines of a small arroyo, or dry gulch. The arroyo, which had long since been buried, originally rose near the southern end of the valley and followed a gently undulating course eastward through a ridge that forms the valley's eastern edge. The section of the arroyo that we excavated was some 200 feet long. Its narrow western end was only about a foot and a half in depth and the same in width, but it grew progressively deeper and wider to the east. Halfway down the arroyo its width was five feet and its depth six; at the point to the east where our excavation stopped it was some 12 feet wide and seven feet deep. At the bottom of the

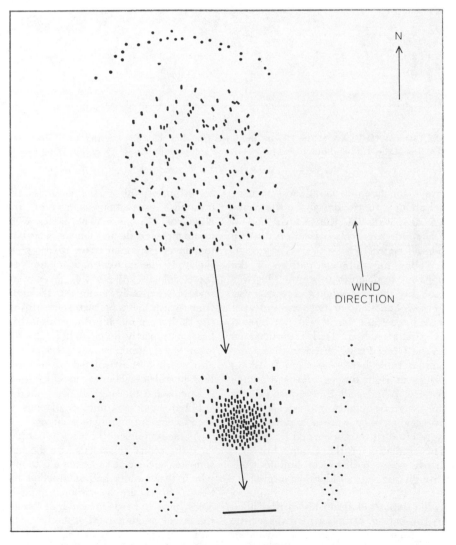

BISON STAMPEDE was probably set off by the Paleo-Indian hunters' close approach to the grazing herd from downwind. Projectile points found among the bones of the animals at the eastern end of the arroyo (*bottom*) suggest that some hunters kept the bison from veering eastward to escape. Other hunters probably did the same at the western end of the arroyo.

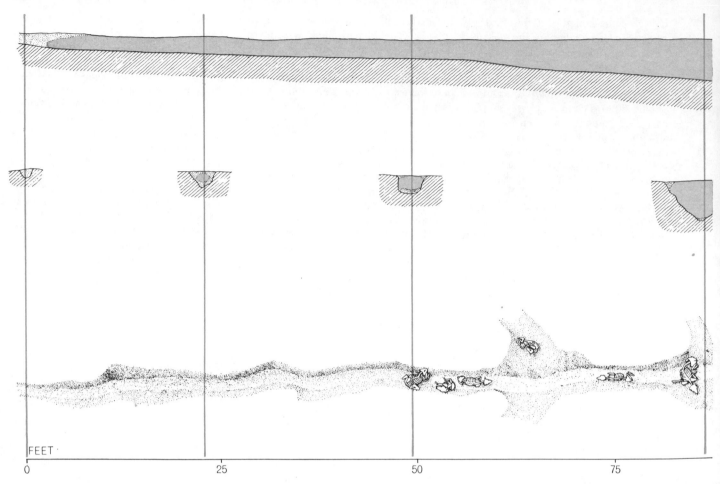

FEET

0   25   50   75

SECTION AND PLAN of the Olsen-Chubbuck site show how the
remains of the dead and butchered bison formed a deposit of bones
that lined the center of the arroyo for a distance of 170 feet (*color
at top*). One part of the site had been excavated by its discoverers

arroyo for its entire length was a channel about a foot wide; above the channel the walls of the arroyo had a
V-shaped cross section [*see top illustration on page 114*].

Today the drainage pattern of the
site runs from north to south. This was
probably the case when the arroyo was
formed, and since it runs east and west
it seems certain that it was not formed
by stream action. Early frontiersmen
on the Great Plains observed that many
buffalo trails led away from watering
places at right angles to the drainage
pattern. Where such trails crossed ridges
they were frequently quite deep; moreover, when they were abandoned they
were often further deepened by erosion.
The similarity of the Olsen-Chubbuck
arroyo to such historical buffalo trails
strongly suggests an identical origin.

The deposit of bison bones that filled
the bottom of the arroyo was a little
more than 170 feet long. It consisted of
the remains of nearly 200 buffaloes of
the species *Bison occidentalis*. Chubbuck and Olsen unearthed the bones of

an estimated 50 of the animals; the
museum's excavations uncovered the
bones of 143 more. The bones were
found in three distinct layers. The bottom layer contained some 13 complete
skeletons; the hunters had not touched
these animals. Above this layer were
several essentially complete skeletons
from which a leg or two, some ribs or
the skull were missing; these bison had
been only partly butchered. In the top
layer were numerous single bones and
also nearly 500 articulated segments of
buffalo skeleton. The way in which these
segments and the single bones were distributed provides a number of clues to
the hunters' butchering techniques.

As the contents of the arroyo—particularly the complete skeletons at the bottom—make clear, it had been a trap into
which the hunters had stampeded the
bison. Bison are gregarious animals.
They move in herds in search of forage;
the usual grazing herd is between 50
and 300 animals. Bison have a keen
sense of smell but relatively poor
vision. Hunters can thus get very close
to a herd as long as they stay down-

wind and largely out of sight. When the
bison are frightened, the herd has a
tendency to close ranks and stampede
in a single mass. If the herd encounters
an abrupt declivity such as the Olsen-
Chubbuck arroyo, the animals in front
cannot stop because they are pushed by
those behind. They can only plunge into
the arroyo, where they are immobilized,
disabled or killed by the animals that fall
on top of them.

The orientation of the skeletons in
the middle and lower layers of the Olsen-Chubbuck site is evidence that the
Paleo-Indian hunters had initiated such
a stampede. Almost without exception
the complete or nearly complete skeletons overlie or are overlain by the skeletons of one, two or even three other
whole or nearly whole animals; the
bones are massed and the skeletons are
contorted. The first animals that fell
into the arroyo had no chance to escape;
those behind them wedged them tighter
into the arroyo with their struggles.
Many of the skeletons are sharply twisted
around the axis of the spinal column.
Three spanned the arroyo, deformed into

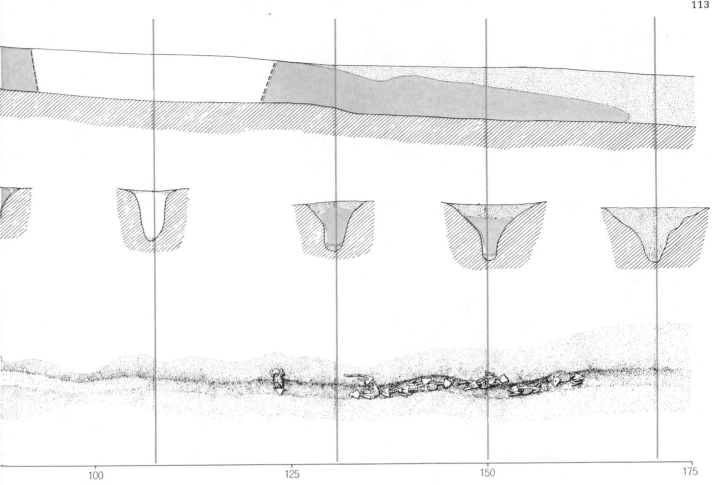

before the author and his associates began work in 1958; this area is represented by the 20-foot gap in the deposit. The shallow inner channel at the bottom of the arroyo can be seen in the plan view (*bottom*); outlines show the locations of 13 intact bison skeletons.

an unnatural U shape. Ten bison were pinned in position with their heads down and their hindquarters up; an equal number had landed with hindquarters down and heads up. At the bottom of the arroyo two skeletons lie on their backs.

The stampeding bison were almost certainly running in a north-south direction, at right angles to the arroyo. Of the 39 whole or nearly whole skeletons, which may be assumed to lie in the positions in which the animals died, not one faces north, northeast or northwest. A few skeletons, confined in the arroyo's narrow inner channel, face due east or west, but all 21 animals whose position at the time of death was not affected in this manner faced southeast, south or southwest. The direction in which the bison stampeded provides a strong clue to the way the wind was blowing on the day of the hunt. The hunters would surely have approached their quarry from downwind; thus the wind must have been from the south.

We have only meager evidence of the extent to which the stampede, once started, was directed and controlled by the hunters. The projectile points found with the bison skeletons in the deepest, most easterly part of the arroyo suggest that a flanking party of hunters was stationed there. It also seems a reasonable inference that, if no hunters had covered the stampede's western flank, the herd could have escaped unscathed around the head of the arroyo. If other hunters pursued the herd from the rear, there is no evidence of it.

Even if the hunters merely started the stampede and did not control it thereafter, it sufficed to kill almost 200 animals in a matter of minutes. The total was 46 adult bulls and 27 immature ones, 63 adult and 38 immature cows and 16 calves. From the fact that the bones include those of calves only a few days old, and from what we know about the breeding season of bison, we can confidently place the date of the kill as being late in May or early in June.

As we excavated the bone deposit we first uncovered the upper layer containing the single bones and articulated segments of skeleton. It was soon apparent that these bones were the end result of a standardized Paleo-Indian butchering procedure. We came to recognize certain "butchering units" such as forelegs, pelvic girdles, hind legs, spinal columns and skulls. Units of the same kind were usually found together in groups numbering from two or three to as many as 27. Similar units also formed distinct vertical sequences. As the hunters had removed the meat from the various units they had discarded the bones in separate piles, each of which contained the remains of a number of individual animals. In all we excavated nine such piles.

Where the order of deposition was clear, the bones at the bottom of each pile were foreleg units. Above these bones were those of pelvic-girdle units. Sometimes one or both hind legs were attached to the pelvic girdle, but by and large the hind-leg units lay separately among or above the pelvic units. The next level was usually composed of spinal-column units. The ribs had been removed from many of the chest vertebrae, but ribs were still attached to some of the other vertebrae. At the top

EXCAVATION at the eastern end of the arroyo reveals its V-shaped cross section and the layers of sand and silt that later filled it. The bone deposit ended at this point; a single bison shoulder blade remains in place at the level where it was unearthed (*lower center*).

BISON SKULL AND STONE POINT lie in close association at one level in the site. The projectile point (*lower left*) is of the Scottsbluff type. The bison skull, labeled 4-F to record its position among the other bones, rests upside down where the hunters threw it.

of nearly every pile were skulls. The jawbones had been removed from most of them, but some still retained a few of the neck vertebrae. In some instances these vertebrae had been pulled forward over the top and down the front of the skull. When the skull still had its jawbone, the hyoid bone of the tongue was missing.

Like the various butchering units, the single bones were found in clusters of the same skeletal part: shoulder blades, upper-foreleg bones, upper-hind-leg bones or jawbones (all broken in two at the front). Nearly all the jawbones were found near the top of the bone deposit. The tongue bones, on the other hand, were distributed throughout the bed. About 75 percent of the single foreleg bones were found in the upper part of the deposit, as were nearly 70 percent of the single vertebrae. Only 60 percent of the shoulder blades and scarcely half of the single ribs were in the upper level.

The hunters' first task had evidently been to get the bison carcasses into a position where they could be cut up. This meant that the animals had to be lifted, pulled, rolled or otherwise moved out of the arroyo to some flat area. It seems to have been impossible to remove the bison that lay at the bottom of the arroyo; perhaps they were too tightly wedged together. Some of them had been left untouched and others had had only a few accessible parts removed. The way in which the butchering units were grouped suggests that several bison were moved into position and cut up simultaneously. Since foreleg units, sometimes in pairs, were found at the bottom of each pile of bones it seems reasonable to assume that the Paleo-Indians followed the same initial steps in butchering that the Plains Indians did in recent times. The first step was to arrange the legs of the animal so that it could be rolled onto its belly. The skin was then cut down the back and pulled down on both sides of the carcass to form a kind of mat on which the meat could be placed. Directly under the skin of the back was a layer of tender meat, the "blanket of flesh"; when this was stripped away, the bison's forelegs and shoulder blades could be cut free, exposing the highly prized "hump" meat, the rib cage and the body cavity.

Having stripped the front legs of meat, the hunters threw the still-articulated bones into the arroyo. If they followed the practice of later Indians, they would next have indulged themselves

BONES OF BISON unearthed at the Olsen-Chubbuck site lie in a long row down the center of the ancient arroyo the Paleo-Indian hunters utilized as a pitfall for the stampeding herd. The bones proved to be the remains of bulls, cows and calves of the extinct species *Bison occidentalis*. Separate piles made up of the same types of bones (for example sets of limb bones, pelvic girdles or skulls) showed that the hunters had butchered several bison at a time and had systematically dumped the bones into the arroyo in the same order in which they were removed from the carcasses. In the foreground is a pile of skulls that was built up in this way.

by cutting into the body cavity, removing some of the internal organs and eating them raw. This, of course, would have left no evidence among the bones. What is certain is that the hunters did remove and eat the tongues of a few bison at this stage of the butchering, presumably in the same way the Plains Indians did: by slitting the throat, pulling the tongue out through the slit and cutting it off. Our evidence for their having eaten the tongues as they went along is that the tongue bones are found throughout the deposit instead of in one layer or another.

The bison's rib cages were attacked as soon as they were exposed by the removal of the overlying meat. Many of the ribs were broken off near the spine. The Plains Indians used as a hammer for this purpose a bison leg bone with the hoof still attached; perhaps the Paleo-Indians did the same. In any case, the next step was to sever the spine at a point behind the rib cage and remove the hindquarters. The meat was cut away from the pelvis (and in some instances simultaneously from the hind legs) and the pelvic girdle was discarded. If the hind legs had been separated from the pelvis, it was now their turn to be stripped of meat and discarded.

After the bison's hindquarters had

been butchered, the neck and skull were cut off as a unit—usually at a point just in front of the rib cage—and set aside. Then the spine was discarded, presumably after it had been completely stripped of meat and sinew. Next the hunters turned to the neck and skull and cut the neck meat away. This is evident from the skulls that had vertebrae draped over the front; this would not have been possible if the neck meat had been in place. The Plains Indians found bison neck meat too tough to eat in its original state. They dried it and made the dried strips into pemmican by pounding them to a powder. The fact that the Paleo-Indians cut off the neck meat strongly suggests that they too preserved some of their kill.

If the tongue had not already been removed, the jawbone was now cut away, broken at the front and the tongue cut out. The horns were broken from a few skulls, but there is little evidence that the Paleo-Indians broke open the skull as the Plains Indians did to take out the brain. Perhaps the most striking difference between the butchering practices of these earlier Indians and those of later ones, however, lies in the high degree of organization displayed by the Paleo-Indians. Historical

accounts of butchering by Plains Indians indicate no such efficient system.

In all, 47 artifacts were found in association with the bones at the Olsen-Chubbuck site. Spherical hammerstones and knives give us some idea of what constituted the hunter's tool kit; stone scrapers suggest that the bison's skins were processed at the site. A bone pin and a piece of the brown rock limonite that shows signs of having been rubbed tell something about Paleo-Indian ornamentation.

The bulk of the artifacts at the site are projectile points. There are 27 of them, and they are particularly significant. Most of them are of the Scottsbluff type. When their range of variation is considered, however, they merge gradually at one end of the curve of variation into Eden points and at the other end into Milnesand points. Moreover, among the projectile points found at the site are one Eden point and a number of Milnesand points. The diversity of the points clearly demonstrates the range of variation that was possible among the weapons of a single hunting group. Their occurrence together at the site is conclusive proof that such divergent forms of weapon could exist contemporaneously.

How many Paleo-Indians were pres-

INTACT SKELETON of an immature bison cow, uncovered in the lowest level of the arroyo, is one of 13 animals the Paleo-Indian hunters left untouched. The direction in which many bison faced suggests that the stampede traveled from north to south.

ent at the kill? The answer to this question need not be completely conjectural. We can start with what we know about the consumption of bison meat by Plains Indians. During a feast a man could consume from 10 to 20 pounds of fresh meat a day; women and children obviously ate less. The Plains Indians also preserved bison meat by drying it; 100 pounds of fresh meat would provide 20 pounds of dried meat. A bison bull of today yields about 550 pounds of edible meat; cows average 400 pounds. For an immature bull one can allow 165 pounds of edible meat, for an immature cow 110 pounds and for a calf 50 pounds. About 75 percent of the bison killed at the Olsen-Chubbuck site were completely butchered; on this basis the total weight of bison meat would have been 45,300 pounds. The *Bison occidentalis* killed by the Paleo-Indian hunters, however, was considerably larger than the *Bison bison* of modern times. To compensate for the difference it seems reasonable to add 25 percent to the weight estimate, bringing it to a total of 56,640 pounds. To this total should be added some 4,000 pounds of edible internal organs and 5,400 pounds of fat.

A Plains Indian could completely butcher a bison in about an hour. If we allow one and a half hours for the dissection of the larger species, the butchering at the Olsen-Chubbuck site would have occupied about 210 man-hours. In other words, 100 people could easily have done the job in half a day.

To carry the analysis further additional assumptions are needed. How long does fresh buffalo meat last? The experience of the Plains Indians (depending, of course, on weather conditions) was that it could be eaten for about a month. Let us now assume that half of the total weight of the Olsen-Chubbuck kill was eaten fresh at an average rate of 10 pounds per person per day, and that the other half was preserved. Such a division would provide enough fresh meat and fat to feed 150 people for 23 days. It seems reasonable to assume that the Paleo-Indian band was about this size. One way to test this assumption is to calculate the load each person would have to carry when camp was broken.

The preserved meat and fat, together with the hides, would have weighed about 7,350 pounds, which represents a burden of 49 pounds for each man, woman and child in the group (in addition to the weight of whatever other necessities they carried). Plains Indians are known to have borne loads as great as 100 pounds. Taking into account the likeli-

hood that small children and active hunters would have carried smaller loads, a 49-pound average appears to be just within the range of possibility.

A band of 150 people could, however, have eaten two-thirds of the kill fresh and preserved only one-third. In that case the fresh meat would have fed them for somewhat more than a month. At the end the meat would have been rather gamy, but the load of preserved meat per person would have been reduced to the more reasonable average of 31 pounds.

One possibility I have left out is that the Paleo-Indians had dogs. If there were dogs available to eat their share of fresh meat and to carry loads of preserved meat, the number of people in the group may have been somewhat less. In the absence of dogs, however, it seems improbable that any fewer than 150 people could have made use of the bison killed at the Olsen-Chubbuck site to the degree that has been revealed by our excavations. Whether or not the group had dogs, the remains of its stay at the site are unmistakable evidence that hunting bands of considerable size and impressive social organization were supporting themselves on the Great Plains some 8,500 years ago.

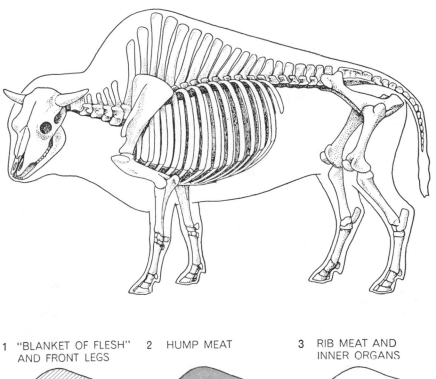

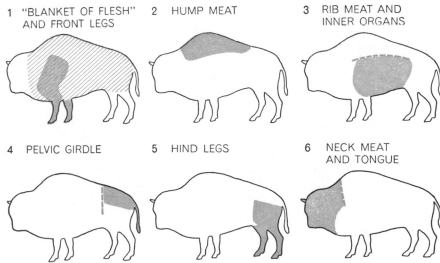

1 "BLANKET OF FLESH" AND FRONT LEGS   2 HUMP MEAT   3 RIB MEAT AND INNER ORGANS

4 PELVIC GIRDLE   5 HIND LEGS   6 NECK MEAT AND TONGUE

BUTCHERING METHODS used by the Paleo-Indians have been reconstructed on the dual basis of bone stratification at the Olsen-Chubbuck site and the practices of the Plains Indians in recent times. Once the carcass of the bison (*skeleton at top*) had been propped up and skinned down the back, a series of "butchering units" probably were removed in the order shown on the numbered outline figures. The hunters ate as they worked.

III

FARMERS
AND PEASANTS

FARMERS AND PEASANTS III

INTRODUCTION

We buy our food from supermarkets without a second thought. Flour comes packaged in white paper bags, meat already butchered and enshrined in plastic wrapping, fruit and vegetables bundled and sorted. The farmer toiling in the fields is a remote and impersonal figure. Children living in cities grow up without ever seeing a farm or even a cow. We take the production of an abundant food supply for granted. Yet agriculture and animal domestication are surprisingly recent innovations, revolutionary developments that may have begun in some limited areas only 15,000 years ago. They had as profound an effect on human history as the Industrial Revolution.

The Agricultural (Neolithic) Revolution

There is a tendency to think of the actual invention of agriculture as a dramatic, unexpected innovation. The early archaeologists conjured up a dramatic, even appealing, scenario of a solitary genius who had the brilliant idea of planting favored wild grains in the hope of assuring a steady food supply. The lone inventor was so successful that everyone adopted agriculture within a few centuries. They forgot that every hunter-gatherer society, however simple, had an intimate knowledge of its environment and was completely familiar with the process of plant germination. What was revolutionary was not the development of food production, but the *consequences* of agriculture and animal domestication. As American archaeologist Kent Flannery writes: "It is vain to hope for the discovery of the first domestic corn cob, the first pottery vessel, the first hieroglyphic, or the first site where several other major breakthroughs occurred."

About forty years ago, V. Gordon Childe formulated his theory of an Agricultural (or Neolithic) Revolution, a revolution that took place, so he believed, in a period of major climatic change at the end of the Pleistocene epoch. With the retreat of the Pleistocene ice sheets, he speculated, the abundant rains that had watered the more temperate Near East shifted northward, and widespread desiccation occurred. Both animals and humans moved into basin areas along rivers and new lakes, where the enforced concentrations of animals, plants, and humans in close association ultimately led to the domestication of plants and animals. Childe believed that farming first developed in the "fertile crescent" of the Near East, a great triangle formed by the Nile Valley, the Jordan River, and Mesopotamia. He thought the "Agricultural Revolution" occurred about 5000 BC.

Childe developed his hypothesis at a time when almost nothing was known about early farming in the Near East, or anywhere else for that matter. Archaeologist Robert J. Braidwood of the University of Chicago decided to test the theory immediately after World War II. He excavated at a series of early village sites in the Zagros mountains on the southern borders of Iraq, believing this was where wild forms of the cereals (oats, barley, wheat) might have grown naturally and provided the basis for the human manipulation of plants that we call domestication. He did not work alone and did not confine his attention to artifacts; he brought into the field a closely knit team of experts, including botanists, geologists, and zoologists, to take an integrated look at every aspect of early agriculture. The team found no evidence of catastrophic climatic change at the end of the Ice Age. Instead, the specialists argued, food production had resulted from more and more specialized hunting and gathering and from the human capacity for experimentation and receptiveness to change that made it possible for domestication to take place. Braidwood was one of the first archaeologists to use radio carbon dates. He was amazed when dates from a village named Jarmo came out as early as the eighth millenium BC. While Braidwood worked in the highlands, British archaeologist Kathleen Kenyon dug deep into the great occupation mounds at the biblical city of Jericho. She electrified the scholarly world by discovering the stone walls of a small town of modest houses that was contemporary with Braidwood's modest Zagros villages.

Current Hypotheses

Today, we are aware of prehistoric societies all over the world that are known to have experimented with agriculture, not only in the Near East, but in Southeast Asia, Northern China, and the Americas as well. Modern research focuses on three major areas of concern: the nature of the environment where the experimentation that led to agriculture took place; the demographic stresses invoved; and the level and type of technology involved in the shift. In other words, investigators are trying to explain *why* food production began rather than proving that it existed. Searching for the causes of the shift means identifying the numerous and complex interactive factors that caused humankind to make what was to become a radical shift in its food getting strategies. The search for these factors requires not only large-scale, multidisciplinary team research, but also sophisticated theoretical models. Highly sophisticated scientific methods like pollen analysis are being used to chronicle vegetational changes that occurred as agriculture took hold. The most effective theoretical models are based on the theories of cultural ecology and assume that the changeover was a slow and undramatic one.

Kent Flannery uses examples of prehistoric hunter-gatherer villages from Mesoamerica to show that their inhabitants exploited a few plant and animal genera whose range cut across several environments. To obtain foods like wild grasses, they had to be in the right place at the right time of year. The timing depended on the plants, not on the people. Once the gatherers came to rely more heavily on specific seasonal foods, their changed schedule might prevent them from exploiting alternative foods whose seasons conflicted with the new schedule. Naturally occurring genetic changes in two food plants, wild corn and beans, made these plants increasingly important to the people who used them (Figure 16). Both plants became slightly more productive, and a positive feedback resulted that reinfored their exploitation. Eventually, the deliberate planting of both crops became the dominant subsistence pattern for the villagers and they became farmers.

Current theories argue that about 20,000 years ago, people began to shift from a hunting and gathering way of life to a more specialized economy that made use of ground stones to crush tough grass seeds, or, in tropical forest

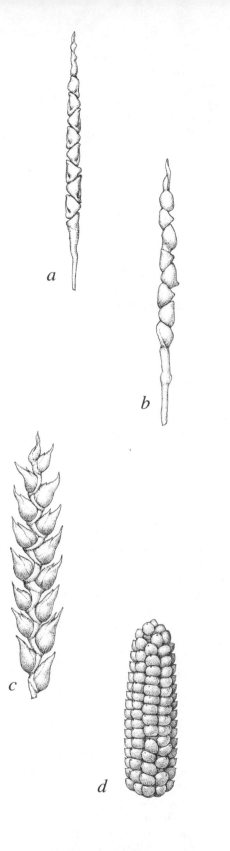
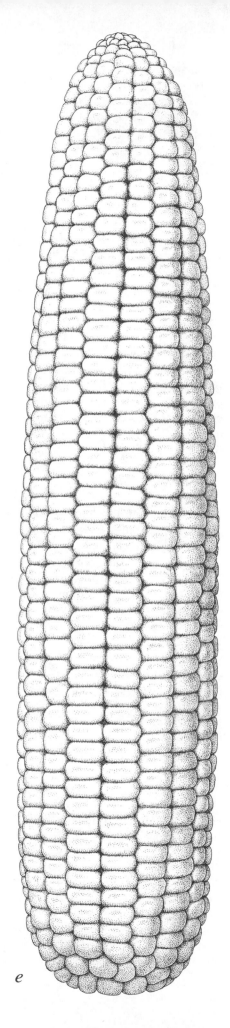

Figure 16   Studying ancient crops. The evolution of corn from the wild grass teosinte has been reconstructed by botanical experiments. All specimens are drawn approximately life size. (a) The "spike" of teosinte is equivalent to the ear of corn and consists of a single row of kernels in hard, shell-like fruit cases. (b) A modified teosinte, from crosses between teosinte and corn, may be similar to an early transitional form. (c) A single mutation in teosinte can give rise to a tunicate variety, in which the hard fruit cases have been converted into soft, husklike glumes from which kernels can be threshed easily. This mutation may well have been a crucial step in the domestication of teosinte. (d) This small primitive ear, from crosses between teosinte and modern corn, is similar to 7000-year-old specimens found in the southwestern United States and Mexico. (e) Modern corn. [From "The Ancestry of Corn" by George W. Beadle. Copyright © 1979 by Scientific American, Inc. All rights reserved.]

areas, to intensive exploitation of root crops like the yam. These specialized economies were successful in the best territories, where wild cereals or root plants were plentiful. Eventually so many people lived in the most favored environments that population densities rose to a point that forced some groups to split off into more marginal areas. There they tried to produce artificially, around the margins of the optimum zones, stands of cereals as dense as those in the heart of the zone.

Wild wheat, barley, maize, and other cereals have qualities quite different from those of their domestic counterparts. In the wild they occur in dense stands that can be harvested by tapping the stem and gathering the falling seeds in a basket. The conversion of these grasses into domestic strains involved selection of desirable properties: the time of harvest had to be controlled and crop yield increased by selecting for a tougher joint (rachis) between grain and stem that prevented the seeds from falling off and re-germinating. The tougher rachis enabled farmers to harvest the crop whenever they wanted. The crops that were bred had to be adaptable enough to grow outside their normal wild habitats. The earliest farmers seem to have grown crops with remarkable success, but probably succeeded only after long experimentation in different locations. By the same token, the domestication of animals implies genetic selection emphasizing special features of continuing use to the farmer. Wild sheep have no wool, wild oxen produce milk only for their offspring, and undomesticated chickens do not produce surplus eggs. Changes in such attributes could be bred by isolating wild populations from a larger gene pool for selective breeding under human care. People then became the selective agents.

Near Eastern Farmers

The archaeological evidence for early agriculture in the Near East is still inadequate. Some 17,000 years ago, some fisherfolk near Aswan on the Upper Nile may have planted wheat and barley in the damp ponds left by the receding river floods, returning some months later to harvest their crops and hunt winter geese. For more than 6000 years, the Ancient Egyptians seem to have utilized cereal grains without any detectable changes in population density or settlement size. Conventional hunting and gathering were still the basic subsistence activities, and the use of cereals was merely another resource in a broad-based food economy. The shift toward full-time agriculture was slow and undramatic, no sudden revolution in human behavior. It was not until after 5000 BC that signs of larger, more densely populated settlements in the Nile Valley appear.

There were gradual settlement shifts in the Kurdish foothills and the Jordan Valley as well. Before about 10,000 BC "Kebaran" hunter-gatherers flourished over much of the region, hunting wild sheep and goats, gazelles, and some large animals, as well as gathering wild cereal grasses in season. These were nomadic peoples, who followed the seasons of game and vegetable foods. After about 12,000 years ago, traces of more sedentary folk, the "Natufians," appear. These were still skilled hunters, who settled in caves and in open-air settlements along the coastal strip from southern Turkey to as far south as the fringes of the Nile Valley. They also relied on fresh and seawater fish. But increasingly their diet came from wild vegetable foods, so that their toolkit included flint-bladed bone sickles for use in harvesting wild grains, and perhaps domestically grown grains as well. Some "Natufians" lived in fairly permanent settlements, some covering more than half an acre. Their burials show enough variety of adornment to suggest that this may be a sign of increased social differentiation among individuals within Natufian communities. Such increasing social complexity prefigures the more elaborate class structures of later urban life. "Natufians" were the first settlers at the spring that was to nourish the city of Jericho in the Jordan Valley.

The gradual transition from hunting and gathering to food production is found at many sites in the Near East. A recent excavation in Syria documents the transition near the Euphrates. In the late tenth and early ninth millennium BC, the small northern Syrian village known to archaeologists as Abu Hureyra lay in a well-wooded area where animals and plants were abundant. Andrew Moore's "A Pre-Neolithic Farmers' Village on the Euphrates" recounts how he used fine screens and flotation equipment, passing soil through water, to recover thousands of wild seeds from the site. These included wild wheat, rye, and barley. Wild vegetable foods were so abundant that the Abu Hureyra people, who were hunters and gatherers, settled down in one place and may have started to plant and harvest wild cereals as part of a deliberate subsistence strategy.

Botanist Gordon Hillman experimented with harvesting stands of wild wheat in eastern Turkey and compared the yields with those estimated for Abu Hureyra. He argues that the inhabitants could have cultivated the wild cereals found in their village with simple techniques for a very long time without changing the morphology of the wild strains. It would have taken centuries for mutations from the wild to the domestic state to occur. There can be little doubt that the Abu Hureyra people were practicing agriculture, for seeds of modern farming weeds like mustard were recovered in the excavations. What happened at Abu Hureyra must have happened at many other villages, for hunter-gatherer communities throughout the Near East may have begun to combine simple cultivation with their age-old subsistence patterns, perhaps thousands of years before agriculture became more prevalent than hunting and gathering.

Trade and Trace Elements

By 7500 BC farming communities were flourishing throughout the Near East, by the Tigris and Euphrates rivers, and in Anatolia. The hunter-gatherers of earlier times had lived for the most part in small bands, isolated from one another for much of the year, their hunting territory restricted by its carrying capacity and the food resources available within it. They were almost entirely self-sufficient in raw materials and foodstuffs, although there are instances, in Australia and elsewhere, of seashells and other ornaments being passed on over long distances. The contacts of the first farming villages extended over much wider territory, for their inhabitants needed all manner of commodities, not only luxuries, but also basic items like salt, surplus grain, and building materials. One of the most prized materials was obsidian, a volcanic glass much valued for its properties in tool- and ornament-making.

Fortunately, obsidian has highly distinctive trace elements that can identify the locality from which it was mined. Few Near Eastern villages between Iran and Ethiopia were close to a natural obsidian outcrop, so every fragment of the rock had to be imported. By using spectrographic analysis of the trace elements in thousands of samples from dozens of sites, archaeologists have been able to show that a widespread obsidian trade sprang up in the Near East after 8000 BC. Most of the sources were located in Anatolia and Armenia, and trade routes connected dozens of villages as far afield as the Euphrates and the Jordan Valley.

Jericho and Çatal Hüyük

These increasing connections encouraged remarkable cultural diversity among the Near Eastern farmers and elevated some initially humble settlements to the status of sizeable towns. The biblical city of Jericho has long been famous as the place stormed by Joshua with the aid of trumpet-sounding priests, whose strident blasts blew down the walls. But Jericho was an important settlement thousands of years before Joshua's army camped before its walls (Figure 17). British archaeologist Kathleen Kenyon dug to the base of the Jericho mounds and unearthed a small town, complete with stone walls, watchtowers, and mud-brick houses that had flourished as early as the eighth millennium BC, more than three millennia before Sumerian cities came into being in Mesopotamia. Jericho lies by a perennial stream. The oasis may have nurtured a town because of its strategic position astride trade routes between the Mediterranean coast and the interior.

Çatal Hüyük in central Turkey was another early town, if not the city that James Mellaart would have us believe. "A Neolithic City in Turkey" describes the town's elaborate architecture, its fine religious art that modeled cattle and humans, and distinctive so-called "fertility-cult" shrines. For more than 1000 years, the economy of the town was based not only on agriculture, but on cattle and sheepherding. The prosperity of Çatal Hüyük was the result not only of efficient agriculture, but also of an extensive obsidian trade supported by outcrops lying within 50 miles of the town. Çatal Hüyük's artisans created finished goods that were traded to villages all over Turkey. At the height of its prosperity, Çatal Hüyük controlled trade over huge areas of Turkey.

This complex settlement was organized it seems by creating ritual and other mechanisms that attempted to retain the close kinship ties of village life while adapting to the new complexities and demands of long-distance trading and growing town populations. Unlike Mesopotamia, where new social and political institutions evolved to handle social change in the new cities, Çatal Hüyük's social system broke down, the town was abandoned, and the people reverted to small village settlements. The world's first experiments in urban living did not last. City dwelling did not come to the fore for another two thousand years.

Figure 17   Jericho. Early Neolithic houses of Jericho had curved walls such as those at left center in this excavation. Running from upper left to lower right are the stones of a Neolithic city wall, probably the oldest in the world. At left is the base of a later structure. [From the British School of Archaeology in Jerusalem, photograph by Kathleen M. Kenyon.]

Figure 18   Stonehenge, England. [Courtesy of the Controller of Her Brittanic Majesty's Stationery Office. British Crown Copyright.]

The new economies spread widely in the West after 7000 BC, into Greece, throughout the Aegean, and eventually into the temperate zones of Europe. The first European farmers moved rapidly northwestwards from the Balkans over the easily compacted soils that stretched from Central Europe to the North Sea coast in the sixth millennium BC. As population densities grew, the cultivators started cultivating heavier soils. By the third and fourth millennia, the Europeans were not only farming and trading, they were erecting sophisticated burial places and centers of worship, known to generations of archaeologists as "megaliths" (Greek: great stones). Glyn Daniel in "Megalithic Monuments" describes how these remarkable monuments were first built about 6000 BP, then used for more than 3000 years. Daniel believes that the farmers first built wooden and stone houses, then transformed the design of these to create large communal tombs, burial chambers covered with earthen mounds. Later a tradition of stone-tomb building spread throughout Europe.

The most famous megaliths are the stone circles of England and Ireland, sacred and secular meeting places originally built in wood, perhaps to replicate forest clearings, and then built in stone. The best known is Stonehenge in southern Britain. Built of great stones imported from many miles away, Stonehenge was erected with its central axis pointing to the midsummer solstice and has been claimed to be a giant astronomical observatory. As Daniel points out, most such claims are little better than extravagant theories. We know next to nothing about the religious rituals and symbolism that moved generations of prehistoric European farmers to their extraordinary architectural efforts.

Early Agriculture in the East

A generation ago, the great geographer Carl Sauer pointed out that agriculture developed quite independently in many parts of the world. He argued that root crops were cultivated very early in tropical rain forest areas in Southeast Asia. Sauer may have been right, for Chester Gorman's excavations at Spirit Cave in the Thai highlands yielded traces of intensive gathering of wild vegetable foods at least 2000 years before agriculture began in Mesopotamia. As recent New Guinea discoveries have shown, it is but a short step from intensive exploitation of wild foods to incipient agriculture and experimentation with root crops. No one is certain that the Spirit Cave seeds in fact come from domesticated plants, but we can be certain that much the same adaptive pressures that triggered a changeover in the Near East were at work in Thailand and elsewhere.

Our knowledge of early agriculture and animal domestication is still hampered by a lamentable lack of field research in many areas. It seems likely that cereal cultivation was developed quite independently in northern China, by 5000 BC and perhaps in sub-Saharan Africa by 2000 BC. Recent pollen researches in highland New Guinea strongly hint at very early food production there as well. Wherever they took hold, agricultural economies were successful, brilliantly so. Farmers not only took over the age-old territories of hunter-gatherers, they penetrated new frontiers and peopled the remotest landmasses of the Pacific. Southeast Asians sailed from island to island in Melanesia and Micronesia and eventually colonized Polynesia, New Zealand, and distant Easter Island and Hawaii. By the time Captain James Cook anchored off Tahiti in 1769, prehistoric farmers had been living in this most remote of tropical paradises for nearly a thousand years.

Precisely the same adaptive pressures that made themselves felt in the Old World surfaced in the New. By 5000 BC, Americans were cultivating a wide range of crops developed from indigenous cultigens. New World agriculture is distinctively American. The domesticated crops grown in the New World were the result of long experimentation and selective breeding of wild cultigens. These included maize (perhaps a grass named teosinte), manioc, sweet and white potatoes, and chili peppers. Tobacco, amaranth, and gourds were in common use. They had no wild cattle, goats, or sheep, but the native Americans domesticated the llama of the Andes, guinea pigs, and dogs. Plowing and riding animals were unknown before European contact; only the llama was available for load-carrying.

The gradual transition in the New World from hunting and gathering to agriculture has been documented in considerable detail in dry areas of Mexico and Peru, where preservation conditions favor the survival of minute seeds. Richard MacNeish's "The Origins of New World Civilization" describes his classic investigations into early agriculture in the Tehuacán Valley of the northern highlands of Mexico. He recounts an exemplary case of meticulous fieldwork designed to investigate the development of food production.

The rock-shelters and open sites of the Tehuacán Valley have yielded a sequence of hunter-gatherer and farming cultures extending over 12,000 years of prehistory, beginning in about 10,000 BC. The small cave of Coxcatlán contained 25 occupation levels, the earliest of which, dating to about 10,000 BC, contained the seeds of wild vegetable foods and the bones of small animals and birds. These "Ajuereado" people were relying heavily on intensive exploitation of vegetable foods. After 7200 BC, plant foods were even more important, and the "El Riego" folk, who succeeded the "Ajuereado," camped throughout the valley during the dry season, gathering and collecting a whole range of vegetable foods, including squashes, chili peppers, and avocados, some of which may have been cultivated.

Between 5200 and 3400 BC the people of the succeeding "Coxcatlan" phase were cultivating a long list of plants, including maize, amaranth, beans, squashes, and chilis. But only about ten percent of their diet came from cultivated plants. The rest was derived from intensive collecting. The maize cobs from the Coxcatlán levels are small and are said to recall the hypothetical wild ancestor of maize (which may never have been seen in the wild). Some experts believe the wild prototype was a grass named *teosinte,* but the evidence is still disputed. After 3000 BC agriculture was well established in the Tehuacán Valley. The history of experimentation and selective breeding of crops in this valley was doubtless repeated at many other locations in Mesoamerica as the new economies were adopted by people accustomed to intensive exploitation of vegetable foods. But, for now, Tehuacán presents us with the most complete history of the development of prehistoric agriculture known anywhere in the world.

Even today, millions of people live off simple, subsistence agriculture, using techniques little modified since prehistoric times. A visitor sailing up the Nile or traveling through the Yucatán can see peasants living in an almost unchanged world, where the annual cycles of planting and harvest provide a timeless backdrop for human existence. The complexities of our industrial civilization seem strangely irrelevant to this almost prehistoric world, yet this was the agricultural base from which the early civilizations arose. The Sumerians, the Ancient Egyptians, the Harappans of the Indus Valley, the Shang of northern China, the Maya and Inca of Mexico and Peru, all these great complex societies flourished because they were based on sophisticated agricultural economies supported by the labor of millions of anonymous peasants. It was these silent farmers whose food surpluses fed the rulers, priests, nobles, soldiers, bureaucrats, and artisans of the first civilizations. Without agriculture, no urban society, not even our own industrial civilization, would have been possible.

REFERENCES

Bender, Barbara. 1977. *Farming in Prehistory*. London: John Murray.

Cohen, Mark. 1977. *The Food Crisis in Prehistory*. New Haven: Yale University Press.

Jennings, Jesse D., ed. 1978. *Ancient Native Americans*. San Francisco: W. H. Freeman and Company.

Mellaart, James. 1975. *The Neolithic of the Near East*. London: Thames and Hudson.

Sauer, Carl O. 1952. *Agricultural Origins and Dispersals*. Washington, D.C.: American Geographical Society.

8

A Pre-Neolithic Farmers' Village on the Euphrates

by Andrew M. T. Moore
August 1979

The Neolithic period is traditionally associated with the emergence of agriculture. At a site in Syria, however, some of the first villagers practiced farming, along with hunting and gathering, even earlier

The stage in human prehistory when man first adopted an agricultural economy is of fundamental interest to archaeologists because it represents the watershed between the hunter-gatherer existence of our ancestors of the Paleolithic period, or Old Stone Age, and the first civilized way of life. For generations scholars have scoured southwestern Asia in an attempt to find out just where and when agriculture began. The pace of exploration and excavation has greatly accelerated in the past 30 years, but archaeologists are now less concerned with where and when an agricultural way of life developed in the region than with how and why. Recent analysis of work at a site in the Euphrates valley of northern Syria has produced data that suggest answers to these last two questions.

The part of southwestern Asia with the largest number of known and excavated sites of Mesolithic (immediately following the Paleolithic) and Neolithic age is the area traditionally known as the Levant. Today the area is shared by the modern states of Syria, Lebanon, Jordan and Israel. The site of the work I shall describe is in northern Syria. By far the largest early Neolithic site anywhere in the Levant, it is a tell: a large mound consisting of the debris of millenniums of human occupation. The mound, known as Tell Abu Hureyra, was destined to be flooded when the water of the Euphrates was impounded by a new dam being constructed a few kilometers downstream at Tabqa. I first saw the mound in March, 1971, three years before it was scheduled to disappear, and was immediately impressed by its size and potential for investigation.

It was obvious that the thick deposit of debris, measuring up to eight meters in height over an area of 11.5 hectares (some 28 acres), must have been built up over a long period. There was thus every hope that excavations at Abu Hureyra would provide abundant evidence on the beginnings of settled life on this eastern frontier of the Levant, where today only an annual 200 millimeters of rain falls on what is mainly an arid steppe.

The surface of the mound was covered by a dense scatter of flint tools and waste similar in type to material that had been excavated some years earlier at the Neolithic site of Buqras, farther down the Euphrates, by Henri de Contenson of the French National Center for Scientific Research (C.N.R.S.). Buqras was dated to about 6000 B.C. (All the dates I shall give here are based on carbon-14 determinations calculated according to the half-life of that radioactive isotope but without calibration.) This places Buqras toward the middle of Neolithic times in the Levant, where the New Stone Age began about 8500 B.C. and continued in most of the region until as late as 4000 to 3500 B.C. If artifacts like those at Buqras were on the surface at Abu Hureyra, one could expect to find below the surface remains from the archaic, or earliest, Neolithic, and perhaps below them remains from the preceding Mesolithic, which here began some 20,000 years ago and continued until about 8500 B.C.

My colleagues and I began work at Abu Hureyra in 1972 under the sponsorship of the Pitt Rivers Museum of the University of Oxford and with the support of a number of other institutions both in the United Kingdom and in North America. By the end of the first season's excavations our optimistic expectation had been fulfilled. Below the levels of archaic and developed Neolithic occupation, dating from about 7500 B.C. to some time after 6000 B.C., appeared evidence of a Mesolithic occupation at the site that had lasted for several centuries in the late 10th and early ninth millenniums B.C. Another season in 1973 saw completion of work at the site, and the great mound was submerged on schedule early in 1974, leaving our group with an immense stockpile of artifacts and animal and plant remains for later examination. Only now, as analysis of the material progresses, is the full significance of the excavation being realized in terms of the transition from a hunting-gathering way of life to a farming one.

The Mesolithic occupation zone at Abu Hureyra is at the northern end of the mound on the edge of the Euphrates floodplain. It consists of a simple village settlement: a series of pit dwellings and other hollows dug into the original ground surface underlying the tell. Each pit dwelling had a framework of upright wood posts; the roofs, of which no trace remains, were probably made of reeds. The pits and hollows had gradually been buried under occupation debris, which had accumulated to a depth of about a meter. Along with the debris were many of the artifacts the Mesolithic occupants had used.

Prominent among the artifacts were stone pestles, rubbing stones and milling stones. Many of them were stained with red ocher, evidence that they had been used for crushing this decorative pigment into powder. The presence of the milling implements in the pit dwellings and hollows suggests that they were also used to process plant foods.

The artifacts found in the greatest numbers were flint tools of two types. Many are so small that they are termed microliths, but a number are heavier flint objects. Also present are immense quantities of waste flint.

By far the commonest of the microliths are small crescent-shaped blades known as lunates; these bladelets could have been set into wood hafts to serve as barbs for an arrow, the cutting edge of a knife or (as is known to be the case elsewhere in the Levant) teeth for a sickle. Other microlith shapes include bladelets blunted along one edge and bladelets chipped to form tiny points for boring holes. Most of the larger stone tools are either hammerstones or scrapers made from sizable flakes of flint. The artisans of this Mesolithic phase also laboriously fashioned dishes of stone other than flint and made notches in the sides of pebbles, possibly to fit them for use as weights for fish nets.

Tools made of bone were also found in abundance. Most of the bone tools are heavy-duty boring points; other bone artifacts include spatulas, needles and double-end points that may have been arrow tips. Among the artifacts of a decorative character were bone beads and pendants, together with beads and pendants made of shell and stone.

The artifacts associated with the Mesolithic village at Abu Hureyra are typical of the later stage of this period elsewhere in the Levant, roughly contemporary with such sites of the Natufian culture in Palestine as Mugharet el Wad, Eynan and Hayonim. During the later Mesolithic period the human population of the Levant was considerably larger than it had been during the preceding several thousand years. The increase in population appears to have been in response to a marked improvement in the environment. Where the earlier stage had been characterized by

TWO OCCUPATION LEVELS at Tell Abu Hureyra appear in this photograph of a test excavation at the northern end of the 28-acre mound. The rectangular mud-brick walls of the dwellings of the archaic Neolithic villagers who settled at the Euphrates River site in about 7500 B.C. are visible at the top. Buried under this Neolithic village until it was exposed by the excavators was a cluster of pit dwellings and work hollows used by sedentary hunter-gatherers of the later Mesolithic period until about 8500 B.C. They evidently raised grain. Postholes around the pits held supports for walls and roofs probably made of reeds. The small holes were made by burrowing rodents.

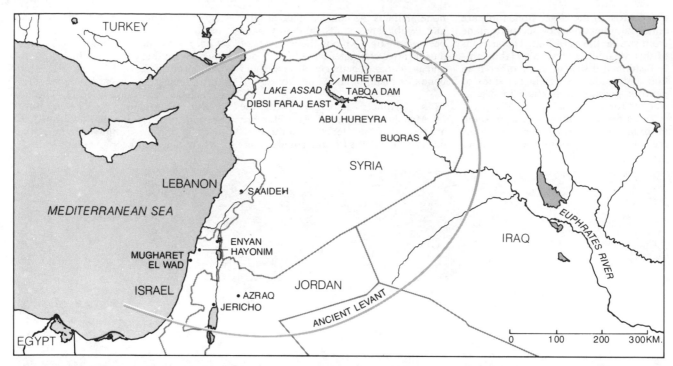

ANCIENT LEVANT, an area now shared by the modern states of Israel, Lebanon, Syria and Jordan, is the part of southwestern Asia that has the largest number of excavated Mesolithic and Neolithic sites. Tell Abu Hureyra (*triangle*) was flooded by damming in 1974.

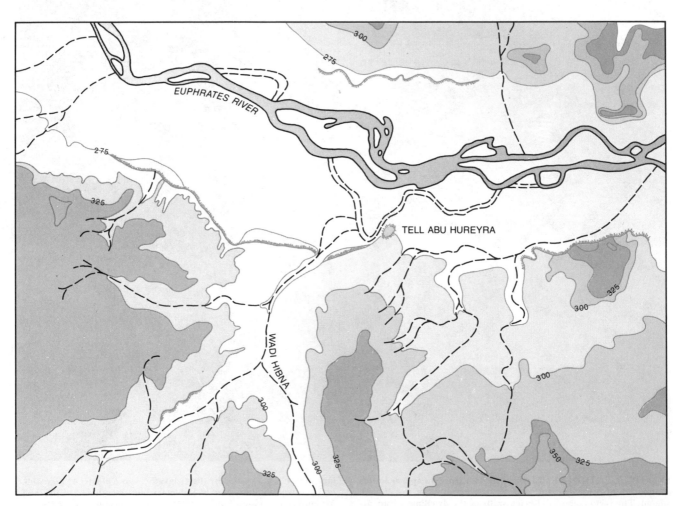

VILLAGE MOUND stands on a low terrace south of the floodplain of the Euphrates. Wadi Hibna, now dry, may have been a perennial stream during archaic Neolithic times that could have been tapped for irrigation. The contour numbers indicate meters above sea level.

cool, dry conditions, the later stage and the following Neolithic period saw a gradual rise in temperature and an increase in rainfall.

The consequence for the Levant was an eastward expansion of the zone of Mediterranean forest that had formerly been confined to the coastal mountains of the region. This wooded zone ultimately reached the edge of the interior plateau. The steppe east and south of the enlarged forest area was separated from the forest proper by an intermediate zone of open woods. During the period of increasingly warm and wet weather the steppe itself became richer in plant and animal species. As a result the intermediate zone between full forest and steppe came to offer particularly attractive opportunities that human populations on the threshold of agriculture were free to exploit.

Abu Hureyra, situated on the edge of the steppe, seems to have been one of a number of settlements that came into being as a result of the improvement in the environment. The process is predictable. The greater rainfall would have brought with it a greater abundance of vegetation, which for small groups of Mesolithic hunter-gatherers would have been a factor of prime importance. Today we would say that the more abundant vegetation was able to support a larger biomass; indeed, this is attested to by the demonstrable growth in the human population. Evidently some of the hunting-gathering groups began to coalesce and set up a sedentary, or at least semisedentary, way of life. The concentration of such enlarged groups at sites such as Abu Hureyra in itself created new circumstances, for example richer social relations. It became advantageous under these circumstances to develop new strategies of subsistence in support of the novel sedentary existence.

Such, at least, seemed a plausible hypothesis to account for the Mesolithic village we discovered at Abu Hureyra. To test the hypothesis the excavators took pains to recover as much evidence on the economy of the settlement as possible. This called for excavation techniques rarely used before in the Levant. First, working with fine-mesh screens the excavators sieved all the soil they had removed from the dig. The dry-sieve technique recovered large quantities of animal bone, more than two tons in all. Second, a flotation method was applied to separate fine plant materials from the sieved soil. Two flotation machines, designed at the University of Cambridge, systematically recovered about 1,000 liters of plant remains from the various levels of the excavation.

Examination of these plant remains, undertaken by Gordon Hillman of the University of Wales, shows that the Mesolithic inhabitants of Abu Hureyra

FLOTATION MACHINE designed at the University of Cambridge was one of two machines used by the excavators at Abu Hureyra to recover some 1,000 liters of plant remains from various site levels. The Mesolithic levels held three kinds of cereal grain: wheat, rye and barley.

collected, if they did not actually cultivate, various pulses, including a wild type of lentil. They also gathered tiny nuts from the turpentine tree (a relative of the pistachio), fruits from hackberry shrubs (plants of the elm family), caper berries and the seeds of wild feather grasses. What came as an exciting and significant surprise was Hillman's discovery of cereal grains. The most numerous of them are grains of a primitive wheat: wild einkorn. Two other cereals are present in less abundance: wild rye and wild barley. Because the cultivation of cereal grains is one of the earliest landmarks of the Neolithic revolution the discovery of three kinds of cereal in the Mesolithic levels at Abu Hureyra raised a crucial question. Were any of the three (and perhaps also the pulses) already being cultivated, or were they too only being collected from the wild?

In considering this question one must first note that neither einkorn wheat nor the other two cereals are found in the wild form anywhere near Abu Hureyra today; the area is too arid. Given the cooler and more humid conditions of the later Mesolithic, however, they might have grown there in the past. This raises another question. Does the fact that the cereal grains recovered from the Mesolithic village at Abu Hureyra are morphologically wild types mean they could not have been cultivated? Not necessarily.

Hillman made use of stands of wild einkorn growing in the Munzur Mountains of eastern Turkey to experiment with various methods of harvesting and with patterns of crop rotation. These experiments were undertaken to determine whether selection pressures favoring mutation from the wild state might operate under such conditions. His conclusion is that as long as the cultivation methods appropriate to simple husbandry were followed the morphology of wild einkorn would remain unaltered even over long periods. Only after unusual cultivation techniques have been applied for many hundreds of years, Hillman asserts, do mutations from the wild to the domestic state appear.

There is evidence suggesting that the

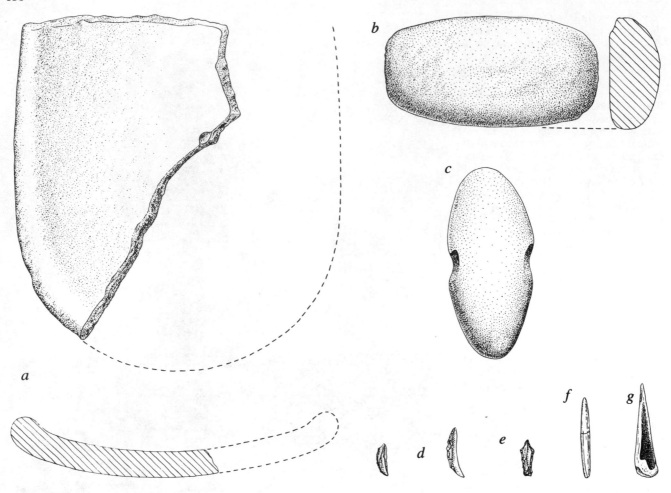

MESOLITHIC ARTIFACTS include basalt milling stones (*a*) and rubbers (*b*) and notched pebbles, possibly net weights (*c*). Among the chipped-flint microliths, lunates (*d*) were the most abundant; micro-borers (*e*) ranked next. Bone tools include double-end points (*f*), possibly points for arrows, and many borers (*g*). Milling stones were certainly used to grind ocher and perhaps also to process plant foods.

inhabitants of Abu Hureyra practiced just such simple methods. For example, the cultivation of cereal grains, even on a small scale, should have disturbed the natural vegetation in the vicinity. This means that the same weed plants characteristic of cultivated areas near the site today should be present in the flotation samples from the Mesolithic levels at the site. It is possible, of course, that tramping of the ground by the Mesolithic inhabitants, or even by their animals, might have opened the way for these same weeds. Be that as it may, the flotation samples show that three such modern weeds (*Atriplex*, one of the steppe-growing members of the goosefoot family, *Alyssum*, a member of the mustard family that is an ornamental plant today, and *Lithospermum*, a member of the borage family) grew close enough to Abu Hureyra in later Mesolithic times to leave their seeds in the excavated soil.

On balance, then, it seems highly likely that the inhabitants of later Mesolithic Abu Hureyra were cultivating three cereal grains (and perhaps also some pulses). This conclusion is strengthened by the similarity between the environment of Abu Hureyra, with much poten-

tially arable land in the vicinity, and the environment of other sites of the later Mesolithic in the Levant: Dibsi Faraj East and Mureybat, sites in the Euphrates valley discovered during the same salvage campaign that saw the excavation of Abu Hureyra, Saaideh in Lebanon and Jericho in Palestine. Sites of the earlier Mesolithic only are not associated with arable land.

A second kind of similarity further strengthens the conclusion that simple husbandry was under way at Abu Hureyra. At least four tells in the Levant that were the sites of flourishing Neolithic agricultural communities have yielded evidence of habitation in later Mesolithic times. Three of them were adjacent to potentially arable land: Jericho, Mureybat and Abu Hureyra.

To turn from the plant remains at Abu Hureyra to the animal remains, Anthony J. Legge of the University of London is in the process of analyzing the two tons of animal bones from the site. His findings show that the inhabitants killed species of game ranging in size from the rabbit to the onager, the wild ass of the Levant. The most popular food animal was the gazelle, but on-

agers, sheep and goats were also killed regularly. The presence among the bones of freshwater-mussel shells and fish vertebrae shows that the Mesolithic population of Abu Hureyra exploited another source of food: the Euphrates.

In summary, the evidence suggests that in later Mesolithic times the inhabitants of Abu Hureyra were already cultivating cereal grains. (Their contemporaries at some other Levant sites were probably doing so too.) They also consumed many plant and animal foods gathered in the wild. Hence the basic Mesolithic tradition of hunting and gathering had here (and to some extent elsewhere) been combined with simple husbandry. The opportunity for such a practice was present in the form of potentially arable land. The motive may well have been to provide the subsistence necessary for a new kind of life, namely the settlement of an increased population in sizable villages.

Midway through the ninth millennium B.C., after several centuries of occupation, the Mesolithic village at Abu Hureyra was abandoned for reasons unknown. The site remained va-

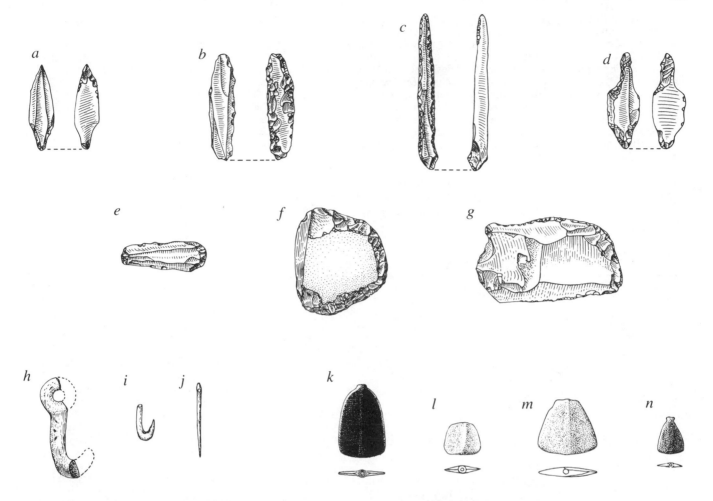

NEOLITHIC ARTIFACTS include points for arrows (*a*), some sickle blades (*b*), reamers (*c*) and borers (*d*), some made of imported obsidian, and many scrapers (*e–g*). Bone objects include a hook-and-eye hook (*h*), a fishhook (*i*) and needles (*j*). Prominent in the graves are "butterfly" beads (*k–n*), usually made of imported agate or serpentine. Several centimeters wide, the beads are only millimeters thick.

cant for about 1,000 years before a new settlement appeared in archaic Neolithic times. By then agriculture was widely practiced both in the Levant and elsewhere in southwestern Asia and sedentary settlements were no novelty. Nevertheless, once Abu Hureyra was reoccupied (in about 7500 B.C.) it soon came to be the largest of all the archaic Neolithic settlements in the Levant. Thousands of people lived on the great tell.

The implications of so many people occupying a space of less than 30 acres are many. For one, the social relations of the inhabitants of the tell must have been considerably more complex than those in the preceding Mesolithic period; indeed, they must have been more complex than the social relations that have been assumed for early Neolithic societies. For another, regulating the affairs of such a settlement would have called for an effective form of communal organization. Hence one may infer the emergence even at this early date of social and political systems that in a more developed form were to become the essential features of the early city states of southwestern Asia, both in the Levant and in Mesopotamia.

Consider one index of interaction of major archaic Neolithic settlements such as Abu Hureyra. That index is trade. Since Abu Hureyra was an unusually large settlement by the second half of the seventh millennium, it can logically be viewed as the focal settlement of a region that embraced many smaller settlements. The archaeological evidence at Abu Hureyra suggests that the components of this regional complex were in contact not only with one another but also, and for the first time, with other regions. Abu Hureyra regularly received the volcanic glass obsidian from several sources in Turkey, along with jadeite, serpentine, agate and malachite. Soapstone came from the Zagros Mountains, turquoise from the Sinai and cowrie shells from the Mediterranean or the Red Sea. As for what Abu Hureyra and its satellite villages offered in exchange for these desirable raw materials, the archaeological record is, alas, silent.

What factors were responsible for the unusual growth of Abu Hureyra as a regional focal point? The single most important factor must have been the development in the Levant of a new kind of agricultural economy. At Abu Hureyra, as at a number of other early Neolithic sites, this new economy rested on the cultivation of cereals and pulses. Whereas it is only probable that the Mesolithic predecessors of the archaic Neolithic villagers cultivated einkorn wheat, barley and lentils, it is certain that the Neolithic villagers did. What is perhaps equally important is that they also cultivated in addition to einkorn a new kind of wheat: emmer. Although certain other crops were grown, four—two wheats, one other cereal and lentils—were the mainstay of cultivation.

Another factor in the growth of Abu Hureyra was its location at the junction of the Euphrates floodplain and the open steppe to the south. This allowed the human population to exploit the resources of two complementary environments. More than that, the people of Neolithic Abu Hureyra may have taken advantage of an accident of local topography to put under irrigation the low ground to the west of the settlement.

In this part of the Euphrates valley today and in the recent past irrigation has been possible only with the aid of pumps or with canals many kilometers long. Neither of these methods was available to the archaic Neolithic population. A little to the west of Abu Hureyra, however, is a small valley, the Wadi Hibna. Today it is dry except after a heavy rain, but under the wetter climatic conditions of archaic Neolithic times it probably carried a perennial stream that might easily have been diverted. By so doing the people of Abu Hureyra could have irrigated both the bottom of the wadi and the floodplain west of their settlement, thereby substantially

increasing crop yields and meeting the demands of a growing population.

As for the animal sector of the archaic Neolithic economy, the same three species that were hunted as game by the Mesolithic occupants of the site are present: gazelle, sheep and goat. Now, however, all three species were probably being herded rather than hunted. The bone remains show that at first many more gazelles than sheep or goats were being slaughtered. Then suddenly the number of gazelles declined and the number of sheep and goats increased proportionately. By the time the de-

veloped phase of the Neolithic had replaced the archaic phase, early in the sixth millennium B.C., cattle and pigs had been added to the settlement's herds and the gazelle had virtually disappeared.

For the remaining centuries of the archaic Neolithic, however, the original three animals were the major source of meat at Abu Hureyra, and the hunting and gathering of supplemental foodstuffs continued to be part of the subsistence strategy. Wild plants and wild game added to the variety of the diet, as did fish and shellfish.

What did Neolithic Abu Hureyra look like? Its numerous rectilinear houses were built close together, with only narrow lanes and little courts between them. Each house, made of mud brick, consisted of several small rooms connected by doorways; some of the doorways were conventional but others had very high sills. Many rooms had burnished plaster floors that were colored black and occasionally had red schematic motifs. The walls of the houses were covered with a mud plaster; some were given a coat of whitewash. It seems likely that each house was occupied by one family.

The artifacts made by this group included flint and, less commonly, obsidian tools with a variety of new shapes. Most were made from blanks produced by removing large blades from a "core." The commonest blade artifacts are arrowheads, knives, end scrapers (tools with the working surface at the end rather than on the side) and burins (blades flaked to retain a sharp angular projection for engraving). A smaller number of blades were made into reamers and sickle edges. The arrowheads must have been intended primarily for hunting, but we found one lodged in the breast of a human skeleton buried in the settlement, suggesting that the bow and arrow also served in combat.

Lawrence H. Keeley of the University of Illinois and Emily Moss of the University of London have examined some of these tools at high magnification for signs of wear indicating the purpose the tools served. They have been able to show that the end scrapers were used for dressing hides, the burins for engraving wood and bone and the reamers for making holes in those same materials.

The roster of flaked stone tools is completed by choppers and scrapers made from large flakes and by stone hammers. Axheads and chisels were made of stone that was not flaked but polished. The rubbing stones and milling stones used to process cereals were pecked or ground into shape. A few fine bowls were made of polished stone; some coarser stone vessels were formed by grinding. Although most Neolithic

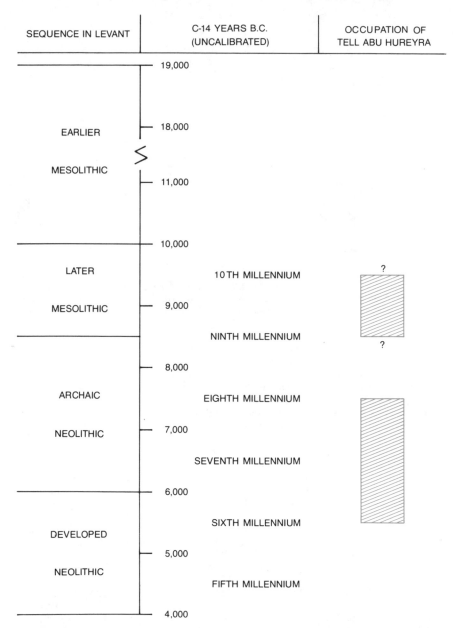

THREE-PHASE OCCUPATION of Abu Hureyra (*colored bars*) began during the later Mesolithic period in the Levant, some 11,500 years ago. The Mesolithic villagers abandoned the site for unknown reasons some 10,500 years ago. About 1,000 years later Abu Hureyra was reoccupied by a group of farmers whose subsistence strategies were characteristic of the archaic Neolithic period. The new settlement soon came to be the largest of its kind in the Levant. A transition from archaic to developed Neolithic came about 1,500 years later. The settlement was deserted not long afterward as a consequence of diminishing rainfall and ecological decline.

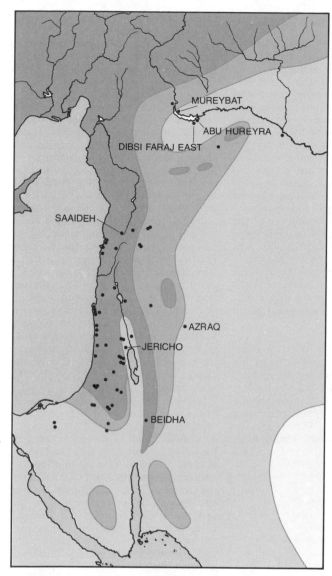 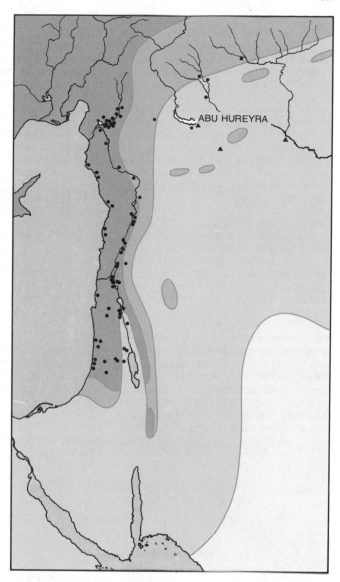

CLIMATIC CHANGE in the Levant between the ninth millennium B.C. (*left*) and the sixth millennium (*right*) is evident from a shift in vegetation zones. Abundant rainfall in later Mesolithic times brought an eastward extension of the Mediterranean forest zone, with more than 300 millimeters of rain per year (*dark color*) and of the intermediate zone of open forest and the steppe beyond, with 300 to 150 millimeters of rain per year (*lighter colors*). Whereas most of the 70 known later Mesolithic sites (*black dots*) were in the zone of greatest rainfall or in the intermediate zone, some were in particularly favorable steppe niches. For example, Abu Hureyra and Dibsi Faraj East were on the Euphrates and Azraq was in an oasis. Three millenniums later the forest, open forest and steppe withdrew westward as rainfall diminished and the desert (*lightest color*) advanced. Even the favorably situated steppe sites (*triangles*) were then abandoned. Of the 80 known sixth-millennium Neolithic sites most were within the area most favorable for mixed farming, the zone of Mediterranean forest.

sites contain pottery, Abu Hureyra and a number of other sites in southwestern Asia show no pottery at all at this stage of their occupation. One of the main functions of pottery is the storage of food, but these Neolithic settlements apparently stored food at least one other way. They had large rectangular vessels made of thick white plaster, so heavy that they must have been permanent fixtures of the rooms in which they were found. It is noteworthy that the proportions of the various kinds of stone tools differ markedly between one part of Abu Hureyra and another, indicating that the archaic Neolithic inhabitants of the site did different things in different parts of the settlement.

The bone artifacts of the archaic Neolithic at the site repeat the Mesolithic inventory of needles, borers and spatulas. A bone fishhook and a bone hook and eye, possibly used to fasten clothing, are archaic Neolithic additions. The excavators also discovered traces of baskets and mats. These must have been among the commonest craft products of the settlement; the baskets would have complemented the rectangular plaster vessels for the storage of food.

Where the repertory of decorative objects in the Mesolithic levels of the site was limited, the number and variety of such artifacts in the archaic Neolithic levels were substantial. There are beads and pendants made of baked clay, bone and shell. Other decorations are fashioned from a variety of stones: simple limestone, various greenstones, including serpentine, and such semiprecious stones as agate, carnelian and turquoise. The finest of all these objects, nearly all of them found in graves, can be described as butterfly beads. Trapezoidal or round in form, they are generally made of serpentine or agate. The beads measure as much as five and a half centimeters in their largest dimension, but they were ground down until they are no more than a few millimeters thick.

The use of such materials, many of them imported, for the manufacture of decorative articles suggests that one incentive for the maintenance of trade with distant communities was pride of person. This suggestion is strengthened by the discovery of an end use for another imported material: malachite. We unearthed one small cockleshell that contained traces of powdered malachite, a popular cosmetic during later periods.

The presence of beads made of baked clay among these decorations is also noteworthy. Other objects made of clay were found in the archaic Neolithic levels of the site, notably figurines in human and animal form. These clay figures, however, were not baked. Nevertheless, if the clay beads were locally made rather than imported, the inhabitants of Abu Hureyra were familiar with two key properties of clay that should have brought them to the threshold of pottery manufacture: plasticity and fire hardening.

The archaic Neolithic settlement reached its maximum size in the seventh millennium B.C. Its growth reflected the sharp increase in the population of the Levant as a whole that accompanied the spread of the new agricultural economy. The occupation of Abu Hureyra continued after the start of the developed Neolithic period in the sixth millennium, but the village shrank to little more than half its former size. Like the preceding settlement, the developed Neolithic village was also built of mud brick. Little is known about its layout, because it has been almost destroyed by thousands of years of exposure to the elements. The buildings seem to have hardly changed in plan from those of the archaic Neolithic, but their inhabitants took to digging numerous pits among the struc-

tures. These they used for a time as hearths and then filled with rubbish.

The artifacts made by the last inhabitants of Abu Hureyra were little different from those of their archaic Neolithic predecessors. One exception is that pottery now appears. Even that innovation seems to have been modest in scale; very few potsherds were found in this part of the excavation. Eventually, in about 5500 B.C. or perhaps a little earlier, the site was abandoned. It remained uninhabited until our group arrived to excavate it.

Why was Abu Hureyra deserted by its inhabitants? The results of the excavation show that over the long life of the settlement its agricultural economy was modified to become increasingly productive. One might seek the answer to the abandonment in purely local terms if it were not for the fact that throughout the Levant other sites in the steppe border zone were also abandoned at about the same time.

I suggest two reasons for these abandonments. The first is that from late in the seventh millennium the overall environment of the Levant was becoming less attractive to a farming population. The temperature had been rising since the retreat of the Pleistocene ice, but the rainfall was now diminishing. The change brought about a gradual

contraction of the zone of Mediterranean forest. The steppe expanded into the forested areas, and the desert in turn began to encroach on the steppe. Thus as the Levant became more arid the pattern of settlement along the border of the steppe was affected.

The second cause of the abandonments, in my view, is that the growth of population during the archaic Neolithic put too great a strain on the delicate balance of the overall economy. As we have seen, that economy had a dual character. The yields of agriculture and animal husbandry provided for much of the population's needs, but at the same time the exploitation of wild resources made its own important contribution. The plant remains at Abu Hureyra show that the natural vegetation (and therefore the soil cover) became steadily more degraded over the life of the settlement. The inhabitants were evidently overgrazing their pasture and overexploiting the natural vegetation as a source of food and fuel. It seems probable that they also seriously reduced the game population at a time when the change in climate was accelerating the same process.

Early in the sixth millennium, possibly in response to the dual pressures of an altered environment and an upset ecological balance, the inhabitants of the Levant settlements, Abu Hureyra included, ceased to rely on hunting and gathering as an important supplement to the farming economy and came instead to depend almost exclusively on the produce derived from mixed farming. In their planting they concentrated on the more productive of the cereal grains and on those pulses that like the lentil were an abundant source of beans and peas. Their herds now included cattle and pigs in addition to the ubiquitous sheep and goats.

This kind of mixed-farming economy was far better suited to those parts of the Levant where the Mediterranean forest still existed, namely the well-watered coast and the northern plains. The inhabitants of the once thriving steppeborder villages gave up their outworn settlements and moved north and west to build new homes in more promising surroundings. The fact that the overall population of the Levant in the sixth millennium B.C. remained about the same as it was at the end of the expansionist seventh millennium indicates that the new adjustment was a successful one, whatever the costs of the dislocation may have been. Although the Neolithic period was already well advanced in the Levant before a mixed-farming economy was developed, the ultimate adoption of that economy early in the sixth millennium B.C. was so successful that it remained the basis of human life in the region until modern times.

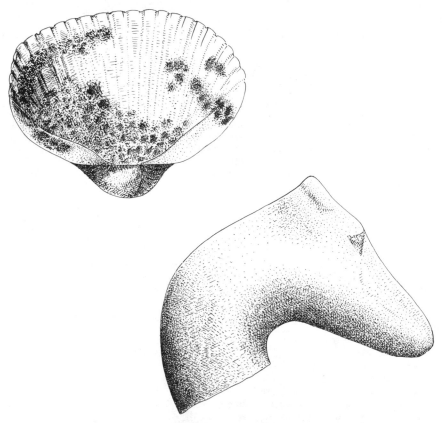

ORNAMENTATION in Neolithic Abu Hureyra is manifested by a cockleshell (*left*) that held powdered malachite, an imported cosmetic, and by a miniature gazelle head made of granite.

A Neolithic City in Turkey

9

April 1964

*An ancient mound now known as Çatal Hüyük has
yielded evidence that communities with highly
developed economic structure, religion and art existed
as long ago as 7000 B.C. and perhaps even earlier*

Excavations on the Anatolian plateau of Turkey a few years ago provided an answer to an archaeological question of long standing about Neolithic culture. The Neolithic is the stage of civilization at which men began to cultivate crops and to domesticate animals and as a result of these activities to dwell in permanent settlements; in the Near East this stage occurred roughly between 7000 B.C. and 5000 B.C. The question was how Neolithic culture had moved from the Near East into Europe. The answer was that the movement was overland, by way of the Anatolian plateau. Such a route had long seemed to archaeologists a logical supposition, but until Neolithic communities were excavated on the plateau there had been no direct evidence to support the supposition [see "Hacilar: A Neolithic Village Site," by James Mellaart, SCIENTIFIC AMERICAN, August, 1961].

In answering one question, however, these excavations raised another: What were the origins of the culture of which Hacilar was representative? The Late Neolithic culture found at Hacilar had arrived there fully developed. The long gap between its arrival, probably about 6000 B.C., and the desertion of a pre-pottery village on the same site some 500 years earlier needed investigation. The gap appeared to correspond to the Early Neolithic period. If an Early Neolithic site could be excavated on the plateau, it might indicate the origin of the Hacilar culture and provide a longer culture sequence.

We had such a site in mind. I had found it about 30 miles southeast of the modern city of Konya in 1958: an ancient mound (*hüyük* in Turkish) bearing the name Çatal. The mound, covered with weeds and thistles, stood in the middle of a great plain. Lying on what

was once the bank of a river (now canalized into other channels to prevent flooding) that flows from the Taurus Mountains onto the plain, it rose gently from the fields to a height of 50 feet.

Çatal Hüyük seemed to be the most promising of some 200 sites we had visited on the Konya plain. A preliminary investigation indicated, to our delight, that the site belonged substantially, if not wholly, to the Early Neolithic period. Small fragments of pottery and broken obsidian arrowheads showed an unmistakable resemblance to those found in the deepest Neolithic levels at Mersin on the southern coast of Turkey, and at Çatal Hüyük they were on top of the mound. Moreover, the pottery looked more primitive than anything we had found at Hacilar.

So it was that Çatal Hüyük's 8,000 years of slumber came to an end on May 17, 1961, when our party began excavations. Ten days later the first Neolithic paintings ever found on man-made walls were exposed, and it was clear that Çatal Hüyük was no ordinary site. Succeeding excavations in 1962 and 1963 have confirmed this impression. With its story only partly revealed by the excavations to date, Çatal Hüyük has already added to the archaeological evidence that the development of towns and cities (as distinct from villages) goes farther back in antiquity than had been thought. Çatal Hüyük deserves the name of city: it was a community with an extensive economic development, specialized crafts, a rich religious life, a surprising attainment in art and an impressive social organization.

For the opportunity to explore this story we are indebted to several organizations. Our excavations have been supported by the Wenner-Gren Foundation for Anthropological Research, the Bol-

lingen Foundation, the British Academy, the University of London, the University of Edinburgh, the Royal Ontario Museum, the Australian Institute of Archaeology, the University of Canterbury in New Zealand and the late Francis Neilson. The Shell Oil Company and British Petroleum Aegean Limited provided technical help. Numerous other institutions have contributed in such ways as sending experts to the site or making analyses of material found at the site.

Çatal Hüyük covers 32 acres and so is easily the largest known Neolithic site, although how much of the site was occupied at any given period cannot be said with certainty. Apparently the settlement grew up from the riverbank, and the substantial part of the mound that spreads back from the river therefore dates from later phases of settlement. Our excavations, covering about one acre, have so far been concentrated on the southwest side of the mound, in a quarter that appears to have been sacred and residential. Because we have found nothing but finished goods in this area, we assume that the bazaar quarter with the workshops lies elsewhere in the mound.

With different quarters for different activities, a clear specialization in crafts and a social stratification that is obvious in both the size of the houses and the quality of burial gifts, this settlement was not a village of farmers, however rich. It was far more than that. In fact, its remains are as urban as those of any site from the succeeding Bronze Age yet excavated in Turkey.

We have found at Çatal Hüyük 12 superimposed building levels, which we have numbered from 0 to VI-A and VI-B to X according to their apparent chronology from latest to earliest [*see illustration on page 145*]. All these levels belong to a single culture that was uninterrupted in development and shows no signs of destruction attributable to outside forces. The entire sequence so far discovered appears to cover the seventh millennium B.C., although radiocarbon dating of Çatal Hüyük materials now in progress at the University of Pennsylvania may provide a more precise time scale. The core of the mound, however, remains to be sounded, and a full 10 meters of deposit there may take the origins of Çatal Hüyük back to the end of the last continental glaciation.

Houses at Çatal Hüyük were built of shaped mud brick of standard sizes. Because the nearest stone was several

miles away and would have been difficult to bring to the site, the foundations of the houses also consist of mud brick, laid in several courses. By these foundations it is possible to recognize buildings even if their floors are gone, as is the case in Level 0. The houses were rectangular, usually with a small storeroom attached [*see the illustration on page 142*]. Apparently these dwellings were one-story structures, perhaps with a wooden veranda.

The houses show a remarkable consistency of plan inside. Along the east wall there were two raised platforms with a higher bench at the southern end. This arrangement constituted a "divan," used for sitting, working and sleeping. The smaller corner platform evidently belonged to the male owner and the

larger central platform to the women and children. This hierarchic convention appears from Level X to Level II and probably existed in Levels I and 0, of which little remains. There are numerous variations on this arrangement of built-in furniture, including situations in which platforms appear along the north or west wall. The hearth was invariably at the south end of the room, sometimes accompanied by an oven and less often by a kiln. There was a reason for this location of the fires: it had to do with the manner in which the houses were entered.

The entrance was, as in some American Indian villages, a hole in the roof, over which there was surely some sort of canopy-like shelter. The roof opening was always on the south side of the

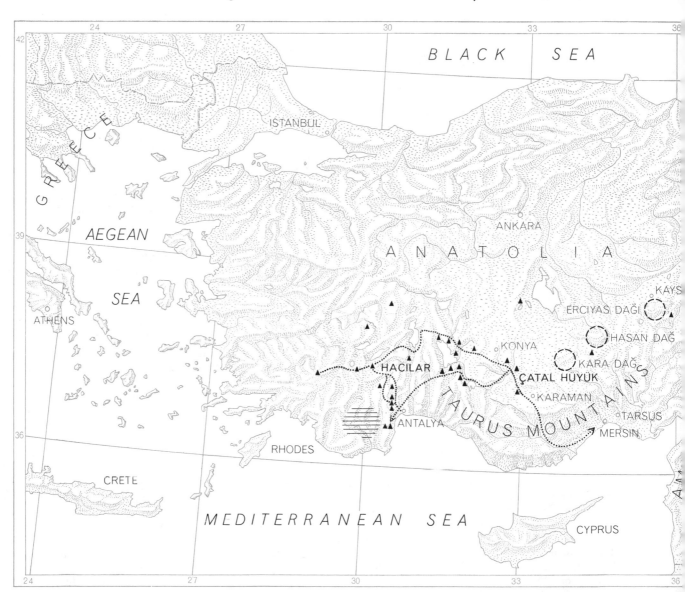

AREA OF NEAR EAST in which the culture represented by Çatal Hüyük was located is shown. Triangular symbols show Neolithic sites; circled areas indicate sources of obsidian; hatched areas, sources of flint. Çatal Hüyük was chosen for extensive archaeological work after excavations at Hacilar revealed a Late Neolithic culture that had arrived fully developed from some other place. Çatal

dwelling; thus it served both as a smoke hole and as an entrance. All access from the outside to the roof was by a movable ladder. From the roof into the dwelling the usual access was by a fixed ladder, although some buildings had another entrance through a well-plastered ventilation shaft that apparently had a movable ladder. Communication between dwellings was accomplished over the rooftops. There is little evidence of lanes and passages, and the courtyards that exist (often merely a ruined house) appear to have been used only for rubbish disposal and excreta.

The system of roof entrances meant that the outside of the settlement presented a solid blank wall. This was a check against enemies and also against

Hüyük apparently represents a culture that was a forerunner of Hacilar's and eventually may be traced back farther than 7000 B.C.

floods. It was evidently a successful defense system, as is indicated by the absence of any signs of massacre. About all any attackers could do—armed as they were with nothing more than bow and arrow, slings and stone tools—was to raid the cattle kept in corrals on the edge of the settlement or to set fire to the roofs. The defenders, in contrast, had the advantage of height and probably of superior numbers. In any case, because of the successful defense the only form of destruction suffered by Çatal Hüyük was fire. Most of the buildings in levels from VI to II were destroyed by fire; but with numerous hearths and ovens and the high winds of the region a disastrous fire about once a century is no more than could be expected.

As a result of these fires the carbonized remains of cereal grains and other foods are plentiful at Çatal Hüyük. There are also many animal bones. The food remains and the bones tell a great deal about the domestic economy of the settlement; the studies being made of them by the paleoethnobiologist Hans Helbaek of the National Museum of Denmark and the zoologist Dexter Perkins, Jr., of Harvard University will probably yield important additional information.

On the basis of what is now known Helbaek has described the grain finds as "the largest, richest and best preserved of all early cereal deposits so far recovered," providing "some of the most significant genetical and cultural" data yet obtained about early civilization. The grains, unlike the finds in other early Near Eastern settlements of cultivated plants little removed from their wild ancestors, include such hybrids and mutants as naked six-row barley and hexaploid free-threshing wheat, which were introduced into Europe from Anatolia in the sixth millennium B.C. The use made of the grains is indicated by the grain bins found in every house and the many mortars for dehusking and querns for grinding. In addition to cereals, peas and lentils the community grew bitter vetch and some other crops; the residents also collected nuts, fruits and berries.

The zoological remains are no less interesting: they show the presence of domesticated sheep even below Level X and cows as early as Level VII. Goats and dogs also appear to have been domesticated, but there is no indication that pigs were. Their absence may be due to religious considerations. Although the domesticated animals provided the community with wool, milk, meat and

skins, the people had by no means abandoned hunting. Wild cattle and red deer were extensively hunted, as were wild asses, wild sheep, boars and leopards.

With such an abundant diet it is not surprising to find from the skeletons that the inhabitants were generally healthy. Bone disease was rare, teeth were good and this dolichocephalic (long-headed) people were fairly tall: the males ranged from about five feet six inches to five feet 10 and the females from five feet to five feet eight. Still, as is to be expected of such an ancient era, few individuals reached middle age.

The burials were inside the houses, beneath the platforms. Most of the skeletons we have found are those of women and children; presumably many of the males died away from home on hunting or fighting forays. The dead were buried in a contracted position, usually lying on their left side with feet toward the wall. Isolated burials were rare; some buildings contain several generations of a family, with 30 or more burials. It appears to have been the practice before final burial to strip the bodies of flesh by a preliminary interment, or by exposure to vultures, insects or microorganisms on an outdoor platform, sheltered by gabled structures built of reeds and mats. Thereafter the bones, still more or less held in position by the ligaments, were wrapped in cloth and given final burial, often being laid out on mats of cloth, skin or fur.

The burials provide information about the dress, weapons and jewelry of the Çatal Hüyük people. Male dress consisted of a loincloth or a leopard skin, fastened by a belt with a bone hook and eye; the men appear also to have worn cloaks fastened with antler toggles in the winter. The women wore sleeveless bodices and jerkins of leopard skin, with fringed skirts or string skirts—the ends of the string being encased in copper tubes for weighting. The women used bone pins for fastening garments.

Weapons buried with the men included polished stone maceheads, obsidian arrowheads and javelin heads and sometimes an obsidian spearhead. Frequently there was a fine flint dagger with a chalk or bone handle and a leather sheath.

Jewelry was mainly for the women and children. They wore the necklaces, armlets, bracelets and anklets we found made of beads and pendants in a great variety of stone, shell, chalk, clay, mother-of-pearl and (as early as Level IX) copper and lead. Cosmetics were

142

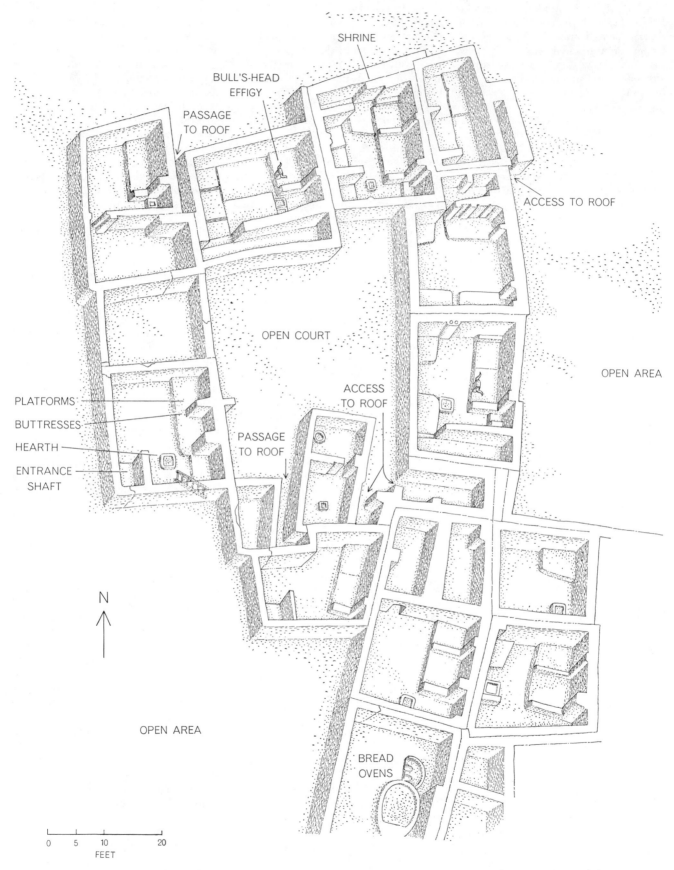

COMMUNITY ARRANGEMENTS of 8,000 years ago in a Neolithic city are depicted on the basis of recent excavations. This is a reconstruction of an area in the fifth of 12 building layers so far found at the Çatal Hüyük site on the Anatolian plateau of Turkey. Access to the buildings was solely from the roof, so that the exterior walls presented a solid blank face, which served effectively as a defense against both attackers and floods. Çatal Hüyük showed a surprising evolution of civilization for so early a community.

SITE OF NEOLITHIC CITY is this mound on the Anatolian plateau of Turkey. The Turkish word for mound is *hüyük*, and this one, which rises 50 feet above the plain, has the modern name of Çatal. After the inhabitants left about 6000 B.C. it lay deserted for 8,000 years; when excavations were started in 1961, it was heavily overgrown. In this photograph the view is from west of the site.

GENERAL VIEW OF EXCAVATIONS at Çatal Hüyük shows work in progress in Level VI, which is near the middle of the 12 levels of construction explored to date. The author chose Çatal Hüyük as the most promising of more than 200 sites he visited on the Anatolian plateau in a search for a representative Early Neolithic community. The site proved to have been a major settlement.

EXCAVATED SHRINE is in Level VI. Three plaster heads of bulls appear atop one another on the west wall, with a half-meter scale below them; on the north wall is a ram's head made of plaster. At bottom right is the remaining part of a small pillar.

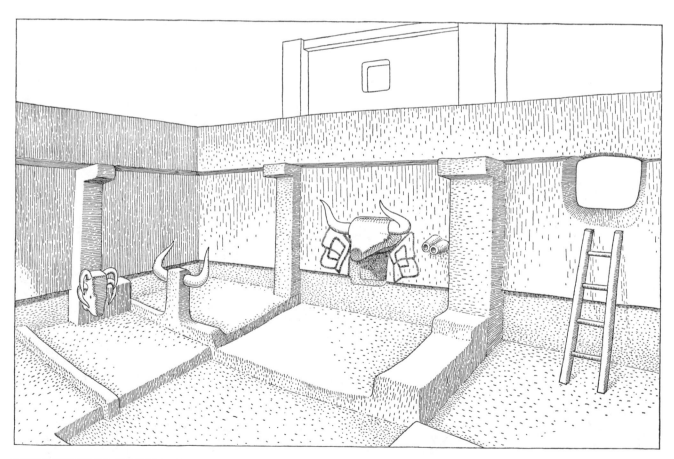

RECONSTRUCTED SHRINE is the same as that shown above. The drawing represents the author's conception, based on excavations of several shrines at Çatal Hüyük, of how the room might have looked in Neolithic times. The stylized heads of animals and women's breasts probably were fertility symbols. Many of the city's shrines also had wall paintings of remarkable sophistication.

widely used, judging from the number of related articles we found, such as palettes and grinders for their preparation, baskets or the shells of fresh-water mussels for their containers and delicate bone pins for their application. The cosmetics probably consisted of red ocher, blue azurite, green malachite and perhaps galena. The women, once arrayed, used mirrors of highly polished obsidian to see the effect.

Several times we found food remains with the dead: berries, peas, lentils, eggs or a joint of meat put next to the deceased in baskets or in wooden bowls and boxes, which are carved with great delicacy. These wooden vessels are a characteristic of the Çatal Hüyük culture, and even when pottery began to appear in quantity around 6500 B.C., baskets and wooden bowls continued in use and had a strong influence on the pottery. The ovals and boat shapes, the lozenges and rectangles that appear in the pottery, not only from Level VI-A upward at Çatal Hüyük but also in the following Late Neolithic of Hacilar, have their origins in the wood-carving tradition of early Çatal Hüyük. In the same way numerous pottery vessels have features such as handles that derive from the earlier basketry.

The first production of pottery at Çatal Hüyük is found in Levels X and IX, but evidently this soft ware could not compete with traditional wood and woven products. It was not until the end of Level VI-A, when technical improvements had led to the production of an excellent hard baked ware, that pottery came into general use. The pottery was handmade and highly burnished. At first it was all dark brown or black; cooking pots were left that way but other objects were soon turned out in red, buff or mottled tones. In the upper levels of the mound animal heads start to appear on oval cups, and an over-all red slip, or coating, is in use, but painting on pottery was apparently never achieved. This pottery develops without a break into that of Late Neolithic Hacilar.

Another area in which Çatal Hüyük shows a people of remarkable technical competence and sophistication is textiles. We found some carbonized textiles in burials as far down as Level VI. They appear to have been wool, and at least three different types of weaving can be distinguished. These are the earliest textiles yet known; Helbaek has written of them that "we shall be hard put to it to find evidence of more perfect work anywhere within the following thousand years."

It is singular that with all these products of human workmanship we have found so few traces of the workmen. None of the 200 houses and shrines excavated so far has shown any evidence that any art or craft other than food preparation was carried on within. We have much fine woolen cloth but only one or two spindle whorls or loom weights, and these are from fill rather than from floor deposits. We have thousands of finely worked obsidian tools but only two small boxes of chips, thousands of bone tools but no piles of waste or splinters. Somewhere in the mound there must be the workshops of the weavers and basketmakers; the matmakers; the carpenters and joiners; the men who made the polished stone tools (axes and adzes, polishers and grinders, chisels, maceheads and palettes); the bead makers who drilled in stone beads holes that no modern steel needle can penetrate and who carved pendants and used stone inlays; the makers of shell beads from dentalium, cowrie and fossil oyster; the flint and obsidian knappers who produced the pressure-flaked daggers, spearheads, lance heads, arrowheads, knives, sickle blades, scrapers and

borers; the merchants of skin, leather and fur; the workers in bone who made the awls, punches, knives, scrapers, ladles, spoons, bowls, scoops, spatulas, bodkins, belt hooks, antler toggles, pins and cosmetic sticks; the carvers of wooden bowls and boxes; the mirror makers; the bowmakers; the men who hammered native copper into sheets and worked it into beads, pendants, rings and other trinkets; the builders; the merchants and traders who obtained all the raw material; and finally the artists—the carvers of statuettes, the modelers and the painters.

The unusual wealth of the city of Çatal Hüyük, as manifested by this great variety of sophisticated workmanship, is a phenomenon as yet without parallel in the Neolithic period. At the base of course lay the new efficiency of food production, transplanted from its probable origin in the hills to the fertile alluvial plain. Although that may account for the unprecedented size of the city, something else is needed to explain the community's almost explosive development in arts and crafts.

The key undoubtedly lies in the community's dependence on the import of

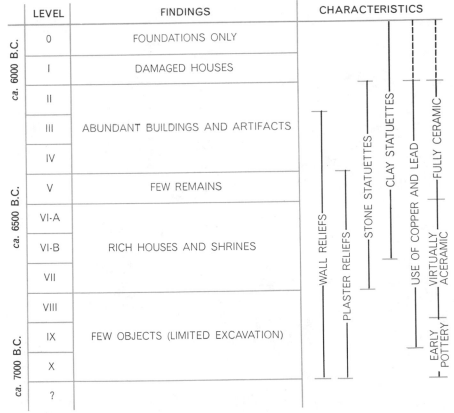

CHRONOLOGY OF HABITATION at Çatal Hüyük is indicated in this chart. Each level above VI-B apparently was built because of fire damage to the preceding level; the site appears to have been deserted after a fire in Level 0. Levels may yet be found below X.

NEOLITHIC ARTIFACTS found at Level VI of Çatal Hüyük and dating from about 6500 B.C. include bone necklace, bone pin, stone beads, limestone bracelet and obsidian mirror.

WALL PAINTING found in Level VI shows children's hands. Çatal Hüyük yielded the earliest known paintings on man-made walls. Most of the painting had a religious purpose.

raw materials (other than clay, timber and food) from near and far. One cannot possibly be wrong in suggesting that it was a well-organized trade that produced the city's wealth. Moreover, it appears likely that the trade in obsidian was at the heart of this extensive commerce. This black volcanic glass, which first appeared in the preceding Mesolithic period, became the most widespread trading commodity during the Neolithic period in the Near East. It has been found in the "proto-Neolithic" and prepottery Neolithic periods at Jericho; it occurs as far south as Beidha near Petra; it reached Cyprus in the sixth millennium. The origin of this obsidian, which was the best material of the time for cutting tools, was almost certainly central Anatolia, and it is extremely likely that the city of Çatal Hüyük controlled this source and organized the trade. The then active volcanoes of Hasan Dağ, Karaca Dağ, Mekke Dağ and others lie on the edge of the Konya plain. The nearest is some 50 miles east of Çatal Hüyük, and all are visible on a clear day. These sources of obsidian were well within the limits of the culture area of which Çatal Hüyük was the undisputed center.

This hegemony was not only economic but also religious and therefore political; in the ancient world no authority could exist without religious sanction. About the political system of Çatal Hüyük one can do little more than guess because there are no writings from the community. It seems likely, however, that at such an early stage of civilization only the priests could have been the bearers of authority.

Of the religious system one can say more because of the shrines and religious art we have found at Çatal Hüyük. In my view they constitute the community's most important archaeological contribution. I would maintain, perhaps wrongly, that the Neolithic religion of Çatal Hüyük (and of Hacilar) was created by women. In contrast to nearly all other earlier and later "fertility cults" of the Near East, it significantly lacks the element of sexual vulgarity and eroticism that is almost automatically associated with fertility and probably is the male's contribution. If the Çatal Hüyük religion is a creation of women, one has the rare opportunity of exploring Neolithic woman's mind by studying the symbolism she used in her effort to comprehend and influence the mysteries of life and death.

Of these symbols there is an abundance. In addition to schematic clay figurines of people and more naturalistic animal figures, there is a unique collection of fine statuettes. Those from the upper layers are modeled in clay; those in the lower layers are carved from stone. Beyond these, which together with burial rites are usually the archaeologist's only sources of information about religion, Çatal Hüyük has produced no fewer than 40 shrines and sanctuaries. They are at every level, but the nine in Level VI-A, the 12 in Level VI-B and the eight in Level VII are particularly rich in information. Wall decorations occur in most: painted scenes with numerous human figures in Levels III and IV; modeled and sometimes painted reliefs in Levels VI-A through X.

The shrines, although frequently large and well appointed, do not differ in plan from the houses, but they are much more lavishly decorated [*see illustration on page 144*]. Even if they were not continuously lived in, they served as burial places, presumably for their priestesses and the priestesses' families. It is only in the shrines that we have found reliefs and symbolism connected with life and death. From these it is possible to reconstruct in some degree the Neolithic pantheon.

The supreme deity was the Great Goddess. Often represented beside her are a daughter and a young son. A bearded god, who is always shown on a bull, was perhaps the Great Goddess' husband. No other deities appear. This group, therefore, probably constitutes the "holy family." Statues and reliefs represent the female deities either as two goddesses or as twins. The idea behind the duplication is evidently that of age and fertility, the whole aim of the religion being to ensure the continuity of life in every aspect: wildlife for the hunter, domesticated life for the civilized communities and finally the life of Neolithic man himself.

It is doubtful that Neolithic thought regarded these as four distinct deities. More likely the representations show aspects of the goddess as mother or as daughter and virgin, with the god as consort or son. The role of the male deity is more pronounced at Çatal Hüyük than it is at Hacilar, perhaps because in Çatal Hüyük hunting and the domestication of wild animals still held major importance, but in general the male plays a subsidiary role.

Scenes dealing with life are generally found on the west wall of the shrines. A typical scene shows the goddess giving birth to a bull or ram. Scenes dealing with death are found on the east

CLAY SEALS, most about the size of a postage stamp, apparently were used for identification. No house had more than one, and all the designs differed. These were in Levels II–IV.

STATUE OF GODDESS, done in clay and about eight inches high, shows her giving birth. Many representations of the goddess were found at Çatal Hüyük; this was in Level II.

wall: in three shrines the east-wall paintings show vultures attacking headless human corpses. Usually, however, the subject of death is expressed in more subtle ways. Representations of women's breasts, for example, which are of course symbolic of life, contained such items as the skulls of vultures, the lower jaws of wild boars and the heads of foxes and weasels—all scavengers and devourers of corpses.

The symbolism of west and east walls, or right and left, is matched by black and red: the red associated with life, the black with death. Panels of red hands are common, and several burial sites show remains of a coating of red ocher, which was evidently intended to be a substitute for blood and so a means of restoring life, at least symbolically. A great black bull covered the vulture paintings; both were symbolic of death. Contrasted with these was another painting of an enormous red bull surrounded by minute jubilant people.

There are some strange figures in the shrines. A stern-looking representation of the goddess was found with a headless bird, probably a vulture. Numerous figures roughly carved out of stalactites suggest a link with the dark world of caves, man's first refuge and sanctuary. An odd painting seems to represent a honeycomb with eggs or chrysalises on boughs and with bees or butterflies, which perhaps symbolize the souls of the dead. It is framed by alternate red and black hands along the top and gray and pink hands along the base. An earlier painting shows alternate red and black lines, resembling a net, similarly framed by hands. Net patterns decorate several other religious scenes, together

with symbols of horns, crosses and hands. Crosses, perhaps a simplified form of a four-petaled flower, were painted on a statuette of the goddess as well as on numerous walls; probably they are to be interpreted as fertility symbols. Rosettes and the double ax (or butterfly) are in the same category.

In several shrines and houses schematized heads of bulls in the form of a pillar serve as a cult symbol for protection. We have found curious benches with one, two, three or seven pairs of the bone cores of horns stuck in the sides. These defy explanation. Perhaps they figured in the burial rites, conceivably serving as a bier while the grave was dug.

Of the rites performed in the shrines little can be said. It is apparent, however, from the absence of blood pits and animal bones that there was no sacrificing of animals in the shrines. There were offerings of other kinds. In a shrine in Level II we found grain that had been burned on the plastered ceremonial altar and then covered by a new coat of plaster; this suggests the first offering after the harvest. In the earlier buildings, particularly in Level VI, there are offerings of all sorts: pots that doubtless contained food and drink; groups of hunting weapons, maces, axes and ceremonial flint daggers; tools; bags of obsidian; beads and many other objects, all unused or in pristine condition.

The wall paintings were mostly created for religious occasions and were covered with white plaster after they had outlived their usefulness. The paint was made of minerals mixed with fat; the painter worked with a brush on a white, cream or pale pink surface. The

range of colors is extensive. Red in all shades, including pink, mauve and orange, is predominant. The other colors are white, lemon yellow, purple, black and (very infrequently) blue. We have yet to find green. In a class apart from the religious paintings are several paintings of textile patterns, which attest the importance attached to weaving. Many of them show kilims, or woven carpets, making carpet weaving an art that can now be traced back to Neolithic times.

Many seasons of work remain at Çatal Hüyük. It is therefore premature to speak definitively about the origins of this remarkable civilization. It can be said, however, that the discovery of the art of Çatal Hüyük has demonstrated that the Upper Paleolithic tradition of naturalistic painting, which died in western Europe with the end of the ice age, not only survived but flourished in Anatolia. The implication is that at least part of the population of Çatal Hüyük was of Upper Paleolithic stock.

These people may not have been the first to learn the arts of cereal cultivation and animal husbandry, but they improved on the techniques to such an extent that they were able to produce the surplus of food that permits the beginning of leisure and specialization. By the seventh millennium they had created the first Mediterranean civilization, of which Çatal Hüyük is such an impressive representative. In time the offshoots of that civilization reached the Aegean shore, and by the sixth millennium Anatolian colonists were laying the foundations for the ultimate development of civilization in Europe.

Megalithic Monuments

by Glyn Daniel
July 1980

*These assemblages of massive stones, of which
Stonehenge is one, are found by the thousands
in Europe. How old they are was long uncertain,
but they have now been dated to the Neolithic period*

Among the most dramatic remains of the ancient cultural landscape of Europe are its many prehistoric stone monuments. These megaliths have long aroused the interest and curiosity both of the general public and of antiquarians and archaeologists, with their interest in correctly describing the nature, purpose, context and age of the structures. To give only two examples, the stone rows of the Carnac region in southern Brittany, where more than 3,000 menhirs stand in parallel lines that extend for nearly four miles, and the Grand Menhir Brisé at nearby Locmariaquer, now broken but originally 22 meters long, are among the most remarkable relics of prehistoric France.

Without doubt the most famous of all megalithic monuments is Stonehenge, on the Wiltshire plain of southern Britain. Visited by thousands yearly, it is second only to the Tower of London as a tourist attraction. It has a larger literature than any other archaeological site in the world, including the pyramids of Egypt and the great statues of Easter Island, as well as mythical sites such as Atlantis. The number of books on Stonehenge and on other megalithic monuments that have poured from the presses in the past decade or so is a measure of the continued interest in these antiquities.

It is also, alas, an all too clear demonstration of the imagination, wishful thinking and credulousness of many authors, and the abysmal ignorance of many alleged archaeologists who can only be described, if uncharitably, as fantasy buffs. This is no new phenomenon. As long ago as 1911 G. Elliot Smith's book *The Ancient Egyptians* brought all these ancient European monuments from the banks of the Nile. Such exercises of the imagination continue. As recently as 1977 Euan MacKie in *The Megalith Builders* declared that they were the work of wise men from predynastic Egypt and Sumeria. There are others, among them Erich von Däniken, who see the megalith builders as voyagers from space. Now there is also a widespread belief that these monuments were built with an astronomical purpose, and such words as "astroarchaeology" and "archaeoastronomy" are freely bandied about. Let us take a sober and balanced look at these structures in the context of our existing detailed knowledge of ancient Europe.

The Study of Megaliths

In 1849 in a book called *Cyclops Christianus* an Oxford don, Algernon Herbert, coined the word megalith (from the Greek *megas*, great, and *lithos*, stone). The word caught on. Although in 1872 James Fergusson, a Scottish architectural scholar, titled his book *Rude Stone Monuments in All Countries*, he too spoke of megaliths. So did T. E. Peet in his *Rough Stone Monuments*, published 40 years later.

These pioneer works established the proper study of megaliths, but they introduced one fundamental confusion. As travelers such as Fergusson journeyed outside Europe they found great stone monuments in Algeria, Palestine, Ethiopia and the Sudan, the Caucasus, Persia, Baluchistan, Kashmir and central and southern India. (In India the megalithic monuments of the Deccan, many of them with "portholes" resembling those of megalithic tombs in Europe, first interested Fergusson in undertaking his comparative researches.) The list does not end there. Megaliths are found in Assam, in Sumatra and on some Pacific islands such as Malekula in the New Hebrides. (The stone figures of Easter Island, although they are certainly large, are not megaliths in the generally accepted sense.) In Japan megalithic tombs were built from the second century B.C. until the seventh century A.D., when the emperor Kotoku forbade them as a waste of labor. The pre-Columbian civilizations of the New World also practiced megalithic construction.

The result of applying the term megalith to all these monuments in different countries, from different periods and in different cultural contexts gave birth to an absurdity: the idea that the structures were genetically connected, that they were the work of a megalithic race or a megalithic people. This notion has long been abandoned, and it is widely realized that the megalithic structures in different parts of the world are similar because they are made of similar materials in similar ways. The parallels are particularly striking in megalithic chambers or rooms that incorporate the basic elements of what is known as trabeate architecture (from the Latin *trabes*, beam). This type of construction is like building a house of cards or of children's blocks: slabs of stone are set upright (orthostats) and other slabs are laid across the uprights as capstones. The architectural possibilities are limited, and so it is not surprising that a megalithic chamber in France or Ireland, dating from the third millennium B.C., should resemble a megalithic chamber in southern India dating from the end of the first millennium B.C.

Another confusion in the minds of many is one between megalithic architecture and cyclopean architecture. The latter also makes use of large stones, but a cyclopean structure is built of stones that are carefully fitted together, even if irregular in shape, and generally set in layers. Cyclopean architecture is found in both the New World (for example the Inca structures of Peru) and the Old (for example the citadels of Mycenae and Tiryns in Greece or the nuraghi, or stone towers, of Sardinia).

The European Megaliths

The megalithic structures of Europe fall into four main categories. First is the menhir, or single standing stone. The word comes from the Welsh *maen*, a stone, and *hir*, long. Brittany is rich in menhirs that range in length from one meter to six meters. A notable exception is the Grand Menhir Brisé, a much larger horizontal stone. No one knows whether this great stone ever stood erect; the earliest records describe it as it is now.

A special kind of menhir, known as a statue menhir, is sculptured so that it bears the representation of a person, hu-

GRAND ARRAY AT CARNAC in southern Brittany includes three separate avenues of menhirs, or standing stones. Seen in this aerial photograph is the Kermario display, consisting of 10 roughly parallel lines of menhirs, hewn from local granite, extending some 4,000 feet.

MOST FAMOUS MONUMENT of the megalithic tradition, Stonehenge is a ring surrounded by a bank and a ditch, situated on the Wiltshire plain of southern Britain. The ring was built in phases, starting in about 2800 B.C., and was completed sometime after 1100 B.C.

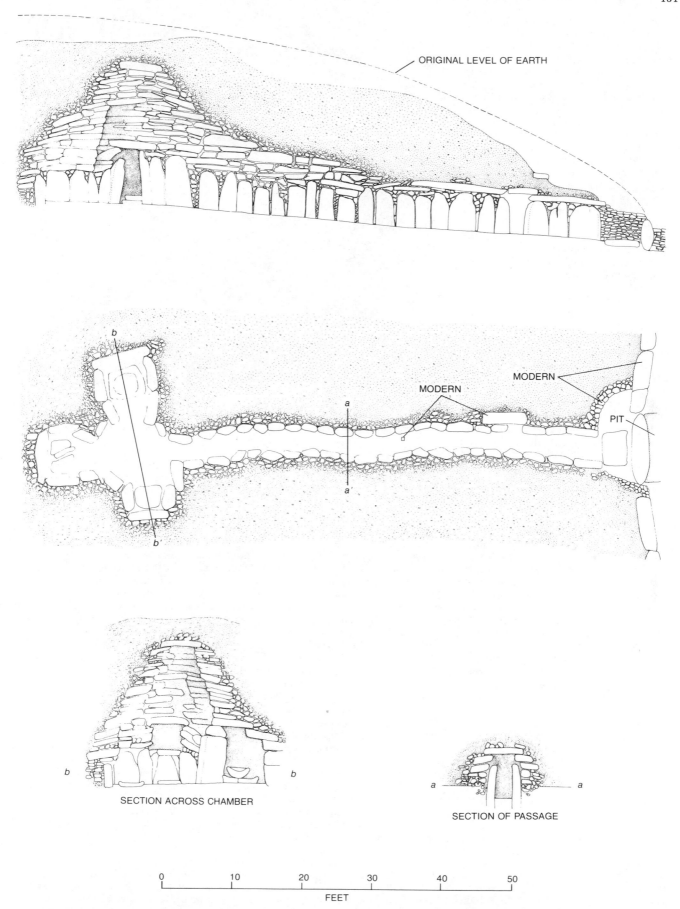

ORIGINAL LEVEL OF EARTH

MODERN

MODERN

PIT

SECTION ACROSS CHAMBER

SECTION OF PASSAGE

0   10   20   30   40   50

FEET

GREATEST BURIAL CHAMBER of the megalithic tradition is Newgrange in County Meath in Eire, shown in elevation at the top and in plan and sections at the bottom. The narrow passage that leads to the burial chamber at the center of the great mound is some 60 feet long; the corbeled vault of the chamber is 20 feet high (*see photograph on following page*).

man or divine. These are found in southern France and northern Italy, with outlying examples both in Spain and on the Channel Islands. These interesting uprights, the earliest monumental sculpture in the round in human history, can be dated to the end of the third millennium B.C. and the beginning of the second. They are not, however, necessarily connected with the undecorated menhirs.

The second category of megalithic structures is made up of grouped standing stones. The stones are set either in rows, as those at Carnac are, or in what used to be called stone circles. The careful surveys of Alexander Thom, retired professor of engineering at the University of Oxford, have shown that many of the latter monuments are not strictly circular: many are in the form of an ellipse or a flattened ellipse. As a result the term now coming into favor as a description of these megalithic enclosures is stone ring. Some stand alone; some surround a burial mound. Some are associated with rows of stones; some, like the famous monuments of Stonehenge and Avebury in southern Britain and Stenness and Brodgar in Orkney, are surrounded by ditches and banks.

The third category, the burial chamber, constitutes the commonest form of European stone monument. There must be 40,000 to 50,000 of these chambers surviving, and originally there were perhaps twice as many. The largest number of them are found in Spain and Portugal, France, Britain and Ireland, Scandinavia and northern Germany. Some are completely buried under large mounds of earth and stone, some bear traces of partially destroyed mounds and others are entirely freestanding. It was thought in the 19th century that all freestanding chambers were the ruins of chambered mounds, but this is not now thought to be so. Some are the remains of denuded burial mounds but others, such as the portal chambers of Ireland and the great stone galleries of western France, were probably always as they are today.

Many burial chambers exhibit a roofing technique more elaborate than the simple capstone; stones were placed on top of the upright orthostats in such a way as to overlap until they formed a corbeled roof, or vault. Among the most famous surviving corbeled vaults are Maes Howe in Orkney and Newgrange in County Meath in Eire. Maes Howe was broken into by the Vikings, but Newgrange, with its vault rising 20 feet above the ground, has remained intact for 4,500 years. It is one of the wonders of prehistoric Europe.

Many of the stones in these chambers are very large. The capstone of the Mount Browne chamber in County Carlow in Eire is estimated to weigh some 100 tons. The great megalithic chamber at Bagneux, near Saumur in western France, is some 20 meters long by five meters wide, and its roof of four

LOOKING UP to the top of the corbeled vault at Newgrange, this photograph reveals its stepped construction. Each successive layer of slabs was placed closer together until capstones could bridge the narrowed gap. A similar corbeled vault was built at Maes Howe in Orkney.

capstones gives three meters of head space to someone standing inside. (It once housed a café!) The capstones are about 60 centimeters thick; the largest of them is estimated to weigh 86 tons.

The fourth category, the megalithic temple, is a limited one. Most of the examples are found in the Mediterranean, on the island of Malta and its neighbor Gozo. The application of the term temple to these great megalithic monuments may conjure up in the minds of some a building comparable in appearance to the pillared structures of dynastic Egypt and Classical Greece. The Maltese monuments are very different. Their solid walls consist of very large slabs of stone, their floor plan includes projecting apses and they were probably roofed with wood beams and thatch. They are certainly among the most impressive prehistoric architectural monuments in the entire Mediterranean area.

That the Maltese structures were temples there is little doubt. They hold no burials and no traces of domestic occupation but do contain many cult objects, including figurines of a female deity and stones decorated with spirals and other designs. There is also no doubt that they date from the fourth millennium B.C. They are thus the earliest example of stone architecture in the Mediterranean and, together with the megalithic chambers of Spain and France, in the entire world.

In medieval times the common folk, and learned men too, thought the great

stone monuments must have been the work of giants of long ago. Indeed, the first recorded excavation of a megalithic chamber in Sweden was for the specific purpose of testing this supposition. It was proved wrong; the remains found in the chamber were not those of giants. Later antiquarians sought to explain the megaliths in terms of written history. The structures were variously ascribed to the Romans, the Anglo-Saxons, the Danes, the Goths and the Huns. For example, Herbert, the coiner of the word megalith, argued that because Stonehenge and other British megaliths were not mentioned by Roman historians and visitors to Britain the structures must be post-Roman.

Who and Why

Gradually it came to be accepted that the megaliths were pre-Roman. The pre-Roman inhabitants of northwestern Europe, namely the ancient Gauls and Britons, had been described by Caesar and others as having a class of wise men called Druids. It is not surprising, then, that the megaliths came to be ascribed to the Druids. Some even took the freestanding chambers for Druidic altars.

Over the past two centuries the growth of archaeological excavation has revealed that megalithic chambers were primarily burial places, used collectively by a community or a family over a period of time. Some large chambers have yielded the remains of 200

DOLMEN, OR "TABLE STONE," is the name given to this form of megalithic monument in Brittany. It consists of a single capstone resting on three or more upright supports and is the simplest form of burial chamber. This monument, situated in Pembrokeshire in Wales, is known as the Carreg Samson cromlech, a Welsh word equivalent to dolmen. Some chambers are freestanding; others are mounded over.

LARGER CHAMBER, also in Pembrokeshire, now has only one capstone. This freestanding burial chamber, at Pentre-Ifan, was first recorded by George Owen in his survey of Pembrokeshire published in 1603. Perhaps 50,000 such burial chambers survive in Europe.

individuals or more. Not all megalith-ic chambers, however, were necessari-ly tombs. Some, like the freestanding chambers of Ireland and the Loire val-ley of France, may have been temples, although scarcely Druidic ones. Indeed, the line between a tomb and a temple is not a hard and fast one, as we realize when we look at Christian churches and cathedrals.

The grave goods found in many meg-alithic chambers are unspectacular: un-decorated pots and polished stone axes. In some areas, however, they are rich and remarkable. In Scandinavia heavily decorated pots with oculi, or eye orna-ments, are found. In Spain many tombs yield large numbers of schist plaques covered with designs, some of them anthropomorphic. Tombs in Brittany have yielded superbly fashioned pol-ished axes and rings of jade, garnet and other precious materials. These date from the third millennium B.C., long an-tedating the Chinese and Maya achieve-ments in jade.

The purpose of the menhirs is more difficult to evaluate. Sometimes burials are found at their foot, but they are not tombs. Moreover, such burials cannot even provide a date for the monument, let alone establish its original purpose. Perhaps these single standing stones were intended as territorial markers. Perhaps alternatively they were meant as memorials for the dead, a prehis-toric version of the Greek cenotaph, or empty tomb.

The purpose of the menhir alignments and the stone rings is clearly neither funerary nor domestic. Perhaps these monuments were places of assembly where tribes or communities met from time to time for both secular and reli-gious purposes. I see them functioning like the Breton *pardons* of the present day: opportunities for priests to conduct sacred rites, for crops and animals to be blessed, for friends and relatives to meet and enjoy a social occasion, a market and a fair, particularly a hiring fair.

Does such a description fit Stone-henge, the best-known stone ring of them all? First it should be remembered that Stonehenge is a complex monu-ment of several periods and many archi-tectural features, including two circles, two horseshoes and carefully shaped "trilithons" that are a far cry from sim-ple orthostats and capstones. The stones themselves are in part sandstone from the Marlborough Downs and in part "foreign" blue stone from the Preseli hills of Pembrokeshire in southern Wales. There are some 80 of the blue stones, weighing up to four tons each; the distance from Preseli to Stonehenge is 135 miles as the crow flies. The sand-stone units, better known as sarsen stones, are also large and were carefully dressed. The largest single component of the sarsen trilithons measures 29 feet eight inches, and the average height of

EROSION OR VANDALISM had stripped away the mound that once concealed this cham-bered tomb by the time the artist recorded the monument in the 1840's. Only one capstone still bears some of the former covering of rubble and earth. The engraving on which this sketch of Bryn Celli Ddu in Anglesey in Wales is based appeared in *Archaeologia Cambrensis*, 1847.

the stones in the sarsen circle is 13 feet six inches. One of the most interesting and architecturally sophisticated devic-es used by the builders of Stonehenge is what is known in Greek architecture as entasis. This consists of shaping an up-right so that the effect of perspective is canceled; when the stones are seen at close range, they do not appear to taper upward but give the optical illusion of being straight-sided.

Measuring the Year

There is no doubt in anyone's mind that Stonehenge was built with its cen-tral axis pointing to the midsummer sun-rise. Many years ago the British astron-omer Sir Norman Lockyer argued that by calculating the exact orientation of Stonehenge he could assign an exact date to the construction of the mon-ument. His conclusion was 1680 B.C. (±200 years). Since then R. J. C. At-kinson of University College, Cardiff, who has done more than anyone by ex-cavation and research to contribute to our modern knowledge of Stonehenge, has pointed out that, owing to errors in Lockyer's original reasoning, his date should be altered slightly. The new read-ing is 1840 B.C. (±200 years).

The astronomical purpose of Stone-henge and other stone rings was not seri-ously argued until after World War II, when Gerald S. Hawkins of Boston Uni-versity proposed in his book *Stonehenge Decoded* (1966) that the monument was a giant calculator for the prediction of eclipses, both lunar and solar. Five years later Thom, in his book *Megalithic Lu-nar Observatories,* postulated that many megalithic monuments served for obser-vation of the movements and phases of

the moon. Thom's surveys had already led him to argue for the existence of a megalithic "yard" measuring 2.72 feet and to suggest that the builders of stone rings had a knowledge of Pythagorean geometry 2,000 years or more before the Greeks. These are extravagant and unconvincing claims; what the builders of megaliths had was a practical knowl-edge of laying out right-angled triangles.

Many people, no doubt bored by the prosaic account of megaliths to be got from archaeological research, jumped on the Hawkins-Thom bandwagon, ac-cepting the builders of megaliths not only as experts in Pythagorean geome-try and possessors of accurate units of mensuration but also as skilled astrono-mers who studied eclipses, the move-ments of the moon and the positions of the stars. To me this is a kind of refined academic version of astronaut archae-ology. The archaeoastronomy buffs, al-though they very properly eschew wise men from outer space, very improperly insist on the presence in ancient Europe of wise men with an apparently religious passion for astronomy. It seems to me that the case for interpreting megalithic monuments as astronomical observato-ries has never been proved. The inter-pretations appear to be subjective and imposed by the observer. Already new surveys are showing the inaccuracy of some of the earlier observations and undermining the hopes of those who believe the builders of megaliths were slaves of an astronomical cult.

The entire study of megaliths in Eu-rope has been revolutionized not by sur-veyors with their eye on the moon and the stars but by advances in prehistor-ic dating. The first of these was the de-velopment by Willard F. Libby and his colleagues of carbon-14 dating. The first carbon-14 dates were published 30 years ago, and since then thousands of them have been determined by laboratories all over the world. A more recent geochronological technique, thermoluminescence dating, has confirmed many carbon-14 findings.

The Question of When

Before the carbon-14 revolution—and it has been no less than revolutionary for the field of prehistoric archaeology—the ages of various ancient works of man had either been guessed at or calculated in a regrettably uncertain way by correlations between the dated civilizations of Egypt and Mesopotamia and undated barbarian Europe. Thus in the period between the two world wars it was customary to assign the earliest European megaliths to the Neolithic period, say between 2500 and 2000 B.C., and the great monuments such as Newgrange and Stonehenge to the Bronze Age, between 1800 and 1500 B.C.

Now, thanks to the carbon-14 revolution, we can confidently state how old the megaliths of Europe actually are. The Maltese temples date from 4000 to 2000 B.C. The megalithic chamber tombs of Spain and Portugal date from 3800 to 2000 B.C. The British and Irish tombs date from just after 3800 to 2000 B.C. and the Scandinavian tombs from before 3000 B.C. to, say, 1800 B.C. In the Irish sequence it is good to have a definite date for Newgrange, showing that it was put up in about 2500 B.C. In the British sequence Atkinson has set down the chronological details of Stonehenge: the first phase was from 2800 to 2200 B.C.; the second phase, including the arrival of the blue stones from Wales, was from 2100 to 2000 B.C.; the third phase, which includes three subphases, was from 2000 to 1100 B.C., when the final phase began.

The dates I have given here, for Stonehenge and for megalithic monuments in general, are what are called calibrated carbon-14 dates. This is to say that they have been adjusted to the corrections based on the study of the rings of the bristlecone pine as displayed in the variation curves plotted by Hans E. Suess of the University of California at San Diego, by R. Malcolm Clark of Monash University in Australia and by others.

How can one explain the origins of these megalithic monuments now that they are accurately dated? There is only one tenable explanation of the menhirs of Brittany and elsewhere in northwestern Europe. They are a local invention; perhaps they represent the translation into stone of an earlier practice of setting up wood posts as cenotaphs or territorial markers or even totem poles.

There is now only one tenable explanation of the Maltese megalithic temples. It used to be argued that they were

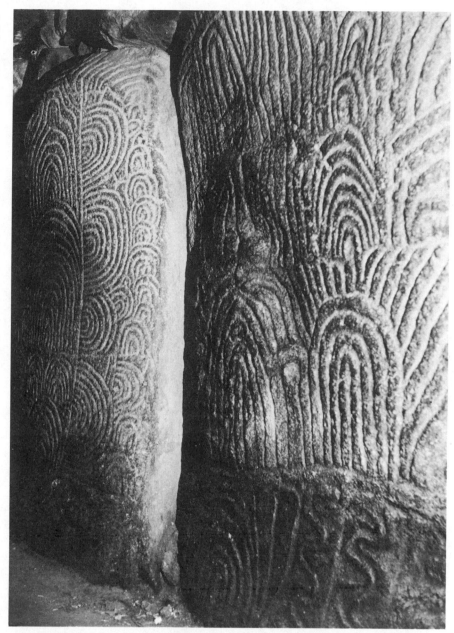

SEMICIRCULAR MOTIF predominates in the low-relief sculpturing of these uprights at the megalithic burial chamber of Gavrinis in France, roughly contemporaneous with Newgrange. Whether the patterns were decorative or whether they had religious meaning is not known.

derived by diffusion from Minoan Crete or from Mycenae or from even farther afield. Carbon-14 chronology now shows them to be earlier than any Minoan, Mycenaean, Egyptian or Sumerian context. The Maltese temples were an indigenous development. Possibly they are aboveground versions of subterranean rock-cut temple tombs. In any event they appear to have no antecedent anywhere, and no structures that can be confidently derived from the Maltese temples have ever been found outside Malta and Gozo.

We now come to the origins of the megalithic chambers and the stone rings. These must not be looked on as isolated phenomena. Instead we must seek to explain them in the context of the Neolithic societies that created them. Elliot Smith's idea that the European megaliths were derived from the mastabas, or stone tombs, of Egypt has no basis in fact and no suggestion of probability. We now know that the megaliths of Europe are older than the mastabas and pyramids of Egypt.

Still another hypothesis, voiced by V. Gordon Childe and others and tenaciously held by most archaeologists during the second quarter of this century, suggested that the megaliths of Europe were built by people who originated in the eastern Mediterranean, particularly in Crete and the islands of the Aegean. Even in the days before carbon-14 dating it was becoming clear that the idea of, for example, deriving great chamber

LARGEST MENHIR in western Europe is this broken specimen at Locmariaquer in Brittany. Three of its four fragments are seen here; the combined length of the four is 22 meters. Whether the menhir ever stood upright is not known; earliest records show it in its present position.

CHRISTIANIZED MENHIR in the Yorkshire village of Rudston, 25 feet high, is the tallest in Britain. The megalithic monument was not thrown down; the graveyard grew up around it.

tombs such as Newgrange and Maes Howe from the domed subterranean tombs of Mycenae was chronologically impossible. As a second line of defense the hypothesis was adjusted backward in time to the vaulted tombs of the Messara in Crete and the rock-cut tombs of the Cyclades. Now both carbon-14 and thermoluminescence determinations show that the European megalithic chambers antedate any of the collective tombs in the eastern Mediterranean.

The New Conclusion

We are therefore forced to conclude that chamber tombs originated independently in at least seven areas of Europe: southern Spain, Portugal, Brittany, northern France, northern Germany, Scandinavia, southern Britain and Scotland. Does this statement appear to be a victory for the "independent evolution" school of archaeological theory over the "diffusionist" school that has held the field for so long?

It is not as simple as that. The Neolithic societies that began to put up megaliths in some areas of Europe in about 4000 B.C. were those that were already building comparable nonlithic or non-megalithic structures, to wit houses and graves. Many of us think at present that an explanation of the appearance of megalithic chamber tombs in many different parts of Europe must take into consideration three successive phases. The first phase postulates an early European Neolithic tradition of building houses of wood or stone. The second phase involves the transformation of these domestic structures into tombs, still constructed of wood, turf or non-megalithic stone. The third phase involves the translation of these widespread Neolithic traditions into megalithic architecture in separate areas of Europe that were without doubt interconnected.

The origin of stone rings may be explained in much the same way, although here the phenomenon does not involve seven separate but interconnected areas. The rings are found only in Britain and Ireland. Just as the chamber tomb translates a simpler precursor, so the stone rings cannot be dissociated from the wood-ring monuments now commonly referred to as woodhenges.

I see the origin of stone rings this way. First there were circular clearings in the forests that covered Neolithic Europe in the fifth and fourth millenniums B.C. We can postulate that sacred and secular gatherings took place in these clearings. Next, owing to the agency of man's domestic animals and man himself, the forests disappeared, whereupon artificial clearings were created by setting posts in a ring as a stage for similar gatherings. The third phase was the translation of the wood rings into stone rings. Then finally, as the tour de ́force of a

REVERSING SPIRALS decorate a low wall in a Maltese megalithic temple at Hal Tarxien, near Valetta. The numerous megalithic tem-ples of Malta and nearby Gozo, once believed to have been inspired by Minoan structures, are now known to be indigenous in origin.

SPIRAL DECORATION is predominant among the motifs executed in low relief on this megalithic column at the entrance to New-grange. The decoration, if it is as old as the burial chamber itself, is at least 1,500 years later than the earliest Maltese megalithic temples.

succession of what one can only call cathedral architects, Stonehenge was built in the middle of the third millennium B.C. and flourished as a temple cum meeting place cum stadium for more than 1,000 years. This brings us back to my earlier question: Does Stonehenge fit the description of megalithic rings in general as sacred and secular meeting places? The answer seems to be emphatically in the affirmative.

Megaliths and Religion

One feels there must have been an impelling faith to inspire the Neolithic people who labored mightily to construct the megaliths of Europe. Tombs, temples, cenotaphs, meeting places—whatever the monuments were—appear to be manifestations of some powerful religious belief including a belief in an afterlife. Was the religion connected with the annual round of the sun, as the orientation of Stonehenge and other stone rings suggests? Was it connected with a mother goddess, as seems to be hinted by the figures from the Maltese temples and those on pottery and on the schist plaques from the tombs in Spain and Portugal? We may never know. Without written sources it is virtually impossible to reconstruct the character-

istics, religious and social, of prehistoric societies. We do not know why the hunters of the Upper Paleolithic created paintings, engravings and sculptures in southern France and northern Spain, and we must admit that we also do not know the social and religious ethos of the megalith builders.

Of the thousands of megalithic tombs in Europe a few are decorated with designs carved in low relief or incised on the stone surface. Some in central Germany seem to be representations of tapestry, perhaps the hangings that may have lined the walls of houses. Others, particularly in the Paris basin, are clear representations of a female in frontal view; the eyes, nose and breasts of the deity are emphasized. The majority of the megalithic designs in the tombs of Brittany and Ireland, however, are geometric patterns: spirals, zigzags, lozenges, concentric circles. Perhaps the finest are at Gavrinis in Brittany and at Newgrange. Some, like the spirals on the great stone at the entrance to Newgrange, seem simply decorative. Others are to our eyes a bewildering confusion of what may be signs and symbols. It is important to remember that some of these geometric decorations are buried in the encompassing mounds of chamber tombs and were never meant to be

seen; they were deliberately hidden at the time of construction. Why? Are they messages or are they sacred symbols? Whatever their meaning, it is set down in a notation we can never decipher.

In this connection it was discovered only 15 years ago that a representation of a dagger had been engraved on one of the uprights at Stonehenge, as had representations of several axes of Early Bronze Age style. Some fancied the dagger to be a Mycenaean one. This kind of art is quite different from that of the chamber tombs, and of course the representations may have been executed late in the history of Stonehenge. To say that they are Bronze Age graffiti, however, is not to say that Stonehenge was a gigantic Bronze Age lavatory.

The practice of building great stone monuments in Europe died out by 1000 B.C., but the general population need not have simultaneously forgotten the nature and significance of the structures. It is by no means impossible that the folk of the first millennium B.C. continued to congregate and worship at the stone rings, and it is more than possible that the Druidic priesthood of the pre-Roman Celts of Gaul and Britain used them as temples. There is, however, no archaeological evidence of it.

At first Christianity strongly disap-

AVEBURY ENCLOSURE, first recognized as a megalithic circle by John Aubrey in the 17th century, caused him to remark that it "does as much exceed in greatness the so renowned Stoneheng as a Cathedral doeth a parish Church." Few of the 190-odd menhirs that made up the circle and its avenues are visible in this aerial photograph, but the bank and ditch, formed by the quarrying of 200,000 tons of chalk, enclose an area of more than 28 acres. The conical mound visible at upper right, called Silbury Hill, is also manmade.

proved of people who worshiped stones, but gradually there came a new tolerance, which was generous enough for certain menhirs to be Christianized. Indeed, in Spain and Brittany a few megalithic monuments have been incorporated into functioning modern Christian churches. I take this to be a sign that the older faith of the builders survived in some shape or form until at least the Middle Ages of western Europe.

The Builders' Skills

It used to be asked: Who are the megalith builders of ancient Europe and where are their houses and settlements? We now think these questions are the wrong way around. It is the Neolithic villagers of Europe in the fourth and third millenniums B.C. who in certain areas built their tombs and temples in enduring stone. There has been much spoken and written recently about a rev-

olution in our picture of the prehistoric past. Archaeologists are described as having thought of Neolithic peoples as savages, and so the new view of the past that shows them having great mathematical, geometrical and astronomical skills and knowledge dramatically changes our image of prehistoric man.

This thesis makes sense only to those who have never understood the archaeological record and who want to sensationalize prehistory. I have never had any doubt that the Neolithic peoples of Europe were good technicians and skilled engineers. They quarried large stones, transported them for considerable distances and erected them with consummate skill and artistry. We can gain some information about their probable techniques by studying the methods used today in areas such as Assam, where megalithic monuments are still being built. We can measure their accomplishments by noting the difficulties present-day farmers and building contractors encounter in trying to break

up the prehistoric structures. For example, late in the past century the capstone of a megalithic chamber near Saumur was moved to be used as a bridge across a local stream. The movers built a number of enormous rollers more than a meter in circumference; each roller was made by lashing the trunks of four oak trees together. Even with the rollers in place 18 pairs of oxen were needed to move the load.

We must never deny the greatness of the megalith builders' achievements. Nor should we deny that from time to time, pausing from their labors at the harvest or at the construction of a monument, they looked as we all do to the sun, the moon and the stars. It is 6,000 years since the first megaliths were built in Malta and Brittany: 4,000 years before the beginning of the Christian Era and 1,000 years before the literate civilizations of Egypt and Mesopotamia. This is a sobering thought when we contemplate, with pride and pleasure, our megalithic patrimony.

The Origins of New World Civilization

by Richard S. MacNeish
November 1964

*In the Mexican valley of Tehuacán bands of hunters
became urban craftsmen in the course of 12,000 years.
Their achievement raises some new questions about the
evolution of high cultures in general*

Perhaps the most significant single occurrence in human history was the development of agriculture and animal husbandry. It has been assumed that this transition from food-gathering to food production took place between 10,000 and 16,000 years ago at a number of places in the highlands of the Middle East. In point of fact the archaeological evidence for the transition, particularly the evidence for domesticated plants, is extremely meager. It is nonetheless widely accepted that the transition represented a "Neolithic Revolution," in which abundant food, a sedentary way of life and an expanding population provided the foundations on which today's high civilizations are built.

The shift from food-gathering to food production did not, however, happen only once. Until comparatively recent times the Old World was for the most part isolated from the New World. Significant contact was confined to a largely one-way migration of culturally primitive Asiatic hunting bands across the Bering Strait. In spite of this almost total absence of traffic between the hemispheres the European adventurers who reached the New World in the 16th century encountered a series of cultures almost as advanced (except in metallurgy and pyrotechnics) and quite as barbarous as their own. Indeed, some of the civilizations from Mexico to Peru possessed a larger variety of domesticated plants than did their European

conquerors and had made agricultural advances far beyond those of the Old World.

At some time, then, the transition from food-gathering to food production occurred in the New World as it had in the Old. In recent years one of the major problems for New World prehistorians has been to test the hypothesis of a Neolithic Revolution against native archaeological evidence and at the same time to document the American stage of man's initial domestication of plants (which remains almost unknown in both hemispheres).

The differences between the ways in which Old World and New World men achieved independence from the nomadic life of the hunter and gatherer are more striking than the similarities. The principal difference lies in the fact that the peoples of the Old World domesticated many animals and comparatively few plants, whereas in the New World the opposite was the case. The abundant and various herds that gave the peoples of Europe, Africa and Asia meat, milk, wool and beasts of burden were matched in the pre-Columbian New World only by a half-domesticated group of Andean cameloids: the llama, the alpaca and the vicuña. The Andean guinea pig can be considered an inferior equivalent of the Old World's domesticated rabbits and hares; elsewhere in the Americas the turkey was an equally inferior counterpart of the Eastern Hemisphere's many

varieties of barnyard fowl. In both the Old World and the New, dogs presumably predated all other domestic animals; in both beekeepers harvested honey and wax. Beyond this the New World list of domestic animals dwindles to nothing. All the cultures of the Americas, high and low alike, depended on their hunters' skill for most of their animal produce: meat and hides, furs and feathers, teeth and claws.

In contrast, the American Indian domesticated a remarkable number of plants. Except for cotton, the "water bottle" gourd, the yam and possibly the coconut (which may have been domesticated independently in each hemisphere), the kinds of crops grown in the Old World and the New were quite different. Both the white and the sweet potato, cultivated in a number of varieties, were unique to the New World. For seasoning, in place of the pepper and mustard of the Old World, the peoples of the New World raised vanilla and at least two kinds of chili. For edible seeds they grew amaranth, chive, panic grass, sunflower, quinoa, apazote, chocolate, the peanut, the common bean and four other kinds of beans: lima, summer, tepary and jack.

In addition to potatoes the Indians cultivated other root crops, including manioc, oca and more than a dozen other South American plants. In place of the Old World melons, the related plants brought to domestication in the New World were the pumpkin, the

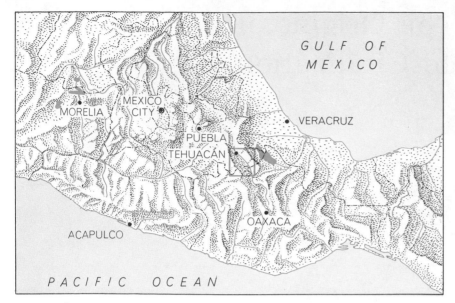

TEHUACÁN VALLEY is a narrow desert zone in the mountains on the boundary between the states of Puebla and Oaxaca. It is one of the three areas in southern Mexico selected during the search for early corn on the grounds of dryness (which helps to preserve ancient plant materials) and highland location (corn originally having been a wild highland grass).

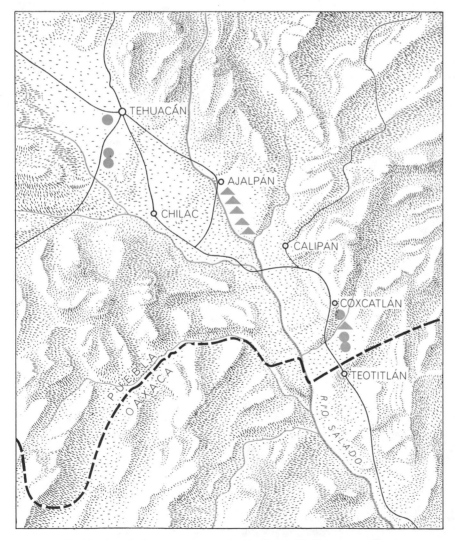

SIX CAVES (dots) and six open-air sites (triangles) have been investigated in detail by the author and his colleagues. Coxcatlán cave (top dot at right), where early corn was found in 1960, has the longest habitation record: from well before 7000 B.C. until A.D. 1500.

gourd, the chayote and three or four distinct species of what we call squash. Fruits brought under cultivation in the Americas included the tomato, avocado, pineapple, guava, elderberry and papaya. The pioneering use of tobacco—smoked in pipes, in the form of cigars and even in the form of cane cigarettes, some of which had one end stuffed with fibers to serve as a filter—must also be credited to the Indians.

Above all of these stood Indian corn, Zea mays, the only important wild grass in the New World to be transformed into a food grain as the peoples of the Old World had transformed their native grasses into wheat, barley, rye, oats and millet. From Chile to the valley of the St. Lawrence in Canada, one or another of 150 varieties of Indian corn was the staple diet of the pre-Columbian peoples. As a food grain or as fodder, corn remains the most important single crop in the Americas today (and the third largest in the world). Because of its dominant position in New World agriculture, prehistorians have long been confident that if they could find out when and where corn was first domesticated, they might also uncover the origins of New World civilization.

Until little more than a generation ago investigators of this question were beset by twin difficulties. First, research in both Central America and South America had failed to show that any New World high culture significantly predated the Christian era. Second, botanical studies of the varieties of corn and its wild relatives had led more to conflict than to clarity in regard to the domesticated plant's most probable wild predecessor [see "The Mystery of Corn," by Paul C. Mangelsdorf; SCIENTIFIC AMERICAN Offprint 26]. Today, thanks to close cooperation between botanists and archaeologists, both difficulties have almost vanished. At least one starting point for New World agricultural activity has been securely established as being between 5,000 and 9,000 years ago. At the same time botanical analysis of fossil corn ears, grains and pollen, together with plain dirt archaeology, have solved a number of the mysteries concerning the wild origin and domestic evolution of corn. What follows is a review of the recent developments that have done so much to increase our understanding of this key period in New World prehistory.

The interest of botanists in the history of corn is largely practical: they study the genetics of corn in order to produce improved hybrids. After the wild ancestors of corn had been sought for nearly a century the search had narrowed to two tassel-bearing New World grasses—teosinte and *Tripsacum*—that had features resembling the domesticated plant. On the basis of crossbreeding experiments and other genetic studies, however, Paul C. Mangelsdorf of Harvard University and other investigators concluded in the 1940's that neither of these plants could be the original ancestor of corn. Instead teosinte appeared to be the product of the accidental crossbreeding of true corn and *Tripsacum*. Mangelsdorf advanced the hypothesis that the wild progenitor of corn was none other than corn itself—probably a popcorn with its kernels encased in pods.

Between 1948 and 1960 a number of discoveries proved Mangelsdorf's contention to be correct. I shall present these discoveries not in their strict chronological order but rather in their order of importance. First in importance, then, were analyses of pollen found in "cores" obtained in 1953 by drilling into the lake beds on which Mexico City is built. At levels that were estimated to be about 80,000 years old—perhaps 50,000 years older than the earliest known human remains in the New World—were found grains of corn

pollen. There could be no doubt that the pollen was from wild corn, and thus two aspects of the ancestry of corn were clarified. First, a form of wild corn has been in existence for 80,000 years, so that corn can indeed be descended from itself. Second, wild corn had flourished in the highlands of Mexico. As related archaeological discoveries will make plain, this geographical fact helped to narrow the potential range—from the southwestern U.S. to Peru—within which corn was probably first domesticated.

The rest of the key discoveries, involving the close cooperation of archaeologist and botanist, all belong to the realm of paleobotany. In the summer of 1948, for example, Herbert Dick, a graduate student in anthropology who had been working with Mangelsdorf, explored a dry rock-shelter in New Mexico called Bat Cave. Digging down through six feet of accumulated deposits, he and his colleagues found numerous remains of ancient corn, culminating in some tiny corncobs at the lowest level. Carbon-14 dating indicated that these cobs were between 4,000 and 5,000 years old. A few months later, exploring the La Perra cave in the state of Tamaulipas far to the north of Mexico City, I found similar corncobs that proved to be about 4,500 years old. The oldest cobs at both sites came close

to fitting the description Mangelsdorf had given of a hypothetical ancestor of the pod-popcorn type. The cobs, however, were clearly those of domesticated corn.

These two finds provided the basis for intensified archaeological efforts to find sites where the first evidences of corn would be even older. The logic was simple: A site old enough should have a level of wild corn remains older than the most ancient domesticated cobs. I continued my explorations near the La Perra cave and excavated a number of other sites in northeastern Mexico. In them I found more samples of ancient corn, but they were no older than those that had already been discovered. Robert Lister, another of Mangelsdorf's coworkers, also found primitive corn in a cave called Swallow's Nest in the Mexican state of Chihuahua, northwest of where I was working, but his finds were no older than mine.

If nothing older than domesticated corn of about 3000 B.C. could be found to the north of Mexico City, it seemed logical to try to the south. In 1958 I went off to look for dry caves and early corn in Guatemala and Honduras. The 1958 diggings produced nothing useful, so in 1959 I moved northward into Chiapas, Mexico's southernmost state. There were no corncobs to be found,

EXCAVATION of Coxcatlán cave required the removal of one-meter squares of cave floor over an area 25 meters long by six meters wide until bedrock was reached at a depth of almost five meters. In this way 28 occupation levels, attributable to seven distinctive culture phases, were discovered. Inhabitants of the three lowest levels lived by hunting and by collecting wild-plant foods.

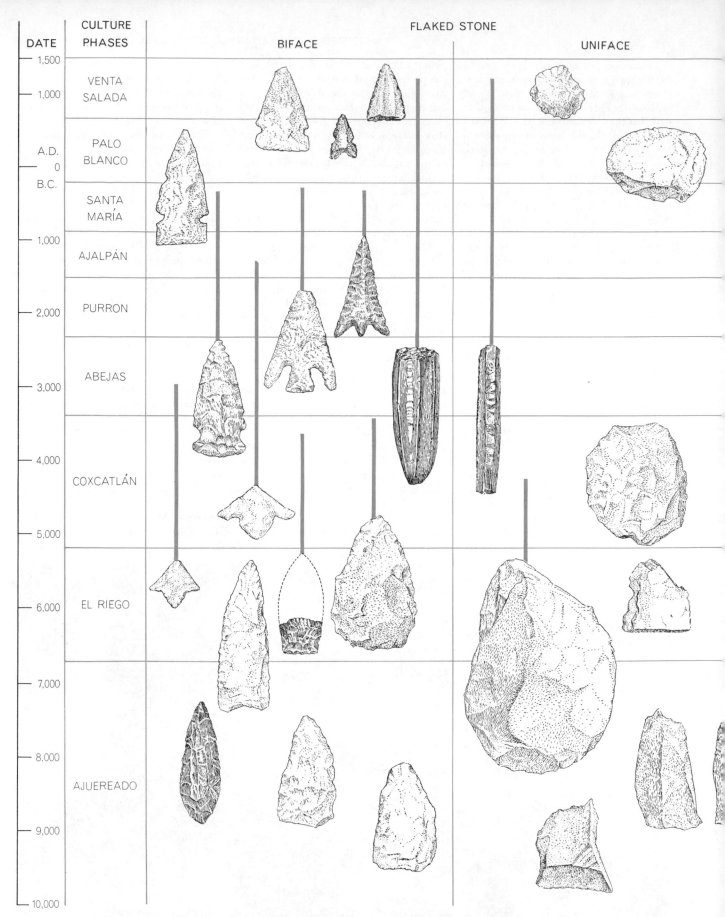

DATE	CULTURE PHASES	FLAKED STONE		
		BIFACE		UNIFACE

STONE ARTIFACTS from various Tehuacán sites are arrayed in two major categories: those shaped by chipping and flaking (*left*) and those shaped by grinding and pecking (*right*). Implements that have been chipped on one face only are separated from those that show bifacial workmanship; both groups are reproduced at half their natural size. The ground stone objects are not drawn to a common scale. The horizontal lines define the nine culture phases thus far distinguished in the valley. Vertical lines (*color*) indicate the extent to which the related artifact is known in cultures other than the one in which it is placed. At Tehuacán the evolution of civilization failed to follow the classic pattern established by the Neolithic Revolution in the Old World. For instance, the mortars,

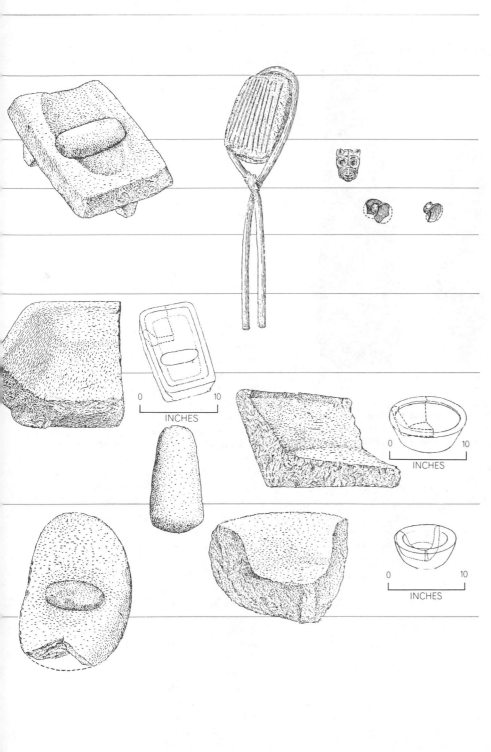

0 10
INCHES

0 10
INCHES

0 10
INCHES

pestles and other ground stone implements that first appear in the El Riego culture phase antedate the first domestication of corn by 1,500 years or more. Not until the Abejas phase, nearly 2,000 years later (marked by sizable obsidian cores and blades and by grinding implements that closely resemble the modern mano and metate), do the earliest village sites appear. More than 1,000 years later, in the Ajalpán phase, earplugs for personal adornment occur. The grooved, withe-bound stone near the top is a pounder for making bark cloth.

but one cave yielded corn pollen that also dated only to about 3000 B.C. The clues provided by paleobotany now appeared plain. Both to the north of Mexico City and in Mexico City itself (as indicated by the pollen of domesticated corn in the upper levels of the drill cores) the oldest evidence of domesticated corn was no more ancient than about 3000 B.C. Well to the south of Mexico City the oldest date was the same. The area that called for further search should therefore lie south of Mexico City but north of Chiapas.

Two additional considerations enabled me to narrow the area of search even more. First, experience had shown that dry locations offered the best chance of finding preserved specimens of corn. Second, the genetic studies of Mangelsdorf and other investigators indicated that wild corn was originally a highland grass, very possibly able to survive the rigorous climate of highland desert areas. Poring over the map of southern Mexico, I singled out three large highland desert areas: one in the southern part of the state of Oaxaca, one in Guerrero and one in southern Puebla.

Oaxaca yielded nothing of interest, so I moved on to Puebla to explore a dry highland valley known as Tehuacán. My local guides and I scrambled in and out of 38 caves and finally struck pay dirt in the 39th. This was a small rock-shelter near the village of Coxcatlán in the southern part of the valley of Tehuacán. On February 21, 1960, we dug up six corncobs, three of which looked more primitive and older than any I had seen before. Analysis in the carbon-14 laboratory at the University of Michigan confirmed my guess by dating these cobs as 5,600 years old—a good 500 years older than any yet found in the New World.

With this find the time seemed ripe for a large-scale, systematic search. If we had indeed arrived at a place where corn had been domesticated and New World civilization had first stirred, the closing stages of the search would require the special knowledge of many experts. Our primary need was to obtain the sponsorship of an institution interested and experienced in such research, and we were fortunate enough to enlist exactly the right sponsor: the Robert S. Peabody Foundation for Archaeology of Andover, Mass. Funds for the project were supplied by the National Science Foundation and by the agricultural branch of the Rockefeller

EVOLUTION OF CORN at Tehuacán starts (*far left*) with a fragmentary cob of wild corn of 5000 B.C. date. Next (*left to right*) are an early domesticated cob of 4000 B.C., an early hybrid variety of 3000 B.C. and an early variety of modern corn of 1000 B.C. Last (*far right*) is an entirely modern cob of the time of Christ. All are shown four-fifths of natural size.

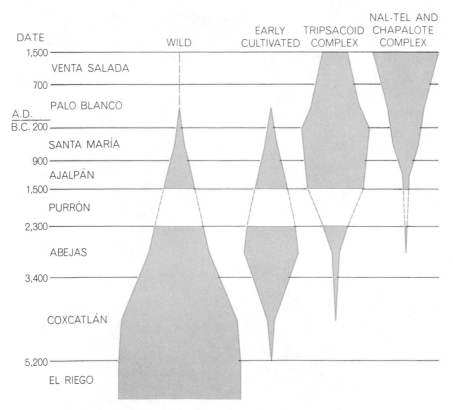

MAIN VARIETIES OF CORN changed in their relative abundance at Tehuacán between the time of initial cultivation during the Coxcatlán culture phase and the arrival of the conquistadors. Abundant at first, wild corn had become virtually extinct by the start of the Christian era, as had the early cultivated (but not hybridized) varieties. Thereafter the hybrids of the tripsacoid complex (produced by interbreeding wild corn with introduced varieties of corn-*Tripsacum* or corn-teosinte hybrids) were steadily replaced by two still extant types of corn, Nal-Tel and Chapalote. Minor varieties of late corn are not shown.

Foundation in Mexico, which is particularly interested in the origins of corn. The project eventually engaged nearly 50 experts in many specialties, not only archaeology and botany (including experts on many plants other than corn) but also zoology, geography, geology, ecology, genetics, ethnology and other disciplines.

The Coxcatlán cave, where the intensive new hunt had begun, turned out to be our richest dig. Working downward, we found that the cave had 28 separate occupation levels, the earliest of which may date to about 10,000 B.C. This remarkably long sequence has one major interruption: the period between 2300 B.C. and 900 B.C. The time from 900 B.C. to A.D. 1500, however, is represented by seven occupation levels. In combination with our findings in the Purrón cave, which contains 25 floors that date from about 7000 B.C. to 500 B.C., we have an almost continuous record (the longest interruption is less than 500 years) of nearly 12,000 years of prehistory. This is by far the longest record for any New World area.

All together we undertook major excavations at 12 sites in the valley of Tehuacán [*see bottom illustration on page 162*]. Of these only five caves—Coxcatlán, Purrón, San Marcos, Tecorral and El Riego East—contained remains of ancient corn. But these and the other stratified sites gave us a wealth of additional information about the people who inhabited the valley over a span of 12,000 years. In four seasons of digging, from 1961 through 1964, we reaped a vast archaeological harvest. This includes nearly a million individual remains of human activity, more than 1,000 animal bones (including those of extinct antelopes and horses), 80,000 individual wild-plant remains and some 25,000 specimens of corn. The artifacts arrange themselves into significant sequences of stone tools, textiles and pottery. They provide an almost continuous picture of the rise of civilization in the valley of Tehuacán. From the valley's geology, from the shells of its land snails, from the pollen and other remains of its plants and from a variety of other relics our group of specialists has traced the changes in climate, physical environment and plant and animal life that took place during the 12,000 years. They have even been able to tell (from the kinds of plant remains in various occupation levels) at what seasons of the year many of the floors in the caves were occupied.

Outstanding among our many finds was a collection of minuscule corncobs that we tenderly extracted from the lowest of five occupation levels at the San Marcos cave. They were only about 20 millimeters long, no bigger than the filter tip of a cigarette [see *top illustration on opposite page*], but under a magnifying lens one could see that they were indeed miniature ears of corn, with sockets that had once contained kernels enclosed in pods. These cobs proved to be some 7,000 years old. Mangelsdorf is convinced that this must be wild corn—the original parent from which modern corn is descended.

Cultivated corn, of course, cannot survive without man's intervention; the dozens of seeds on each cob are enveloped by a tough, thick husk that prevents them from scattering. Mangelsdorf has concluded that corn's wild progenitor probably consisted of a single seed spike on the stalk, with a few pod-covered ovules arrayed on the spike and a pollen-bearing tassel attached to the spike's end [see *bottom illustration at right*]. The most primitive cobs we unearthed in the valley of Tehuacán fulfilled these specifications. Each had the stump of a tassel at the end, each had borne kernels of the pod-popcorn type and each had been covered with only a light husk consisting of two leaves. These characteristics would have allowed the plant to disperse its seeds at maturity; the pods would then have protected the seeds until conditions were appropriate for germination.

The people of the valley of Tehuacán lived for thousands of years as collectors of wild vegetable and animal foods before they made their first timid efforts as agriculturists. It would therefore be foolhardy to suggest that the inhabitants of this arid highland pocket of Mexico were the first or the only people in the Western Hemisphere to bring wild corn under cultivation. On the contrary, the New World's invention of agriculture will probably prove to be geographically fragmented. What can be said for the people of Tehuacán is that they are the first whose evolution from primitive food collectors to civilized agriculturists has been traced in detail. As yet we have no such complete story either for the Old World or for other parts of the New World. This story is as follows.

From a hazy beginning some 12,000 years ago until about 7000 B.C. the people of Tehuacán were few in number. They wandered the valley from season to season in search of jackrabbits, rats, birds, turtles and other small animals, as well as such plant foods as be-

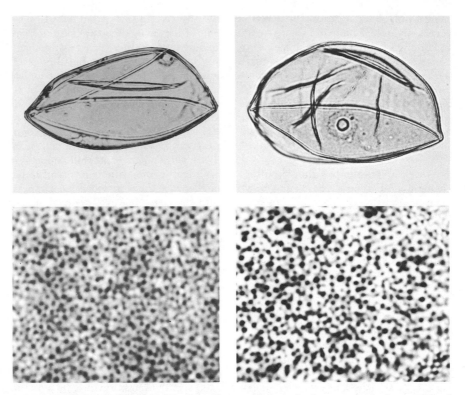

ANTIQUITY OF CORN in the New World was conclusively demonstrated when grains of pollen were found in drilling cores taken from Mexico City lake-bottom strata estimated to be 80,000 years old. Top two photographs (*magnification 435 diameters*) compare the ancient corn pollen (*left*) with modern pollen (*right*). Lower photographs (*magnification 4,500 diameters*) reveal similar ancient (*left*) and modern (*right*) pollen surface markings. The analysis and photographs are the work of Elso S. Barghoorn of Harvard University.

THREE NEW WORLD GRASSES are involved in the history of domesticated corn. Wild corn (*reconstruction at left*) was a pod-pop variety in which the male efflorescence grew from the end of the cob. Teosinte (*center*) and *Tripsacum* (*right*) are corn relatives that readily hybridized with wild and cultivated corn. Modern corn came from such crosses.

came available at different times of the year. Only occasionally did they manage to kill one of the now extinct species of horses and antelopes whose bones mark the lowest cave strata. These people used only a few simple implements of flaked stone: leaf-shaped projectile points, scrapers and engraving tools. We have named this earliest culture period the Ajuereado phase [*see illustration on pages 164 and 165*].

Around 6700 B.C. this simple pattern changed and a new phase—which we have named the El Riego culture from the cave where its first evidences appear—came into being. From then until about 5000 B.C. the people shifted from being predominantly trappers and hunters to being predominantly collectors of plant foods. Most of the plants they collected were wild, but they had domesticated squashes (starting with the species *Cucurbita mixta*) and avocados, and they also ate wild varieties of beans, amaranth and chili peppers. Among the flaked-stone implements, choppers appear. Entirely new kinds of stone tools—grinders, mortars, pestles and pounders of polished stone—are found in large numbers. During the growing season some families evidently gathered in temporary settlements, but these groups broke up into one-family bands during the leaner periods of the year. A number of burials dating from this culture phase hint at the possibility of part-time priests or witch doctors who directed the ceremonies involving the dead. The El Riego culture, however, had no corn.

By about 5000 B.C. a new phase, which we call the Coxcatlán culture,

had evolved. In this period only 10 percent of the valley's foodstuffs came from domestication rather than from collecting, hunting or trapping, but the list of domesticated plants is long. It includes corn, the water-bottle gourd, two species of squash, the amaranth, black and white zapotes, the tepary bean (*Phaseolus acutifolius*), the jack bean (*Canavalia ensiformis*), probably the common bean (*Phaseolus vulgaris*) and chili peppers.

Coxcatlán projectile points tend to be smaller than their predecessors; scrapers and choppers, however, remain much the same. The polished stone implements include forerunners of the classic New World roller-and-stone device for grinding grain: the mano and metate. There was evidently enough surplus energy among the people to allow the laborious hollowing out of stone water jugs and bowls.

It was in the phase following the Coxcatlán that the people of Tehuacán made the fundamental shift. By about 3400 B.C. the food provided by agriculture rose to about 30 percent of the total, domesticated animals (starting with the dog) made their appearance, and the people formed their first fixed settlements—small pit-house villages. By this stage (which we call the Abejas culture) they lived at a subsistence level that can be regarded as a foundation for the beginning of civilization. In about 2300 B.C. this gave way to the Purrón culture, marked by the cultivation of more hybridized types of corn and the manufacture of pottery.

Thereafter the pace of civilization in

the valley speeded up greatly. The descendants of the Purrón people developed a culture (called Ajalpán) that from about 1500 B.C. on involved a more complex village life, refinements of pottery and more elaborate ceremonialism, including the development of a figurine cult, perhaps representing family gods. This culture led in turn to an even more sophisticated one (which we call Santa María) that started about 850 B.C. Taking advantage of the valley's streams, the Santa María peoples of Tehuacán began to grow their hybrid corn in irrigated fields. Our surveys indicate a sharp rise in population. Temple mounds were built, and artifacts show signs of numerous contacts with cultures outside the valley. The Tehuacán culture in this period seems to have been strongly influenced by that of the Olmec people who lived to the southeast along the coast of Veracruz.

By about 200 B.C. the outside influence on Tehuacán affairs shifted from that of the Olmec of the east coast to that of Monte Alban to the south and west. The valley now had large irrigation projects and substantial hilltop ceremonial centers surrounded by villages. In this Palo Blanco phase some of the population proceeded to full-time specialization in various occupations, including the development of a salt industry. New domesticated food products appeared—the turkey, the tomato, the peanut and the guava. In the next period—Venta Salada, starting about A.D. 700—Monte Alban influences gave way to the influence of the Mixtecs. This period saw the rise of true

COXCATLÁN CAVE BURIAL, dating to about A.D. 100, contained the extended body of an adolescent American Indian, wrapped in a pair of cotton blankets with brightly colored stripes. This bundle in turn rested on sticks and the whole was wrapped in bark cloth.

cities in the valley, of an agricultural system that provided some 85 percent of the total food supply, of trade and commerce, a standing army, large-scale irrigation projects and a complex religion. Finally, just before the Spanish Conquest, the Aztecs took over from the Mixtecs.

Our archaeological study of the valley of Tehuacán, carried forward in collaboration with workers in so many other disciplines, has been gratifyingly productive. Not only have we documented one example of the origin of domesticated corn but also comparative studies of other domesticated plants have indicated that there were multiple centers of plant domestication in the Americas. At least for the moment we have at Tehuacán not only evidence of the earliest village life in the New World but also the first (and worst) pottery in Mexico and a fairly large sample of skeletons of some of the earliest Indians yet known.

Even more important is the fact that we at last have one New World example of the development of a culture from savagery to civilization. Preliminary analysis of the Tehuacán materials indicate that the traditional hypothesis about the evolution of high cultures may have to be reexamined and modified. In southern Mexico many of the characteristic elements of the Old World's Neolithic Revolution fail to appear suddenly in the form of a new culture complex or a revolutionized way of life. For example, tools of ground (rather than chipped) stone first occur at Tehuacán about 6700 B.C., and plant domestication begins at least by 5000 B.C. The other classic elements of the Old World Neolithic, however, are slow to appear. Villages are not found until around 3000 B.C., nor pottery until around 2300 B.C., and a sudden increase in population is delayed until 500 B.C. Reviewing this record, I think more in terms of Neolithic "evolution" than "revolution."

Our preliminary researches at Tehuacán suggest rich fields for further exploration. There is need not only for detailed investigations of the domestication and development of other New World food plants but also for attempts to obtain similar data for the Old World. Then—perhaps most challenging of all —there is the need for comparative studies of the similarities and differences between evolving cultures in the Old World and the New to determine the hows and whys of the rise of civilization itself.

SOPHISTICATED FIGURINE of painted pottery is one example of the artistic capacity of Tehuacán village craftsmen. This specimen, 2,900 years old, shows Olmec influences.

IV

CITIES
AND CIVILIZATIONS

CITIES AND CIVILIZATIONS IV

INTRODUCTION

"The Country Life is to be preferred," wrote William Penn in the seventeenth century, "for there we see the works of God, but in the cities little else but the works of men." The city is truly a people-designed institution, one that has but a 5000-year history, beginning in Egypt and Mesopotamia and stretching into modern times. City life is the dominant settlement pattern in the world today, so dominant that the demands of the urban environment have torn apart the millennia-old patterns of social and cultural behavior associated with humankind.

What Is Civilization?

The emergence of urban civilization was, along with the beginnings of food production, one of the most significant events in human history and prehistory. But what exactly *is* civilization? So far no one has succeeded in defining it, and a uniform definition seems impossible. The historian Arnold Toynbee tried to explain the origins of civilization in terms of successful responses to challenging difficulties. He thought in terms of at least 21 civilizations, each a species of the "genus" human society. The orientalist Henri Frankfort spoke of the "form" of a civilization—the style that shaped its political and judicial institutions and its art, literature, religion, and morals. The form of a civilization changes through time, he wrote, as a result both of continuous internal change and of external forces. And the anthropologist Robert Redfield made a sharp distinction between the folk society of prehistoric and later times and the literate civilization. Folk societies are based on the notion that the moral order is more important than the technological one. Technology in these societies is simple; no formal religion or state regulations control the behavior of the members of a folk society.

Redfield regards civilization as the exact opposite of the folk society with respect to the relationship between technology and morality. He defines civilization as a single state—a state of society in which the community has become much larger and less self-sufficient. The simple division of labor between males and females is replaced by more complex, much more impersonal relationships. Larger affiliations of social class or religious belief take the place of the closely knit family and kin relationships of earlier times. Social thinking becomes more systematic as its dominant attitudes and philosophies result from more reflective postures about the human condition. Civilizations usually want to justify their existence and their place in the world; folk societies are more concerned with a state of equilibrium, with simply "being." They have a reasonable expectation that life in the future will be the same as it always has been.

Civilization is, of course, mostly things added to society: writing, public works, cities, markets, long-distance trading, and so on. A whole new and elaborate social structure comes into being, based on a state organized into social or economic classes, with power in the hands of an aristocratic elite, and often a divine ruler or a group of military leaders and priests. To study the origins of civilization is to trace the evolution of human societies away from folk societies. Not all societies depart completely from the norms of folk society. Chinese civilization, for example, retained much of the social organization of earlier times, but Chinese art and philosophy underwent dramatic refinement.

Perhaps the best working definition of civilization to adopt is that formulated by anthropologist Clyde Kluckhohn many years ago. He defined three essential criteria for civilization: towns with a population of more than 5000 persons; writing; and monumental ceremonial architecture, including ceremonial centers.

The Urban Revolution

Redfield's way of looking at civilization involves the study of both the technological and intangible aspects of human society. Archaeologists must, perforce, work with the material remains of ancient civilizations—artifacts and houses, food remains, and art objects. It is hardly surprising that the first modern hypotheses about the rise of civilization were based on the emergence of the city and major technological innovations. V. Gordon Childe thought that his Urban Revolution began in the Near East, following closely on the heels of the Agricultural Revolution. He centered his definition of the Urban Revolution on the development of the city, a densely populated settlement whose farmers furnished food surpluses to support a small army of artisans, priests, and traders. Metallurgical industries emerged, which provided superior weapons and led to the emergence of a class society, including both an elite and full-time specialists. Writing was essential for record-keeping and the development of exact sciences and astronomy. "A unifying religious force" dominated urban life, as priest-kings and despots rose to power over huge populations of peasants and artisans.

Childe believed that the Urban Revolution was a critical turning point in human cultural, economic, and social change. This bold concept dominated archaeological thinking for years, but was eventually shown to have serious flaws. Some of Childe's criteria for cities and civilization are far from universal, for some civilizations, among them the Minoans of Crete and the Mycenaeans of mainland Greece, did not have cities. Others, like the Inca of Peru, never developed writing. The only characteristics common to all civilizations seem to be a degree of craft specialization, a well-formulated and integrating religious structure, and a complex social organization.

Social Processes

The debate about the origin of cities and civilization has been concerned both with critiques of Childe's Urban Revolution hypothesis and with attempts to understand the actual processes that led to the emergence of the city. Robert Adams, whose article "The Origin of Cities" leads off this section, has emphasized the significance of the development of social organization and craft specialization during the Urban Revolution. He believes that the emergence of civilization was predominantly a social process, more an expression of changes in the ways people interacted with one another than in the ways they interacted with the environment. The rise of civilizations may have depended on the availability of abundant food surpluses, but the real innovations were a whole series of institutions and the vastly greater size and complexity of the urban society. In other words, civilization resulted from a variety of interacting political and economic human forces.

Adams describes changes in social organization in Mesopotamia and in central Mexico, where millennia-old kin-based folk societies were replaced by class societies whose elaborate political and religious hierarchies controlled every aspect of public and private life. The new, complex urban states depended on a complex division of labor, on a strongly centralized supreme secular and religious authority that had the ability to organize not only the labor of favored artisans, but the labor of a standing army and hundreds of traders. Those who controlled the destinies of such societies had acquired the ability to muster thousands of people, either free citizens paying taxes through obligatory labor, or slaves, to carry out ambitious public works— temples, palaces, major irrigation projects—for the benefit of all. Thus, argues Adams, a correct theory of the rise of civilization depends on an understanding not of material innovations, but of all manner of subtle and intangible decisions and social processes that affected the way people lived in close juxtaposition.

Processes, Mechanisms, Stresses

Generations of archaeologists have searched for the primary causes of civilization. Some have cited the development of trade, metallurgy, and writing as "prime movers," major causes for the rise of cities. Population growth, the development of irrigation agriculture, even warfare, or the growth of organized religion, have been cited as primary factors. The trouble with all these single-cause explanations is that what actually occurred was far more complex than a simple explanation allows. For example, one ecological theory argued that the exceptional fertility of the Mesopotamian floodplain and the Nile Valley accounted for the emergence of civilization in the Near East. This fertility, and a benign climate, continued the hypothesis, led to food surpluses that could support the craftworkers and other specialists who formed the fabric of civilization. Reality is, of course, much more complex, for these fertile environments were in fact patchworks of different ecological zones, each with its own subsistence potential. What was new was not the exploitation of the different zones, but the *integration* of the process of exploitation by a single society with control over all of them. This is not the same thing as saying that favorable ecological conditions caused civilization to flourish. Rather, ecology was but one component in a close network of ecological, economic, social, and technological changes that eventually led in some places to the rise of civilization.

Today's archaeologists draw on models of cultural ecology and systems theory to examine early civilization. They think of societies like that of the Ancient Egyptians as elaborate cultural systems made up of many subsystems, such as subsistence, technology, religion, social organization, that interact with one another. And the cultural system in turn interacts with the wider ecological system of which it is part. Under this notion, complex mechanisms involving both decision-making and societal policy keep the system as a whole in equilibrium. Those who favor the systems approach think in terms of three abstractions: the processes of cultural change by which the early civilizations developed their new complexity; the mechanisms—the actual ways in which these processes of increasing complexity occurred; and the socioenvironmental stresses that led to the selection of these mechanisms. These stresses include food shortages, warfare, population growth, and are by no means common to all states.

Recently, geographer Karl Butzer has used the systems approach to study the cultural ecology of Ancient Egyptian civilization. He argues that it can be regarded as an ecosystem that emerged in response to sets of ecological

opportunities. Over time, the Egyptians made a series of inevitable adjustments, some successful, leading to population growth, others unsuccessful,
leading to population decline. These demographic adjustments were commonly associated with the ups and down of political power. Thus, the political structures of Ancient Egypt were not nearly so durable as the basic
adaptive system to the Nile environment they purported to control, or as the
cultural identity of which they were part. Butzer compares civilization to the
ecological concept of trophic levels among biotic communities, in which
organisms with similar feeding habits, like herbivores and carnivores, define
successive tiers interlinked in a vertical chain. Likewise, he hypothesizes, an
efficient social hierarchy comprises several trophic levels arranged in what he
calls a "low angle pyramid." This is supported by a broad base of farmers and
linked to the peak of the pyramid by a middle-level bureaucracy. The vertical
structure channels food and information through the system, and an efficient
energy flow allows each trophic level to flourish in a steady state.

Under this rubric, a flatter pyramid with little vertical structure would
provide less information flow and limit the potential productivity of the lower
levels. But this pyramid would allow growth at the lower levels, with new
technologies or organizational devices favoring an expanded generation of
energy at the lower level. A steep, top-heavy pyramid laden with nobles and
bureaucrats places excessive burdens on the lowest levels, so much so that
external and internal forces can undermine the stability of society. This
model shows how the Egyptians persisted in adjusting to their floodplain
environment for thousands of years: they overcame external and internal
crises by reorganizing their state and economic structure. The key variables
were the fluctuations of the Nile itself, occasional foreign intervention, the
character of royal leadership, and a progressively more pathological class of
elite nonfarmers who persisted in exploiting the common farmer, a process
that led to eventual social collapse. But, through all these variables, the
essential components of the village sociopolitical system survived more or
less intact, right up to the nineteenth century AD.

Writing

The earliest civilizations developed in the Near East, along the Tigris and
Euphrates and the Nile. By 3200 BC the Mesopotamian delta was dotted with
villages, small towns, and a few major communities with imposing temples
and fortified walls that could be called cities. The Sumerian city of Uruk and
its satellite villages extended out for at least six miles from the urban core.
This teeming city of narrow, winding alleys and mud-brick houses had its
own bazaars and artisans' workshops. Uruk traded with communities hundreds of miles away. Each Mesopotamian city depended on its neighbors, at
first because each provided things essential for a well-balanced existence.
Later, they needed each other for protection from outsiders who would have
plundered their goods. The Mesopotamian city had developed a complex
management system with a well-defined hierarchy of rulers, priests, land-
owners and bureaucrats, traders and peasants. This system organized and
regulated society, meted out reward and punishment, and made policy decisions for the thousands of people who lived under it.

By 3400 BC the Sumerians' trade and commercial transactions had become
so complex that the possibilities for thievery and accounting mistakes were
endless. The state bureaucrats had the enormous task of keeping track of
shipments of metal ore, thousands of bales of wool, and a myriad of other
commodities held in official storerooms. No one could possibly keep all the
details in their heads, so many people began to use small clay tokens as
counters. Denise Schmandt-Besserat in "The Earliest Precursor of Writing"
describes how Mesopotamian writing may have arisen. She points out that

written records developed quite independently in many places, among them China, where the first writing was scratched on the shoulder blades of oxen. Schmandt-Besserat studied clay tokens from dozens of prehistoric Near Eastern villages and towns. She found they assumed various shapes, among them spheres, disks, and cones. She speculates that the different sizes and shapes of the tokens formed a universal accounting system that functioned somewhat like the old-fashioned abacus counting device seen in Near Eastern bazaars to this day.

Perhaps these three-dimensional counters were first devised to inventory stored food supplies. Eventually the marked clay tokens became small clay tablets scratched with incised markings that depicted familiar objects like pots and animals. From there it was a short step to conventionalized, simple, wedge-shaped (cuneiform) signs that were written equivalents of phonetic syllables and spoken language. Now trade could expand, unfettered by the limitations of human memory. At first specially trained scribes used cuneiform to record inventories and commercial transactions. Soon they began to explore the limitless opportunities to express oneself in writing. Sumerian writings include not only official records and the boastings of kings, but love stories, great epics, hymns, and poetry—the first literature in the world.

Trade

The beginnings of writing mirror a massive expansion of trade between cities and distant societies. The decision to acquire commodities from afar depended on the urgency of the need for goods and on the difficulty of acquiring and transporting them. Much early trade was based on specific commodities such as copper ore and salt, which involved peculiar problems of acquisition and transport. In the early civilizations, the ruler and his immediate followers were generally entitled to trade and to initiate the steps leading to the acquisition of goods from a distance. The king might employ merchants or traders to do the work for him, but the trade was in the royal name. Not that early Near Eastern trade was unsophisticated, far from it. If later historical records are any guide, the early Sumerians floated loans and engaged in wholesaling and contracting—and individual profit may have been the all-important motive behind their enterprise.

Long-distance trade was carefully coordinated with fluctuating supply and demand. It is not enough to think of trade as simply the distribution of exports and imports. Changes in the volume and nature of trade influenced and modified not only production, but social and economic structure as well. For example, we know that the Aztec merchants (*pochteca*) of Mexico could purchase the title "Lord," presumably as a measure of their status as successful traders. The Aztecs were so dependent on foreign trade that their merchants acted as official spies as well as entrepreneurs.

The Tepe Yahyā mound in southeastern Iran was excavated by C. C. Lamberg-Karlovsky and provided evidence of widespread connections between several centers of early civilization. Lamberg-Karlovsky believes that the Sumerians, their eastern, Proto-Elamite neighbors, the Egyptians, and the Harappans of the Indus Valley were already maintaining a pattern of cultural and economic exchange among themselves by 3500 BC. Tepe Yahyā stood halfway between the Euphrates and the Indus, a city that controlled rich sources of chlorite, a soapstone easily worked into fine vases, also gold, silver, tin, and lead. Lamberg-Karlovsky argues that Tepe Yahyā was an important "central place" of manufacture and distribution of raw materials and finished objects in a trading network that linked hundreds of towns, cities, and villages into one of the world's first truly global commercial chains. There is a tendency to think of the early civilizations as isolated phenomena, societies that functioned within the narrow confines of their own homelands,

Figure 19 Fragments of soapstone bowls from Tepe Yahyā. Soapstone bowls, many of them elaborately decorated, were among the numerous objects made at Tepe Yahyā and traded eastward and westward during the first half of the third millennium BC. [From the Peabody Museum, photograph by Alexander D. Kernan.]

unaware of more distant societies. The Tepe Yahyā excavations show that the mercantile world of the Near East was far more sophisticated than one might have believed.

Writing and Daily Life

The nineteenth-century archaeologists who uncovered the Assyrians and recovered thousands of Ancient Egyptian papyri were hampered in their understanding of early civilization by the difficulties of deciphering cuneiform and hieroglyphs. The first breakthrough came in 1799, when a French officer serving with Napoleon's army in Egypt found the trilingual Rosetta Stone. The celebrated philologist Jean François Champollion used it to decipher hieroglyphs in 1822, enabling scholars to read the names of the pharaohs and to study many details of Ancient Egyptian life. Mesopotamian cuneiform was a far more formidable proposition, partly because there was no convenient trilingual inscription, only a vast proclamation in Persian, Elamite, and Babylonian script on a rock face near Behistun in Iran. British cavalry-officer-turned-diplomat Henry Crewicke Rawlinson succeeded in copying the precipitous inscription in 1847, just as Austen Henry Layard discovered the Assyrian monarch Ashur-bani-pal's royal library in his palace at Nineveh.

It took a tiny group of experts most of the rest of the century to sort and decipher this vast archive of clay tablets. The philologists were astonished to find a rich literature of epics and laments that included the now famous account of a great flood that bears a remarkable resemblance to the Flood in Genesis. Subsequent excavations in Sumerian cities like Nippur, Ur-of-the-Chaldees, and Lagash have yielded a mass of information on Sumerian daily life—everything from farmers' almanacs to schoolboys' scribbles. Above all, the clay tablets throw light on Sumerian cosmology and religion and reveal many resemblances to the beliefs of modern faiths. The order of the creation of the universe, the resignation of sinful humans to the will of the gods, and death and resurrection are only a few features of the Sumerian's creed that survived without much change in later religions. The Sumerian's own written records show that there is hardly an area of Western civilization—mathematics, philosophy, literature, architecture, finance, education, religion, folklore—that does not owe something to the Sumerians.

Even more formidable linguistic problems were posed by the mysterious script found by Sir Arthur Evans in the storerooms of the palace of the legendary King Minos at Knossos, Crete, in 1900. He uncovered a hitherto unknown civilization that flourished the length and breadth of the Aegean Sea for at least five centuries after 2000 BC. The excavations revealed a multistoried palace, covered with brilliantly colored frescoes. There were vast storage magazines for wine and olive oil and thousands of clay tablets inscribed in a totally unfamiliar script. Evans spent the rest of his long life poring over Minoan script. He identified two forms, an earlier writing he named Linear A and a more refined version called Linear B, also found on the mainland. To his chagrin, he was unable to decipher either of them. It was not until the 1950s that a young scholar named Michael Ventris identified the language of Linear B as archaic Greek and translated the first Minoan and Mycenaean tablets. Most of them turned out to be inventories of equipment and supplies.

By this time a huge archive of Linear B tablets was issuing from excavations at the palace of the legendary Homeric hero Nestor at Pylos in western Greece. These thirteenth-century BC royal archives turned out to be a mine of information on Mycenaean life that had to be pieced together from hundreds of arid, long forgotten records, most of them little more than incomplete lists. John Chadwick's "Life in Mycenaean Greece" describes some of the insights obtained from these remarkable archives. The article discusses some of the theories that lead philologists to compile detailed statistics of such arcane matters as crop yields and slave inventories. Particularly fascinating are the descriptions of the early warning systems against attack from the sea and the estimates of rations and livestock censuses made from the tablets. Chadwick shows how our knowledge of early civilizations is derived from many archaeological sources and how it can be enriched enormously by scientific use of documentary records, however obscure.

The Decline of Civilization

We live in a world where doomsday prophecies are fashionable, even lucrative. Prophets forecast that the world will end, that our civilization is in imminent danger of blowing itself into space or plunging into decadence. The record of prehistory does nothing to reinforce an optimism that any one civilization will last forever, but it does show that humankind always creates new alternatives from the ashes of earlier societies. The early civilizations declined for many reasons. The Sumerians overirrigated their fields and fought each other continuously until their northern neighbors annexed their lands. The Ancient Egyptian state fell apart when the pharaohs were unable to mine the gold to pay their armies and laborers. The Minoans of Crete were weakened by devastating earthquakes and eruptions about 1500 BC, while the Mycenaeans succumbed to invaders about three centuries later. The Harappans of the Indus Valley were confronted with constant perils from uncontrolled flooding.

The Harappan civilization arose during the third millennium BC on the fertile Indus Valley floodplain. Even today, as the summer floods recede, the people plant wheat and barley on the alluvial plains, using extensive irrigation canals to bring water to their fields. By 2700 BC the Indus farmers had mastered the arts of irrigation and flood control. They now proceeded to alter the environment of the valley beyond recognition. As population densities rose and people settled on the floodplain, their villages and fields were vulnerable to seasonal floods that could sometimes reach disastrous proportions. Confronted with what may have seemed like the wrath of the gods, the people had but one defense—cooperative flood works and tightly controlled agriculture that would feed more mouths and provide at least a degree of security against the vagaries of the elements.

Like the Sumerians, the Harappans adopted the city as the means of organizing and controlling their civilization. We have knowledge of at least four major Harappan cities, of which Harappa and Moenjo-daro are the best known. Vast regimented communities with great citadels and gridlike streets of drab, mud-brick houses, both were built on artificial mounds above the floods, but at the cost of herculean effort. Moenjo-daro was rebuilt at least nine times, but to no avail, for the civilization was eventually overwhelmed not by foreign invasion, but by catastrophic inundations. Each individual flood may not have amounted to a death blow, but the cumulative effects of years of seasonal flooding may have assisted in the slow decline of the southern parts of Harappan domains. The political and economic control of the tiny elite that governed the cities may have been insufficient to prevent fragmentation of the once enormous polity they ruled for centuries.

New World Civilizations

"These great towns . . . and buildings rising from the water, all made of stone, seemed like an enchanted vision . . . . Indeed some of our soldiers asked if it were not all a dream," wrote one of the hardy Spanish adventurers who accompanied Hernando Cortés to Mexico in 1519. This handful of *conquistadores* were some of the few westerners ever to see a preindustrial civilization at the peak of its prosperity. They were astounded at the Aztec capital, Tenochtitlán, the center of the Aztec world. Yet, two short years later, Tenochtitlán was in ruins and the Aztec civilization dismantled, overwhelmed by superior technology and fatal weaknesses in its political system. A tradition of urban civilization extending back more than 3000 years melted away literally overnight.

Teotihuacán and the Highlands

The Aztecs themselves boasted that they were the masters of Mexico and that their civilization had its origins in the sacred but ruined city of Teotihuacán that lay to the northeast of their own capital. They believed that they lived in the world of the Fifth Sun, a world created by the quarreling gods just as Teotihuacán was abandoned. They also believed that their civilization was doomed to eventual extinction through terrible catastrophe, a prophecy that seemed to come true with the arrival of the *conquistadores*. Aztec legends take the story of Mexican civilization back as far as the time of the Toltecs, who reigned over the Valley of Mexico in the twelfth century AD. There are vague references to Teotihuacán, but we have to rely on archaeology for a dispassionate account of the origins of Mesoamerican civilization. The seeds of highland civilization may have been first sown in the Veracruz lowlands among the Olmec ("rubber") people of the twelfth to fifteenth centuries BC, who founded a remarkable religious tradition and enjoyed a distinctive art style that depicted jaguars and other savage beasts. The new beliefs spread widely, to the Maya lowlands and also to the highlands, where the city of

Teotihuacán came into dominance in a dramatic spurt of urban development about 2000 years ago.

It was here that the long cherished features of later Mexican civilization came into full flower: a complicated and intensely symbolic religious cosmology guided by a sophisticated secular and religious calendar, vast centers that were the settings for elaborate public ceremonies, and, toward the end of the city's life-span, an ardent militarism that was to nurture the Aztecs' later frenzied belief in human sacrifice as a means of appeasing the gods. Rene Millon, in "Teotihuacán," describes the vast city from its humble beginnings as a village of modest size to its heyday as a metropolis housing more than 120,000 people. What is remarkable is that Teotihuacán was built according to a master plan conceived in the early centuries of the city and adhered to for generations.

Recent settlement surveys throughout the Basin of Mexico have shown that Teotihuacán was such an important center that in the early stages of its prosperity something like eighty to ninety percent of the total population of the Basin lived within a short distance of the city. Other planned communities were placed near strategic resources, such as salt deposits. Teotihuacán's rulers presided over a densely cultivated and partly irrigated landscape and over an urban population of farmers whose labors provided most of the city's food from lands within a radius of 20 square kilometers. This was a highly organized civilization, where thousands of people labored in unquestioning obedience to the great gods of the city, among them Tlaloc, the god of rain, and the feathered serpent Quetzalcoatl, god of Venus and of the Creation. Teotihuacán was the blueprint for all subsequent Mexican civilizations, a city whose influence was felt centuries after its decline in the eighth century AD.

The Origins of Maya Civilization

The Maya peoples of the Mexican and Guatemalan lowlands created perhaps the most celebrated of all Mesoamerican civilizations, celebrated in part for its spectacular ceremonial centers that rise above the all-encompassing rain forests of the Yucatán. Recent researches have revolutionized our knowledge of the Maya, once thought by archaeologists to have been a civilization of rural villagers who came together to erect huge ceremonial centers where only a few people lived. Large scale investigations at such famous centers in Tikal and El Mirador are changing this picture dramatically. The Maya ceremonial centers, we now know, were large cities with extensive satellite settlements. By using side-scan radar and other remote sensing devices, archaeologists have shown that the Maya drained swamps and devised enormous canal systems that enabled them to support not only high population densities, but large numbers of non-food-producers as well. The great pyramids of Tikal and other centers are testimony to the organizational abilities of the Maya, a people with a sophisticated calendar and a hieroglyphic script that is only now being deciphered to reveal a patchwork of genealogies and rulers' names.

Norman Hammond has studied the origins of the Maya in lowland Belize. He points out in his article "The Earliest Maya" that the Classic period of Maya civilization flourished between about AD 250 and 900. But the origins of this remarkable society are still little known. Hammond discovered a site named Cuello, a ceremonial precinct with residential compounds. The lower levels of the evolving center yielded a characteristic pottery found in association with earthen platforms radiocarbon-dated to the mid-third-millennium BC, far earlier than the previous reading for Maya pottery of about 900 BC. The Cuello finds identify Maya culture as one of the most important formative cultures of Mexican civilization. It may even be that Maya civilization predated that of the Olmecs. Clearly, the traditions of Mexican civilization extend back far into prehistory, for at least 3000 years before the Classic Maya erected their magnificent cities in the rainforests of the Yucatán and the Peten.

Mound Builders: Complex Societies in North America

When pioneer farmers and missionaries made their way westward into the Midwest and the great Ohio River valley in the late eighteenth century, they found many signs of ancient human activity. The fertile tracts of plain and woodland were dotted with earthen mounds and extensive earthworks that followed the floodplain and adorned the low hills overlooking the river. Once the settlers fanned out over the Midwest, across the Alleghenies and into the Mississippi valley, even more mounds appeared, some of them enormous, like the complex of mounds at Cahokia, Illinois, on the east bank of the Mississippi near present-day St. Louis. Others came to light along the southern shores of the Great Lakes, and as far west as Nebraska, and throughout the southeast. Some farmers thought of the mounds as a nuisance and plowed them flat. Others dug into them for buried treasure but were disappointed to find little more than human bones, carved soapstone pipes, and occasional copper artifacts.

It was not long before intellectuals in the East began to take an interest in the mysterious people who had built such extensive earthworks long before Europeans arrived. A few scholars, Thomas Jefferson among them, believed they were the work of Indian tribes. Jefferson had taken the trouble to excavate a burial mound and observe its various layers (in one of the first applications of archaeological stratigraphy) and concluded that it was an Indian sepulcher. But most people thought that "highly civilized nations" had lived in the Midwest long before even the Indians had arrived, nations that had created a spectacular civilization, extending from the Mississippi to the Ohio, and from Florida to the Great Lakes. Imaginative novelists out to make a quick dollar jumped on the bandwagon and churned out epic tales of bloody battles and gleaming cities that perished in a holocaust of destruction before the modern Indian inhabitants settled among the silent earthworks. The human bones in the mounds were said to be the remains of thousands of war victims buried in the mounds with lavish ceremony. Thus was born the "Myth of the Mound Builders," a myth that is perpetuated to this day in the Book of Mormon, as a tenet of religious faith. An attractive theory, but there was no archaeological evidence whatsoever to support the hypothesis of the mound builder civilization. There were, however, Spanish and French explorers' accounts of Indians using temple mounds that were conveniently ignored by the myth-makers.

Mound fervor reached such a pitch in 1881 that a special rider was added to the congressional appropriation for the Bureau of Ethnology at the Smithsonian Institution for the investigation of "mound builders and prehistoric mounds." Between 1881 and 1887, archaeologist Cyrus Thomas excavated over 2000 mounds of every known type and subjected their contents to meticulous analysis. He was able to show that every artifact from his excavations—potsherd, mica ornament, soapstone pipebowl, hammered copper axe—was of identifiable Indian manufacture; indeed, the species of animals carved on soapstone pipes were of forms still living in the Midwest. His massive 730-page monograph showed cultural continuity between the culture of the mound builders and that of the modern Indians. He rescued early European accounts of the mound builders from historical oblivion. All modern research into the mound builder cultures has been based on this solid work.

Hopewell

The final two articles in *Prehistoric Times* survey contemporary knowledge about the mound builders, derived from excavations in hundreds of burial mounds and at the great ceremonial center of Cahokia on the Mississippi. The origins of the mound builders go back thousands of years into prehistory, to a time over 3000 years ago, when Indian groups in the Midwest lived by hunting and by gathering wild vegetable foods. So abundant were the natural resources of the Illinois River valley and other floodplain locations that many Indian communities were able to live more or less sedentary lives, subsisting off freshwater molluscs, migrating wildfowl, hunting, and intensive plant collecting. Stuart Struever's excavations at Koster and other prehistoric settlements in the Illinois valley have shown how the size of what archaeologists call "Woodland" Indian communities rose gradually from about 3000 years ago. Eventually, at about the time of Christ, populations had risen to the point that agriculture was a viable subsistence strategy. By AD 900, the peoples of the Midwest were dependent on maize cultivation for much of their diet. It was during this period of population growth that new burial cults took hold among the Indians, beliefs that involved both mound building and elaborate ceremonials.

Olaf Prufer, in "The Hopewell Cult," describes the beginnings of mound building with the Adena culture in the first millennium BC. The Hopewell people built enormous earthworks and traded magnificent cult objects like mica figures, masks, and hammered copper ornaments, throughout an area of hundreds of miles. The cult objects probably passed from individual to individual in a series of intricate gift exchanges that reinforced kin links between clan chieftains and other important leaders. The prized artifacts were then buried with the same chieftains in communal mounds, where the kin members were also deposited. Prufer describes the simple economy of the Hopewell people and the defensive earthworks they erected after AD 550, when their villages apparently came under external threat. The Hopewell cult faded away and the focus of spiritual and secular authority passed westward to the Mississippi valley, where a new and powerful series of chieftaincies arose about AD 1000.

Cahokia and the Mississippian

Melvin Fowler, "A Pre-Columbian Urban Center on the Mississippi," takes up the story with a description of excavations at Cahokia. The "Mississippian" culture was centered on the rich floodplains of the river north and south of St. Louis. Cahokia itself is a vast complex of earthworks, dominated by Monk's Mound, a huge stepped earthwork covering about 15 acres and rising over 100 feet above the floodplain. Cahokia in turn is the largest of 10 large and small Mississippian population centers and at least 50 farming villages known from the 125-square miles designated as American Bottoms, the densest concentration of prehistoric population in North America.

The Mississippian was a society of indigenous origins whose complexity was an adaptation to highly fertile, annually flooded arable soils, in which maize and beans flourished and where huge yields of wild vegetable foods could be gathered. Fish and waterfowl may have comprised up to fifty percent of the diet of the villagers living on the floodplain. Most of the population lived in small villages and probably rarely visited the large centers like Cahokia or Moundville, Alabama. These were far more than ceremonial precincts. Like Mexican centers, they were markets and focal points for powerful chieftaincies. Cahokia was an important nexus for salt and axe-blade trading, but, above all, it was the place where the Mississippian chieftains displayed their political and religious power for all to behold.

We know little about how Mississippian society functioned, but judging from eighteenth-century explorers' accounts of late mound builder societies, people were divided into rigid social classes. Only the elite could engage in long-distance trade. They also enjoyed the privilege of elaborate burial. Unfortunately, we have few clues as to the public ceremonies and rituals of the Mississippians. Many ceremonial objects bear distinctive motifs, such as sunbursts and weeping eyes, that are linked by experts into a "Southern Cult" that flourished throughout Mississippian country. The cult appears to be an amalgam of indigenous Indian and Mexican themes. Wind, fire, sun, and human sacrifice are common motifs in both Mississippian and Mexican cosmology as we know them. It is possible that Aztec *pochteca,* itinerant merchants, introduced their religious beliefs to the distant Mississippi valley. But is it only fair to say that no Mexican artifacts have yet come from Mississippian settlements.

This remarkable society—perhaps one should say near-civilization—flourished right up to the sixteenth century. Then in 1541–42 Spanish *conquistador* Hernando de Soto encountered Creek Indian chiefs who still lived in fortified towns with temple mounds and plazas in the South. The smallpox he brought with him decimated center after center, weakening Mississippian culture beyond recovery. The first missionaries who worked among the Indians of the southeast recorded only dim memories of the great mound builders of earlier centuries.

The Industrial Civilization

For most of the past 5000 years, human civilization was a tentative and often fragile experiment, supported by relatively simple technologies and abundant cheap labor. In many areas where early civilizations flourished and empires waxed and waned, large and prosperous civilizations could not survive the collapse of the political and economic structure that begat them. More permanent traditions of civilization emerged in the West, with the Roman cities and military camps, with the rebuilding of Carthage by its new masters only a short time after they destroyed it, and with the survival of Roman provincial towns after the collapse of the Empire. But not until medieval times did the explosion of city building begin that has continued unabated. This explosion led to a demand for goods, materials, and services on such a large scale that only major technological innovation could satisfy them. The preindustrial civilization, with its many innovations stemming from repeated experimentation and from artisans' accumulated experience with new technologies, was the ancestor of the industrial civilization, its mechanized technologies and almost infinite capacity for expansion and production.

The industrial civilization was the product of the Industrial Revolution of the eighteenth and nineteenth centuries. Mechanized technologies powered by fossil fuels, scientific experimentation, and vastly expanded commercial activity were among the factors that led to a quantum jump in the global population, worldwide trade, scientific knowledge, and large-scale migration. Today most Americans—and an increasing portion of the world's population—live in industrial civilizations, in economic, political, and social contexts that were unimagined even 500 years ago. The industrial civilization has given millions of people a higher standard of living and vastly expanded material and philosophical expectations. But the same civilization, with its insatiable demand for natural resources, has extended its tentacles to every corner of the world. Hundreds of hunter-gatherer and peasant societies have fallen victim to its demands and been submerged in tawdry, watered-down versions of Western Civilization. In a sense, humankind has peopled the world twice, once with small bands of hunter-gatherers who lived as part of the natural environment, whatever its local variations, and a second time with a global civilization that cares little for ecological balance and the local adaptations of prehistoric times. It remains to be seen what form human biological and cultural diversity will take in the world of the universal industrial civilization.

REFERENCES

Adams, Robert M. 1966 *The Evolution of Urban Society*. Chicago: University of Chicago Press.

Bankes, George. 1977. *Peru Before Pizarro*. Oxford, England: Phaidon.

Chang, Kwang-Chin. 1980. *The Shang Civilization*. New Haven: Yale University Press.

Diringer, David. 1963. *Writing*. London: Thames and Hudson.

Hammond, Norman. 1982. *Ancient Maya Civilization*. New Brunswick, N.J.: Rutgers University Press.

Hood, Sinclair. 1973. *The Minoans*. London: Thames and Hudson.

Jennings, Jesse D., ed. 1978. *Ancient Native Americans*. San Francisco: W. H. Freeman and Company.

Johnson, Paul. 1978. *The Civilization of Ancient Egypt*. London: Weidenfeld and Nicholson.

Kramer, Samuel. 1963. *The Sumerians*. Chicago: University of Chicago Press.

Lloyd, Seton. 1979. *The Archaeology of Mesopotamia*. London: Thames and Hudson.

Redman, Charles L. 1978. *The Rise of Civilization*. San Francisco: W. H. Freeman and Company.

Renfrew, Colin. 1973. *Before Civilization*. New York: Knopf.

Taylour, Lord William, 1969. *The Mycenaeans*. London: Thames and Hudson.

Weaver, Muriel Porter. 1982. *The Aztecs, Maya, and Their Predecessors*, 2nd ed. New York: Academic Press.

Wheeler, Mortimer. 1968. *Early India and Pakistan*. New York: Frederick Praeger.

12

The Origin of Cities

by Robert M. Adams
September 1960

The agricultural revolution ultimately made it possible for men to congregate in large communities and to take up specialized tasks. The first cities almost certainly arose in Mesopotamia

The rise of cities, the second great "revolution" in human culture, was pre-eminently a social process, an expression more of changes in man's interaction with his fellows than in his interaction with his environment. For this reason it marks not only a turning but also a branching point in the history of the human species.

Earlier steps are closely identified with an increasing breadth or intensity in the exploitation of the environment. Their distinguishing features are new tools and techniques and the discovery of new and more dependable resources for subsistence. Even in so advanced an achievement as the invention of agriculture, much of the variation from region to region was simply a reflection of local differences in subsistence potential.

In contrast the urban revolution was

MAP OF NIPPUR on a clay tablet dates from about 1500 B.C. Two lines at far left trace the course of Euphrates River; adjacent lines show one wall of the city. Square structures at far right are temples; the two vertical lines at right center represent a canal.

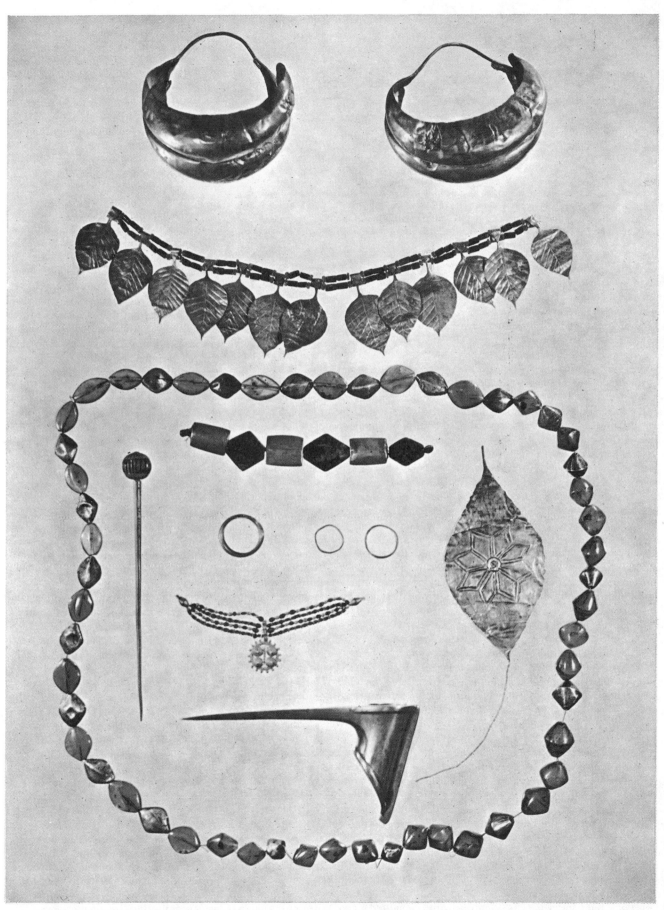

ROYAL GRAVE OFFERINGS from later tombs at Ur indicate the concentration of wealth that accompanied the emergence of a kingly class. Dated at about 2500 B.C., the objects include large gold earrings (*top*); a headdress with gold leaves; beads of gold, lapis and carnelian; gold rings; a gold leaf; a hairpin of gold and lapis; an ornament with a gold pendant; an adz head of electrum.

188

EARLY GRAVE OFFERINGS from Mesopotamian tombs of about 3900 B.C. consist mainly of painted pottery such as two vessels at left. Vessels of diorite (*center and right center*) and alabaster (*far right*), found in tombs of about 3500 B.C. and later, reflect growth of trade with other regions and increasing specialization of crafts. These vessels and objects on opposite page are in the University Museum of the University of Pennsylvania.

a decisive cultural and social change that was less directly linked to changes in the exploitation of the environment. To be sure, it rested ultimately on food surpluses obtained by agricultural producers above their own requirements and somehow made available to city dwellers engaged in other activities. But its essential element was a whole series of new institutions and the vastly greater size and complexity of the social unit, rather than basic innovations in subsistence. In short, the different forms that early urban societies assumed are essentially the products of differently interacting political and economic—human—forces. And the interpretive skills required to understand them are correspondingly rooted more in the social sciences and humanities than in the natural sciences.

Even the term urban needs qualification. Many of the qualities we think of as civilized have been attained by societies that failed to organize cities. At least some Egyptologists believe that civilization advanced for almost 2,000 years under the Pharaohs before true cities appeared in Egypt. The period was marked by the development of monumental public works, a formal state superstructure, written records and the beginnings of exact science. In the New World, too, scholars are still searching the jungles around Maya temple centers in Guatemala and Yucatán for recognizably urban agglomerations of dwellings. For all its temple architecture and high art, and the intellectual achievement represented by its hieroglyphic writing and accurate long-count calendar, classic Maya civilization apparently was not based on the city.

These facts do not detract from the fundamental importance of the urban revolution, but underline its complex character. Every high civilization other than possibly the Mayan did ultimately

produce cities. And in most civilizations urbanization began early.

There is little doubt that this was the case for the oldest civilization and the earliest cities: those of ancient Mesopotamia. The story of their development, which we will sketch here, is still a very tentative one. In large part the uncertainties are due to the state of the archeological record, which is as yet both scanty and unrepresentative. The archeologist's preoccupation with early temple-furnishings and architecture, for example, has probably exaggerated their importance, and has certainly given us little information about contemporary secular life in neighboring precincts of the same towns.

Eventually written records help overcome these deficiencies. However, 500 or more years elapsed between the onset of the first trends toward urbanism and the earliest known examples of cuneiform script. And then for the succeeding 700 or 800 years the available texts are laconic, few in number and poorly understood. To a degree, they can be supplemented by cautious inferences drawn from later documents. But the earliest chapters rest primarily on archeological data.

Let us pick up the narrative where Robert J. Braidwood left it in *The Agricultural Revolution*, with the emergence of a fully agricultural people, many of them grouped together in villages of perhaps 200 to 500 individuals. Until almost the end of our own story, dating finds little corroboration in written records. Moreover, few dates based on the decay of radioactive carbon are yet available in Mesopotamia for this crucial period. But by 5500 B.C., or even earlier, it appears that the village-farming community had fully matured in southwestern Asia. As a way of life it then stabilized internally for 1,500 years or more, although it con-

tinued to spread downward from the hills and piedmont where it had first crystallized in the great river valleys.

Then came a sharp increase in tempo. In the next 1,000 years some of the small agricultural communities on the alluvial plain between the Tigris and Euphrates rivers not only increased greatly in size, but changed decisively in structure. They culminated in the Sumerian city-state with tens of thousands of inhabitants, elaborate religious, political and military establishments, stratified social classes, advanced technology and widely extended trading contacts [see the article "The Sumerians," by Samuel Noah Kramer, beginning on page 179]. The river-valley agriculture on which the early Mesopotamian cities were established differed considerably from that of the uplands where domestication had begun. Wheat and barley remained the staple crops, but they were supplemented by dates. The date palm yielded not only prodigious and dependable supplies of fruit but also wood. Marshes and estuaries teemed with fish, and their reeds provided another building material. There was almost no stone, however; before the establishment of trade with surrounding areas, hard-fired clay served for such necessary agricultural tools as sickles.

The domestic animals—sheep, goats, donkeys, cattle and pigs by the time of the first textual evidence—may have differed little from those known earlier in the foothills and northern plains. But they were harder to keep, particularly the cattle and the donkeys which were needed as draft animals for plowing. During the hot summers all vegetation withered except for narrow strips along the watercourses. Fodder had to be cultivated and distributed, and pastureland was at a premium. These problems of management may help explain why the herds rapidly became a responsibility of people associated with the temples. And control of the herds in turn may have provided the stimulus that led temple officials frequently to assume broader control over the economy and agriculture.

Most important, agriculture in the alluvium depended on irrigation, which had not been necessary in the uplands. For a long time the farmers made do with small-scale systems, involving breaches in the natural embankments of the streams and uncontrolled local flooding. The beginnings of large-scale canal networks seem clearly later than the advent of fully established cities.

In short, the immediately pre-urban society of southern Mesopotamia consisted of small communities scattered along natural watercourses. Flocks had to forage widely, but cultivation was confined to narrow enclaves of irrigated plots along swamp margins and stream banks. In general the swamps and rivers provided an important part of the raw materials and diet.

Where in this pattern were the inducements, perhaps even preconditions, for urbanization that explain the precocity of the Mesopotamian achievement? First, there was the productivity of irrigation agriculture. In spite of chronic water-shortage during the earlier part of the growing season and periodic floods around the time of the harvest, in spite of a debilitating summer climate and the ever present danger of salinity in flooded or over-irrigated fields, farming yielded a clear and dependable surplus of food.

Second, the very practice of irrigation must have helped induce the growth of cities. It is sometimes maintained that the inducement lay in a need for centralized control over the building and maintaining of elaborate irrigation systems, but this does not seem to have been the case. As we have seen, such systems came after the cities themselves. However, by engendering inequalities in access to productive land, irrigation contributed to the formation of a stratified society. And by furnishing a reason for border disputes between neighboring communities, it surely promoted a warlike atmosphere that drew people together in offensive and defensive concentrations.

Finally, the complexity of subsistence pursuits on the flood plains may have indirectly aided the movement toward cities. Institutions were needed to medi-

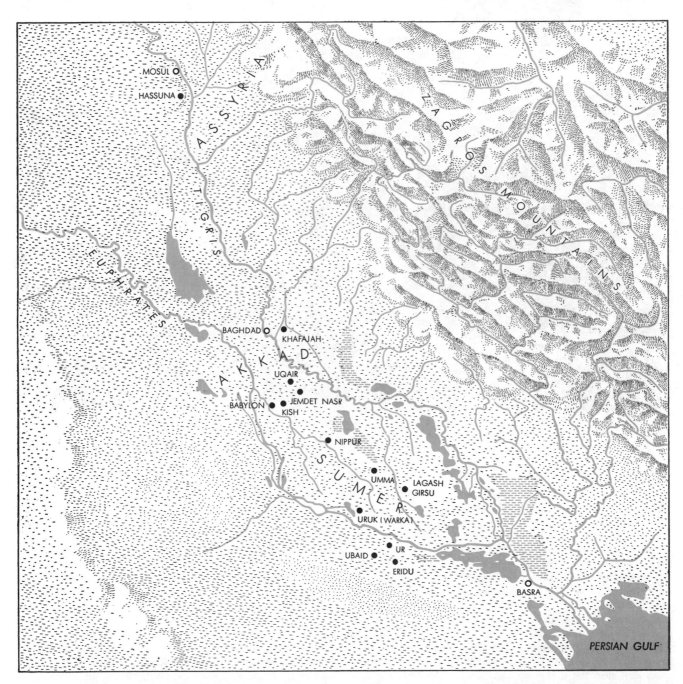

ANCIENT CITIES of Mesopotamia (*black dots*) were located mainly along Tigris and Euphrates rivers and their tributaries. In ancient times these rivers followed different courses from those shown on this modern map. Modern cities are shown as open dots.

CITY OF ERBIL in northern Iraq is built on the site of ancient city of Arbela. This aerial view suggests the character and appearance of Mesopotamian cities of thousands of years ago, with streets and houses closely packed around central public buildings.

ate between herdsman and cultivator; between fisherman and sailor; between plowmaker and plowman. Whether through a system of rationing, palace largesse or a market that would be recognizable to us, the city provided a logical and necessary setting for storage, exchange and redistribution. Not surprisingly, one of the recurrent themes in early myths is a rather didactic demonstration that the welfare of the city goddess is founded upon the harmonious interdependence of the shepherd and the farmer.

In any case the gathering forces for urbanization first become evident around 4000 B.C. Which of them furnished the

initial impetus is impossible to say, if indeed any single factor was responsible. We do not even know as yet whether the onset of the process was signaled by a growth in the size of settlements. And of course mere increase in size would not necessarily imply technological or economic advance beyond the level of the village-farming community. In our own time we have seen primitive agricultural peoples, such as the Yoruba of western Nigeria, who maintained sizable cities that were in fact little more than overgrown village-farming settlements. They were largely self-sustaining because most of the productive inhabitants were full-time farmers.

The evidence suggests that at the beginning the same was true of Mesopotamian urbanization: immediate economic change was not its central characteristic. As we shall see shortly, the first clear-cut trend to appear in the archeological record is the rise of temples. Conceivably new patterns of thought and social organization crystallizing within the temples served as the primary force in bringing people together and setting the process in motion.

Whatever the initial stimulus to growth and reorganization, the process itself clearly involved the interaction of many different factors. Certainly the institutions of the city evolved in different directions and at different rates, rather than as a smoothly emerging totality. Considering the present fragmentary state of knowledge, it is more reasonable here to follow some of these trends individually rather than to speculate from the shreds (or, rather, sherds!) and patches of data about how the complete organizational pattern developed.

Four archeological periods can be distinguished in the tentative chronology of the rise of the Mesopotamian city-state. The earliest is the Ubaid, named for the first site where remains of this period were uncovered [*see map on page 189*]. At little more than a guess, it may have lasted for a century or two past 4000 B.C., giving way to the relatively brief Warka period. Following this the first written records appeared during the Protoliterate period, which spanned the remainder of the fourth millennium. The final part of our story is the Early Dynastic period, which saw the full flowering of independent city-states between about 3000 and 2500 B.C.

Of all the currents that run through the whole interval, we know most about religious institutions. Small shrines existed in the early villages of the northern plains and were included in the cultural inventory of the earliest known agriculturalists in the alluvium. Before the end of the Ubaid period the free-standing shrine had lost its original fluidity of plan and adopted architectural features that afterward permanently characterized Mesopotamian temples. The development continued into the Early Dynastic period, when we see a complex of workshops and storehouses surrounding a greatly enlarged but rigidly traditional arrangement of cult chambers. No known contemporary structures were remotely comparable in size or complexity to these establishments until almost the end of the Protoliterate period.

At some point specialized priests appeared, probably the first persons released from direct subsistence labor. Their ritual activities are depicted in Protoliterate seals and stone carvings. If not immediately, then quite early, the priests also assumed the role of economic administrators, as attested by ration or wage lists found in temple premises among the earliest known examples of writing. The priestly hierarchies continued to supervise a multitude of economic as well as ritual activities into (and beyond) the Early Dynastic period, although by then more explicitly political forms of organization had perhaps become dominant. For a long time, however, temples seem to have been the

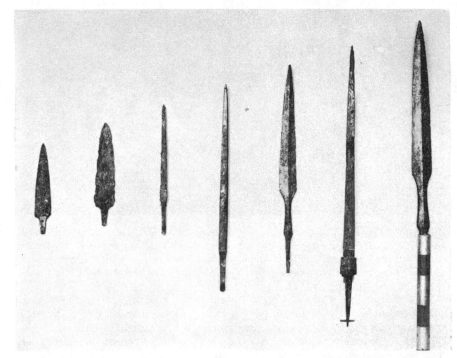

SPEARHEADS of copper and bronze from the royal cemetery at Ur date back to the third millennium B.C. The workmanship of these weapons matches that of the jewelry shown on page 170.

largest and most complex institutions that existed in the communities growing up around them.

The beginnings of dynastic political regimes are much harder to trace. Monumental palaces, rivaling the temples in size, appear in the Early Dynastic period, but not earlier. The term for "king" has not yet been found in Protoliterate texts. Even so-called royal tombs apparently began only in the Early Dynastic period.

Lacking contemporary historical or archeological evidence, we must seek the origins of dynastic institutions primarily in later written versions of traditional myths. Thorkild Jacobsen of the

University of Chicago has argued persuasively that Sumerian myths describing the world of the gods reflect political institutions as they existed in human society just prior to the rise of dynastic authority. If so, they show that political authority in the Protoliterate period rested in an assembly of the adult male members of the community. Convoked only to meet sporadic external threat, the assembly's task was merely to select a short-term war leader.

Eventually, as the myths themselves suggest, successful war leaders were retained even in times of peace. Herein lies the apparent origin of kingship. At times springing up outside the priestly corporations, at times coming from them,

ROYAL WAR-CHARIOT carved on limestone plaque from city of Ur reflects increasing concern of Mesopotamian cities about methods of warfare in middle of third millennium B.C.

RELIGIONS of ancient Mesopotamia were dominated by the idea that man was fashioned to serve the gods. Here a worshipper followed by figure with pail brings a goat as an offering to goddess seated at right. A divine attendant kneels before her. This impression and the one below were made from stone cylinder-seals of Akkadian period (about 2400 B.C.).

new leaders emerged who were preoccupied with, and committed to, both defensive and offensive warfare against neighboring city-states.

The traditional concerns of the temples were not immediately affected by the new political leadership. Palace officials acquired great landed estates of their own, but the palace itself was occupied chiefly with such novel activities as raising and supplying its army, maintaining a large retinue of servants and entertainers and constructing a defensive wall around the city.

These undertakings took a heavy toll of the resources of the young city-states, perhaps too heavy to exact by the old "democratic" processes. Hence it is not surprising that as permanent, hereditary royal authority became established, the position of the assembly declined. In the famous epic of Gilgamesh, an Early Dynastic king of Uruk, the story opens with the protests of the citizenry over their forced labor on the city walls. Another episode shows Gilgamesh manipulating the assembly, obviously no longer

depending on its approval for his power. Rooted in war, the institution of kingship intensified a pattern of predatory expansionism and shifting military rivalries. The early Mesopotamian king could trace his origin to the need for military leadership. But the increasingly militaristic flavor of the Early Dynastic period also can be traced at least in part to the interests and activities of kings and their retinues as they proceeded to consolidate their power.

As society shifted its central focus from temple to palace it also separated into classes. Archeologically, the process can best be followed through the increasing differentiation in grave offerings in successively later cemeteries. Graves of the Ubaid period, at the time when monumental temples were first appearing, hold little more than a variable number of pottery vessels. Those in the cemetery at Ur, dating from the latter part of the Early Dynastic period, show a great disparity in the wealth they contain. A small proportion, the royal tombs

(not all of whose principal occupants may have belonged to royal families), are richly furnished with beautifully wrought weapons, ornaments and utensils of gold and lapis lazuli. A larger number contain a few copper vessels or an occasional bead of precious metal, but the majority have only pottery vessels or even nothing at all. Both texts and archeological evidence indicate that copper and bronze agricultural tools were beyond the reach of the ordinary peasant until after the Early Dynastic period, while graves of the well-to-do show "conspicuous consumption" of copper in the form of superfluous stands for pottery vessels even from the beginning of the period.

Early Dynastic texts likewise record social and economic stratification. Records from the main archive of the Baba Temple in Girsu, for example, show substantial differences in the allotments from that temple's lands to its parishioners. Other texts describe the sale of houseplots or fields, often to form great estates held by palace officials and worked by communities of dependent clients who may originally have owned the land. Still others record the sale of slaves, and the rations allotted to slaves producing textiles under the supervision of temple officials. As a group, however, slaves constituted only a small minority of the population until long after the Early Dynastic period.

Turning to the development of technology, we find a major creative burst in early Protoliterate times, involving very rapid stylistic and technical advance in the manufacture of seals, statuary and ornate vessels of carved stone, cast copper or precious metals. But the number of craft specialists apparently was very small, and the bulk of their products seems to have been intended only for cult purposes. In contrast the Early Dynastic period saw a great increase in production of nonagricultural commodities, and almost certainly a corresponding increase in the proportion of the population that was freed from the tasks of primary subsistence to pursue their craft on a full-time basis. Both stylistically and technologically, however, this expansion was rooted in the accomplishments of the previous period and produced few innovations of its own.

Production was largely stimulated by three new classes of demand. First, the burgeoning military establishment of the palace required armaments, including not only metal weapons and armor but also more elaborate equipment such as chariots. Second, a considerable vol-

GILGAMESH, early Mesopotamian king and hero of legend, may be figure attacking water buffalo (right center). Figure stabbing lion may be his companion, the bull-man Enkidu.

ume of luxury goods was commissioned for the palace retinue. And third, a moderate private demand for these goods seems to have developed also. The mass production of pottery, the prevalence of such articles as cylinder seals and metal utensils, the existence of a few vendors' stalls and the hoards of objects in some of the more substantial houses all imply at least a small middle class. Most of these commodities, it is clear, were fabricated in the major Mesopotamian towns from raw materials brought from considerable distance. Copper, for example, came from Oman and the Anatolian plateau, more than 1,000 miles from the Sumerian cities. The need for imports stimulated the manufacture of such articles as textiles, which could be offered in exchange, and also motivated the expansion of territorial control by conquest.

Some authorities have considered that technological advance, which they usually equate with the development of metallurgy, was a major stimulant or even a precondition of urban growth. Yet, in southern Mesopotamia at least, the major quantitative expansion of metallurgy, and of specialized crafts in general, came only after dynastic city-states were well advanced. While the spread of technology probably contributed further to the development of militarism and social stratification, it was less a cause than a consequence of city growth. The same situation is found in New World civilizations. Particularly in aboriginal Middle America the technological level remained very nearly static before and after the urban period.

Finally we come to the general forms of the developing cities, perhaps the most obscure aspect of the whole process of urbanization. Unhappily even Early Dynastic accounts do not oblige us with extensive descriptions of the towns where they were written, nor even with useful estimates of population. Contemporary maps also are unknown; if they were made, they still elude us. References to towns in the myths and epics are at best vague and allegorical. Ultimately archeological studies can supply most of these deficiencies, but at present we have little to go on.

The farming villages of the pre-urban era covered at most a few acres. Whether the villages scattered over the alluvial plain in Ubaid times were much different from the earlier ones in the north is unclear; certainly most were no larger, but the superficial appearance of one largely unexcavated site indicates that they may have been more densely built up and more formally laid out along a regular grid of streets or lanes. By the end of the Ubaid period the temples had begun to expand; a continuation of this trend is about all that the remains of Warka and early Protoliterate periods can tell us thus far. Substantial growth seems to have begun toward the end of the Protoliterate period and to have continued through several centuries of the Early Dynastic. During this time the first battlemented ring-walls were built around at least the larger towns.

A few Early Dynastic sites have been excavated sufficiently to give a fairly full picture of their general layout. Radiating out from the massive public buildings of these cities, toward the outer gates, were streets, unpaved and dusty, but straight and wide enough for the passage of solid-wheeled carts or chariots. Along the streets lay the residences of the well-to-do citizenry, usually arranged around spacious courts and sometimes provided with latrines draining into sewage conduits below the streets. The houses of the city's poorer inhabitants were located behind or between the large multiroomed dwellings. They were approached by tortuous, narrow alleys, were more haphazard in plan, were less well built and very much smaller. Mercantile activities were probably concentrated along the quays of the adjoining river or at the city gates. The marketplace or bazaar devoted to private commerce had not yet appeared.

Around every important urban center rose the massive fortifications that guarded the city against nomadic raids and the usually more formidable campaigns of neighboring rulers. Outside the walls clustered sheepfolds and irrigated tracts, interspersed with subsidiary villages and ultimately disappearing into the desert. And in the desert dwelt only the nomad, an object of mixed fear and scorn to the sophisticated court poet. By the latter part of the Early Dynastic period several of the important capitals of lower Mesopotamia included more than 250 acres within their fortifications. The city of Uruk extended over 1,100 acres and contained possibly 50,000 people.

For these later cities there are written records from which the make-up of the population can be estimated. The overwhelming majority of the able-bodied adults still were engaged in primary agricultural production on their own holdings, on allotments of land received from the temples or as dependent retainers on large estates. But many who were engaged in subsistence agriculture also had other roles. One temple archive, for example, records that 90 herdsmen, 80 soldier-laborers, 100 fishermen, 125 sailors, pilots and oarsmen, 25 scribes, 20 or 25 craftsmen (carpenters, smiths, potters, leather-workers, stonecutters, and mat- or basket-weavers) and probably 250 to 300 slaves were numbered among its parish of around 1,200 persons. In addition to providing for its own subsistence and engaging in a variety of specialized pursuits, most of this group was expected to serve in the army in time of crisis.

Earlier figures can only be guessed at from such data as the size of temple establishments and the quantity of craft-produced articles. Toward the end of the Protoliterate period probably less than a fifth of the labor force was substantially occupied with economic activities outside of subsistence pursuits; in Ubaid times a likely figure is 5 per cent.

It is not easy to say at what stage in the whole progression the word "city" becomes applicable. By any standard Uruk and its contemporaries were cities. Yet they still lacked some of the urban characteristics of later eras. In particular, the development of municipal politics, of a self-conscious corporate body with at least partially autonomous, secular institutions for its own administration, was not consummated until classical times.

Many of the currents we have traced must have flowed repeatedly in urban civilizations. But not necessarily all of them. The growth of the Mesopotamian city was closely related to the rising tempo of warfare. For their own protection people must have tended to congregate under powerful rulers and behind strong fortifications; moreover, they may have been consciously and forcibly drawn together by the elite in the towns in order to centralize political and economic controls. On the other hand, both in aboriginal Central America and in the Indus Valley (in what is now Pakistan) great population centers grew up without comprehensive systems of fortification, and with relatively little emphasis on weapons or on warlike motifs in art.

There is not one origin of cities, but as many as there are independent cultural traditions with an urban way of life. Southern Mesopotamia merely provides the earliest example of a process that, with refinements introduced by the industrial revolution and the rise of national states, is still going on today.

13

The Earliest Precursor of Writing

by Denise Schmandt-Besserat
June 1978

Long before the Sumerians invented writing, accounts in western Asia were kept with clay tokens of various distinctive shapes. It appears that the tokens gave rise to the Sumerian ideographs

What led to writing? The art itself is a good example of what students of the past call independent invention, since systems of writing have evolved in isolation at different times in different parts of the world. For example, one system—the Chinese ideogram—can be traced to its origin in archaic signs engraved on the scapular bones of sheep or the shells of turtles in the second millennium B.C. as a means of asking questions of heaven. Roughly 1,000 years later an entirely independent system of writing arose halfway around the world in Mesoamerica. It combined a simple system of numerical notation with complex hieroglyphs and was principally used to indicate the dates of various events according to an elaborate calendrical system.

Both Chinese and Maya writing were relatively late inventions. Some one system of writing must have been the earliest, and it is from such an initial point that we may begin the search for the antecedents of the art. The credit for being the first to write texts is usually given to the Sumerians of Mesopotamia. By the last century of the fourth millennium B.C. the officials of such Sumerian city-states as Uruk had developed a system of recording numerals, pictographs and ideographs on specially prepared clay surfaces. (A pictograph is a more or less realistic portrayal of the object it is supposed to represent; an ideograph is an abstract sign.)

At Uruk a team of German archaeologists directed by Julius Jordan turned up many examples of these archaic records in 1929 and 1930. The texts, about 1,000 of them, were first analyzed by Adam Falkenstein and his students. Today additional discoveries have increased the total number of Uruk and Uruk-style texts to about 4,000, and Falkenstein's pioneer efforts are being continued mainly by Hans J. Nissen of the Free University of Berlin and his associate Margaret W. Green.

Although the clay blanks used by the Uruk scribes are universally referred to as tablets, a word with the connotation of flatness, they are actually convex. Individual characters were inscribed in the clay by means of a stylus made of wood, bone or ivory, with one end blunt and the other pointed. The characters were basically of two kinds. Numerical signs were impressed into the clay; all other signs, pictographs and ideographs alike, were incised with the pointed end of the stylus. The repertory of characters used by the Uruk scribes was large; it is estimated at no fewer than 1,500 separate signs.

Hypotheses about the origin of writing generally postulate an evolution from the concrete to the abstract: an initial pictographic stage that in the course of time and perhaps because of the carelessness of scribes becomes increasingly schematic. The Uruk tablets contradict this line of thought. Most of the 1,500 signs (Falkenstein compiled 950 of them) are totally abstract ideographs; the few pictographs represent such wild animals as the wolf and the fox or items of advanced technology such as the chariot and the sledge. Indeed, the Uruk texts remain largely undeciphered and an enigma to epigraphers. The few ideographic signs that have been identified are those that can be traced back stage by stage from a known cuneiform character of later times to an archaic Sumerian prototype. From the fragmentary textual contents that such identities allow it appears that the scribes of Uruk mainly recorded such matters as business transactions and land sales. Some of the terms that appear most frequently are those for bread, beer, sheep, cattle and clothing.

After Jordan's discovery at Uruk other archaeologists found similar texts elsewhere in Mesopotamia. More were found in Iran: at Susa, at Chogha Mish and as far off as Godin Tepe, some 350 kilometers north of Uruk. In recent years tablets in the Uruk style have been unearthed in Syria at Habuba Kabira and Jebel Aruda, nearly 800 kilometers to the northwest. At Uruk the tablets had been found in a temple complex; most of the others came to light in the ruins of private houses, where the presence of seals and the seal-marked clay stoppers for jars indicate some kind of mercantile activity.

The fact that the Uruk texts contradict the hypothesis that the earliest form of writing would be pictographic has inclined many epigraphers to the view that the tablets, even though they bear the earliest-known writing, must represent a stage in the evolution of the art that is already advanced. The pictographic hypothesis has been revived anew. The fact that no writing of this kind has yet appeared at sites of the fourth millennium B.C. and even earlier is explained away by postulating that the writing of earlier millenniums was recorded exclusively on perishable mediums that vanished long ago, such as parchment, papyrus or wood.

I have an alternative proposal. Research into the first uses of clay in the Near East over the past several years suggests that several characteristics of the Uruk material provide important clues to what kinds of visible symbols actually preceded the archaic Sumerian texts. These clues include the choice of clay as a material for documents, the convex profile of the Uruk tablets and the appearance of the characters recorded on them.

Nuzi, a city site of the second mil-

CLAY TOKENS FROM SUSA, a city site in Iran, are seen in the composite photograph on the opposite page. The tokens, in the collection of the Musée du Louvre, are about 5,000 years old. The five tokens in the top row represent some of the commonest shapes: a sphere, a half-sphere, a disk, a cone and a tetrahedron. The more elaborate tokens in the next row have been marked with incisions or impressions. Unperforated and perforated versions of similar tokens appear in the third and fourth rows. Tokens in the bottom two rows vary in shape and marking; some can be equated with early Sumerian ideographs (*see illustration on pages 200 and 201*).

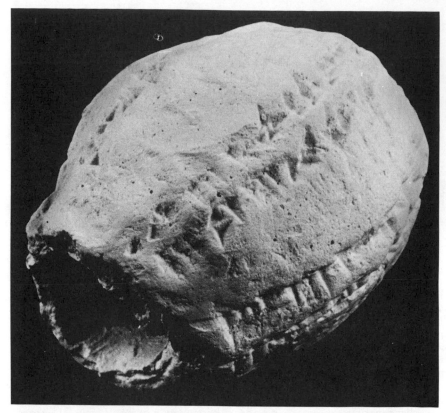

EGG-SHAPED HOLLOW TABLET was found in the palace ruins at Nuzi, a Mesopotamian city site of the second millennium B.C. The cuneiform inscription on its surface lists 48 animals. On being opened the tablet was found to contain 48 counters. The counters were lost before an accurate description had been prepared, but Nuzi texts suggest their use for reckoning.

SPHERICAL BULLA, an envelope of clay with tokens enclosed, was excavated from levels of the third millennium B.C. at Tepe Yahya, a site in south-central Iran halfway between the Indus Valley and lower Mesopotamia. Three tokens (*right*) were enclosed: a cone and two spheres.

lennium B.C. in Iraq, was excavated by the American School of Oriental Research in Baghdad between 1927 and 1931. Nearly 30 years later, reviewing an analysis of the Nuzi palace archives, A. Leo Oppenheim of the Oriental Institute of the University of Chicago reported the existence of a recording system that made use of "counters," or tokens. According to the Nuzi texts, such tokens were used for accounting purposes; they were spoken of as being "deposited," "transferred" and "removed."

Oppenheim visualized a kind of dual bookkeeping system in the Nuzi texts; in addition to the scribes' elaborate cuneiform records the palace administration had parallel tangible accounts. For example, one token of a particular kind might represent each of the animals in the palace herds. When new animals were born in the spring, the appropriate number of new tokens would be added; when animals were slaughtered, the appropriate number of tokens would be withdrawn. The tokens were probably also moved from one shelf to another when animals were moved from one herder or pasture to another, when sheep were shorn and so forth.

The discovery of a hollow egg-shaped tablet in the palace ruins supported Oppenheim's hypothesis. The inscription on the face of the tablet turned out to be a list of 48 animals. The hollow tablet rattled, and when one end of it was carefully opened, 48 tokens were found inside. Presumably the combination of a written list and countable tokens represented a transfer of animals from one palace service to another. Unfortunately we have no accurate description of the tokens; they were subsequently lost.

The Nuzi archives are dated to about 1500 B.C. The great Elamite site, Susa, has levels that are more than 1,500 years older. The digging at Susa, undertaken by French investigators, began in the 1880's and continues to this day. Six years after Oppenheim's 1958 report Pierre Amiet of the Musée du Louvre was able to confirm the existence of a similar accounting system at Susa. The token containers at Susa, unlike the container from Nuzi, were hollow clay spheres. Amiet called them "bullae"; so far about 70 of them have been found. The tokens they contain are clay modeled in a variety of geometric forms, including spheres, disks, cylinders, cones and tetrahedrons.

Amiet's finding was one of great significance; not only did it demonstrate that bullae and tokens were in existence at least a millennium and a half before they appeared at Nuzi but also it showed that they were as old or older than the earliest written records at Uruk. Indeed, it later became clear that the tokens, at least, were very much older.

In 1969 I began a research project

197

BULLA FROM SUSA shows two rows of surface impressions that
match in number and shape the tokens it contained (*foreground*): one
large cone, three small cones (*bottom row*) and three disks (*top row*).
Tablets with incised representations of tokens probably evolved next.

with the objective of discovering when
and in what ways clay first came to be
used in the Near East. The making of
pottery is of course the most familiar
use of clay, but before the appearance of
pottery man was making clay beads,
modeling clay figurines, molding bricks
out of clay and using clay for mortar. As
a start on my project I visited museums
in the U.S., in Europe and in various
Near Eastern cities that had collections
of clay artifacts dating back to the seventh, eighth and ninth millenniums B.C.
This interval of time, beginning around
11,000 years ago and ending a little
more than 8,000 years ago, saw the firm
establishment of the first farming settlements in western Asia.

In the museum collections, along with
the beads, bricks and figurines I had expected to find, I encountered what was
to me an unforeseen category of objects:
small clay artifacts of various forms. As
I later came to realize, the forms were
like those Amiet had found inside his
Susa bullae: spheres, disks, cones, tetrahedrons, ovoids, triangles (or crescents),
biconoids (double cones joined at the
base), rectangles and other odd shapes
difficult to describe. Could these artifacts, some of them 5,000 years older
than the tokens from Susa, also have
served as tokens?

I began to compile my own master
catalogue of these oddities, listing each

token that was known to have come
from a specific site. In summary, I found
that whereas all of them were small,
measuring on the average from one
centimeter to two centimeters in their
greatest dimension, many were of two
distinct sizes. For example, there were
small cones about a centimeter high and
large cones three to four centimeters
high. There were also thin disks, only
three millimeters thick, and thick ones,
as much as two centimeters thick. Other
variations were evident. For example, in
addition to whole spheres I found quar-
ter-, half- and three-quarter spheres.
Some of the tokens had additional features. Many were incised with deep
lines; some had small clay pellets or
coils on them and others bore shallow
circular punch marks.

The tokens had all been modeled by
hand. Either a small lump of clay had
been rolled between the palms of the
hands or the lump had been pinched between the fingertips. The clay was of a
fine texture but showed no sign of special preparation (such as the addition of
tempering substances, a practice in pottery making that enhances hardness after firing). All the tokens had, however,
been fired to ensure their durability.
Most of them varied in color from buff
to red, but some had become gray and
even blackish.

I found that the tokens were present

in virtually all museum collections of
artifacts from the Neolithic period in
western Asia. An extreme example of
abundance is provided by the early village site of Jarmo in Iraq, first occupied
some 8,500 years ago. Jarmo has yielded a total of 1,153 spheres, 206 disks and
106 cones. Reports generally indicate
that the excavators found the tokens
scattered over the floors of houses located in various parts of a site. If the tokens
had once been kept in containers, such
as baskets or pouches, these had disintegrated long ago. Nevertheless, there is
evidence suggesting that the tokens were
segregated from other artifacts and even
implying what their function was. The
reports indicate that many were found
in clusters numbering 15 or more and
that the clusters were located in storage
areas within the houses.

As I reviewed the museum collections and the related site reports I became increasingly puzzled by the apparent omnipresence of the tokens. They
had been found in sites from as far west
as Beldibi in what is now southwestern
Turkey to as far east as Chanhu Daro in
what is now Pakistan. Tokens had even
been unearthed at an eighth-millenni-
um-B.C. site on the Nile near Khartoum.

At the same time I found that some
site reports failed to take note of the
tokens that had been collected, or men-

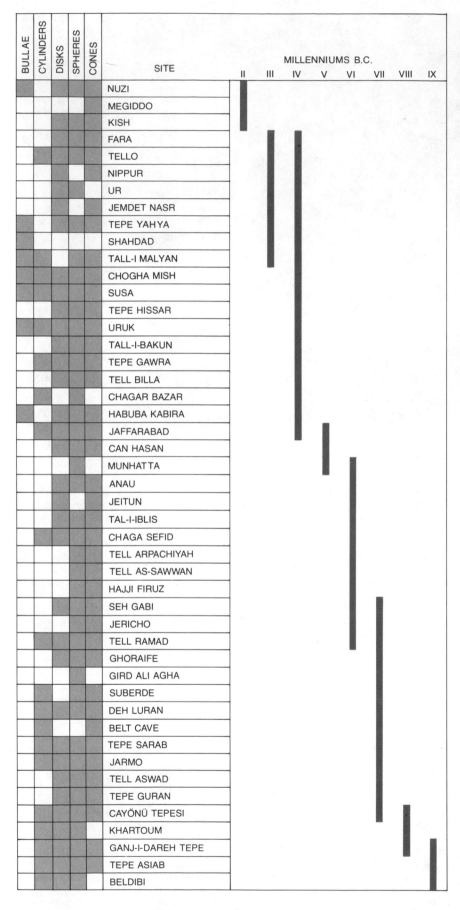

SITES WHERE TOKENS APPEAR represent a span of time from the ninth millennium B.C. to the second. As many as 20 variations on four basic token shapes are present at the earliest sites. Clay envelopes as containers for tokens do not appear before the fourth millennium B.C.

tioned them only casually. When the tokens were noted, the heading might read "objects of uncertain purpose," "children's playthings," "game pieces" or "amulets." As an example, the tokens from Tello in Iraq were interpreted by their discoverer, Henri de Genouillac, as amulets that expressed the residents' desire for "personal identification." Another example appears in Carleton S. Coon's report on Belt Cave in Iran: "From levels 11 and 12 come five mysterious...clay objects, looking like nothing in the world but suppositories. What they were used for is anyone's guess."

The realization that the tokens were all artifacts of the same kind was also hampered because, when they were listed at all in the site reports, they usually appeared under not one heading but several headings depending on their shape. For example, cones have been described as schematic female figurines, as phallic symbols, as gaming pieces and as nails, and spheres were mostly interpreted as marbles or as sling missiles.

Having studied at the École du Louvre, I was familiar with the work of Amiet. Nevertheless, I had compiled a catalogue of hundreds of tokens before I at last realized how much like Amiet's tokens from Susa these far earlier clay artifacts were. At first it seemed impossible that the two groups could be related; a minimum of 5,000 years separated the tokens of Neolithic times from those of Bronze Age Susa. As I extended my investigations to include later clay artifacts, dating from the seventh millennium B.C. to the fourth millennium and later, I found to my surprise that similar clay tokens had been found in substantial numbers at sites representative of the entire time span. Evidently a system of accounting that made use of tokens was widely used not only at Nuzi and Susa but throughout western Asia from as long ago as the ninth millennium B.C. to as recently as the second millennium.

The system appears to have been much the same as many other early, and even not so early, methods of account keeping. Classical scholars are familiar with the Roman system of making "calculations" with pebbles (*calculi* in Latin). Up to the end of the 18th century the British treasury still worked with counters to calculate taxes. For that matter, the shepherds of Iraq to this day use pebbles to account for the animals in their flocks, and the abacus is still the standard calculator in the markets of Asia. The archaic token system of western Asia was if anything only somewhat more complex than its later counterparts.

Considered overall, the system had some 15 major classes of tokens, further divided into some 200 subclasses on the basis of size, marking or fractional vari-

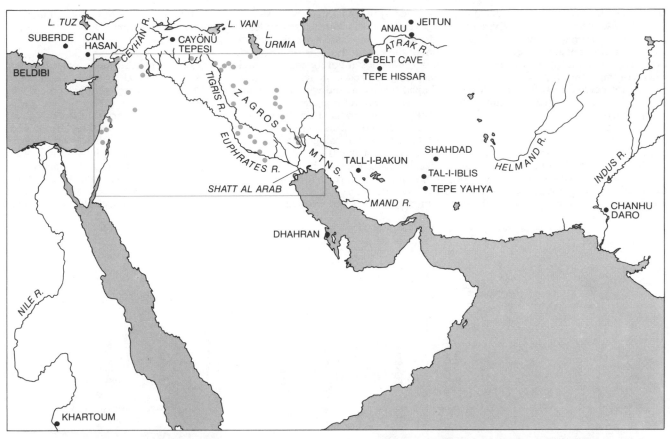

GEOGRAPHICAL DISTRIBUTION of tokens extends from as far north as the Caspian border of Iran to as far south as Khartoum and from Asia Minor eastward to the Indus Valley. Sites identified only by dots (*color*) within a rectangle here are named in the map below.

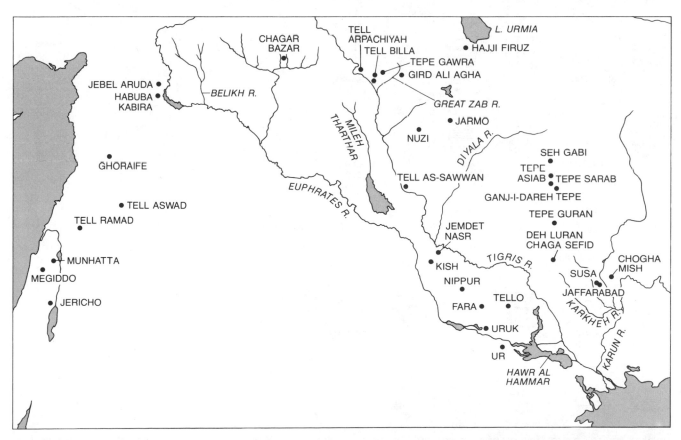

CLUSTERING OF SITES in the drainage of the upper and lower Tigris and the lower Euphrates and in the Zagros region of Iran is more a reflection of the availability of study collections than a measure of the actual extent and frequency of token use in the area.

ation, as in the case of the quarter-, half- and three-quarter spheres. Evidently each particular shape had a meaning of its own; a few appear to represent numerical values and others specific objects, commodities in particular.

It is not necessary to theorize about some of these meanings; a number of ideographs on the Uruk tablets almost exactly reproduce in two dimensions many of the tokens. For example, Uruk arbitrary signs for numerals, such as a small cone-shaped impression for the number one, a circular impression for the number 10 and a larger cone-shaped impression for the number 60 are

matched by tokens: small cones, spheres and large cones. Further examples of ideographs that match tokens include, under the general heading of commodities, the Uruk symbol for sheep (a circle enclosing a cross), matched by disk-shaped tokens incised with a cross, and the Uruk symbol for a garment (a circle enclosing four parallel lines), matched by disk-shaped tokens incised with four parallel lines. Still other examples are ideographs for metal and oil and more clearly pictographic symbols for cattle, dogs and what are evidently vessels; each tablet sign can be matched with a similarly shaped and marked token. In

addition, the forms of many still unread Sumerian ideographs appear to match other tokens.

Why did such a repertory of three-dimensional symbols come into existence? It cannot simply be a coincidence that the first tokens appear early in the Neolithic period, a time of profound change in human society. It was then that an earlier subsistence pattern, based on hunting and gathering, was transformed by the impact of plant and animal domestication and the development of a farming way of life. The new agricultural economy, although it un-

FIFTY-TWO TOKENS, representative of 12 major categories of token types, have been matched here with incised characters that appear in the earliest Sumerian inscriptions. Most of the inscriptions cannot be read. Here, if the meaning of the symbol is known, the

doubtedly increased the production of food, would have been accompanied by new problems.

Perhaps the most crucial would have been food storage. Some portion of each annual yield had to be allocated for the farm family's own subsistence and some portion had to be set aside as seed for the next year's crop. Still another portion could have been reserved for barter with those who were ready to provide exotic products and raw materials in exchange for foodstuffs. It seems possible that the need to keep track of such allocations and transactions was enough to stimulate development of a recording system.

The earliest tokens now known are those from two sites in the Zagros region of Iran: Tepe Asiab and Ganj-i-Dareh Tepe. The people of both communities seem to have tended flocks and were possibly experimenting with crops around 8500 B.C., although at the same time they continued to hunt game and gather wild plants. The clay tokens they made were quite sophisticated in form. There were four basic types of token: spheres, disks, cones and cylinders. In addition there were tetrahedrons, ovoids, triangles, rectangles, bent coils and schematic animal forms. Subtypes included half-spheres and cones, spheres and disks with incisions and with punch marks. The set totaled 20 individual symbols.

The Neolithic period and the succeeding Chalcolithic period, or Copper Age, in western Asia lasted about 5,000 years. Over this substantial span one finds surprisingly few changes in the tokens, a fact that may indicate how well suited to the needs of an early agricultural economy this recording system was. In about 6500 B.C., 2,000 years after the rise of the first Zagros farming communities, another Iranian village, Tepe Sarab, began to flourish. The token inventory from excavations at Tepe

VII CYLINDER		IX TRIANGLE		XI RECTANGLE		XIII VESSEL		XIV ANIMAL		XV MISCELLANEOUS	
TOKENS	SUMERIAN PICTOGRAPHS	TOKENS	SUMERIAN PICTOGRAPHS	TOKENS	SUMERIAN PICTOGRAPHS	TOKENS	SUMERIAN PICTOGRAPHS	TOKENS	SUMERIAN PICTOGRAPHS	TOKENS	SUMERIAN PICTOGRAPHS
WOOD						TYPE OF VESSEL		DOG		BED	
		STONE VESSEL			GRANARY	SHEEP'S MILK VESSEL		COW			
		METAL				TYPE OF VESSEL		LION			
		HILL				TYPE OF VESSEL					
				MAT, RUG							

equivalent word in English appears. The Sumerian numerical symbols equated with the various spherical and conical tokens are actual impressions in the surface of the tablet. In two instances (*sphere*) incised lines are added; in a third (*cone*) a circular punch mark is added.

Sarab shows no increase in the number of main types and an increase in subtypes from 20 only to 28, among them a four-sided pyramid and a stylized ox skull that is probably representative of cattle.

Perhaps it was during the Chalcolithic period that the agricultural surpluses of individual community members came to be pooled by means of taxes in kind, with the supervision of the surplus put into the hands of public officials such as temple attendants. If that is the case, the need to keep track of individual contributions evidently failed to bring any significant modification in the recording system. The tokens unearthed at four sites that flourished between 5500 and 4500 B.C.—Tell Arpachiyah and Tell as-Sawwan in Iraq and Chaga Sefid and Jaffarabad in Iran—reflect no more than minor developments. A new type of token, the biconoid, appears, and among some of the subtypes painted black lines and dots have taken the place of incisions and punch marks.

Early in the Bronze Age, between 3500 and 3100 B.C., there were significant changes in the recording system. This period saw an economic advance quite as remarkable in its own way as the rise of the farming economy that laid the foundation for it. The new development was the emergence of cities. Surveys of ancient sites in western Asia indicate a drastic increase in the population of Iraq and Iran; urban centers with many inhabitants begin to appear close to the earlier village settlements.

Craft specialization and the beginnings of mass production appear at this time. The bronze smithies and their products gave the age its name, but craftsmen other than smiths also arose, concentrated in various areas. The invention of the potter's wheel allowed the development of a pottery industry, and the output of various mass-production kilns came to be distributed over great distances. A similar trend is apparent in the manufacture of stone vessels, and the development of an expanded trade network is indicated by the appearance in Iraq of such exotic materials as lapis lazuli.

The development of an urban economy, rooted in trade, must have multiplied the demands on the traditional recording system. Not only production but also inventories, shipments and wage payments had to be noted, and merchants needed to preserve records of their transactions. By the last century of the fourth millennium B.C. the pressure of complex business accountancy on the token system becomes apparent both in the symbols and in how the tokens were used.

To consider the symbols first, six sites

of the late fourth millennium B.C. in Iraq (Uruk, Tello and Fara), in Iran (Susa and Chogha Mish) and in Syria (Habuba Kabira) have yielded tokens representative of the full range of early shapes. In addition, some new shapes appear, among them parabolas, rhomboids and replicas of vessels. Even more significant than the appearance of new shapes, however, is the great proliferation of subtypes indicated by a variety of incised markings on the tokens. It is also now that a few of the tokens begin to have appliqué markings: added pellets or coils of clay.

The six sites have yielded a total of 660 tokens dating to about 3100 B.C. Of this number 363, or 55 percent, are marked with incisions. Most of the incisions are deep grooves made with the pointed end of a stylus; the grooves are placed conspicuously and with a clear concern for symmetry. On rounded tokens such as spheres, cones, ovoids and cylinders the incisions usually run around the equator and are thus visible from any aspect. On flat tokens such as disks, triangles and rectangles the incisions appear only on one face.

Most of the incisions present a pattern of parallel lines, although incised crosses and crisscross patterns are also found. The number of parallel lines would not seem to be random: there can be as many as 10 incisions, and the frequency of one-stroke, two-stroke, three-stroke and five-stroke patterns is conspicuous. It is noteworthy that with the exception of two-stroke patterns odd-numbered patterns are the most frequent.

Although incised patterns are by far the most abundant, 26 of the tokens (some 4 percent of the total) show circular impressions apparently made by punching the clay with the blunt end of a stylus. Some of the punched tokens bear a single impression. Others show a cluster of six punches, arranged either in a single row or in two rows with three impressions each.

As for changes in how the tokens were used, it is significant that 198 of them, or 30 percent of the total, are perforated. The perforated tokens run the gamut of types and include subtypes of the unmarked, incised and punched variety. In effect this means that tokens of any type or subtype were available in both unperforated and perforated forms. The perforations are so small that only a thin string could have passed through them. Of the explanations that come to mind one is that all 15 types of tokens and their 250 subtypes are nothing more than individual amulets that the early Bronze Age urban folk of western Asia wore on strings around their neck or wrist. I reject this explanation on two grounds. First, none of the perforated tokens that I have examined shows any evidence of being used as an amulet, such as wear polish or erosion around

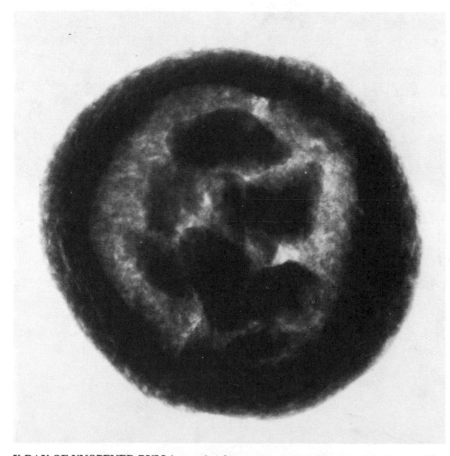

X RAY OF UNOPENED BULLA reveals tokens, some apparently cones and others ovoids. Age of the bulla is unknown; it was an isolated surface find near Dhahran in Saudi Arabia.

the string hole. Second, it seems preposterous that such a complex repertory of forms, so widespread in geographical distribution and manufactured with such remarkable uniformity, should have served as personal adornment in 30 percent of the cases and for some other purpose in the remaining 70 percent.

I prefer the hypothesis that some tokens representative of a specific transaction were strung together as a record. It seems at least plausible that the complexity of record keeping in an urban economy might have given rise to duplicate tokens suitable for stringing.

The stringing of tokens, if that is what the perforated tokens imply, would be only one change in how these symbolic bits of clay were used at the end of the fourth millennium B.C. A much more significant change is the first appearance at this time of clay bullae, or envelopes, such as those Amiet found as containers of tokens at Susa. The existence of a bulla is clear-cut direct evidence of the user's desire to segregate the tokens representing one or another transaction. The envelope could easily be made by pressing the fingers into a lump of clay about the size of a tennis ball, creating a cavity large enough to hold several tokens; the envelope could then be sealed with a patch of clay.

There is no doubt in my mind that such bullae were invented to provide the parties to a transaction with the kind of smooth clay surface that according to Sumerian custom could be marked by the personal seals of the individuals concerned as a validation of the event. The fact that most of the 350 bullae so far discovered bear the impressions of two different seals lends support to my conviction. Amiet has suggested that the Susa bullae may have served as bills of lading. In this view a rural producer of, say, textiles would consign a shipment of goods to an urban middleman, sending along with the shipment a bulla that contained a number of tokens descriptive of the kind and quantity of merchandise shipped. By breaking the bulla the recipient of the shipment could verify the makeup of the shipment; moreover, the need to deliver an intact bulla would inhibit the carrier from tampering with the merchandise in transit. This sealed transfer of tokens between trade partners represents an entirely new way of using the ancient recording system.

The innovation had one serious drawback. The seals impressed on the smooth exterior of the bulla served to validate each transmission, but if the seal impressions were to be preserved, the bulla had to remain intact. How, then, could one determine what tokens were enclosed and how many? A solution to the problem was soon found. The surface of the bulla was marked so that in addition to the validating seal impressions, it bore images of all the enclosed tokens.

TABLETS FROM URUK show the convex shape that may reflect their evolution from hollow bullae. Impressions represent numerals. Tablets are in the Pergamon Museum in Berlin.

The most striking example of this stratagem is a bulla that proved to contain six grooved ovoid tokens. Each of the six tokens had been pressed into the surface of the bulla before being stored inside it; they fit the surface imprints exactly. This means of recording the contents of a bulla on its exterior was not, however, universally practiced. On most bullae the impression was made with a thumb or a stylus; a circular impression stood for a sphere or a disk, a semicircular or triangular impression stood for a cone, and so forth.

The bulla markings were clearly not invented to take the place of the token system of record keeping. Nevertheless, that is what happened. One can visualize the process. At first the innovation flourished because of its convenience; anyone could "read" what tokens a bulla contained and how many without destroying the envelope and its seal impressions. What then happened was virtually inevitable, and the substitution of two-dimensional portrayals of the tokens for the tokens themselves would seem to have been the crucial link between the archaic recording system and writing. The hollow bullae with their enclosed tokens would have been replaced by inscribed solid clay objects: tablets. The strings, baskets and shelf loads of tokens in the archives would have given way to representative signs inscribed on tablets, that is, to written records.

The convex profile of the early Uruk tablets may well be a morphological feature inherited from the spherical bullae. Much the same may be true of the

selection as a writing surface of a material as unsuitable as clay, a soft and easily smeared medium that must be dried or baked if it is to be preserved. There can be little doubt about the relation between the shapes and markings of the tokens and the supposed arbitrary forms of many Uruk ideographs. No fewer than 33 clear-cut identities exist between the ideographs and two-dimensional representations of tokens and more than twice that many are possible.

To summarize, the earliest examples of writing in Mesopotamia may not, as many have assumed, be the result of pure invention. Instead they appear to be a novel application late in the fourth millennium B.C. of a recording system that was indigenous to western Asia from early Neolithic times onward. In this view the appearance of writing in Mesopotamia represents a logical step in the evolution of a system of record keeping that originated some 11,000 years ago.

On this hypothesis the fact that the system was used without significant modification until late in the fourth millennium B.C. seems attributable to the comparatively simple record-keeping requirements of the preceding 5,000 years. With the rise of cities and the development of large-scale trade the system was pushed onto a new track. Images of the tokens soon supplanted the tokens themselves, and the evolution of symbolic objects into ideographs led to the rapid adoption of writing all across western Asia.

14

Life in Mycenaean Greece

by John Chadwick
October 1972

When Pylos and Knossos were burned some 3,000 years ago, the notes written on clay by palace scribes were preserved by baking. These jottings provide a glimpse of how the Greeks lived before classical times

"Rowers bound for Pleuron.... Female slaves of the priestess on account of sacred gold.... Smiths with an allotment of bronze.... Masons who are to build.... Thus the woodcutters will contribute.... Thus Phygepris saw when the King appointed Augeas to be *damokoros*.... The private estate of Amaryntas...." These are some of the more striking phrases we can read on clay tablets written by the earliest literate inhabitants of Greece. What motivated their literacy? Why did the Greeks, long before they borrowed the Phoenician alphabet, adopt a clumsy and complex form of syllabic writing based on the Cretan system? The answer is simple: They needed to keep accounts.

No man willingly keeps accounts. So long as he can, he carries the figures in his head and guesses. A small farm can be run adequately, if not very efficiently, by an illiterate farmer. But if a number of small farms are united in a big one, and even more urgently if a number of tiny principalities are united in a small kingdom, the need for an accounting system arises and an expert who knows how to keep adequate records must be employed.

Although we can only guess at the details, small kingdoms seem to have begun to grow up in Greece around the 16th century B.C. All we can say for certain is that, at some time before the beginning of the 14th century B.C., the growth of these small states created the conditions that require bookkeeping. The requirement was met by borrowing a system of notation from nearby Crete, which was then the home of an alien and more advanced civilization. The Cretan system of writing, which we call Linear A, was crude but it was adequate for keeping rough accounts. The Greeks adopted and modified it. Using some 90 Cretan signs, they wrote down for the first time the sounds of their own language, syllable by syllable. The notation on the tablets these prehistoric Greeks left behind them we call Linear B. It seems safe to assume that by the 14th and 13th centuries B.C. every major Greek palace had a large staff of trained clerks who meticulously recorded in Linear B every transaction that concerned the palace stores.

It is an unlucky chance that once a method of recording accounts had been devised its users never chose to employ the system for any other purpose. Indeed, it seems very odd to us who are literate that other literate men never jotted down a private thought, never carved their name on a durable object and never even ordered that their name be engraved on their tomb. The fault lies as much in the script as in its users. The system at their disposal was slow and complicated and its meanings were often ambiguous. It was adequate for the headings of lists, such as the ones quoted above, and it was admirably suited for recording the numbers in a flock of sheep. But it was hardly suitable for a letter, much less a line or two of verse. All things considered, it may be that the attitude of the Greek kings toward their bookkeepers resembled the one attributed, apocryphally no doubt, to the American delegates at an international conference in the far-off days when the language of all such proceedings was French. Asked how, when none of them understood French, they could follow what was going on, one of them replied: "Aw, we've got secretaries."

This much at least is certain. Every Linear B tablet thus far uncovered by the patient work of archaeologists is a piece of the bureaucratic machinery that kept the prehistoric Greek economy operating. So far as the entire corpus of inscriptions is concerned, it is as if we had salvaged the contents of a few wastebaskets at four different state capitals. I call these collections wastebaskets rather than archives advisedly; there is good reason to believe that what we have unearthed are not the permanent palace ledgers at all. Instead they seem to be temporary records, notes written for immediate use and kept on file only until the end of the current year. Moreover, the notes are incomplete; the various series to which they belong have not been preserved intact. To make things harder for us, the individual tablets have not escaped damage, both at the time when the buildings that housed them were destroyed by fire and during the more than 30 centuries they were buried.

Even in those instances where the records happen to be complete, we cannot hope to translate them perfectly. They are not elegantly phrased reports but abbreviated jottings of economic data. To the writers the only matters of importance were the tallies; all the rest consisted of rough headings designed to ensure that the writer, or perhaps another clerk in the same office, remembered what the figures referred to. To those of us who attempt to penetrate the minds of these prehistoric bureaucrats the task is as baffling as it is fascinating. Still, areas of meaning are little by little beginning to appear, and we can already give some account of the facts that underlie the fragmentary records.

Four significant sets of Linear B tablets are known. The first that was found is also the earliest. It was unearthed at Knossos in central Crete in a context that assigns it to the early part of the

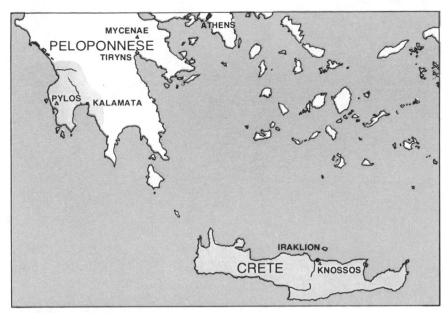

MYCENAEAN SITES where tablets with Linear B inscriptions have been unearthed in the greatest numbers are Knossos on the island of Crete and Pylos in southwestern Peloponnese. A few tablets have also been found at Thebes, north of Athens, and at two other sites: the ruins of Mycenae itself and of Tiryns, which may have been seaport for Mycenae.

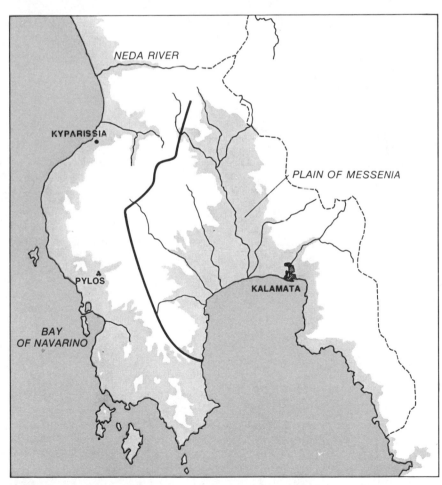

KINGDOM OF PYLOS consisted of two provinces. The western province, running along the coast, was separated from the eastern province by a mountain chain that probably provided a natural boundary (*heavy line*). The royal palace of Pylos was located in the western province, just north of the Bay of Navarino. The eastern province embraced the rich valley of Messenia; the southern frontier of the kingdom was probably near modern Kalamata. All areas lower than 200 meters in this map and the map on the opposite page are in gray.

14th century B.C. The second set of tablets was discovered at Pylos, in southwestern Greece; they are perhaps the most recent of any known, having been written late in the 13th century. Two very small collections of tablets fall between these extremes. One is from Thebes in Boeotia, about 30 miles northwest of Athens, and the other is from Mycenae in the northeastern part of the Peloponnese. There are now reports of fragments of tablets from Tiryns, which was probably the seaport for Mycenae, and clay jars bearing short, painted inscriptions in Linear B have been discovered at a number of Greek sites. Most of our conclusions concerning the earliest literate civilization in Greece are necessarily based on the relatively large collections of tablets at Pylos and Knossos. Regardless of the scarcity of the finds elsewhere, however, we are doubtless justified in believing that during this period of Greek prehistory a secretariat, busy recording economic statistics, was a fixture of every Greek state. The period itself is called by archaeologists the Mycenaean period after the famous site excavated by Heinrich Schliemann in the 19th century.

One feature common to the tablets from all the sites is the absence of any year date. Moreover, the tablets have an irritating tendency to refer to "this year" and "last year," which makes sense only if one assumes that they were meant to be scrapped at the year's end. An abstract of the rough information they contained was probably transferred to a "permanent" ledger at each year's end. By a fine irony the archives that housed these permanent records, evidently written in pen and ink on perishable material, appear to have been destroyed by the same catastrophic fires that baked the temporary records, jotted on raw clay, into hard pottery and thereby preserved them.

Although year dates are absent, we occasionally find month dates. For example, a month date is almost always present on tablets that record offerings to the gods. A typical superscription might be "In the month of *Diwios*." No day dates within the month are included. The names of five months are found in the collection of tablets at Knossos. Those at Pylos probably bear the names of three months; the identification of one of these, however, is uncertain.

If we knew at what point in the year the Greek calendar of the period began, we should be able to calculate the approximate date when each palace was

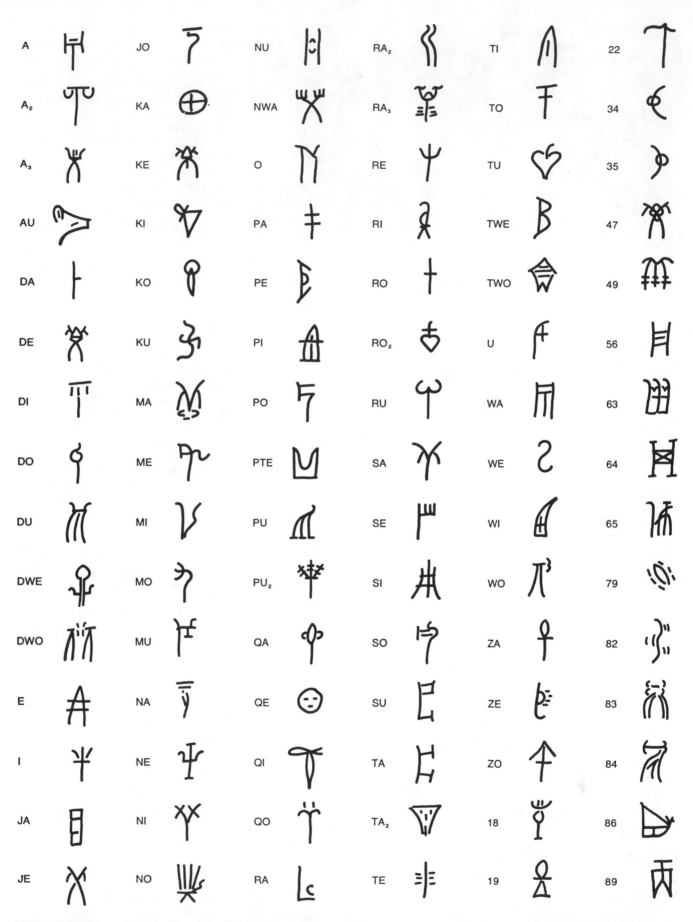

NINETY SIGNS comprise the Linear B syllabary. Seventeen are not yet conclusively deciphered; numerals appear beside them.

The vowel or vowel-consonant sounds of the other 73 signs are shown in alphabetical notation. Linear B also has 110 ideograms.

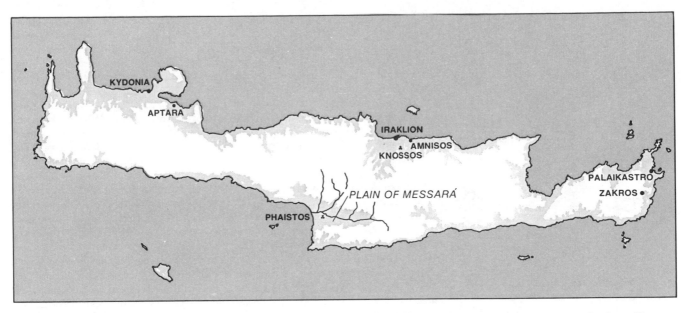

KINGDOM OF CRETE embraced the entire island but apparently did not include any overseas possessions. The mountainous interior of Crete minimized all but coastwise communications. Knossos, close to the coast, was thus a good location for the royal palace.

destroyed. The four natural points at which a year may begin are the solstices and the equinoxes, and we know that later Greek calendars favored starting with the autumnal equinox. Actually the Knossos and Pylos tablets do offer some clues to when the year began in Mycenaean times. For example, it cannot have begun with the vernal equinox because the Pylos tablets record nothing about the midsummer grain harvest and the Knossos tablets touch on harvest activities scarcely if at all. At the same time it is quite clear that at Knossos the spring shearing had been done and the wool clip had been gathered. This means that at least the month of April lay behind. Because the name of the current month may not have been recorded before the destruction of Knossos, a date for this event sometime during June appears plausible. This date in turn suggests that the Mycenaean year began with the winter solstice.

The Pylos tablets offer support for this hypothesis, particularly if they do record the names of three months. The third of these months seems to have been named "Sailing." Now, ancient navigators did not sail during the winter. Consequently a month that marked the start of the sailing season would come in early spring. Some confirmation of this conjecture is provided by other Pylos tablets, which contain numerous records of sheep but none of lambing or of shearing. This would accord well with a date in late March or early April for the destruction of Pylos. If the 1,400 tablets we have from Pylos indeed repre-

sent a mere three months' work by the palace clerks, we must deplore the fact that the burning of Pylos was not postponed until November.

That Knossos and Pylos were the seats of monarchies might be deduced merely from the size of the ruined palaces. The tablets confirm this (the Mycenaean word for "king" was wanax), but regrettably they fail to tell us the proper name of either monarch. The king's name was the kind of fact that would have been known to every inhabitant in each capital and therefore was not worth putting down in temporary records.

The tablets do reveal something of the organization below the ruler. There was a class of royal officers called "Followers," a term not unlike the European title "Count" in its original sense of "companion." At the local level there were other officials (and their deputies) who played a more restricted role. For example, these officials are directed to make contributions in bronze and gold. It seems likely that the local authorities were successors to the petty rulers, originally independent, whose principalities had been amalgamated into the royal kingdom.

How large were the kingdoms? In the case of Knossos this question is not hard to answer. Crete is a large island: some 160 miles long and up to 40 miles wide. It is also quite mountainous, with heights exceeding 7,000 feet. Apart from strips along the coast it has only one large level area: the fertile plain of Messará in the south-central part of the island [see illustration above]. Knossos

was situated a few miles inland from the northern coast, along which the island's lines of communication run, and thus it was well placed to administer the whole of Crete.

The size of the kingdom administered from Knossos is further documented by numerous place-names contained in the tablets. Eleven of the names are easily identifiable. They include Knossos itself; its port, Amnisos; the chief site in the Messará, Phaistos, and various other sites in the central sector. Two placenames belong to towns in the west of Crete: Kydonia (now Khania) and Aptara.

There is now reason to believe that two more names among the several on the Knossos tablets that are not yet geographically identified belong to sites in eastern Crete. This conclusion is the result of a remarkable feat of technology. The story is as follows. Two place-names appear both on the Knossos tablets and on pottery jars that have been unearthed at Thebes, the Boeotian site on the Greek mainland. H. W. Catling and A. Millett of the Ashmolean Museum in Oxford have analyzed the clay of these Theban jars. Its composition is not the same as that of other Theban clays, but it does match the material available from two contemporary sites in eastern Crete now known as Zákros and Palaikastro. The clay-analysis method is too new to give results that are beyond challenge, but the coincidence is at the least remarkable. In any event the general weight of evidence suggests that at this time,

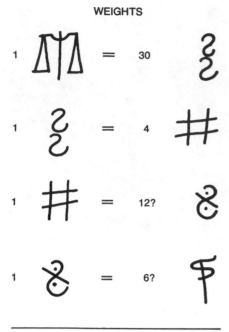

WEIGHTS

1 ⚖ = 30 ⟨sign⟩

1 ⟨sign⟩ = 4 #

1 # = 12? ⟨sign⟩

1 ⟨sign⟩ = 6? ⟨sign⟩

DRY MEASURE

1 ⟨sign⟩ = 10 T

1 T = 6 ⟨sign⟩

1 ⟨sign⟩ = 4 ⟨sign⟩

LIQUID MEASURE

1 ⟨sign⟩ = 3 ⟨sign⟩

1 ⟨sign⟩ = 6 ⟨sign⟩

1 ⟨sign⟩ = 4 ⟨sign⟩

TABLES OF EQUIVALENTS show signs used to record weights and volumes. The top unit in each table is the largest. For dry and liquid volumes these signs identified the commodity. Shown here are wheat and wine.

around 1375 B.C., the ruler at Knossos controlled the whole of Crete.

The Knossos tablets are lacking, however, in place-names that can be identified with Mycenaean sites outside the island, which suggests that the kingdom had no major overseas possessions. In this connection the sudden destruction that befell the palace at Knossos does not, in spite of earlier opinion, seem to have been the result of a foreign invasion. It appears increasingly possible that the kingdom was overthrown by a revolt originating on the island itself. Perhaps the rural population grew rebellious because it was weary of filling out endless reports for the benefit of the central administration.

In calculating the size of the domain ruled from Pylos we cannot apply the place-name method with much success. This mainland region seems to have changed more radically with respect to names during the interval separating the Mycenaean period from the classical period that followed it. Apart from Pylos itself, few of the place-names in the Pylos tablets can be located with any certainty. Even Pylos, although the name has been preserved down to the present, has twice been moved to a new location. It was shifted in classical times to a point on the north side of the Bay of Navarino and again in medieval times to its present location at the southern end of the bay.

Mycenaean Pylos was clearly a site well suited to the control of much of southwestern Peloponnese. The question is: How far did the kingdom's control extend to the north and east? We can start to answer this question by building up a picture of the relationships that existed between the place-names listed on the Pylos tablets, even though their locations are not known. This enables us to create a model of the kingdom's political organization and then see if the model can be fitted to the map. For example, we know that the kingdom was divided into two provinces and that the more distant of the two was located beyond some landmark visible from the palace. The outlook from the palace ruins today reveals a very evident mountain barrier that separates the strip of land along the west coast from the rich valley of Messenia to the east [see bottom illustration on page 205]. It therefore seems a reasonable assumption that the two provinces of Pylos, broadly speaking, probably corresponded to the western coastal region and to the valley beyond the mountains.

The area we shall call the Hither Province, that is, the coastal region, was subdivided into nine districts; each district included a main town. The tablets always enumerate the nine towns in the same order, and it can be shown that the order of enumeration runs from north to south. Where, then, was the northern boundary of the Hither Province? There are four clues. First, no place-name that can be identified is located more than 25 miles north of Pylos. Second, if the northern frontier had been more than 30 miles to the north, the palace itself would have been eccentrically located within the kingdom. Third, high mountains come close to the sea some 25 miles north of Pylos, providing a good natural line of defense. Fourth, there is archaeological evidence suggesting that this natural line of defense did form the kingdom's northern boundary. Indeed, no one would hesitate to accept this conclusion if it were not that Homer, recording events that had taken place 500 years before his time, placed the frontier of Pylos much farther to the north. Homer's geography, however, was clearly anachronistic if not entirely fictional, so that his evidence need not be taken too seriously.

As for the boundaries of the Further Province, the valley of Messenia is bordered on its eastern flank by another mountain range, the vast Taÿgetos, which includes peaks rising above 7,000 feet. This obstacle establishes a natural eastern frontier for the kingdom. What is less clear is just how far to the south the Further Province ran along the western shore of the Mani Peninsula, the central finger of the three south-pointing fingers of land that comprise the southern Peloponnese. Communications by land along the Mani coast have been notoriously difficult until recently. Adding this fact to the suggestion, contained in the Pylos tablets, that the Further Province had a short coastline, it seems logical to assume that the kingdom's southern boundary on the Mani coast lay somewhere near the modern town of Kalamata. If these frontiers of the Hither and Further provinces are the right ones, Pylos was a tidy kingdom that measured 50 miles at the most from north to south and about 30 miles from east to west.

The economic base of prehistoric Greek kingdoms such as Pylos must of course have been agricultural. In Mycenaean times currency was unknown, and we have no evidence that com-

BROKEN TABLET seen reassembled here is an example of how contexts help to establish the identity between Mycenaean syllable sequences and words in classical Greek. This is the only tablet from Knossos that records horses in a context unconnected with chariots. A part of the tablet (*right*), obviously a tally, was found by the first excavator of Knossos, Sir Arthur Evans, but the part bearing four syllabic signs (*left*) was not studied until the 1950's. The two syllables on the top line read "i-qo," equivalent to the classical *hippoi*, or "horses." The two syllables on the bottom line read "o-no," which is equivalent to "asses."

modities had their relative value fixed in terms of any common unit. Trade must have been by barter. That exchanges of this kind did take place is suggested by some entries on the tablets.

The agricultural year was not far advanced when Pylos fell. One result of this is that the tablets do not give any clear indication of how the land was farmed. What deductions we can make about the crops in Pylos come from records of the rations issued by the palace. These records make it clear that the chief cereals were wheat and barley. The relative values of the two (rations of barley, a coarser grain, are nearly double those of wheat) suggest that the wheat grown in Pylos was not primitive emmer but the modern form *Triticum vulgare*.

Because no obvious equivalent to the Mycenaean volumetric system exists today it has not been easy to determine the exact quantities of the rations. By reference to similar values in other societies, however, one can estimate a range of magnitudes that ought to include the Mycenaean ones. The estimates can be further refined by a study of the containers the Mycenaeans used, because some of the vessels probably served as measures. For example, eight-tenths of a liter appears to be one standard Mycenaean unit of volume. Exactly which unit this is, however, remains uncertain. It could be twice as much or (less likely) four times as much as the smallest of the Mycenaean units of volume.

One Pylos tablet gives what is apparently an equation between 18 large units of olive oil and 38 storage jars; the figures allow us to cross-check the assumption that the Mycenaean minimum unit of volume was four-tenths of a liter. To judge from the tablet, the average capacity of a storage jar works out to 34 minimum units, or 13.6 liters if the minimum value is .4 liter. This

fits nicely with the fact that one kind of jar widely used for liquids in Mycenaean times ranged from 12 to 14 liters in capacity.

Using estimates like this, we reckon that the minimum daily ration for a slave was .64 liter of wheat or 1.2 liters of barley. Larger amounts were often provided, and the basic grain ration was supplemented with foodstuffs such as figs or olives. We know little of how the grain was prepared and cooked. It was evidently ground into meal with stone hand mills; the Pylos tablets refer to women assigned to this task. We do know that spices, among them coriander, fennel and mint, were used to season what must otherwise have been a rather uninteresting cereal diet. Wine was drunk, although in what quantities we cannot tell.

The management of livestock is rather better known. From Crete come very extensive records concerning sheep. J. T. Killen of the University of Cambridge has analyzed these records and deduces that some 100,000 sheep were under the direct control of the palace. There may also have been other flocks under private ownership. The sheep population consisted mainly of castrated males, kept for their wool; smaller breeding flocks served to provide replacements. The annual wool clip was carefully measured against a predicted norm. Any shortfall was duly recorded, but we are not told what the consequences of a deficiency were for the shepherd. The scale of wool production was considerable, although of course the yield per head was much smaller than it is with today's breeds of sheep.

An interesting series of tablets from Crete lists pairs of working oxen by name. The names are the equivalent, in Greek, of the descriptive names commonly given to animals. The important point here is that the names are Greek.

This indicates that Greek was the language of the peasantry in Crete and not, as has been suggested, exclusively the language of the palace.

At Pylos oxen are rarely mentioned, but an annual tribute of ox hides suggests that the cattle herds in the kingdom must have totaled at least 1,500 head. There is also evidence for large flocks of sheep and goats at Pylos. Records of pigs are few and list only small numbers.

Deer were hunted, possible for venison and certainly for skins. The hides of oxen, goats and pigs also were made into leather, some of which was used for footwear and some for straps. The native wild goat of Crete was hunted for its large horns. The horns seem to have been used to make composite bows; attaching a layer of horn to the wood gives a bow more power.

We do not read much about the husbandry of horses. At this time the domestic horse in Greece was quite small and not strong enough to make a good mount. Instead horses were used in pairs to draw two-wheeled chariots of light construction. It is most unlikely that the prehistoric Greeks used their chariots in mass military formations as did their contemporaries, the Hittites of Asia Minor. The plains almost everywhere in Greece are rather narrow and are usually intersected by watercourses, if not cluttered with olive trees and vines. As a result the light Mycenaean vehicles would rarely have been able to move freely cross-country except along well-built roads.

There is good archaeological evidence that an extensive Mycenaean road system did in fact exist. The primary function of the chariot must therefore have been road transportation, and indeed this is implied by later Greek tradition. The story of Oedipus' murder of his father is the first recorded instance of a fight developing out of a traffic incident; each driver, it will be remembered, refused to give way to the other. Even in the *Iliad* the chariot was mainly used to carry warriors in and out of battle. They dismounted to fight.

The wool clip of Crete was spun and woven. We have some of the records that enabled the ruler at Knossos to control the output of textile workshops all over Crete, and they suggest that a surplus of wool cloth was available for export. Pylos produced both wool and flax, a crop that is still grown on a considerable scale in this part of Greece. The palace seems to have assessed the local villages for a certain number of bales of

PLEA FOR DIVINE HELP comprises the text scribbled hastily on this clay tablet discovered in the palace ruins at Pylos in the Greek Peloponnese. Only the reverse of the tablet is shown; the syllabic system of writing used for the inscription is the one known as Linear B. The tablet lists sacrifices to 13 gods and goddesses of the Mycenaean pantheon. Each deity will receive a gold vessel; a man will be dedicated (and probably sacrificed) to each of the two chief gods and a woman to each of the eight chief goddesses.

prepared flax fiber; the flax was collected in depots, where a labor force of women made it into linen thread. There is mention of fine linen cloth, no doubt worn by the rich, but much of the linen may have gone into ropes and canvas. The canvas may have been used for sails and perhaps for padded armor. Craftsmen were employed to produce luxury goods other than fine linen. We have descriptions of ornate furniture, richly carved and inlaid with gold and ivory. A favorite material for ornament was a blue glass paste, an inexpensive substitute for lapis lazuli.

The principal metal was bronze. Although iron was known to the Mycenaeans, the techniques of working it were not. Bronze was made not only into tools and weapons but also, at least in the palaces, into cups, cauldrons and other vessels. Ordinary folk no doubt drank from and cooked in pottery. The main weapon was a heavy bronze slashing sword. A series of tablets listing such swords was found at Knossos near the king's private apartments, perhaps in the quarters of the royal bodyguard. Bronze body armor was also known but was not widely used.

There is evidence that at Pylos the working of bronze was a major industry. The ores required to make the alloy are not known to exist in quantity in southwestern Greece. The necessary raw materials must therefore have been imported from overseas, the copper doubtless from Cyprus and the tin probably from central or western Europe. Some of the bronzesmiths in Pylos may have originally been refugees who fled from Crete at the time of the Minoan collapse in the 15th century B.C. This is suggested by Pylos tablets that list tripod cauldrons "of Cretan work." Moreover, some smiths are listed as being "in the service of the Mistress." The Mistress is often mentioned in the tablets; the word must refer to the important female deity who is so often depicted in the religious scenes that appear in murals and vase paintings of the period. We know that in Crete groups of smiths had combined religion with craft, somewhat in the fashion of the guilds of Europe in medieval times. The excavations at Mycenae show that there too groups of craftsmen maintained shrines near their workshops.

The most curious aspect of the bronze metallurgy at Pylos is the large discrepancy between the number of smiths and the quantity of bronze issued to them. Making some allowance for the incomplete preservation of the Pylos tablets, we can estimate that there were nearly 400 smiths in the kingdom. If that number of smiths had been fully occupied, they should have been able to produce bronze objects in large quantities. The amounts of bronze they actually received from palace stores, however, are

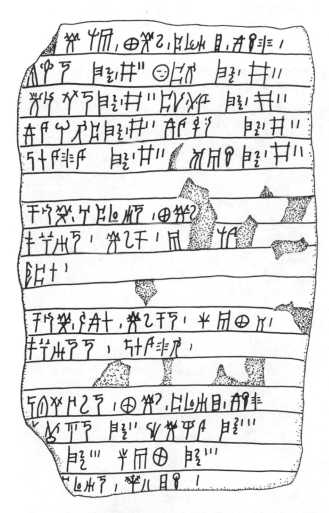

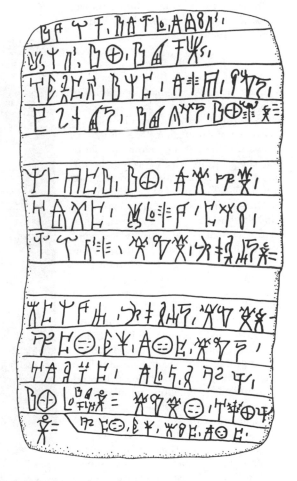

TWO TABLETS FROM PYLOS reflect the troubled last days of the kingdom in the late 13th century B.C. The tablet at left is a tally of the bronzesmiths at Akerewa, a town that was probably on the Bay of Navarino. Like the other Pylos bronzesmith tablets, it indicates underemployment, probably because there was a shortage of ores imported from abroad. The tablet at right is the first of a series concerning a coast-watcher force amounting to some five men per kilometer of shoreline, presumably deployed to bring news of any invasion from the sea. Introductory phrase reads "Thus the watchers are guarding the coastal regions." Soon afterward Pylos fell.

remarkably small The total for all the smiths together is only about a ton. Some individuals received as little as 1.5 kilograms, and others are listed as receiving no bronze at all. In other words, the metallurgical labor force must have been partly unemployed and largely underemployed. Finally, there is evidence that the palace was calling on the principal local officials throughout the kingdom for the collection of bronze to be made into armaments (an interesting parallel to the British appeal for aluminum saucepans to be made into fighter planes during World War II).

All of this makes sense if we take two facts into account. First, in order to make bronze, Pylos had to import raw materials from abroad. Second, overseas travel must have been perilous just at this time. We know the second fact from Egyptian historical records that report major attacks on the Nile delta toward the end of the 13th century B.C. and at the beginning of the 12th century. The attackers, called by the Egyptians the "Sea Peoples," seem to have been an alliance of miscellaneous Mediterranean tribes who, by joining together, had assembled a powerful fleet.

A third fact is that Pylos was living in fear of attack from the sea. This is made clear by a remarkable series of tablets that describe a kind of coastal early-warning system: small units of guards spread out along the kingdom's seacoast. There is no reason to doubt that the king of Pylos expected the enemy to come by sea; the kingdom's natural defenses on its land frontiers made any attack from that quarter extremely difficult. The king's fears were fully justified. Soon afterward his palace went up in flames, and the absence of valuable objects among the artifacts unearthed at Pylos strongly suggests that the royal residence was looted before being put to the torch.

The evident shortage of the ores needed to make bronze at Pylos therefore ties in neatly with other evidence that the seas had become unsafe. The reason Mycenaean civilization collapsed is still unknown. The long popular theory that it was caused by a new wave of Greek invaders pressing down from the north is no longer tenable. All we are sure of is that nearly every major Mycenaean site so far excavated shows traces of fire and destruction around this date. Even at Mycenae itself a raid seems to have penetrated as far as the massive fortifications of the citadel, even if it did not actually breach them.

We can well imagine the scene at Pylos as news arrived of raiders scouring the shores of the Aegean. The king hastily organized his coastal-watch system. He must also have disposed his army so as best to block the approaches to the palace; Pylos, unlike Mycenae, had no fortifications. The tablets that speak of the coast-watchers also specify the whereabouts of 11 officers of the royal court. Although one function of these officers was liaison and communication, their disposition strongly suggests that each may have been accompanied by a regiment of the royal army. We can thus deduce that small forces were disposed to protect the north, south and east of the kingdom, while the main weight of defense was concentrated around the Bay of Navarino, by far the most likely place for an enemy landing.

Of course, divine help was also sought. A large, badly written tablet, bearing evidence of several false starts, changes of mind and simple errors, lists an offering to be made to an entire pantheon of deities [see illustration on page 210]. Some are the familiar Olympians of classical Greece: Zeus, Poseidon, Hermes and Hera. There are also names that later were entirely forgotten. The offering consists of 13 gold vessels and eight women and two men. This is surely too rich a treasure for any ordinary ceremony. Both the hasty writing and the fact that the tablet was never recopied in a more seemly fashion suggest that it was written only a short time before disaster struck. The ceremony must have been a last desperate attempt to secure the protection of heaven. The men and women were probably destined not to become slaves of the deities named but to be outright human sacrifices. In addition to numerous instances of this practice recorded in classical myth, there is now some archaeological evidence that such offerings were made in Mycenaean Greece under exceptional circumstances. Whether or not these 10 individuals actually fell victim to the priest's knife, the king's cry for help went unanswered. The palace was reduced to ruins and remained forgotten until it was brought to light by American excavators more than 3,000 years later.

FUNERARY MASK made of gold exemplifies the Mycenaean craftsmen's more elaborate work. The mask, presumably that of a chief, was discovered in a shaft grave at Mycenae.

Teotihuacán

by René Millon
June 1967

The first and largest city of the pre-Columbian New World arose in the Valley of Mexico during the first millennium A.D. At its height the metropolis covered a larger area than imperial Rome

When the Spaniards conquered Mexico, they described Montezuma's capital Tenochtitlán in such vivid terms that for centuries it seemed that the Aztec stronghold must have been the greatest city of pre-Columbian America. Yet only 25 miles to the north of Tenochtitlán was the site of a city that had once been even more impressive. Known as Teotihuacán, it had risen, flourished and fallen hundreds of years before the conquistadors entered Mexico. At the height of its power, around A.D. 500, Teotihuacán was larger than imperial Rome. For more than half a millennium it was to Middle America what Rome, Benares or Mecca have been to the Old World: at once a religious and cultural capital and a major economic and political center.

Unlike many of the Maya settlements to the south, in both Mexico and Guatemala, Teotihuacán was never a "lost" city. The Aztecs were still worshiping at its sacred monuments at the time of the Spanish Conquest, and scholarly studies of its ruins have been made since the middle of the 19th century. Over the past five years, however, a concerted program of investigation has yielded much new information about this early American urban center.

In the Old World the first civilizations were associated with the first cities, but both in Middle America and in Peru the rise of civilization does not seem to have occurred in an urban setting. As far as we can tell today, the foundation for the earliest civilization in Middle America was laid in the first millennium B.C. by a people we know as the Olmecs. None of the major Olmec centers discovered so far is a city. Instead these centers—the most important of which are located in the forested lowlands along the Gulf of Mexico on the narrow Isthmus of Tehuantepec—were of a ceremonial character, with small permanent populations probably consisting of priests and their attendants.

The Olmecs and those who followed them left to many other peoples of Middle America, among them the builders of Teotihuacán, a heritage of religious beliefs, artistic symbolism and other cultural traditions. Only the Teotihuacanos, however, created an urban civilization of such vigor that it significantly influenced the subsequent development of most other Middle American civilizations—urban and nonurban—down to the time of the Aztecs. It is hard to say exactly why this happened, but at least some of the contributing factors are evident. The archaeological record suggests the following sequence of events.

A settlement of moderate size existed at Teotihuacán fairly early in the first century B.C. At about the same time a number of neighboring religious centers were flourishing. One was Cuicuilco, to the southwest of Teotihuacán in the Valley of Mexico; another was Cholula, to the east in the Valley of Puebla. The most important influences shaping the "Teotihuacán way" probably stemmed from centers such as these. Around the time of Christ, Teotihuacán began to grow rapidly, and between A.D. 100 and 200 its largest religious monument was raised on the site of an earlier shrine. Known today as the Pyramid of the Sun, it was as large at the base as the great pyramid of Cheops in Egypt [*see bottom illustration on page 220*].

The powerful attraction of a famous holy place is not enough, of course, to explain Teotihuacán's early growth or later importance. The city's strategic location was one of a number of material factors that contributed to its rise. Teotihuacán lies astride the narrow waist of a valley that is the best route between the Valley of Mexico and the Valley of Puebla. The Valley of Puebla, in turn, is the gateway to the lowlands along the Gulf of Mexico.

The lower part of Teotihuacán's valley is a rich alluvial plain, watered by permanent springs and thus independent of the uncertainties of highland rainfall. The inhabitants of the valley seem early to have dug channels to create an irrigation system and to provide their growing city with water. Even today a formerly swampy section at the edge of the ancient city is carved by channels into "chinampas": small artificial islands that are intensively farmed. Indeed, it is possible that this form of agriculture, which is much better known as it was practiced in Aztec times near Tenochtitlán, was invented centuries earlier by the people of Teotihuacán.

The valley had major deposits of obsidian, the volcanic glass used all over ancient Middle America to make cutting and scraping tools and projectile points. Obsidian mining in the valley was apparently most intensive during the city's early years. Later the Teotihuacanos appear to have gained control of deposits of obsidian north of the Valley of Mexico that were better suited than the local material to the mass production of blade implements. Trade in raw obsidian and obsidian implements became increasingly important to the economy of Teotihuacán, reaching a peak toward the middle of the first millennium A.D.

The recent investigation of Teotihuacán has been carried forward by specialists working on three independent but related projects. One project was a monumental program of excavation and reconstruction undertaken by Mexico's National Institute of Anthropology, headed by Eusebio Dávalos. From 1962 to 1964 archaeologists under the direction of Ignacio Bernal, director of the

National Museum of Anthropology, unearthed and rebuilt a number of the
structures that lie along the city's principal avenue ("the Street of the Dead");
they have also restored Teotihuacán's
second main pyramid ("the Pyramid of
the Moon"), which lies at the avenue's
northern end. Two of the city's four largest structures, the Pyramid of the Sun
and the Citadel, within which stands
the Temple of Quetzalcoatl, had been
cleared and restored in the 1900's and
the 1920's respectively. Among other
notable achievements, the National Institute's work brought to light some of
the city's finest mural paintings.

As the Mexican archaeologists were
at work a group under the direction of
William T. Sanders of Pennsylvania
State University conducted an intensive
study of the ecology and the rural-settle-
ment patterns of the valley. Another
group, from the University of Rochester,
initiated a mapping project under my
direction. This last effort, which is still
under way, involves preparing a detailed
topographic map on which all the city's
several thousand structures will be located. The necessary information is being secured by the examination of surface remains, supplemented by small-
scale excavations. One result of our work
has been to demonstrate how radically
different Teotihuacán was from all other
settlements of its time in Middle America. It was here that the New World's
urban revolution exploded into being.

It had long been clear that the center
of Teotihuacán was planned, but it soon
became apparent to us that the extent
and magnitude of the planning went far
beyond the center. Our mapping revealed that the city's streets and the
large majority of its buildings had been
laid out along the lines of a precise grid
aligned with the city center. The grid
was established in Teotihuacán's formative days, but it may have been more
intensively exploited later, perhaps in
relation to "urban renewal" projects undertaken when the city had become rich
and powerful.

The prime direction of the grid is
slightly east of north (15.5 degrees). The
basic modular unit of the plan is close
to 57 meters. A number of residential
structures are squares of this size. The
plan of many of the streets seems to repeat various multiples of the 57-meter
unit. The city's major avenues, which run
parallel to the north-south axis, are
spaced at regular intervals. Even the
river running through the center of the
city was canalized to conform to the grid.
Miles from the city center the remains of
buildings are oriented to the grid, even
when they were built on slopes that ran
counter to it. A small design composed
of concentric circles divided into quadrants may have served as a standard
surveyor's mark; it is sometimes pecked
into the floors of buildings and sometimes into bare bedrock. One such pair
of marks two miles apart forms a line

exactly perpendicular to the city's north-
south axis. The achievement of this kind
of order obviously calls for an initial
vision that is both audacious and self-
confident.

A city planner's description of Teotihuacán would begin not with the
monumental Pyramid of the Sun but
with the two complexes of structures that
form the city center. These are the Citadel and the Great Compound, lying
respectively to the east and west of
the city's main north-south avenue, the
Street of the Dead. The names given the
various structures and features of Teotihuacán are not, incidentally, the names
by which the Teotihuacanos knew them.
Some come from Spanish translations of
Aztec names; others were bestowed by
earlier archaeologists or by our mappers
and are often the place names used by
the local people.

The Street of the Dead forms the
main axis of the city. At its northern end
it stops at the Pyramid of the Moon, and

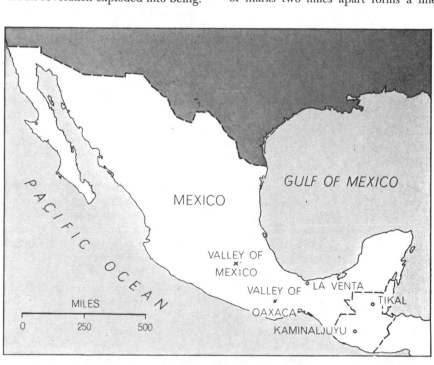

EARLY CIVILIZATION in Middle America appeared first in the lowlands along the Gulf
of Mexico at such major centers of Olmec culture as La Venta. Soon thereafter a number of
ceremonial centers appeared in the highlands, particularly in the valleys of Oaxaca, Puebla
and Mexico. Kaminaljuyu and Tikal, Maya centers respectively in highlands and lowlands
of what is now Guatemala, came under Teotihuacán's influence at the height of its power.

CEREMONIAL HEART of Teotihuacán is
seen in an aerial photograph looking southeast toward Cerro Patlachique, one of a pair
of mountains that flank the narrow valley
dominated by the city. The large pyramid in

we have found that to the south it extends for two miles beyond the Citadel-Compound complex. The existence of a subordinate axis running east and west had not been suspected until our mappers discovered one broad avenue running more than two miles to the east of the Citadel and a matching avenue extending the same distance westward from the Compound.

To make it easier to locate buildings over so large an area we imposed our own 500-meter grid on the city, orienting it to the Street of the Dead and using the center of the city as the zero point of the system [see bottom illustration, p. 219]. The heavy line defining the limits of the city was determined by walking around the perimeter of the city and examining evidence on the surface to establish where its outermost remains end. The line traces a zone free of such remains that is at least 300 meters wide and that sharply separates the city from the countryside. The Street of the Dead,

East Avenue and West Avenue divide Teotihuacán into quadrants centered on the Citadel-Compound complex. We do not know if these were formally recognized as administrative quarters of the city, as they were in Tenochtitlán. It is nonetheless possible that they may have been, since there are a number of other similarities between the two cities.

Indeed, during the past 25 years Mexican scholars have argued for a high degree of continuity in customs and beliefs from the Aztecs back to the Teotihuacanos, based partly on an assumed continuity in language. This hypothetical continuity, which extends through the intervening Toltec times, provides valuable clues in interpreting archaeological evidence. For example, the unity of religion and politics that archaeologists postulate at Teotihuacán is reinforced by what is known of Aztec society.

The public entrance of the Citadel is a monumental staircase on the Street of the Dead. Inside the Citadel a plaza

opens onto the Temple of Quetzalcoatl, the principal sacred building in this area. The temple's façade represents the most successful integration of architecture and sculpture so far discovered at Teotihuacán [see bottom illustration on page 222].

The Great Compound, across the street from the Citadel, had gone unrecognized as a major structure until our survey. We found that it differs from all other known structures at Teotihuacán and that in area it is the city's largest. Its main components are two great raised platforms. These form a north and a south wing and are separated by broad entrances at the level of the street on the east and west. The two wings thus flank a plaza somewhat larger than the one within the Citadel. Few of the structures on the platforms seem to have been temples or other religious buildings. Most of them face away from the Street of the Dead, whereas almost all the other known structures along the avenue face toward it.

the foreground is the Pyramid of the Moon. The larger one beyond it is the Pyramid of the Sun. Many of the more than 100 smaller religious structures that line the city's central avenue, the Street of the Dead, are visible in the photograph. South of the Pyramid of the Sun and east of the central avenue is the large enclosure known

as the Citadel. It and the Great Compound, a matching structure not visible in the photograph, formed the city's center. More than 4,000 additional buildings, most no longer visible, spread for miles beyond the center. At the peak of Teotihuacán's power, around A.D. 500, the population of the city was more than 50,000.

One therefore has the impression that the Compound was not devoted to religious affairs. In the Citadel there are clusters of rooms to the north and south of the Temple of Quetzalcoatl, but the overall effect conveyed by the temples and the other buildings that surround the Citadel's plaza is one of a political center in a sacred setting. Perhaps some of its rooms housed the high priests of Teotihuacán.

The plaza of the Compound is a strategically located open space that could have been the city's largest marketplace. The buildings that overlook this plaza could have been at least partly devoted to the administration of the economic affairs of the city. Whatever their functions were, the Citadel and the Compound are the heart of the city. Together they form a majestic spatial unit,

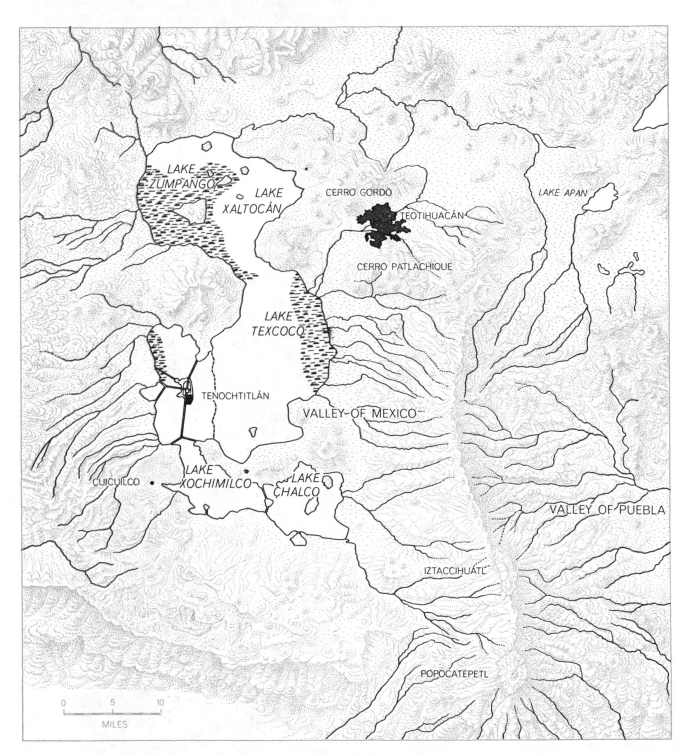

VALLEY OF MEXICO was dominated by shallow lakes in late pre-Hispanic times; in the rainy season they coalesced into a single body of water. Teotihuacán was strategically located; it commanded a narrow valley a few miles northeast of the lakes that provided the best route between the Valley of Mexico and the Valley of Puebla, which leads to the lowlands along the Gulf of Mexico (*see map at bottom of page 214.*). It was an important center of trade and worship from 100 B.C. until about A.D. 750. Centuries after its fall the Aztec capital of Tenochtitlán grew up in the western shallows of Lake Texcoco, 25 miles from the earlier metropolis.

a central island surrounded by more open ground than is found in any other part of Teotihuacán.

The total area of the city was eight square miles. Not counting ritual structures, more than 4,000 buildings, most of them apartment houses, were built to shelter the population. At the height of Teotihuacán's power, in the middle of the first millennium A.D., the population certainly exceeded 50,000 and was probably closer to 100,000. This is not a particularly high figure compared with Old World religious-political centers; today the population of Mecca is some 130,000 and that of Benares more than 250,000 (to which is added an annual influx of a million pilgrims). One reason Teotihuacán did not have a larger population was that its gleaming lime-plastered residential structures were only

SOUTH ELEVATION

APARTMENT HOUSE typical of the city's many multiroomed dwellings was excavated in 1961 by Laurette Séjourné. The outer walls of the compound conform with the 57-meter module favored by the city's planners. Within its forbidding exterior (*see south façade at bottom of illustration*) individual apartments comprised several rooms grouped around unroofed patios (*smaller white areas*).

218

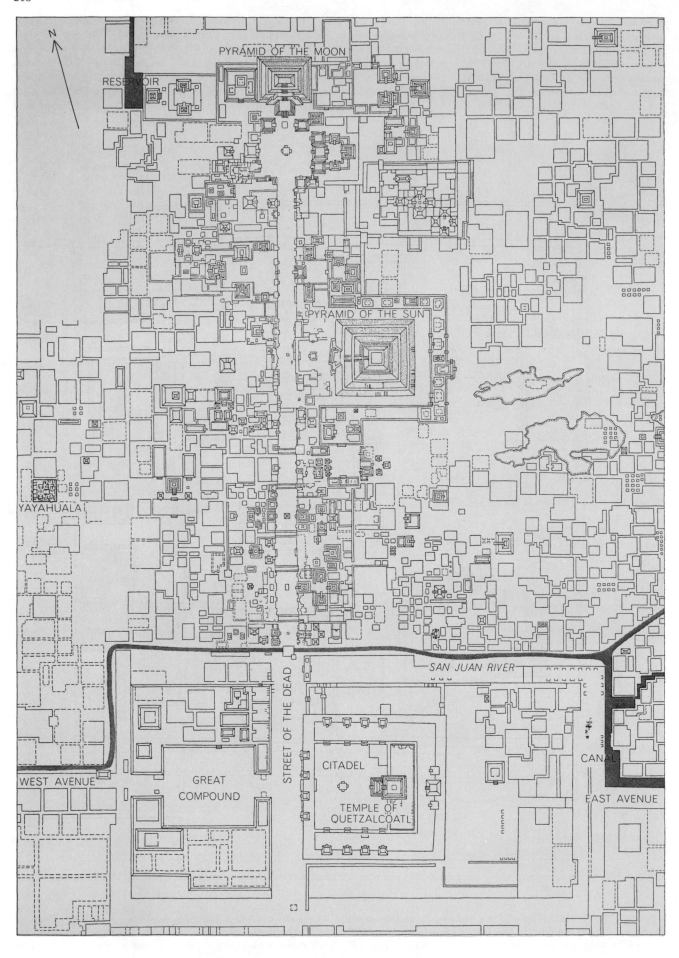

PYRAMID OF THE MOON

RESERVOIR

PYRAMID OF THE SUN

YAYAHUALA

SAN JUAN RIVER

STREET OF THE DEAD

CITADEL

WEST AVENUE

GREAT
COMPOUND

TEMPLE OF
QUETZALCOATL

CANAL

EAST AVENUE

one story high. Although most of the inhabitants lived in apartments, the buildings were "ranch-style" rather than "high-rise."

The architects of Teotihuacán designed apartments to offer a maximum of privacy within the crowded city, using a concept similar to the Old World's classical atrium house [see illustration on page 217]. The rooms of each apartment surrounded a central patio; each building consisted of a series of rooms, patios, porticoes and passageways, all secluded from the street. This pattern was also characteristic of the city's palaces. The residential areas of Teotihuacán must have presented a somewhat forbidding aspect from the outside: high windowless walls facing on narrow streets. Within the buildings, however, the occupants were assured of privacy. Each patio had its own drainage system; each admitted light and air to the surrounding apartments; each made it possible for the inhabitants to be out of doors yet alone. It may be that this architectural style contributed to Teotihuacán's permanence as a focus of urban life for more than 500 years.

The basic building materials of Teotihuacán were of local origin. Outcrops of porous volcanic rock in the valley were quarried and the stone was crushed and mixed with lime and earth to provide a kind of moisture-resistant concrete that was used as the foundation for floors and walls. The same material was used for roofing; wooden posts spaced at intervals bore much of the weight of the roof. Walls were made of stone and mortar or of sunbaked adobe brick. Floors and wall surfaces were then usually finished with highly polished plaster.

What kinds of people lived in Teotihuacán? Religious potentates, priestly bureaucrats and military leaders presumably occupied the top strata of the city's society, but their number could not have been large. Many of the inhabitants tilled lands outside the city

and many others must have been artisans: potters, workers in obsidian and stone and craftsmen dealing with more perishable materials such as cloth, leather, feathers and wood (traces of which are occasionally preserved). Well-defined concentrations of surface remains suggest that craft groups such as potters and workers in stone and obsidian tended to live together in their own neighborhoods. This lends weight to the hypothesis that each apartment building was solely occupied by a "corporate" group, its families related on the basis of occupation, kinship or both. An arrangement of this kind, linking the apartment dwellers to one another by webs of joint interest and activity, would have promoted social stability.

If groups with joint interests lived not only in the same apartment building but also in the same general neighborhood, the problem of governing the city would have been substantially simplified. Such organization of neighborhood groups could have provided an intermediate level between the individual and the state. Ties of cooperation, competition or even conflict between people in different neighborhoods could have

created the kind of social network that is favorable to cohesion.

The marketplace would similarly have made an important contribution to the integration of Teotihuacán society. If the greater part of the exchange of goods and services in the city took place in one or more major markets (such as the one that may have occupied the plaza of the Great Compound), then not only the Teotihuacanos but also the outsiders who used the markets would have felt a vested interest in maintaining "the peace of the market." Moreover, the religion of Teotihuacán would have imbued the city's economic institutions with a sacred quality.

The various social groups in the city left some evidence of their identity. For example, we located a walled area, associated with the west side of the Pyramid of the Moon, where large quantities of waste obsidian suggest that obsidian workers may have formed part of a larger temple community. We also found what looks like a foreign neighborhood. Occupied by people who apparently came to Teotihuacán from the Valley of Oaxaca, the area lies in the western part of the city. It is currently under study by

CITY CENTER is composed of two sets of structures, the Great Compound and the Citadel (bottom illustration on opposite page). They stand on either side of the Street of the Dead, the main north-south axis of the city. A pair of avenues approaching the center of the city from east and west form the secondary axis. The city's largest religious monuments were the Pyramid of the Sun, the Pyramid of the Moon and the Temple of Quetzalcoatl, which lies inside the Citadel. Yayahuala (left of center) was one of many residential compounds. Its architecture is shown in detail on page 217.

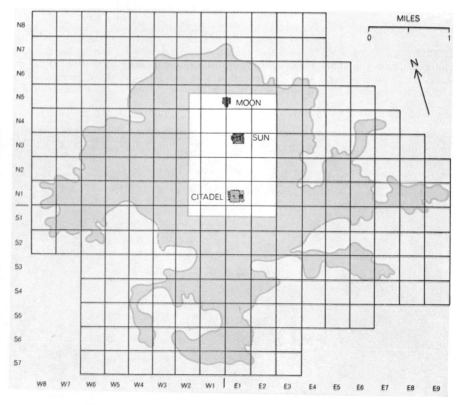

IRREGULAR BOUNDARY of Teotihuacán is shown by a solid line that approaches the edges of a grid, composed of 500-meter squares, surveyed by the author's team. The grid parallels the north-south direction of the Street of the Dead, the city's main avenue. One extension of the city in its early period, which is only partly known, has been omitted. A map of Teotihuacán's north-central zone (light color) is reproduced on page 218.

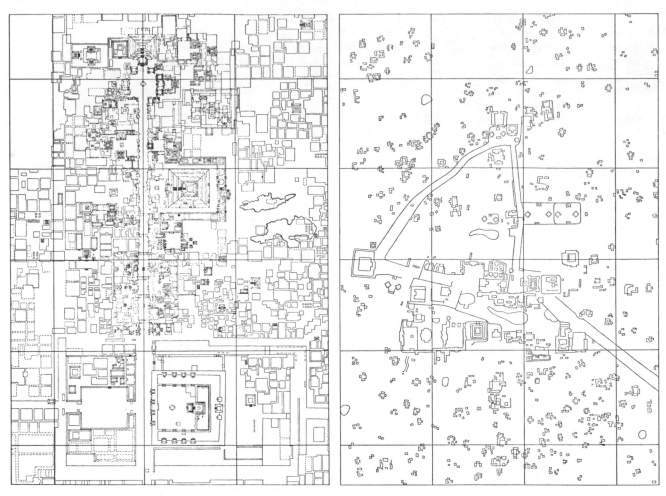

DENSITY OF SETTLEMENT at Teotihuacán is compared with that at Tikal, largest of the lowland Maya ceremonial centers in Middle America. The maps show the central area of each settlement at the same scale. The data for Teotihuacán (*left*) are from surveys by the author and the Mexican government. Those for Tikal (*right*) are from a survey by the University of Pennsylvania. Even though its center included many public structures, Teotihuacán's concentrated residential pattern shows its urban character.

PYRAMID OF THE SUN is as broad at the base as the great pyramid of Cheops in Egypt, although it is only half as high. It was built over the site of an earlier shrine during Teotihuacán's first major period of growth, in the early centuries of the Christian era.

John Paddock of the University of the Americas, a specialist in the prehistory of Oaxaca. Near the eastern edge of the city quantities of potsherds have been found that are characteristic of Maya areas and the Veracruz region along the Gulf of Mexico. These fragments suggest that the neighborhood was inhabited either by people from those areas or by local merchants who specialized in such wares.

We have found evidence that as the centuries passed two of the city's important crafts—the making of pottery and obsidian tools—became increasingly specialized. From the third century A.D. on some obsidian workshops contain a high proportion of tools made by striking blades from a "core" of obsidian; others have a high proportion of tools made by chipping a piece of obsidian until the desired shape was obtained. Similar evidence of specialization among potters is found in the southwestern part of the city. There during Teotihuacán's period of greatest expansion one group of potters concentrated on the mass production of the most common type of cooking ware.

The crafts of Teotihuacán must have helped to enrich the city. So also, no doubt, did the pilgrim traffic. In addition to the three major religious structures more than 100 other temples and shrines line the Street of the Dead. Those who visited the city's sacred buildings must have included not only peasants and townspeople from the entire Valley of Mexico but also pilgrims from as far away as Guatemala. When one adds to these worshipers the visiting merchants, traders and peddlers attracted by the markets of Teotihuacán, it seems likely that many people would have been occupied catering to the needs of those who were merely visiting the city.

Radical social transformations took place during the growth of the city. As Teotihuacán increased in size there was first a relative and then an absolute decline in the surrounding rural population. This is indicated by both our data from the city and Sanders' from the countryside. Apparently many rural populations left their villages and were concentrated in the city. The process seems to have accelerated around A.D. 500, when the population of the city approached its peak. Yet the marked increase in density within the city was accompanied by a reduction in the city's size. It was at this time, during the sixth century, that urban renewal programs may have been undertaken in areas

HUMAN FIGURE, wearing a feather headdress, face paint and sandals, decorates the side of a vase dating from the sixth century A.D. Similar figures often appear in the city's murals.

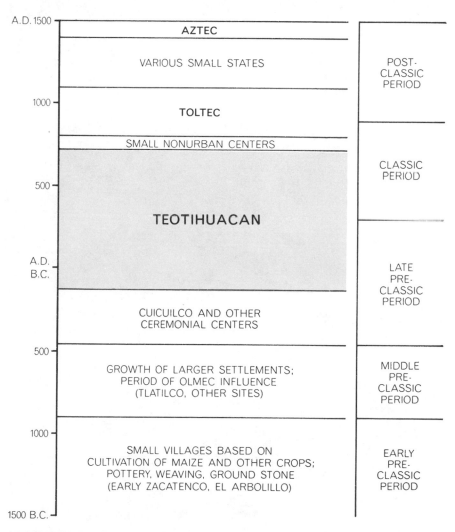

CITY'S BIRTH took place during the late pre-Classic Period in the Valley of Mexico, about a century before the beginning of the Christian era. Other highland ceremonial centers such as Cuicuilco in the Valley of Mexico and Cholula in the Valley of Puebla were influential at that time. Although Teotihuacán fell in about A.D. 750, near the end of the Classic Period, its religious monuments were deemed sacred by the Aztecs until Hispanic times.

PYRAMID OF THE MOON, excavated in the early 1960's by a Mexican government group under the direction of Ignacio Bernal, stands at the northern end of the Street of the Dead. The façade presented to the avenue (*above*) consists of several interlocking, truncated pyramids thrusting toward the sky. The structure, 150 feet high and 490 feet wide at the base, is smaller than the Pyramid of the Sun but is architecturally more sophisticated.

TEMPLE OF QUETZALCOATL is the major religious structure within the Citadel, the eastern half of Teotihuacán's city center. The building is believed to represent the most successful integration of sculpture and architecture to be achieved throughout the city's long history. A covering layer of later construction protected the ornate façade from damage.

where density was on the rise.

Such movements of rural and urban populations must have conflicted with local interests. That they were carried out successfully demonstrates the prestige and power of the hierarchy in Teotihuacán. Traditional loyalties to the religion of Teotihuacán were doubtless invoked. Nevertheless, one wonders if the power of the military would not have been increasingly involved. There is evidence both in Teotihuacán and beyond its borders that its soldiers became more and more important from the fifth century on. It may well be that at the peak of its power and influence Teotihuacán itself was becoming an increasingly oppressive place in which to live.

The best evidence of the power and influence that the leaders of Teotihuacán exercised elsewhere in Middle America comes from Maya areas. One ancient religious center in the Maya highlands—Kaminaljuyu, the site of modern Guatemala City—appears to have been occupied at one time by priests and soldiers from Teotihuacán. Highland Guatemala received a massive infusion of Teotihuacán cultural influences, with Teotihuacán temple architecture replacing older styles. This has been recognized for some time, but only recently has it become clear that Teotihuacán also influenced the Maya lowlands. The people of Tikal in Guatemala, largest of the lowland Maya centers, are now known to have been under strong influence from Teotihuacán. The people of Tikal adopted some of Teotihuacán's artistic traditions and erected a massive stone monument to Teotihuacán's rain god. William R. Coe of the University of Pennsylvania and his colleagues, who are working at Tikal, are in the midst of evaluating the nature and significance of this influence.

Tikal provides an instructive measure of the difference in the density of construction in Maya population centers and those in central Mexico. It was estimated recently that Tikal supported a population of about 10,000. As the illustration at the top of page 92 shows, the density of Teotihuacán's central area is strikingly different from that of Tikal's. Not only was Teotihuacán's population at least five times larger than Tikal's but also it was far less dispersed. In such a crowded urban center problems of integration, cohesion and social control must have been of a totally different order of magnitude than those of a less populous and less compact ceremonial center such as Tikal.

What were the circumstances of Teotihuacán's decline and fall? Almost certainly both environmental and social factors were involved. The climate of the region is semiarid today, and there is evidence that a long-term decline in annual rainfall brought the city to a similar condition in the latter half of the first millennium A.D. Even before then deforestation of the surrounding hills may have begun a process of erosion that caused a decrease in the soil moisture available for crops. Although persistent drought would have presented increasingly serious problems for those who fed the city, this might have been the lesser of its consequences. More ominous would have been the effect of increasing aridity on the cultivators of marginal lands and the semisedentary tribesmen in the highlands north of the Valley of Mexico. As worsening conditions forced these peoples to move, the Teotihuacanos might have found themselves not only short of food but also under military pressure along their northern frontier.

Whether or not climatic change was a factor, some signs of decline—such as the lowering of standards of construction and pottery-making—are evident during the last century of Teotihuacán's existence. Both a reduction in population and a tendency toward dispersion suggest that the fabric of society was suffering from strains and weaknesses. Once such a process of deterioration passed a critical point the city would have become vulnerable to attack.

No evidence has been found that Teotihuacán as a whole had formal defenses. Nonetheless, the valley's drainage pattern provides some natural barriers, large parts of the city were surrounded by walls or massive platforms and its buildings were formidable ready-made fortresses. Perhaps the metropolis was comparatively unprotected because it had for so long had an unchallenged supremacy.

In any case, archaeological evidence indicates that around A.D. 750 much of central Teotihuacán was looted and burned, possibly with the help of the city's own people. The repercussions of Teotihuacán's fall seem to have been felt throughout civilized Middle America. The subsequent fall of Monte Alban, the capital of the Oaxaca region, and of many Maya ceremonial centers in Guatemala and the surrounding area may reasonably be associated with dislocations set in motion by the fall of Teotihuacán. Indeed, the appropriate epitaph for the New World's first major metropolis may be that it was as influential in its collapse as in its long and brilliant flowering.

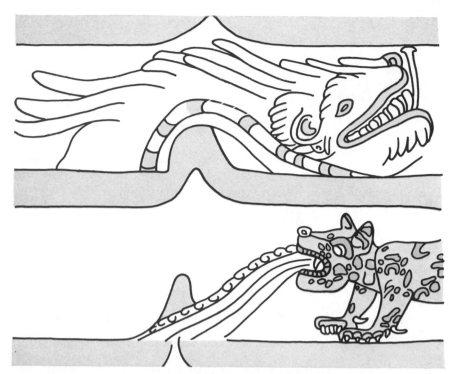

FEATHERED SERPENT, from one of the earlier murals found at Teotihuacán, has a free, flowing appearance. The animal below the serpent is a jaguar; the entire mural, which is not shown, was probably painted around A.D. 400. It may portray a cyclical myth of creation and destruction. The city's principal gods were often represented in the form of animals.

LATER SERPENT GOD, with a rattlesnake tail, is from a mural probably painted less than a century before the fall of Teotihuacán. The figure is rendered in a highly formal manner. A trend toward formalism is apparent in the paintings produced during the city's final years.

16

The Earliest Maya

by Norman Hammond
March 1977

Archaeological excavations in Belize in Central America have pushed back the origins of the Maya to 2500 B.C. The buildings and pottery uncovered clearly foreshadow the splendor of the Classic Maya period

The collapse of Maya civilization, culturally the most advanced of any in the pre-Columbian New World, has inspired almost as many explanations as there are students of American prehistory. An unanswered question of equal importance is how Maya civilization first arose. Until recently that question has received relatively little attention, but its cogency is now greatly increased. Work over the past two seasons on the eastern margin of the Maya area in Belize (formerly British Honduras), often regarded as a backwater, has pushed the beginnings of the Maya Formative (or Preclassic) period back by more than 1,500 years, from about 900 B.C. to perhaps as long ago as 2600 B.C. The new findings place this Early Formative Maya culture among the oldest settled societies in Mesoamerica or, for that matter, in the entire New World.

The term Mesoamerica is often mistakenly thought to be synonymous with Central America: the region extending from southern Mexico to Panama. The term is actually much narrower. Prehistorians define it as the culturally unified area that in pre-Columbian times embraced southern Mexico (including Yucatán), Guatemala, Belize and the western parts of Honduras and El Salvador. The last and politically the most developed of the Mesoamerican civilizations was the Aztec, which the Spanish conquistadors overthrew in 1521. The Aztec capital, Tenochtitlán, was situated where Mexico City stands today, and Aztec political power was centered on the high plateau of Mexico.

Not all Mesoamerican civilizations had this highland focus. The Olmec, one of the earliest of the complex societies in the region, built major ceremonial centers on the low-lying coastal plain of the Gulf of Mexico; examples are San Lorenzo and La Venta. At the same time the Olmec zone of cultural influence and Olmec trade extended into much of the high plateau.

To the east of both the Aztec and the Olmec area in Mexico lies the peninsula of Yucatán and, south of the peninsula, the northern lowlands of Guatemala (the Petén) and Belize. In this southern area during the first millennium of the Christian Era what are regarded as the outstanding characteristics of Maya civilization emerged. This was the start of the Maya Classic period. Extending from about A.D. 250 to 900, the Classic period witnessed the development of mathematics, nontelescopic astronomy and calendrical calculations more advanced than any in other parts of the New World. The data were expressed in a hieroglyphic script utilizing more than 800 characters, many of which still defy decipherment. Paralleling these purely intellectual achievements the Classic Maya civilization gave employment to a school of vase painters as talented as those of Classical Greece and to architects whose great temple pyramids and sacred precincts still amaze the visitor of today.

In common with a number of other students of Mesoamerican prehistory I have been concerned in recent years with the factors underlying the rise of Maya civilization. My own work has taken the form of a series of field studies examining the demographic and economic aspects of the Maya Formative period. The geographical focus of our project, established jointly by the British Museum and the Centre of Latin American Studies at the University of Cam-

MAYA ARCHITECTURE OF THE EARLY FORMATIVE PERIOD is shown in reconstructions based on the partial excavation at Cuello, a site in northern Belize, of two plaster-covered earth platforms that were the foundations for timbered superstructures. The two small superstructures, one circular and one oblong, are alternative conceptions of the timber-and-thatch building that occupied the older of the two platforms, which was probably circular in plan and some six meters in diameter. The platform was built directly on an old soil surface that included burned wood suitable for carbon-14 analysis; the date of construction appears to fall

bridge in 1973, was inspired by the late Sir Eric Thompson, who pointed out the archaeological importance of northern Belize. Physiographically the region is a continuation of the lowlands. To the south and west the Petén, the Classic Maya heartland in northern Guatemala, forms a rain-forest zone with numerous rivers and lakes. To the north the Yucatán peninsula forms an arid zone: a karst landscape of sinkholes, caverns and underground streams. Northern Belize lies within the rain-forest zone but borders on the arid zone. Two of its major valleys are those of the Rio Hondo and the New River. Following the two rivers upstream, one moves south and west toward the Petén heartland [*see illustration on page 227*].

A second reason for selecting the area is that decades of intermittent exploration (mainly by Thomas Gann, a physician and amateur archaelogist, between 1896 and 1936) have uncovered a number of major and minor archaeological sites that evidently were occupied in Late Formative times, a period extending from about 300 B.C. to A.D. 250. Finally, the people of Belize are greatly interested in their country's past, and the government encourages archaeological research. As a result we have enjoyed the friendliest cooperation not only with the government, through the Archaeological Commissioner, Joseph O. Palacio, but also with such representatives of the private sector as Belize Sugar Industries, Maya Airways and G. A. Roe Insurance Services, all of which are generous sponsors of our work.

A line drawn along the 18th parallel defines the southern boundary of our research area in northern Belize; the eastern boundary is the Caribbean, and the western and northern boundaries are the Mexican border along the Rio Hondo and across Chetumal Bay. The entire research area covers some 3,500 square kilometers. During our first field season, in 1973, we concentrated on locating as many archaeological sites as possible. These we classified in terms of size and complexity: scattered, informal residential clusters; formal clusters grouped around a central plaza, and ceremonial precincts, minor or major, surrounded by residential areas of varying extent. We also established a rough regional chronology based on the pottery uncovered in test excavations at several sites. The pottery chronology was achieved by comparing styles and style changes with those already established for pottery from elsewhere in the Maya region, either discovered in association with dated inscriptions (which first appear in about A.D. 250) or dated by means of carbon-14 analysis.

All together we plotted some 60 sites, most of them last occupied during the Classic period and most located in the higher and drier western part of the region: areas of raised ground between the Rio Hondo and the New River and between the New River and Freshwater Creek. Three sites included ceremonial precincts ranging in size from medium to large, and one of them, Nohmul, was surrounded by more than 20 square kilometers of residential settlements. Each of the three ceremonial precincts included a large elevated acropolis, building foundations surrounding large plazas, several tall temple pyramids and at least one parallel-sided court where the sacred ball game had been played.

All three of the major sites, Nohmul, Aventura and El Pozito, are located along the same stretch of high ground, the ridge between the Rio Hondo and the New River. It is easy to visualize the three as the capitals of separate Classic Maya principalities. The lesser sites that surround them are comparable to the towns and villages around the cathedral cities of medieval Europe. One of these lesser sites, located almost exactly midway between Nohmul and El Pozito, stands on land owned by the Cuello family, who hospitably gave us permission to investigate it.

We named the site after its owners. Examination in 1974 of a partially destroyed mound at the site revealed pottery of an unfamiliar type that we had also encountered in the lowest levels of our test excavations at Nohmul and elsewhere. At those sites the unfamiliar pottery was associated with recognizable wares of the Maya Middle Formative period (from 900 to 300 B.C.). The Cuello sherds, however, had no such associations. Was the unfamiliar ware perhaps even older and indigenous? Or had

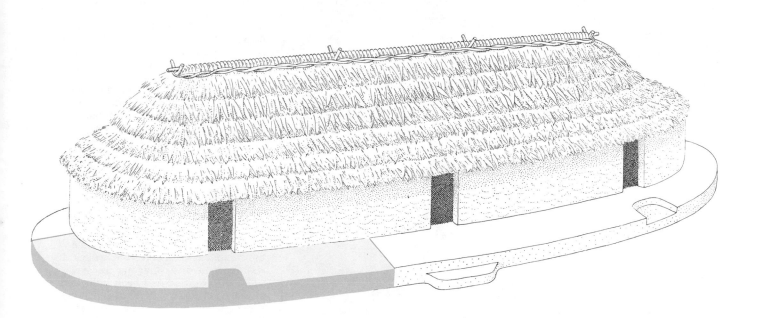

between 2500 and 2400 B.C., making the platform the oldest architectural endeavor known in Mesoamerica. That a superstructure of some kind once stood on the platform is evident from numerous postholes (*see illustration on page 234*). The larger and more recent platform (*above*) was apparently oblong, some five meters wide and more than 10 meters long, with rounded ends. At the point where one end begins to curve a niche was built into the side of the platform; evidence that the plaster lining of the niche had been renewed suggests that it served as a step for mounting the platform from the patio in front. The platform was probably built between 1700 and 1500 B.C. Considerations of symmetry suggest the second niche shown here, and the small size of both niches suggests the centrally located additional step. The restoration, however, is conjectural; indeed, only those parts of both platforms shown in color have been excavated.

AGES OF EARLY POTTERY IN THE NEW WORLD vary from site to site over a range of 1,200 years. In Mesoamerica (*colored rectangle*) pottery from the Tehuacán valley is estimated to be 4,800 years old and pottery from Puerto Marquez 5,200 years old. Pottery superior in quality to both, recently found in Belize, includes some that is 4,600 years old. One site in the U.S., Stallings Island, has yielded pottery nearly that old, but the most ancient New World pottery now known is from sites in South America: the pottery from Real Alto averages 5,000 years in age, and that from Valdivia and Puerto Hormiga respectively averages 5,600 and 5,800 years.

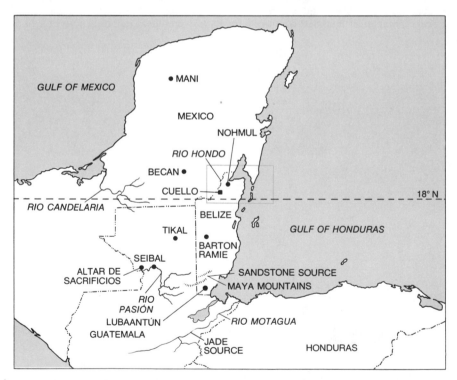

MAYA LOWLANDS consist of three parts of Mesoamerica: the Yucatán peninsula of Mexico, the Petén region of Guatemala and Belize. Classic Maya civilization reached its apogee in about A.D. 700 in the tropical forest of the Petén; Tikal was a major Classic ceremonial center. Until recently the earliest lowland pottery known was from sites on the Rio Pasión. Ascribed to the Maya Middle Formative period, the wares are dated at about 900 B.C. The earliest lowland pottery now known is that of the Swasey ceramic complex, unearthed at Cuello. Carbon-14 dates for Swasey wares extend from 1250 to 2600 B.C. Swasey pottery, unearthed at four other sites in northern Belize, has also been found at two sites in Yucatán: Becan and Mani.

it been made elsewhere in the first millennium B.C. and reached the sites in northern Belize as an import?

The question could be answered only by excavation. Moreover, the location of Cuello midway between two major ceremonial sites suggested other possible benefits that might accrue from further investigation. What was the nature of the contacts between Nohmul and El Pozito in the Classic period? If the major centers were indeed the capitals of principalities, where was the frontier between them? With questions of this kind in mind we decided to carry out a small-scale excavation at Cuello during our next field season, in 1975.

Cuello lies five kilometers west of Orange Walk Town, capital of the district of Orange Walk. The most obvious part of the uncleared site is a small ceremonial precinct of the Classic period consisting of two linked plazas, each with a small temple pyramid. No stone superstructures survive anywhere at the site, and it is probable that not only the temples but also the many residences and other structures were built of perishable materials: timber frames with palm-thatch roofs.

To the south of the ceremonial precinct we located a series of large platforms. One of them, about four meters high and 80 meters long, particularly attracted our attention because on it was a small temple pyramid, about eight meters high. The pyramid was simply too small for such a large platform. This architectural discontinuity suggested that the temple was a late addition, perhaps built after the platform had been abandoned for some time. On the eroded sides of the temple pyramid we found potsherds of the Classic period. Perhaps, like the unfamiliar pottery we had found in 1973, the platform belonged to the earlier Formative period. Certainly its four meters of material should contain traces of a long period of growth; such had proved to be the case with the large platform at the North Acropolis in Tikal, the great Maya ceremonial center in the Petén.

Work began early in 1975 on the selected structure, designated Platform 34 on the Cuello site map, under the supervision of Duncan Pring, then a graduate student at the University of London and the ceramic specialist for the project. It soon became clear that our guess was right; the pyramid had been built long after the platform. A layer of debris had accumulated on the plaster surface of the platform, evidence that the structure had been out of service for some time, before the pyramid was built directly on top of the debris.

We cut down into the platform, exposing a succession of well-preserved plaster floors. Between the successive layers of plaster we found thin deposits

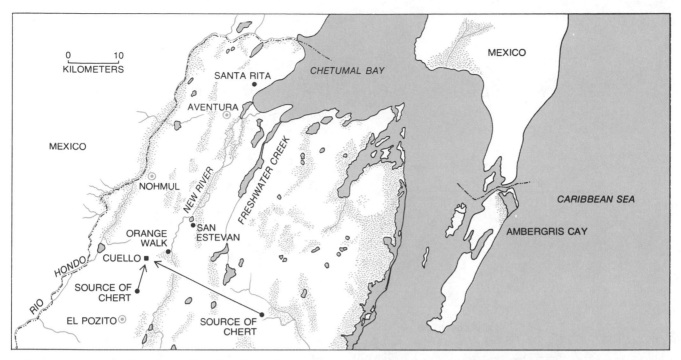

MAYA SITES IN NORTHERN BELIZE include three large enough to rank as regional ceremonial centers (*color*): Aventura, El Pozito and Nohmul. All are situated on the higher ground between two streams, the Rio Hondo and the New River, that empty into Chetumal Bay. The Cuello site is midway between El Pozito and Nohmul, about five kilometers west of Orange Walk Town. The inhabitants of the site early in the Maya Formative period brought the colored chert they preferred as a raw material for edged tools from two nearby sources, seven and 27 kilometers away. To collect the marine shells they made into ornaments required a minimum round trip of 100 kilometers.

of debris and an occasional thicker layer containing potsherds, animal bones, snail shells and small quantities of burned wood. Two meters down the potsherds included some of the unfamiliar type, this time in association with the remains of pottery identifiable as products of the Middle Formative period. Some 70 centimeters below this the potsherds were all of the unfamiliar type; this was the case thereafter until the excavation reached bedrock at a depth of about four meters.

The finding settled one of our hypothetical questions. The examples of the unfamiliar ware that we had encountered in the early levels of Belize sites elsewhere were not imports. The presence of the ware signified that each site had an even longer history than had been supposed. Until the time of our probes the earliest-known kinds of pottery in the Maya lowlands had been products of the Middle Formative period unearthed at two sites in the Petén: Seibal and Altar de Sacrificios on the Rio Pasión. There Gordon R. Willey of Harvard University had turned up pottery of an early phase of the Middle Formative associated with material that yielded carbon-14 dates equivalent to slightly later than 900 B.C. Nowhere in the lowlands had any pottery been unearthed that unquestionably belonged to the Early Formative period (then estimated to run from 1500 to 900 B.C.).

All the ceramic complexes of northern Belize are named after local rivers or lagoons, and so we designated our unknown pottery the Swasey ceramic complex after a nearby tributary of the New River. Obviously the sherds from the lower levels in the Cuello platform were older than the pottery from Seibal and Altar de Sacrificios The question was, how much older? In the traditional view of early influences in Mesoamerica the Olmec civilization, centered on the Gulf Coast of Mexico west of the Maya area, is considered a probable source of the stimuli affecting the earliest aspects of Maya culture. The period of Olmec influence began around 1300 B.C. Was the Swasey complex early enough to have predated possible Olmec contacts and thus to have inaugurated a cultural tradition independent of Olmec influences?

This remained the question foremost in our minds during the summer and fall of 1975 as two laboratories, one at the University of Cambridge and the other at the University of California at Los Angeles, undertook to make carbon-14 determinations on samples of burned wood from the platform excavation at Cuello. Here two points should be made about carbon-14 dates. First, the dates I am citing are "calibrated." That is, the variations in the regularity of carbon-14 readings, revealed by the analysis of samples of known age from the long-lived bristlecone pine, have been eliminated. Hence the dates represent true calendar years, A.D. or B.C.,

rather than carbon-14 laboratory years.

Second, there is a degree of statistical uncertainty in carbon-14 dating, as is apparent in the laboratory notation. Take as an example the notation 1000 B.C. ± 100. The 1000 B.C. date, usually a mean figure that combines the results of two or more tests of the sample material, is known as the "central" figure; the ± 100 indicates odds of roughly two to one in favor of the specimen's age falling somewhere between 1100 and 900 B.C. Statistically this range on each side of the central figure constitutes one standard deviation. If one extends the range to two standard deviations, which in this example would be from 1200 to 800 B.C., the likelihood that the age of the specimen will fall somewhere between these extremes is increased from 68 percent to 97 percent. Extensions of this kind appear in the illustration on page 121. When two such extensions overlap, the two carbon-14 dates are said to be statistically inseparable.

The first carbon-14 date to come through was from Roy Switsur and Alan Ward at Cambridge. It was for a specimen of wood found in a midden deposit representing the transition between the earlier, or Swasey, phase at Cuello and its successor Middle Formative phase, Lopez Mamom. The date of this level proved to be about 1250 B.C., or more than three centuries earlier than the pottery from Willey's Middle Formative sites in the Petén.

The date suggested not only that the

228

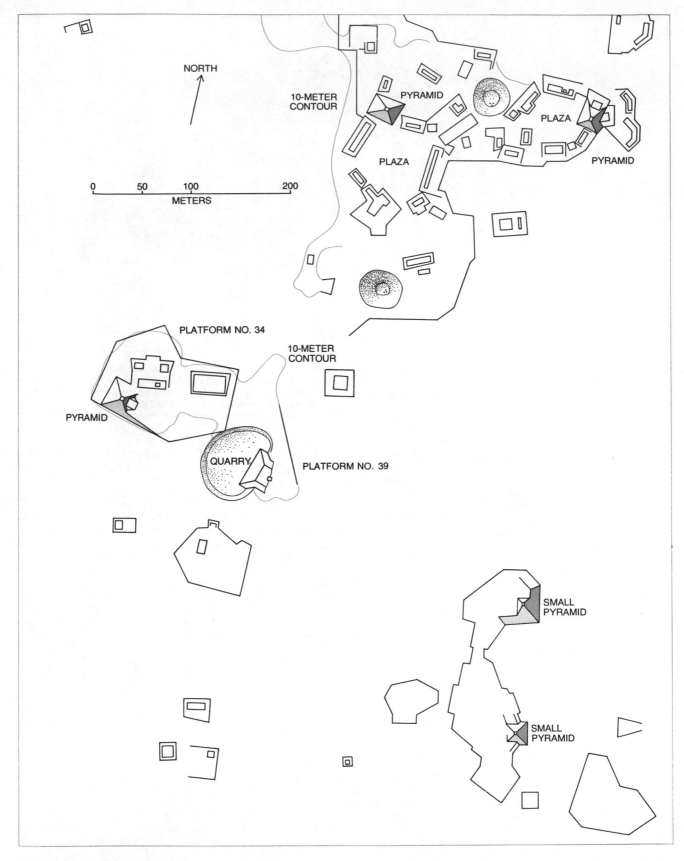

NORTH

10-METER
CONTOUR

PYRAMID

PLAZA

PLAZA

PYRAMID

PYRAMID

0   50   100   200
METERS

PLATFORM NO. 34

10-METER
CONTOUR

PYRAMID

QUARRY

PLATFORM NO. 39

SMALL
PYRAMID

SMALL
PYRAMID

NORTHERN BELIZE SITE, Cuello, is outlined in part; the plan is taken from a survey still in progress. In Classic Maya times Cuello was a minor ceremonial center, its principal focus being two adjacent plazas flanked by pyramids (top). Earlier, during the Formative period, the focus was to the south and west and included a massive platform identified by the mappers of the site as Platform No. 34. It was built in the Late Formative period, as was a second, partially destroyed platform, No. 39, situated some 180 meters to the east of No. 34. The area excavated in 1976 (color), overlapping a test trench dug during the previous season, bordered on a small pyramid on Platform No. 34 that was not added to the structure until Classic times. Age of the platforms and pyramids at lower right is not yet known.

Middle Formative period began earlier than had been supposed but also that the Swasey complex could well represent a hitherto unknown lowland Maya Early Formative period. Moreover, the Swasey upper levels were at least contemporaneous with the Olmec. Two additional dates from Cambridge, one for a Middle Formative layer of the platform and one for a Late Formative layer, reinforced our confidence in the antiquity of the transition deposit.

In November we received the carbon-14 determinations from Rainer Berger at U.C.L.A. A sample from a level immediately below the transition deposit yielded an almost identical reading; a sample from a somewhat lower level indicated a date perhaps two centuries earlier. The agreement between the findings of the two laboratories gave us confidence in the most surprising determination of all. Wood from the lowest midden uncovered in the probe of the Cuello platform, located just above bedrock, was assigned a carbon-14 date by the U.C.L.A. laboratory that ranged from 2450 to 2750 B.C. and thus had a central value equivalent to 2600 B.C. In effect one season of work at Cuello had pushed back the antiquity of the Maya by a full millennium and the prehistory of the lowlands by more than 1,600 years. Moreover, the establishment of such an early date for the possible inception of the Maya Formative period had effectively removed the Olmec civilization from further consideration as the initial stimulus of Maya culture and even suggested the possibility that Maya culture acted as an influence on the emergent Olmec society.

The great antiquity of the Swasey pottery complex had even wider implications. Up to the time of our discovery the earliest-known examples of a ceramic tradition in Mesoamerica had been pottery from two areas in Mexico west of the Maya zone: the Purrón ware of the Tehuacán valley and the Pox pottery of Puerto Marquez on the Pacific coast. Broadly speaking, the Tehuacán pottery (about 2800 B.C.) appears to be coeval with Swasey ware, and the Puerto Marquez pottery, although a good deal earlier (about 3200 B.C.), is statistically inseparable from Swasey because the dates overlap when they are extended by two standard deviations.

Stylistically, however, the Swasey ware is much more sophisticated than either the Purrón or the Pox. In contrast to their limited repertory the Swasey ware has a wide range of forms, finishes and decorations. Could these lowland products of the Early Formative period in the Maya area represent the starting point of a pottery tradition that later expanded over much of Mesoamerica?

Our single very early carbon-14 date from Cuello was clearly in urgent need of confirmation. Furthermore, the nar-

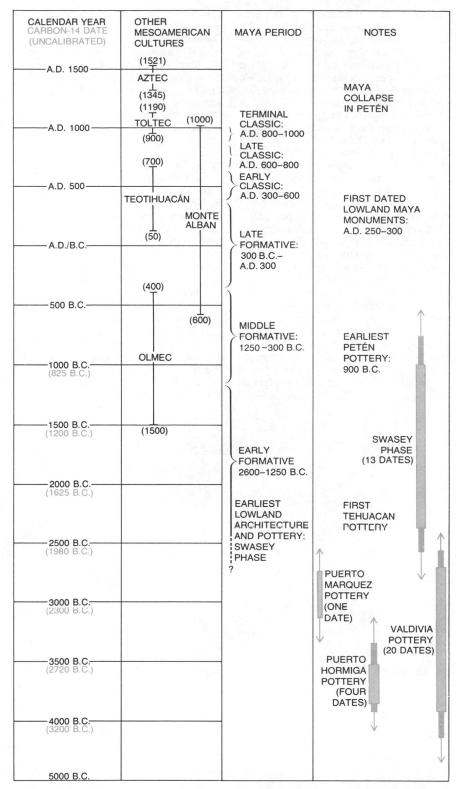

MAYA CHRONOLOGY over a span of 3,500 years is seen against the perspective of other contemporary and later Mesoamerican civilizations' rise and decline. Dates in black (*left*) show calendar years; dates in color are the equivalent carbon-14 years; these have not been calibrated to eliminate their inconsistency, which increases with samples of increasing age. The range of sample age determinations is indicated in four instances by arrows of varying thickness (*color*): for the Swasey ceramic complex at Cuello, for the Mexican Pacific site Puerto Marquez, where pottery slightly earlier than Swasey has been found, and for two South American sites with even earlier pottery. Heads of arrows show maximum ranges of dates, extended from the central carbon-14 reading by ±20 percent (two standard deviations). Wider line measures a one-deviation extension. Where several dates are known the widest line (*light color*) shows the dates' central range. The lowland Formative period was formerly thought to begin in about 900 B.C.

row shaft cut into Platform 34 had provided virtually no information about the economy or the cultural repertory of the Swasey-phase inhabitants of the site, a population that seemed to have a good claim to being the earliest Maya. We therefore decided to put in a short season of further excavations at Cuello in March and April of last year.

That excavation season was supervised by Sara Donaghey of the York Archaeological Trust, which also supplied our group with a drafter, Sheena Howarth, and a conservator, Jim Spriggs. A prime necessity was an accurate map of the site, and work on it had been undertaken in the 1975 season by Michael Walton, an English architect, and Basilio Ah, a Mopan Maya from southern Belize. The two had previously mapped the Maya ceremonial center of Lubaantún [see "The Planning of a Maya Ceremonial Center," by Norman Hammond; SCIENTIFIC AMERICAN, May, 1972]. Ah continued the mapping in 1976, working with another architect, Frederick Johnson of Honolulu. In its present state the map shows the ceremonial precinct at Cuello, surrounded by a scatter of residential compounds [see illustration on page 228]. Three massive

platforms, spaced several hundred meters apart, lie south of the later center of Cuello along a line running a little south of east. The westernmost of the three is Platform 34, which reached its present dimensions in Late Formative times. The final construction work on the central structure, Platform 39, also took place in the Late Formative period; the age of the easternmost platform has not yet been determined.

The 1976 excavation was confined to a '10-by-10-meter square on Platform 34, its four sides facing the four cardinal directions. Two quadrants of the square were excavated: a five-meter square at the northeast corner and another at the southwest corner. The western side of the southwest quadrant incorporated the 1975 shaft, so that we knew roughly what old floors and midden layers to expect at what depths in the new parts of the excavation. By digging diagonally opposed quadrants we also had the benefit of exposing continuous 10-meter vertical sections through the platform, one running from north to south and the other from east to west.

The 1975 shaft provided excellent guidance during the first two weeks of

the season, a time devoted to peeling away successive plaster floor surfaces and screening accumulations of debris. As we passed a floor at a depth of about a meter, however, we encountered two features unlike any we had unearthed in 1975. The first was a layer of rubble, burned plaster and earth, evidence that some structure or structures even older than the platform had been deliberately destroyed. The second, to the south and east of the first, was the surface of a massive rubble dump. Its rough lumps of limestone and chert filled these two sides of the excavation.

Further digging revealed that the layer of rubble, burned plaster and earth covered the remains of two structures that had stood just beyond the rubble dump. We then turned to the task of removing the one-meter layer of rubble. It soon became clear that the rubble had been used to fill up a sunken patio and that the two structures had once stood on individual platforms on the north and west sides of the patio. (We reached the limits of our grid before the south and east sides of the patio were exposed.) The plaster floor of the patio was found to be in a good state of preservation under the rubble.

EXAMPLES OF SWASEY WARES include two of the most abundant variety, Consejo Red (a, b). The pots have a cream underslip and a red surface slip. The second shallow dish (c), incised with a series of chevrons, is also representative of the Consejo group; its rim and interior are decorated with a red slip. The last two vessels are assigned to other groups of the eight within the Swasey complex. Pot d carries a "reserved" design, produced by applying a red slip over an orange underslip. The third dish (e), covered inside and out with a buff slip, has been further decorated with fine incisions that form a repeated X pattern and frame a false suspension lug. The Swasey-complex groups include 25 ceramic varieties; most of the ones seen here were reconstructed by Louise Christianson from sherd studies.

The 1975 shaft had missed both the west edge of the patio and the rubble fill by about a meter; what we had taken to be earlier floors of the great platform were in fact the interior floors of successive buildings that had stood on the west side of the patio. Further excavation made it plain that in this part of the site the construction of Platform 34 had been preceded by the deliberate razing of the buildings bordering the patio and the filling of the sunken area with rubble.

We were able to place the time of the remodeling toward the end of the Middle Formative period, about 400 B.C. The work had involved a considerable communal effort. Two facts make this clear. First, the limestone available locally at Cuello differs in texture from the limestone used to fill in the sunken patio. Second, there is no chert at all available at Cuello. The nearest source of both fill materials is at least two kilometers from the site.

Platform 34, like the other two great platforms, is obviously a ceremonial structure rather than a residential one. The communal aspect of its construction would thus also seem to involve ceremonial behavior. But what about the structures that had been burned and buried earlier? Were they temples or perhaps residences for a social elite? Or had they been some ordinary cluster of dwellings, razed to make way for the great platform? The evidently ritual nature of the demolition and covering up suggests that the razed structures had been ceremonial ones.

The more impressive of the two buildings had stood on the north side of the patio. A stairway led from the patio up to an open terrace at the front. The front wall of the building, which has been so far only partly excavated, was constructed of small, rounded limestone boulders, laid in courses and covered with a facing of plaster. The doorframe was made out of stiff, perhaps pounded, earth with a core of rubble to give it added strength. The terrace, of similar earth-and-rubble construction, was covered with plaster. Except in the staircase area the plaster finish ran down the face of the terrace and blended into the plaster floor of the patio.

As we dug down, exposing the floor of the building, we found a human burial sealed under the threshold. Such graves are not uncommonly associated with Maya structures and have come to be known as foundation burials. The skeleton was that of a young male, lying on its right side with its head pointing west. In the grave was a small, plain pottery jar and a string of beads made out of mollusk shells and jade.

The second building, on the west side of the patio, had been razed level with the patio floor. Only the outline of its entrance stairway and front wall could

be seen, and the plaster patio floor near it showed signs of intense fire. As we extended our excavation of the area we found that the west edge of the patio at the time of the razing (about 400 B.C.) had in preceding periods been shifted somewhat to the east. Preserved under the Middle Formative buildings and the patio floor were the remains of structures representing three successive periods of construction during the Swasey phase; they constitute the earliest Maya architecture known.

The most recent of the three Swasey buildings is represented by a structure with a poorly preserved floor. Its plaster surface had covered an earlier hole that had once supported the butt of a large timber upright. Remnants of the upright timber, still present in the hole, yielded a carbon-14 reading some three centuries earlier than the readings for samples from this construction period located elsewhere. This suggests that the upright had been a quite mature tree when it was cut down and set in place. On balance the carbon-14 determinations suggest a date of from 1700 to 1500 B.C. for this final Swasey construction period.

The structure was evidently a low platform; its straight east façade had been at least 10 meters long and perhaps substantially longer. At its south end it swept around to the west in a curve, and

to judge from what we can see of this feature the platform had been at least five meters wide. Where the curve begins a niche was set into the edge of the platform near the top. Indications that the plaster lining of the niche had been renewed suggest that it was used as a step by those climbing from the sunken patio to the top of the platform. A similar niche may exist at the unexcavated north end of the platform. The small size of the niche we uncovered seems also to argue for the existence of a central stair. The top of the platform had supported a timber superstructure, as was evident from a series of postholes, but no certain plan for the timber structure could be determined.

The structure that represents the next Swasey architectural phase was buried under the last one. It fronts on the same line, but its façade was curved rather than straight. A modest earth-filled platform, it was a mere 30 centimeters high. From what we can see we estimate that it was some seven meters long and four to five meters wide. It had a plaster top and a plaster facing, reinforced along its upper edge with a line of rough stones probably intended to minimize erosion. Like the platform that succeeded it, it had supported timber-framed superstructures; the evidence of the postholes indicates that two such structures had occupied the platform in succession. Both had rounded sides rather than

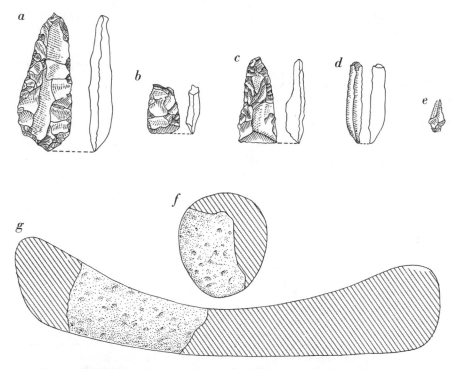

STONE IMPLEMENTS UNEARTHED AT CUELLO were made chiefly by flaking chert (*top*) or by grinding sandstone (*bottom*). The large tool (*a*) is 15 centimeters long; it is typical of the general-utility choppers of the Formative period. Next (*b, c*) are small axe-adzes that may have served for finer work. The long parallel-sided blade (*d*) is much like later Maya work in obsidian. The small point (*e*) probably was used as a drill or punch rather than as a projectile. Fragments of pinkish sandstone (*f, g*) imported from the Maya Mountains 150 kilometers away are shown in restoration here: a mano and metate, the Mesoamerican corn mill.

straight ones, and the earlier of the two was the larger one. Carbon-14 determinations from numerous samples, some contemporaneous with the platform and some from a succeeding layer, suggest a date for the platform between 2300 and 2000 B.C. Both platforms fronted a plaster-floored patio that covered essentially the same area as the Middle Formative patio had.

The oldest of the three Swasey structures came to light at the juncture of our two five-by-five-meter quadrants and had evidently been built at a time before the Early Formative pattern of constructing platforms around a patio perimeter had become established. So far we have uncovered what appears to be part of a circular platform with a three-meter radius. If our preliminary interpretation is correct, the surface area of the platform would have exceeded 28 square meters.

Like the later Swasey structures the platform was built of earth and had a plaster surface; it supported a timber superstructure and rested directly on a substrate of long-buried soil. The soil is mixed with quantities of trash and other debris of occupation apparently derived from dwelling sites that stood outside our area of excavation. Burned wood from this buried soil has yielded a carbon-14 date that falls between 2500 and 2400 B.C. This would place the date of construction of the earliest platform at Cuello substantially more than 4,000 years ago, making it the earliest example of architecture known in Mesoamerica and one of the earliest in the New World.

The three successive examples of Early Formative architecture unearthed at Cuello may be said, if we take the liberty of rounding the dates, to be roughly 4,400, 4,100 and 3,600 years old. The existence of architectural traditions typical of Classic Maya dwellings, such as plastered floors and platforms with timber-framed superstructures, in the lowlands that long ago is indicative of a developmental period for Maya culture of far greater duration than has been supposed.

Our excavations last year provided significant data on the economy of the lowland Maya during the Early Formative period. For example, we found five more human burials, all associated with the Swasey structures. One was a child four or five years old, three were adult males and the fifth was a young adult female. The biological anthropologist for the project, Frank P. Saul of the Medical College of Ohio, concludes that all four adults show abnormally advanced tooth wear, suggesting the presence of an abrasive substance in their daily diet.

The abrasive could have been either of two abrasives that are found in the diet of the Maya today. One is lime, which is in the diet because the Maya steep the kernels of maize in slaked lime before boiling them; the process softens the hard coating of the kernel and also releases certain amino acids in the maize that would otherwise be unassimilable. The other abrasive is grit derived from the stone roller (mano) and milling table (metate) that are still used today to crush the maize kernels into corn meal. Fragments of these grinding stones, which can also be used to grind seeds other than maize, have been unearthed in the earliest of the kitchen middens at Cuello. They were made out of two distinctive kinds of sandstone that were not of local origin.

For the present it is only an assumption that maize was cultivated at Cuello in the Early Formative period. We recovered a large sample of carbonized plant remains at the site, but they are still being analyzed by Barbara Pickersgill of the University of Reading and their identity is not yet known. It is possible that the lowland economy at this period included such root crops as manioc and sweet potato, but proof is unlikely to be forthcoming because identifiable remains of these plants seldom survive prolonged burial in a tropical lowland soil.

Hunting amplified the diet of the early Maya at Cuello. The bones of both the white-tailed deer (*Odocoileus virginianus*) and the agouti (*Dasyprocta* sp.), unearthed from Swasey-phase middens, have been identified by Elizabeth S. Wing of the Florida State Museum. Snails are also represented; the shells of five edible species, the swamp-dwelling *Pomacea flagellata* in particular, have been identified by Lawrence Feldman of the University of Missouri at Columbia. Between 40 and 60 percent of the snail shells were found in deposits of kitchen refuse.

Among the snails are a number of species, seldom if ever eaten, that are common to forest, freshwater and marine environments. Entirely unrepresented in the Swasey material, however, is one snail subspecies (*Neocyclotus dysoni cookei*) that is characteristic of areas that have been burned over and are rich in leaf humus. This suggests that if the Swasey-phase Maya of Cuello did cultivate maize, they did not practice milpa agriculture: planting corn in a field that is prepared by felling and burning the natural brush. Quite the opposite evidence is found in the Middle Formative phase that followed: shells of the swamp snail *Pomacea* decrease in number until they account for only 16 percent of the total, whereas the proportion of the milpa-dwelling *Neocyclotus* rises from zero to 55 percent.

Feldman interprets this change in the snail sample as evidence that the Maya of the succeeding phase were draining swampy land, thereby diminishing the area suitable for *Pomacea* and bringing the drained land under cultivation. Support for his view comes from the findings of a survey group under the direction of Alfred Siemens of the University of British Columbia and Dennis E. Puleston of the University of Minnesota. This group, working just west of us along the Rio Hondo, on the boundary between Mexico and Belize, has mapped a series of raised-field complexes. The fields were formed in riverside swamps by digging drainage canals and using the spoil from the canals to construct platforms that stand above water level. A wood post retrieved from the bank of one of the Rio Hondo canals has yielded a carbon-14 date that falls at about the end of the Swasey phase at Cuello, or about the time of the decline of the swamp snails.

What was grown on these platforms? Perhaps corn, perhaps root crops, perhaps even a "cash" crop such as cacao. Certainly the construction and maintenance of the raised-field complexes would have required some degree of communal cooperation not inconsistent with a structured society and an elite class. As for the need for a cash crop, the presence of imported materials at Cuello suggests that the early Maya there had reason to produce something with which to barter. (In later centuries the cacao bean was a widely accepted form of currency throughout Mesoamerica.)

The foundation burial on the north side of the patio under Platform 34 and two of the five earlier graves included beads of jade and shell among the burial offerings. In addition one of the Swasey graves contained a lump of hematite, the hard iron-ore pigment used in powdered form for pottery decoration and body painting. The shells and the hematite could have been obtained within the Maya lowlands and perhaps even in northern Belize, but the jade could not. The nearest known source of the distinctive green gemstone is some 350 kilometers away, in the Motagua valley on the margin of the Guatemala highlands. The presence of jade beads in these early graves is proof of the existence of an extensive exchange network in this part of Mesoamerica more than 3,500 years ago.

Other materials utilized by the Swasey-phase inhabitants of Cuello may also have been obtained through exchange, but the sources were closer. The Maya Mountains of Belize, some 150 kilometers south of Cuello, were evidently the source of the pink-hued kinds of sandstone used to make manos and metates. Richard Wilk of the University of Arizona traced the brightly colored chert the inhabitants favored as a raw material for edged tools to two nearby sources; one, a notable chert workshop at Colha. is 27 kilometers from Cuello and the other, at Richmond Hill, is seven kilometers away. The shells of marine mollusks found at the site must have been transported over a minimum distance of 50 kilometers.

The high quality of the early pottery at Cuello calls for a brief description of the Swasey ceramic inventory. All in all, the variety of vessel forms and surface finishes is considerable, and the workmanship is consistently expert. In type the pots range from rough, unslipped pieces—"earthenware" in modern terminology—to thinner-walled pieces with smooth and glossy surfaces, probably comparable in prestige value and in function to today's porcelains. As the ceramics specialist with the project, Pring has surveyed the Cuello findings from the Early Formative period through the Late Formative, and he sees in them a record of a single, continuous process of development.

The earliest entity in the sequence, the Swasey ceramic complex, can be subdivided into some 25 varieties on the basis of combinations of vessel shape and surface appearance [see illustration on page 230]. The commonest are plain, smooth-slipped red bowls: Ramgoat Red and Consejo Red. Ramgoat Red bowls, the earlier of the two varieties, have only a single layer of red slip on their surface. The Consejo Red bowls, which gradually replace the Ramgoat

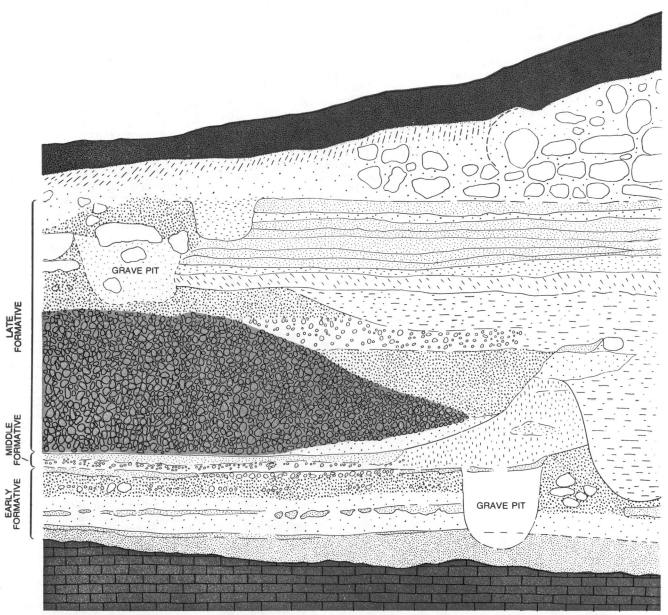

LATE FORMATIVE

MIDDLE FORMATIVE

EARLY FORMATIVE

GRAVE PIT

GRAVE PIT

CROSS SECTION of the southwestern five-meter square excavated at Cuello shows the southern exposure of successive strata, from a layer of soil (*color, top*) that accumulated after the site was deserted in about A.D. 900 to bedrock (*color, bottom*) some five meters below the surface. Rock-filled area at right, just below the soil, is the stair platform of the Classic-period pyramid that was built on top of a platform of the Late Formative period in about A.D. 600; the stippled layers under the Classic pyramid represent the successive renewals of the plaster floors that formed the surface of the Late Formative platform. A wood sample from the third of these floors yielded a carbon-14 date equivalent to 200 B.C. The massive rubble fill (*light color, left*), which was not exposed by a 1975 test trench, rests on the plaster floor of a patio built in Middle Formative times. This floor and the one under it end abruptly at the right, evidence that structures facing the patio were razed in about 425 B.C. to clear the way for the Late Formative construction. Samples of wood from the stratum between the two floors date to about 800 B.C. The lowest plaster floor of all, covering an ancient soil that rests on bedrock, is 4,500 years old.

Red as the commonest ceramics, have a cream-colored underslip under the red surface, which gives them a glossier, lighter and more consistent tone.

Other notable Swasey-complex varieties include vessels with two-tone surfaces—red on cream, black on red and red on orange—and vessels with surface colors other than red: cream, black, orange, brown and buff. Still others have incised surface decorations: bold chevrons or multiple incisions forming an X pattern. A few have animal heads modeled in the round on the rim or on the wall; so far Pring has recognized a frog or toad, a monkey and a turtle.

One particularly striking type of vessel is a long-necked bottle with burnished decorations on an unslipped gray surface. None of the bottles found at Cuello are intact, but the overall character of the material is quite similar to that of ceramics found at Mani in northern Yucatán in 1942 by the late George Brainerd. That was in the days before carbon-14 dating, but Brainerd nonetheless assigned the pottery to the period of about 1500 B.C. His accuracy must be accounted an inspired guess.

The overall impression conveyed by the Swasey ceramic complex is one of liveliness and variety in both color and decoration. The vessels are indisputably the product of a mature technology rather than an emerging one. Yet these are the earliest ceramics from the Maya lowlands and among the earliest in all Mesoamerica. Where did this technology evolve?

The earliest Swasey-phase remains known are some 4,500 years old. Any answer to the pottery puzzle must therefore be sought in areas where ceramics were known before that time. One possible answer is that the precursor or precursors of the Swasey ceramic complex are to be found in the Maya lowlands, perhaps at Cuello itself or perhaps at other equally early sites. In addition to being uncovered at Mani, well to the north, Swasey-complex pottery has been found at four adjacent sites in Belize: Nohmul, El Pozito, Santa Rita and San Estevan. A few sherds have also come from Becan, a site located almost in the center of the Yucatán peninsula. At none of these other sites has the age of the Swasey-complex pottery been established by carbon-14 dating. A recent carbon-14 date, however, is available from the central Belize site of Barton Ramie, more than 100 kilometers south of Cuello. The date is about 1500 B.C., which falls within the range of the Swasey carbon-14 dates at Cuello. If one also accepts the probability that the earliest Maya occupation of Mani, some 270 kilometers northeast of Cuello, was contemporary with the earliest-known Swasey phase, then a swath of the lowlands some 400 kilometers in length from north to south (from Mani to Barton Ramie), would seem to have been settled by the Maya of the Formative period, no matter how sparsely, at least 600 years earlier than was formerly believed.

What are the prospects that further work at Cuello will uncover still earlier horizons of occupation? Three carbon-14 determinations made at U.C.L.A. late last year provide an ambiguous hint. Samples of burned wood, from layers at the site that have already yielded a sequence of carbon-14 dates firmly linked to the Cuello stratigraphic succession, give considerably earlier readings. The ages of the samples range from early in the fourth millennium B.C. to the middle of the millennium, or from about 6,000 to 5,500 years ago. It is clear from the archaeological context that the much older wood was trash, swept up for construction fill more than a millennium after it had been burned. The fire that burned the wood could have been either a forest fire due to natural causes or the result of human activity in the Cuello area. We calculate the chance that the site was occupied more than 4,750 years ago at about 50–50.

There are alternatives to the possibility of an early evolution of Mesoamerican ceramics centered in the Maya lowlands. One is that ceramics are known to have been made in central and Pacific-coast Mexico and even in the southeastern U.S. some 4,500 years ago. None of the ceramics from these areas, however, have either the variety or the sheer panache of the Swasey ceramic complex.

Pottery 4,500 years old is also known from Monagrillo in Panama, and in northwestern South America pottery has been unearthed that is at least 6,000 years old. The principal South American sites are Puerto Hormiga on the coast of Colombia and Valdivia in southern Ecuador, but it seems likely that during the millennium before the oldest examples of the Swasey ceramic complex first appeared pottery was being made in South America all the way from the Gulf of Guayaquil to the Gulf of Venezuela, both along the coast and in the highlands of the Andes. As for possible relations between this early New World ceramic focus and Mesoamerica, Donald Lathrap of the University of Illinois maintains that there are close resemblances between 4,500-year-old pottery from Real Alto, a site in southern Ecuador that he excavated recently, and the Swasey-complex pottery from Cuello.

For the moment it seems prudent to leave the question open. The origins of Maya pottery may have been local or they may have been exotic. If it was the latter, then a South American stimulus seems more likely than any other now in evidence. What can be said unequivocally is that in the Swasey phase at Cuello we see not only in the pottery but also in the architecture and in the use of stone artifacts the beginning of the cultural tradition that is known as Classic Maya nearly 3,000 years later. Where its creators came from, and when, are questions we hope one day to answer.

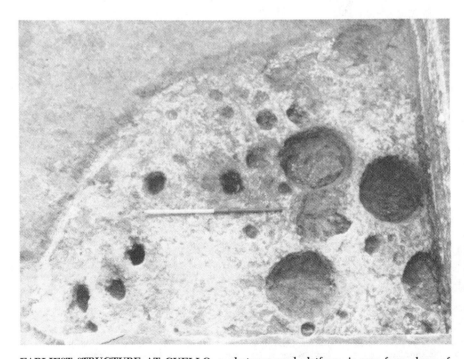

EARLIEST STRUCTURE AT CUELLO, a plaster-covered platform, is seen from above after partial excavation. It was constructed some 4,500 years ago. Its curved edge suggests that the platform was circular in overall shape; two possible reconstructions of the timber structure that stood on it are shown on page 128. The postholes in the plaster surface offer little guidance on the shape of the structure. Large holes are ovens dug into the platform at a slightly later date.

17

The Hopewell Cult

by Olaf H. Prufer
December 1964

A 1,500-year-old rubbish heap unearthed in southern Ohio holds the answers to some key questions about the ancient Indians who lived there and built huge funeral mounds filled with offerings

As Europeans explored North America, they found that many of the continent's river valleys were dotted with ancient earthworks. Scattered from western New York to North Dakota and south to Louisiana and the Florida Keys were uncounted thousands of burial mounds, temple mounds, hilltop ramparts surrounded by ditches, and earthen walls enclosing scores of acres. Some Colonial scholars were so impressed by these works that they thought they must have been built by an unknown civilized people that had been exterminated by the savage Indians. In due course it became clear that the earthworks had been put up by the Indians' own ancestors, and that they belonged not to one culture but to a series of separate cultural traditions spanning a period of 3,000 years.

Perhaps the most striking assemblage of these works is located in southern Ohio in the valleys of the Muskingum, Scioto and Miami rivers. It consists of clusters of large mounds surrounded by earthworks laid out in elaborate geometric patterns. As early as 1786 one such group of mounds at the confluence of the Muskingum and the Ohio (the present site of Marietta, Ohio) was excavated; it was found to be rich in graves and mortuary offerings. It was not until the 1890's, however, that the contents of the Ohio mounds attracted public attention. At that time many of them were excavated to provide an anthropological exhibit for the Chicago world's fair of 1893. One of the richest sites was on the farm of M. C. Hopewell, and the name Hopewell has been assigned to this particular type of mortuary complex ever since.

More recent excavations have shown that the Hopewell complex extends far beyond southern Ohio. Hopewell re-

mains are found in Michigan and Wisconsin and throughout the Mississippi valley; there are Hopewell sites in Illinois that are probably older than any in Ohio. Typical Hopewell artifacts have been unearthed as far west as Minnesota and as far south as Florida. The mounds of southern Ohio are nonetheless the most numerous and the richest in mortuary offerings.

Thanks to carbon-14 dating it is known that the Hopewell complex first materialized in southern Ohio about 100 B.C. and that the last elaborate valley earthwork was constructed about A.D. 550. Until recently, however, there were other questions to which only conjectural answers could be given. Among them were the following: In what kinds of settlements did the people of southern Ohio live during this period? Where were their habitations located? On what foundation did their economy rest? Answers to these questions can now be given, but first it is necessary to say exactly what the Hopewell complex is.

What is known about the Hopewell complex of Ohio has been learned almost exclusively from the nature and contents of burial mounds. In many places these structures are found in groups enclosed by earthworks linked in a pattern of squares, circles, octagons and parallel lines [*see top illustration on page 242*]. The dimensions of some of the enclosures are immense: the largest known Hopewell earthworks in Ohio—the Newark Works in Licking County—covered four square miles. Many of the burial mounds are also large: the central mounds on the Hopewell farm and at the Seip and Harness sites, all of which are in Ross County, range from 160 to 470 feet in length and from 20 to 32 feet in height. Within the mounds are

the remains of numerous human bodies, some of them alone and some in groups. If the bodies were simply interred, they rest on earthen platforms surrounded by log cribs; if they were cremated, the bones are found in shallow basins of baked earth.

The sequence of events in the construction of a major mound seems to have been as follows. Bare ground was first covered with a layer of sand; then a large wooden structure was raised on this prepared floor. Some of the structures were so extensive that it is doubtful that they had roofs; they were probably stockades open to the sky. Individual graves were prepared inside these enclosures; in many cases the burials were covered with low mounds of earth. When the enclosure was filled with graves, the wooden structure was set afire and burned to the ground. Then the entire burial area was covered with layer on layer of earth and stone, forming the final large mound.

The quantity and quality of the grave goods accompanying the burials indicate that the people of the period devoted a great deal of time and effort to making these articles. A marked preference for exotic raw materials is evident. Mica, frequently cut into geometric or animate shapes, was imported from the mountains of Virginia, North Carolina and Alabama [*see illustration on page 236*]. Conch shells, used as ceremonial cups, came from the Gulf

SILHOUETTED HAND made from a sheet of mica (*following page*) is typical of the elaborate grave offerings found at the Hopewell site near Chillicothe, Ohio. Human, animal and geometric figures of mica are characteristic Hopewell funerary goods; they are particularly abundant in southern Ohio.

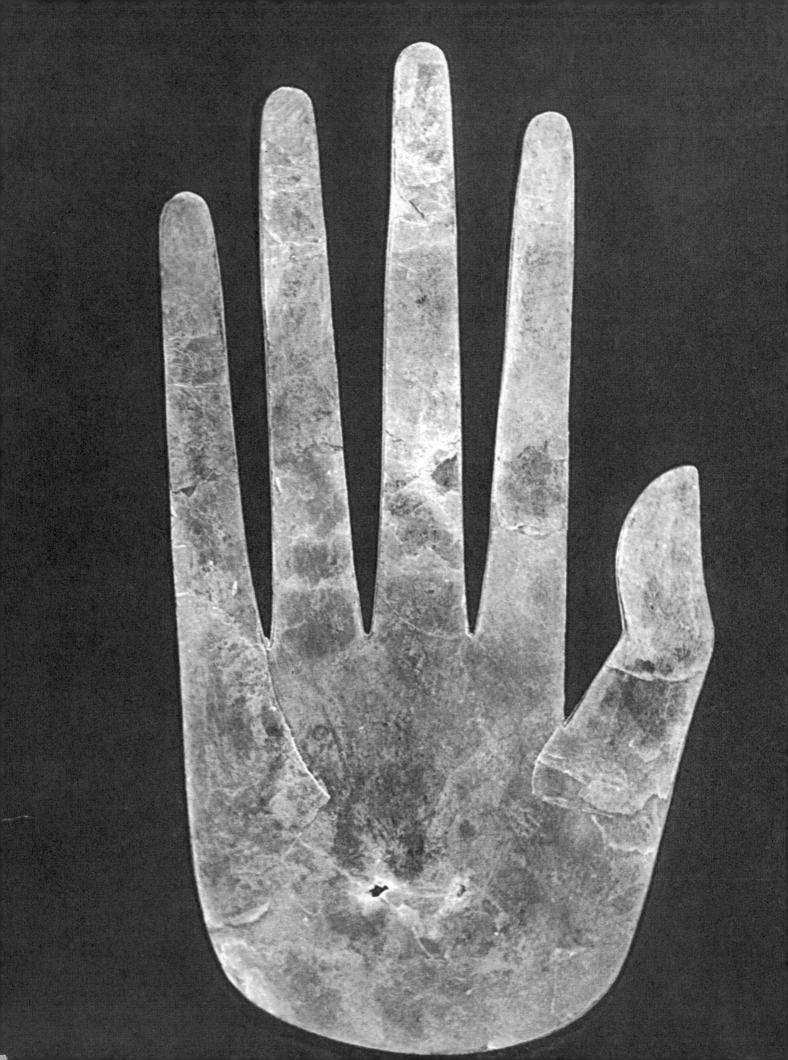

Coast. Obsidian, exquisitely flaked into large ritual knives, was obtained either from what is now the U.S. Southwest or from the Yellowstone region of the Rocky Mountains. The canine teeth of grizzly bears, frequently inlaid with freshwater pearls, may also have been imported from the Rockies. Copper, artfully hammered into heavy ax blades and into ornaments such as ear spools, breastplates and geometric or animate silhouettes, was obtained from the upper Great Lakes.

Even in their choice of local raw materials the Hopewell craftsmen of Ohio favored the precious and the unusual. Much of their work in stone utilized the colorful varieties of flint available in the Flint Ridge deposits of Licking County. The freshwater pearls came from the shellfish of local rivers, and they were literally heaped into some of the burials. The tombs of the Hopewell site contained an estimated 100,000 pearls; a single deposit at the Turner site in Hamilton County has yielded more than 48,000.

Other typical Hopewell grave furnishings are "platform" pipes [*see lower illustration on page 240*], elaborately engraved bones of animals and men, clay figurines and highly distinctive kinds of decorated pottery. Projectile points of flint show characteristic forms; the flint-workers also struck delicate parallel-sided blades from prepared "cores."

For the most part these characteristic objects of the Hopewell complex are the same wherever they are found. In spite of this fact the Hopewell complex cannot be classed as a "culture" in the anthropological sense of the word, that is, as a distinct society together with its attendant material and spiritual manifestations. On the contrary, the Hopewell complex was only one segment of the cultural totality in each area where it is encountered. A reconstruction of life in eastern North America from 500 B.C. to A.D. 900 reveals the existence of distinct cultural traditions in separate regions, each rooted in its own past. During the Hopewell phase each of these regional traditions was independently influenced by the new and dynamic religious complex. The new funeral customs did not, however, take the place of the local culture; they were simply grafted onto it. Although the word "cult" has some unfortunate connotations in common usage, it is more appropriate to speak of a Hopewell cult than of a Hopewell culture.

The exact religious concepts that

EARTHWORKS characteristic of the burial cult are found throughout eastern North America. Major Hopewell centers, from the Gulf Coast to the Great Lakes, are named on the map.

SOUTHERN OHIO is the locale of the most abundant and richest Hopewell sites. The majority are found along the Miami, Scioto and Muskingum rivers and range in date from 100 B.C. to A.D. 550. After that no more lowland centers were built; instead hilltops were fortified (*colored dots locate three major examples*). The McGraw site was excavated by the author.

238

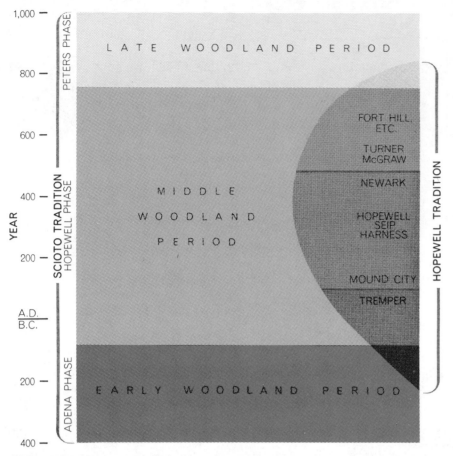

SEQUENCE OF CULTURES in southern Ohio during the rise and decline of the Hopewell funeral complex indicates that a local tradition of Woodland culture, called Scioto, was present in the area before the Hopewell cult appeared and continued both during and after it. The earliest of the Woodland culture periods began about 1200 B.C. in southern Ohio.

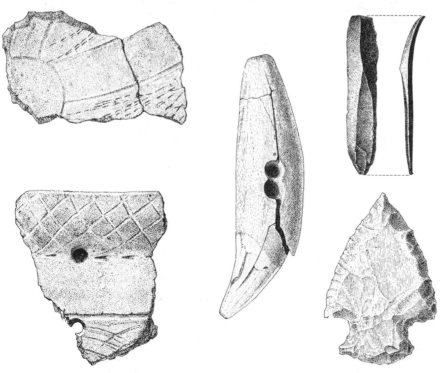

IDENTITY OF FARMSTEAD discovered at the McGraw site as the residence of Indians who participated in the burial cult is proved by the presence of characteristic Hopewell tools and ceremonial objects. The fine, parallel-sided flint blade is typically Hopewell, as is the "Snyders" projectile point. The bear canine and the pottery are standard burial finds.

permitted the successful diffusion of the Hopewell cult necessarily remain unknown. Curiously enough, however, the cult's consumption of exotic materials for grave goods may have provided a mechanism for its diffusion. Procurement of raw materials entailed an exchange system of almost continental proportions; many widely separated areas in North America must have been brought into contact as their natural resources were tapped by practitioners of the Hopewell rites.

Students of the Hopewell remains in southern Ohio have been disturbed for more than a century by the lack of evidence for any habitation sites linked to the great funerary centers. In other Hopewell areas, notably Illinois, large villages are clearly associated with the local ceremonial sites. Years of patient fieldwork in Ohio had failed to produce anything that could legitimately be called a settlement. The extensive enclosures and their associated clusters of burial mounds contain no evidence of habitation to speak of. The little that has been found seems to mark brief squatters' tenancies, probably associated with the construction of the final mounds or with ceremonies that may have been performed from time to time. Clearly the nature of Hopewell society and its settlement patterns in Ohio were markedly different from those in Illinois.

Still another puzzle was the fact that remains of corn have been found at only two Ohio Hopewell sites—Harness and Turner—and in both cases under doubtful circumstances. It was therefore supposed that the Hopewell phase in Ohio was one of simple hunting and collecting and no agriculture. Whether because of this supposition or because earlier investigators were looking for sizable villages, most of the search for Hopewell habitation sites has been confined to regions near the ceremonial centers, leaving the rich bottomlands along the rivers largely unexplored.

While reflecting on all these factors in 1962 I was struck by a possible parallel between the Ohio Hopewell sites and the classic ceremonial sites of certain areas in Middle America, where the religious center remained vacant except on ritual occasions and the population lived in scattered hamlets surrounding the center. To apply such an assumption to the Ohio Hopewell complex meant granting the people agriculture; it meant, furthermore, that the bottomlands were the very zones in which to look for small farming communities. Survey work along the floodplain of the middle and lower Scioto River during the past two years has amply demonstrated the validity of this assumption. Our survey teams from the Case Institute of Technology have turned up 37 small sites—the largest of them little more than 100 feet in diameter—marked by thinly scattered objects on the surface. These objects include sherds of cord-marked pottery, chips of flint, fragments of shell and bone and, most important, the fine, parallel-edged bladelets that are among the characteristic artifacts of the Hopewell complex.

It is certain that many such habitation sites are now lost forever under the accumulated silt of river floodplains and that others have been destroyed by river meandering. A perfect example of flood burial in the making is provided by the McGraw site, which is located on bottomland near an ancient meander of the Scioto River two miles south of Chillicothe. Alva McGraw, the owner of the land, brought the site to our attention in 1962. Surface indications were scanty; over an area 10 feet square we found only a few potsherds, some shell fragments, bits of flint and fire-cracked rocks. The site was on a nearly imperceptible rise of land, the remnant of a knoll that had been almost covered by river silts.

Under ordinary circumstances no archaeologist would have been attracted by such an impoverished find. It happened, however, that this site and similar ones on the McGraw farm were soon to be destroyed by road construction. We therefore decided without much enthusiasm to sound the area with a modest trench. Where the trench cut into the ancient knoll we found no remains at depths lower than the plow zone: eight inches below the surface. But where the trench extended beyond the knoll, proceeding down its slope to the adjacent silt-covered low ground, we struck a dense deposit of residential debris, evidently the refuse heap of an ancient farmstead.

This deposit, a foot thick and 95 by 140 feet in extent, was packed with material. There were more than 10,000 pottery fragments, some 6,000 animal bones, nearly 2,000 identifiable mollusk shells, abundant remains of wild plants and both an ear and individual kernels of corn. In fact, this single rubbish heap contained enough material to answer the questions posed at the beginning of this article.

First, in spite of the pattern of organized village life associated with the Hopewell cult 400 miles to the west in Illinois, the people of southern Ohio lived in small, scattered farm dwellings. This does not mean that the population was sparse; indeed, the size and complexity of the ceremonial earthworks in Ohio imply ample manpower. The significant fact is that the two groups shared a religion but lived quite different secular lives. In seeking parallels for this phenomenon one turns to the early, expansionist days of Christianity or of Islam, when a religion was shared by peoples with sharply contrasting cultures.

Second, the Ohio Hopewell people built their dwellings not near ceremonial centers but on the floodplains of the

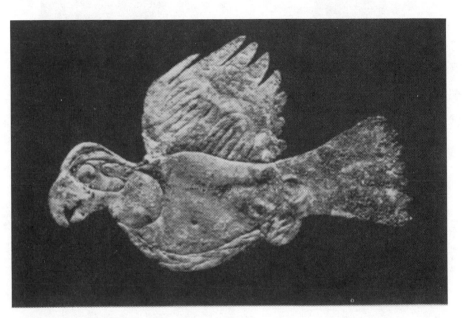

BIRD EFFIGY from Mound City combines cutout and repoussé techniques in copper work. The metal was imported from outcroppings at Isle Royale in Lake Superior. Hopewell funeral offerings of copper include rings, ear spools, breastplates and headdresses, many geometric forms, copper-plated wooden objects and large ax blades, evidently cold-forged.

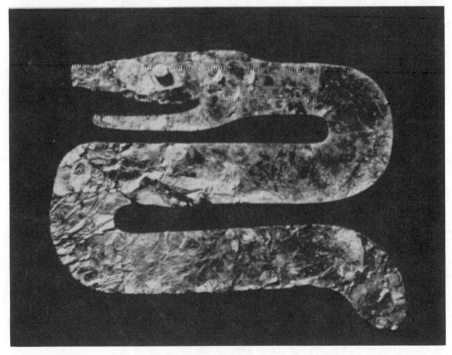

SNAKE EFFIGY from the Turner site is a foot-wide mica silhouette cut from a sheet imported from Virginia or North Carolina. Some Ohio burials were literally blanketed by mica.

HUMAN FIGURES representing a kneeling man and a standing woman are modeled in terra-cotta. Unearthed at the Turner site, they were ritually broken, or "killed," before burial.

PLATFORM PIPE from the Mound City site has a bowl carved to represent a toad. Pipes showing birds, fishes, mammals and human figures were also made for Hopewell burials.

nuts, walnuts and acorns. Other wild plants that have been identified are the hackberry and the wild plum. Apparently corn was the only plant the people cultivated, but the remains make it clear that their knowledge of corn-raising had not been recently acquired. The charred ear of corn from the McGraw site, still bearing a number of kernels, is of a 12-row variety. It appears to be of a type intermediate between the northern flint corn grown in Ohio in late pre-European times and the ancient flint corns and popcorns known from elsewhere in the Western Hemisphere. One of the isolated kernels from the deposit has been identified as belonging to an eight-row or 10-row variety of corn; it possibly represents a full-fledged, although small, member of the northern flint type. These relatively advanced types of corn imply a long period of agricultural activity before the site was first occupied.

The date of the McGraw site's occupation can be estimated both from the style of its artifacts and from carbon-14 determinations; it is roughly A.D. 450. The bulk of the artifacts could have come from any pre-Hopewell site in Ohio; for example, less than 4 percent of the pottery fragments found in the deposit are characteristic of the Hopewell complex. This reinforces the point made earlier: Whenever the influences of the Hopewell cult appear, they are imposed on an already existing culture that for the most part continues in its own ways.

The McGraw site is nevertheless clearly identified as belonging to the Hopewell complex not only by the few Hopewell potsherds but also by other characteristic Hopewell artifacts. Parallel-sided flint bladelets were found in large numbers, and the bulk of the projectile points were of the classic Hopewell type known as "Snyders," after the site of that name in Illinois. The inhabitants of the McGraw farmstead evidently included craftsmen engaged in the production of grave goods for the Hopewell cult: cut and uncut mica was found in abundance. One bear tooth turned up in the midden, with typical countersunk perforations but without any inlay of pearls. There were also two ornaments made of slate that, like the bear-tooth ornament, were unfinished. Perhaps all these objects were discards; this would help to explain their presence in a refuse heap.

The McGraw site therefore casts considerable light on life in southern Ohio

rivers, presumably because the bottomland was most suitable for agriculture. As for their economy in general, they raised corn, but a substantial part of their food came from hunting, fishing and collecting. Analysis of the animal bones in the McGraw deposit shows that the commonest source of meat was the white-tailed deer. Other game animals that have been identified in the deposit

are the cottontail rabbit and the turkey. River produce was of equal or perhaps greater importance for the larder; we found the bones and shells of a variety of turtles, the bones of nine species of fish and the shells of 25 species of mollusk.

Among the wild-plant foods these people collected were nuts: the deposit contained charred remains of hickory

CEREMONIAL BLADES unearthed at the Hopewell site are of obsidian, probably from the Yellowstone area of the Rocky Mountains. The largest (*center*) is 13 inches in length.

In southern Ohio the people of the Early Woodland period were mound builders long before the Hopewell cult arose. They belonged to the Adena culture (which takes its name from a mound site near Chillicothe). The remains of the Adena people show that they were roundheaded rather than longheaded. They lived without contact with the Hopewell cult until about 100 B.C.; at that time, according to carbon-14 determinations, the Tremper mound of Scioto County was raised. This mound contained some 300 crematory burials. Many of the grave offerings are typical of the Adena culture, but some of them show Hopewell influences.

As skulls from later burials indicate, the arrival of the Hopewell cult in Ohio (presumably from Illinois) was accompanied by the arrival of a new population; these people were longheaded rather than roundheaded. How many immigrants arrived is an open question. The total number of individuals found in Ohio Hopewell mounds—an estimated 1,000—can represent only a fraction of the population of this region during the Middle Woodland period. It seems probable that most of the local inhabitants were the roundheaded Adena folk, many of whom may well have continued to live typical Adena lives untroubled by the neighboring Hopewell cultists. The fact that numerous Adena mounds continued to be built during Hopewell times is strong evidence for this.

To judge from their production of Hopewell ceremonial objects, the residents of the McGraw site would not have been undisturbed Adena folk. It is equally unlikely that they were immigrants from Illinois. It seems more probable that the immigrants were a privileged minority who in some way had come to dominate some of Ohio's Adena people, among whom were the farmers of the McGraw site.

during the latter days of the Hopewell phase. Skilled hunters and food-collectors, gifted artisans in a wide range of materials, the people who manufactured the rich grave goods for the ritual burials lived in small scattered farmsteads on the river bottoms.

But were the people who made the grave goods the same as those who were buried in the great Hopewell mounds? Curiously this appears to be unlikely, at least in southern Ohio. To explain why, it is necessary to sketch what is known about the rise and decline of the Hopewell complex against

the general background of the various prehistoric cultures in eastern North America.

Of the four successive major culture stages in this part of the New World—Paleo-Indian, Archaic, Woodland and Mississippian—only the third is involved here. In southern Ohio the Woodland stage begins about 1200 B.C. and ends shortly before the arrival of the Europeans. In the entire eastern part of North America, southern Ohio included, the Woodland stage is divided into Early, Middle and Late periods.

Why did the Hopewell complex ultimately disappear? It may be that one part of the answer is plain to see. From their first arrival in southern Ohio until A.D. 550 these cultists evidently not only felt secure in themselves but also appear to have taken no steps to guard from raiders the treasures buried with their dead. After that time, however, no more ceremonial centers were built in open valleys. Instead it seems that every inaccessible hilltop in southern Ohio was suddenly crowned by earthworks that appear to have served a defensive function.

This does not mean that such sites as

MYTHICAL BEAST with four horns and feet with five talons decorates the surface of a narrow stone object 10 inches long. It was found at the Turner site. Its purpose is unknown.

OCTAGON AND CIRCLE in this aerial photograph are a portion of the earthworks marking the most extensive known Hopewell construction: the site at Newark, Ohio. Most of the four-square-mile array (*see original plan below*) has now been obliterated by modern building. Only these figures (now part of a golf course) and another circle (used for years as a fairground) have been preserved.

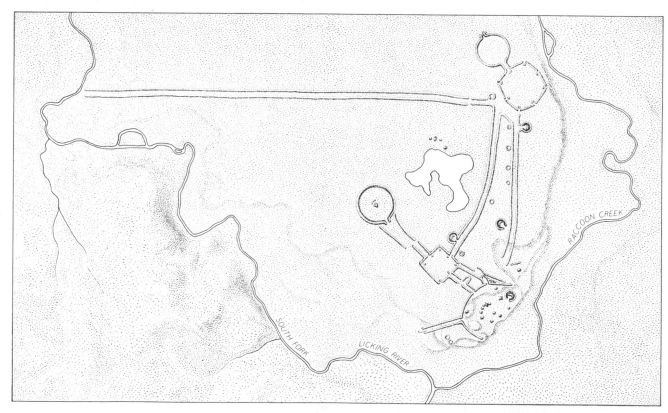

LONG AVENUES bounded by parallel earthen walls constitute the major parts of the Newark site. When first surveyed, the longest parallels (*top*) extended from the paired figures shown in the photograph at top of page to the Licking River, two and a half miles distant. Both circles are quite precise: the fairground circle (*center*) diverges at most 13 feet from a mean diameter of 1,175 feet, and the golf course circle only 4.5 feet from a mean diameter of 1,045 feet. The Newark site has never been systematically excavated.

Fort Hill, Fort Ancient and Fort Miami were permanently inhabited strongholds. Quite the contrary; at Fort Hill, for example, a survey of the land surrounding the foot of the hill has revealed several small farmsteads resembling the McGraw site. It is probable that the hilltop earthworks were places of refuge that were occupied only in time of danger. That there were such times is demonstrated by the evidence of fires and massacres at the Fort Hill, Fort Ancient and Fort Miami sites.

What was the nature of the danger? As yet there is no answer, but it is interesting to note that at about this same time the Indian population in more northerly areas first began to protect their villages with stockades. Unrest of some kind appears to have been afoot throughout eastern North America.

This being the case, it is not hard to envision the doom of the Hopewell cult. Whatever its basic religious tenets, the tangible elements of the ceremony were the celebrated grave goods, and the most notable of the goods were produced from imported raw materials. The grave goods were of course cherished for their part in the religious scheme; could the scheme itself be kept alive when the goods were no longer available? I suggest that the Hopewell cult could survive only as long as its trade network remained intact and, further, that the postulated current of unrest in eastern North America during the seventh and eighth centuries A.D. was sufficient to disrupt that network.

Whether or not this caused the collapse of the Hopewell cult, there is no question that it did collapse. By the beginning of the Late Woodland period, about A.D. 750, elaborate burial mounds containing rich funeral offerings were no longer built. For the very reason that Hopewell was only a cult and not an entire culture, however, the distinctive local traditions that had participated in the Hopewell ceremonies now reasserted themselves.

In Ohio this regional tradition is named Scioto [see top illustration on page 238]. Because of the alien nature of the Hopewell ceremonial complex, the phase of the Scioto tradition—called Hopewell—during which the funeral centers were built has a dual status. In terms of chronology the Hopewell phase was only one subdivision of the Scioto tradition. At the same time the Hopewell religious cult must be granted the status of a full-fledged tradition in its own right.

A Pre-Columbian Urban Center on the Mississippi

by Melvin L. Fowler
August 1975

*About A.D. 1000 there arose in the area north and south
of what is now St. Louis the most populous Indian
settlements north of Mexico. Foremost among them
was Cahokia, which included some 120 mounds*

One of the largest earthworks built by ancient man anywhere in the world rises in the U.S. Middle West not far from where the Illinois and Missouri rivers join the Mississippi. Relatively few people other than prehistorians are aware of this colossal monument, and even prehistorians have only recently learned that it marks the center of a 125-square-mile area that contained the most populous pre-Columbian settlements in the New World north of Mexico. Today the area, which includes a floodplain, alluvial terraces and low bluffs along the east bank of the Mississippi north and south of St. Louis, is called American Bottoms. The huge earthwork at its center, a few miles east-northeast of East St. Louis, Ill., is known as Monks Mound. The aggregation of some 120 lesser earthworks that surround it is called Cahokia: the name of an Indian group living in the area at the time of the French colonization early in the 18th century.

Monks Mound, which got its name from a short-lived Trappist settlement, is still an impressive affair [*see illustration on page 253*]. Its base, which rises from a plain lying 417 feet above sea level, measures 1,000 feet from north to south and more than 700 feet from east to west, covering an area of about 15 acres. Its volume is estimated to be 22 million cubic feet; in North America only the Pyramid of the Sun at Teotihuacán and the great pyramid at Cholula are larger. It rises in four steps to a maximum height of 100 feet above the plain. The first terrace, occupying about a fourth of the surface area at that level, is 40 feet high. Three lobelike protrusions in the northwest quadrant of the mound collectively form the second ter-

race, which is some 62 feet high. The third and fourth terraces occupy the northeast quadrant; the fourth terrace, at an elevation of 100 feet, is three feet higher than the third.

For all its impressiveness, Monks Mound is only a part of the even more impressive Cahokia group, and Cahokia in turn is only one, albeit the largest, of 10 large and small population centers and 50-odd farming villages that flourished in American Bottoms about the start of the second millennium (A.D. 1000).

How did these North American population centers arise? The best answer at present is that a complex feedback interaction involving population growth and an advance in agricultural productivity was responsible. Sometime late in the eighth century, it appears, the hoe re-

placed the digging stick in maize agriculture and a variety of maize became available that was better suited to the climate of the Middle West than the southern varieties that had been grown there up to that time.

Archaeologists, both amateur and professional, have worked in American Bottoms for a century, and in recent decades some of the sites that lacked official protection have been partially excavated before local construction destroyed them. Since 1950 at Cahokia alone individual or joint efforts by five universities and at least two museums have resulted in soundings and excavations at a score of localities. Yet only two or three of the 120 Cahokia mounds have been adequately excavated. Meanwhile the mounds that marked prehistoric popula-

CLOSE-UP OF MONKS MOUND, looking to the northwest, gives a sense of its dimensions: 1,000 feet at the base from north to south, more than 700 feet from east to west and 100 feet above the plain at the highest point. The mound is the largest pre-Columbian structure in the New World north of Mexico; it was built in successive stages between A.D. 900 and 1250.

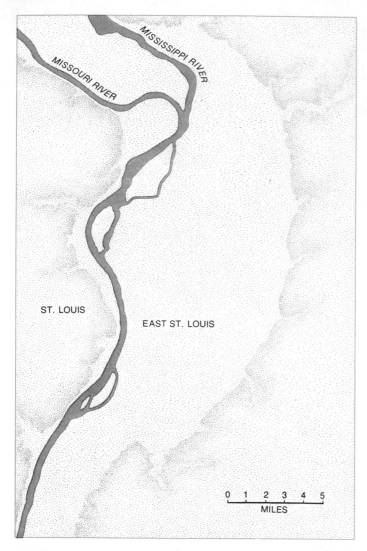

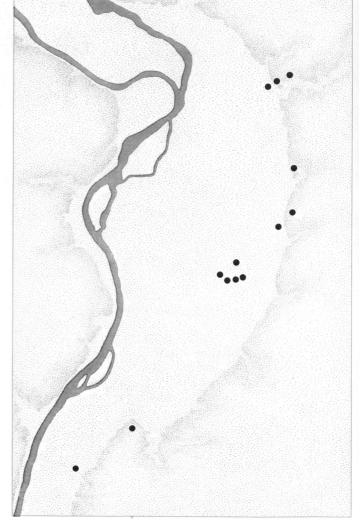

LINE OF BLUFFS (*left*) on both sides of a low floodplain outlines the American Bottoms region at and below the confluence of the Mississippi and Missouri rivers. The river channels shown are the present ones; the numerous lakes, creeks and sloughs occupying much of the bottomland have been omitted. About A.D. 800 (*right*) there were at least 13 Late Woodland habitation sites (*black dots*) in the region. Eight have been recognized on or near the upland bluffs; five, including one where Monks Mound would later rise, have so far been located in the richer bottomland. Farm productivity increased in American Bottoms soon thereafter.

tion centers of equal interest in St. Louis and East St. Louis have been obliterated by urban expansion. Nevertheless, it is possible, thanks to the work of recent years, to trace the evolution of the pre-Columbian settlements in American Bottoms with some degree of confidence.

The sophisticated kind of social and economic organization that is reflected by the construction of earthworks in American Bottoms was not the first to arise in the region. For several hundred years before that people belonging to a widespread culture, known as the Hopewell culture after a site in Ohio, had undertaken the construction of scores of earth enclosures, effigy mounds and other earthworks all through the Middle West. Another feature of the Hopewell culture was a widespread trade in exotic materials from as far away as the Rocky Mountains. Hopewell was a flowering of

what is called the Middle Woodland period in this part of America. After A.D. 500, however, this cultural integration of a large area came to an end. The farming hamlets that thrived in the vicinity of American Bottoms about A.D. 800 were representative of the subsequent Late Woodland period.

The initial phase of the settlement at American Bottoms that led to the rise of Cahokia extended from A.D. 600 to 800. It is called the Patrick phase after A. J. R. Patrick, a physician of Belleville, Ill., who was a pioneer investigator of Cahokia in the latter half of the 19th century. Archaeologists from the University of Illinois at Urbana have excavated Patrick-phase pit deposits at a site at the western extremity of the Cahokia settlement, and our group from the University of Wisconsin at Milwaukee found

Patrick-phase materials in the bottom occupation levels we uncovered below the eastern margin of Monks Mound. Other Patrick-phase remains have been found outside the Cahokia area.

The people of the Patrick phase appear to have been newcomers to American Bottoms, perhaps attracted there from the more typical river-bluff and upland farms by the fertile sandy loams that form the natural terraces and levees of the river valley. The information now available about the Patrick phase and an unnamed century-long phase that followed it is largely obtained from the analysis of pottery fragments gathered by surface collecting and the excavation of refuse heaps. Patrick-phase house sites indicate that residences at this time were rectangular and that the house posts were set in pits. There is little evidence of mound building between 600

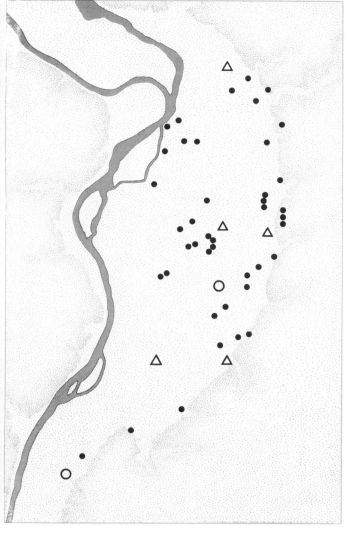
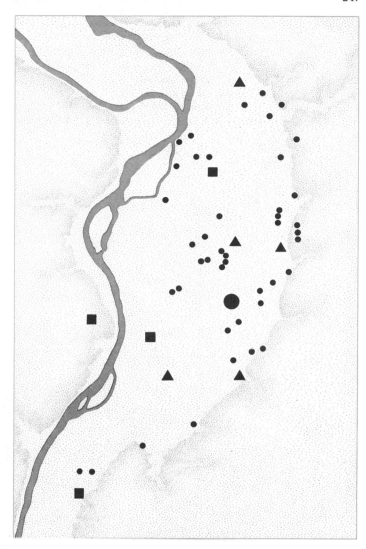

FAIRMOUNT PHASE at Cahokia (*left*), which extended from A.D. 900 to 1050, brought many changes to American Bottoms. Two sites, Cahokia and Lunsford-Pulcher (*open circles*), came to include a number of earth mounds. Farm villages (*dots*) increased in number from 13 to 42. In addition five sites larger than villages arose, four of them near Cahokia (*triangles*); each included at least one platform mound. In the following 200 years (*right*), embracing the Stirling and Moorehead phases at Cahokia, other sites with plazas and platform mounds arose (*squares*). During this time Cahokia (*solid circle*) became the largest community in American Bottoms.

and 900, nor is it clear just how, sometime about 900, people of the Late Woodland period here adopted what American archaeologists call Mississippian culture.

The occupation phase that followed, called Fairmount, continued for 150 years. It was typically Mississippian in culture and includes ample evidence, in the form of mound construction and elaborate burials, that sharp social stratification and a centralized control of resources had arisen among the inhabitants of American Bottoms. Soil cores taken by investigators from Washington University indicate that the first work at Monks Mound probably began at this time. My group's excavation of a small "ridgetop" earthwork, Mound 72 near the middle of the Cahokia group, produced indications that the builders of other mounds in the vicinity followed a

plan calling for the overall orientation of the settlement along a north-south axis.

In view of the enormous quantities of fill required for the construction of the Cahokia earthworks, one immediate question is where did the soil come from? The answer is that the builders followed a procedure still used today: they dug "borrow pits." So far nine borrow pits have been located at Cahokia. The largest, about 800 yards southwest of Monks Mound, covered a 17-acre area and was about six feet deep. The second-largest pit covered nearly eight acres and the others ranged from about two acres to less than one acre. A group from the University of Illinois at Urbana has investigated one of the borrow pits that probably supplied the earth fill for an early phase in the construction of Monks Mound. The pit had later served as a

trash dump; when it was full, the area was leveled and a large platform mound was built on top of the former excavation.

The builders did some of their digging with tools made from the hard, fine-grained stone known as chert. Quite probably they also worked with wood tools that have long since disintegrated, and they carried the earth fill from the pits to the construction sites in baskets.

Among the earthworks at Cahokia, Monks Mound is unique in shape. Mound 72 is one of six known ridgetop mounds in the group. By far the most common mound shape at Cahokia, however, is the platform mound; 28 square, oblong or oval single-platform mounds and four stepped, or double-platform, mounds have been identified [*see illustration on next two pages*]. In some instances excavation has shown that wood structures were built on the tops of the platform mounds, and so it is generally assumed that all the platform mounds served as building sites. The double-platform mounds presumably were used for structures more important than those on the mounds with only one platform. Just which platforms supported ceremonial buildings and which were residential sites occupied by the Cahokia elite is a question that only additional excavation can answer. A fourth kind of mound was also built; it is conical. There were seven of these mounds at Cahokia, and their shape makes it improbable that they were used as building foundations. They may have been used as burial mounds.

Other mound-building communities arose in American Bottoms during the Fairmount phase. One of them, the Lunsford-Pulcher site some 10 miles south of Cahokia, may even have approached Cahokia in size and importance at the time. Five other sites, four

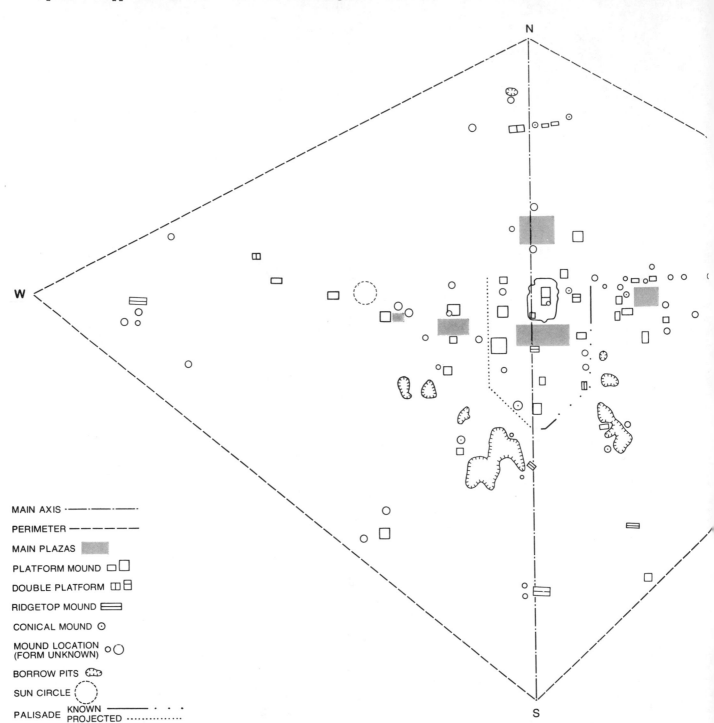

CAHOKIA MOUNDS once extended three miles from the East Group (*right*) to the Powell Group (*left*), both now destroyed, and 2.25 miles from the Kunneman Group (*top*) to the Rattlesnake Group (*bottom*). When the four cardinal points are bounded (*broken colored line*), the area enclosed is some five square miles. Many of the 120 or so mounds at Cahokia have been obliterated by plowing or construction. Only 92 appear on this plan, and the original shape of 47 of them can no longer be determined. The remaining 45 fall into four classes. There are 28 single platforms and four double platforms; all 32 probably had buildings on them. Seven mounds are conical and six are classified as "ridgetop." Four of the ridgetop mounds may have been intended to mark the two axes of the site. Open colored circles locate the 47 mounds of unknown shape; irregular black areas mark eight of the nine known "borof them quite near Cahokia, are characterized by the construction of at least one platform mound. Elsewhere in the bottomland the number of farming hamlets and villages, all of them without mounds, had increased from a known total of 13 during the Patrick phase to more than three times that number [see illustration on page 247]. Two carbon-14 dates, both based on wood samples excavated at Cahokia, have helped to define the duration of the Fairmount phase. A house site excavated by workers from the University of Illinois at Urbana produced a carbon-14 age reading in the range between A.D. 685 and 985, and wood recovered from a ceremonial posthole underlying Mound 72 produced a reading in the range between A.D. 925 and 1035.

The most intriguing information unearthed so far concerning the intellectual and societal complexity of Mississippian culture about the end of the first millennium is associated with the Fairmount phase. In 1961 archaeologists from the Illinois State Museum undertook salvage archaeology in advance of Federal highway construction at Cahokia. They came on a series of soil stains some 900 yards west of Monks Mound. Tracing the stains, they found that many large upright timbers had once been arrayed in a circle. Within the circular enclosure the inhabitants of Cahokia were probably able, by sighting along certain marker posts, to observe the annual sequence of the solstices and the equinoxes. Solar observations of this kind, of course, can be the basis of a useful agricultural calendar. Several of these woodhenges were built in the same part of Cahokia over the centuries, but the first was built during the Fairmount phase.

Our group from Milwaukee had been struck by the fact that three of the six ridgetop mounds at Cahokia were located respectively at the eastern, southern and western extremities of the settlement. A fourth ridgetop mound, Mound 72, was located at the edge of the largest borrow pit, 800 yards south of Monks Mound. We found the position of Mound 72 suggestive. If one draws a line from Mound 72 to a ridgetop mound in the Rattlesnake group, some 600 yards farther south, a northward extension of the line crosses the southwest corner of the first terrace of Monks Mound. It seemed plausible to us that Mound 72 had served to mark a carefully calculated north-south center line at Cahokia.

To test our hypothesis we excavated a trench at the point in Mound 72 where, according to our prediction, the north-south center line would have crossed the structure. We uncovered a pit that extended well below ground level. At the bottom of the pit we found the impression of the butt of a very large upright timber. The timber itself was gone; perhaps the Fairmount-phase inhabitants had later removed it for use elsewhere. Still present, however, were the remains

of logs that had been used to hold the large timber in position. A sample of this wood provided the carbon-14 date mentioned above.

As we continued to excavate Mound 72 it became clear that at the time the marker post was first erected, and continuously thereafter, the locale had served as a burial ground. It was no ordinary cemetery but one evidently reserved for the burial of the elite, perhaps even several generations of the same elite family. It was many years before the mound grew to its final ridgetop shape. We could recognize a succession of building phases; they included no fewer than six separate episodes of burial involving a total of at least 200 individuals.

The first episode, which was probably contemporaneous with the raising of the timber upright, began with the construction of a timber building on level ground. The lack of refuse in association with the building suggests that it was used as a mortuary, or charnel house. Early accounts of European contacts with some Indian groups in the Southeast include descriptions of the storage of the dead in such buildings and of their final burial only at a time that was ceremonially determined. In any event the building was eventually dismantled, and a mound was raised over a group of burials that included the body of one individual who had just died and the bundled bones of several others who had been dead for a long time. This kind of interment is suggestive of a ritual that postpones the burial of lesser kin until a kinsman of high status dies, whereupon all are buried as a group.

The earthwork that was built over this first mass burial was a small platform mound. Nothing was added to the mound for some time, but one pit was dug on the east side and another on the south to accommodate group burials. These pit burials comprised the second episode of burial at the site.

The third episode involved two further excavations and additional construction. One of the excavations was a pit that intruded into the fill covering the pit dug earlier on the south side of the mound. No bodies were buried in the new hole; instead the diggers placed pottery, shell beads and projectile points in the pit and then refilled it. At about the same time a rectangular pit was dug at the southeast corner of the mound and 24 individuals were buried there. Work did not stop with the refilling of the pit but was continued until a mound was raised above it that extended the initial platform mound to the southeast.

Just as the erection of a north-south

on page 247

row pits" that furnished earth to the builders. A broken colored circle locates the Cahokia woodhenge. Shaded areas outline five possible main plazas. The perimeter palisade surrounding the center of the site has been traced only in part; a dotted line (color) suggests its possible further extension.

0   500   1,000

YARDS

marker post suggests sophisticated planning, so the fourth episode of burial at Mound 72 indicates that the social system of Fairmount-phase Cahokia was a distinctly stratified one. First a large pit was excavated about 10 yards southeast of the extension that had been added to the platform mound during the previous episode. Between the pit and the mound extension a small earth mound was raised, and the bodies of four men, with head and hands missing, were placed on top of it. In the pit the bodies of more than 50 young women, all between the ages of 18 and 23, were placed side by side. Finally earth was heaped over both group burials so that the platform mound was extended still farther to the southeast.

Although there is no physical evidence that the young women met a violent death, their closeness in age argues strongly against their having died from disease or from some common disaster. It is difficult to avoid the conclusion that, like the four mutilated men, the women were sacrificed, probably as a part of some kind of funeral ritual.

On whose behalf was the sacrifice made? Not far from the pit, at the place where the timber upright had once stood, we uncovered another group burial. It contained the remains of an individual of obvious importance who had been buried soon after his death. His

TAPERED BEAKER from Cahokia is some nine inches high. Its spiral scroll design is more sophisticated than most of the pottery motifs encountered at the site. The pot is in the collection of the Illinois State Museum.

body had been placed on a platform made up of thousands of shell beads; nearby were a number of bone bundles and the partly disarticulated remains of other individuals.

Not far from this group burial were the remains of three men and three women; buried with them was a wealth of grave goods [see *illustration on page 252*]. A sheet of rolled-up copper, roughly three feet long and two feet wide, had probably come from the Lake Superior region. Several bushels of sheet mica may have been imported from as far to the east as North Carolina. Quantities of arrowheads were present. Some had been freshly flaked from a variety of local materials. Others, including arrowheads made of a black chert found in Arkansas and Oklahoma, had evidently been imported ready-made. None of the arrowheads showed any sign of ever having been used. Finally, there were 15 beautifully polished double-concave stone disks of the kind European visitors later saw used in a sporting event that the Indians of that time called "chunky."

These rich burials were covered by a mound that stood to the southeast of the original (and now twice extended) platform mound. They constitute the fifth episode of burial at Mound 72. It seems reasonable to suppose this episode was contemporaneous with the sacrifice of the young women.

The sixth episode of burial is less spectacular. Ten oblong pits were dug in an area that was then probably near the southwestern edge of the multiple mound. The pits were used for mass burials and in most instances the individuals were buried soon after death. When the last oblong grave was filled, the builders of Mound 72 covered the multiple structure with fresh earth, giving it the ridgetop form that had initially attracted our attention. From the first episode to the last the sequence of burials and mound building seems to have occupied less than 100 years out of the 150-year Fairmount phase.

About A.D. 1050 the Fairmount phase was succeeded by a 100-year phase that has been named Stirling. Cahokia continued to grow during this phase, until the settlement covered between four and five square miles. Excavations of the fourth terrace at Monks Mound by groups from Washington University indicate that about A.D. 1100 the terrace was walled and was the site of one large building and several lesser ones. Work by our group has revealed that other buildings stood on the southwest corner of the lowest terrace at that time.

Elsewhere in American Bottoms other centers marked by mounds, in particular the Lunsford-Pulcher site to the south, began to assume increased stature. The mounds of St. Louis and East St. Louis appear to have been started during the Stirling phase, and another multiple-mound community, the Mitchell site, grew up some eight miles north of Cahokia. All four communities were located close to the major waterways of the region. This suggests that waterborne commerce of the kind indicated by the exotic Fairmount-phase grave goods may by then have become as important to the prosperity of American Bottoms as the high-yield harvests from the bottomland farms.

At some time about A.D. 1150 the Stirling phase at Cahokia was succeeded by the Moorehead phase, named after Warren K. Moorehead of the University of Illinois, who studied the Cahokia mounds almost half a century ago. The Cahokia community attained its highest development during that 100-year phase. At Monks Mound a succession of platform mounds, topped by timber buildings, were built on the lowest terrace. Construction activity is also evident elsewhere. One Moorehead-phase project was the rebuilding of an elaborate timber stockade, probably defensive in nature, that at least partly surrounded both Monks Mound and 16 other mounds in its vicinity.

Traces of this structure were first detected in aerial photographs; they appear as white lines running in a north-south direction to the east of Monks Mound. Our group conducted test excavations of the traces in the latter 1960's and discovered evidence of at least four consecutively constructed stockade systems. The first one, apparently built during the Stirling phase, was a wall made of large logs set on end. At intervals the wall incorporated circular projections, or bastions. The second stockade, probably built early in the Moorehead phase, was similar in design except that the bastions, located at the same points as those of the first stockade, were square rather than circular. A third stockade differed from the second only in minor details, and a fourth phase of construction involved an extensive remodeling of the third stockade.

It proved possible to trace the north-south line of the stockade for about 700 yards in the aerial photographs before it turned toward the southwest. Photo-interpretation suggests that the stockade, after turning, continued to a point some 300 yards due north of Mound 72 and

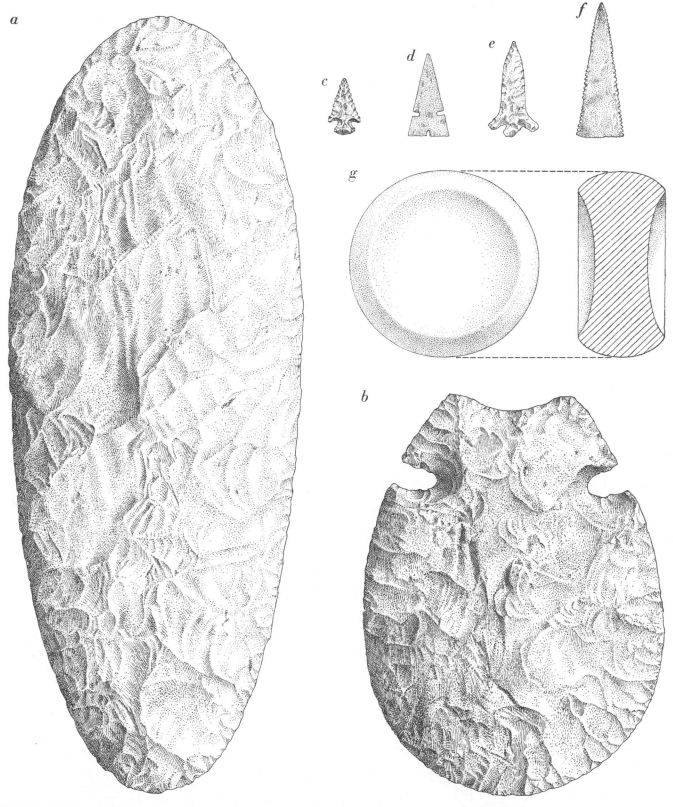

STONE ARTIFACTS from Cahokia, mostly chipped out of flint, range in size from large farm tools to small points. All are shown here at 60 percent actual size. The narrow cutting tool (a) is more than a foot long and may have been used like a hoe. The notched oval (b) more closely resembles a conventional hoe blade; it is some eight inches long. The smallest point (c) is one of several found in Mound 72 that were made from a black chert that is not locally available; the points were probably made in Arkansas or Oklahoma and imported to Cahokia. This example is 1.2 inches long. The triply notched point (d), 1.5 inches long, is also from Mound 72, as is the peculiarly tanged point (e), 1.7 inches long, that may be an import from Arkansas. The largest point (f), 2.5 inches long, is also from Mound 72; it is made from a kind of chert found in southern Illinois. The polished stone that resembles a concave hockey puck (g) is identical with those used in historical times by the Indians of the Southeast in the game of "chunky." The specimen, 3.5 inches in diameter, is in the Illinois State Museum. The large tools are in the St. Louis Museum of Science and Natural History. The points, unearthed during the author's excavation of Mound 72, are now at the University of Wisconsin at Milwaukee.

then angled back along a northwest leg, roughly equal to the southwest leg in length, before turning due north again. So far nothing is known about the stockade's northern terminus. If its northern limit was located exactly where the northernmost traces of its east side now seem to end, it would have enclosed some 200 acres in the central part of Cahokia.

The stockade has been called a fortification because it incorporated bastions or perhaps towers. Another interpretation of the structure is possible. Monks Mound and 16 other earthworks, including some of the largest platform mounds at the site, lie within the area more or less enclosed by the stockade. Did the structure perhaps screen off and isolate a central core of the community that had a higher status than the periphery? In the absence of the kinds of data that only further excavation can provide, such questions remain unanswered. In any event evidence other than maintenance of the stockade supports the view that the Moorehead phase saw Mississippian culture reach its peak at American Bottoms. For example, the woodhenge excavations suggest that the last of the

solar observatories was built at this time. Again, to judge by the number of house sites in areas where such sites have been found, the Moorehead-phase population of Cahokia may have approached 40,000.

How was this substantial population distributed? The area outside the stockade, with its many mounds, suggests a pattern. The mounds appear to have been organized in clusters, and each cluster includes platform mounds, plazas and what are probably burial mounds. The clusters suggest the existence of subcommunities located within the larger metropolis.

The distribution of house sites at Cahokia is also suggestive of a pattern of community organization. A ridge runs through the site from east to west; it is along this ridge line, over an area of some 2,000 acres, that the main concentration of housing is found. The houses were spaced at regular intervals, several to an acre. Of pole-and-thatch construction, they were mostly rectangular in floor plan. Evidently once a building site was chosen a succession of structures were built in the same place, suggesting several generations of occu-

pation. The houses show substantial variations in size. Some could have been the residences of persons of high status, while others may have sheltered craftsmen or even farmers.

Finally, evidence of change in the pattern of land utilization, particularly close to the stockade, hints at the social complexity of Cahokia at its height. In one location some 400 yards west of Monks Mound land that was residential at an earlier time was transformed during the Stirling phase into an area of walled enclosures and large public structures. The area was not returned to residential use until after A.D. 1250. The construction of the stockade provides another example. A part of the timber wall appears to have been built through the middle of an active residential area without regard for the residents. All these findings hint at the power of the central authority that directed the destiny of the Cahokia community.

The next phase at American Bottoms, named Sand Prairie, continued from A.D. 1250 until about 1500. The data from Cahokia for this period give the impression of a far lower level of activity. It was now that the area to the west of Monks Mound was reconverted from public uses to private ones and that minor additions were made to the lower part of Monks Mound. At least one mound still supported a public building. This is the Murdock mound, a double-platform structure located at the angle where the east wall of the stockade turns to the southwest. Excavation there by workers from the Illinois State Museum in 1941 uncovered timbers from what was apparently the last stage of construction of a large building. Wood samples gave a carbon-14 age ranging from A.D. 1270 to 1470.

No name has yet been chosen for the final phase at American Bottoms, which extends from A.D. 1500 to 1700, or about the time of contact with Europeans. The pattern, insofar as it has been traced, is one of continuing decline. About all that is certain, as excavations have shown, is that local Indians sometimes visited Monks Mound at the beginning of the 18th century to bury their dead.

Why did the remarkably successful Mississippian culture at American Bottoms fade away? Perhaps the decline was related to the exhaustion of local resources: a lack of timber for public and private buildings, for the stockade and for the sun circle, and the disappearance of the game animals (mainly deer) in the immediate hinterland that had provided a vital part of the inhabi-

RICH CACHE OF GRAVE GOODS was found at Mound 72 together with the bones of six individuals. Above the marker arrow (*lower left*) are a cluster of arrowheads, including many imported from the Ozarks. Above them (*center*) is a group of chunky stones. The cylindrical mass to their right is a rolled sheet of copper from the region of Lake Superior. Parallel with the roll of copper is a row of large and small shell beads; they are from the Gulf coast. The rounded pile just above the chunky stones is a mass of imported sheet mica.

AREA OF CENTRAL PLAZA at Cahokia is seen in this aerial photograph. The view is to the north; the shadows cast by the late afternoon sun accentuate the relief. The conical mound at left is No. 57; the platform mound at right is No. 60. Both were once enclosed by the timber wall that surrounded the plaza and Monks Mound, the 100-foot-high earthwork at upper right that dominated Cahokia.

tants' diet. Even the fertility of the bottomland loam, where the maize was grown, was not inexhaustible. Evidence from elsewhere in North America, for example at Chaco Canyon in New Mexico, indicates that population concentrations and the overuse of local resources go hand in hand.

It is also possible that the decline of the large settlements at American Bottoms, Cahokia in particular, was related to the growing strength of other centers of Mississippian culture. Cahokia had been the largest single Mississippian center and also perhaps the earliest. Its role in the evolution of the Mississippian way of life must have been dominant for centuries. At the same time American Bottoms was a major crossroads, particularly for travel by water. Its northern extremity was marked by the confluence of the Illinois and Mississippi rivers; the Illinois was a highway to the north-northeast and the upper Mississippi was a highway to the north and north-northwest. Just to the south of this confluence the Missouri River, a highway to the west and northwest, also joins the Mississippi. Toward the southern end of American Bottoms a highway into the Ozarks, the Meramec River, enters the Mississippi from the west. And some 150 miles to the south is the confluence of the Mississippi with the second-greatest of North American rivers, the Ohio, a major highway leading to the east and northeast.

The exotic materials found at sites in American Bottoms (for example black chert, probably from the Ozarks; native copper, almost certainly from Lake Superior; sheet mica, possibly from North Carolina; salt from southern Illinois or Missouri; lead from northern Illinois, and marine shells from the Gulf coast) are concrete evidence of the waterborne commerce that presumably kept American Bottoms in contact with other Mississippian or proto-Mississippian areas of North America. In addition many perishable goods, of which no archaeological trace remains, probably moved through Cahokia in the course of this commerce. Meanwhile Mississippian culture expanded to other areas and thrived. When the first Europeans traveled through southeastern North America, even though Cahokia was by then abandoned and unknown, they found many flourishing Mississippian regional centers. The young warriors were playing games with chunky stones, their elders were tending charnel houses and preparing bundles of bones for final burial and (among the Natchez Indians) an elaborate social hierarchy, headed by

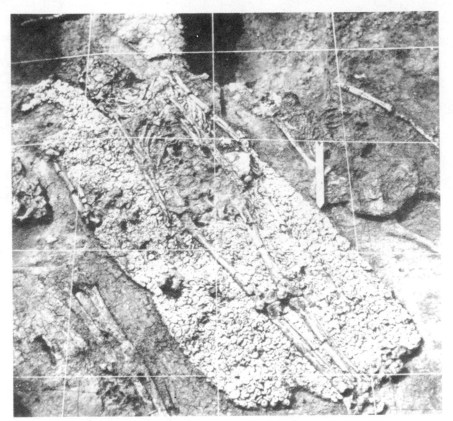

BURIAL PLATFORM made of thousands of shell beads, drilled for stringing, supports the skeleton of a man who was buried in the extended position. The burial was found in the part of Mound 72 near where a large post had once stood to mark the north-south axis of Cahokia. The interred man probably held an important social position. All the burials in and under Mound 72 date from the Fairmount phase at Cahokia: A.D. 900 to A.D. 1050.

chiefs called suns, still built mounds and lived on top of them and regularly offered human sacrifices in the ceremonies that attended the burial of people of high status.

It is plausible to suppose that in addition to the handicap of diminishing resources the Mississippians of American Bottoms suffered from a loss of social status and economic power as the other regional centers of Mississippian culture developed their own hinterlands and spheres of influence. This does not alter the fact that the settlements at American Bottoms and at Cahokia in particular offer a nearly unique opportunity to study the rise of a complex society that for centuries controlled the natural resources of an immediate hinterland and also oversaw the distribution of highly valued resources drawn from more distant areas. The processes that led to the rise of such a society, although they are not yet understood in detail, can be suggested in broad outline.

The initial stimulus seems to have been the population expansion and the jump in agricultural productivity. High crop yields and sedentary communities in turn combined to foster further in-

creases in population density; perhaps it was competition for available farmland and the resulting conflict between rival communities that stimulated the evolution of social controls and societal hierarchies.

The fact that one community in American Bottoms, Cahokia, became the dominant community can be understood in these terms. First, Cahokia stands on some of the best agricultural land in the region. Second, a network of sloughs, lakes and creeks gave Cahokia easy access both to the rest of American Bottoms and to the long-distance transport network formed by the big rivers. Cahokia was thus a central place ideally situated both to exploit the resources of the immediate hinterland and to dominate the trade in exotic goods.

So much for the rise of Cahokia, at least in the light of present knowledge. The processes involved in its decline, however, need to be understood quite as much as the processes involved in its rise. Those who plan future studies of American Bottoms should recognize that the question of why Cahokia was abandoned is among the most significant questions that remain unanswered.

BIBLIOGRAPHIES

I HUMAN ORIGINS

1. The Evolution of Man

PHYLOGENY OF THE PRIMATES: A MULTIDISCIPLINARY APPROACH. Edited by W. Patrick Luckett and Frederick S. Szalay. Plenum Press, 1975.

EVOLUTION AT TWO LEVELS IN HUMANS AND CHIMPANZEES. Mary-Claire King and A. C. Wilson in *Science*, Vol. 188, No. 4184, pages 107–116; April 11, 1975.

HUMAN ORIGINS: LOUIS LEAKEY AND THE EAST AFRICAN EVIDENCE. Edited by Glynn Ll. Isaac and Elizabeth R. McCown. W. A. Benjamin, 1976.

MOLECULAR ANTHROPOLOGY: EVOLVING INFORMATION MOLECULES IN THE ASCENT OF THE PRIMATES. Edited by Morris Goodman and Richard E. Tashian. Plenum Press. 1976.

ORIGINS. Richard Leakey and Roger Lewin. E. P. Dutton, 1977.

HUMAN EVOLUTION: BIOSOCIAL PERSPECTIVES. Edited by Sherwood L. Washburn and Elizabeth R. McCown. Benjamin/Cummings, 1978.

2. The Fossil Footprints of Laetoli

FOSSIL HOMINIDS FROM THE LAETOLIL BEDS. M. D. Leakey, R. L. Hay, G. H. Curtis, R. E. Drake, M. K. Jackes and T. D. White in *Nature*, Vol. 262, No. 5568; August 5, 1976.

MELILITITE-CARBONATITE TUFFS IN THE LAETOLIL BEDS OF TANZANIA. Richard L. Hay in *Contributions to Mineralogy and Petrology, Vol. 67, No. 4, pages 357–367; December 15, 1978*.

PLIOCENE FOOTPRINTS IN THE LAETOLIL BEDS AT LAETOLI, NORTHERN TANZANIA. M. D. Leakey and R. L. Hay in *Nature*, Vol. 278, No. 5702, pages 317–323; March 22, 1979.

PALEOENVIRONMENT OF THE LAETOLIL BEDS, NORTHERN TANZANIA. R. L. Hay in *Hominid Sites: Their Geologic Settings*, edited by G. Rapp, Jr., and C. F. Vondra. Western Press, 1981.

3. The Food-Sharing Behavior of Protohuman Hominids

PRIMATE BEHAVIOR AND THE EMERGENCE OF HUMAN CULTURE. Jane B. Lancaster. Holt, Rinehart & Winston, 1975.

EARLIEST MAN AND ENVIRONMENTS IN THE LAKE RUDOLF BASIN: STRATIGRAPHY, PALEOECOLOGY AND EVOLUTION. Edited by Yves Coppens, F. C. Howell, Glynn Ll. Isaac and Richard E. F. Leakey. University of Chicago Press, 1976.

HUMANKIND EMERGING. Edited by Bernard G. Campbell. Little, Brown, 1976.

HUMAN ORIGINS: LOUIS LEAKEY AND THE EAST AFRICAN EVIDENCE. Edited by Glynn Ll. Isaac and Elizabeth R. McCown. W. A. Benjamin, 1976.

II HUNTER-GATHERERS

4. A Paleolithic Camp at Nice

LES NIVEAUX QUATERNAIRES MARINS DES ALPES-MARITIMES: CORRÉLATIONS AVEC LES INDUSTRIES PRÉHISTORIQUE. Henry de Lumley in *Compte rendu sommaire des Séances de la Société Géologique de France*, Vol. 5, 7th Series, pages 163–164; 1963.

LES FOUILLES DE TERRA AMATA À NICE: PREMIERS RÉSULTATS. H. de Lumley in *Bulletin du Musée d' Anthropologie préhistorique de Monaco*, No. 13, pages 29–51; 1966.

5. The Neanderthals

EVOLUTION OF THE GENUS *HOMO*. William W. Howells. Addison-Wesley, 1973.

NEANDERTHAL MAN: FACTS AND FIGURES. William W. Howells in *Paleoanthropology: Morphology and Paleoecology*, edited by Russell H. Tuttle. Mouton, 1975.

HUMAN EVOLUTION. C. L. Brace and M. F. Ashley Montagu. Macmillan, 1977.

LES ORIGINES HUMAINES ET LES ÉPOQUES DE L'INTELLIGENCE. Edited by J. Piveteau. Masson et Cie., 1978.

III FARMERS AND PEASANTS

8. A Pre-Neolithic Farmers' Village on the Euphrates

PAPERS IN ECONOMIC PREHISTORY. Edited by E. S. Higgs. Cambridge University Press, 1972.

FARMING IN PREHISTORY. Barbara Bender, St. Martin's Press, 1975.

THE EXCAVATION OF TELL ABU HUREYRA IN SYRIA: A PRELIMINARY REPORT. A. M. T. Moore in *Proceedings of the Prehistoric Society*, Vol. 41, pages 50–77; December, 1975.

THE NEOLITHIC OF THE NEAR EAST. James Mellaart. Scribner's, 1976.

9. A Neolithic City in Turkey

THE EARLIEST CIVILIZATIONS OF THE NEAR EAST. James Mellaart. McGraw-Hill, 1965.

CATAL HÜYÜK, James Mellaart. McGraw-Hill, 1967. (The most complete account available.)

6. The Archaeology of Lascaux Cave

LASCAUX. H. Breuil in *Bulletin de la Société préhistorique française*, Vol. 47, pages 355–363; 1950.

LASCAUX: PAINTINGS AND ENGRAVINGS. Annette Laming. Penguin Books, 1959.

DÉBRIS DE CORDE PALÉOLITHIQUE À LA GROTTE DE LASCAUX (DORDOGNE). A. Glory in *Mémoires de la Société préhistorique française*, Vol. 5, pages 135–169; 1959.

LASCAUX INCONNU: XIIᵉ SUPPLÉMENT À "GALLIA PRÉHISTOIRE." Arl. Leroi-Gourhan, J. Allain, L. Balout, C. Bassier, R. Bouchez, J. Bouchud, C. Couraud, B. and D. Delluc, J. Evin, M. Girard, A. Laming-Emperaire, A. Leroi-Gourhan, M. Sarradet, F. Schweingruber, Y. Taborin, D. Vialou and J. Vouvé. Éditions du Centre National de la Recherche Scientifique, 1979.

7. A Paleo-Indian Bison Kill

ANCIENT MAN IN NORTH AMERICA. H. M. Wormington. The Denver Museum of Natural History, 1949.

EARLY MAN IN THE NEW WORLD. Kenneth Macgowan and Joseph A. Hester, Jr. Doubleday, 1962.

THE HIGH PLAINS AND THEIR UTILIZATION BY THE INDIAN. Waldo R. Wedel in *American Antiquity*, Vol. 29, No. 1, pages 1–16; July, 1963.

10. Megalithic Monuments

STONEHENGE. R. J. C. Atkinson. Macmillan, 1956.

THE MEGALITH BUILDERS OF WESTERN EUROPE. Glyn L. Daniel. Praeger, 1958.

BRITTANY. P. R. Giot. Praeger, 1960.

ANCIENT EUROPE FROM THE BEGINNINGS OF AGRICULTURE TO CLASSICAL ANTIQUITY. Stuart Piggott. Edinburgh University Press, 1965.

BEFORE CIVILIZATION: THE RADIOCARBON REVOLUTION AND PREHISTORIC EUROPE. Colin Renfrew. 1973.

11. The Origins of New World Civilization

ANCIENT MESOAMERICAN CIVILIZATION. Richard S. MacNeish in *Science*, Vol. 143, No. 3606, pages 531–537; February, 1964.

DOMESTICATION OF CORN. Paul C. Mangelsdorf, Richard S. MacNeish and Walton C. Galinat in *Science*,

Vol. 143, No. 3606, pages 538–545; February, 1964.

FIRST ANNUAL REPORT OF THE TEHUACAN ARCHAE-OLOGICAL-BOTANICAL PROJECT. Richard Stockton MacNeish. Robert S. Peabody Foundation for Archaeology, 1961.

MEXICO. Michael D. Coe. Frederick A. Praeger, 1962.

SECOND ANNUAL REPORT OF THE TEHUACAN ARCHAE-OLOGICAL-BOTANICAL PROJECT. Richard Stockton MacNeish. Robert S. Peabody Foundation for Archaeology, 1962.

IV CITIES AND CIVILIZATIONS

12. The Origin of Cities

LA CITÉ-TEMPLE SUMÉRIENNE. A Falkenstein in *Cahiers D'Histoire Mondiale*, Vol. I, No. 4, pages 784–814; April, 1954.

CITY INVINCIBLE: A SYMPOSIUM ON URBANIZATION AND CULTURAL DEVELOPMENT IN THE ANCIENT NEAR EAST. Oriental Institute Special Publication, 1960.

EARLY POLITICAL DEVELOPMENT IN MESOPOTAMIA. Thorkild Jacobsen in *Zeitschrift für Assyriologie und Vorderasiatische Archäologie*, Vol. 52, No. 18, pages 91–140; August, 1957.

THE PREINDUSTRIAL CITY. Gideon Sjoberg in *American Journal of Sociology*, Vol. I, No. 5, pages 438–445; March, 1955.

WHAT HAPPENED IN HISTORY. V. Gordon Childe. Penguin Books, 1946.

13. The Earliest Precursor of Writing

AN OPERATIONAL DEVICE IN MESOPOTAMIAN BUREAU-CRACY. A. Leo Oppenheim in *Journal of Near Eastern Studies*, Vol. 17, pages 121–128; 1958.

GLYPTIQUE SUSIENNE. Pierre Amiet in *Mémories de la Délégation archéologique en Iran*, Vol. 43; 1972.

AN ARCHAIC RECORDING SYSTEM AND THE ORIGIN OF WRITING. Denise Schmandt-Besserat in *Syro-Mesopotamian Studies*, Vol. 1, No. 2; July, 1977.

14. Life in Mycenaean Greece

DOCUMENTS IN MYCENAEAN GREEK. Michael Ventris and John Chadwick. Cambridge University Press, 1956.

GREECE IN THE BRONZE AGE. Emily Vermeule. The University of Chicago Press, 1964.

THE DECIPHERMENT OF LINEAR B. John Chadwick. Cambridge University Press, 1970.

THE LINEAR SCRIPTS AND THE TABLETS AS HISTORICAL DOCUMENTS. Sterling Dow and John Chadwick in *The Cambridge Ancient History*. Cambridge University Press, 1971.

15. Teotihuacán

THE CULTURAL ECOLOGY OF THE TEOTIHUACÁN VALLEY. William T. Sanders. Department of Sociology and Anthropology, Pennsylvania State University, 1965.

INDIAN ART OF MEXICO AND CENTRAL AMERICA. Miguel Covarrubias. Knopf, 1957.

AN INTRODUCTION TO AMERICAN ARCHAEOLOGY, Vol. I: NORTH AND MIDDLE AMERICA. Gordon R. Willey. Prentice-Hall, 1969.

MESOAMERICA BEFORE THE TOLTECS. Wigberto Jiménez Moreno in *In Ancient Oaxaca*, edited by John Paddock. Stanford University Press, 1966.

MEXICO BEFORE CORTEZ: ART, HISTORY AND LEGEND. Ignacio Bernal. Doubleday, 1963.

NORTHERN MESOAMERICA. Pedro Armillas in *Prehistoric Man in the New World*, edited by Jesse D. Jennings and Edward Norbeck. The University of Chicago Press, 1964.

16. The Earliest Maya

THE RISE AND FALL OF MAYA CIVILIZATION. John Eric Sidney Thompson. University of Oklahoma Press, 1966.

THE LOST CIVILIZATION: THE STORY OF THE CLASSIC MAYA. T. Patrick Culbert. Harper & Row, 1974.

PRECLASSIC TO POSTCLASSIC IN NORTHERN BELIZE. Norman Hammond in *Antiquity*, Vol. 48, No. 191, pages 177–189; September, 1974.

RADIOCARBON CHRONOLOGY FOR EARLY MAYA OCCU-PATION AT CUELLO, BELIZE. Norman Hammond, Duncan Pring, Rainer Berger, V. R. Switsur and A. P. Ward in *Nature*, Vol. 260, No. 5552, pages 579–581; April 15, 1976.

THE ORIGINS OF MAYA CIVILIZATION. Edited by Richard E. W. Adams. University of New Mexico Press. 1978.

17. The Hopewell Cult

EXPLORATION OF THE MOUND CITY GROUP. William C. Mills in *Ohio Archaeological and Historical Quarterly*, Vol. 31, No. 4, pages 423–584; October, 1922.

EXPLORATIONS OF THE SEIP GROUP OF PRE-HISTORIC EARTHWORKS. Henry C. Shetrone and Emerson F. Greenman in *Ohio Archaeological and Historical Quarterly*, Vol. 40, No. 3, pages 349–509; July, 1931.

18. A Pre-Columbian Urban Center on the Mississippi

ARCHAEOLOGICAL PHASES AT CAHOKIA. Melvin L. Fowler. Papers in Anthropology No. 1, Illinois State Museum Research Series, 1972.

EXPLORATIONS INTO CAHOKIA ARCHAEOLOGY. Edited by Melvin L. Fowler. Bulletin No. 7, Illinois Archaeological Survey, Inc., 1973.

CAHOKIA: ANCIENT CAPITOL OF THE MIDWEST. Melvin L. Fowler. Addison-Wesley Module in Anthropology No. 48, 1974.

INDEX